On Stone and Scroll

Beihefte zur Zeitschrift für die alttestamentliche Wissenschaft

Herausgegeben von
John Barton · Reinhard G. Kratz
Choon-Leong Seow · Markus Witte

Band 420

De Gruyter

On Stone and Scroll

Essays in Honour of Graham Ivor Davies

Edited by
James K. Aitken, Katharine J. Dell
and Brian A. Mastin

De Gruyter

G

ISBN 978-3-11-022805-2

e-ISBN 978-3-11-022806-9

ISSN 0934-2575

Library of Congress Cataloging-in-Publication Data

A CIP catalogue record for this book is available from the Library of Congress.

Bibliographic information published by the Deutsche Nationalbibliothek

The Deutsche Nationalbibliothek lists this publication in the Deutsche
Nationalbibliografie; detailed bibliographic data are available in the Internet
at http://dnb.d-nb.de.

© 2011 Walter de Gruyter GmbH & Co. KG, Berlin/Boston

Printing: Hubert & Co. GmbH & Co. KG, Göttingen
∞ Printed on acid-free paper

Printed in Germany

www.degruyter.com

Preface

The sheer number of contributors to this volume from all over the world is in itself testimony to the esteem in which we all hold the honorand of this volume, Professor Graham Davies. Contributors know Graham in many contexts—as fellow scholar, as colleague, as teacher, as supervisor and, unanimously, as friend. He is a leading Old Testament expert who has deservedly reached the top of his field. A lasting focus of his work has been the combination of sources that he has utilized in the interpretation of the biblical text. His approach has been distinctive in biblical studies in his combining of archaeological, inscriptional, linguistic, and theological evidence for a deeper understanding of texts. His work has ranged from archaeological studies through an edition of Hebrew inscriptions, contributions to Hebrew semantics and biblical theology, to exegesis of the Pentateuch and Prophets. His academic work in the field has been expertly summarized for us by Professor John Emerton in the opening paper of this volume. *On Stone and Scroll* falls into three parts—archaeology, biblical texts, and language and literacy—and these all reflect main areas central to Graham's work and interests. This volume is to be presented to Graham on his retirement—but we know that this will not be his retirement from the field, just from his distinguished career lecturing and teaching in the Faculty of Divinity in Cambridge, which spans over 30 years. The editors would like to thank the Managers of the Bethune-Baker Fund in the Faculty of Divinity for a grant to support this project. They would also like to thank the Faculty of Asian and Middle Eastern Studies for their financial support.

The editors were all responsible for commissioning and editing, but special thanks should go to Brian Mastin for his very meticulous preliminary editing work on almost all the articles and to James Aitken for his work on producing camera-ready copy for approximately half of the articles. The camera-ready copy of the other half of the articles was efficiently produced by three Cambridge postgraduates, Joshua Harper, Max Kramer, and Chris Thomson (a current PhD student of Graham's). Particular thanks go to Chris Thomson for his attention to detail and hard work which has contributed greatly to the production of the high-quality camera-ready copy required by De Gruyter. Our thanks also go to the publishers, especially to Dr Albrecht Döhnert for enthusiastically agreeing to publish this book. Graham's long-standing association with De Gruyter and his membership of the *ZAW* board make this a very fitting publishing connection.

The editors decided to tell Graham about this project in very general terms a couple of years ago and so arranged by email to meet him "to discuss a publication." We met in the ancient University Combination Room in Cambridge and Graham nervously said, "If you are wanting me to be involved in another publication, I am afraid I am fully booked up." Imagine his surprise and pleasure when we revealed our real purpose! We hope that Graham enjoys the articles in this volume, itself but a small token of our esteem for him.

James Aitken
Katharine Dell
Brian Mastin
Cambridge, February 2011

Table of Contents

Part I: Archaeology

Part II: Biblical Texts

List of Contributors

JAMES K. AITKEN, Lecturer in Hebrew, Old Testament, and Second Temple Studies, University of Cambridge, and Fellow of Fitzwilliam College, Cambridge

JAMES ATWELL, Dean of Winchester Cathedral

GRAEME AULD, Professor Emeritus of Hebrew Bible, University of Edinburgh

DAVID L. BAKER, Senior Lecturer in Old Testament, Trinity Theological College, Perth, Australia

JOHN R. BARTLETT, Former Associate Professor of Biblical Studies and Fellow Emeritus of Trinity College Dublin

JOSEPH BLENKINSOPP, John A. O'Brien Professor Emeritus, University of Notre Dame, Indiana, U.S.A.

MARK J. BODA, Professor of Old Testament, McMaster Divinity College, and Professor, Faculty of Theology, McMaster University

GEORGE J. BROOKE, Rylands Professor of Biblical Criticism and Exegesis, University of Manchester

KEVIN J. CATHCART, Emeritus Professor of Near Eastern Languages, University College, Dublin, and Member of Campion Hall, Oxford

RONALD E. CLEMENTS, Emeritus Professor of Old Testament Studies, King's College, University of London

JOHN DAY, Professor of Old Testament Studies in the University of Oxford, and Fellow and Tutor of Lady Margaret Hall, Oxford

KATHARINE J. DELL, Senior Lecturer in Old Testament Studies in the Faculty of Divinity, University of Cambridge, and Fellow of St Catharine's College, Cambridge

J. A. EMERTON, Fellow of St John's College, Cambridge, and Emeritus Regius Professor of Hebrew, University of Cambridge

ANTHONY GELSTON, Emeritus Reader in Theology, University of Durham

JOHN GOLDINGAY, David Allan Hubbard Professor of Old Testament, Fuller Theological Seminary, Pasadena, California

ROBERT P. GORDON, Regius Professor of Hebrew in the University of Cambridge, and Fellow of St Catharine's College, Cambridge

JOHN W. HILBER, Associate Professor of Old Testament, Dallas Theological Seminary

WILLIAM HORBURY, Professor Emeritus of Jewish and Early Christian Studies, University of Cambridge, and Life Fellow of Corpus Christi College, Cambridge

PHILIP JENSON, Lecturer in Old Testament, Ridley Hall, Cambridge

WILLIAM JOHNSTONE, Professor Emeritus of Hebrew and Semitic Languages, University of Aberdeen

JAN JOOSTEN, Professeur d'Ancien Testament, Faculté de Théologie Protestante, Université de Strasbourg and Institut Universitaire de France

JAMES KINNIER WILSON, Emeritus Fellow of Wolfson College, Cambridge, and Sometime Eric Yarrow Lecturer in Assyriology, University of Cambridge

ARIE VAN DER KOOIJ, Professor Emeritus at the Institute for Religious Studies of Leiden University

ARMIN LANGE, Professor for Second Temple Judaism at the University of Vienna, Institute for Jewish Studies

A. A. MACINTOSH, Fellow of St. John's College, Cambridge

B. A. MASTIN, Sometime Senior Lecturer in Hebrew, University of Wales, Bangor; Affiliated Lecturer, Faculty of Asian and Middle Eastern Studies, University of Cambridge

A. D. H. MAYES, Emeritus Erasmus Smith's Professor of Hebrew and Fellow Emeritus of Trinity College, Dublin

ALAN MILLARD, Emeritus Rankin Professor of Hebrew and Ancient Semitic Languages, University of Liverpool

WALTER MOBERLY, Professor of Theology and Biblical Interpretation at the University of Durham

ERNEST NICHOLSON, Formerly Oriel Professor of the Interpretation of Holy Scripture in the University of Oxford, and Provost of Oriel College, Oxford

PAUL NOBLE, Independent scholar resident in Cambridge

ROBERT B. SALTERS, Visiting Professor in the Department of Old Testament and Ancient Near Eastern Studies, University of South Africa

ALISON SALVESEN, University Research Lecturer, Oriental Institute, University of Oxford, and Polonsky Fellow in Jewish Bible Versions, Oxford Centre for Hebrew and Jewish Studies

JOACHIM SCHAPER, Chair in Hebrew, Old Testament, and Early Jewish Studies, University of Aberdeen

KLAAS A. D. SMELIK, Professor of Hebrew and Jewish Studies and Director of the Etty Hillesum Research Centre at Ghent University, Belgium

STUART D. WEEKS, Senior Lecturer in Old Testament and Hebrew, University of Durham

PETER J. WILLIAMS, Warden, Tyndale House, Cambridge

H. G. M. WILLIAMSON, Regius Professor of Hebrew in the University of Oxford, and Student of Christ Church, Oxford

Table of Abbreviations

11QApPsᵃ	*Apocryphal Psalmsᵃ*
1QapGen	*Genesis Apocryphon*
2QSir	2QSirach
8ḤevXIIgr	The Greek Minor Prophets Scroll from Naḥal Ḥever
A.	Tablet signature of texts from Mari
AASF	Annales Academiae Scientiarum Fennicae
AASOR	Annual of the American Schools of Oriental Research
AB	Anchor Bible
ABD	*Anchor Bible Dictionary*. Edited by D. N. Freedman. 6 vols. New York, 1992
ABRL	Anchor Bible Reference Library
ADPV	Abhandlungen des Deutschen Palästina-Vereins
AfOB	Archiv für Orientforschung: Beiheft
ÄgAbh	Ägyptologische Abhandlungen
AION	*Annali dell'Istituto Orientale di Napoli*
AJSL	*American Journal of Semitic Languages and Literature*
AnBib	Analecta biblica
ANET	*Ancient Near Eastern Texts Relating to the Old Testament*. Edited by J. B. Pritchard. 3d ed. Princeton, 1969
AnOr	Analecta orientalia
AnSt	*Anatolian Studies*
Ant.	*Jewish Antiquities*
AOAT	Alter Orient und Altes Testament
AOTC	Apollos Old Testament Commentary
APOT	*The Apocrypha and Pseudepigrapha of the Old Testament*. Edited by R. H. Charles. 2 vols. Oxford, 1913
Aq.	Aquila
ArBib	The Aramaic Bible
Arch	*Archaeology*
ARES	Archivi reali di Ebla: Studi
ARM	Archives royales de Mari
ASP	American Studies in Papyrology
ASV	Amercian Standard Version
ATANT	Abhandlungen zur Theologie des Alten und Neuen Testaments
ATD	Das Alte Testament Deutsch
ATDan	Acta theologica danica

AuOr	*Aula orientalis*
AUSS	*Andrews University Seminary Studies*
AV	Authorized Version
b. Ber.	*Babylonian Talmud, Tractate Berakot*
b. Meg.	*Babylonian Talmud, Tractate Megillah*
b. Šabb.	*Babylonian Talmud, Tractate Šabbat*
b. Sanh.	*Babylonian Talmud, Tractate Sanhedrin*
b. Šebu.	*Babylonian Talmud, Tractate Šebuʿot*
b. Yoma	*Babylonian Talmud, Tractate Yoma*
BA	*Biblical Archaeologist*
BAIAS	*Bulletin of the Anglo-Israel Archeological Society*
BAR	*Biblical Archaeology Review*
BASOR	*Bulletin of the American Schools of Oriental Research*
BASP	*Bulletin of the American Society of Papyrologists*
BC	before Christ
BCE	before the Common Era
BDB	Brown, F., S. R. Driver, and C. A. Briggs. *A Hebrew and English Lexicon of the Old Testament*. Oxford, 1907
BEL	Biblical Encyclopaedia Library
BETL	Bibliotheca ephemeridum theologicarum lovaniensium
BEvT	Beiträge zur evangelischen Theologie
BH	Biblical Hebrew
BHS	*Biblia Hebraica Stuttgartensia*. Edited by K. Elliger and W. Rudolph. Stuttgart, 1983
BHT	Beiträge zur historischen Theologie
Bib	*Biblica*
BibInt	*Biblical Interpretation*
BibOr	Biblica et orientalia
BIOSCS	*Bulletin of the International Organization for Septuagint and Cognate Studies*
BIS	Biblical Interpretation Series
B.J.	*Bellum judaicum*
BKAT	Biblischer Kommentar, Altes Testament. Edited by M. Noth and H. W. Wolff
BLMJ	Bible Lands Museum, Jerusalem
BN	*Biblische Notizen*
BO	*Bibliotheca orientalis*
BTB	*Biblical Theology Bulletin*
BWANT	Beiträge zur Wissenschaft vom Alten und Neuen Testament
BZ	*Biblische Zeitschrift*

BZAR	Beihefte zur Zeitschrift für altorientalische und biblische Rechtsgeschichte
BZAW	Beihefte zur Zeitschrift für die alttestamentliche Wissenschaft
ca.	circa
CAD	*The Assyrian Dictionary of the Oriental Institute of the University of Chicago.* Chicago, 1956–
CaESup	Suppléments aux Cahiers évangile
CAT	Commentaire de l'Ancien Testament
CBET	Contributions to Biblical Exegesis and Theology
CBH	Classical Biblical Hebrew
CBQ	*Catholic Biblical Quarterly*
CBQMS	Catholic Biblical Quarterly Monograph Series
CC	Continental Commentaries
CCEM	Contributions to the Chronology of the Eastern Mediterranean
CCSL	Corpus Christianorum: Series latina. Turnhout, 1953–
CDA	*Concise Dictionary of Akkadian.* Edited by J. Black, A. George, and N. Postgate. Wiesbaden, 1999
CE	Common Era
cf.	*confer*, compare
CHJ	*Cambridge History of Judaism.* Edited by W. D. Davies and Louis Finkelstein. Cambridge, 1984–
ChrEg	*Chronique d'Egypte*
CIS	*Corpus inscriptionum semiticarum*
col(s).	column(s)
ConBOT	Coniectanea biblica: Old Testament Series
COS	*The Context of Scripture.* Edited by W. W. Hallo. 3 vols. Leiden, 1997–2002
COut	Commentaar op het Oude Testament
CTA	*Corpus des tablettes en cunéiformes alphabétiques découvertes à Ras Shamra-Ugarit de 1929 à 1939.* Edited by A. Herdner. Mission de Ras Shamra 10. Paris, 1963
Cyr.	*Cyropaedia*
DBAT	*Dielheimer Blätter zum Alten Testament und seiner Rezeption in der alten Kirche*
DCH	*Dictionary of Classical Hebrew.* Edited by D. J. A. Clines. Sheffield, 1993–
DDD[1]	*Dictionary of Deities and Demons in the Bible.* Edited by K. van der Toorn, B. Becking, and P. W. van der Horst. 1st ed. Leiden, 1995

*DDD*²	*Dictionary of Deities and Demons in the Bible.* Edited by K. van der Toorn, B. Becking, and P. W. van der Horst. 2d ed. Leiden, 1999
diss.	dissertation
DJD	Discoveries in the Judaean Desert
DNWSI	*Dictionary of the North-West Semitic Inscriptions.* J. Hoftijzer and K. Jongeling. 2 vols. Leiden, 1995
DOTT	*Documents from Old Testament Times.* Edited by D. W. Thomas. London, 1958
DSD	*Dead Sea Discoveries*
Ṣe	Naḥal Ṣeʾelim
EA	El-Amarna tablets. According to the edition of J. A. Knudtzon. *Die el-Amarna-Tafeln.* Leipzig, 1908–1915. Reprint, Aalen, 1964. Continued in A. F. Rainey, *El-Amarna Tablets,* 359–379. 2d revised ed. Kevelaer, 1978
EBib	Études bibliques
ed.	editor(s), edition
e.g.	*exempli gratia,* for example
Enc	*Encounter*
ERE	*Encyclopedia of Religion and Ethics.* Edited by J. Hastings. 13 vols. New York, 1908–1927. Reprint, 7 vols., 1951
ErIsr	*Eretz-Israel*
esp.	especially
ESV	English Standard Version
ET	English translation
Ḥev	Naḥal Ḥever
Ḥev/Se	Naḥal Ḥever documents earlier attributed to Seiyal
EVV	English Versions
Expl. Dan.	*Explanatio in Danielem*
ExpTim	*Expository Times*
f.	folio
FAT	Forschungen zum Alten Testament
fig(s).	figure(s)
FOTL	Forms of the Old Testament Literature
Frg. Tg	*Fragment Targum*
FRLANT	Forschungen zur Religion und Literatur des Alten und Neuen Testaments
GKC	*Gesenius' Hebrew Grammar.* Edited by E. Kautzsch. Translated by A. E. Cowley. 2d. ed. Oxford, 1910
GNB	Good News Bible
GRBS	*Greek, Roman, and Byzantine Studies*

HAL	Koehler, L., W. Baumgartner, and J. J. Stamm. *Hebräisches und aramäisches Lexikon zum Alten Testament*. 5 fascicles. Leiden, 1967–1995 (KBL3). ET: *HALOT*
HALOT	Koehler, L., W. Baumgartner, and J. J. Stamm, *The Hebrew and Aramaic Lexicon of the Old Testament*. Translated and edited under the supervision of M. E. J. Richardson. 5 vols. Leiden, 1994–2000
HAR	*Hebrew Annual Review*
HAT	Handbuch zum Alten Testament
Hist.	*History*
HKAT	Handkommentar zum Alten Testament
HSAT	Die Heilige Schrift des Alten Testaments. Edited by Franz Feldmann and Heinrich Herkenne
HSS	Harvard Semitic Studies
HTKAT	Herders theologischer Kommentar zum Alten Testament
HTR	*Harvard Theological Review*
HUCA	*Hebrew Union College Annual*
HUCM	Monographs of the Hebrew Union College
IBC	Interpretation: A Bible Commentary for Teaching and Preaching
IBHS	*An Introduction to Biblical Hebrew Syntax*. B. K. Waltke and M. O'Connor. Winona Lake, Indiana, 1990
IBS	*Irish Biblical Studies*
ICC	International Critical Commentary
IDBSup	*Interpreter's Dictionary of the Bible: Supplementary Volume*. Edited by K. Crim. Nashville, 1976
idem	the same
i.e.	*id est*, that is
IEJ	*Israel Exploration Journal*
Il.	*Iliad*
illus.	illustration
Inst.	*Institutio oratoria*
Int	*Interpretation*
IRT	Issues in Religion and Theology
JAAR	*Journal of the American Academy of Religion*
JAOS	*Journal of the American Oriental Society*
JARCE	*Journal of the American Research Center in Egypt*
Jastrow	Jastrow, M. *A Dictionary of the Targumim, the Talmud Babli and Yerushalmi, and the Midrashic Literature*. 2d ed. New York, 1903
JBL	*Journal of Biblical Literature*
JCS	*Journal of Cuneiform Studies*

JDS	Jewish Desert Studies
JE	*The Jewish Encyclopedia.* Edited by I. Singer. 12 vols. New York, 1925
JEA	*Journal of Egyptian Archaeology*
JEOL	*Jaarbericht van het Vooraziatisch-Egyptisch Gezelschap (Genootschap) Ex oriente lux*
JETS	*Journal of the Evangelical Theological Society*
JJS	*Journal of Jewish Studies*
JNES	*Journal of Near Eastern Studies*
JNSL	*Journal of Northwest Semitic Languages*
JPS	*The Holy Scriptures According to the Masoretic Text: A New Translation.* Jewish Publication Society of America
JPS	Jewish Publication Society
JQR	*Jewish Quarterly Review*
JRAS	*Journal of the Royal Asiatic Society*
JRS	*Journal of Roman Studies*
JSJSup	Supplements to the Journal for the Study of Judaism
JSNTSup	Journal for the Study of the New Testament: Supplement Series
JSOT	*Journal for the Study of the Old Testament*
JSOTSup	Journal for the Study of the Old Testament: Supplement Series
JSPSup	Journal for the Study of the Pseudepigrapha: Supplement Series
JSS	*Journal of Semitic Studies*
JSSEA	*Journal of the Society for the Study of Egyptian Antiquities*
JTS	*Journal of Theological Studies*
K	Kouyunjik Collection, British Museum
KAgr	Kuntillet 'Ajrud
KAI	*Kanaanäische und aramäische Inschriften.* H. Donner and W. Röllig. 2d ed. Wiesbaden, 1966–1969
KAT	Kommentar zum Alten Testament
KBL	Koehler, L., and W. Baumgartner, *Lexicon in Veteris Testamenti libros.* 2d ed. Leiden, 1958
KEHAT	Kurzgefasstes exegetisches Handbuch zum Alten Testament
KHC	Kurzer Hand-Commentar zum Alten Testament
KJV	King James Version
KlPauly	*Der kleine Pauly*
KRI	Kitchen, K. A. *Ramesside Inscriptions: Historical and Biographical.* 8 vols. Oxford, 1975–1990

KTU	*Die keilalphabetischen Texte aus Ugarit.* Edited by M. Dietrich, O. Loretz, and J. Sanmartín. AOAT 24/1. Neukirchen-Vluyn, 1976. 2d, enlarged ed.: *The Cuneiform Alphabetic Texts from Ugarit, Ras Ibn Hani, and Other Places.* Münster, 1995
LÄ	*Lexikon der Ägyptologie.* Edited by W. Helck, E. Otto, and W. Westendorf. Wiesbaden, 1972
Lane	Lane, E. W. *An Arabic-English Lexicon.* 8 vols. London. Reprint, 1968
LBH	Late Biblical Hebrew
LCL	Loeb Classical Library
Lev. Rab.	*Leviticus Rabbah*
LHBOTS	Library of Hebrew Bible/Old Testament Studies
LSJ	Liddell, H. G., R. Scott, H. S. Jones, *A Greek-English Lexicon.* 9th ed. with revised supplement. Oxford, 1996
LXX	Septuagint
LXX.D	*Septuaginta Deutsch: Das griechische Alte Testament in deutscher Übersetzung.* Deutsche Bibelgesellschaft, 2009
m. Meg.	*Mishnah, Tractate Megillah*
MARI	*Mari: Annales de recherches interdisciplinaires*
Mas	Masada
MdB	Le Monde de la Bible
Midr.	Midrash
MS(S)	Manuscript(s)
MSU	Mitteilungen des Septuaginta-Unternehmens
MT	Masoretic Text
Mur	Murabbaʿat
MUSJ	*Mélanges de l'Université Saint-Joseph*
n.	note
NAB	New American Bible
NASB	New American Standard Bible
NCB	New Century Bible
NEAEHL	*The New Encyclopedia of Archaeological Excavations in the Holy Land.* Edited by E. Stern. 4 vols. Jerusalem, 1993
NEB	New English Bible
NETS	*A New English Translation of the Septuagint.* Edited by A. Pietersma and B. G. Wright. Oxford, 2007
NF	neue Folge
NICOT	New International Commentary on the Old Testament
Nin.	Nineveh King lists, numbered A–R
NIV	New International Version
NJB	New Jerusalem Bible

NJPS *Tanakh: The Holy Scriptures: The New JPS Translation according to the Traditional Hebrew Text*
NKJV New King James Version
NLT New Living Translation
no(s). number(s)
NovTSup Novum Testamentum Supplements
NRSV New Revised Standard Version
NS new series
NTOA Novum Testamentum et Orbis Antiquus
OBO Orbis biblicus et orientalis
OBT Overtures to Biblical Theology
Od. *Odyssey*
OLA Orientalia lovaniensia analecta
OLZ *Orientalische Literaturzeitung*
Or *Orientalia*
OT Old Testament
OTE *Old Testament Essays*
OTG Old Testament Guides
OTL Old Testament Library
OTP *Old Testament Pseudepigrapha.* Edited by J. H. Charlesworth. 2 vols. New York, 1983
OtSt Oudtestamentische studiën
p. page
P Pyramid Texts, according to J. P. Allen, *The Ancient Egyptian Pyramid Texts.* Atlanta, Ga., 2005
P.Amh.Eg. *The Amherst Papyri, Being an Account of the Egyptian Papyri in the Collection of the Right Hon. Lord Amherst of Hackney, F.S.A. at Didlington Hall, Norfolk.* Edited by P. E. Newberry. London, 1899
P.Cair.Zen. *Zenon Papyri, Catalogue général des antiquités égyptiennes du Musée du Caire.* Edited by C. C. Edgar. Cairo
P.Lond. *Greek Papyri in the British Museum.* London
P.Oxy. *The Oxyrhynchus Papyri.* Published by the Egypt Exploration Society in Graeco-Roman Memoirs. London
P.Petaus *Das Archiv des Petaus (P. Petaus).* Edited by U. Hagedorn, D. Hagedorn, L. C. Youtie, and H. C. Youtie. Cologne, 1969
PAAJR *Proceedings of the American Academy of Jewish Research*
PAM Palestine Archaeological Museum
PEQ *Palestine Exploration Quarterly*
Pesaḥ. *Pesaḥim*

PG	Patrologia graeca [= Patrologiae cursus completus: Series graeca]. Edited by J.-P. Migne. 162 vols. Paris, 1857–1886
Phil	*Philologus*
pl.	plural
pl(s).	plate(s)
Praem.	*De praemiis et poenis*
PSI	*Papiri greci e latini*. Pubblicazioni della Società Italiana per la ricerca dei papiri greci e latini in Egitto. Florence
PT	Pyramid Texts, according to K. Sethe, *Die altaegyptischen Pyramidentexte: Nach den Papierabdrücken und Photographien des Berliner Museums*. Leipzig, 1908–1922
PW	Pauly, A. F. *Paulys Realencyclopädie der classischen Altertumswissenschaft*. G. Wissowa. Munich, 1894–1980
Q	Qumran
QD	Quaestiones disputatae
RA	*Revue d'assyriologie et d'archéologie orientale*
RÄR	*Reallexikon der ägyptischen Religionsgeschichte*. H. Bonnet. Berlin, 1952.
RB	*Revue biblique*
RBL	*Review of Biblical Literature*
REB	Revised English Bible
REg	*Revue d'égyptologie*
REJ	*Revue des études juives*
RelSRev	*Religious Studies Review*
repr.	reprint
rev.	revised
RevQ	*Revue de Qumran*
RGG	*Religion in Geschichte und Gegenwart*. Edited by Hans Dieter Betz. 9 vols. 4th ed. Tübingen, 1998–2007
RIH	Ras Ibn Ḥani
RIMA	The Royal Inscriptions of Mesopotamia, Assyrian Periods
RlA	*Reallexikon der Assyriologie*. Edited by Erich Ebeling et al. Berlin, 1928–
RS	Ras Shamra
RSO	*Rivista degli studi orientali*
RSR	*Recherches de science religieuse*
RSV	Revised Standard Version
RTL	*Revue théologique de Louvain*
RV	Revised Version
S. Eli. Rab.	*Seder Eliyahu Rabbah*
SAA	State Archives of Assyria
SAAS	State Archives of Assyria Studies

SAOC	Studies in Ancient Oriental Civilizations
SAT	Die Schriften des Alten Testaments
SB	Sources bibliques
SBB	Stuttgarter biblische Beiträge
SBLAIL	Society of Biblical Literature Ancient Israel and Its Literature
SBLDS	Society of Biblical Literature Dissertation Series
SBLEJL	Society of Biblical Literature Early Judaism and Its Literature
SBLRBS	Society of Biblical Literature Resources for Biblical Study
SBLSCS	Society of Biblical Literature Septuagint and Cognate Studies
SBLSymS	Society of Biblical Literature Symposium Series
SBLWAW	Society of Biblical Literature Writings from the Ancient World
SBT	Studies in Biblical Theology
SC	Sources chrétiennes. Paris: Cerf, 1943–
SEL	*Studi epigrafici e linguistici*
SemeiaSt	Semeia Studies
sg.	singular
SHANE	Studies in the History of the Ancient Near East
Sib. Or.	*Sibylline Oracles*
SJOT	*Scandinavian Journal of the Old Testament*
SJT	*Scottish Journal of Theology*
SOTS	Society for Old Testament Study
SOTSMS	Society for Old Testament Study Monograph Series
SSN	Studia semitica neerlandica
STAR	Studies in Theology and Religion
STDJ	*Studies on the Texts of the Desert of Judah*
StPh	Studia Phoenicia
StudBib	Studia biblica
SubBi	Subsidia biblica
s.v.	*sub verbo*, under the word
Sym.	Symmachus
TA	*Tel Aviv*
TADAE	*Textbook of Aramaic Documents from Ancient Egypt*. Edited by Bezalel Porten and Ada Yardeni. 4 vols. Jerusalem, 1986–1999
TAOP	Tel Aviv Occasional Publications
TDOT	*Theological Dictionary of the Old Testament*. Edited by G. J. Botterweck and H. Ringgren. Translated by J. T. Willis, G. W. Bromiley, and D. E. Green. Grand Rapids, 1974–

Tg.	Targum
Tg. Neof.	*Targum Neofiti*
Tg. Onq.	*Targum Onqelos*
Tg. Ps.-J.	*Targum Pseudo-Jonathan*
TGI	*Textbuch zur Geschichte Israels.* Edited by K. Galling. 2d ed. Tübingen, 1968
Th.	Theodotion
Them	*Themelios*
ThWAT	*Theologisches Wörterbuch zum Alten Testament.* Edited by G. J. Botterweck and H. Ringgren. Stuttgart, 1970–
TLOT	*Theological Lexicon of the Old Testament.* Edited by E. Jenni, with assistance from C. Westermann. Translated by M. E. Biddle. 3 vols. Peabody, Mass., 1997
TNIV	Today's New International Version
TOTC	Tyndale Old Testament Commentaries
TQ	*Theologische Quartalschrift*
trans.	translation, translated by
Transeu	*Transeuphratène*
TU	Texte und Untersuchungen
TUAT	*Texte aus der Umwelt des Alten Testaments.* Edited by Otto Kaiser. Gütersloh, 1984–
TWNT	*Theologische Wörterbuch zum Neuen Testament.* Edited by G. Kittel and G. Friedrich. Stuttgart, 1932–1979
TynBul	*Tyndale Bulletin*
UCBC	University of California, Berkeley Cuneiform collection
UCOP	University of Cambridge Oriental Publications
UF	*Ugarit-Forschungen*
UT	*Ugaritic Textbook.* C. H. Gordon. AnOr 38. Rome, 1965
v(v).	verse(s)
VL	Vetus Latina
vol(s).	volume(s)
VT	*Vetus Testamentum*
VTSup	Supplements to Vetus Testamentum
Vulg.	Vulgate
W	Texts from Warka (Uruk)
WB	Weld-Blundell Prism, Ashmolean Museum
WBC	Word Biblical Commentary
Wehr	Wehr, H. *A Dictionary of Modern Written Arabic.* Edited by J. M. Cowan. Ithaca, 1961, 1976[3]
WMANT	Wissenschaftliche Monographien zum Alten und Neuen Testament
WO	*Die Welt des Orients*

y. Meg.	*Jerusalem Talmud, Tractate Megillah*
y. Qidd.	*Jerusalem Talmud, Tractate Qidduśin*
y. Ta'an.	*Jerusalem Talmud, Tractate Ta'anit*
Yal.	*Yalquṭ*
ZAH	*Zeitschrift für Althebräistik*
ZÄS	*Zeitschrift für ägyptische Sprache und Altertumskunde*
ZAW	*Zeitschrift für die alttestamentliche Wissenschaft*
ZDMG	*Zeitschrift der Deutschen Morgenländischen Gesellschaft*
ZDMGSup	Zeitschrift der Deutschen Morgenländischen Gesellschaft: Supplementbände
ZDPV	*Zeitschrift des Deutschen Palästina-Vereins*
ZPE	*Zeitschrift für Papyrologie und Epigraphik*
ZTK	*Zeitschrift für Theologie und Kirche*

Biographical Note: Graham Ivor Davies

1944	26th September. Born in Liskeard, Cornwall
1955–1963	Educated at King's College School, Wimbledon
1963	Admitted to Merton College, Oxford, as Postmaster in Classics
1965	First Class, Honour Classical Moderations
1967	B.A. (Oxon.), First Class, Honour School of Literae Humaniores
1969	First Class, Honour School of Theology
	Canon Hall Senior New Testament Prize
	Pusey and Ellerton Senior Prize for Hebrew
	Admitted as a Research Student to Peterhouse, Cambridge
1970	Hall-Houghton Senior Septuagint Prize (Oxford)
	M.A. (Oxon.)
	Jeremie Septuagint Prize (Cambridge)
1971–1978	Assistant Lecturer, then Lecturer, in Old Testament Studies, University of Nottingham
1975	Ph.D. (Cantab.)
	Visiting Lecturer, St. George's College, Jerusalem
	Participated in archaeological excavations at Tell es-Sebaʿ (Beersheba)
1977	Licensed as Lay Reader, Diocese of Southwell
1977 and 1980	Participated in archaeological excavations at Tell ed-Duweir (Lachish)
1979–1993	Lecturer in Divinity (Old Testament and Intertestamental Studies), University of Cambridge

1979–1987	Director of Studies in Theology, Pembroke College, Cambridge
1979–1988	Director of Studies in Theology, Peterhouse, Cambridge
1983	Fellow, Fitzwilliam College, Cambridge
1983–2008	Director of Studies in Theology, Fitzwilliam College, Cambridge
1985	Visiting Research Fellow, Merton College, Oxford (Hilary Term)
1986	Macbride Sermon, University of Oxford
1987	Fellow of the Society of Antiquaries
1991–1995	Secretary of the Coordinating Committee of the European Science Foundation Scientific Network on "The Semantics of Classical Hebrew"
1993–2001	Reader in Old Testament Studies, University of Cambridge
1995	Secretary, Fifteenth Congress of the International Organization for the Study of the Old Testament, Cambridge, 16th–21st July
1998	D.D. (Oxon.)
	Consultant on Hebrew language for a new edition of the Authorised Version of the Bible (*The New Cambridge Paragraph Bible* [ed. David Norton; Cambridge: Cambridge University Press, 2005])
2001–2011	Professor of Old Testament Studies, University of Cambridge
2003	Fellow of the British Academy
2006–2009	Chairman, Theology and Religious Studies Section, British Academy
2008	Schweich Centenary Lecture, British Academy

Publications of Graham Ivor Davies

A. Books

The Way of the Wilderness: A Geographical Study of the Wilderness Itineraries in the Old Testament. SOTSMS 5. Cambridge: Cambridge University Press, 1979.

Megiddo. Cities of the Biblical World. Cambridge: Lutterworth, 1986.

Ancient Hebrew Inscriptions: Corpus and Concordance. With the assistance of M. N. A. Bockmuehl, D. R. de Lacey, and A. J. Poulter. Cambridge: Cambridge University Press, 1991.

K. A. D. Smelik. *Writings from Ancient Israel*. Translated (from Dutch) by G. I. Davies. Edinburgh: T&T Clark, 1991. Translation of *Behouden schrift: Historische documenten uit het oude Israel*. Baarn: Ten Have, 1984.

Hosea. NCB. London: Harper Collins, 1992.

Hosea. OTG. Sheffield: Sheffield Academic Press, 1993.

J. Calvin. *The Bondage and Liberation of the Will: A Defence of the Orthodox Doctrine of Human Choice against Pighius (1543)*. Edited by A. N. S. Lane. Translated (from Latin) by G. I. Davies. Texts and Studies in Reformation and Post-Reformation Thought 2. Grand Rapids, Mich.: Baker, 1996.

Ancient Hebrew Inscriptions Volume 2: Corpus and Concordance. Cambridge: Cambridge University Press, 2004.

J. Calvin. *Defensio sanae et orthodoxae doctrinae de servitute et liberatione humani arbitrii*. Volume 3 of *Scripta didactica et polemica*. Edited by A. N. S. Lane with the assistance of G. I. Davies. Geneva: Droz, 2008.

Forthcoming:

The Schweich Lectures and Biblical Archaeology. Oxford: Oxford University Press for the British Academy, 2011.

B. Editorships

Editor, Cities of the Biblical World series (Lutterworth).

Editor of *Palestine Exploration Quarterly*, from vol. 122 (1990) to vol. 132 (2000).

Editor, International Critical Commentary (Old Testament volumes), from 2004.

Editorial Board, *Palestine Exploration Quarterly*, from 2001.

Editorial Board, *Zeitschrift für die alttestamentliche Wissenschaft*, from 2007.

Co-editor (with K. J. Dell and Y. V. Koh), *Genesis, Isaiah and Psalms: A Festschrift to Honour Professor John Emerton for his Eightieth Birthday.* VTSup 135. Leiden: Brill, 2010.

C. Articles

"Hagar, el-Heğra and the Location of Mount Sinai." *VT* 22 (1972): 152–63.

"The Hebrew Text of Exodus VIII 19 (EVV. 23): An Emendation." *VT* 24 (1974): 489–92.

"The Wilderness Itineraries: A Comparative Study." *TynBul* 25 (1974): 46–81.

"The Uses of *r⁶⁶* Qal and the Meaning of Jonah IV 1." *VT* 27 (1977): 105–11.

"A New Solution to a Crux in Obadiah 7." *VT* 27 (1977): 484–87.

"Apocalyptic and Historiography." *JSOT* 5 (1978): 15–28.

"The Significance of Deuteronomy I.2 for the Location of Mount Horeb." *PEQ* 111 (1979): 87–101.

"A Note on the Etymology of *hištaḥᵃwāh*." *VT* 29 (1979): 493–95.

"A Fragment of an Early Recension of the Greek Exodus." Pages 151–56 in *Papers Presented to the Fifth International Congress on Biblical Studies Held at Oxford, 1973.* Edited by E. A. Livingstone. TU 126. Berlin: Akademie-Verlag, 1982.

"Tell ed-Duweir: Ancient Lachish: A Response to G. W. Ahlström." *PEQ* 114 (1982): 25–28.

"The Wilderness Itineraries and the Composition of the Pentateuch." *VT* 33 (1983): 1–13.

"Tell ed-Duweir: Not Libnah but Lachish." *PEQ* 117 (1985): 92–96.

"Megiddo in the Period of the Judges." Pages 34–53 in *Crises and Perspectives: Ancient Near Eastern Polytheism, Biblical Theology, Palestin-*

ian Archaeology and Intertestamental Literature. Edited by A. S. van der Woude. OtSt 24. Leiden: Brill, 1986.

"British Archaeologists." Pages 37–62 in *Benchmarks in Time and Culture: An Introduction to Palestinian Archaeology Dedicated to Joseph A. Callaway*. Edited by J. F. Drinkard, G. L. Mattingly, and J. Maxwell Miller. Atlanta, Ga.: Scholars Press, 1988.

"The Destiny of the Nations in the Book of Isaiah." Pages 93–120 in *Le livre d'Isaïe: Les oracles et leurs relectures: Unité et complexité de l'ouvrage*. Edited by J. Vermeylen. BETL 81. Leuven: Peeters, 1989.

"*ʾUrwōt* in 1 Kings 5:6 (EVV. 4:26) and the Assyrian Horse Lists." *JSS* 34 (1989): 25–38.

"Solomonic Stables at Megiddo after all?" *PEQ* 120 (1988): 130–41.

"The Samaria Ostraca: Two Onomastic Notes" (with A. J. Poulter), *VT* 40 (1990): 237–40.

"The Wilderness Itineraries and Recent Archaeological Research." Pages 161–75 in *Studies in the Pentateuch*. Edited by J. A. Emerton. VTSup 41. Leiden: Brill, 1990.

"Response to J. Greenfield and J. Hoftijzer." Pages 143–48 in *The Balaam Text from Deir Alla Re-Evaluated*. Edited by J. Hoftijzer and G. van der Kooij. Leiden: Brill, 1991.

"The Presence of God in the Second Temple and Rabbinic Doctrine." Pages 32–36 in *Templum Amicitiae: Essays on the Second Temple Presented to Ernst Bammel*. Edited by W. Horbury. JSNTSup 48. Sheffield: JSOT Press, 1991.

"The Use and Non-Use of the Particle *ʾet* in Hebrew Inscriptions." Pages 14–26 in *Studies in Hebrew and Aramaic Syntax: Presented to Professor J. Hoftijzer on the Occasion of his Sixty-Fifth Birthday*. Edited by K. Jongeling, H. L. Murre-van den Berg, and L. van Rompay. Studies in Semitic Languages and Linguistics 17. Leiden: Brill, 1991.

"Pragmalinguistics and Classical Hebrew: A Response to I. Zatelli." *ZAH* 6 (1993): 73–78.

"An Archaeological Commentary on Ezekiel 13." Pages 108–25 in *Scripture and Other Artifacts: Essays on the Bible and Archaeology in Honor of Philip J. King*. Edited by M. D. Coogan, J. C. Exum, and L. E. Stager. Louisville, Ky.: Westminster John Knox, 1994.

"King Solomon's Stables: Still at Megiddo?" *BAR* 20, no. 1 (January/February 1994): 44–49.

"Were there Schools in Ancient Israel?" Pages 199–211 in *Wisdom in Ancient Israel: Essays in Honour of J. A. Emerton*. Edited by J. Day, R. P. Gordon, and H. G. M. Williamson. Cambridge: Cambridge University Press, 1995.

"The Composition of the Book of Exodus: Reflections on the Theses of E. Blum." Pages 71–85 in *Texts, Temples and Tradition: A Tribute to Menahem Haran*. Edited by M. Fox, V. A. Hurowitz, A. Hurvitz, M. L. Klein, B. J. Schwartz, and N. Shupak. Winona Lake, Ind.: Eisenbrauns, 1996.

"K^D in Exodus: An Assessment of E. Blum's Proposal." Pages 407–20 in *Deuteronomy and Deuteronomic Literature: Festschrift C. H. W. Brekelmans*. Edited by M. Vervenne and J. Lust. BETL 133. Leuven: Peeters, 1997.

"A Samaritan Inscription with an Expanded Text of the Shemaᶜ." *PEQ* 131 (1999): 3–19.

"Some Points of Interest in Sixteenth-Century Translations of Exodus 15." Pages 247–55 in *Hebrew Study from Ezra to Ben-Yehuda*. Edited by W. Horbury. Edinburgh: T&T Clark, 1999.

"Three Christian Commentators on Hosea." Pages 129–50 in *New Heaven and New Earth: Prophecy and the Millennium: Essays in Honour of Anthony Gelston*. Edited by P. J. Harland and C. T. R. Hayward. VTSup 77. Leiden: Brill, 1999.

"The Theology of Exodus." Pages 137–52 in *In Search of True Wisdom: Essays in Old Testament Interpretation in Honour of Ronald E. Clements*. Edited by E. Ball. JSOTSup 300. Sheffield: Sheffield Academic Press, 1999.

"Introduction to the Pentateuch." Pages 12–38 in *The Oxford Bible Commentary*. Edited by J. Barton and J. Muddiman. Oxford: Oxford University Press, 2001.

"Genesis and the Early History of Israel." Pages 105–34 in *Studies in the Book of Genesis*. Edited by A. Wénin. BETL 155. Leuven: Peeters, 2001.

"Hebrew Inscriptions." Pages 270–86 in *The Biblical World*. Edited by J. Barton. London: Routledge, 2002.

"Some Christian Uses and Interpretations of the Song of Moses (Exodus 15:1–18)." Pages 179–95 in *Vergegenwärtigung des Alten Testaments: Beiträge zur biblischen Hermeneutik: Festschrift für Rudolf Smend zum 70. Geburtstag*. Edited by C. Bultmann, W. Dietrich, and C. Levin. Göttingen: Vandenhoeck & Ruprecht, 2002.

"Covenant, Oath and the Composition of the Pentateuch." Pages 71–89 in *Covenant as Context: Essays in Honour of E. W. Nicholson*. Edited by A. D. H. Mayes and R. B. Salters. Oxford: Oxford University Press, 2003.

"Prophecy and Tradition: Response to Christopher R. Seitz." Pages 53–58 in *Prophetie in Israel*. Edited by I. Fischer, K. Schmid, and H. G.

M. Williamson. Altes Testament und Moderne 11. Münster: Lit-Verlag, 2003.

"Fresh Evidence for E. H. Palmer's Travels from Cambridge Libraries." Pages 331–40 in *Biblical and Near Eastern Essays: Studies in Honour of Kevin J. Cathcart*. Edited by C. McCarthy and J. F. Healey. JSOTSup 375. London: T&T Clark, 2004.

"Was There an Exodus?" Pages 23–40 in *In Search of Pre-exilic Israel*. Edited by J. Day. JSOTSup 400. London: T&T Clark, 2004.

"Some Uses of Writing in Ancient Israel in the Light of Recently Published Inscriptions." Pages 155–74 in *Writing in Ancient Near Eastern Society: Festschrift for A. R. Millard*. Edited by P. Bienkowski, C. Mee, and E. Slater. LHBOTS 426. London: T&T Clark, 2005.

"'God' in Old Testament Theology." Pages 175–94 in *Congress Volume: Leiden 2004*. Edited by A. Lemaire. VTSup 109. Leiden: Brill, 2006.

"The Contribution of the Palestine Exploration Fund to Research on the Holy Land." Pages 53–64 in *Palaestina exploranda: Studien zur Erforschung Palästinas im 19. und 20. Jahrhundert anlässlich des 125jährigen Bestehens des Deutschen Vereins zur Erforschung Palästinas*. Edited by U. Hübner. ADPV 34. Wiesbaden: Harrassowitz, 2006.

"The Exegesis of the Name of God in Exodus." Pages 139–56 in *The God of Israel: Studies of an Inimitable Deity*. Edited by R. P. Gordon. UCOP 64. Cambridge: Cambridge University Press, 2007.

"Leopold Schweich and his Family." *British Academy Review* 12 (January 2009): 53–57.

"The Transition from Genesis to Exodus." Pages 59–78 in *Genesis, Isaiah and Psalms: A Festschrift to Honour Professor John Emerton for his Eightieth Birthday*. Edited by K. J. Dell, G. Davies, and Y. V. Koh. VTSup 135. Leiden: Brill, 2010.

"The Ethics of Friendship in Wisdom Literature." Pages 135–50 in *Ethical and Unethical in the Old Testament: God and Humans in Dialogue*. Edited by K. J. Dell. LHBOTS 528. London: T&T Clark, 2010.

Forthcoming:

"The Friendship of Jonathan and David." In a Festschrift edited by G. A. Khan and D. Lipton. 2011.

"The Reception of Gesenius' Dictionary in England." In *Gesenius Bicentenary Conference Volume*. Edited by S. Schorch. 2011.

"Dividing Up the Text of the Pentateuch: Some Remarks on the Jewish Tradition." In *Leshon limmudim*, a Festschrift edited by D. A. Baer and R. P. Gordon. 2011/2012.

"The Beginnings of Biblical Archaeology." In a Festschrift edited by M. J. Boda and I. W. Provan. 2011/2012.

D. Dictionary Articles, etc.

"Abarim," "Abel," "Bene-jaakan," "Dedan," "Dizahab," "Ebal (Mount)," "Eleazar," "Eshcol," "Gudgodah," "Kenath," "Marah," "Massah," "Oaths," "Shittim," "Socoh," "Zamzummim," and "Zedad." Pages 2, 3, 184, 380, 392, 404, 435, 477, 595, 847–48, 945, 961, 1105–6, 1446, 1468, 1672–73, and 1679 in *The Illustrated Bible Dictionary.* Edited by J. D. Douglas, N. Hillyer, F. F. Bruce, et al. 3 vols. Leicester: Inter-Varsity Press, 1980.

"Exodus and the Wanderings" (map and text). Pages 56–57 in *The Times Atlas of the Bible.* Edited by J. B. Pritchard. London: Times Books, 1987.

"Sinai, Mount," and "Wilderness Wanderings." Pages 47–49 and 912–14 in vol. 6 of *The Anchor Bible Dictionary.* Edited by David Noel Freedman. 6 vols. New York: Doubleday, 1992.

"Megiddo." Pages 47–48 in vol. 21 of *The Dictionary of Art.* Edited by J. Turner. 34 vols. London: Macmillan, 1996.

"Exodus." Pages 228–29 in *The Oxford Companion to Christian Thought.* Edited by A. Hastings. Oxford: Oxford University Press, 2000.

E. Longer Reviews

D. Hagner, *The Use of the Old and New Testaments in Clement of Rome. JTS* NS 28 (1977): 170–76.

H. Cazelles, *A la recherche de Moïse. JTS* NS 31 (1980): 113–16.

K.Galling, *Textbuch zur Geschichte Israels*; S. I. L. Norin, *Er spaltete das Meer*; and H. Valentin, *Aaron. VT* 31 (1981): 109–20.

U. Koppel, *Das deuteronomistische Geschichtswerk und seine Quellen. VT* 31 (1981): 498–99.

R. North, *A History of Biblical Map-Making. VT* 32 (1982): 368–71.

A. G. Auld, *Joshua, Moses and the Land. JTS* NS 33 (1982): 209–13.

H.-P. Müller, *Das Hiobproblem: Seine Stellung und Entstehung im alten Orient und im Alten Testament. VT* 33 (1983): 366–68.

R. E. Friedman, *The Exile and Biblical Narrative. JTS* NS 34 (1983): 222–26.

O. Camponovo, *Königtum, Königsherrschaft und Reich Gottes in den frühjüdischen Schriften. JTS* NS 37 (1986): 505–6.

J. H. Tigay, *You Shall Have No Other Gods. JTS* NS 40 (1989): 143–46.

R. B. Coote and K. W. Whitelam, *The Emergence of Early Israel in Historical Perspective*. *JTS* NS 41 (1990): 129–31.

Y. Yadin et al., *Hazor III–IV: Text*. *BO* 52 (1994): 151–53.

J. Renz and W. Röllig, *Handbuch der althebräischen Epigraphik*, vols. 1, 2/1 and 3. *JSS* 44 (1999): 112–15.

M. Vervenne, ed., *Studies in the Book of Exodus*. *JTS* NS 50 (1999): 631–33.

J. C. Gertz, *Tradition und Redaktion in der Exoduserzählung*. *JTS* NS 53 (2002): 571–75.

E. Stern, *The Archaeology of the Land of the Bible*. Volume 2, *The Assyrian, Babylonian and Persian Periods*. *JTS* NS 55 (2004): 162–65.

J. C. Gertz, K. Schmid, and M. Witte, eds., *Abschied vom Jahwisten: Die Komposition des Hexateuch in der jüngsten Diskussion*. *BO* 62 (2005): 315–17.

J. Renz and W. Röllig, *Handbuch der althebräischen Epigraphik*, vol. 2/2. *JSS* 52 (2007): 141–43.

S. L. Gogel, *A Grammar of Epigraphic Hebrew*. *JNES* 66 (2007): 227–29.

J. Van Seters, *A Law Book for the Diaspora*. *JTS* NS 59 (2008): 214–16.

M. S. Smith, *The Origins of Biblical Monotheism*. *JTS* NS 59 (2008): 208–10.

The Contribution by Graham Davies to Old Testament Studies*

J. A. EMERTON

The following description of the contribution made by the publications of Graham Davies to Old Testament studies is intended to be read alongside the list of his books and articles printed on the immediately preceding pages, where full bibliographical information will be found.

It is impossible within the limits of the present article to consider all his publications, but it is hoped that the article will give a clear and adequate account of the substantial contribution made by him to biblical and related subjects. His earlier publications, on which his later work is founded, will be sketched in greater detail than his more recent books and articles.

Davies's first publications arose from his work as a research student at Cambridge. His book, *The Way of the Wilderness* (1979), is a revised version of Part 2 of his PhD dissertation.[1] It is a study of Num 33:1–49 and related passages in the Pentateuch (especially Num 21:12–20 and Deut 10:6–7) concerned with itineraries of the wanderings of the Israelites in the Sinai peninsula under the leadership of Moses. The passages discussed "belong, from the point of view of their form, to a widely attested literary genre of the ancient world, which survives mainly in official documents," and this way of presenting a route was probably "borrowed . . . from the repertoire of the archives of the Israelite royal court."[2]

Chapters are devoted to the Jewish interpretations of the relevant passages in Greek and also in Hebrew and Aramaic, to Christian interpretations, and to interpretations in Arabic. Davies correctly insists that "the history of the tradition (or rather, traditions) of interpretation" deserves attention "as a subject in its own right," for "[i]t is only when the tradition and its own processes of development have been investigated that its value for a modern historical (or historico-geographical)

---

*　　I should like to thank the Revd Brian Mastin for reading a draft of this article and making a number of helpful suggestions.

1　　Davies, *The Way of the Wilderness*, vi.

2　　Davies, *The Way of the Wilderness*, 1.

inquiry can be adequately assessed."[3] This is followed by an investigation of what lay behind the written traditions. The material is not all to
be treated as derived from the same source, although itinerary routes
that parallel Num 33:1–49 (apart from those belonging to the Priestly
writing) were probably taken from it. The itinerary routes were incorporated into the Sinai narratives most likely by a Deuteronomistic
redactor, and places now named in the individual episodes cannot confidently be located by references in the stories. The itineraries are to be
regarded as routes, and not as lists of places visited by the Israelites.
They normally give a complete account of the route and the distance to
be covered by each day's journey between two places, and periods of
time beyond a single day are not to be envisaged except where support
for the idea is found in the text. In a further chapter, Davies considers
the locations of key points on the routes: Mount Sinai, whose traditional identification with Jebel Musa is thought by Davies to be
"approximately correct";[4] and Yam Suf, that is, "the Gulfs of Suez and
Akaba, but not . . . separate stretches of water further . . . north."[5] The
word *sûp* "refers to some kind of vegetation," but does not always
mean "reeds," which "do not grow in either of the gulfs."[6] As is now
generally recognized, Kadesh is located "at or near Ain Qadeis."[7]
Attention is paid to the statement in Deut 1:2 that "It is eleven days'
journey from Horeb by way of Mount Seir to Kadesh-barnea." The
various routes in the Sinai peninsula are listed and described, and their
relevance to biblical passages is assessed. The theory of J. Koenig that
Sinai is to be identified with Hala'l-Bedr in north-west Arabia is discussed and rejected. The book is rightly described by John R. Bartlett
elsewhere in this Festschrift as "an indispensable resource for research
into this area of Old Testament topography."

A number of other articles by Davies on the same or related subjects were published in 1972, 1974, and 1979, and he has returned to
such questions in later publications. An article in 1983 discusses the
place of the itineraries in the composition of the Pentateuch. Davies
begins by referring to G. W. Coats's argument that notes of departure
and arrival in the wilderness narratives "constitute an important structural element" in the Pentateuch.[8] He comments that relatively few of
the notes are to be ascribed to the Priestly source, and argues that most

---

3   Davies, *The Way of the Wilderness*, 2.
4   Davies, *The Way of the Wilderness*, 69.
5   Davies, *The Way of the Wilderness*, 74.
6   Davies, *The Way of the Wilderness*, 71, 74.
7   Davies, *The Way of the Wilderness*, 74.
8   Davies, "The Wilderness Itineraries and the Composition of the Pentateuch," 1.

of the non-P material is derived from Num 33:1–49. The itinerary notes were inserted by the Deuteronomistic redactor to link the various narratives in the form of a journey. The motive for turning the traditions into a journey was to make them fresh presentations of the nation's "divinely directed origins" as a "contribution to the task of restoring the morale of the Judaean people, both in Palestine and in the Diaspora, as they were encouraged by others to expect a new Exodus and a new entry into the land of promise."[9]

The bearing of recent archaeological research on the wilderness itineraries is examined by Davies in 1990, with special reference to two theories. The first is the association of the Israelite crossing of the sea with Lake Sirbonis on the northern coast of Egypt on the Mediterranean, to the east of Port Said. This forms part of a theory that has attracted some writers since it was expounded by Otto Eissfeldt in 1932; and it was already discussed by Davies in his book of 1979. In this later article Davies continues to reject the theory, noting, among other things, that the region was not geologically stable at the time, and that it is uncertain whether Lake Sirbonis existed in its present form at the supposed time of the exodus.

The second theory examined by Davies is the identification proposed by E. Anati of Mount Sinai with Har Karkom between Kadesh-barnea and Eilat, against which Davies advances strong arguments. Finally, Davies contributes an account of the wilderness wanderings and an article on Mount Sinai in *The Anchor Bible Dictionary* in 1992.

Davies's earlier work was not confined to the study of the Sinai peninsula and Israelite traditions of the wilderness wanderings. An article in 1978 discussed the place of historiography in apocalyptic. Apocalyptic thinking was not concerned only with the future. The "preoccupation of the apocalyptic writers with historiography is a major element of their activity whose neglect leads to a distorted picture of them being drawn."[10] This interest in Old Testament theology is a further dimension to his work, which will be met again in some of his later publications.

The publications arising from the work of Davies as a research student and young lecturer cover a range of subjects. His research centred on passages in Exodus and Numbers, but touched on other parts of the Pentateuch and the remainder of the Old Testament, and even extended to apocalyptic. Attention was paid to the ancient versions and to Jewish sources in Greek and Semitic languages, to Christian writers,

---

9   Davies, "The Wilderness Itineraries and the Composition of the Pentateuch," 13.
10   Davies, "Apocalyptic and Historiography," 15.

and to geographical matters. In addition he showed his ability to mar-
shal evidence, to see the weakness of some arguments and to develop
positive arguments, and to present his material clearly. Such expertise
and skills of presentation were to be extended and further developed in
the future.

The work of archaeologists is mentioned from time to time by
Davies in his book of 1979 and related publications, and it was to play
an important part in his future work. His interest in Biblical Archaeology, indeed, existed even before he became a research student. He
chose to study the subject while reading for the Final Honour School of
Theology at Oxford, and was fortunate enough to have as his tutor
Kathleen Kenyon, one of the most distinguished British archaeologists
to work in Palestine. It was not until some years later that he was able
to learn in the field more about archaeology in Israel while working
with Yohanan Aharoni and David Ussishkin.

Davies's second book (1986) was a study of Megiddo, which
appeared in the series Cities of the Biblical World, of which he was
editor. The first chapter discusses the identification of the site of Tell el-
Mutesellim with that of the city. Incidentally, Bienkowski, in a review
of Davies's book, notes that he does not mention in the book who first
made the identification, but that he has supplied the information to
Bienkowski and has agreed to its publication in the review. The person
responsible "seems to be C. W. M. van de Velde" in 1858.[11] Davies's
second chapter writes of the first excavation of the site by Gottlieb
Schumacher in the early twentieth century, and then the longer period
of work there in the 1920s and 1930s by the Oriental Institute of Chicago. It is characteristic of the thoroughness of Davies as a scholar that
he travelled to Chicago to study unpublished notes on the archaeological work. Further work was done by Yigael Yadin and others from the
Hebrew University of Jerusalem in the 1960s and 1970s.

The remaining chapters examine in turn the earliest settlements on
the site, Canaanite Megiddo, Israelite Megiddo, and finally Megiddo
under the Persians and afterwards. This book provides a clear and
well-informed record of the results of archaeological work in Megiddo,
and of the history of the city. Moreover, Bienkowski comments that,
though the book "is aimed primarily at non-specialists," it contains
some new suggestions which "are stimulating and offer fresh
insights."[12]

---

11   Piotr Bienkowski, review of G. I. Davies, Megiddo, PEQ 120 (1988): 150–51 (150).
12   Bienkowski, review of G. I. Davies, Megiddo, 150–51.

One of the questions arising from the excavations at Megiddo is discussed by Davies in an article in 1988. The Chicago archaeologists working at Megiddo in 1930 identified the remains of certain buildings with stalls in which horses for Solomon's chariots were kept. However, Yadin's work on the sites led him to conclude that they belonged to the age of Omri and Ahab in the ninth century, not to that of Solomon in the tenth. J. B. Pritchard argued in 1970 that buildings on these sites would not have been suitable as stables for horses, and even claimed that "the very idea that stables were used at all in the ancient Near East was an unproved assumption."[13] The fact that similar buildings at Tell es-Seba were found to be stacked with pottery appeared to favour the view that the buildings in Megiddo were storehouses, rather than stables. Yadin responded that there was archaeological evidence that stables were used in the ancient Near East, and later J. S. Holladay produced both literary and archaeological evidence for stables. There must have been stables at Megiddo, and the only question is which of the excavated sites best fits the requirements. Holladay also refuted Pritchard's arguments that the use of the sites at Megiddo as stables would not have been a practical possibility. "The Megiddo buildings of Stratum IV were very likely stables after all."[14] Still, Yadin had shown that the sites for the stables belonged to the ninth century, not the tenth. Davies asks, however, whether they were preceded by buildings of the tenth century. He argues on the basis of the excavation reports in Chicago which, as noted above, he had studied, that there is evidence that the buildings of the ninth century were preceded by buildings of the tenth. "Although the evidence is unavoidably fragmentary . . . it is sufficient, I believe, to establish with a high degree of probability that Solomon did indeed have stables at Megiddo."[15]

Another article (1989) by Davies is relevant to Megiddo, although he believes that 1 Kgs 5:6 [4:26] should be interpreted in a different way from what has been customary. The RSV, as is usual in English translations, understands the verse to say "Solomon also had forty thousand stalls of horses (ʾurwôt sûsîm) for his chariots, and twelve thousand horsemen" (presumably as crew for the chariots). The corresponding verse in 2 Chr 9:25 is somewhat different. It says that "Solomon had four thousand stalls for horses and chariots, and twelve thousand horsemen, whom he stationed in the chariot cities and with the king in Jerusalem." The figure of four thousand stalls has seemed to a number of commentators to be more probable than forty thousand, and its

---

13 Davies, "Solomonic Stables at Megiddo after all?", 130.
14 Davies, "Solomonic Stables at Megiddo after all?", 132.
15 Davies, "Solomonic Stables at Megiddo after all?", 140.

relation to twelve thousand men points to each chariot having a crew of three. On the other hand, it has seemed strange to speak of stalls for chariots as well as for horses. A Hebrew word for "stall," which has long been recognized here, is cognate with Akkadian *urû*, which has that meaning as well as several others. The same meaning fits 2 Chr 32:28, where it appears in the phrase "stalls for all kinds of cattle" (RSV). W. von Soden believes that the meaning "stallion" in Akkadian is primary in relation to another meaning of the noun, namely, "a team (of horses)." Davies, however, believes that "it is more probable that the meaning 'team' should be seen as a secondary development from the meaning 'stall, stable, manger.'"[16] He also discusses the ancient versions of the Hebrew Bible for the relevant verses. His discussion leads him to conclude that 1 Kgs 5:6 [4:26] originally read "four thousand" and referred, not to stalls, but to teams of horses, each with a crew of three men to each chariot. In 2 Chr 32:28, however, the meaning "stalls" fits the context and reflects another meaning of the Akkadian cognate. 1 Kings 5:6, where it is understood as a reference to teams of horses, is compared by Davies to well-attested Assyrian horse-lists.

Two articles by Davies in 1982 and 1985 defend the identification of Lachish with Tell ed-Duweir against G. W. Ahlström's challenge, and point out that the challenge overlooks the discussion by K. Elliger in 1934. Davies's view has since continued to prevail.

The work of British archaeologists in Palestine especially since 1900 is surveyed by Davies in 1988, soon to be followed by other studies in the history of archaeological work. It is not surprising that he was invited to become the editor of the *Palestine Exploration Quarterly*, a task which he performed with the assistance of several scholars. His concise summary of the contribution of the Palestine Exploration Fund to research on the Holy Land between 1865 and 2002 was published as an article in 2006.

An important series of twentieth-century monographs on Palestinian archaeology, but also on other kindred subjects, was based on the Schweich Lectures delivered under the auspices of the British Academy. The centenary of the first lecture was celebrated by the Academy in 2008 in a lecture delivered by Graham Davies, himself a Fellow of the Academy. This account of the founder and the circumstances of the foundation, and the early years of its series, is to be published in the form of a book, but a short account of the subject matter of the lecture was published in an article in 2009.

---

16   Davies, "ʾUrwōt in 1 Kings 5:6 (EVV. 4:26)," 35.

One of the valuable results of Palestinian archaeology has been the discovery of inscriptions, and a major contribution to Hebrew and biblical studies has been *Ancient Hebrew Inscriptions: Corpus and Concordance* (1991), followed in 2004 by a further volume which added another 750 inscriptions, most of which had been published for the first time in the previous ten years. This work, prepared by Davies with the assistance of several scholars, aimed to publish, as far as possible, all Hebrew inscriptions known to have been written before 200 BC. The introduction to the first volume comments on some of the problems facing the compilers, such as deciding which inscriptions whose Palestinian provenance is unknown are in Hebrew, and which are in a closely related language, and which way of reading a text should be adopted when opinions are divided. The Hebrew text is printed in transliteration, and the inscriptions are arranged according to the date of discovery wherever possible. The concordance facilitates study of the inscriptions and is an invaluable help in assessing their contribution to our understanding of the Hebrew language. In the concordance the nature of the words is defined: for example, *adv.* = adverb; *DN* = divine name; *LN* = place-name (local name).

Davies is the author of a number of articles about inscriptions; for example, two notes on the Samaria ostraca (1990); "The Use and Non-use of the Particle *'et* in Hebrew Inscriptions" (1991); and "A Samaritan Inscription with an Expanded Text of the Shema'" (1999). He also translated into English from the Dutch a book by K. A. D. Smelik: *Writings from Ancient Israel* (1991).

It was stated in the second paragraph of the present article that the more recent publications of Graham Davies would be considered in less detail than his earlier publications (though much more could have been written about them). His scholarly achievements have been traced from his time as a research student until he became an established scholar with an international standing. The range of his scholarly interests has been amply illustrated in what has already been said, and the remainder of this article will be highly selective.

Two books on the prophet Hosea by Davies were published in 1992 and 1993. The first of these books is a commentary in the New Century Bible series. The second is in the Old Testament Guides series, and is only 122 pages long. This series is intended to help students to understand the composition and the subject matter of individual Old Testament books, and to learn the principal questions that arise in scholarly study. Both books serve their purpose well, and the latter acts as a supplement to the former. According to Davies, Gomer, in Hosea 1, who may not have been Hosea's wife, was already a prostitute, and she symbolizes "the improper association of Israel with Baal." On the other hand, Hosea 3 is about a different woman, who was also sexually promiscuous, and the prophet's loving her "stands for Yahweh's seeking out of faithless Israel."[17]

The book of Exodus has had a special interest for Davies since his work on the wilderness wanderings. He has for some time been preparing to write a volume on it for the International Critical Commentary series, and his studies on the subject have led to a number of articles. He suggested in 1974 that *pĕdūt* in Exod 8:19[23] should be emended to **prdt*, "separation." In 1982 he discussed "A Fragment of an Early Recension of the Greek Exodus," and in 1996 he assessed the work on the composition of Exodus by Erhard Blum, who has suggested an analysis of the Pentateuch that differs from the familiar Graf-Wellhausen analysis. A further assessment of Blum's work was offered by Davies in the following year. He recognizes Blum's great ability as a scholar, but advances some critical questions about his work. The theology of the book of Exodus is discussed in 2000, and in 2004 Davies offered a generally positive answer to the question, "Was there an Exodus?"

A closely-reasoned study of the exegesis of the divine name in Exodus (2007) considers three passages. First, 34:5–8, in which there "are no major text-critical problems," is examined, and it is maintained that qr° + *b* here means, not "to call upon," but "to make a declaration about," and that Yahweh is the speaker.[18] The possibility of a liturgical origin is considered. The suggestions that it may be an original part of the J source or that it is a later addition are considered, but the question is left open. Second, Exod 6:2–8 comes from the Priestly source, which holds that the name Yahweh was previously unknown to Israel, and the claim that it is compatible with the view that the divine name was already known is refuted. The passage combines "a theology of divine action with the theology of divine presence that is evident later in Exodus."[19] Third, Exod 3:13–15 with *'ehyeh 'ăšer 'ehyeh* is examined. The theory that the verb was originally *'ahyeh* and was understood in a causative sense is not accepted, nor is the view that the name Yahweh originally meant "something like 'Creator.'"[20] Finally, the three passages are compared with others in Exodus, and there is an appendix on the history of the interpretation of Exod 3:13–15 in both the ancient

---

17   Davies, *Hosea* (1993), 90.
18   Davies, "The Exegesis of the Divine Name in Exodus," 143.
19   Davies, "The Exegesis of the Divine Name in Exodus," 147.
20   Davies, "The Exegesis of the Divine Name in Exodus," 149.

versions and sixteenth- and seventeenth-century translations as well as more modern translations.

A further discussion of "God" in Old Testament theology was read by Davies at the Congress of the International Organization for the Study of the Old Testament which was held at Leiden in 2004 (2006). Davies discusses the use of different words for "God" (ʾēl, ʾĕlōah, and ʾĕlōhîm), and their significance.

Articles on a range of subjects may be further illustrated. In 1995, for example, he discussed the disputed question "Were there Schools in Ancient Israel?" He concluded that "[f]ormal instruction may only have been given in the capital cities and the administrative centres that were dependent on them. Even this may only have been on a limited scale until the eighth century."[21] There have also been articles on individual verses and some on Christian interpreters of the Old Testament, and even a translation from the Latin of a treatise by John Calvin, one of Davies's rare publications outside the field of Old Testament studies.

It is to that field that he has made a substantial and a varied contribution.

---

21   Davies, "Were there Schools in Ancient Israel?", 210.

Part I

Archaeology

Treasures of Merenptah in the Karnak Temple at Luxor

The Record of the Walls of the Cour de la Cachette*

JAMES ATWELL

In January 2003 I was fortunate that my companion on a visit to the great Karnak Temple at Luxor was Graham Davies. Graham took me through the massive Hyperstyle Hall and then guided me to the external west wall of the Cour de la Cachette. It is an unprepossessing, rather neglected, corner of the temple where the dust and the sand blow around fallen blocks of stone. We looked at a wall that had lost the top courses of its masonry in a rather haphazard way, and seemed to contain a jumble of partly-faded and damaged reliefs. Graham pointed to one of them and said: "That may be the earliest known picture of the Israelites." He had enabled the stones to speak. Remembering the wonder of that moment, it is a privilege to dedicate this short essay to him with enormous appreciation of a friendship that has lasted over several decades and opened for me many doors of understanding.

What are those reliefs that we were gazing at? What is their significance? A central formal inscription, partly mutilated, records the peace treaty drawn up between Ramesses II and the Hittite King Hattusilis III in 1259 BC after a long period of warfare between Egypt and the Hittite Empire. It had seemed to define the significance of the tableaux that surrounded it and present a likely context. However, Yurco, while working at Luxor in 1976/77 with the University of Chicago's Epigraphic Survey, studied these reliefs and the accompanying hieroglyphic inscriptions. In particular, he investigated the cartouches attached to the murals. Rather to his surprise "it became clear that Merenptah was the pharaoh originally named in the cartouches, and

* The editors and the author of this article are grateful to Professor K. A. Kitchen for permission to reproduce four passages from his *Ramesside Inscriptions: Historical and Biographical*, vol. 4 (Oxford: Blackwell, 1982) (= *KRI*).

that Ramesses II was not named in them at all."[1] They had subsequently been usurped by Merenptah's son and eventual successor, Seti II.[2] This is confirmed by Kitchen.[3] Wall space largely unused by the long-lived Ramesses II[4] was available to his thirteenth son and successor, who in turn wished to have his achievements remembered before heaven.

Cartouches of Merenptah from the Victory Stela (*KRI* 4:13)

If these murals are to be associated with Merenptah, then they are to be interpreted primarily not by comparison with other texts from the reign of Ramesses II, but in conjunction with Merenptah's nearby legacy on the east interior wall of the Cour de la Cachette, which also, by the quirk of circumstances, is close by another copy of the Hittite Peace Treaty. The clutch of records on the walls of the Cour de la Cachette associated with Merenptah are threefold. First, there are the reliefs on the external wall already noted. Second, there is the Great Karnak Inscription on the east internal wall.[5] This relates to the Pharaoh's repulsion and defeat of the Libyan incursion into the Delta. Thirdly, there is, south of the inscription just identified, a fragmentary copy of the Victory Stela, which again celebrates Merenptah's victory over the Libyans, but sets it in a greater context in the final poetic lines. Those final lines, complete in the original text, name "Israel," and so have often won the whole inscription the name of the Israel Stela. The original was found in 1896 by Flinders Petrie in Merenptah's Mortuary

---

1   Frank J. Yurco, "Merenptah's Canaanite Campaign," *JARCE* 23 (1986): 189–215 (196).

2   Yurco, "Merenptah's Canaanite Campaign," 196–99; idem, "3,200-Year-Old Picture of Israelites Found in Egypt," *BAR* 16/5 (1990): 20–38 (22, 24–25).

3   K. A. Kitchen, review of Hourig Sourouzian, *Les monuments du roi Merenptah*, *JEA* 79 (1993): 303–6 (304).

4   Yurco, "Picture of Israelites," 26. Traces of a not-completely-erased relief of the Battle of Kadesh are visible under the scenes to the left (north) of the Peace Treaty on the outer wall of the Cour de la Cachette.

5   *KRI* 4:2–12; Colleen Manassa, *The Great Karnak Inscription of Merneptah: Grand Strategy in the 13th Century BC* (Yale Egyptological Studies 5; New Haven, Conn.: Yale Egyptological Seminar, 2003), 154–69.

Temple on the West Bank of Thebes and is now in the Cairo Museum.[6] The Stela records the first mention of Israel in history, and the only mention in Egyptian antiquity. These three texts inform each other.

We must consider first the Great Karnak Inscription. It consists of 79 vertical lines of which, unfortunately, the top third is missing. It is written within the conventions of its period. Scribes have often been blamed for grammatical errors, but the reality is:

> As with most, if not all, historical texts of the Ramesside Period, the Karnak Inscription is a complex mixture of Middle Egyptian, Late Egyptian, and transitional forms peculiar to the corpora of "late" Middle Egyptian.[7]

The text bears witness to the most significant crisis of Merenptah's reign, a crisis he saw off, but which did not bode well for the future. The Libyans were set to return, and the Sea Peoples, who on this occasion were perhaps Libyan mercenaries,[8] were eventually to ring down the curtain on the settled Bronze Age status quo of the ancient Near Eastern Mediterranean world.

The inscription relates that in 1208 BC (Merenptah, year 5), the Libyan chief of the Rebu, "Merey, Son of Dedy," allied with the Sea Peoples, had entered the Delta "at the fields of Perire" (line 15). That Merey had come to stay is clear from the record: "he bringing his wife, his children . . ." (line 14). Although it is not mentioned here, the Libyan invasion seems to have been co-ordinated with a Nubian attack from the south, as the report of the latter was received only two days before the confrontation with Merey, according to an additional source known as the Amada Stela.[9] There was a real crisis that confronted Merenptah.

Within fourteen days of the intelligence having reached the Pharaoh, the army was summoned, and, equally important, divine sanction was given by oracle and by dream. "The army of His Majesty together with his chariotry went forth" (line 32). After a battle lasting six hours, the enemy fled, leaving everything behind. The official report is made to the Palace: "The enemy Merey has gone. It is because of his baseness that his limbs fled, having passed by me deep in the night" (line 41). The inscription accurately records the booty, evidence of the scribal Civil Service employed to capture the military detail. The number of slain was recorded in the haul of 6,359 uncircumcised phalli and, in addition, from the Libyans' allies, 2,362 severed hands. These were

---

6   *KRI* 4:12–19. The text is laid out in parallel for the Karnak Stela and the Cairo Stela (Catalogue 34025 verso).

7   Manassa, *Great Karnak Inscription*, 4.

8   Manassa, *Great Karnak Inscription*, 3.

9   *KRI* 4:34 lines 5–7 (Temple of Amada, Nubia).

gathered not only as an accurate accounting device, but also as an offering to the Egyptian gods. Other trophies accurately enumerated included swords, chariots, silver drinking vessels, cattle, and goats. "The entire land was rejoicing to heaven" (line 47). However, Merenptah was taking no risks for the future; he intended a lesson for those who threatened the royal order. Captured Libyans were impaled south of Memphis.[10]

The inscription is far from being a prosaic military record. It is cast as a celebration of Merenptah's kingship in which, as the Son of Re, he has a cosmic role to overcome disorder and establish order (ma'at). Merey is, therefore, wretched and despicable as the disturber of cosmic order and enemy of the good. Merenptah's victory has a global context.

There is some evidence from the Great Karnak Inscription that the theologically global implications of Merenptah's triumph were also worked out in a foreign policy that was more strategic than simply responding to a single crisis. The Battle of Perire may have been for Merenptah what Kadesh had been for his father, but it was part of a greater plan for Egyptian national security. The Libyan incursion has dominated the historical record of what was a more complex set of circumstances. There is reference in line 24 to foreign aid, which is included as evidence of the positive and life-giving order the king champions: "It is in order to vivify this Hittite land that I have caused grain to be sent in ships." Clearly the Hittites were in trouble, and the Pharaoh perceived it to be to his advantage to have a powerful ally to help maintain order in the face of aggressive incursions which might destabilise the familiar balance of power.

There is evidence from outside the Great Karnak Inscription which throws light on that aid initiative, and sets it in a wider Canaanite context. The bronze sword with Merenptah's cartouche found at Ugarit (Ras Shamra) may indicate more substantial support for that city.[11] Ugarit was part of the trading establishment of the Mediterranean world, and one of those cities at risk from the Sea Peoples. Wainwright has suggested that Merenptah sent mercenaries to Ugarit along with grain to the Hittites.[12]

Line 12 of the Great Karnak Inscription provides a further hook to another circumstance: "[Pharaoh] does not heed hundreds of thousands on the day of battle. Having returned bearing plunder, his army

---

10   *KRI* 4:34 lines 13–14.
11   C. Schaeffer, "Une épée de bronze d'Ugarit (Ras Shamra) portant le cartouche de Mineptah," *REg* 11 (1957): 139–43.
12   G. A. Wainwright, "Meneptaḥ's Aid to the Hittites," *JEA* 46 (1960): 24–28.

proceeded."[13] Where has the army returned from? Clearly, there has been another piece of significant military activity. For that we must consider our next text.

The Victory Stela[14] also celebrates the triumph of Merenptah over the Libyans. It is described by Wilson as "a poetic eulogy of a universally victorious pharaoh."[15] It does, nonetheless, have a core of historical report, but with less detail than the Karnak Inscription. It does not identify the battlefield, report the battle, or record the plunder; nor is Merey named. However, as an "abomination" and "anathematised," he is cast as the antipathy of wholesome order. There is a vivid account of how the Libyans dropped everything, even their water skins, and fled from the battle scene. There is an echo of the watchman's report in the previous inscription in the mention that: "The vile enemy chief of Libya fled all alone in the deep of night."[16]

The Libyans or "Tjehenu" (Cairo Stela Line 11; *KRI* 4:15 lines 9 and 11) here have the determinatives both for foreign land and people.

For the eulogy heaped upon Merenptah we must once again remember the nature and significance of ancient Near Eastern kingship, particularly as it was manifested in Egypt. The king's profile was enormous and next to the gods. His actions and his decisions affected the well-being and security of the nation; responsible kingship guaranteed the order of society, which was perceived as seamless with cosmic order. When Merenptah went to battle it was not simply a matter of military strategy; it was an honouring of the moral grain of the universe. Its abuse by Merey had provoked an ethical recoil:

---

13   Manassa, *Great Karnak Inscription*, 155.
14   J. A. Wilson, "Hymn of Victory of Mer-ne-Ptah (The 'Israel Stela')," *ANET*, 376–78; E. F. Wente, Jr., "The Israel Stela," in *The Literature of Ancient Egypt: An Anthology of Stories, Instructions, Stelae, Autobiographies, and Poetry* (ed. W. K. Simpson; New Haven, Conn.: Yale University Press, 2003), 356–60.
15   Wilson, "Hymn of Victory," 376.
16   Wente, "Israel Stela," 357.

> Ptah said regarding the Libyan enemy,
> "Collect all his crimes to be turned back upon his head. Place him in the hand of Merenptah-hetephimaat that he may cause him to disgorge what he has swallowed like a crocodile."[17]

The Pharaoh, in ridding Egypt of the Libyan threat, is "the Sun who has cleared away the storm cloud that had been over the Black Land and who has caused Egypt to see the rays of the solar disk." Indeed, of the divine Re it may be said: "it is his son who is upon the throne of the sun god." It is in that context we must understand a genuine relief that the king's victory has refreshed the primeval equilibrium of *ma'at* and seen off the threat of disorder: "It is with song that one goes and comes."[18] It is a song which rejoices in universal victory.

The Victory Stela concludes with a poem which makes explicit the clues recognized in the Great Karnak Inscription. That is, the Libyan crisis has to be seen within the context of a greater foreign policy framework that Merenptah was working to achieve. That greater vision, as we have noted, was built into the concept of kingship which relates to parameters that are global and universal. It seems that Merenptah was well aware that security, and its prize which was order, for Egypt involved a vigilance to the east as well as to the west. There has been some debate about the way this poem should be set out.[19] Wente's translation captures its symmetry and balance:

> Princes are prostrate saying, "*Shalom!*"
> Not one lifts up his head among the Nine Bows.
> Now that Tjehenu has come to ruin,
> > Khatti is pacified;
> > The Canaan has been plundered into every sort of woe:
> > > Askalon has been overcome;
> > > Gezer has been captured;
> > > Yanoam is made nonexistent.
> > > Israel is laid waste; his seed is no longer;
> > Khor is become a widow because of Egypt.
> All lands combined, they are at peace.
> Whoever roams about gets subdued
> > by the King of Upper and Lower Egypt, Baenre-miamon;
> > the Son of Re, Merenptah-hetephimaat,
> > given life like Re every day.[20]

---

17 Wente, "Israel Stela," 359.

18 Wente, "Israel Stela," 357, 358, 360.

19 E.g., Michael G. Hasel, *Domination and Resistance: Egyptian Military Activity in the Southern Levant, ca. 1300–1185 B.C.* (Probleme der Ägyptologie 11; Leiden: Brill, 1998), 260–71.

20 Wente, "Israel Stela," 360.

The fact that the first line of the poem uses the Canaanite word *shalom* transliterated directly into hieroglyphs (*š-l-m*) is remarkable.

The Canaanite word *shalom* is transliterated into the hieroglyphic text of the final poem of the Victory Stela (Karnak Version, *KRI* 4:19 line 4)

We have already noted the significance of *ma^cat* for ancient Egypt. It represented "right order" in every layer of society and nature, and had its counterpart in the vocabulary of Canaan,[21] including the associated concept *shalom*. If *ma^cat* represented "right order," the product of respect for *ma^cat* was harmony/*shalom*; that is, peace and prosperity across an ordered universe. *Shalom* cleverly turns attention towards the region of Canaan, as well as, at the same time, asserting that *ma^cat* is universally established by the Pharaoh's action. All have had their crimes turned back upon their own heads, and the world, as Egypt saw it, was as the Creator intended: at peace with itself.

The "Nine Bows" refers to the totality of the traditional enemies of Egypt. The "Tjehenu," that is the Libyans, are mentioned first in the list of those who come to ruin. The primacy of that victory is acknowledged, and its significance balanced with the major power at the opposite end of the geographical spectrum: "Khatti is pacified." That is, the Hittites, who were the recipients of Pharaoh's grain-aid in the Great Karnak Inscription. Next "the Canaan" and "Khor" enclose the four named Palestinian communities. There has been some debate about whether "the Canaan" refers to Palestine and "Khor" to Syria.[22] In this circumstance the two appear to be synonymous, and to act as "bookends" for the enclosed names. The listed names are clearly ranked as of equal significance and represent the key military campaigns that have subdued Palestine: Ashkelon, Gezer, Yanoam, and Israel. The verbs used denote serious punishment: "overcome," "captured," "made nonexistent," and, doubly for Israel, "laid waste" and "his seed is no

---

21   The key to this vocabulary is "righteousness," *ṣedeq*; see H. H. Schmid, *Gerechtigkeit als Weltordnung* (BHT 40; Tübingen: Mohr [Siebeck], 1968).
22   Cf. Hasel, *Domination and Resistance*, 257–60; A. F. Rainey, "Israel in Merenptah's Inscription and Reliefs," *IEJ* 51 (2001): 57–75 (63–64).

longer."[23] Here we have an indication from whence Pharaoh's army had returned "bringing plunder" before confronting the Libyans.

Israel is named with the determinative for foreign people in the Victory Stela
(*KRI* 4:19 line 7)

The flow of the poem next sums up the total situation: "All lands combined, they are at peace." The credit, of course, goes to Egyptian Kingship as manifested by Merenptah. There could not be a clearer indication of the totality of the Pharaoh's foreign policy and the universal order he could claim to have achieved successfully. The poem is a fitting summary of the Victory Stela, setting the Libyan victory within a global context and resonating to the fruit of *ma'at* in world *shalom*.

We may now return to the reliefs on the external west wall of the Cour de la Cachette. At this stage a plan is helpful, and Yurco's numbering of the scenes is given:[24]

North					South
3	(Hittite	4	6	9	10
2	Treaty)	1	5	7	8	(Triumph Scene)

Of the four scenes around the Peace Treaty, scenes 1, 2, and 3 share a single artistic convention. The colossal form of the Pharaoh dominates the representation of the advancing Egyptians on the right of the picture, confronting the fortified city on the left with a battle raging beneath. Scene 1, to the right hand side of the peace treaty on the lower register, has retained its hieroglyphic description: "The vile town which his majesty overcame when it was wicked, Ashkelon."[25] On the right there is a huge representation of the rearing horses of the Pharaoh's chariot team with the Pharaoh, bow drawn, alert and lethal upon his chariot. On the left are the crenellated walls, tower, and gates of Ashkelon. The Egyptians are putting scaling ladders against the walls while the people of the town on top of the walls and tower are praying

---

23 Rainey, "Israel in Merenptah's Inscription," 57–63, dismisses the interpretation of "seed" as "grain."

24 Yurco, "Picture of Israelites," 23.

25 Yurco, "Merenptah's Canaanite Campaign," 208, cf. *KRI* 2:166 lines 2–3.

with hands outstretched to heaven. Two people are dangling children from the top of the tower, which may be a last desperate act of sacrifice (cf. 2 Kgs 3:27), and was certainly a vivid memory recorded. A Canaanite falls headlong from the tower. Beneath the city the infantry are being wiped out at the Egyptian advance, but the archers behind are still holding firm. A Canaanite chariot is in retreat.

Scene 2, continuing in the lower register to the left of the peace treaty, depicts the defeat of another fortified city. In the centre of the picture is a gigantic image of Pharaoh on foot, scimitar raised, seemingly attacking the city single-handed. Behind the Pharaoh a figure identified as Prince Khaemwaset holds the horses of the chariot team. The horses, too, are identified as of the royal stable and named "Beloved of Amun" (Mry-ʾImn). Beneath the Pharaoh's feet are the corpses of the defeated enemy. Beneath the waiting horses archers leave the scene of battle with prisoners of war identified by their ankle-length Canaanite dress.

Scene 3, to the left of the peace treaty upper register, is a snapshot of an animated moment of the mêlée of battle. The rearing horses of the Pharaoh's chariot team frame the carnage of a battle scene beneath. Canaanite infantry are in the process of being dispatched, and a Canaanite soldier on horseback seems to be beckoning the others to flee the scene of devastation. The Pharaoh confronts a crenellated tower and gate. From the battlements, the inhabitants lift up praying hands. People are in various stages of falling headlong from the tower. Despite its damaged state, the tableau still captures in a frighteningly vivid way the very moment when the siege turns in favour of the Egyptians.

Scene 4 may be different in that it does not seem to have the set-piece of the Pharaoh confronting a fortified city. However, interpretation is made difficult because of its fragmented state. The top half and more of the scene is missing as well as the right-hand end. The back legs of the Pharaoh's rearing chariot horses may clearly be discerned, which indicates that, once again, the battle scene was dwarfed by a huge image of the Pharaoh in his chariot, much like scene 3. However, in this instance it seems that the image would virtually reach right across the whole canvas if reconstructed and leave no room for a balancing fortress. Beneath the Pharaoh's horse is a chariot belonging to Egypt's enemies with one horse stumbling and the other looking back. Bodies are strewn along the base of the picture and others are in the process of being added to that number. The forward march of battle continues; the ankles and feet of the infantry are framed by long Canaanite-style robes. Yurco would add to this scene a loose block, found nearby, that fits at the top of a scene. It is the top half of the image of a prince in a chariot fitted with an umbrella-shade. The horses are visible from the neck upwards and the prince controls the reins. He seems to be one of two, as the text refers to an adjacent missing picture, which is identified with the name "Seti," that is Seti-merenptah, the Crown Prince of Merenptah.[26]

Encounter with the four scenes in their original state, even after millennia of weathering, communicates a vibrance which speaks of vivid historical reality. These are not stereotype battle scenes available like rolls of wallpaper to cover any eventuality. The man on horseback fleeing, the children held headlong over the battlement, the Canaanite falling to his doom, the men scaling the city wall with ladders, the citizens imploring the mercy of heaven, all capture an eyewitness record. Clearly the royal scribes who accompanied the army were charged to record a visual image of the triumphs as carefully as their numerate colleagues monitored the booty and the dead. Here we have the fruits of Pharaoh's war correspondents. The record says a great deal for the first-hand intelligence assembled by the Egyptian bureaucracy and the dependability of the information it gathered.

By contrast, the rest of the scenes are more stereotyped.[27] They relate to the binding of captives (scene 5), their collecting and the return to Egypt (scenes 6–9), and a concluding scene (scene 10) now totally missing which has been reconstructed as a triumph scene involving "prisoner smiting" stretching across both registers.[28] Fragments of the latter in a nearby field include one identified by Yurco which contains an image of the Pharaoh, who is clearly Merenptah.[29] It corroborates the evidence from the cartouches. The lower register of these additional scenes is dominated by the captured Shasu (scenes 5, 7, and 8). They were nomadic groups living in Canaan and Sinai. Judging by the inscriptions some had harried the army and others had been "plundered." They receive no mention in the Victory Stela. They can be clearly identified as they wear kilt and turban. In different circumstances they were allowed into Egypt peacefully to water their livestock.[30]

---

26   Yurco, "Merenptah's Canaanite Campaign," 205.

27   Yurco, "Merenptah's Canaanite Campaign," 209.

28   F. Le Saout, "Reconstitution des murs de la Cour de la Cachette," *Cahiers de Karnak VII (1978–1981)* (Paris: Editions Recherche sur les civilisations, 1982): 213–57 (252 pl. IV 4a and b; 257 pl. IX 4c).

29   Yurco, "Picture of Israelites," 26; idem, "Merenptah's Canaanite Campaign," 207 n. 24.

30   J. A. Wilson, "The Report of a Frontier Official," *ANET*, 259.

The interlocking significance of this clutch of Merenptah's records, both written and illustrated, is certainly to establish a holistic perspective on the military activities of his reign. In particular, the scenes on the outer wall rebalance the record. The naming of Ashkelon, the Canaanite long robes, the binding of the Shasu, all turn the spotlight towards Syria-Palestine. They flesh out the stark, yet tantalisingly brief, evidence of the poem at the end of the Victory Stela. The significance of the devastation topped and tailed by "the Canaan" and "Khor" is vividly brought to life. This is no stereotype memory transferred from a previous era. There was a campaign into Canaan during Merenptah's reign, and before the Libyan repulsion in year 5 of that reign. The fact that the dated Victory Stela,[31] which celebrates the Libyan victory, includes the retrospective synopsis of the Palestinian military campaign provides the boundary. The foreign policy concerns of Merenptah's reign looked eastwards as well as westwards. Wilson's scepticism in referring to Merenptah's "real or figurative triumph over Asiatic peoples"[32] has not proved warranted.

Contrary to the evidence, the echoes of scepticism continue to reverberate the scholarly world. Redford, who refers to the "decrepit Merneptah," maintains that "there is absolutely no evidence that Merneptah attacked all these places [in Palestine] during his short reign."[33] It is true that Merenptah must have been in his sixties as Pharaoh, but no one doubts that the Libyan campaign was undertaken under his auspices. Redford also thinks the mention of Prince Khaemwaset, who holds the chariot horses in scene 2, relates the scene to Ramesses II. A well-known son of Ramesses did indeed bear that name. Redford further identifies the name of the horses in the chariot team, "Beloved of Amun," as the favourite team of Ramesses II.[34] These points are answered by Kitchen, who notes that a Prince Khaemwaset II would not necessarily appear in the historical record, and that such names for the chariot span are commonplace "in reign after reign." He suggests that Crown Prince Seti, encountered above in the summary of scene 4, may have led the Palestinian campaign on his father's behalf. That could account for his confidence, that it was quite appropriate to usurp his father's cartouches relating to the Palestinian campaign when he eventually became Seti II.[35]

---

31   Wente, "Israel Stela," 356.
32   Wilson, "Hymn of Victory," 376.
33   D. B. Redford, "The Ashkelon Relief at Karnak and the Israel Stela," *IEJ* 36 (1986): 188–200 (199, 197).
34   Redford, "The Ashkelon Relief," 194–96.
35   Kitchen, review of Hourig Sourouzian, 305.

More recently, Frendo continues to link the Palestinian victories to Ramesses II.[36] That can no longer be sustained in view of the evidence of the scenes on the outer wall of the Cour de la Cachette. The title claimed by Merenptah in the Amada Stela has to be given full credence: "binder of Geza";[37] in that text it balances "vanquisher of Libu." Further evidence of the impact of Merenptah's reign on Palestine, this time in the hill country, is probably to be found in the biblical geographical reference that "the boundary (of Judah) extends from the top of the mountain to the spring of the Waters of Nephtoah" (Josh 15:9; cf. 18:15). The redundant reference to "spring of waters" is explained if the original reading was "the Fountain of Mer-ne-Ptah."[38]

Yurco goes beyond the general identification of the scenes on the outer wall of the Cour de la Cachette as relating to a Palestinian campaign in Merenptah's reign, and identifies the four scenes around the Peace Treaty with the four names contained in the geographical area Canaan/Khor in the Victory Stela poem: Ashkelon, Gezer, Yanoam (in the north of Palestine), and Israel.[39] The genius of Yurco's observation is to note the correspondence between the two records. Both are registers of four significant victories that mark the same campaign. There is a *prima facie* case for expecting consistency between the lists; both are, doubtless, dependent upon the same scribal intelligence travelling with the army on the campaign. The name Ashkelon is identified in both lists. There are two further fortified communities identified in both. Given the evidence of the Amada Stela, one of the additional fortified towns must be Gezer. The case is strengthened by a further crucial parallel observation.

Israel seems to be singled out in a particular way within the list of the four Canaanite communities named in the Victory Stela poem. Each of the communities named is followed by a determinative, that is, a hieroglyphic sign which is not pronounced but helps to define the word it accompanies. Ashkelon, Gezer, and Yanoam are all followed by a throw stick ⌐ (= foreign [country or person]) and three hills ⌒⌒⌒ (= foreign country).[40] By contrast, Israel is followed by a man-woman sign with plural strokes 𓀀𓁐 (= people)[41] and a throw stick ⌐ (= foreign

---

36 Anthony J. Frendo, "Back to Basics: A Holistic Approach to the Problem of the Emergence of Ancient Israel," in *In Search of Pre-exilic Israel* (ed. John Day; JSOTSup 406; London: T&T Clark International, 2004), 41–64 (51).

37 *KRI* 4:33 line 9.

38 Cf. J. A. Wilson, "The Journal of a Frontier Official," *ANET*, 258–59 (258 n. 6).

39 Yurco, "Merenptah's Canaanite Campaign"; idem, "Picture of Israelites."

40 Sir Alan Gardiner, *Egyptian Grammar* (3d ed.; London: Oxford University Press, 1957), 33.

41 Gardiner, *Egyptian Grammar*, 31.

[country or person]). The determinatives attached to Ashkelon, Gezer, and Yanoam are appropriately used to describe foreign city states. They identify an area with territorial boundaries. By contrast, Israel is described not in terms of location, but as an ethnic group. Israel is a people. "The group thus designated might be living on the level of village culture, or could be pastoralists still in the nomadic stage."[42] Israel is distinct in the list as the only one that has not embraced the Canaanite city state way of life but is living outside urban culture.

There is a striking parallel with scene 4 on the outer wall of the Cour de la Cachette. Although only the lower part of the scene remains and it requires careful interpretation, we noted above that it does not seem to have the set-piece of the Pharaoh confronting a fortified city. Pharaoh and his chariot seem to be in the middle of the scene. This representation would fit well with the scenario of a battle in open country-side in a non-urban context. Yurco even identifies the landscape as "with low hills,"[43] which could correspond well with the location of the "Wells of Merenptah." This rural context is a strong indication that the fourth scene should indeed be identified as Israel. It presents a final and persuasive correspondence between the two records. The pieces fit seamlessly.

The correspondence enables Yurco to locate the four scenes around the Peace Treaty; scene 1 (identified by the inscription) as Ashkelon, scene 2 as Gezer, scene 3 as Yanoam, scene 4 as Israel. He does this on the grounds that the text should be read anti-clockwise, and that it works geographically and probably represents the progress of the campaign.[44] Kitchen makes the same identification with different logic, suggesting the text works "outwards" (in this case right to left), and that the military action against first Ashkelon and then Gezer was followed by a confrontation with Israel in the Judean hills near Jerusalem (Wells of Nephtoah) and finally the subduing of Yanoam in the north.[45] Whatever the military strategy, the identifications seem fairly secure, with Ashkelon as the anchor.

Not everyone agrees. Just as Wilson was reticent to endorse the historicity of the campaign into Canaan under Merenptah, he has been cautious as regards the reliability of evidence based on the accuracy of the royal scribes. He refers to "the notorious carelessness of Late-

42   Rainey, "Israel in Merenptah's Inscription," 66.
43   Yurco, "Picture of Israelites," 32.
44   Yurco, "Merenptah's Canaanite Campaign," 199, 206–7.
45   G. Gilmour and K. A. Kitchen, "The Pharaoh Sety II and Egyptian Political Relations with Canaan at the End of the Late Bronze Age" (forthcoming).

Egyptian scribes and several blunders of writing in this stela."[46] This has become received wisdom and tended to influence later verdicts.[47] It must be acknowledged that there can be a variation in the use of the determinatives which could be interpreted as carelessness. The Libyans appear both with and without the people determinative in the Victory Stela.[48] However, the thorough analysis by Kitchen of this Stela does not bear out Wilson's assessment.[49] Kitchen concludes:

> There is no reason whatever to doubt the accuracy and appositeness of the determinative signs used both for the towns in Canaan (Ascalon, Gezer, Yenoam) and for one equally modest group of people (Israel).[50]

A possible grammatical issue with Merenptah's scribes has been identified with the use of the masculine singular suffix (translation "his") with the word "seed" to refer back to a collective noun "Israel."[51] However, if the Egyptian scribe was aware that a people called Israel claimed descent from a single ancestor as "children of Israel" it would make complete sense.[52]

Rainey would rather identify Israel with the Shasu,[53] whom we noted are very evident in the subsequent wall scenes of the military activities in Canaan under Merenptah. In fact, Shasu is a generic term for a varied collection of nomadic groups, and cannot simply be equated with Israel. There is no ready identification of Israel with any particular Shasu group depicted in the scenes on the outer wall of the Cour de la Cachette. As we commented above, these scenes in any case seem to be less specific and more stereotyped than scenes 1–4.

The fact is that Israel has turned up in this evidence named alongside Canaanite cities, with Canaanite dress and even in possession of a chariot. The latter indicates reasonable prosperity at this time, and the Canaanite clothing confirms archaeological evidence that settlements in

---

46   Wilson, "Hymn of Victory," 378 n. 18.
47   Cf. H. Emily Stein, "The Israel Stele," *Papers for Discussion Presented by the Department of Egyptology, the Hebrew University, Jerusalem, 1981–1982*, vol. 1 (ed. Sarah Groll and H. Emily Stein; Jerusalem: Hebrew University, 1982), 156–65 (157).
48   *KRI* 4:15 lines 9, 11, compared with 4:19 line 3.
49   K. A. Kitchen, "The Physical Text of Merenptah's Victory Hymn (The 'Israel Stela')," *JSSEA* 24 (1994 [published 1997]): 71–76 (75): "A rate of error at most of 0.85% but really of only a significant 0.21% (between less than one per cent and less than one-quarter of one per cent) is, frankly, minute; it is totally wrong to think that this text in any way swarms with errors."
50   Kitchen, "The Physical Text," 75–76.
51   W. Spiegelberg, "Zu der Erwähnung Israels in dem Merneptah-Hymnus," *OLZ* 11 (1908): cols. 403–5. He interprets "grain" as harvest rather than seed as in human offspring (col. 404 n. 5), but see above, n. 23.
52   Yurco, "Merenptah's Canaanite Campaign," 211.
53   Rainey, "Israel in Merenptah's Inscription," 74.

the hill country of Palestine show cultural conformity with Canaan.[54] It leaves open whether this is through assimilation or whether the residents of the hill country were disaffected Canaanite migrants, or indeed a mixture of both possibilities. It also leaves open to what extent Israel is to be identified with all or part of the highland settlements and their village culture.

The treasures of Merenptah which we have identified as associated with the walls of the Cour de la Cachette have included the naming of "Israel." We have been able to locate that mention within a vivid and reliable historical context. Its uniqueness makes evaluation of its significance both more difficult and more significant. There is some substance to the deductions that we are now able to draw. We are on firm ground in maintaining that Israel is of sufficient significance to leave its imprint on the wheel of history in the years immediately following the accession of Merenptah to the throne of Egypt in 1212 BC. Already there is evidence of Israel's distinct identity that was robust enough to attract the Pharaoh's attention and punitive military activity. The significance of Israel rated alongside that of moderately-sized city states as were Ashkelon, Gezer, and Yanoam, and was recorded in that context. They were all thought to be of sufficient warrant to number among the Pharaoh's trophies of victory.

Further, Israel was recognized by Egyptian intelligence as different from the city states named alongside it. Israel was identified ethnically rather than geographically, defined not by land or geographical location, but as a people or community. They were "children of Israel," who claimed familial identity. Consequently, their political structure would not have been based on kingship as is the case for Canaanite cities, but there must have been some mutual affiliation which was recognizably coherent. There are indicators that they were not nomads (Shasu), but living at the level of village culture which was at home in the hill country. Further, Israel is compounded from the divine name El, the high god of the Canaanite pantheon. That reflects a pre-Yahwistic phase.

This is a significant amount of information to be able to claim about Israel at the end of the thirteenth century BC. It must be taken seriously by those who would seek to re-evaluate the legacy of ancient Israel and to reassign its origins to a later date.[55] There are still plenty of mysteries

---

54 I. Finkelstein and N. A. Silberman, *The Bible Unearthed: Archaeology's New Vision of Ancient Israel and the Origin of its Sacred Texts* (New York: Free Press, 2001), 118.

55 K. W. Whitelam, *The Invention of Ancient Israel: The Silencing of Palestinian History* (London: Routledge, 1996); T. L. Thompson, *Early History of the Israelite People: From the Written and Archaeological Sources* (SHANE 4; Leiden: Brill, 1992).

to unravel, but the story of Israel has now made its indelible mark on the pages of history.

In continuing beyond the assured conclusions above, further reflection cannot claim the same status. However, an inevitable question arises. If there were an historical Exodus, how does that event relate to the Israel of the Stela? That the question is worth pursuing is suggested by the fact that Yahweh, who became identified with the God of Israel, seems to have come from outside of Canaan. All the indications are that Yahweh is associated with tribes who inhabited the mountainous regions to the south of Palestine.[56] That Yahweh was brought with, and felt to be responsible for, the Exodus migration satisfactorily explains what is otherwise an anachronism.

The reign of Merenptah is surprisingly early to find Israel post-Exodus established and clearly flourishing in Palestine. We have to allow for the Exodus from Egypt, the infusion into the local population in Canaan, and the emergence of Israel from that centrifuge. Could it be that, in the mention on the Stela, Israel is captured at the stage before the Exodus contingent arrived?

We have to take seriously the state to which Israel was reduced under Merenptah — "his seed is no longer." Consequent on that decimation, Israel would have been open to and receptive of a renewing influx that could revitalise its languishing condition. Indeed, that Israel survived Merenptah's punishment at all may be due to the injection of confidence and energy that the Exodus population brought, based upon a sense of divine election. In that case, ironically, one might speculate that as Merenptah or Crown Prince Seti was pounding the Israelites in Palestine, the remnant of Hebrew slaves was escaping Egypt. They had endured bondage under Ramesses II, who was intent on founding the store cities Pi-Ramesse and Pithom. The confusion leading up to the Libyan invasion may well have given them their cue.

---

56   Frendo, "Back to Basics," 51; J. E. Atwell, *The Sources of the Old Testament* (London: T&T Clark International, 2004), 43–44.

Prophetic Speech in the Egyptian Royal Cult[*]

John W. Hilber

Defining Prophecy

Shortly after completing my dissertation in 2004 under Prof. Davies on Assyrian prophecy and the Psalms, he asked me for my opinion on the origin of divine speech in Ramesside texts, which he had been reading in conjunction with his research on Exodus. This essay is the result of a more carefully considered answer to his question, however long delayed! With great admiration I dedicate this essay in his honour.

"Prophecy" is a divine message intuitively received for transmission to a third party.[1] Its intuitive nature distinguishes it from inductive divination (e.g., extispicy).[2] Prophecy also differs from "literary predictive texts," which are not messenger speech, rather compositions of a more historiographical nature (e.g., *Prophecy of Marduk*).[3] DeJong Ellis stresses that prophetic texts are both literary phenomena and "products of cultic or other cultural activity."[4] This essay explores whether certain

---

[*]   I would like to express my appreciation to Daniel Fleming and especially to James Hoffmeier for their helpful comments on an earlier draft of this paper, read at the 2008 Annual Meeting of SBL. Any errors or omissions are solely mine.

1   Manfred Weippert, "Aspekte israelitischer Prophetie im Lichte verwandter Erscheinungen des Alten Orients," in *Ad bene et fideliter seminandum: Festgabe für Karlheinz Deller zum 21. Februar 1987* (ed. Gerlinde Mauer and Ursula Magen; AOAT 220; Kevelaer: Butzon & Bercker, 1988), 287–319 (289–90); idem, "Prophetie im Alten Orient," in *Neues Bibel-Lexikon* (ed. Manfred Görg and Bernhard Lang; 3 vols.; Düsseldorf: Benziger, 1991–2001), 3, cols. 196–200 (197).

2   Martti Nissinen, "Die Relevanz der neuassyrischen Prophetie für die alttestamentliche Forschung," in *Mesopotamica, Ugaritica, Biblica: Festschrift für Kurt Bergerhof zur Vollendung seines 70. Lebensjahres am 7. Mai 1992* (ed. Manfried Dietrich and Oswald Loretz; AOAT 232; Kevelaer: Butzon & Bercker, 1993), 217–58 (221); Martti Nissinen, *References to Prophecy in Neo-Assyrian Sources* (SAAS 7; Helsinki: University of Helsinki Press, 1998), 6.

3   Maria deJong Ellis, "Observations on Mesopotamian Oracles and Prophetic Texts: Literary and Historiographical Considerations," *JCS* 41 (1989): 127–86.

4   DeJong Ellis, "Observations," 160–61.

Egyptian royal texts might qualify as the product of what the ancient
audience would have judged to be prophetic activity.

Defining Egyptian "Prophecy"

Past discussion of Egyptian prophecy has been dominated by comparison with biblical prophecy, with foretelling future events and social
criticism setting the primary criteria for potential Egyptian examples.
Bonnet focused on texts involving future-telling (e.g., *Prophecies of Ner-
ferti*, *Prophecies of the Lamb*) and concluded that the term "prophetic" is
inappropriate, since these texts only record the prognostications of wise
men commanding secret knowledge through magic.[5] Lanczkowski
criticized the exclusive focus on foretelling, arguing that social critique
is equally valid, illustrated by comparison between the *Eloquent Peasant*
and Old Testament texts.[6] In Hermann's exploration of the boundaries
between Israelite and Egyptian prophecy, he searched Egyptian sources
for evidence of a charismatic prophetic class similar to that of the Old
Testament seer and for parallels in literary genre and content, including
texts with social criticism as well as future-telling (e.g., *Prophecies of
Neferti*, *Complaints of Khakheperre-Sonb*, *Eloquent Peasant*).[7] In his view,
none of these texts are prophetic, due to the absence of an authoritative,
charismatic messenger.

Shupak's discussion of Middle Kingdom texts examined those containing either future-telling or ethical admonition.[8] In her assessment,
prose narratives such as *Tale of the Shipwrecked Sailor* or *King Kheops and
the Magicians* offer "evidence of the custom and practice of foretelling
the future in ancient Egypt" but are akin to the genre of legend (like
Elijah and Elisha stories) and quite different from those of the Hebrew
canonical prophets. In addition, verse compositions that only address
social ethics, such as *Eloquent Peasant*, *Complaints of Khakheperre-Sonb*,
and *Dispute Between a Man and His Ba*, resemble biblical prophecy only
in the *theme* of ethical admonition. These, together with texts that
include motifs of both future-telling and social rebuke (*Admonitions of*

---

5   Hans Bonnet, "Prophezeiung," in *RÄR*, 608–9; similarly, Robert Schlichting,
     "Prophetie," in *LÄ* 4:1122–25 (1122).
6   Günter Lanczkowski, *Altägyptischer Prophetismus* (ÄgAbh 4; Wiesbaden: Harras-
     sowitz, 1960), 8–9, 11.
7   Siegfried Herrmann, "Prophetie in Israel und Ägypten: Recht und Grenze eines
     Vergleichs," in *Congress Volume: Bonn 1962* (VTSup 9; Leiden: Brill, 1963), 47–65 (56–
     60, 63–64).
8   Nili Shupak, "Egyptian 'Prophecy' and Biblical Prophecy: Did the Phenomenon of
     Prophecy, in the Biblical Sense, Exist in Ancient Egypt?" *JEOL* 31 (1989–1990): 5–40.

Ipuwer, Prophecies of Neferti), properly belong in the class of wisdom literature.[9] Most important in her analysis is the absence of divine messenger speech and the observation that the element of prediction stems from the employment of magic by priests and sages.[10] While the studies of Ritner and Lloyd suggest that the boundary between magic and intuitive prophecy might be unclear,[11] a consensus remains that these texts originated in a wisdom tradition.

Several Ptolemaic texts have been mentioned above (*The Demotic Chronicle, Prophecy of the Lamb,* and *Prophecy of the Potter*).[12] Like the *Prophecies of Neferti,* these texts utilize prophecy *ex eventu* for political purposes and share many features with apocalyptic literature. The origin and performance setting of these texts is unknown, and, given their late date and possible Hellenistic influence, their contribution to the question of prophetic speech in Egypt before Ptolemaic times is questionable.[13]

In summary, these studies correctly express the expectation that "prophecy" necessitates messenger speech arising from an intuitive consciousness of divine revelation, and none of the Egyptian texts under consideration satisfies this definition. Were it not for the element of foretelling in some of these texts, it seems likely that the question of prophecy might never have arisen.

---

9   More recently defined, "admonitory (or critical) wisdom literature" (Nili Shupak, "The Egyptian 'Prophecy'—A Reconsideration," in *Von reichlich aegyptischem Verstande: Festschrift für Waltraud Guglielmi zum 65. Geburtstag* [ed. Hans-W. Fischer-Elfert and Karol Zibelius-Chen; Wiesbaden: Harrassowitz, 2006], 133–44 [143]).

10 Shupak, "Egyptian 'Prophecy' and Biblical Prophecy," 24, 27. Cf. Bernd Ulrich Schipper, "'Apokalyptik,' 'Messianismus,' 'Prophetie'—Eine Begriffsbestimmung," in *Apokalyptik und Ägypten: Eine kritische Analyse der relevanten Texte aus dem griechisch-römischen Ägypten* (ed. Andreas Blasius and Bernd Ulrich Schipper; OLA 107; Leuven: Peeters, 2002), 21–40 (38).

11 Robert K. Ritner, *The Mechanics of Ancient Egyptian Magical Practice* (SAOC 54; Chicago: The Oriental Institute, 1993), 36–38; Alan B. Lloyd, "Heka, Dreams, and Prophecy in Ancient Egyptian Stories," in *Through a Glass Darkly: Magic, Dreams and Prophecy in Ancient Egypt* (ed. Kasia Szpakowska; Swansea: Classical Press of Wales, 2006), 71–94.

12 For text and commentary, see Didier Devauchelle, "Les Prophéties en Égypte Ancienne," in *Prophéties et oracles, II: En Égypte et en Grèce* (CaESup 89; Paris: Cerf, 1994), 6–30 (6–9, 18–30); H. Felber "Die Demotische Chronik," H.-J. Thissen, "Das Lamm des Bokchoris," L. Koenen with A. Blassius, "Die Apologie des Töpfers an König Amenophis oder das Töpferorakel," and J. F. Quack, "Ein neuer prophetischer Text aus Tebtynis," in Blasius and Schipper, *Apokalyptik und Ägypten:* 65–111, 113–38, 139–87, 253–74.

13 Regarding international influence, see Bernd Ulrich Schipper, "Apokalyptik und Ägypten?—Erkenntnisse und Perspektiven," in Blasius and Schipper, *Apokalyptik und Ägypten,* 277–302 (301–2).

Widening the Search

Nissinen argues that a text be considered "prophetic" when it explicitly mentions a prophet or when there is a quotation or paraphrase of divine words that otherwise can be characterized as prophetic. The *absence* of evidence that other methods of divination are at play is also important.[14] While the presence of first-person divine speech is helpful, this element is also manifest in other non-prophetic genres where divine beings are in conversation (e.g., divine love poetry, city laments, cosmic epics). Introductory speech formulas are important; but since messenger speech is a critical test, one can also search the original setting for a probable performance scenario in which a divine message would be conveyed to a third party.[15]

In the light of these criteria, a class of Egyptian texts have, to the best of my knowledge, been overlooked in previous discussions on Egyptian prophecy. Numerous royal inscriptions feature introductory speech formulas accompanying first-person divine speech with direct address to the king. In either a Mesopotamian or Levantine context, this type of text would be considered of prophetic origin, but Mesopotamian and Levantine contexts also witness prophetic functionaries to whom such texts are easily attributed. The problem with the Egyptian setting is the absence of such clear descriptions. Therefore, the next part of this article explores the Egyptian context for plausible performance scenarios of prophetic speech.

Revelatory Settings

Oracles

The Egyptian custom of consulting gods during bark processions was common.[16] The topics of inquiry included matters of state as well as

---

14   Nissinen, *References to Prophecy*, 9–10.

15   Because of the generic sense of words used to introduce divine speech and oracles (*ḫr/dd* "say"; *nd* "consult," "greet"; *bȝw* "manifestation"; *sr* "foretell"; *šm* "babble") the context is determinative for the nature of the communication.

16   Jaroslav Černý, "Egyptian Oracles," in *A Saite Oracle Papyrus from Thebes in the Brooklyn Museum* (ed. Richard A. Parker; Providence: Brown University Press, 1962), 35–48; Lászlo Kákosy, "Orakel," *LÄ* 4:600–606; A. G. McDowell, *Jurisdiction in the Workmen's Community of Deir El-Medîna* (Leiden: Nederlands Instituut voor het Nabije Oosten, 1990), 107–28; Bonnet, "Prophezeiung," 608–9; Jean-Marie Kruchten, "Oracles," in *The Oxford Encyclopedia of Ancient Egypt* (ed. Donald B. Redford; 3 vols.;

resolution of legal issues and advice to commoners.[17] Questions placed before the god could be either oral or written, and the deity's response most likely came in the form of movement of the bark.[18] This binary inquiry appears to be a form of technical divination and not prophecy. On the literary level, differentiating the two can be difficult, since expanded binary responses might appear to be prophetic speech. But the written record of the oracle could be a scribe echoing the words of the original question rather than recording an auditory phenomenon,[19] or perhaps a priest simply reframed the question as a response.[20] Both possibilities are illustrated in Mesopotamian and biblical records of divine response to binary inquiries.[21]

Several royal texts, usually discussed in connection with binary oracles, might also involve prophetic speech. The selection of Thutmosis III for kingship during a procession of Amun appears to involve movements of the bark;[22] but in response to the proclamation of his royal titulary, the court replies, "The oracle of the god himself, is like the word of Re at the first beginning. Thoth is he who makes the writing speak."[23] Breasted suggests that this refers to the oracle which decreed Thutmose III as king, a phenomenon similar to the query and reply regarding Hatshepsut's Punt expedition, where the phrase, "oracle of the god," also appears.[24] The latter could be a binary response. Similar difficulties face analysis of the oracle to Thutmosis IV, who

---

Oxford: Oxford University Press, 2001), 2:609–12. On pre-New Kingdom oracles, see John Baines, "Practical Religion and Piety," *JEA* 73 (1987): 79–98 (89–90).

17   James H. Breasted, *Ancient Records of Egypt* (5 vols.; Chicago: University of Chicago Press, 1906), vol. 2, §§140, 606, 827; vol. 3, §§174, 580 line 26; K. A. Kitchen, *Ramesside Inscriptions Translated and Annotated: Translations* (5 vols., in progress; Oxford: Blackwell, 1993–), vol. 3, no. 146, §283:10.

18   Černý, "Egyptian Oracles," 43–45; Kákosy, "Orakel," 600.

19   McDowell, *Jurisdiction in the Workmen's Community of Deir El-Medîna*, 109.

20   Kákosy, "Orakel," 600–601. There is evidence from Ptolemaic times of voice projection mechanisms (Kruchten, "Oracles," 611), but in general, fraudulent practices are unlikely (Černý, "Egyptian Oracles," 44; McDowell, *Jurisdiction in the Workmen's Community of Deir El-Medîna*, 110; Bonnet, "Prophezeiung," 562–63).

21   For Mesopotamia, see Nissinen, *References to Prophecy*, 33; Riekele Borger, *Die Inschriften Asarhaddons Königs von Assyrien* (AfOB 9; Osnabrück: Biblio-Verlag, 1967), §27 (Nin. A i 14); J.-M. Durand, *Archives épistolaires de Mari I/1* (ARM 26; Paris: Éditions Recherche sur les Civilisations, 1988), 54–55; and Ivan Starr, *Queries to the Sungod: Divination and Politics in Sargonid Assyria* (SAA 4; Helsinki: University of Helsinki Press, 1990), nos. 305 9–r.5, 320 r.11–13. For biblical examples, see Karel van der Toorn, "L'oracle de victoire comme expression prophétique au Proche-Orient ancien," *RB* 94 (1987): 63–97 (68–71).

22   Breasted, *Ancient Records of Egypt*, vol. 2, §140.

23   Breasted, *Ancient Records of Egypt*, vol. 2, §151.

24   Breasted, *Ancient Records of Egypt*, vol. 2, §151 note a, §285 line 5.

sought counsel of Amun in the face of the Nubian rebellion. Breasted notes that the description of this oracle, "as a father speaks to a son," is identical to that describing Thutmosis IV's dream recorded on the Sphinx Stela.[25] As Černý observes, the descriptions of these oracles are too vague to reconstruct the proceedings.[26] He suggests that Thutmosis IV, for example, might only be reporting a private revelation. This would be similar to the claim in Ramesses II's lament at the Battle of Kadesh.[27] However, it will be argued below that the proclamation of Thutmosis III's titulary is best understood as prophetic speech.

Dreams

Neo-Assyrian and Mari texts report dream experiences that contain divine messages to be delivered to a third party, thereby overlapping with prophecy.[28] Egyptian dreams, on the other hand, report divine speech only as private revelation.[29] One exception appears in the Ptolemaic *Archive of Ḥor*, where divine instructions in a dream regarding cultic matters are conveyed to temple officials.[30] Other utterances in

25   Breasted, *Ancient Records of Egypt*, vol. 2, §827 note b, §815 line 9.

26   Černý, "Egyptian Oracles," 36.

27   John L. Foster, *Hymns, Prayers, and Songs: An Anthology of Ancient Egyptian Lyric Poetry* (SBLWAW 8; Atlanta, Ga.: Scholars Press, 1995), no. 91: "Have I not gone and listened to your voice that I might not disobey the counsel which you gave?"

28   Neo-Assyrian: Simo Parpola, *Assyrian Prophecies* (SAA 9; Helsinki: University of Helsinki Press, 1997), xlvi–xlvii; Nissinen, *References to Prophecy*, 53–54 (cf. Simo Parpola, *Letters from Assyrian and Babylonian Scholars* [SAA 10; Helsinki: University of Helsinki Press, 1993], no. 174). Mari: Martti Nissinen, C. L. Seow, and Robert K. Ritner, *Prophets and Prophecy in the Ancient Near East* (SBLWAW 12; Atlanta, Ga.: Society of Biblical Literature, 2003), nos. 35 (ARM 26 227), 37 (ARM 26 232), 38 (ARM 26 233), 39 (ARM 26 234), 42 (ARM 26 237).

29   For Egyptian dreams in general, see Kasia Szpakowska, *Behind Closed Eyes: Dreams and Nightmares in Ancient Egypt* (Swansea: Classical Press of Wales, 2003). For examples, see Breasted, *Ancient Records of Egypt*, vol. 2, §815; 3:§582; *COS* 2.21–22, and §2.3 lines 20b–22a. The category of private revelation also applies to sending one's soul to the netherworld in order to obtain an oracle, or sending a dream to another (see John Gee, "Oracle by Image: Coffin Text 103 in Context," in *Magic and Divination in the Ancient World* [ed. Leda Ciraolo and Jonathan Seidel; Ancient Magic and Divination 2; Leiden: Brill, 2002], 83–88 [86–88]).

30   John D. Ray, *The Archive of Ḥor* (London: Egypt Exploration Society, 1976), no. 23 recto 6–23, verso 15–26. If delivered in a Mesopotamian or Israelite context, this would constitute cultic prophecy. Cf. Nissinen, Seow, and Ritner, *Prophets and Prophecy in the Ancient Near East*, §§1 (A. 1121+A. 2731), 4 (ARM 26 194); Parpola, *Assyrian Prophecies*, nos. 2.3, 3.5; Steven W. Cole and Peter Machinist, *Letters from Priests to the Kings Esarhaddon and Assurbanipal* (SAA 13; Helsinki: University of Helsinki Press, 1998), no. 144; Isa 1:11–17; Haggai; Mal 1:7–8.

this archive are potentially prophetic speech unrelated to dreams, however the circumstances are too vague to draw firm conclusions.[31] Since Hellenistic prophecy may have influenced the practices recorded in this Ptolemaic archive, these examples are less valuable in assessing the practice of prophecy in earlier periods. But even apart from the *Archive of Ḥor*, the earlier Egyptian dream reports and narratives incorporating dreams contribute to our understanding of broader cultural expectations regarding divine messages. Interpretation of dreams depended on an interconnectedness between dream experience and the events of the real world,[32] implying that free speech from a deity to a human was known. This reinforces the possibility of intuitive prophecy in Egypt.

Communication with the Dead

Ritner cites evidence of intercessory expectations, including conveyance of hidden information, through contact with the dead in all periods of Egyptian history.[33] Because these are *private* revelations from the realm of the gods, usually in dreams, they do not constitute prophecy. Nevertheless, receiving revelatory messages from the deceased affirms the socio-religious prerequisite for intuitive prophecy. After all, it is not accidental that King Saul conjures from the dead the prophet Samuel, because he hopes for a continuation of Samuel's prophetic services (1 Samuel 28).[34]

Narrative Literature

The most well-known story regarding prophecy in Egyptian literature is the *Report of Wenamun*. However, as is often observed, while this

---

31   Ray, *The Archive of Ḥor*, no. 31B lines 5–8 and no. 33, and Ray's comments on pp. 133–34.

32   Szpakowska, *Behind Closed Eyes*, 69 and 72 (cf. A. Spalinger, "A Lost Dream Episode?," in Szpakowska, *Through a Glass Darkly*, 227–42 [234]).

33   Robert K. Ritner, "Necromancy in Ancient Egypt," in Ciraolo and Seidel, *Magic and Divination in the Ancient World*, 89–96 (90). For sources, see Edward Wente, *Letters from Ancient Egypt* (SBLWAW 1; Atlanta, Ga.: Scholars Press, 1990), nos. 340–53 and Baines, "Practical Religion and Piety," 86–88. Examples that might press the boundaries of prophecy include Seti I (Breasted, *Ancient Records of Egypt*, vol. 3, §§279–81), Setne Khamwas, and *The Instruction of Amenemhat* (Ritner, "Necromancy in Ancient Egypt," 91–92). Priestly inquiries through visions and dreams in the Roman period (Ritner, *The Mechanics of Ancient Egyptian Magical Practice*, 215) are too late to inform earlier practices.

34   Ritner, "Necromancy in Ancient Egypt," 95.

shows that Egyptians acknowledged the validity of prophecy in other cultures, it is not a witness to the phenomenon in Egypt.[35] Lloyd highlights other narratives describing the foretelling of an individual's fate (*Doomed Prince, Tale of Two Brothers,* and *Papyrus Westcar*),[36] and Pinch suggests that women serving in the Hathor temple functioned as seers for this purpose.[37] Not enough is known of this setting to draw conclusions. Perhaps it is through means of magic. But, as Lloyd writes, "the references to *heka*, dreams, and prophecy in our stories will reflect in some degree the social reality of their use and function."[38]

Seers

Baines draws attention to the consultation of a "seer" (*t3 rḫt,* "the wise woman"), attested from Deir el-Medina, a phenomenon he argues was normal.[39] Although she predicts the movement of the divine bark, Borghouts notes that her means of acquiring knowledge is unknown.[40] So, the contribution to a search for prophecy is unclear.

Royal Inscriptions

Funeral Texts

Although the *Pyramid Texts* are predominantly incantations spoken on behalf of the deceased king or recorded for his own use in the afterlife, in some instances the gods themselves address the deceased.[41] The important question is whether the priests reciting these words are functioning as intermediaries for the gods, which would constitute prophecy. Depictions of priests wearing masks, impersonating various deities

---

35   See also William L. Moran, ed., *The Amarna Letters* (Baltimore: Johns Hopkins University Press, 1992), no. 23.

36   Lloyd, "Heka, Dreams, and Prophecy in Ancient Egyptian Stories," 71–94.

37   Geraldine Pinch, *Magic in Ancient Egypt* (Austin: University of Texas Press, 1994), 56, 116–17.

38   Lloyd, "Heka, Dreams, and Prophecy in Ancient Egyptian Stories," 88.

39   Baines, "Practical Religion and Piety," 93.

40   J. F. Borghouts, "Divine Intervention in Ancient Egypt and Its Manifestation (*b3w*)," in *Gleanings from Deir el-Medîna* (ed. R. J. Demarée and Jac J. Janssen; Leiden: Nederlands Instituut voor het Nabije Oosten, 1982), 1–70 (26–27).

41   James P. Allen, *The Ancient Egyptian Pyramid Texts* (SBLWAW 23; Atlanta, Ga.: Society of Biblical Literature, 2005), P 14 (=PT 535), P 325 (=PT 474), P 357 (=PT 508), P 483 (=PT 534), P 484 (=PT 536), P 489-495 (=PT 542-548), P 515 (=PT307), P 522 (=PT 580).

in ritual, might support this conception,[42] as does the suggestion that pyramid texts originated from shamanistic oral tradition.[43]

Coronation Texts

The words of the court at Thutmosis III's coronation bear repeating: "this word which has been spoken to us; which we have heard in the court. . . . The oracle of the god himself, is like the word of Re at the beginning. Thoth is he who makes the writing speak."[44] As noted above, the oracle might refer to the bark's movements in selecting Thutmosis; but in view of the announcement of the royal titulary immediately preceding the court's reply, it should not be restricted to bark movements. A similar description of divine speech in the court is reflected in the coronation of Hatshepsut.

Hatshepsut's birth and coronation reliefs feature addresses to the queen from the gods as well as conversations within the divine council.[45] While the birth sequence is fictive, one might speculate about ritual re-enactments during kingship renewal at the Festival of Opet. But in the case of her coronation narrative, ritual performance of divine words seems likely—the iconography portrays goddesses holding crowns as Amun addresses the queen regarding their presentation. Later, the text states that Thutmosis I "commanded that the ritual

---

42 For illustrations see Othmar Keel, *The Symbolism of the Biblical World: Ancient Near Eastern Iconography and the Book of Psalms* (New York: Seabury Press, 1978), illus. 264b; Sue D'Auria, Peter Lacovara, and Catharine Roehrig, eds., *Mummies and Magic: The Funerary Arts of Ancient Egypt* (Boston: Museum of Fine Arts, 1988), fig. 24 and catalogue illus. 86, north wall; Salima Ikram and Aidan Dodson, *The Mummy in Ancient Egypt: Equipping the Dead for Eternity* (London: Thames & Hudson, 1998), illus. 4 and 19. Arelene Wolinski ("Egyptian Masks: The Priest and His Role," *Arch* 40, no. 1 [January/February 1987]: 22–29) perhaps overstates the evidence, particularly from the details of lappets, as does the earlier work of M. A. Murray ("Ritual Masking," in *Mélanges Maspero I* [Orient Ancien 66; Cairo: French Archaeological Institute of Cairo, 1935–1938], 251–55). Whether priests actually wore masks in these rituals before the first millennium is unclear; however, later archaeological evidence supports this (see Ian Shaw and Paul Nicholson, "Masks," in *The Dictionary of Ancient Egypt* [New York: Harry N. Abrams, Inc., 1995], 171–72; Lorelie H. Corcoran, "Masks," in *The Oxford Encyclopedia of Ancient Egypt*, 2:345–46). For divine impersonation in non-royal burials, see John A. Wilson, "Funeral Services of the Egyptian Old Kingdom," *JNES* 3 (1944): 201–18 (218). Women impersonating goddesses in lament ritual are attested in *The Lamentations of Isis and Nephthys* (Miriam Lichtheim, *Ancient Egyptian Literature*, 3 vols. [Berkeley: University of California Press, 1973–1980], 3:116–21). I thank John Ray for suggesting the possible association between priestly masks and prophetic performance.

43 Pinch, *Magic in Ancient Egypt*, 51.

44 Breasted, *Ancient Records of Egypt*, vol. 2, §151.

45 Breasted, *Ancient Records of Egypt*, vol. 2, §§192–242.

priests be brought to [proclaim] her great names. . . . They proclaimed
her royal names, for the god caused that it should be in their hearts to
make her names according to the form with which he had made them
before."[46] Even if fictive, this report probably corresponds with actual
custom in order to give a credible portrait, parallel to the example from
Thutmosis III mentioned above.

Horemheb's coronation texts describe Amun-Re coming forth in
procession to meet the crown prince, and one fragment preserves the
common, divine declaration of sonship in this context: "You are my
son, my heir, who issued from my body. . . ."[47] Texts accompanying the
representation of Tutankhamen's Opet Festival, later usurped by
Horemheb, are particularly interesting. They set divine address to the
king in context with descriptions of ritual procession, including the
towing of the divine bark, presentation of offerings, dancers and musi-
cians, and records of human speeches and songs celebrating the event.[48]
It is unlikely that performance of these divine speeches played no role
in the otherwise real-life ritual being portrayed.

Bell argues that the coronation rituals undertaken by Hatshepsut
and Horemheb at the Luxor temple served successive Egyptian kings
from the New Kingdom onwards.[49] The reliefs of Ramesses III's Opet
Festival at Karnak are similar to those just described, featuring divine
speeches in context with ritual details.[50] In Ramesses II's purported
prayer on behalf of Ramesses III in *Payprus Harris*, he praises Amun
who declared to him a reign of 200 years.[51] Both Breasted and more
recently Kákosy comment that this may refer to a priestly oracle.[52] The
variation from the stereotypical "millions" gives it a ring of authenticity. In summary, the conferral of royal titularies and affirmations of

46   Breasted, *Ancient Records of Egypt*, vol. 2, §§229–230, 239. Breasted (p. 99 n. a) writes,
     "They were inspired to announce the same names which the god had already con-
     ferred upon her before (§230)." The coronation texts of Amenhotep III reflect similar
     rituals and speeches; see Barbara Cumming and Benedict G. Davies, *Egyptian His-
     torical Records of the Later Eighteenth Dynasty* (6 vols.; Warminster: Aris & Phillips,
     1982–1985), vol. 4, no. 573.
47   William J. Murnane and Edmund S. Meltzer, *Texts from the Amarna Period in Egypt*
     (SBLWAW 5; Atlanta, Ga.: Scholars Press, 1995), §§106–107A (cf. Cumming and
     Davies, *Egyptian Historical Records*, vol. 6, no. 826).
48   Cumming and Davies, *Egyptian Historical Records*, vol. 6, no. 775. For iconography
     and texts, see Walter Wreszinski, *Atlas zur Altaegyptischen Kulturgeschichte* (3 vols.;
     Leipzig: J. C. Hinrichs, 1932–1936), vol. 2, folios 189–202.
49   Lanny Bell, "Luxor Temple and the Cult of the Royal *Ka*," *JNES* 44 (1985): 251–94
     (270, 280).
50   Kitchen, *Ramesside Inscriptions: Translations*, vol. 5, no. 47, §§186:1–189:15.
51   Breasted, *Ancient Records of Egypt*, vol. 4, §246.
52   Breasted, *Ancient Records of Egypt*, vol. 4, 141 n. a; Kákosy, "Orakel," 602.

divine relationship at coronations cannot be understood as replies to a binary query; and they were probably communicated orally through human agency, reflected in some manner in temple ritual. Both Assyrian and Israelite coronation texts have been linked to prophecy with a similar cultic backdrop in view;[53] and prophets spoke at the Akitu festival, including the ritual of kingship renewal.[54]

Building Inscriptions

In a prayer to Amun, Seti I anticipates that the god would speak to future generations, urging the continuation of his own building initiatives begun by oracle.[55] Would he have expected only affirmative "nods" from future binary inquiries? The dedication inscription of Ramesses II for Seti's temple at Abydos extols Ramesses as one who "championed his father." After Ramesses's dedication speech, which he claims to have delivered personally,[56] the inscription reports an affirmation from Seti, speaking to Ramesses "face to face."[57] Other divine speeches also feature in the opening scenes of this inscription. Another dedication inscription, possibly of Ramesses II, for the temple of Ptah in Memphis, is recorded on a stela for the "Station of the King" marking his position in temple ritual. It contains divine speech similar to coronation inscriptions.[58] Ramesses II's *The Blessing of Ptah* features an extended speech by the god enumerating his many favours upon the king, to which Ramesses replies with a list of his own pious acts.[59] Such conversation reports are common in texts of this period.[60] It is possible that divine words in these inscriptions are scribal creations offering silent testimony to the pleasure of the gods; however, it seems likely

53 E.g., 1 Samuel 9–10; 16; 1 Kings 1; Psalms 2; 110; and the coronation/re-enthronement rituals of Esarhaddon (John W. Hilber, *Cultic Prophecy in the Psalms* [BZAW 352; Berlin: Walter de Gruyter, 2005], 47–50, 61, 76–127).

54 Alasdair Livingstone, *Court Poetry and Literary Miscellanea* (SAA 3; Helsinki: University of Helsinki Press, 1989), nos. 34:28–29 and 35:31 and Nissinen, Seow, and Ritner, *Prophets and Prophecy in the Ancient Near East*, no. 133.

55 Breasted, *Ancient Records of Egypt*, vol. 3, §174; Kitchen, *Ramesside Inscriptions: Translations*, vol. 1, no. 32, §67:5–9.

56 "I have come myself in person" (Kitchen, *Ramesside Inscriptions: Translations*, vol. 2, no. 103, §§331:15–332:1, and esp. 332:9). Cf. Breasted, *Ancient Records of Egypt*, vol. 3, §§272–81.

57 Kitchen, *Ramesside Inscriptions: Translations*, vol. 2, §§334:10–336:11.

58 Breasted, *Ancient Records of Egypt*, vol. 3, §§533–37.

59 Breasted, *Ancient Records of Egypt*, vol. 3, §§398–414; Kitchen, *Ramesside Inscriptions: Translations*, vol. 2, no. 68, §258:1–281:12.

60 K. A. Kitchen, *Ramesside Inscriptions Translated and Annotated: Notes and Comments* (2 vols., in progress; Oxford: Blackwell, 1993–), 2:161, §252.

that such words were actually spoken through human agency in the rituals of dedication.[61] Mesopotamian and biblical counterparts exist for prophetic authorization of building projects as well, although none are preserved pertaining to building dedication ceremonies.[62]

Triumph Hymns

Thutmosis III's "Poetic Stela" opens with an introductory speech formula, "Words spoken by Amen-Re," and continues throughout with first-person divine speech.[63] The ritual setting is indicated by the accompanying offering scene and references in the poem to Thutmosis's visit to the temple.[64] Kitchen notes that another stela at Karnak bears substantially the same introductory address by Amun.[65]

Amenhotep III's triumph hymn appears in the context of a longer building inscription, originally from his mortuary temple behind the Memnon Colossi at Thebes. It concludes with an extensive speech of Amun, affirming the king's universal rule and extolling him for his projects.[66] The top of the stela shows Amenhotep offering libations before Amun. The inscription mentions another stela from this same temple, which marked the "Station of the King," where the king's part in rituals would have been performed. It consists of an exchange of words between the king and Amun, similar to the conclusion of the

---

61 In the temple of Khonsu at Karnak is a dedication inscription of the then high priest, Herihor. It features a scene of the priest walking backwards in front of a bark procession, offering incense. Recorded in this context is an address to him from Amun (Breasted, *Ancient Records of Egypt*, vol. 4, §§611, 620). The address of Amun to Herihor's grandson, Paynozem (at the time high priest), who is portrayed standing before the god, adorns another building inscription (Breasted, *Ancient Records of Egypt*, vol. 4, §633). However, the repeated references to the god's "nod" to inquiries recorded elsewhere in these inscriptions raises a question as to what extent they might be expansions of binary responses (cf. §§615–618).

62 2 Sam 7:5–17; Ps 132:11–18; Haggai; Ezra 6:14; Assurbanipal Prism T ii 7–24 (Hilber, *Cultic Prophecy in the Psalms*, 101–12; Nissinen, *References to Prophecy*, 35–42).

63 For the text, see K. A. Kitchen, *Poetry of Ancient Egypt* (Documenta Mundi: Aegyptiaca 1; Jonsered: Paul Åströms, 1999), §28 (cf. Lichtheim, *Ancient Egyptian Literature*, 2:35–38 and Breasted, *Ancient Records of Egypt*, vol. 2, §§655–62).

64 See Adolf Erman, *The Ancient Egyptians: A Sourcebook of their Writings* (London: Methuen, 1927; repr., Gloucester, MA: Peter Smith, 1978), 254 nn. 2 and 4, 256 n. 1; trans. of *Die Literatur de Aegypter* (Leipzig: J. C. Hinrichs, 1923).

65 Kitchen, *Poetry of Ancient Egypt*, 165.

66 For text, see Kitchen, *Poetry of Ancient Egypt*, §29 (cf. Lichtheim, *Ancient Egyptian Literature*, 2:43–48 and Breasted, *Ancient Records of Egypt*, vol. 2, §§882–92). This is not a literary adaptation of Thutmosis III's "Poetic Stela" (Kitchen, *Poetry of Ancient Egypt*, 177).

second stela of Thutmosis III mentioned above.[67] For a ritual exchange of words, a priestly intermediary (i.e., a "prophet") would be necessary to perform the divine counterpart to the king's role at his "station."

Later manifestations of this type of triumph hymn offer further evidence that the speeches were part of live ritual. The campaign inscriptions of Seti I echo the wording found in Thutmosis's and Amenhotep's triumph hymns, as the god responds to Seti's offering of prisoners and tribute.[68] Later Ramesside texts featuring comparable wording are accompanied by reliefs depicting sword conferral and the presentation and ritual killing of prisoners before the gods.[69] The tradition extended over 500 years, drawing to a close with the reliefs of Shoshenq I.[70] Some have argued that priests actually played the part of the gods in the sword ceremony, uttering the divine words recorded in the reliefs. Schulman, for example, notes that the sword presentation depicted at Medinet Habu is followed by other scenes that illustrate a real event; and he compares the impersonation of deities at the sword conferral to their role wearing divine masks in funeral rites.[71] Müller claims that the offering of incense depicted in a relief of the much earlier Kamose can only point to a temple setting and a real ritual of sword conferral presented in the accompanying text.[72] Since presentation of weapons, offerings, and ceremonial execution are part of actual ritual, it is reasonable to suppose that royal and divine speeches recorded on

---

67 Breasted, *Ancient Records of Egypt*, vol. 2, §§905–10. For a more complete text, see Cumming and Davies, *Egyptian Historical Records*, vol. 4, no. 569. This specific "station" is mentioned in the stela containing Amenhotep III's victory hymn (Breasted, *Ancient Records of Egypt*, vol. 2, §883 line 5, cf. Breasted's link on p. 368, n. d). Cf. the "station of the king" in the selection narrative of Thutmosis III (Breasted, *Ancient Records of Egypt*, vol. 2, §140, n. b) and a similar stela of Amenhotep II at Elephantine and Amada (Breasted, *Ancient Records of Egypt*, vol. 2, 791). An ancient Israelite counterpart might be the king's pillar in the temple (2 Kgs 11:14; 23:3; 2 Chr 34:31).

68 Breasted, *Ancient Records of Egypt*, vol. 3, §§105, 110, 116 (borrowed from Amenhotep III), 117 (borrowed from Thutmosis III), 136, 150, 155 (all from Karnak), and §§164–65 (from Redesiyeh); Kitchen, *Ramesside Inscriptions: Translations*, vol. 1, no. 1, §§6:15–11:9, no. 3, §§13:1–15:14, no. 6, §§17:7–20:11 (cf. *COS* 2, §§2.4a, c, e, f).

69 K. A. Kitchen and G. A. Gaballa, "Ramesside Varia II," *ZÄS* 96 (1969–1970): 14–28 (23–28).

70 Kitchen, *Poetry of Ancient Egypt*, §64, see comments p. 433.

71 Alan R. Schulman, "Take for Yourself the Sword," in *Essays in Egyptology in Honor of Hans Goedicke* (ed. Betsy M. Bryan and David Lorton; San Antonio: Van Siclen, 1994), 265–95 (269–70). Cf. Othmar Keel, *Wirkmächtige Siegeszeichen im Alten Testament* (OBO 5; Fribourg, Switzerland: Universitätsverlag, 1974), 62–63, 74–76; Othmar Keel, "Powerful Symbols of Victory: The Parts Stay the Same, the Actors Change," *JNSL* 25/2 (1999): 204–40 (209).

72 Hans Wolfgang Müller, *Der Waffenfund von Balata-Sichem und die Sichelschwerter* (Munich: Der Bayerischen Akademie der Wissenschaft, 1987), 144–45.

these reliefs were actually performed, which would constitute prophecy.

Scribes and Prophecy

The length, literary artistry, and repeated use of divine speeches might suggest scribal composition; however, one must be careful not to set prophet and scribe in mutually exclusive roles. The priests in Egypt who would have functioned in the prophetic role were highly literate, and scribal activity in the "House of Life" was considered "inspired."[73] Other ancient Near Eastern parallels also caution against an unnecessary dichotomy between scribe and prophet. Parpola argues that prophetic oracle collection SAA 9 3, with scribal editing, was read at the coronation celebration of Esarhaddon conducted at the Aššur temple and publicly delivered by a prophet.[74] Similarly, on the basis of the inclusion of a prophetic oracle in the Akitu kingship ritual, van der Toorn suggests that such oracles were placed into frozen liturgical form for such occasions.[75] Floyd stresses that composition, transmission, and performance of biblical prophecy were all variations of orality so that scribe and prophet converge.[76] Some psalms incorporating prophetic speech were no less "intuitive prophecy" if composed initially in written form.[77]

Similar to divine letters in Mesopotamia, a speech could be composed in the voice of the deity and read publicly to the king. Indeed, written communication in general was composed for oral performance, which in the Egyptian context extended to royal inscriptions.[78] While

---

73 Alan H. Gardiner, "The House of Life," *JEA* 24 (1938): 157–79 (168).

74 Parpola, *Assyrian Prophecies*, lxiv, lxx. Cf. Martti Nissinen, "Spoken, Written, Quoted, and Invented: Orality and Writtenness in Ancient Near Eastern Prophecy," in *Writings and Speech in Israelite and Ancient Near Eastern Prophecy* (ed. Ehud Ben Zvi and Michael H. Floyd; SBLSymS 10; Atlanta, Ga.: Society of Biblical Literature, 2000), 235–72 (251–53).

75 Van der Toorn, "L'oracle de victoire," 93. For text, see Nissinen, Seow, and Ritner, *Prophets and Prophecy in the Ancient Near East,* no. 133.

76 Michael H. Floyd, "'Write the Revelation!' (Hab 2:2): Re-imagining the Cultural History of Prophecy," in *Writings and Speech*, 103–43.

77 Hilber, *Cultic Prophecy in the Psalms*, 221–24.

78 Christopher J. Eyre, "Is Egyptian Historical Literature 'Historical' or 'Literary'?" in *Ancient Egyptian Literature: History and Forms* (ed. A. Loprieno; Probleme der Ägyptologie 10; Leiden: Brill, 1996), 420–29. Redford suggests that courtly communication might have provided the impetus for divine address to the king, and divine response to royal prayer may have "roots in oral practice," but that the certainty of

Assyrian divine letters are generally of a different genre than reports of prophecy,[79] one example (SAA 3 47) is indistinguishable, form-critically, from prophetic speech.[80] The Eshnunna oracles of Kititum are probably divine letters written from oral communication,[81] and at least one Mari text appears to be a divine letter to the king rather than a report of prophetic speech embedded within royal correspondence.[82] Thus, some Egyptian reliefs citing divine speeches to the king could have been construed by the original audience as "prophetic," whether delivered through oral, prophetic performance or simply read aloud by a priest in the cult in the manner of a divine letter.

Conclusion

The critical test for prophecy is evidence of a divine message intuitively received and conveyed by a human intermediary. In the absence of a description in the text explicitly mentioning a prophetic functionary,[83] prophetic speech is likely when other means of divination are ruled out and a plausible performance scenario is evident. There is evidence from diverse Egyptian texts of the socio-religious prerequisite for prophecy, and royal ritual-texts present good evidence of prophetic speech performance in the Egyptian cult.

---

this deduction is unclear to him (Donald B. Redford, "Scribe and Speaker," in *Writings and Speech*, 161–63, 186–88).

79   Livingstone, *Court Poetry and Literary Miscellanea,* nos. 44–46. For the genre comparison, see p. xxx.

80   Beate Pongratz-Leisten, *Herrschaftswissen in Mesopotamien: Formen der Kommunikation zwischen Gott und König im 2. und 1. Jahrtausend v. Chr.* (SAAS 10; Helsinki: University of Helsinki Press, 1999), 232; Livingstone, *Court Poetry and Literary Miscellanea,* no. 47.

81   Maria deJong Ellis, "The Goddess Kititum Speaks to King Ibalpiel: Oracle Texts from Ishchali," *MARI* 5 (1987): 250, 256; William L. Moran, "An Ancient Prophetic Oracle," in *Biblische Theologie und gesellschaftlicher Wandel (Festschrift N. Lohfink)* (ed. G. Braulik, W. Groß, and S. McEvenue; Freiburg, Germany: Herder, 1993), 252–59.

82   Pongratz-Leisten, *Herrschaftswissen in Mesopotamien,* 204 (ARM 26 194).

83   The absence of such descriptions in Egyptian texts is not surprising in view of the dominating focus on the royal person. Indeed, the king is always portrayed as the sole priestly functionary even though in actual practice, others performed the service to the gods (Barry J. Kemp, *Ancient Egypt: Anatomy of a Civilization* [London: Routledge, 1991], 190; John Baines, "Ancient Egyptian Kingship: Official Forms, Rhetoric, Context," in *King and Messiah in Israel and the Ancient Near East: Proceedings of the Oxford Old Testament Seminar* [ed. John Day; JSOTSup 270; Sheffield: Sheffield Academic Press, 1998], 16–53 [28]).

The Palestinian Campaign of Pharaoh Shishak

A. D. H. Mayes

I. Introduction

1 Kings 14:25–28 records an invasion of Palestine by Shishak of Egypt, in which the threat to Jerusalem was, it is implied, lifted only at the cost of a large payment. No capture of Jerusalem is reported, but the Egyptian ruler "took away the treasures of the house of the Lord and the treasures of the king's house; he took away everything. He also took away all the shields of gold which Solomon had made." The Chronicler, in 2 Chr 12:1–12, preserves the record, while elaborating on the size of Shishak's army and on the Egyptian destruction of fortified cities in Judah, and setting the whole in the context of Rehoboam's faithlessness and subsequent repentance. In the case of both Kings and Chronicles, the focus of Shishak's military attention is the Judean capital city, Jerusalem.

The great temple at Karnak was adorned by Pharaoh Shoshenq I (945–924 BC), the first king of the 22nd Dynasty, through the addition of a triumphal gateway between the small temple of Rameses III and the then front of the Karnak temple, the present second pylon. This gate, known as the Bubastite Portal, commemorates the Bubastite family in Thebes to which Shoshenq belonged. Shoshenq's family was Libyan in origin, belonging to those settled by Rameses III in the twelfth century as conscripted troops in the eastern Nile delta. Bubastis, halfway between Memphis and Tanis, Egypt's capitals in the 21st Dynasty, was the site at which Shoshenq's family emerged as a local chiefdom of the Libyan Meshwesh, a family which was able to forge links with the priests at Memphis and the royal family at Tanis.[1] Shoshenq's uncle Osorkon briefly ruled during the 21st Dynasty, while Shoshenq himself married the daughter of Psusennes II, the last king of that dynasty. On the death of Psusennes II without an heir, Shoshenq was able to take

---

1   Cf. Amélie Kuhrt, *The Ancient Near East c. 3000–330 BC* (2 vols.; London: Routledge, 1995), 2:626–27.

the throne. The wall, just east of the Bubastite Portal, forming a westward extension of the hypostyle hall of the temple of Amun, bears Shoshenq's record of his Palestinian campaign.

The record left by Shoshenq, or, to use the version of his name preserved in the Old Testament, Shishak,[2] provides the Egyptian version of the event recorded in 1 Kings. The date and context of this campaign are matters of considerable dispute. 1 Kings 14 relates it to the reign of Rehoboam, and the Egyptian evidence is widely held to support a date late in the reign of Shishak.[3] The stone used for Shishak's building work at the Karnak temple, including probably the Bubastite portal, was quarried, according to an inscription cut into the sandstone walls of the quarry at Silsileh,[4] in Shishak's twenty-first year, that is, near the end of his reign, and it is unlikely that the event commemorated in the inscription had taken place many years earlier and gone unrecorded.[5] Moreover, given the weakness of Egypt at the end of the 21st Dynasty, the beginning of the Third Intermediate Period, and given also the foreign Libyan origin of Shishak, it is likely that, for all that Shishak may have wished to prove himself as a capable ruler through a Palestinian campaign, this venture took some years to prepare for; it was only on the basis of having consolidated his rule at home that Shishak, late in his reign, could undertake a military campaign abroad. The lack of any apparent follow-up campaign also points to its having taken place not many years before the end of Shishak's reign.

The correlation of Egyptian and Israelite monarchic history at this point is problematic. In general, Egyptian chronology has two fixed points serving as relatively secure dates: the reign of Rameses II (1279–1213 BC) and the accession of Psammetichus I (664 BC). Between these

---

2   The name Shoshenq is variously written in Egyptian as *ssnq* and *ssq*, the loss of the *n* being common in the Libyan period; cf. Kenneth A. Kitchen, *The Third Intermediate Period in Egypt (1100–650 B.C.)* (2d ed.; Warminster: Aris & Phillips, 1986), 73 n. 356. The "o" vowel, yielding the pronunciation "Shoshenq," is attested by the Kethib in 1 Kgs 14:25 and also by the Septuagint.

3   Though for a date early in Shishak's reign cf. Donald B. Redford, *Egypt, Canaan, and Israel in Ancient Times* (Princeton: Princeton University Press, 1992), 312–15.

4   Cf. James H. Breasted, *Ancient Records of Egypt* (5 vols.; Chicago: University of Chicago Press, 1906; repr., London: Histories and Mysteries of Man, 1988), 4:344–47 (§§701–8).

5   Kenneth A. Kitchen, "Egyptian Interventions in the Levant in Iron Age II," in *Symbiosis, Symbolism, and the Power of the Past* (ed. William G. Dever and Seymour Gitin; Winona Lake, Ind.: Eisenbrauns, 2003), 113–32 (121–25), suggests that it was in fact the wealth acquired by Shishak in his Palestinian campaign that provided the resources for his going on a "building spree" not seen in Egypt since the time of Rameses II. Undoubtedly such building activities were facilitated by the spoils of war, but a specific connection with the gold of Solomon, as recorded in 1 Kings 14, must remain uncertain.

dates there is uncertainty, with the synchronism of Shishak and Rehoboam having a significant role in the search for further fixed points.[6] The different chronological systems, however, that are widely used for Egyptian and Israelite chronology, do not always allow for a degree of overlap in the reigns of Shishak and Rehoboam sufficient to provide for an invasion of Palestine by Shishak in Rehoboam's fifth year,[7] and Shishak's invasion is sometimes dated to the reign of Solomon rather than that of Rehoboam.[8] On the other hand, Van Seters has suggested that one of the sources used by the Deuteronomist in 1 Kings 14 was a record of temple income and its use;[9] this, if true, would suggest that 1 Kings 14 is reliable in dating Shishak's invasion to the fifth year of Rehoboam. Even though the similarity of the record in 1 Kgs 14:26 and 2 Kgs 24:13 might indicate that the handing over of temple treasure as a ransom is more a late deuteronomistic literary topos than a historical record,[10] its attachment to Rehoboam could still reflect the memory, or indeed record, of an Egyptian invasion at that time. A question mark must remain, but the balance of probability seems to lie in favour of dating this invasion to the reign of Rehoboam in the middle of the second half of the tenth century BC.

---

6 Cf. Bernd U. Schipper, *Israel und Ägypten in der Königszeit* (OBO 170; Fribourg, Switzerland: Universitätsverlag Freiburg Schweiz; Göttingen: Vandenhoeck & Ruprecht, 1999), 119–21.

7 Cf. the chronological table in John H. Hayes and J. Maxwell Miller, eds., *Israelite and Judaean History* (London: SCM, 1977), 682–83.

8 Cf. Giovanni Garbini, *History and Ideology in Ancient Israel* (London: SCM, 1988), 29–30, who believes that the Deuteronomist, wishing to exculpate Solomon the temple builder of sacrilege relating to the temple, transferred to Rehoboam an event that properly belonged to Solomon's reign; cf. also Hermann M. Nieman, "The Socio-Political Shadow Cast by the Biblical Solomon," in *The Age of Solomon* (ed. Lowell K. Handy; Leiden: Brill, 1997), 252–99 (296–97); Ernst Axel Knauf, "Le roi est mort, vive le roi! A Biblical Argument for the Historicity of Solomon," in Handy, *The Age of Solomon,* 81–95 (93–95)

9 John Van Seters, *In Search of History* (New Haven, Conn.: Yale University Press, 1983), 301; cf. also Marc Z. Brettler, "Method in the Application of Biblical Source Material to Historical Writing (with Particular Reference to the Ninth Century BCE)," in *Understanding the History of Ancient Israel* (ed. H. G. M. Williamson; Oxford: Oxford University Press, 2007), 305–36 (320–22); Nadav Naʾaman, "The Northern Kingdom in the Late Tenth–Ninth Centuries BCE," in Williamson, *Understanding the History of Ancient Israel,* 399–418 (399–400).

10 Cf. T. E. Mullen, "Crime and Punishment: The Sins of the King and the Despoliation of the Treasuries," *CBQ* 54 (1992): 231–48, who believes that the story is a deuteronomistic genre created in the light of events in the time of the Deuteronomist; cf. also Israel Finkelstein, "The Campaign of Shoshenq I to Palestine: A Guide to the 10th Century BCE Polity," *ZDPV* 118 (2002): 109–35 (112–13).

II. Interpretation of the Shishak Record

The Shishak record belongs within an Egyptian tradition which also forms an essential context for its interpretation. To this tradition there belong especially the triumphal reliefs of the New Kingdom Pharaohs Thutmosis III, Seti I, Rameses II, and Rameses III, the first three of these also being found at Karnak, and the fourth at Medinet Habu.[11] All, including the Shishak record, have a tripartite structure comprising a relief scene, a topographical list, and an inscription: in the relief the Pharaoh is depicted in a highly conventional form smiting his foreign enemies,[12] and including the representation of a god presenting a sword to the king; the enemies of the king are depicted bound by lead ropes held by the god or another god or goddess, and on these enemies oval rings contain the names of the places conquered by the Pharaoh; the third part, the inscription, identifies the king, the gods, and the defeated enemies, but is dominated by a speech, in stereotypical language, by the god Amun to the king, in which the might of the king is praised.

It is important to recognize the conventional nature of these records in general. That this is the nature of the relief and the inscription is easy to establish: the smiting scenes and the language in praise of the Pharaoh appear frequently in Egyptian history, and so cannot be interpreted simplistically as descriptive of and relating to particular historical occasions. But this is largely true also of the topographical lists, at least those of the New Kingdom Pharaohs. In the case of the topographical lists of Thutmosis III and Rameses III, they are complemented by annals and other historical records, but the route taken by the army according to the latter is not reflected in the topographical lists; in the case of Seti I's topographical list, and that of Rameses III, name rings often do not refer to particular places but rather to regions such as Hatti, Upper Retenu, and Lower Retenu, while Seti I's list includes locations, such as Babylon, where Seti did not campaign. The lists are repetitive, the same place being sometimes repeated even within the same list; they refer not just to places or regions but also to groups: the Sand-Dwellers, the Nine Bows, Asiatics, Bedouin, Nubians. The interpretation of the nature and purpose of these lists given by Wilson[13] is

---

11 Detailed descriptions of these will be found in Kevin A. Wilson, *The Campaign of Pharaoh Shoshenq I into Palestine* (FAT 2/9; Tübingen: Mohr Siebeck, 2005), 16–47.

12 For a sophisticated treatment of this canonical element in Egyptian art, cf. Whitney Davis, *Masking the Blow* (Berkeley and Los Angeles: University of California Press, 1992).

13 Wilson, *Campaign*, esp. 36–40.

convincing: their intention is to present the king as victorious over all foreign lands, and, just as in the reliefs and in the inscriptions, this victory is given by Amun. Their primary purpose is not that of preserving historical information, nor indeed simply that of royal propaganda, but is rather to be understood within the temple context where they are to be found. These topographical inscriptions are located on the exterior temple walls and doorways. In so far as the temple is the dwelling place of the gods, where *maat* prevails, outside the temple lies the threat of chaos; the temple walls are, therefore, the dividing line between order and chaos, and these topographical inscriptions, proclaiming the victory of the Pharaoh over his enemies as the gift of Amun, function to hold chaos at bay. Clearly the names are those of real places and groups, but the origin of their usage in any particular instance is not any specific military victory which is being commemorated; rather, those who carved these topographical lists used scribal military records of actual and potential enemies, and indeed probably also Egyptian onomastic lists, those early attempts at classification of items in an encyclopedic manner, one group of which consists of towns and cities.[14] This is the tradition to which the later topographical inscription of Shishak I must also be related; the question must be whether it provides an adequate interpretive context for that inscription.

The Shishak topographical inscription, like its predecessors, consists of a relief, an inscription, and a topographical list. As with the others, so too in this instance the relief scene includes gods, king, and kneeling captives: Amun is again portrayed holding out a sword to the king and, along with Wast the goddess of Thebes, as holding the lead ropes binding the captive enemies; the king adopts the conventional striding pose with arms upraised and holding a weapon with which to smite his foes; the kneeling captives carry oval rings containing the topographical list. The inscription includes the titulary of the king and also describes him as "the great god, great of power, who strikes the foreign lands who attack him," and credits him with the "smiting of the chiefs of the tribesmen of Nubia, all inaccessible foreign lands, all the lands of Fenkhu (Syria-Palestine), the lands of the northern border of Asia." In this, the inscription takes up much of the language of earlier topographical inscriptions, and expresses the universal nature of Shishak's victories. This idealization of Shishak is reflected also in the speech of Amun which, though not simply a copy of the Amun speech in other reliefs, similarly describes the king as having defeated all his foes. These enemies are the traditional enemies of Egypt, and, in the

14   Wilson, *Campaign,* 44.

case of the Shishak inscription, reference is made even to Mitanni, a nation that had long ceased to exist. The conventional nature of the presentation in both relief and inscription links the Shishak topographical inscription closely to the established tradition.

The topographical list of the Shishak inscription originally had about 175 names, but many of these have been erased and only 127 can now be read. They are in three sections: first, at the beginning of the first row, the list is introduced by the Nine Bows, the traditional lands and peoples of the Pharaoh's rule; secondly, in the rest of the first row and rows two to five, are the names of places located primarily in the coastal plain, the plain of Megiddo and the Jezreel valley, the Ephraimite hill country, and Gilead; thirdly, in rows six to ten, are the names of places located apparently in the Negeb. Most of the identifiable toponyms are found in the second section; that the toponyms of the third section belong to the Negeb is indicated by the threefold occurrence of reference to the Negeb in the toponyms.

It is clear that in many respects, especially with reference to the relief and inscription, Shishak's topographical inscription reflects Egyptian convention and has no particular historical reference. This is hardly surprising. As a pharaoh of Libyan origin, Shishak's major concern would have been his integration into Egyptian tradition as the basis for his legitimacy. Undoubtedly for this reason one element of his titulary, as given in the inscription, is Hedj-Kheper-Re, a prenomen first used by Smendes the founder of the 21st Dynasty.[15] Yet this element in itself also suggests that an adequate interpretation of the Shishak topographical inscription must go beyond seeing it purely in terms of Egyptian convention. Shishak's use of a prenomen of Smendes indicates precisely the intention to ensure that the particularities of his rule are legitimated through being linked with the identifiable Egyptian past. This is true also of the relief, for while the superscription to the representation of the defeated enemies refers to the "smiting of the chiefs of the tribesmen of Nubia, all inaccessible foreign lands, all the lands of Fenkhu, the lands of the northern borders of Asia," thus presenting Shishak as universal ruler, the relief presents all the defeated foes as Asiatics.[16] This is not just something distinguishing this topographical inscription from others where the reliefs depict more than one ethnic group, but it also suggests that Shishak is consciously using

---

15   Cf. also John D. Currid, *Ancient Egypt and the Old Testament* (Grand Rapids, Mich.: Baker Books, 1997), 177.

16   Wilson, *Campaign*, 58; the relief scenes of Thutmosis III, Seti I, Rameses II, and Rameses III, by contrast, depict variously Asiatics, Nubians, and Libyans (22, 24).

a particular well-established genre in order to depict and validate his own specific achievement.

This aim of the Shishak topographical inscription is borne out by its topographical list, for the latter carries a superscription which is partly conventional but to some extent unique, and which is also at some variance with the actual list of toponyms itself. The superscription is conventional in presenting Shishak's conquest as universal ("southern and northern foreign lands"), but it is almost unique[17] in that it refers to a particular campaign ("his first expedition of victory"); it is at variance with the actual list itself in that the latter contains the names of places only in Palestine. Moreover, whereas the topographical lists of the New Kingdom Pharaohs repeat the same toponyms through many lists, the Shishak list contains many place names, such as Arad, Taanach, and Rehob, that do not occur in the other lists.[18] Both the internal tension and the unique characteristics of the Shishak topographical list suggest once again that Shishak's topographical inscription is to be interpreted in terms of an attempt on the part of Shishak to integrate his specific Palestinian campaign into Egyptian tradition, so legitimizing his rule as Pharaoh, by presenting it in terms of the conventional genre established in the New Kingdom topographical inscriptions.[19] Thus, the Shishak topographical list should be credited with considerable significance in terms of its reflecting the campaign of Shishak I into Palestine at a late stage in his reign. Through this topographical inscription Shishak not only connects himself with the glorious Egyptian past but also imparts significant historical information about the historical basis for his doing so.

Any attempt to understand the Shishak topographical list encounters the major difficulty that not only have many of its place names

---

17   Cf. below on the Thutmosis III topographical list.

18   Cf. Anson F. Rainey and R. Steven Notley, *The Sacred Bridge* (Jerusalem: Carta, 2006), 185, who also point out that the forms of names, such as Megiddo and Socoh, are different in the Shishak list when compared with the 18th Dynasty lists; cf. also Amihai Mazar, "The Spade and the Text: The Interaction between Archaeology and Israelite History Relating to the Tenth–Ninth Centuries BCE," in Williamson, *Understanding the History of Ancient Israel*, 143–71 (149–51).

19   On the uniqueness of the Shishak list as the basis for accepting its historical reliability, cf. also Martin Noth, "Die Wege der Pharaonenheere in Palästina und Syrien IV," *ZDPV* 61 (1938): 277–304 (281); Kitchen, *Third Intermediate Period*, 432; Schipper, *Israel und Ägypten*, 125–26. Wilson (whose work has been used here extensively), *Campaign*, 60–65, argues the opposite case, but unconvincingly. Wilson does not give adequate importance to the fact that the Thutmosis III list makes reference to a specific campaign and also seems to be the basis of the other New Kingdom topographical lists, which suggests that the conventional genre is in fact rooted in a particular historical situation, that of the campaign of Thutmosis III.

been effaced or preserved only in part, but very many of those that remain cannot be identified. The list falls into two parts, an upper and a lower register. The upper register is in five lines, each line containing thirteen name-rings.[20] The first nine of line one are the "Nine Bows"; of the remaining fifty-five names,[21] some fourteen have been more or less completely lost; at least two others require a degree of restoration that makes their reading uncertain; and of the remainder, only some twenty-four may be identified with known sites in Palestine. The two uncertain readings are two of the three in line one, following the "Nine Bows." That they should be read as "Gaza" and "Gezer"[22] is not improbable: the restorations suit their immediate context; the resulting connection of Gezer with the third place name, "Rubate," is a conjunction found in the earlier list of Thutmosis III; the restored names have a general fit with the others in the upper register. All the names in this register belong to west Jordan Palestine and the immediately adjoining areas east of the Jordan. Several attempts have been made to discover here a coherent route followed by Shishak's army in the invasion. Invariably, however, these have involved a boustrophedon reading of the upper register and/or a rearrangement of some of the place names mentioned.[23] The lack of any analogy for a boustrophedon reading in other Egyptian texts, and the fact that it does not fit throughout the topographical list,[24] inevitably weakens the case for it here, and, in any case, the proposal proceeds on the assumption that a single route march of some sort is here preserved. What is indisputable is that there are certain clusters of place names which point to concerted military

---

20   On this and what follows, cf. Wilson, *Campaign*, 101–33; Rainey and Notley, *Sacred Bridge*, 186–88.

21   The tenth "name-ring" in line one contains probably a heading to the list rather than a place name; so the actual place names of the upper register are numbered 11–65; cf. Nadav Naʾaman, *Ancient Israel's History and Historiography* (Winona Lake, Ind.: Eisenbrauns, 2006), 127.

22   So Rainey and Notley, *Sacred Bridge*, 186, who admit, however, that "the uncertainty of the readings precludes the drawing of substantive military or political conclusions." Wilson, *Campaign*, 105, argues that the restoration of "Gaza" (of which only the first letter is preserved) assumes that the list is an itinerary and that Gaza would have been the first city in Canaan to be reached. His own reading of "Makkedah," however, rests on extremely flimsy grounds.

23   Cf. especially the review in Wilson, *Campaign*, 5, 7–11; also Gösta W. Ahlström, "Pharaoh Shoshenq's Campaign to Palestine," in *History and Traditions of Early Israel: Studies Presented to Eduard Nielsen* (ed. André Lemaire and Benedikt Otzen; VTSup 50; Leiden: Brill, 1993), 1–16 (4–7).

24   Indeed, even in those lines for which it has been proposed it does not fit with the direction of reading indicated by the hieroglyphs themselves.

activity in certain areas,[25] suggesting perhaps that Shishak's campaign was effected not solely by successive conquests on the part of a single army but also through the operations of separate detachments sent out to specific areas.[26] Either Gaza or Megiddo, particularly given their significance in Egyptian relations with Palestine, may have been the base from which such units were despatched into the central hill country, the Jordan valley and beyond the Jordan, and especially the plain of Jezreel. In any case, there is no doubt but that the focus of the attack, as reflected in the upper register, is on the territory of, and particularly the routes through, the northern kingdom of Israel.

An advantage of this approach to the record in the upper register is that, on the probable assumption that Gaza rather than Megiddo was Shishak's base, it allows for a better understanding of the place names in the lower register. That register comprises rows six to ten, containing eighty-five names, with an additional five names at the end of what may be an otherwise effaced bottom line.[27] Even within this section there are more than thirty missing name rings, and these gaps must leave a question mark over the precise area to which the place names refer. The problem is exacerbated by the fact that so few of the places mentioned in the lower register can be identified anyway.[28] Nevertheless, two points may be made. First, it is clear, especially from the three references to "the Negeb (of)," and from the identification of a few of the toponyms,[29] that it is the Negeb that is the focus of attention here. Secondly, it is remarkable, even given the number of missing or effaced name rings, that there is no reference to Jerusalem or to other significant sites of the highlands of Judah. These are indeed settlements in the southern part of the territory of the kingdom of Judah, but it cannot be claimed that the kingdom of Judah as such was the object of Shishak's interest. Shishak's attention was focused in the south not on the highlands of Judah but on the desert area south of the Judean highlands.

---

25 Rainey and Notley, *Sacred Bridge*, 187, find two "sequences," one to be traced from west to east-south-east and embracing Taanach, Shunem, Bethshean, Rehob, Hapharaim, and Adoraim, and the other from north to south, including Megiddo, Tell Ara, Kh. Burin, Jett, Kh. Yemma, Socoh, and Tappuah, and other sites as yet unidentified.

26 As proposed, though with too precise detail to be wholly convincing, by Siegfried Herrmann, "Operationen Pharao Schoschenks I. im östlichen Ephraim," *ZDPV* 80 (1964): 55–79, and Ahlström, "Pharaoh Shoshenq's Campaign to Palestine."

27 Na'aman, *Ancient Israel's History and Historiography*, 128–29, notes that, since many of the names are compounded, the actual number of places should be reduced by at least twenty.

28 So Wilson, *Campaign*, 118–33, lists only some ten which are either almost certain or probable identifications.

29 Especially Arad and Sharuhen, cf. nos. 108–10, 125 in Wilson, *Campaign*, 127, 129.

III. The Significance of the Shishak Invasion

The interpretation of the Shishak invasion has inevitably been strongly influenced by the biblical record. An extreme form of this is the view which denies any specific historical value to the Shishak record, seeing it simply in terms of being a conventional Egyptian genre, so that the Old Testament is then left as the sole source for historical reconstruction.[30] Thus Wilson is able to claim that, in line with the biblical report, Shishak's campaign was aimed at Jerusalem alone, and, having been bought off by Rehoboam, he was able to carry away the treasures of the temple and palace. Had Israel also been an objective there is no reason to think that the deuteronomistic account would have omitted to mention it. The only real evidence in favour of an Egyptian campaign against Israel, according to this view, is the fragment of a stele of Shishak found at Megiddo, but all this shows is that at some point Megiddo did recognize the authority of Shishak; it does not prove the capture and destruction of Megiddo by Shishak.[31] The wider historical context here is Shishak's support for his vassal Jeroboam, who had earlier taken refuge with Shishak after having fled to Egypt to escape Solomon (1 Kgs 11:40). On Solomon's death, Jeroboam returned to Israel and was made king at Shechem, so beginning a period of constant warfare with Judah.[32] This is the historical framework of Shishak's interference on his vassal's behalf.

This reconstruction, however, cannot stand if the Shishak topographical inscription is, as here argued, more than a conventional account, for this shows that Judah was not a focus of Egyptian attention. The lack of reference to Jerusalem is not to be explained by the suggestion that it may have featured among those now lost names in the record, for the general areas of Egyptian activity are clear, and these do not include the highlands of Judah. Judah and Jerusalem were not within Shishak's particular sphere of interest.[33]

---

30 So Wilson, *Campaign*, esp. 63–65. For Breasted, *Ancient Records of Egypt*, 4:348–49 (§§709–10), also, the inscription is a conventional record using stereotyped language drawn from earlier monuments, leaving only the record of 1 Kings 14 for historical reconstruction, though Breasted does credit the list of towns and localities with historical veracity.

31 Wilson, *Campaign*, 74.

32 Wilson, *Campaign*, 97–99.

33 Cf. also Finkelstein, "Campaign of Shoshenq I," 111–13. As Knauf ("Le roi est mort, vive le roi!", 93 n. 54) notes, none of the gaps in the Shishak list have a geographical context suggesting an original reference to Jerusalem. The closest the list comes to Jerusalem is lines 2–3, where Gibeon, Beth-horon, Kiriath-jearim, and Aijalon are

At somewhere near the other end of the spectrum from Wilson lies a recent account by Finkelstein,[34] in which the Egyptian account is the basis for at least one aspect of a critical reconstruction of Israelite history. Noting that those toponyms that may be safely identified belong to the Jezreel Valley, the international road in the plain of Sharon, the area of Gibeon in the highlands, the area of Penuel and Mahanaim east of the Jordan, and, in the south, the Beersheba Valley, the southern coast, the Besor region, and the Negeb highlands, Finkelstein significantly also points out the missing territories: the highlands of Judah, the hill country of northern Samaria, the Shephelah, the Galilee and the northern Jordan valley, the central and northern coastal plain, and the plateau of Gilead. This suggests a fairly precisely targeted operation with specific objectives: Shishak's campaign was in fact focused on three regions: the desert area south of Judah, the Jezreel Valley in the north, and the highland area to the north of Jerusalem centred on Gibeon.

Finkelstein claims that, from an archaeological perspective, Judah emerged to full statehood only in the eighth century,[35] while in the time of Shishak it was only a small chiefdom ruled from the poor highland settlement of Jerusalem. The object of Shishak's interest in the south was not the sparsely inhabited highlands of Judah, but a tenth-century desert chiefdom further south, identified archaeologically, and comprising Arad, Khirbet el-Meshash, Tell es-Sebaʿ and the Nahal Besor and Negeb highland sites, and his intention was to take control over the trade related prosperity which had brought about the sedentarization of nomads to form this chiefdom.

In the north, according to Finkelstein, Shishak took over the Jezreel Valley cities from their Canaanite inhabitants; it was only the subsequent Egyptian withdrawal that allowed for the expansion of the northern kingdom of Israel into the Valley.[36] The highland areas attacked by Shishak, the area of Gibeon including the cities of Gibeon, Beth-horon, and Zemaraim, must be understood as an Egyptian assault on the hub of an emerging polity that endangered Egyptian interests in Palestine. This is the core of the territory that the biblical tradition assigns to Saul. The historical background proposed by Finkelstein is

---

mentioned, but the immediately adjoining places at each end of this list are Mahanaim and Megiddo.

34 Finkelstein, "Campaign of Shoshenq I."

35 Cf. also David W. Jamieson-Drake, *Scribes and Schools in Monarchic Judah* (JSOTSup 109; Sheffield: Almond Press, 1991).

36 Cf. also Mario Liverani, *Israel's History and the History of Israel* (London: Equinox, 2005), 101–3.

that a strong Israelite political entity developed here, parallel to the chiefdom of the early Davidides in Jerusalem. It was the core of this Israelite polity that Shishak attacked, and, on his withdrawal, he allowed it to be taken over by the Jerusalem rulers. This is the background to the deuteronomistic picture of the greater Davidic united monarchy. The more remote highland parts of the Israelite polity centred on Gibeon, which Shishak had not entered, became the centre for the Israelite kingdom which expanded into the plain of Jezreel on the Egyptian withdrawal. The hostile relationships between this emergent Israel and Jerusalem are reflected in 1 Kings 15, and Jerusalemite occupation of the northern areas was brought to an end by the rise of the powerful Omride dynasty in Israel.

Attractive and persuasively argued as Finkelstein's proposal is, it reflects a reconstruction of Israelite history which is wholly dependent on a contentious argument on chronology in Palestinian archaeology. Finkelstein's low chronology has not only shifted the dating of the monumental structures at Gezer, Hazor, and Megiddo down to the ninth century, thus removing them as potential witnesses to an earlier state formation,[37] but has also, in so far as it portrays an arid and sparsely settled tenth-century Judah, and a Jerusalem of less than imperial significance, cast fundamental doubt on the historical reality of a tenth-century united monarchy of Israel and Judah.[38] Yet even apart from the contentious nature of the proposal,[39] it must be asked if even here there is too quick a correlation of Egyptian and biblical records. Such a correlation inevitably involves the ascription of relationships and motives to the actors involved about which we can have little or no knowledge. The variety of interpretations proposed, often mutually

---

37   That they do provide such evidence, even if dated to the tenth century, cannot be taken as certain. The city gate structures at Gezer and Hazor show differences from that at Megiddo, and, moreover, similar gates are to be found elsewhere in much later periods and at non-Israelite sites such as Ashdod; cf. Israel Finkelstein and Neil Asher Silberman, *David and Solomon* (New York: Free Press, 2006), 275–81; Knauf, "Le roi est mort, vive le roi!", 91 n. 40.

38   Cf. also Margreet Steiner, "Jerusalem in the Tenth and Seventh Centuries BCE: From Administrative Town to Commercial City," in *Studies in the Archaeology of the Iron Age in Israel and Jordan* (ed. Amihai Mazar; JSOTSup 331; Sheffield: Sheffield Academic, 2001), 280–88 (281–83).

39   For a discussion cf., e.g., the various essays in V. Fritz and P. R. Davies, eds., *The Origins of the Ancient Israelite States* (JSOTSup 228; Sheffield: Sheffield Academic, 1996), and William G. Dever, "Histories and Non-Histories of Ancient Israel: The Question of the United Monarchy," in *In Search of Pre-exilic Israel* (ed. John Day; JSOTSup 406; London: T&T Clark International, 2004), 65–94.

incompatible,[40] is in fact not only a reflection of the futility of engaging with the event at this level of detail, but also a neglect of the primary task: the understanding of the event within an Egyptian frame of reference. At least here basic results can be achieved which are not dependent on a resolution to the difficulties surrounding Israelite early monarchic history.

Egypt's relationship with Syria-Palestine was marked by a considerable tension between ideology and reality. The ideology may have proclaimed that the rule of Amun was universal and so presupposed Egypt's domination of Syria-Palestine,[41] but the reality was different: by contrast with its relationship with Nubia, where total Egyptian control of this tribal area was secured by the imposition of a provincial administrative system,[42] Egypt was confronted in Syria-Palestine by an established system of city-states, each with its king and governing officials. No bureaucracy had to be created *de novo*. Although certain cities, such

---

40 So, while Wilson, as noted, argues that Shishak was concerned to support Jeroboam, for others, such as Benjamin Mazar ("Pharaoh Shishak's Campaign to the Land of Israel," in *Volume du Congrès: Strasbourg 1956* [VTSup 4; Leiden: Brill, 1957], 57–66), his intention was to punish Jeroboam as a rebellious vassal.

41 Tutankhamun's "Restoration Inscription," in lamenting the state of affairs under the earlier regime of Akhenaten, declared: "The gods were ignoring this land: if an army was sent to Djahy [Palestine] to broaden the boundaries of Egypt, no success of theirs came to pass"; cf. William J. Murnane, *Texts from the Amarna Period in Egypt* (Atlanta, Ga.: Scholars Press, 1995), 213. The "Story of Wenamun," while deriving from the beginning of the 21st Dynasty, has been plausibly interpreted by Bernd U. Schipper, *Die Erzählung des Wenamun* (OBO 209; Fribourg, Switzerland: Academic Press Fribourg; Göttingen: Vandenhoeck & Ruprecht, 2005), 299–324, as a politico-religious document of the reign of Shishak, serving as the religious ideology foundational to his rule in Egypt and his invasion of Palestine. In this story, Amun's claim to Syria-Palestine is presupposed, but stands in basic tension with the reality of Wenamun's difficult experiences in fulfilling his mission to secure timber for the barge of Amun.

42 Nubia was included under the authority of "a king's son of the southern lands," under whom were two deputies, one for Nubia and the other for Kush, parallel to the system of two viziers in Egypt; cf. D. O'Connor, "New Kingdom and Third Intermediate Period, 1552–664 BC," in *Ancient Egypt: A Social History* (ed. B. G. Trigger, B. J. Kemp, D. O'Connor, and A. B. Lloyd; Cambridge: Cambridge University Press, 1983), 204–18, and especially the table illustrating the Egyptian structure of government (208). See also J. K. Hoffmeier, "Aspects of Egyptian Foreign Policy in the 18th Dynasty in Western Asia and Nubia," in *Egypt, Israel, and the Ancient Mediterranean World: Studies in Honor of Donald B. Redford* (ed. G. N. Knoppers and A. Hirsch; Leiden: Brill, 2004), 121–41. Nubia's incorporation into Egypt is presupposed in the reported complaint of Kamose, the last ruler of the 17th Dynasty, who initiated the expulsion of the Hyksos, to his nobles: "Let me understand what this strength of mine is for! One prince is in Avaris, another is in Kush, and here I sit associated with an Asiatic and a Nubian! Each man has his slice of this Egypt, dividing up the land with me"; cf. "The War Against the Hyksos," translated by John A. Wilson (*ANET*, 232).

as Gaza, Sumer, and Kumidi, were set aside as residences for Egyptian commissioners, there was little attempt outside the southern coastal plain at colonization, through implanting Egyptian elements and insinuating Egyptian cult practices, as in Nubia. Palestine was valued primarily for its trade routes, and, secondly, for the few resources it could directly contribute to Egyptian wealth. If, even at the height of Egyptian power, there was no attempt at incorporation of Syria-Palestine,[43] this was even more the case in a time of internal Egyptian weakness at the beginning of the 22nd Dynasty. Whether or not there had been a united kingdom of David and Solomon, whether or not Solomon had earlier contracted a marriage with an Egyptian princess,[44] the motivation behind the Shishak invasion should be understood in the context of the limited practical objectives that marked Egyptian relations with Palestine, particularly since the decline of the New Kingdom.[45] In the case of all the major areas affected by the invasion, the Negeb, the international coastal route, the Jezreel valley, and even the area of Gibeon in the highlands, which belongs to the direct route linking the southern coastal region to the Jordan valley, it is clear that it is the protection of trade routes that the invasion was designed to secure.[46] A study of the consequences of the invasion, on the other hand, and especially perhaps its unintended consequences, may give it a significance with wider implications.

---

43   For a detailed study of Egyptian imperialism in the New Kingdom, cf. B. J. Kemp, "Imperialism and Empire in New Kingdom Egypt (c. 1575–1087 B.C.)," in *Imperialism in the Ancient World* (ed. P. D. A. Garnsey and C. R. Whittaker; Cambridge: Cambridge University Press, 1978), 7–57.

44   Independently of the question of a united monarchy, on this at least there must be considerable doubt; cf. Schipper, *Israel und Ägypten*, 84–107.

45   For a survey, cf. especially Paul S. Ash, *David, Solomon and Egypt: A Reassessment* (JSOTSup 297; Sheffield: Sheffield Academic, 1999).

46   Cf. also Ahlström, "Pharaoh Shoshenq's Campaign to Palestine," 13–16; Schipper, *Die Erzählung des Wenamun*, 315.

Who Built and Who Used the Buildings at Kuntillet ʿAjrud?

B. A. MASTIN

Kuntillet ʿAjrud in northern Sinai was occupied during the first third of the eighth century BC. No consensus has been reached about the identity of those who built and used the buildings here, though the question is important, since some of them were responsible for the inscriptions which mention "Yahweh and his asherah."[1] Thus, for example, Meshel claims that the site's "construction should be attributed to the kingdom of Israel . . . or to one of the Judean kings closely aligned with the Israelite kingdom,"[2] Lemaire that it was a joint Phoenician and Israelite enterprise,[3] and Zevit that "it was conceived, maintained, and defended" by the authorities in Jerusalem.[4] The purpose of this essay is to re-examine the evidence on which a decision has to be based.

I. Was There a Phoenician Presence at Kuntillet ʿAjrud?

1. The Inscriptions Written on Plaster

Meshel says that fragments of three inscriptions written in ink on plaster were discovered at Kuntillet ʿAjrud, and that they are "in Phoenician script but in the Hebrew language."[5] One inscription is illegible.[6]

---

1   G. I. Davies, *Ancient Hebrew Inscriptions: Corpus and Concordance* (Cambridge: Cambridge University Press, 1991), 80–81 (§§8.016.1; 8.017.2; 8.021.1–2), cf. *ʾšrt[h]* in §8.015.1, as corrected, together with §8.017, in idem, *Ancient Hebrew Inscriptions Volume 2: Corpus and Concordance* (Cambridge: Cambridge University Press, 2004), 233; J. Renz, *Die althebräischen Inschriften, Teil 1: Text und Kommentar* (J. Renz and W. Röllig, *Handbuch der althebräischen Epigraphik*, vol. 1; Darmstadt: Wissenschaftliche Buchgesellschaft, 1995), 61–62, 64 (§§KAgr(9):8.2; KAgr(9):9.6; KAgr(9):10.2), cf. *ʾšrt* in §KAgr(9):6.b (p. 58).

2   Z. Meshel, "Teman, Ḥorvat," *NEAEHL* 4:1458–64 (1464).

3   A. Lemaire, "Date et origine des inscriptions hébraïques et phéniciennes de Kuntillet ʿAjrud," *SEL* 1 (1984): 131–43 (131–33, 136–39).

4   Z. Zevit, *The Religions of Ancient Israel: A Synthesis of Parallactic Approaches* (London: Continuum, 2001), 378.

5   Z. Meshel, "Kuntillet ʿAjrud," *ABD* 4:103–9 (107).

Parts of the other two inscriptions have been transcribed,[7] and a photograph of portions of two lines of one of these has been published.[8] I have argued in detail elsewhere that, on the basis of the available evidence, there is no reason to doubt that these texts were composed in Hebrew. There is nothing in what has so far been published which cannot be Hebrew, and the use of vowel letters in three words, and the two examples of *wāw* consecutive + the imperfect, strongly suggest that the language is not Phoenician.[9] One inscription refers to El (or God) and Baal.[10] Some Phoenician texts mention a god Baal, but the way in which this inscription speaks of El is not in accordance with what is known about Phoenician practice. It is therefore unlikely that this is a Phoenician religious text.[11] If the letters which can be studied on a photograph are typical, the script of these texts is neither exclusively Phoenician nor exclusively Hebrew. They would therefore have been written by men who had been in either direct or indirect contact with Phoenicians, but who were not themselves Phoenician. A comparison with contemporary inscriptions in Phoenician script which were found in Palestine points to a link with northern Palestine or with an area with which the Phoenicians traded, but not with Judah.[12]

2. The Reading *lśrˁr*

Many scholars think that four inscriptions on storage jars should be read *lśrˁr*, "belonging to/for the governor of the city."[13] Catastini,

---

6   Davies, *Ancient Hebrew Inscriptions,* 80 (§8.014); Renz, *Die althebräischen Inschriften,* 58 (Nr. 1).

7   Davies, *Ancient Hebrew Inscriptions,* 80, 82 (§§8.015; 8.023); cf. idem, *Ancient Hebrew Inscriptions Volume 2,* 233–34; Renz, *Die althebräischen Inschriften,* 58–59 (§§KAgr(9):6; KAgr(9):7).

8   S. Aḥituv, *Handbook of Ancient Hebrew Inscriptions* [in Hebrew] (BEL 7; Jerusalem: Bialik Institute, 1992), 159; Meshel, "Teman, Ḥorvat," 1462.

9   B. A. Mastin, "The Inscriptions Written on Plaster at Kuntillet ˁAjrud," *VT* 59 (2009): 99–115 (105–9, 114).

10   Davies, *Ancient Hebrew Inscriptions,* 82 (§8.023.1, 2, 3, to be corrected to lines 1, 5, and 6; cf. idem, *Ancient Hebrew Inscriptions Volume 2,* 234); Renz, *Die althebräischen Inschriften,* 59 (§KAgr(9):7.1, 2, 3).

11   Mastin, "Inscriptions Written on Plaster," 111–14.

12   Mastin, "Inscriptions Written on Plaster," 100–105, 114.

13   Davies (*Ancient Hebrew Inscriptions,* 79–80 [§§8.007–8.010]) and Renz (*Die althebräischen Inschriften,* 55 [§KAgr(9):2.3]) mistakenly insert a space between *lśr* and *ˁr*; cf., e.g., J. Gunneweg, I. Perlman, and Z. Meshel, "The Origin of the Pottery of Kuntillet ˁAjrud," *IEJ* 35 (1985): 270–83 and pl. 33 (pl. 33:D). As is customary in transcribing inscriptions, here and elsewhere Davies uses *š* instead of *ś*.

however, reads a Phoenician *dālet* instead of the *ʿayin* and translates "to the head of the community."[14] His hypothesis that a community of prophets lived at Kuntillet ʿAjrud has received little support, but conclusions about the reading must remain provisional until all four inscriptions have been fully published.

It is surprising that the inscriptions read *ʿr*, and not *hʿr*. Davies lists five examples of *śr hʿr*, all of which are on bullae, but does not report any other instance without the definite article.[15] Although Hadley states that Hestrin[16] provides "other examples of *śr ʿr*,"[17] this is not the case. Gogel observes that some of the Samaria Ostraca, and perhaps Lachish Letter 13.3 and Tell Arad Ostracon 40.10–11, have no definite article where one might have been expected,[18] but there is no parallel to the phrase *śr ʿr* in these texts. In Phoenician, however, the definite article was not employed regularly until ca. 700 BC, and even then it was omitted in titles.[19] Catastini relies on this as a further indication that his reading is correct.[20] Yet Renz suggests that the definite article may have been used in an identical way in both Phoenician and Hebrew at this stage in the development of the Hebrew language.[21] Moreover, Joüon and Muraoka, who cite 2 Sam 2:8; 19:14; 1 Kgs 16:16; 2 Kgs 25:8; Jer 39:9, say that "[w]ith nouns of titles there is a certain tendency to omit the article" in biblical Hebrew.[22] They do not refer to the texts from Kuntillet ʿAjrud, though Sarfatti maintains that "the determinate form in the bullae agrees with standard Biblical Hebrew, while the indeter-

---

14   A. Catastini, "Le iscrizioni di Kuntillet ʿAjrud e il profetismo," *AION* NS 42 (1982): 127–34 (128–29). He is followed, for example, by F. Scagliarini, "Osservazioni sulle iscrizioni di Kuntillet ʿAǧrud," *RSO* 63 (1989): 199–212 (203–4).

15   Davies, *Ancient Hebrew Inscriptions*, 171 (§100.402.1); 187 (§100.510.1); idem, *Ancient Hebrew Inscriptions Volume 2*, 77 (§§101.191.2; 101.192.2; 101.193.1); cf. W. Röllig, *Siegel und Gewichte*, in J. Renz and W. Röllig, *Handbuch der althebräischen Epigraphik*, vol. 2/2 (Darmstadt: Wissenschaftliche Buchgesellschaft, 2003), 230 (§9.8.2), 364 (§17.35.2), 418 (§§30.9.1; 30.10.1).

16   R. Hestrin, "Hebrew Seals of Officials," in *Ancient Seals and the Bible* (ed. L. Gorelick and E. Williams-Forte; Occasional Papers on the Near East 2/1; Malibu, Calif.: Undena Publications, 1983), 50–54 (51).

17   J. M. Hadley, *The Cult of Asherah in Ancient Israel and Judah: Evidence for a Hebrew Goddess* (UCOP 57; Cambridge: Cambridge University Press, 2000), 112.

18   S. L. Gogel, *A Grammar of Epigraphic Hebrew* (SBLRBS 23; Atlanta, Ga.: Scholars Press, 1998), 174–75; 174 n. 206.

19   J. Friedrich, W. Röllig, M. G. Amadasi Guzzo, and W. R. Mayer, *Phönizisch-Punische Grammatik* (3d ed.; AnOr 55; Rome: Pontifical Biblical Institute, 1999), 210–11 (§§296, 297[3]).

20   Catastini, "Le iscrizioni di Kuntillet ʿAjrud," 128.

21   Renz, *Die althebräischen Inschriften*, 55 n. 3.

22   P. Joüon and T. Muraoka, *A Grammar of Biblical Hebrew* (rev. ed.; SubBi 27; Rome: Pontifical Biblical Institute, 2006), 480 (§137r).

minate form of Kuntillet ʿAjrud reveals a more colloquial style."[23] This
theory cannot be discussed here. Whatever its merits, while the absence
of the definite article in *śr ʿr* might be due to Phoenician influence, it
might equally well have a place in the history of Hebrew usage. If it
could be established that one of the letters is a Phoenician *dālet*, this
would, of course, be decisive.

Gunneweg, Perlman, and Meshel state that neutron activation
analysis shows that the clay from which three jars found at Kuntillet
ʿAjrud were made "may have come from the [Tel] Miqne region."
Greater precision is unattainable because this "region has not been well
documented by pottery analyses." There are inscriptions on all three
jars, one of which reads *lśrʿr*, but we are not told whether the inscriptions on the other two jars are identical.[24] Thus at least one, and perhaps more, of the jars on which *lśrʿr* was incised was presumably sent
to Kuntillet ʿAjrud from the Shephelah. It must, however, remain an
open question whether this was done by Phoenicians.

3. The Term *ʾšrh*

At Kuntillet ʿAjrud the word *ʾšrth* is of central importance in at least
three Hebrew inscriptions,[25] and Meshel says that, if it "derives from
ʾšrt, it . . . is Phoenician."[26] Two Phoenician inscriptions contain the
noun *ʾšrt*. It is likely that one should be dated palaeographically to the
early part of the fifth century BC.[27] The other is from 222 BC.[28] Hoftijzer
and Jongeling state that *ʾšrt* probably signifies "a sanctuary," though
they note that some scholars prefer "sacred pole (of wood)" or "divine
female consort,"[29] and Tomback tentatively suggests "sacred grove."[30]
It is unnecessary to review theories about the meaning of *ʾšrh* at Kuntil-

---

23   G. B. Sarfatti, "Hebrew Inscriptions of the First Temple Period: A Survey and some
     Linguistic Comments," *Maarav* 3 (1982): 55–83 (71–73).
24   Gunneweg, Perlman, and Meshel, "The Origin of the Pottery," 280 and pl. 33:D.
25   See n. 1 above.
26   Z. Meshel, "Two Aspects in the Excavation of Kuntillet ʿAǧrud," in *Ein Gott allein?
     JHWH-Verehrung und biblischer Monotheismus im Kontext der israelitischen und altorien-
     talischen Religionsgeschichte* (ed. W. Dietrich and M. A. Klopfenstein; OBO 139; Fri-
     bourg, Switzerland: Universitätsverlag Freiburg Schweiz; Göttingen: Vandenhoeck
     & Ruprecht, 1994), 99–104 (102).
27   M. Dothan, "A Phoenician Inscription from ʿAkko," *IEJ* 35 (1985): 81–94 and pl.
     13:A–B (83 line 2 [text], 92, but cf. 93 n. 93 [date]).
28   *KAI* 1:4, §19.4 (text), and *KAI* 2:27 (date).
29   *DNWSI* 1:129.
30   R. S. Tomback, *A Comparative Semitic Lexicon of the Phoenician and Punic Languages*
     (SBLDS 32; Missoula, Mont.: Scholars Press, 1978), 36.

let ʿAjrud and in the Old Testament, since they have been discussed in detail by Emerton.[31] He argues convincingly that the *ʾšrh* is "likely to have been some kind of wooden symbol of the goddess Asherah," though not a living tree, and rightly claims that "it seems best ... to interpret [the] Hebrew inscriptions [from Kuntillet ʿAjrud and the inscription from Khirbet el-Qom which include the word *ʾšrth*] in the light of known Hebrew usage, rather than to appeal to cognate languages and to postulate a meaning not established in the Old Testament."[32] The goddess Asherah is never mentioned in Phoenician or Punic texts,[33] but is, of course, prominent in the myths from Ugarit. If, as is probable, the *ʾšrh* is the cult symbol of this goddess and bears her name, the term did not enter Hebrew as a Phoenician loanword.

4. The Absence of Phoenician Pottery

Ayalon observes that the "ceramic finds [at Kuntillet ʿAjrud] ... represent virtually a complete assemblage." He does not discuss the seventeen vessels found in the eastern building, but in his comprehensive study of the remainder of the pottery he identifies Phoenician influence on some items. He also comments that Phoenician pottery "differs in form and finish from the ʿAjrud vessels," and so he concludes that none of these "can be defined with certainty as Phoenician, except possibly a jug ... and additional decorated fragments."[34] Petrographic analysis, however, shows that this jug was made in central or northern Israel.[35] If Kuntillet ʿAjrud was regularly visited by Phoenicians, it is strange that so little Phoenician pottery has been found.

---

31   J. A. Emerton, "New Light on Israelite Religion: The Implications of the Inscriptions from Kuntillet ʿAjrud," *ZAW* 94 (1982): 2–20 (13–19).

32   Emerton, "New Light on Israelite Religion," 15, 18; cf. idem, "'Yahweh and His Asherah': The Goddess or Her Symbol?" *VT* 49 (1999): 315–37.

33   E. Lipiński, *Dieux et déesses de l'univers Phénicien et Punique* (OLA 64; StPh 14; Leuven: Peeters, 1995), 225.

34   E. Ayalon, "The Iron Age II Pottery Assemblage from Ḥorvat Teiman (Kuntillet ʿAjrud)," *TA* 22 (1995): 141–205 (142, 141, 191, 193, 196, 194 n. 11, 194).

35   Y. Goren, "Petrographic Analyses of Ḥorvat Teiman (Kuntillet ʿAjrud) Pottery," Appendix A to Ayalon, "Iron Age II Pottery Assemblage," *TA* 22 (1995): 206–7 (§12); cf. Ayalon, "Iron Age II Pottery Assemblage," 173–74.

5. Art

Wall paintings and drawings on two pithoi were discovered at Kuntillet ʿAjrud. Beck maintains that "[t]he majority of the motifs on both surfaces are derived from the Phoenician-Syrian world, with perhaps a certain admixture of the desert art."[36] She believes that both the murals and the drawings on the pithoi may have been produced by "itinerant artisans,"[37] but she thinks that the "national affiliation" of those responsible for the drawings (and by implication also of those responsible for the murals) cannot be determined "on the basis of the present evidence."[38] It should be noted, however, that some motifs which were "in fashion in Judah from the 9th century onwards" are not "reflected in the ʿAjrud drawings."[39] Similarly Keel and Uehlinger state that the artist who drew the animals on the pithoi may have come from either north Syria or Phoenicia, but that, though he might have been an Israelite, this is unlikely.[40] It is impossible to be sure whether Phoenicians were among the artists who worked at Kuntillet ʿAjrud.

6. Summary

The belief that the construction of the buildings at Kuntillet ʿAjrud was a joint Phoenician and Israelite enterprise goes beyond the evidence. If there had been a substantial Phoenician presence at Kuntillet ʿAjrud, it might be expected that much more Phoenician pottery would have

---

36   P. Beck, "The Drawings from Ḥorvat Teiman (Kuntillet ʿAjrud)," *TA* 9 (1982): 3–68 and pls. 1–16 (60–61, cf. 27, 36, 39–40, 44–45, 49, 50, 52, 58); repr. in idem, *Imagery and Representation: Studies in the Art and Iconography of Ancient Palestine: Collected Articles* (TAOP 3; Tel Aviv: Emery and Claire Yass Publications in Archaeology, 2002), 94–170, without the plates but with additional illustrations (161, cf. 122, 132, 136–37, 141–42, 148, 150, 157).

37   Beck, "The Drawings from Ḥorvat Teiman," 62; repr. in idem, *Imagery and Representation*, 163.

38   P. Beck, "The Art of Palestine during the Iron Age II: Local Traditions and External Influences (10th–8th Centuries BCE)," in *Images as Media: Sources for the Cultural History of the Near East and the Eastern Mediterranean (1st Millennium BCE)* (ed. C. Uehlinger; OBO 175; Fribourg, Switzerland: Universitätsverlag Freiburg Schweiz; Göttingen: Vandenhoeck & Ruprecht, 2000), 165–83 (180); repr. in idem, *Imagery and Representation*, 203–222 (218).

39   Beck, "The Drawings from Ḥorvat Teiman," 44; repr. in idem, *Imagery and Representation*, 142.

40   O. Keel and C. Uehlinger, *Göttinnen, Götter und Gottessymbole: Neue Erkenntnisse zur Religionsgeschichte Kanaans und Israels aufgrund bislang unerschlossener ikonographischer Quellen* (QD 134; Freiburg im Breisgau: Herder, 1992), 244; ET *Gods, Goddesses, and Images of God in Ancient Israel* (Edinburgh: T&T Clark, 1998), 217.

been found. Phoenician artists may have worked there, and some of its supplies may have been purchased from Phoenician merchants, who may also have used the route past Kuntillet ʿAjrud and have stopped there, but Phoenicians do not seem to have had a major involvement in the business of the site. It is unlikely that the term *ʾšrh* is a Phoenician loanword. Other inscriptional material suggests, however, that some Israelites who came to Kuntillet ʿAjrud had been in direct or indirect contact with Phoenicians and had been influenced by them, perhaps in northern Palestine, or in an area with which the Phoenicians traded.

II. The Pottery

1. The Absence of Local Pottery

Meshel says that "not a single sherd of the rough hand-made pottery typical of the Israelite sites of the Negev was found" at Kuntillet ʿAjrud.[41] For Ayalon, this "raises the question of whether the nomads of the desert (if they were indeed the makers of these vessels) were banned from settling at the site."[42] This may or may not have been the case, though the absence of local pottery tells against Hadley's claim that the person who was in charge at Kuntillet ʿAjrud "could have been a member of a tribe living in the vicinity."[43] Moreover, according to Keel and Uehlinger, the wall paintings, which appear to have been deliberately planned, and whose subjects include a city which may be under siege and a prince sitting on a throne and holding a lotus blossom, point to the official character of the establishment.[44] In addition, the construction of these buildings in a very inhospitable area must have required careful organization and considerable expenditure. The authority which was responsible for this might have been expected to send its own officials to run the site. It may be presumed that those who were in charge at Kuntillet ʿAjrud came from elsewhere.

---

41   Z. Meshel, "Kuntilat ʿAjrud, 1975–1976," *IEJ* 27 (1977): 52–53 (52).

42   Ayalon, "Iron Age II Pottery Assemblage," 199.

43   Hadley, *The Cult of Asherah*, 112.

44   Keel and Uehlinger, *Göttinnen, Götter und Gottessymbole*, 278 and figs. 237, 238a; ET *Gods, Goddesses, and Images of God*, 245 and figs. 237, 238a. See also Beck, "The Drawings from Ḥorvat Teiman," figs. 18, 21, and 21a, and pls. 7.1 and 10, partially reproduced in idem, *Imagery and Representation*, figs. 19, 23, and 23a.

2. Pottery from the Northern Kingdom of Israel

It is significant that the types of pottery discovered at Kuntillet ʿAjrud which came from Israel differ from those which came from Judah. Ayalon observes that "the identifiable sources of the parallels to many of the small vessels are in Israel." In particular, he notes that "a group of more than twenty identical cooking-pots," out of thirty which were found, are the same "in shape, clay and finish" as cooking-pots from Samaria, "while in Judea and along the coast cooking-pots in use differed in form and clay." He concludes that "they were brought to ʿAjrud from Israel," and comments that, "[a]s the simplest vessel in daily use, the cooking-pot represents reliable testimony for the origin . . . of vessels."[45] Zevit believes that the so-called "Samaria Ware" could, "at least theoretically, . . . have been manufactured somewhere in Judah,"[46] but he appears to have overlooked Gunneweg, Perlman, and Meshel's demonstration that "[t]he southern and central regions, both coastal and inland, can be ruled out with confidence" as the source of the two items of this ware which were submitted for neutron activation analysis.[47] It is, however, perhaps incautious of Ayalon to assert that "there was not even one single small vessel at ʿAjrud for which the source of its parallels was Judea." Although there may not be many parallels from Judah, he adduces examples of bowls from Arad, Jerusalem, Tell en-Naṣbeh, Beer-sheba, and Tel Halif, of jugs, juglets, and lamps from Beer-sheba, and of flasks from Jerusalem and Beer-sheba.[48] Nonetheless, the "vessels whose forms originate in Israel" are "mainly small everyday types," while the "large containers for transporting and storing supplies" came from "Judea, the Shephelah and the Southern Coast."[49] It will be suggested below that practical considerations explain why these vessels were not brought from the north.

Hadley says that, "[a]s the site was in Judaean territory, and as trade through this area would greatly benefit Judah, perhaps the Judaean kings built it and stocked it initially, but other provisions and pottery were left by the travellers themselves."[50] Similarly Ayalon asks whether "the site [was] established and maintained jointly by the people of Israel, Judea and the Southern Coast."[51] But both scholars fail to

---

45   Ayalon, "Iron Age II Pottery Assemblage," 193, 155.
46   Zevit, *The Religions of Ancient Israel*, 378.
47   Gunneweg, Perlman, and Meshel, "The Origin of the Pottery," 282.
48   Ayalon, "Iron Age II Pottery Assemblage," 194, 144–45, 148–49, 168, 176–78.
49   Ayalon, "Iron Age II Pottery Assemblage," 194.
50   Hadley, *The Cult of Asherah*, 112.
51   Ayalon, "Iron Age II Pottery Assemblage," 198–99.

reckon with the absence of small pottery vessels which can be traced to Judah. If the Judean authorities had thought it worthwhile to set up a post at Kuntillet ʿAjrud, or if they had participated in such a venture, a number of travellers from Judah might have been expected to visit the site. It would be strange if they left nothing behind to reveal their presence except "large containers for transporting and storing supplies." By contrast, there is ample evidence for the presence of men from the northern kingdom of Israel.

3. The Storage Vessels

Twenty-six pithoi, 182 storage jars, and three holemouth jars were excavated at Kuntillet ʿAjrud.[52] Gunneweg, Perlman, and Meshel have shown that the eleven pithoi which were tested by neutron activation analysis were manufactured in or near Jerusalem, that four of the seven storage jars which were tested "were almost certainly made in the southern coastal region," and that the other three, which were discussed above in Section I.2, "may have come from the [Tel] Miqne region."[53] According to Ayalon, there are no parallels to the pithoi or the holemouth jars from any site to the north of Judah or the Shephelah.[54] As was noted above, he considers that the "containers for transporting and storing supplies" came from "Judea, the Shephelah and the Southern Coast." He rightly comments that "[t]he large quantity of storage vessels," which comprise 51.5% of the assemblage, "is reasonable in light of the distance between the site and the centres of settlement in the Land of Israel, which required bringing supplies from afar and storing them at the site." Moreover, "no granaries, milling devices or sickle blades were found at ʿAjrud."[55] Each of the two pithoi which were embellished with drawings and inscriptions was over three feet high and when empty weighed almost 30 pounds.[56] Five other "complete vessels and 14 sherds of this type" of pithos were discovered, and Ayalon records others of comparable size.[57] Zevit pertinently observes that "[t]heir fragility coupled with their loaded weight must have rendered them difficult to transport, and under general circumstances

---

52   Ayalon, "Iron Age II Pottery Assemblage," 187.

53   Gunneweg, Perlman, and Meshel, "The Origin of the Pottery," 272–76, 278–81.

54   Ayalon, "Iron Age II Pottery Assemblage," 156–58.

55   Ayalon, "Iron Age II Pottery Assemblage," 187–88 and n. 7.

56   Z. Meshel, "Did Yahweh Have a Consort? The New Religious Inscriptions from the Sinai," *BAR* 5, no. 2 (March/April 1979): 24–35 (27).

57   Ayalon, "Iron Age II Pottery Assemblage," 157–58, 160.

made their transportation highly impractical."[58] In view of the problems involved in provisioning Kuntillet ʿAjrud, it might have seemed convenient to transport the supplies which were needed for as short a distance as possible. It is likely that the large storage vessels came from Judah, the Shephelah, and the southern coastal region because these areas are close to Kuntillet ʿAjrud. If this was the extent of the link between Judah and Kuntillet ʿAjrud, the absence of other vessels from Judah would be accounted for.

Meshel supposes that "[t]he site . . . was inhabited by a small group of priests, perhaps sent from the kingdom of Israel," which "subsisted on tithes and donations, including supplies, sent mostly from Judah."[59] It might, however, be expected that those who had dispatched priests some distance to an inhospitable region would have been responsible for maintaining them.[60] Meshel says that "most of the pithoi . . . bore one or two incised letters on their shoulders." The letters are ʾālep, yôd, or the combination qôp rêš.[61] He believes that they "are abbreviations indicating offerings and tithes,"[62] though Zevit thinks that the pithoi may have contained wine or oil which was "of a special purity or manufactured under special supervision for use within the sacred precincts" at cult centres and that the letters "may have been 'brand' labels."[63] A number of theories about the meaning of these letters are discussed by Renz, who gives convincing reasons why none is satisfactory.[64] It would be unwise to rely on these inscriptions as evidence for a cultic link between Jerusalem and Kuntillet ʿAjrud.

4. Further Data

Ayalon observes that "[a]n additional group of vessels," which includes bowls and jars of types which are also found in Israel, "finds most of its parallels at sites in the Shephelah," and he comments, "[i]t is interesting that the overlap in the sources of parallels is between the Shephelah and Israel, and not between the Shephelah and Judea or the Southern Coast, which are closer." He also notes that "[p]arallels to

---

58 Zevit, *The Religions of Ancient Israel*, 379.
59 Meshel, "Teman, Ḥorvat," 1464.
60 Hadley, *The Cult of Asherah*, 111.
61 Davies, *Ancient Hebrew Inscriptions*, 78–79 (§§8.001–8.003); cf. idem, *Ancient Hebrew Inscriptions Volume 2*, 232; cf. Renz, *Die althebräischen Inschriften*, 54 (§KAgr(9):1).
62 Meshel, "Teman, Ḥorvat," 1461.
63 Zevit, *The Religions of Ancient Israel*, 379–80.
64 Renz, *Die althebräischen Inschriften*, 52–54, 52 nn. 2, 3, 53 nn. 1, 2.

certain large and small vessels," among which are jars which represent "the dominant type at ʿAjrud," "can be found at sites on the Southern Coast (such as Ashdod)."[65] Travellers who had passed through the southern coastal region may have brought vessels acquired on their journey to Kuntillet ʿAjrud, which may also have been visited by traders from this area and from the Shephelah. Ayalon asks whether "the people of . . . the Southern Coast" were among those who "established and maintained" the buildings at Kuntillet ʿAjrud.[66] Since, however, there is a satisfactory alternative explanation for the presence of this pottery, which is the only evidence on which Ayalon relies, it is impossible to tell whether his conjecture is likely to be correct.

5. Summary

The evidence provided by the pottery is consistent with, and gives strong support to, the view that Israel was the authority which constructed and ran the establishment at Kuntillet ʿAjrud. The difference between the kinds of vessel from Israel and those from Judah is significant, and indicates that Judah was one of the places from which supplies were obtained, but that it did not have an important role in running the site. Travellers from the southern coastal region and from the Shephelah may have used the facilities at Kuntillet ʿAjrud, but the pottery record leaves open the question whether, and, if so, how far, the authorities or the people of these areas were involved.

III. Proper Names

At Kuntillet ʿAjrud there are nine, or possibly ten, theophorous names which include the divine name Yahweh. In each case it is spelt *yw* and not *yhw*. Examples are *šknyw*, *šmryw*, and *ʿzyw*.[67] I have discussed elsewhere the evidence for the spellings *yw* and *yhw* in eighth-century Palestine.[68] The Divine Name is spelt *yw* in texts from the kingdom of Israel, while in Judah it is normally spelt *yhw*. Meshel says that the

---

65 Ayalon, "Iron Age II Pottery Assemblage," 194.

66 Ayalon, "Iron Age II Pottery Assemblage," 198–99.

67 Davies, *Ancient Hebrew Inscriptions Volume 2*, 11 (§8.026.1, 3, 4). There is a full listing in B. A. Mastin, "The Theophoric Elements *yw* and *yhw* in Proper Names in Eighth-Century Hebrew Inscriptions and the Proper Names at Kuntillet ʿAjrud," *ZAH* 17–20 (2004–2007): 109–35 (111).

68 Mastin, "The Theophoric Elements *yw* and *yhw*," 109–28.

spelling found at Kuntillet ʿAjrud is an indication that "the site reflects a strong northern (Israelite, not Judean) influence,"[69] though this is disputed by Zevit, who emphasizes that *yw* is the spelling in some Judean names.[70] Since, however, the concentration of such a large number of theophorous names compounded with *yw* at Kuntillet ʿAjrud, together with the absence of names compounded with *yhw*, is unlike the overall pattern of usage in Judah, it is probable that these are the names of men who came from the kingdom of Israel.[71]

I have examined elsewhere other names which have been thought to be Judean, and have argued that there is no sufficient reason for supposing this. They are the names of men who may have come from either Judah or Israel.[72] I failed, however, to consider ʿyrʾ, which Renz rightly regards as the name of a man from Judah because the diphthong indicated by the *yôd* is a characteristic of the south Palestinian dialect.[73] Some eighteen names are attested at Kuntillet ʿAjrud. There may have been more than one Judean among the eight men whose names were not compounded with the divine name Yahweh, but even so the presence of a relatively large number of men from Israel in the short time the site was occupied is striking.

IV. The Titles "Yahweh of Samaria" and "Yahweh of Teman"

Despite the hesitations of some scholars,[74] there is a consensus that the phrase *yhwh. šmrn* in a blessing from Kuntillet ʿAjrud[75] should be translated "Yahweh of Samaria." It is probable that a blessing which invokes Yahweh in this way would have been written by someone from the northern kingdom of Israel.[76]

---

69   Meshel, "Teman, Ḥorvat," 1464.
70   Zevit, *The Religions of Ancient Israel*, 378, 381, 398.
71   Mastin, "The Theophoric Elements *yw* and *yhw*," 128–31.
72   Mastin, "The Theophoric Elements *yw* and *yhw*," 129–30.
73   J. Renz, *Schrift und Schreibertradition: Eine paläographische Studie zum kulturgeschicht-lichen Verhältnis von israelitischem Nordreich und Südreich* (ADPV 23; Wiesbaden: Otto Harrassowitz, 1997), 6. For the text, see Davies, *Ancient Hebrew Inscriptions*, 79 (§8.004.1); Renz, *Die althebräischen Inschriften*, 55 (§KAgr(9):2.1) and 55 n. 1 (on the diphthong).
74   So, e.g., Renz, *Die althebräischen Inschriften*, 61 and 61 n. 2.
75   Davies, *Ancient Hebrew Inscriptions*, 81 (§8.017.2); Renz, *Die althebräischen Inschriften*, 61 (§KAgr(9):8.2).
76   Emerton, "New Light on Israelite Religion," 9, 12–13, 19.

Although reservations have sometimes been expressed,[77] it is generally agreed that the phrase *yhwh tmn*, "Yahweh of Teman," should be read in a second blessing.[78] The phrase *yhwh. htṁn*, "Yahweh of the Teman," may well occur in another inscription.[79] Whatever the reason for associating Yahweh with Teman, all hypotheses about its location, as far as I know, place it to the south or south-east of Judah. McCarter notes, however, that the spelling *tmn*, to be vocalised *têmān*, is that of "the Israelite (northern) dialect of Hebrew."[80] Moreover, the blessing is pronounced by *ʾmryw*, who presumably came from north Palestine.[81] Thus, despite the use in them of the title "Yahweh of (the) Teman," these inscriptions are evidence for the presence of men from the kingdom of Israel.

According to Meshel, Teman is spelt *tymn* in a further inscription from Kuntillet ʿAjrud. He reads [*y*]*hwh* [ ] *tymn* in line 1 and restores *yhwh. hty*[*mn*] in line 2.[82] McCarter observes that *tymn*, to be vocalised *taymān*, is "the Judahite (southern) form" of the name.[83] Though it would be unwise to base far-reaching conclusions on Meshel's preliminary publication of this text, it would not be surprising if worshippers of Yahweh from Judah were to have come to Kuntillet ʿAjrud.

V. Other Deities at Kuntillet ʿAjrud

Meshel thinks that northern influence can "perhaps" be seen "in the mention of several deities, along with the combinations 'YHWH of Samaria and his Asherah' and 'YHWH of Teman and his Asherah.'"[84] Four deities at most fall to be considered: El, Baal, Asherah, and Bes.

El (or God) and Baal are referred to in one of the inscriptions written on plaster.[85] As was noted in Section I above, I have argued elsewhere that these inscriptions are the work of men from Israel or from

---

77   So, e.g., Renz, *Die althebräischen Inschriften*, 62 (§KAgr(9):9.5) and 62 n. 5.

78   Davies, *Ancient Hebrew Inscriptions*, 81 (§8.021.1).

79   Davies, *Ancient Hebrew Inscriptions*, 80 (§8.016.1); Renz, *Die althebräischen Inschriften*, 64 (§KAgr(9):10.2); but cf. Hadley, *The Cult of Asherah*, 130.

80   P. K. McCarter, "Kuntillet ʿAjrud," *COS* 2.47:171–73 (2.47B:172 n. 1).

81   See Section III above.

82   Meshel, "Teman, Ḥorvat," 1462, accepted by Davies, *Ancient Hebrew Inscriptions*, 80 (§8.015), as emended in idem, *Ancient Hebrew Inscriptions Volume 2*, 233. S. Aḥituv, in a personal communication cited by Zevit (*The Religions of Ancient Israel*, 373 n. 45), and Hadley (*The Cult of Asherah*, 135), differ about the reliability of this restoration.

83   McCarter, "Kuntillet ʿAjrud," 2.47B:172 n. 1.

84   Meshel, "Teman, Ḥorvat," 1464.

85   See n. 10.

an area with which the Phoenicians traded, but not from Judah. In this text El and Baal may be either titles of Yahweh or the names of Canaanite gods. Baal was worshipped in Israel and Judah until after the establishment at Kuntillet ʿAjrud had been abandoned (Hos 2:10[8]; 13:1; 2 Kgs 21:3; 23:4–5; Jer 2:8), though the evidence for Baal as a designation of Yahweh is restricted to the north (Hos 2:18[16]). It is harder to obtain information about the worship of El in either Israel or Judah. Yahweh is, however, referred to simply as ʾl, "God," in Ps 78:7, 8, 18, 19, 34, 41. This psalm has "an anti-northern bias" and was presumably composed in Judah before 722 BC.[86] Because northern traditions in the Old Testament have been transmitted through the south, it is difficult to identify a similar usage in the north. Although the likelihood is that beliefs held in the northern kingdom would have been reflected in this text, greater certainty is unattainable.

Since "[Yahweh's] asherah" belonged to both the cult of Yahweh of Teman and that of Yahweh of Samaria, Asherah was worshipped in the south as well as the north. This is confirmed by the reference to Yahweh's asherah in an inscription assigned by Davies to the mid-eighth century BC. It comes from Khirbet el-Qom in Judah, and in it the theophorous element *yhw* in the names of two men identifies them as Judeans.[87]

There is widespread agreement that two Bes-type figures are depicted on Pithos A,[88] though some scholars consider that the drawings represent Yahweh and Asherah.[89] Murray observes that figurines of Bes were one of "the chief amulets of the ninth and eighth centuries" BC at Lachish.[90]

Thus Asherah and Bes were known in Judah. Although the inscriptions written on plaster reveal northern influence at Kuntillet ʿAjrud, this cannot be deduced from their content.

---

86   J. Day, *Psalms* (OTG; Sheffield: JSOT Press, 1990), 58.
87   Davies, *Ancient Hebrew Inscriptions*, 106 (§25.003.1–6); Renz, *Die althebräischen Inschriften*, 207–11 (§Kom(8):3.1–6).
88   Beck, "The Drawings from Ḥorvat Teiman," 27–31; repr. in idem, *Imagery and Representation*, 122–26; Hadley, *The Cult of Asherah*, 136–44, 152 .
89   So, e.g., McCarter, "Kuntillet ʿAjrud," 2.47A:171.
90   Margaret A. Murray, "Faience Amulets," in *Lachish III (Tell ed-Duweir): The Iron Age: Text* (Olga Tufnell et al.; London: Oxford University Press, 1953), 378–81 (381, cf. 379).

VI. The Palaeography of the Inscriptions

In the course of a discussion of the scripts used in Israel down to 722 BC and in Judah until the third quarter of the eighth century BC, Renz examines in detail the links between these scribal traditions and the scripts used at Kuntillet ʿAjrud. He leaves out of account the inscriptions written on plaster, which he characterizes as Phoenician. The forms of the letters in the other inscriptions are classified under four headings: those which are also found in the south in the ninth century BC; those which continued in use in the south from the first quarter of the eighth century BC, but not in the north; those which continued in use in both the north and the south; and those which continued in use only in the north. Renz distinguishes innovative and conservative features in this material. The innovative features have parallels in the north, or in both north and south, but are not present in inscriptions from the south which are older than, or contemporary with, the inscriptions from Kuntillet ʿAjrud. Renz therefore concludes that it is most likely that these inscriptions belong with northern scribal traditions.[91]

VII. The Spelling of the Divine Name

In the published texts from Kuntillet ʿAjrud the Divine Name is spelt *yhwh* five times and *yhw* twice.[92] Renz states that it is unclear whether *yhw* is followed by a badly damaged *hê* in KAgr(9):3.1,[93] and the correctness of the reading in KAgr(9):10.1 is questioned by McCarter.[94] It has also been thought that both examples could be due to scribal error.[95] Despite these uncertainties, it remains possible that the spelling *yhw* is attested in these two texts. Meshel comments that "[p]ossibly, the form of the Tetragrammaton" in KAgr(9):3.1 "may be Israelite rather than Judahite," though he adds that "no definite conclusion can be drawn, since all other occurences [*sic*] have the Tetragrammaton in

---

91 Renz, *Schrift und Schreibertradition*, 3, 5–6.

92 Davies, *Ancient Hebrew Inscriptions*, 80–81 (§§8.015.2; 8.016.1; 8.017.2; 8.021.1) and idem, *Ancient Hebrew Inscriptions Volume 2*, 233 (on §§8.015.1; 8.017) for *yhwh*; idem, *Ancient Hebrew Inscriptions*, 80–81(§§8.011.1; 8.022.1) for *yhw*; Renz, *Die althebräischen Inschriften*, 58, 61, 62, 64 (§§KAgr(9):6.2; KAgr(9):8.2; KAgr(9):9.4–5; KAgr(9):10.2) for *yhwh* and 56, 64 (§§KAgr(9):3.1; KAgr(9):10.1) for *yhw*.

93 Renz, *Die althebräischen Inschriften*, 56 and n. a.

94 McCarter, "Kuntillet ʿAjrud," 2.47B:172 n. 4.

95 Lemaire ("Date et origine des inscriptions," 134–35), probably, for KAgr(9):3.1, and Zevit (*The Religions of Ancient Israel*, 399 n. 102), possibly, for KAgr(9):10.1.

full."[96] He refers to Aḥituv's opinion that *yhw* and *yhwh* are the spellings found respectively in Israel and Judah. But all Aḥituv says in support of this assertion is that the theophorous element in proper nouns in Israel is *yw*.[97] There are no other instances of *yhw* recorded by Davies.[98] This spelling is, however, common at Elephantine,[99] and it is frequently supposed that at least some of the religious traditions of this colony had their origin in Israel at Bethel. Moreover, Steiner believes that the divine name Yaho (*yhw*) occurs as part of what he terms "a Psalm from Bethel" in P.Amh.Eg. 63 XI.17, a text which he dates to perhaps the beginning of the third century BC.[100] In addition, Pardee suggests as a possible alternative to the theory of scribal error in the inscriptions from Kuntillet ʿAjrud that "*yhw* could be simply phonetic writing, according to the North Israelite/Phoenician tradition, for a pronunciation /yahwê/."[101] It was noted in Section IV above that it was someone from the northern kingdom who presumably composed the blessing by *yhwh tmn*. The evidence is far from conclusive, but the spelling *yhw* may also have been used by men from Israel.

VIII. Conclusion

Phoenician merchants and artists may have visited Kuntillet ʿAjrud, but it is unlikely that there was a substantial Phoenician presence. Taken together, the pottery, the North Palestinian names, the blessing by Yahweh of Samaria, the spelling *tmn*, the palaeography of the inscriptions, and possibly the spelling *yhw*, point to the kingdom of Israel as the authority which constructed and maintained the establishment. Some Judeans came there, and supplies were brought from Judah, but there is only limited evidence for the presence of Judeans at Kuntillet ʿAjrud.

I have known Graham Davies since he entered Peterhouse as a Research Student in 1969, and am grateful for his friendship over the

---

96 Meshel, "Two Aspects in the Excavation," 102.

97 Aḥituv, *Handbook of Ancient Hebrew Inscriptions*, 153.

98 Davies, *Ancient Hebrew Inscriptions*, 365; idem, *Ancient Hebrew Inscriptions Volume 2*, 164.

99 E.g., *TADAE* 1, §4.7:6, 24, 26; 2, §§2.10:6; 3.4:10.

100 R. C. Steiner, "The Aramaic Text in Demotic Script," *COS* 1.99:309–27 (310, 318). It is not possible to discuss other interpretations of this difficult text here.

101 D. Pardee, "An Evaluation of the Proper Names from Ebla from a West Semitic Perspective: Pantheon Distribution according to *Genre*," in *Eblaite Personal Names and Semitic Name-Giving* (ed. A. Archi; ARES 1; Rome: Missione Archeologica Italiana in Siria, 1988), 119–51 (125 n. 32).

years. I am glad to pay tribute here to his outstanding contribution to the study of Hebrew inscriptions, among so much else.

The Phoenician Inscriptions from Arslan Tash and Some Old Testament Texts

(Exodus 12; Micah 5:4–5[5–6]; Psalm 91)

Kevin J. Cathcart

Forty-five years ago, when I was a postgraduate student in Rome, I wrote a short article on the Hebrew text of Mic 5:4–5[5–6], noting in particular some interesting linguistic parallels with the Phoenician inscriptions from Arslan Tash.[1] Exactly ten years later I published another article on the same biblical passage, this time paying more attention to the genre of the text in the light of the same inscriptions and other Semitic incantations.[2] From a new collation of the artefacts in 1983, Teixidor suggested that the Arslan Tash inscriptions were fakes,[3] and Amiet arrived at the same view after his examination of the iconography.[4] However, van Dijk rebutted Amiet's arguments.[5] Following this controversy, Pardee carried out a new examination of the artefacts and published a detailed epigraphic and philological commentary on the texts that upholds the authenticity of the inscriptions.[6]

Scholars have mentioned several Old Testament texts in their interpretations of the Arslan Tash inscriptions, most notably Exodus 12 and Deut 6:4–9. For example, Conklin has published a useful study in which he presents evidence for the presence of the incantational elements of the Arslan Tash inscriptions in Ugarit, New Kingdom Egypt,

---

1   K. J. Cathcart, "Notes on Micah 5,4–5," *Bib* 49 (1968): 511–14.
2   K. J. Cathcart, "Micah 5,4–5 and Semitic Incantations," *Bib* 59 (1978): 38–48.
3   J. Teixidor, "Les tablettes d'Arslan Tash au Musée d'Alep," *AuOr* 1 (1983): 105–8.
4   P. Amiet, "Observations sur les 'Tablettes magiques' d'Arslan Tash," *AuOr* 1 (1983): 109.
5   J. van Dijk, "The Authenticity of the Arslan Tash Amulets," *Iraq* 54 (1992): 65–68.
6   D. Pardee, "Les documents d'Arslan Tash: authentiques ou faux?" *Syria* 75 (1998): 15–54. See also Y. Avishur, *Phoenician Inscriptions and the Bible* (Tel Aviv-Jaffa: Archaeological Center Publication, 2000), 240–43; F. M. Cross, *Leaves from an Epigrapher's Notebook: Collected Papers in Hebrew and West Semitic Palaeography and Epigraphy* (HSS 51; Winona Lake, Ind.: Eisenbrauns, 2003), 269.

and the Passover account in Exodus 12.[7] In my earlier studies I mentioned the parallel pair of verbs *tidrōk*, "you shall tread" // *tirmōs*, "you shall trample" in Ps 91:13 but did not appreciate the significance of my observation for the interpretation of the psalm.[8] So in this short study I shall assess the relevance of the inscriptions from Arslan Tash for the study of Exodus 12, Mic 5:4–5[5–6] and Psalm 91. Graham Davies has contributed impressively to the study of ancient Hebrew inscriptions and I know that he is particularly interested in Exodus. It is a pleasure to dedicate my contribution to him, with gratitude for his friendship over many years.

The Arslan Tash inscriptions first came to light in 1933 but were not published until 1939 and 1971.[9] The language of the inscriptions is Phoenician but the script is Aramaic and can be dated to the seventh century BC. The two limestone plaques on which the inscriptions are written also bear reliefs, which are variously interpreted as deities or demons. The first plaque contains an incantation to keep harmful night-creatures from entering the house until the sun rises. Protection is provided with the help of the gods Ashur, Ḥoron, and Shamsh. Since the first inscription (hereafter Arslan Tash I) is the one that concerns us most, a translation of it follows.[10]

1. An incantation against ʿApta; the conjuration of
2. Sasm son of Padrisha.
3. Utter (it) for his benefit,
4. and say to the stranglers:
5. the house I enter,
6. you shall not enter;
7. and the courtyard I tread,
8. you shall not tread.
9. An eternal treaty has been made with us,
10. Ashur has made it with us,
11. (he) and all the sons of the gods,
12. and the chief(s) of the assembly of all our holy ones;[11]

---

7   B. Conklin, "Arslan Tash I and Other Vestiges of a Particular Syrian Incantatory Thread," *Bib* 84 (2003): 89–101.

8   Cathcart, "Micah 5,4–5 and Semitic Incantations," 40.

9   R. du Mesnil du Buisson, "Une tablette magique de la région du Moyen Euphrate," in *Mélanges syriens offerts à Monsieur René Dussaud* (2 vols.; Bibliothèque archéologique et historique 30; Paris: Geuthner, 1939), 1:421–34; A. Caquot and R. du Mesnil du Buisson, "La seconde tablette ou 'petite amulette' d'Arslan Tash," *Syria* 48 (1971): 391–406.

10   I follow the text established by Pardee, "Les documents d'Arslan Tash," 18–19.

11   Here, like other scholars, I follow H. Torczyner, "A Hebrew Incantation against Night-Demons from Biblical Times," *JNES* 6 (1947): 18–29 (23), who understands the *n* of *qdšn* as a first person plural suffix. This effectively removes an alleged Aramaism. Of course Torczyner was wrong in his view that the language was Hebrew. See

13. and it is a treaty (witnessed by) heaven and earth
14. [for]ever, by the oath of the lord [of]
15. [. . .] the earth, by the oath of
16. [the w]ife of Ḥoron, whose utterance is perfect,
17. and (by that) of his seven other wives,
18. and the eight wives of the holy lord.

(Drawing)

19. (Incantation) against ʿApta: from the dark room
20. she has passed immediately tonight.
21. From my house into the street she has gone.
22. [. . .] to
23. my door,
24. and he has il-
25. luminated
26. the doorposts. Shamsh has risen . . .

Exodus 12

Cross and Saley were the first to recognize the potential significance of *mzzt*, "the doorposts," in Arslan Tash I, 26.[12] Their reading of lines 22–29 is noticeably different from Pardee's but *mzzt* is clear in any case. In both interpretations, the rising sun drives away a nocturnal prowler. Cross and Saley point out that the plaque is too large to be worn around the neck and suggest that it was hung in the house, most probably at the doorway. They see a parallel between the plaque and its function and the blood of the Passover lamb on the doorposts of the Israelites in Exod 12:22–27 and they also mention the instruction in Deut 6:4–9 to write the words of the law on doorposts. The question is, are they claiming too much when they say that "the Arslan Tash plaque was a pagan prototype of the *mĕzūzāh*, the Israelite portal inscription"?[13]

In his commentary on Exodus, Propp briefly introduces the Arslan Tash inscriptions into the discussion of the apotropaic aspects of the

---

the remarks by S. D. Sperling, "An Arslan Tash Incantation: Interpretations and Implications," *HUCA* 53 (1982): 1–10 (7); Pardee, "Les documents d'Arslan Tash," 40.

12 F. M. Cross and R. J. Saley, "Phoenician Incantations on a Plaque of the Seventh Century B.C. from Arslan Tash in Upper Syria," *BASOR* 197 (1970): 42–49 (48–49); repr. in Cross, *Leaves from an Epigrapher's Notebook*, 265–69 (269).

13 Cross and Saley, "Phoenician Incantations," 49; repr. in Cross, *Leaves from an Epigrapher's Notebook*, 269. T. H. Gaster accepts Cross and Saley's observations on the *mezuzot*. See "A Hang-Up for Hang-Ups: The Second Amuletic Plaque from Arslan Tash," *BASOR* 209 (1973): 18–26 (26).

application of blood to the doorposts and the lintel.[14] Unfortunately, Pardee's new study of the inscriptions was not yet available to him and, following Cross and Saley, he mentions female "lamb-stranglers" (for *l ḫnqt ʾmr* in lines 4–5, which really means "say to the stranglers") and a male demon "Sasam" (probably a personal name in line 2) which he calls "close cousins of the original paschal demon."[15] It seems to me that this claim can be no more than tentative given the fragmentary nature of the inscription at the place where *mzzt* occurs. Nevertheless, Propp has highlighted some interesting aspects of the Passover account. For example, he notes that the ritual is celebrated just before nightfall, since night was the time when hostile forces were thought to be most dangerous. Taking advantage of Pardee's new collation of the inscription, Conklin has been able to make the telling point that the new reading *ll z*, "this night" in line 20 underlines the "night-time aspect" of Arslan Tash I. He argues further that Exod 12:22, "None of you shall go outside the door of your house *until morning*" makes clearer sense when it is observed that at the end of Arslan Tash I "Shamsh emerges," that is, "Sun rises" (lines 25–26). The hostile powers of the night have gone and it is safe to go outside.[16]

Blood was applied to the doorposts because doorways and thresholds were areas of vulnerability, marking the boundary between the safety of home and the dangers lurking outside. This supports the view that *pesaḥ* may mean "protection." Yahweh protects the houses of the Israelites. Propp suggests that Exod 12:27, *wĕʾet battênû hiṣṣîl*, "but (Yahweh) saved our houses" is the Elohist's comment on Exod 12:23, *ûpāsaḥ yahweh ʿal happetaḥ*, "and Yahweh will protect over the doorway."[17] It should be noted that the verb *hiṣṣîl*, "saved," in Exod 12:27 also occurs in Mic 5:5[6] and Ps 91:3 which will be discussed below. It must be mentioned that in Exod 12:23 the "destroyer" (*mašḥît*) appears as an independent agent of Yahweh.[18] The blood on the doorposts

---

14 W. H. C. Propp, *Exodus 1–18* (AB 2; New York: Doubleday, 2001), 441.

15 Propp, *Exodus 1–18*, 441.

16 Conklin, "Arslan Tash I," 98.

17 Propp, *Exodus 1–18*, 401. The concern with the doorway of a house in incantations is noted by Conklin in his comparison of Arslan Tash I with RS 24.244 (= KTU 1.100), a mythological story dealing with the search for a cure for snake venom. Although the Ugaritic text is not an incantation, it contains some striking incantatory language. See Conklin, "Arslan Tash I," 94–95. Conklin's analysis is well done and he makes good observations. Notice especially his remarks on the deity Ḥoron (found in lines 58, 61, 67), an important figure in protective magic. In lines 71–72, the following tricolon occurs: *ptḥ bt mnt / ptḥ bt wuba / hkl wištql*, "Open the house of incantation, open the house that I may enter, the palace that I may come in."

18 Propp, *Exodus 1–18*, 408–9.

ensures that the "destroyer" does not enter the houses of the Israelites. In Ezek 9:1 the six executioners (*pĕquddôt*), agents of Yahweh, who carry out the killing of those without marks on their foreheads, each have "a destroying weapon" (*kĕlî mašḥētô bĕyādô*), which recalls the *mašḥît* of Exod 12:23. Zimmerli finds an analogy to the destroying group in Ezekiel 9 in the seven evil spirits or seven demons of Mesopotamian incantations.[19]

Recently Frey-Anthes has suggested that scholars avoid the use of the word "demon" for the interpretation of Old Testament texts.[20] She points out with reference to the harmful *mašḥît* in Exod 12:23, for example, that the term has been used for beings that "are placed at border-situations of life and they are fought against by apotropaic rituals."[21] Whether or not her proposal for the abandonment of the term "demon" is acceptable, her remarks about "border-situations" and "border-crossings" are noteworthy. The demarcation between sacred space or domestic space and hostile areas will be mentioned again in this article. Clements remarks that the slaughter in Ezekiel 9 begins at the sanctuary, "the very place to which everyone looks for protection and help."[22] Furthermore, the language of Ezek 9:7 is almost incantatory: "Defile the house (*habbayit*) and fill the courtyards (*haḥăṣērôt*) with the slain." Compare *bt* // *ḥṣr* in Arslan Tash I, 5–7.

Micah 5:4–5[5–6]

4   If the Assyrians come into our land,
     if they tread in our fortresses,
        we shall raise against them seven princes (shepherds),
        eight chiefs of men;
5   and they will rule the land of Assyria with the sword
     and the land of Nimrod with the drawn blade.
     They will deliver us from the Assyrians,
     if they come into our land,
     If they tread in our country.

---

19   W. Zimmerli, *Ezekiel* (2 vols.; Hermeneia; Philadelphia, Pa.: Fortress, 1979–83), 1:246; trans. of *Ezechiel* (2 vols.; BKAT 13/1 and 2; Neukirchen-Vluyn: Neukirchener Verlag, 1969).

20   H. Frey-Anthes, "Concepts of 'Demons' in Ancient Israel," *WO* 38 (2008): 38–52 (38). The article is based on the author's Bonn dissertation, *Unheilsmächte und Schutzgenien, Antiwesen und Grenzgänger: Vorstellungen von "Dämonen" im alten Israel* (OBO 227; Fribourg, Switzerland: Academic Press Fribourg; Göttingen: Vanden-hoeck & Ruprecht, 2007).

21   Frey-Anthes, "Concepts of 'Demons,'" 38.

22   R. E. Clements, *Ezekiel* (Louisville, Ky.: Westminster John Knox, 1996), 40.

This passage is usually dated to the post-exilic period. There can be little doubt that the whole of Mic 5:1–5[2–6] has been reworked by later editors, though v. 1 probably derives from Micah and there was probably an earlier form of vv. 4–5 which can be attributed to the prophet. In any event the passage as we have it now concerns a new order in which God's rule will be exercised by a new Davidic figure. Assyria of the earlier, pre-exilic form of the text was seen in later times as an epithet for world powers. Although I have discussed in some detail elsewhere the striking linguistic parallels between Arslan Tash I and Mic 5:4–5[5–6], I have found several recent scholarly discussions of Mic 5:4–5[5–6] most interesting and further comment is required.

"The Assyrians," literally "Assyria" (*ʾaššûr*), are the subject of the opening conditional clauses and as such may stand before the conjunction *kî*. Compare 1 Kgs 8:37, *rāʿāb kî yihyeh bāʾāreṣ*, "if there is famine in the land." R. P. Gordon has drawn attention to the use of *k* [*kî*] at the beginning of the Ugaritic prayer in RS 24.266:26'–36' (= KTU 1.119, 26'–36') and has compared the usage there with that in Mic 5:4–5[5–6].[23]

> If (k) a strong one attacks your gate,
> a warrior your walls,
> you shall lift your eyes to Baʿal and say:
> "O Baʿal, if you drive the strong one from our gate,
> the warrior from our walls,
> a bull, O Baʿal, we shall sanctify,
> a vow, O Baʿal, we shall fulfil;
> a firstborn, O Baʿal, we shall sanctify,
> a htp-offering, O Baʿal, we shall fulfil,
> a feast, O Baʿal, we shall offer;
> to the sanctuary, O Baʿal, we shall go up,
> that path, O Ba[ʿal], we shall take."
> Then Baʿal will hear your prayer:
> he will drive the strong one from your gate,
> the warrior from your walls.

The parallel with Mic 5:4–5[5–6] is interesting because both texts mention the circumstances in which action will be taken or prayer should be offered. The remarkable similarity of the form and structure of the Ugaritic prayer was first noticed by Saracino[24] and is discussed further by Wagenaar.[25] Saracino astutely draws attention to the end of the

---

23 R. P. Gordon, "*K/kî/ky* in Incantational Incipits," *UF* 23 (1991): 161–63. For the text, see D. Pardee, *Ritual and Cult at Ugarit* (SBLWAW 10; Atlanta, Ga.: Society of Biblical Literature, 2002), 149–50.

24 F. Saracino, "A State of Siege: Mi 5, 4–5 and an Ugaritic Prayer," *ZAW* 95 (1983): 263–69.

25 J. A. Wagenaar, *Judgement and Salvation: The Composition and Redaction of Micah 2–5* (VTSup 85; Leiden: Brill, 2001), 294–95.

prayer, lines 34–35: "Then Baʿal will hear your prayer: he will drive the strong one from your gate, the warrior from your walls." These lines form an inclusio just like the tricolon at the end of Mic 5:5[6].[26]

In the Arslan Tash inscription Ashur is the eponymous god of Assyria. The presence of this divine name can be explained by the fact that Arslan Tash, where the inscription was found, is in ancient Hadattu, the seat of an Assyrian governor in the eighth century. In the inscription Ashur, Ḥoron, and Shamsh are the deities who cooperate in keeping harmful night-time creatures from entering the house. In Mic 5:4–5[5–6], however, the princes and chieftains will keep out ʾaššûr, "Assyria" or "the Assyrians."

The parallel pair of verbs yābôʾ, "come" // yidrōk, "tread," which occurs twice in Mic 5:4–5[5–6], has striking counterparts in Arslan Tash I, 5–8: ʾbʾ, "I enter" // ʾdrk, "I tread"; bl tbʾn, "you shall not enter" // bl tdrkn, "you shall not tread."[27] This parallel pair is not found elsewhere in the Bible but we shall have reason to comment below on tidrōk, "you will tread" // tirmōs, "you will trample" in Ps 91:13. In Arslan Tash I the "stranglers" and any other hostile force are forbidden to enter the house or courtyard. In Mic 5:4–5[5–6] force is threatened against the Assyrians if they enter the land and the fortresses. The collocation of the verbs bwʾ and drk is found in 1 Sam 5:5, a text of interest for our discussion: "This is why all the priests of Dagon and all who enter (habbāʾîm) Dagon's temple do not tread (yidrĕkû) on the threshold of Dagon in Ashdod to this day." It was thought that the threshold had been contaminated by the pieces of the god Dagon, shattered by the presence of the Ark. Tsumura comments: "Temple thresholds were considered especially worthy of respect because they separated sacred and common areas."[28] Finally, it is instructive to compare the hostile sense of the verbs in Jer 9:20: "Death has climbed up (ʿālâ) through our windows, he has entered (bāʾ) our palaces; cutting off the youths from the streets, the young men from the squares." Death is portrayed as a demon that slays.

---

26 Saracino, "A State of Siege," 268.

27 See Cathcart, "Notes on Micah 5,4–5," 512; idem, "Micah 5,4–5 and Semitic Incantations," 40. Note the words addressed to a harmful entity in a Ugaritic incantation from Ras Ibn Ḥani, RIH 78/20:18 (= KTU 1.169:18), [b]t ubu al tbi, "The house I enter you must not enter." See Pardee, "Les documents d'Arslan Tash," 36.

28 D. T. Tsumura, The First Book of Samuel (NICOT; Grand Rapids, Mich.: Eerdmans, 2007), 206. See also P. K. McCarter, I Samuel (AB 8; Garden City, N.Y.: Doubleday, 1980), 122.

I still retain MT *bĕ'armĕnōtênû*, "our fortresses," in Mic 5:4[5] and do not need to repeat the arguments here.[29] Hillers finds my defence of the MT unconvincing and champions the long-standing emendation to *bĕ'admātēnû* on the basis of the LXX ἐπὶ τὴν χώραν ὑμῶν.[30] Waltke also dismisses my "dubious arguments" and favours the emendation of the MT. Unfortunately, his text-critical commentary is confusing and does not inspire confidence. He says that the MT "should be rejected in favor of LXX's *chōrān hymōn* (= Heb. *'admantēnû* [sic]) 'our lands' because it constitutes a better parallel with 'into our country.' . . . The confusion of *d* and *r* is common."[31] Actually LXX ἐπὶ τὴν χώραν ὑμῶν = *bĕ'admatĕkem*, "in your land." I assume that the strange *'admantēnû* is a printing error and that Waltke meant to omit the *n* between *m* and *t*. The error is compounded pages later in the hybrid form *"'adm^enōtênû."*[32]

Wagenaar has taken my previously published view that Mic 5:4–5[5–6] contains incantatory language much further than I would.[33] I refer in particular to his discussion of *r‘ym* and *nsyky 'dm* in v. 4. MT *rō‘îm*, "shepherds," is commonly used for "kings" or "princes." See, for example, Nah 3:18, *rō‘êkā*, "your princes" // *'addîrêkā*, "your nobles." *Nāsîk*, "leader, chieftain" (cf. Akk. *nasīku*), occurs only four times in the Old Testament. In Josh 13:21 *nĕsîkê sîḥôn*, "chieftains of Sihon," follows *nĕsî'ê midyān*, "leaders of Midian," and in Ezek 32:29–30 *nĕsîkê ṣāpôn*, "chieftains of the north," follows *'ĕdôm mĕlākêhā wĕkol-nĕsî'êhā*, "Edom, its kings and all its leaders." In Ps 83:12, *nĕsîkēmô*, "their chieftains," is parallel with *nĕdîbēmô*, "their nobles." The LXX usually translates *nĕsîkê* by ἄρχοντες, "rulers," and this is the word used for the version of Mic 5:4 in 8ḤevXIIgr. Micah 5:4 LXX, however, has δήγματα ἀνθρώπων, "biters of men" (see VL *morsus hominum*), apparently understanding consonantal *nsyky* as *nšky* from *nāšak*, "to bite." Sellin,[34] following Riessler,[35] preferred the LXX reading and in recent years Saracino and

29 Cathcart, "Micah 5,4–5 and Semitic Incantations," 40–41. My arguments are accepted by H. W. Wolff, *Dodekapropheton 4: Micha* (BKAT 14/4; Neukirchen-Vluyn: Neukirchener Verlag, 1982), 104; H. G. M. Williamson, "Marginalia in Micah," *VT* 47 (1997): 360–72 (365–67).

30 D. R. Hillers, "Imperial Dream: Text and Sense of Mic 5:4b–5," in *The Quest for the Kingdom of God: Studies in Honor of George E. Mendenhall* (ed. H. B. Huffmon, F. A. Spina, and A. R. W. Green; Winona Lake, Ind.: Eisenbrauns, 1983), 137–39 (138); idem, *Micah* (Hermeneia; Fortress, 1984), 68.

31 B. K. Waltke, *A Commentary on Micah* (Grand Rapids, Mich.: Eerdmans, 2007), 288.

32 Waltke, *A Commentary on Micah*, 293.

33 Wagenaar, *Judgement and Salvation*, 180–88, 294–300.

34 E. Sellin, *Das Zwölfprophetenbuch* (KAT 12; Leipzig: Deichert, 1922), 290.

35 P. Riessler, *Die kleinen Propheten oder das Zwölfprophetenbuch* (Rottenburg: W. Bader, 1911), 118.

Wagenaar have agreed with him.[36] These scholars read *rāʿîm*, "evil spirits" or "wicked men" for MT *roʿîm*, "shepherds, princes," and argue that their proposed parallel *nōšĕkê ʾādām*, "biters of men" (Wagenaar), "biters of the Earth [hell])" (Saracino), are demonic beings. Wagenaar thinks that the LXX "may have retained a vague memory of the original meaning."[37] This is not convincing and the most likely explanation is that the LXX translator of Micah simply did not grasp the sense of *nāsîk*. The confusion of *sāmek* and *šîn* is not unusual in the LXX of the Twelve.[38] The final cola of v. 4 in which the "seven princes, eight chiefs of men" are found and the first part of v. 5 are probably post-exilic additions to the text. The numerical pair 7//8 is rare in the Old Testament, the only other occurrence being in Qoh 11:2. Its presence in a Phoenician incantation (Arslan Tash I, 17–18) is noteworthy; it is found several times in later Aramaic and Mandaic incantations.[39]

Finally, the verb in v. 5 *wĕhiṣṣîlû* (for MT *wĕhiṣṣîl*) *mēʾaššûr*, "They will save us from the Assyrians," is the same as that in Exod 12:27, *wĕʾet battênû hiṣṣîl*, "but (Yahweh) saved our houses." I understand the princes and leaders in v. 4 to be the subject of *hiṣṣîlû*, but a good case has also been made for taking *zeh šālôm*, "the one of peace," in v. 4 as the subject of the singular form *hiṣṣîl*.[40]

Psalm 91

The relevance of the Arslan Tash inscriptions for the interpretation of Psalm 91 may not seem apparent. The psalm, which is frequently called a wisdom psalm, has all the appearances of a prayer of personal piety and devotion. In it God appears as the protector of a person who seeks refuge in him. This is evident in the first verses in which the person

---

36   Saracino, "A State of Siege," 266; Wagenaar, *Judgement and Salvation*, 184–85.

37   Wagenaar, *Judgement and Salvation*, 186. Saracino and Wagenaar link the seven demons of Mesopotamian incantations, which Zimmerli associated with the executioners in Ezekiel 9, to seven evil spirits in Mic 5:4[5], a possibility I considered but rejected in 1978. See Cathcart, "Micah 5,4–5 and Semitic Incantations," 46–47.

38   There are no grounds for the view that *nāšak*, "bite," had a dialectal form with *šîn*.

39   In addition to the inscriptions which I listed in Cathcart, "Micah 5,4–5 and Semitic Incantations," 41–43, I should mention an inscription published by C. Müller-Kessler, "A Mandaic Gold Amulet in the British Museum," *BASOR* 311 (1998): 83–88 (85). In lines 33–35 there is an unusual distribution of seven and eight: "the seven tongues of the sorcerers, of the sorceresses and of the eight liliths."

40   For the emendation *wĕhiṣṣîlû*, see J. M. P. Smith, *A Critical and Exegetical Commentary on the Books of Micah, Zephaniah and Nahum* in J. M. P. Smith, W. H. Ward, and J. A. Bewer, *A Critical and Exegetical Commentary on Micah, Zephaniah, Nahum, Habakkuk, Obadiah and Joel* (ICC; Edinburgh: T&T Clark, 1911), 108–9.

expresses his complete trust in God and seeks his protection. Verses 3–13 are replete with metaphors and images of the dangers and hostile forces from which God will rescue the one taking refuge in Him. In the final verses of the psalm, vv. 14–16, God affirms the promises of protection and assures the one who trusts in him that he will be rewarded with fullness of life and salvation.

Some commentators have seen a background for the psalm in the temple liturgy. Kraus thinks that an individual has entered the protective area of the temple sanctuary.[41] Zenger too discusses the protective function of the temple, pointing out how the sacral space with its special protective function is set apart from the profane and hostile world.[42] In the discussion of Arslan Tash I and Exodus 12 we noted the importance of the protection of the house. In Mic 5:4–5[5–6] the space to be protected from Assyria is the land and its fortresses. In Psalm 91 the temple offers protection from a hostile world of which, as Zenger well describes it, "pictures full of treacherous, monstrous, indeed demonic dangers are contrasted with powerful images of protection and of a victorious battle against this world."[43]

The language of Psalm 91 is interesting. I have already referred to *tidrōk*, "you will tread" // *tirmōs*, "you will trample" in v. 13. These and similar verbs are often incantatory when they are used of the intrusion of hostile elements but in the psalm they are employed in the reverse action of subduing the hostile serpents and lions, thought by some commentators to represent dangers in general or perhaps the monster of chaos.[44] The verb *hiṣṣîl*, "save, deliver from, rescue" in Exod 12:27 and Mic 5:5[6] is also found in Ps 91:3, *yaṣṣîlěkā*, "He will rescue you." The language of v. 10 is also very much like that of incantations: *lōʾ těʾunneh ʾēlêkā rāʿâ wěnegaʿ lōʾ yiqrab běʾohŏlêkā*, "No evil shall befall you, no scourge come near your tent." Not only does God provide protection in the sanctuary of the temple, he also ensures safety in the house. Perhaps the most interesting part of the psalm for our discussion is at vv. 5–6 which mention *paḥad laylâ*, "the terror of the night," and *deber bāʾōpel yahǎlōk*, "pestilence that goes about in the darkness." These hostile elements bring to mind the nocturnal dangers mentioned in Arslan

41   H.-J. Kraus, *Psalms 60–150* (Minneapolis, Minn.: Fortress, 1993), 221; trans. of *Psalmen 2: Psalmen 60–150* (5th rev. ed.; BKAT 15/2; Neukirchen-Vluyn: Neukirchener Verlag, 1978).

42   E. Zenger, in F.-L. Hossfeld and E. Zenger, *Psalms 2: A Commentary on Psalms 51–100* (Hermeneia; Minneapolis, Minn.: Fortress, 2005), 430; trans. of *Psalmen 51–100* (HTKAT; Freiburg im Breisgau: Herder, 2000).

43   Zenger in Hossfeld and Zenger, *Psalms 2*, 430.

44   See A. Weiser, *The Psalms* (OTL; London: SCM, 1962), 611–12; trans. of *Die Psalmen* (2 vols.; ATD 14–15; 5th rev. ed.; Göttingen: Vandenhoeck & Ruprecht, 1959).

Tash I, 19–20 and Exod 12:12–13. The Targum of Ps 91:5–6 expands the MT as follows:

> You will not be afraid of the terror of the demons that go about in the night, of the arrow of the angel of death which he looses during the day; nor of the pestilence that goes about in darkness, nor of the band of demons that attacks at noon.

It is not surprising, therefore, to find that in a fragmentary manuscript of so-called apocryphal psalms from Qumran (11QApPs[a]), Psalm 91 is one of a collection of three (or four) apotropaic psalms (the others did not become part of the canon). The community at Qumran recited these psalms to ward off evil spirits ready to cause harm.[45] Ps 91:11–12 is quoted in the Matthean and Lukan accounts of the temptation of Jesus in the desert and some scholars have seen an allusion to Ps 91:13 in Luke 10:17–20 where Jesus says he has given the disciples "authority to tread upon serpents and scorpions and over all the power of the enemy."[46] It is possible, however, that Deut 8:15, "an arid wasteland with poisonous snakes and scorpions," is in the mind of the New Testament writer here.[47] However, given the mingling of texts from Deuteronomy 6–8 and Psalm 91 in Matt 4:1–11 and Luke 4:1–13, it is not impossible that there are allusions to both Deut 8:15 and Ps 91:13 in Luke 10:19. Deuteronomy and Psalms are two of the most often quoted

---

45   M. Henze, "Psalm 91 in Premodern Interpretation and at Qumran," in *Biblical Interpretation at Qumran* (ed. M. Henze; Grand Rapids, Mich.: Eerdmans, 2005), 168–93 (186–93); M. S. Pajunen, "Qumranic Psalm 91: A Structural Analysis," in *Scripture in Transition: Essays on Septuagint, Hebrew Bible, and Dead Sea Scrolls in Honour of Raija Sollamo* (ed. A. Voitila and J. Jokirata; JSJSup 126; Leiden: Brill, 2008), 591–605; idem, "The Function of 11QPsAp[a] as a Ritual," in *Text and Ritual* (ed. A. K. Gudme; Copenhagen: Department of Biblical Studies, University of Copenhagen, 2009), 50–60. For a similar use of Psalm 91 in Jewish tradition, see the Babylonian Talmud, *b. Šebu.* 15b.

46   J. A. Fitzmyer, *The Gospel according to Luke (X–XXIV)* (AB 28A; Garden City, N.Y.: Doubleday, 1985), 863, regards an alleged allusion to Ps 91:13 in Luke 10:19 as "far-fetched." For a more positive view, see C. A. Evans, "The Aramaic Psalter and the New Testament: Praising the Lord in History and Prophecy," in *From Prophecy to Testament: The Function of the Old Testament in the New* (ed. C. A. Evans; Peabody, Mass.: Hendrickson, 2004), 80. Dealing with the threat from snakes and scorpions has a long history. In an incantation from Ugarit (RS 92.2014:6–7) we read: *ʕly l tʕl bṯn ʕlk qn l tqnn ʕqrb tḥtk*, "The serpent will indeed not come up against you, the scorpion will indeed not stand under you." See Pardee, *Ritual and Cult at Ugarit*, 159. For even earlier incantations directed against snakes and scorpions, see G. Cunningham, *Deliver Me from Evil: Mesopotamian Incantations: 2500–1500 B.C.* (Studia Pohl, series maior 17; Rome: Pontifical Biblical Institute, 1997), 21, 35, 105–6. For the patristic interpretation of Ps 91:13, see A. Quacquarelli, *Il leone e il drago nella simbolica dell'età patristica* (Quaderni di vetera christianorum; Bari: Istituto di Letteratura Cristiana Antica, Università di Bari, 1975).

47   P. Grelot, "Étude critique de Luc 10, 19," *RSR* 69 (1981): 87–100 (90).

Old Testament books in the New Testament and two of the most frequently attested among the Dead Sea Scrolls.

In Late Antiquity and the medieval period, Exodus 12,
Deuteronomy 6, Ezekiel 9, and Psalm 91 all appear in instructive
combinations. For example, Deut 6:4 and Ps 91:1 are found joined
together into a single text in a Jewish incantation bowl.[48] The text is
interwoven with a word from Deut 6:4 followed by a word drawn from
Ps 91:1 and so on: *šmᶜ ywšb yyśrʾl* [sic] *bstr yhwh*, etc. Deut 6:5 and
Ps 91:1 are woven together in three Aramaic magical bowls and a Genizah fragment.[49] A large number of Greek papyri containing Psalm 91 or
parts of it have been found in Egypt. They were widely used as amulets
by Christians from early times until the medieval period. One published recently measures 11.5 x 26.8 cm and dates from the late sixth or
early seventh century AD. It contains Psalm 91 (LXX 90), the heading of
Psalm 92 (LXX 91), the Lord's Prayer, and a doxology.[50] Throughout the
history of Judaism and Christianity, Psalm 91 has been interpreted as
an apotropaic song used to protect the faithful from malevolent spirits.
Although Wellhausen thought Psalm 91 could have served as a talis-
man in Old Testament times, this is unproven.[51]

In the Middle Ages, preachers for the Crusades combined some of
these texts in their sermons. Eudes of Châteauroux (b. ca. 1190) cited
Exod 12:23, Ps 91:13, and Ezek 9:6 in close proximity.[52] Gilbert of
Tournai (b. 1200) drew attention to Exod 12:22–23 and Ezek 9:4, 6,
where he and other preachers found scriptural support for the view

---

48   J. Naveh and S. Shaked, *Amulets and Magic Bowls: Aramaic Incantations of Late
     Antiquity* (Jerusalem: Magnes, 1985), 184–87, bowl 11.

49   See the references for these three previously published Aramaic magical bowls in
     Naveh and Shaked, *Amulets and Magical Bowls*, 187. The Geniza text has been pub-
     lished by S. Shaked, "An Early Geniza Fragment in an Unknown Iranian Dialect," in
     Barg-i sabz: A Green Leaf: Papers in Honour of Professor Jes P. Asmussen (ed. W. Sun-
     dermann, J. Duchesne-Guillemin, and F. Vahman; Acta Iranica 28; Leiden: Brill,
     1988), 219–35 (228–30). The incantation and spells are in Aramaic, and the inter-
     woven text of Deut 6:4 and Psalm 91 is followed by Deut 6:5. The mixing of verses is
     meant to confuse demons. In another incantation text from the Cairo Geniza, a long
     magical name is composed of the initial letters of Ps 91:1–9. See L. H. Schiffman and
     M. D. Swartz, *Hebrew and Aramaic Incantation Texts from the Cairo Geniza* (Semitic
     Texts and Studies 1; Sheffield: JSOT Press, 1992), 71 (text), 78 (commentary).

50   C. A. Laʾda, "A Greek Papyrus Amulet from the Duke Collection with Biblical
     Excerpts," *BASP* 41 (2004): 93–113. A convenient list of attestations of Psalm 91 (LXX
     Psalm 90) in Greek manuscripts is provided on pp. 107–10.

51   J. Wellhausen, *The Book of Psalms* (The Polychrome Bible; London: J. Clarke, 1898),
     201. See also N. Nicolsky, *Spuren magischer Formeln in den Psalmen* (BZAW 46; Gies-
     sen: Alfred Töpelmann, 1927), 14–29.

52   C. Maier, *Crusade Propaganda and Ideology: Model Sermons for the Preaching of the Cross*
     (Cambridge: Cambridge University Press, 2000), 170–73, §§9–11.

that the Crusader soldiers would be liberated from the demons by the "letter tau," that is, the cross sign.[53]

In this short study we have paid particular attention to Exodus 12, Mic 5:4–5[5–6] and Psalm 91. On several occasions Deuteronomy 6–8 and Ezekiel 9 also figured in the discussion. We found affinities between the language of several of these biblical texts and that of the Arslan Tash inscriptions. The significance of the "threshold" or "border-crossing" and the importance of the protection of the house or land (domestic space) were also highlighted. The threat of hostile forces at night is present in Arslan Tash I, Exodus 12, and Psalm 91. My previous arguments in 1978 notwithstanding, the evidence for incantatory aspects of Mic 5:4–5[5–6] is less compelling, but the language is striking nevertheless and worthy of attention.

---

53   Maier, *Crusade Propaganda and Ideology*, 180–83, §§10, 13; see also 186–87, §19.

A Literary Analysis of the Shiloah (Siloam) Tunnel Inscription

KLAAS A. D. SMELIK

This contribution is dedicated to my dear friend and colleague Graham Davies, to whom I owe a magnificent English translation of my book on Hebrew inscriptions.

The digging of the Shiloah Tunnel beneath the City of David around 700 BCE was an exceptional feat of engineering. It was a blind dig, unlike the water tunnels at Megiddo and Hazor, which were line of sight digs. The engineer did not make use of intermediate shafts for the excavation work either—the method utilized in Urartu and Mesopotamia. He had developed his own approach to the problem, unique for his time, and was successful in making a tunnel with what was for his time a unique length.

The inscription made in the Shiloah Tunnel in the same period[1] is likewise exceptional. It does not mention the name of a king or a god—unlike the other building inscriptions from the ancient Near East.[2] The text of this inscription concentrates on the stonemasons, who were cutting the rock with their pick-axes. Not even the engineer in charge of the project is mentioned. The inscription could be considered as a

---

[1] The proposal to date the Shiloah Tunnel Inscription in the Hasmonean period made by J. Rogerson and P. R. Davies in 1996 has met strong opposition from colleagues. Cf. J. Rogerson and P. R. Davies, "Was the Siloam Tunnel built by Hezekiah?" *BA* 59 (1996). 138–48; R. Hendel, "The Date of the Siloam Inscription: A Rejoinder to Rogerson and Davies," *BA* 59 (1996): 233–37; J. A. Hackett, F. M. Cross, P. Kyle McCarter, Jr., A. Yardeni, A. Lemaire, E. Eshel, and A. Hurvitz, "Defusing Pseudo-Scholarship: The Siloam Inscription Ain't Hasmonean," *BAR* 23, no. 2 (March/April 1997): 41–50, 68.

[2] William H. Shea draws our attention to texts of the Assyrian king Sennacherib, the same king who attacked Judah in Hezekiah's time. In these dedications, the great accomplishments of the king are recited in the first person. He is the one who digs canals with an iron pick-axe. The people who work in the king's service are not mentioned at all. See W. H. Shea, "Commemorating the Final Breakthrough of the Siloam Tunnel," in *Fucus: A Semitic/Afrasian Gathering in Remembrance of Albert Ehrman* (ed. Yoël L. Arbeitman; Current Issues in Linguistic Theory 58; Philadelphia, Pa.: John Benjamins Publishing, 1988), 431–42 (441–42).

unique example of "proletarian consciousness"[3] in antiquity, and this has inspired some scholars to ascribe the text to the tunnel workers themselves.

There are more peculiarities to note. Building inscriptions are usually placed on a spot where they can easily be seen. The Shiloah Tunnel Inscription, however, has been located six metres from the current outlet of the tunnel. Since the text concentrates on the meeting of the two crews who were making the tunnel, one would expect the inscription to have been placed at this juncture point, but it was not. Altman suggests that "the inscription is at the place where the inspiration for the solution to the engineering problem of how to build a blind tunnel through solid rock without intermediate shafts was received from his [the engineer's] god."[4] But in the inscription we find no mention of any divine inspiration, neither does the engineer figure in the text (as remarked before). Altman's explanation is based on mere speculation. The same applies to Faust's thesis that the present spot for the inscription was the place where the two teams of stonemasons met.[5] Judging from the traces in the tunnel, it is clear that the juncture point was at a quite different spot, approximately in the middle of the tunnel. Neither explanation is therefore convincing. Another proposal was made by Parker. The inscription was deliberately placed here because "it was not designed for public display. . . . Such a display might be dangerous, since it was generally only kings who recorded such accomplishments."[6] But why bother to chisel an inscription in a place where no one is supposed to see it?

The Shiloah Tunnel is exceptional in other respects too. The tunnel was not cut in a straight line but in something like an S-bend. As the crow flies, it involves a distance of some 320 m but because of the many bends in its line, the tunnel measures approximately 533 m. Why was so much extra work carried out? This is an interesting problem and various explanations have been brought forward. In my book *Writings*

---

3   Cf. the following lines from the poem by Bertolt Brecht, "Fragen eines lesenden Arbeiters" (1935):
        Wer baute das siebentorige Theben
        In den Büchern stehen die Namen von Königen.
        Haben die Könige die Felsbrocken herbeigeschleppt?

4   Rochelle I. Altman, "Some Notes on Inscriptional Genres and the Siloam Tunnel Inscription," *Antiguo Oriente* 5 (2007): 35–88 (80).

5   Avraham Faust, "A Note on Hezekiah's Tunnel and the Shiloah Inscription," *JSOT* 90 (2000): 3–11.

6   Simon B. Parker, "Siloam Inscription Memorializes Engineering Achievement," *BAR* 20, no. 4 (July/August 1994): 36–38 (38).

from Ancient Israel,[7] superbly translated into English by Graham Davies in 1991, I have favoured the theory that the tunnel builders made use of tapped signals from above. The thorough investigation published by Frumkin and Shimron in 2006 has shown beyond doubt that this is the most probable solution[8]—notwithstanding the study by Gill favouring the explanation that the diggers followed the course of a subterranean watercourse.[9] Frumkin and Shimron stress, however, that the tunnel "must have been engineered and hewn by man without a pre-existing natural conduit." They base their conclusion on "two lines of evidence: (a) the natural features of ST [= the Shiloah Tunnel]—the lack of any continuous fissure or remnant of a karst passage, and the natural sediments covering the ancient plaster, and (b) the artificial features—the plaster covering bare bedrock, and the false starts and hewing deviations."[10]

When the engineers had no fissure to lead them, how did they manage to communicate to the stonemasons in which direction they had to dig? Frumkin and Shimron suggest that at first "acoustic messages from the surface must have been the dominant technique which controlled the complex proceedings underneath." They observe, "[o]ur acoustic experiments between surface and the central portion of ST demonstrate that tapping with a hammer on bedrock is well effective to depths of about 15 m, and detectable up to about 20–25 m." But when the stonecutters reached deeper levels, they were at a loss: "it can also be assumed that the subsurface teams were out of *effective* mutual acoustic range until a few meters of each other."[11] This explains the chaotic excavation along the central portion of the tunnel, where the two teams of stonemasons made many deviations and false starts before they could finally hear each other and adjust their direction (as can be derived from the traces in the tunnel). Thanks to Frumkin and Shimron's detailed examination of the tunnel, we now know how the

---

7   Klaas A. D. Smelik, *Writings from Ancient Israel: A Handbook of Historical and Religious Documents;* trans. G. I. Davies (Edinburgh: T&T Clark, 1991; American edition: Louisville, Ky.: Westminster John Knox, 1991), 67. A completely revised and updated edition was published in Dutch in 2006: Klaas A. D. Smelik, *Neem een boekrol en schrijf: Tekstvondsten uit het oude Israël* (Zoetermeer: Boekencentrum, 2006).

8   A. Frumkin and A. Shimron, "Tunnel Engineering in the Iron Age: Geoarchaeology of the Siloam Tunnel, Jerusalem," *Journal of Archaeological Science* 33 (2006): 227–37.

9   D. Gill, "Subterranean Waterworks of Biblical Jerusalem: Adaptation of a Karst System," *Science* 254 (1991): 1467–71. See also his article "How They Met," *BAR* 20, no. 4 (July/August 1994): 20–33, 64, and S. Lancaster and G. Long, "Where They Met: Separations in the Rock Mass near the Siloam Tunnel's Meeting Point," *BASOR* 315 (1999): 15–26.

10   Frumkin and Shimron, "Tunnel Engineering in the Iron Age," 235.

11   Frumkin and Shimron, "Tunnel Engineering in the Iron Age," 233 (their italics).

tunnel was made. This information is very useful for the right interpretation of the Shiloah Tunnel Inscription, to which we turn now.

History of the Discovery

The history of the discovery of the Shiloah Tunnel Inscription is as exceptional as the text itself. In the summer of 1880, one of the native pupils of Conrad Schick, a German Protestant missionary and architect, already long resident in Jerusalem, was playing with some other lads in the Siloam Pool, and while wading up the subterranean channel he slipped and fell into the water. On rising to the surface, he noticed, in spite of the darkness, what looked like letters on the rock which formed the southern wall of the channel. Schick, on being told of them, visited the spot and found that an ancient inscription, concealed for the most part by the water, actually existed there. The first thing to be done was to lower the level of the water, so as to expose the inscription to view. But Schick's efforts to copy the text were not very successful, because he was not a specialist in ancient Hebrew epigraphy. Since the letters of the inscription, as well as every crack and flaw in the stone, had been filled by the water with a deposit of lime, it was impossible for him to distinguish between characters and accidental markings on the rock, or to make out the exact forms of the letters. I have studied a copy made by Schick that is kept in the Biblical Museum in Amsterdam. It is very difficult to distinguish the actual writing, because Schick has noted everything he saw on the surface of the rock.

During his visit to Jerusalem in 1881, Sayce made a new copy of the inscription. He describes his labour as follows: "I had to sit for hours in the mud and water, working by the dim light of a candle."[12] Then he enlisted the assistance of his colleague H. Guthe, who removed the deposit of lime by the application of an acid and so revealed the original appearance of the inscription. A cast of it was taken and squeezes were made from the cast, that could be studied at leisure and in a good light.

These actions turned out to have been a wise precaution because in 1890 the Shiloah Inscription was surreptitiously cut from the wall of the tunnel and broken into fragments. These were, however, recovered by the efforts of the British Consul at Jerusalem. The pieces were brought to Constantinople, where the inscription was reconstructed with the

---

12   A. H. Sayce, ed., *Records of the Past*, NS vol. 1 (London: Samuel Bagster & Sons, 1888), 169.

help of the squeezes. Since then, it has been kept in the Istanbul Archaeological Museum, although Israel has asked the Turkish Government to return the inscription to Jerusalem, where it belongs.

Who Wrote the Text?

We turn now to the question: who wrote this text? We have mentioned already the rather romantic view that the stonemasons chiselled this text in the tunnel wall after completing their demanding task. The most convincing argument for this identification is the fact that the text concentrates on them and their labour, and not on the king, who is not even mentioned. In Sir 48:17 we read (probably in relation to the same achievement): "Hezekiah fortified his city, directing water into it; with bronze [LXX: iron] he hacked through the rocks and dammed up the water into a pool." In the Shiloah Tunnel Inscription, however, it is not the king who is hacking but the stonemasons. This is a realistic but exceptional way of describing a building operation ordered by a king.

Nevertheless, this identification is rather improbable, as appears from the execution of the inscription. It was made by "someone who was accustomed to writing on a regular basis."[13] It is important to note that the text was not written in monumental but in a cursive script. This points to a person who was accustomed to write on papyrus or on shards (ostraca). It is unlikely that the stonemasons had this experience.

In my article on the literary structure of the Yavneh Yam inscription,[14] I have shown that a literary analysis of an inscription can be helpful in establishing the identity of the writer of the text. In this case too, a literary analysis can help us to get a clearer understanding of the way the text was composed. But let us first have a look at the text itself.[15] I suggest the following translation:

[Concerning][16] the breakthrough.
And this was the story of the breakthrough.

---

13   Altman, "Some Notes on Inscriptional Genres and the Siloam Tunnel Inscription," 79.

14   K. A. D. Smelik, "The Literary Structure of the Yavneh-Yam Ostracon," *IEJ* 42 (1992): 55–61.

15   G. I. Davies, *Ancient Hebrew Inscriptions: Corpus and Concordance* (Cambridge: Cambridge University Press, 1991), 68 (§4.116); cf. idem, *Ancient Hebrew Inscriptions Volume 2: Corpus and Concordance* (Cambridge: Cambridge University Press, 2004), 231.

16   Several suggestions have been made about the word with which the inscription originally began. There is space for only two or three letters. To these suggestions, I add here another possibility: the Hebrew preposition עַל. The first two words of the

While the [stonemasons were] still [striking with] the pick-axe,
each man towards his comrade,
and while there were still three ells to br[eak through,]
[there was hear]d the voice of a man
shouting towards his comrade,
for there was a *resonance*[17] in the rock,
from the right [to the lef]t.[18]
And on the day of the breakthrough
the stonemasons struck
each man in the direction of his comrade
pick-axe against [pick-]axe.
Then the water ran from the spring to the pool
for two hundred and a thousand ells.
And a hundred ells was the height of the rock over the head of the stone-
mason[s].

Literary Structure

The Shiloah Tunnel Inscription can be outlined as follows:

    a.   Title: "Concerning the breakthrough"
    b.   Summary: "And this was the story of the breakthrough"
    c.   First event: "there was heard the voice"
    d.   Second event: striking "pick-axe against pick-axe"
    e.   Third event: "the water ran from the spring to the pool"
    f.   Conclusion: size of the tunnel.

The outline shows clearly that the inscription "is not concerned with
the recounting of the complete history of the excavation of the tunnel.
Rather, the text is very much preoccupied with *a specific moment on a
specific day*—the culmination of a great and exciting engineering

---

inscription constitute the title of the text. In Jer 14:1 we see a comparable use of עַל:
"The word of the LORD which came to Jeremiah concerning (עַל) the drought."

17   Hebrew: זדה. Since this is the only time the word occurs in Classical Hebrew, we do
not know its meaning. Several translations have been proposed; cf. the detailed discussion by J. Renz, *Die althebräischen Inschriften, Teil 1: Text und Kommentar* (vol. 1 of
Handbuch der althebräischen Epigraphik; ed. J. Renz and W. Röllig; Darmstadt: Wissenschaftliche Buchgesellschaft, 1995), 184–85. The translation "resonance," proposed
by É. Puech, "L'inscription du Tunnel de Siloé," *RB* 81 (1974): 196–214, is in my opinion the most probable rendering, since there is no indication that there was a fissure
here before making the tunnel: "Close observation of the headward face of bedrock
in the false starts shows no evidence of a karst conduit which could guide the hew-
ers for any distance" (Frumkin and Shimron, "Tunnel Engineering in the Iron Age,"
232).

18   It is also possible to translate: "in the south and i[n the north]"; cf. Shea, "Commemorating the Final Breakthrough of the Siloam Tunnel," 434.

project."[19] In this respect, the translation "the breakthrough" for Hebrew הנקבה is better than the other suggested translations like "the tunnel."[20] The final moment of breaking through the last part of the rock from both sides is the main subject of the inscription, not the engineering project as such. The title and summary of the inscription make it clear to the reader that not the whole story will be told in the text, only the event of the breakthrough. The triple repetition of נקבה in this rather short text indicates that נקבה has the function of a *Leitwort*, a literary device that is rather common in the Hebrew Bible.

The situation of both teams of stonemasons is described in the first lines of section c. Here we note the repetition of the conjunctive complex בוד, "while still" (second time with the conjunction ו). This is another literary device;[21] it serves to stress the contrast between the initial situation in which the stonemasons were trying to work in the direction of the other team but were very uncertain whether they were digging the right way or not, and the final result described in section e. Evidence of how awkward the situation actually was has been given by Frumkin and Shimron: several times both teams were at a loss. The uncertainty ended, however, as soon as "the voice of a man shouting towards his comrade was heard." At that moment, the tunnel workers knew for sure in which direction they had to dig.[22] The reason that the voices of the other team could be heard at this moment, and not before, is explained by a subordinate clause introduced by the conjunction כי. Unfortunately, the explanation does not make sense to us because we do not know the meaning of the Hebrew word זדה, but this did not, of course, apply to the first readers of the text who must have been familiar with the word.

Before describing the next stage of the event, the author inserts "And on the day of the breakthrough" at the beginning of section d, stressing the importance of the moment. After many days of hard labour, this will be the final day—"the day of the breakthrough." Until now, the stonemasons had struck only rock, but on this special day they struck their pick-axes against the axes of the other team that

---

19 V. Sasson, "The Siloam Tunnel Inscription," *PEQ* 114 (1982): 111–17 (113, his emphasis).

20 For this translation, see Parker, "Siloam Inscription Memorializes Engineering Achievement," 37.

21 Cf. F. W. Dobbs-Allsopp, J. J. M. Roberts, C. L. Seow, and R. E. Whitaker, *Hebrew Inscriptions: Texts from the Biblical Period of the Monarchy with Concordance* (New Haven: Yale University Press, 2005), 502: "The literary style it evinces, when taken with other elements, indicates that the inscription was composed by a skilled writer, not just put together by a workman."

22 Frumkin and Shimron, "Tunnel Engineering in the Iron Age," 232–35.

appeared through the rock in the last phase of the breakthrough. They
did not only hear the sound of breaking rock, but also that of metal
striking metal.

The climax of the whole project was the moment that the water
started to flow not only in the northern part of the tunnel but also in the
southern part, as soon as the last pieces of smashed rock had been
removed. This moment is described in section e. Note the use of the
imperfectum consecutivum instead of the perfect—the perfect serves as
the normal narrative tense in this inscription. The *imperfectum consecuti-*
vum indicates the beginning of the movement of the water (inchoative).
Finally, "the water ran from the spring to the pool" (to wit: from the
Gihon Spring to the Siloam Pool). The work had been completed.

By way of conclusion, two measurements are given: the length of
the tunnel and the distance between the ceiling of the tunnel and the
surface. The last statement is only partly true: the figure of 100 ells
given here represents the maximum distance reached at a few places.
Still, it is striking that the text ends in this way. It reflects a keen interest
in the exact measurements of the tunnel project, although it is not a nice
ending from a literary point of view.

Let us now pay attention to two other details in the text that reveal
the writer's literary skill. The threefold repetition of "each man towards
his comrade" is a literary device well-known from the Bible, but note
the variation in the expression in sections c and d:

> each man towards his comrade
> the voice of a man shouting towards his comrade (section c)
> each man in the direction of his comrade (section d).

A variation in a repetition is another literary device typical of biblical
narrative in order to enliven the text.

Let us conclude the analysis with noting another literary device: the
inclusio around the text formed by the twofold appearance of the word
חצבם, "stonemasons" (the first time, however, in a reconstructed part of
the text).

Again: Who Wrote the Text?

We have already dismissed the possibility that the inscription was written by the stonemasons. We have to search for other solutions. Coote
and Altman suggest that the inscription was made by the chief engineer of this project. This is also the opinion of Parker.[23] Coote states:

---

23   Parker, "Siloam Inscription Memorializes Engineering Achievement," 36–38.

"The success of the moment enabled and induced the engineer to commemorate the event by an inscription."[24] An argument for this identification is the special interest in numbers typical of this text.[25] But was an engineer in ancient Judah "someone who was accustomed to writing on a regular basis" (to quote Altman)?[26] Can we suppose that he was really able to chisel an inscription in such a professional way?

Another possibility is to assume that a royal scribe connected to the Judahite court was the author of this text.[27] Levi della Vida even suggested that the text was transcribed from a Judahite chronicle. A pointer to this may be the fact that, as appears from 2 Kgs 20:20, a passage about the Shiloah Tunnel was included in the Book of the Chronicles of the Kings of Judah. We quote the biblical text:

> The rest of the deeds of Hezekiah, and all his might, and how he made the pool and the conduit and brought water into the city, are they not written in the Book of the Chronicles of the Kings of Judah?[28]

But from this very succinct summary,[29] it is clear that the (lost) Book of the Chronicles of the Kings of Judah focused on King Hezekiah and his achievements as a ruler. And that is not the case in the Shiloah Tunnel Inscription, as we have stressed before. Due to the absence of any reference to the royal sponsor, the hypothesis that a scribe connected with the Judahite court has made this text can be ruled out. The assumption that it was an abstract taken from the royal Judahite chronicles is, moreover, contradictory to the nature of this text, which is a self-contained unit: "the composition appears to be whole and intact as it stands."[30]

In my opinion, we have to look for an author outside the royal court. In ancient Judah there were scribes who did not work for the king and his court but for the ordinary citizens of Jerusalem. An

---

24 R. B. Coote, "Siloam Inscription," *ABD* 6:23–24 (24).

25 Parker, "Siloam Inscription Memorializes Engineering Achievement," 37.

26 Altman, "Some Notes on Inscriptional Genres and the Siloam Tunnel Inscription," 79.

27 "In jedem Fall wird wohl an den Königshof und den dazugehörigen Beamtenapparat als Entstehungsort zu denken sein" (Renz, *Die althebräischen Inschriften,* 182 n. 1).

28 G. Levi della Vida, "The Shiloah Inscription Reconsidered," in *In Memoriam Paul Kahle* (ed. M. Black and G. Fohrer; BZAW 103; Berlin: Alfred Töpelmann, 1968), 162–66.

29 Most scholars assume that the main reason for making this tunnel was the impending campaign by the Assyrian king Sennacherib, but another solution is more probable (as I have explained in my book *Writings from Ancient Israel,* 66): the tunnel was made in connection with the water-supply for the new quarter of Jerusalem built in Hezekiah's days. In that case, there was no reason to hasten the project (*pace* Faust, "A Note on Hezekiah's Tunnel and the Shiloah Inscription," 4).

30 Shea, "Commemorating the Final Breakthrough of the Siloam Tunnel," 441.

example is Baruch, the son of Neriah. He is well-known as the prophet Jeremiah's secretary, but in Jerusalem a bulla was found with the following inscription: "Belonging to Berechiah, the son of Neriah, the scribe."[31] The papyrus on which this seal-impression had been fixed is gone, but the text on the bulla shows that Baruch had his own office as a scribe and that he was not working for Jeremiah alone. People could hire him (and other scribes) when they needed a text to be written. The same is still happening in the modern Near East—I saw it in Amman. But the work of a scribe was not limited to writing letters and requests, as the example of Baruch shows. Several parts of the book of Jeremiah are ascribed to him. Texts of a more literary nature were also written by the scribes of ancient Judah.

Therefore, I propose that the engineer(s) of the Shiloah Tunnel project hired a professional scribe to write an inscription. In this text, the final stage of the project was described in a literary way, in "poetic prose" to quote Shea,[32] but with the addition of the measurements so important for the engineer(s)—although they disturb the structure of the text to a certain degree, as we have already noted. The scribe did his job as ghost-writer in such a convincing manner that scholars have assumed that the stonemasons themselves had written the text—notwithstanding the professional way the inscription was chiselled in cursive writing and the literary devices in the text. It is the magic of a good writer to give readers the feeling that they have a report of an eye-witness in front of them. But it is only magic. . . .[33]

---

31   Davies, *Ancient Hebrew Inscriptions*, 186 (§100.509); N. Avigad and B. Sass, *Corpus of West Semitic Stamp Seals* (Jerusalem: Israel Exploration Society, 1997), 175–76 (§417A).

32   Shea, "Commemorating the Final Breakthrough of the Siloam Tunnel," 441.

33   This article was completed in June 2009, and I was therefore unable to take account of the article by A. Sneh, R. Weinberger, and E. Shalev, "The Why, How, and When of the Siloam Tunnel Reevaluated," *BASOR* 359 (2010): 57–65.

Incense—the Ancient Room Freshener

The Exegesis of Daniel 2:46*

ALAN MILLARD

When Atrahasis, the Babylonian Noah, left his boat, he sacrificed to the gods, who smelt the offering and gathered like flies over it. In describing it, according to an Old Babylonian manuscript copied in 1635 BC, the Mother-goddess asked, "Has the god Enlil come to the incense [*qutrinu*]?"[1] Incense was an integral part of worship of the gods across the ancient Near East from the earliest periods. We may assume that in prehistoric times people noticed that certain things gave off a pleasant smell when put on a fire. (More recently, in the eighteenth century, Egyptian peasants noticed that old papyri did so!) Observing that wood, or sap, or resin from particular trees were productive, they experimented with others, so that some were sought especially for the purpose. What human beings enjoyed, they would expect their gods to enjoy also, and, as usual, they lavished that on their deities. By the end of the third millennium BC, documents from Babylonia record a wide variety of materials used for perfumes and incense, derived from various vegetable substances—resins, shavings, twigs—and incense burners occur in cuneiform texts from the Early Bronze Age into the Iron Age.[2] Lists of materials for making perfumes in cuneiform texts at Mari include cedar, cypress, juniper, myrtle—either the woods themselves or the resins—and various resins hard to identify.[3] Although these lists

---

*   This essay expands some paragraphs of "The Value and Limitations of the Bible and Archaeology for Understanding the History of Israel—Some Examples," in *Israel: Ancient Kingdom of Late Invention* (ed. Daniel I. Block; Nashville, Tenn.: B&H Academic, 2008), 9–24, originally read at the International Meeting of the Society of Biblical Literature in Edinburgh, July 2006.
1   Atrahasis III v 34–41. W. G. Lambert and A. R. Millard, *Atra-ḫasīs: The Babylonian Story of the Flood* (Oxford: Clarendon, 1969), 98–99; Benjamin R. Foster, *Before the Muses: An Anthology of Akkadian Literature* (3d ed.; Bethesda, Md.: CDL Press, 2005), 251.
2   K. Nielsen, *Incense in Ancient Israel* (VTSup 38; Leiden: Brill, 1986).
3   F. Joannès, "La culture matérielle à Mari (V): Les parfums," *MARI* 7 (1993): 251–70.

and recipes for making perfumes[4] are not specifically for incense, they show the variety of ingredients available from within the Fertile Crescent. The materials burnt as incense vary from the readily available to the exotic. It is a mistake to suppose that the ingredients of every type of incense were the rare and expensive frankincense and myrrh, imported from Southern Arabia or the Horn of Africa and available only to the wealthy classes.

From Egypt there are pictures of incense burners and records of incense brought from the distant land of Punt in the 5th Dynasty (ca. 2500–2350 BC). One word, *sntr*, seems to mean "incense" in general, and it is sometimes qualified by the evidently West Semitic *qdrt* (קטרת) in the Ramesside Papyrus Harris I.[5] Analyses of residues in jars of New Kingdom date labelled *sntr* show it "consisted predominantly, if not exclusively, of pistacia resin."[6] Another term, *ꜥntyw*, denotes the product of Punt, which may be both myrrh and frankincense.[7]

The import of myrrh into Egypt is attested from the Old Kingdom onwards; in one of the "Harper" Songs, the hearer is encouraged to be happy, "put myrrh on your head, dress you(rself) in fine linen."[8] It was a substance desired from Egypt by Milk-ilu of Gezer, and, conversely, sent to Egypt as part of his daughter's dowry by Tushratta of Mitanni (EA 269:16, 22 iii 29, and 25 iv 51). It was also known at Ugarit. Frankincense was less common, but small quantities were found in the tomb of Tutankhamun.[9] Until the end of the New Kingdom, incense, with other exotic goods, was brought to Egypt along the Red Sea coast from Punt. That link broke early in the twelfth century BC, to be replaced by expanding use of the overland route through Arabia from the Yemen, consequent upon the expansion of camel caravans.[10] Exactly when that route was opened is unknown, but there were evidently contacts

---

4   E. Ebeling, *Parfümrezepte und kultische Texte aus Assur* (Rome: Pontifical Biblical Institute, 1950).

5   J. E. Hoch, *Semitic Words in Egyptian Texts* (Princeton: Princeton University Press, 1994), 305.

6   M. Serpico, J. Bourriau, L. Smith, Y. Goren, B. Stern, and C. Heron, "Commodities and Containers: A Project to Study Canaanite Amphorae Imported into Egypt During the New Kingdom," in *The Synchronisation of Civilisations in the Eastern Mediterranean in the Second Millennium B.C. II* (ed. M. Bietak; CCEM 4; Vienna: Verlag der Österreichischen Akademie der Wissenschaften, 2003), 365–75 (368).

7   Nielsen, *Incense in Ancient Israel*, 13–15.

8   K. A. Kitchen, *Poetry of Ancient Egypt* (Documenta Mundi, Aegyptiaca 1; Jonsered: Paul Åström, 1999), 137–42.

9   A. Lucas, *Ancient Egyptian Materials and Industries* (4th ed.; London: Arnold, 1962), 111–13.

10   M. Jasmin, "Les conditions d'émergence de la route de l'encens à la fin du IIe millénaire avant notre ère," *Syria* 82 (2005): 49–62.

between the Levant and southern Arabia during the second millennium BC. Liverani has demonstrated, on the basis of Assyrian texts, that trade was moving between Sheba and Mesopotamia by about 900 BC. The earliest relevant text, an inscription of Tukulti-Ninurta II (ca. 891–884 BC), mentions myrrh (*murru*).[11] The word for frankincense (*labānatu*) is absent from Assyrian and Babylonian texts, except for one occurrence in a medical compilation and one in a medical commentary, so it may never have displaced other fragrant resins there. The term is assumed to be a loanword from West Semitic.[12]

The instructions for preparing the sacred incense in Exod 30:34–38 end with a prohibition on anyone making the same incense for their own use, prescribing the most severe punishment for anyone who might do so. Yet, as commonly observed, that implies there were other types of incense which Israelites could use in "secular" situations; Prov 27:9, "Perfume and incense bring joy to the heart," may indicate that, and Ps 45:9[8] refers to the wafting of the smoke of incense into clothes, as is still done to-day (see below).

Not surprisingly, most of the information about incense in the ancient Near East is related to formal or royal cults. It is kings and their officials who are usually shown offering incense and it is in religious scenes that priests burn incense. In texts the same figures are the ones who deal with incense, whether in Egypt, or in Babylonia, or in Israel. There are several pictures from Assyria, many on cylinder seals,[13] some on sculptures, like the relief of Ashurbanipal honouring the lions he had killed, and a coloured scene on a faience vessel from Ashur, 36 cm high.[14] A Babylonian boundary stone of Meli-shipak, ca. 1175 BC, shows the king before a god with an incense burner between them.[15] All these incense burners share the same form, a tall, tapering stand with a bowl on top, sometimes with flames flaring from it, sometimes perhaps with a cover (as in Achaemenid examples, see below).

However, incense burning was not confined to those rituals. In both Babylonia and Egypt texts prescribe incense as a fumigant in medical

---

11   M. Liverani, "Early Caravan Trade between South-Arabia and Mesopotamia," *Yemen* 1 (1992): 111–15. The texts from Suḫu, which supplied the fresh information, are translated by K. Lawson Younger in *COS* 2:279–83 (281–82).

12   *CAD* L, 8b.

13   D. Collon, *Catalogue of the Western Asiatic Seals in the British Museum: Cylinder Seals V: Neo-Assyrian and Neo-Babylonian Periods* (London: British Museum, 2001), nos. 130–34; A. Moortgat, *Vorderasiatische Rollsiegel* (Berlin: Mann, 1940), no. 655.

14   R. D. Barnett, *Sculptures from the North Palace of Ashurbanipal at Nineveh* (London: British Museum, 1976), 54, pl. 57; W. Andrae, *Coloured Ceramics from Ashur* (London: Kegan Paul, 1925), pl. 29.

15   P. Amiet, *Art of the Ancient Near East* (New York: Abrams, 1980), no. 516.

processes, as a counter to the stench of putrefaction and as a counter to domestic smells, perfuming houses and clothes.[16] The two last uses continue to the present day. Over thirty years ago, a British journalist reported how a Saʿudi sheikh stood over an incense burner to allow the aromatic smoke to seep into his robes and almost simultaneously the same habit was reported among the Marsh Arabs.[17] Albright, too, drew attention to the burning of incense as a means of freshening houses in recent times.[18] In the Yemen frankincense perfumed houses, where, in living memory, it was burnt "on small pottery burners that are still made in the pattern of those recovered from the remains of the Hellenic period, being square with square legs."[19]

Those ancient incense burners were the subjects of a survey undertaken in 1979, published in 1983.[20] Scores of examples in stone or pottery were registered from sites in Arabia, Palestine, and Babylonia. The Bible Lands Museum, Jerusalem, possesses an example of gilded silver, dated to the Achaemenid era, 11.0 cm high, 8.4 cm wide, 8.6 cm deep, decorated with rosettes, palmettes, and four-pointed stars in low relief (BLMJ 1339).[21] All are dated in the first millennium BC, from the seventh century to Roman times. There were exceptions. Sir Leonard Woolley excavated three specimens at Ur which he dated to the second millennium BC. The survey concluded that the archaeologist's dating was mistaken; the form of the allegedly second millennium incense burners is identical with forms found in the first millennium and the exact provenance in Ur was doubted. Hardly had that study been published when an exhibition was staged in Paris to display finds from Emar on the mid-Euphrates where excavations were made in advance

16   Nielsen, *Incense in Ancient Israel*, 89–94.

17   G. Robyns, *Woman 76*, no. 1986 (14 June, 1975), 24; E. Ochsenschlager, *Archaeology* 27.3 (1974), 165.

18   William F. Albright, "The Lachish Cosmetic Burner and Esther 2, 12," in *A Light unto My Path: Old Testament Studies in Honor of Jacob M. Myers* (ed. H. N. Bream et al.; Philadelphia, Pa.: Temple University Press, 1974), 25–32; see my notes in a review of E. Lipiński, *Studies in Aramaic Inscriptions and Onomastics, JSS* 21 (1976): 174–78 (177), and M. D. Fowler, "Excavated Incense Burners: A Case for Identifying a Site as Sacred?" *PEQ* 117 (1985): 25–29; idem, "Excavated Incense Burners," *BA* 47 (1984): 183–86.

19   N. Hepper, *Illustrated Encyclopedia of Bible Plants* (Leicester: Inter-Varsity, 1992), 137.

20   M. O'Dwyer Shea, "The Small Cuboid Incense-Burner of the Ancient Near East," *Levant* 15 (1983): 76–109.

21   *Bible Lands Museum, Jerusalem: Guide to the Collection* (Tel Aviv: Sirkis, 1992), 104 and W. Seipel and A. Wieczorek, eds., *Von Babylon bis Jerusalem: Die Welt der altorientalischen Königsstädte* (2 vols.; Vienna: Kunsthistorisches Museum; Mannheim: Reiss-Museum, 1999), 2:119. I am indebted to Dr F. Vukosavović, Bible Lands Museum, for details of this piece.

of the flood waters of Lake Assad. The town was a settlement of the Late Bronze Age which had been abandoned soon after 1200 BC. Among the objects recovered from the make-up of the terraces on which the buildings stood, therefore earlier in date, were several of the "small cuboid incense burners." Thus their age was extended back well into the second millennium BC, beyond question. At the same time, publication of the results of excavations at Tell Kannas, some 20 km upstream from Emar, disclosed the existence of the same type of incense burner earlier still, in the Middle Bronze Age, the first half of the second millennium BC. Now the isolated examples from Ur, which their excavator placed in the second millennium, could be re-assessed. Although few of the objects have come from second millennium levels in southern Babylonia (there are some from Kassite deposits at Nippur), they can be assigned to the period originally claimed.[22] All of these discoveries were duly catalogued in another, more detailed, survey which was undertaken in 1988–89 and published in 1990.[23] A later assessment of examples excavated at Tell Jemmeh concluded that at least one could be dated "to about 1100 to 1050 BC."[24]

This is no new story, but it bears repeating because it offers a good warning against what may be called "the lowest common denominator syndrome," that is, assuming that an aberrant or eccentric feature has to be brought into line with all others of the same class. This is significant for biblical studies. Where the Bible or any other ancient text reports something for a period earlier than other sources attest, or an object is discovered which apparently pre-dates all others of the same kind, its witness should not be automatically assigned to that later time, or taken to reflect it. Where the report refers to something which no other source confirms, or the object is without parallel, dismissing its testimony runs the danger of destroying evidence which may be correct and valuable. A prime example of that from the past is the case of the "kings of the Hittites" whom Ben-Hadad's army thought Israel had hired to fight against them (2 Kgs 7:6). Before A. H. Sayce's recognition of the Hittite kingdoms in 1876, those Hittites were dismissed as unhistorical.[25] Another case is the characterization of the use of iron at an

---

22 A. R. Millard, "The Small Cuboid Incense-Burners: A Note on their Age," *Levant* 16 (1984): 172–73.

23 W. Zwickel, *Räucherkult und Räuchergeräte* (OBO 97; Fribourg, Switzerland: Universitätsverlag Freiburg Schweiz, 1990).

24 J. Hassell, "A Re-examination of the Cuboid Incense-burning Altars from Tell Jemmeh," *Levant* 37 (2005): 133–62 (155).

25 W. Wright, *The Empire of the Hittites* (2d ed.; London: James Nisbet, 1886), 116–17, citing F. W. Newman, *A History of the Hebrew Monarchy* (2d ed.; London: J. Chapman, 1853), 178–79. I owe the precise reference to my friend K. A. Kitchen.

early period in Israel's history as "historically highly improbable"
because, it is alleged, the occurrences "do not fit the archaeological
evidence." A survey of references to, and examples of, ironmongery
from the Late Bronze Age reveals adequate evidence for treating the
biblical references as sound reflections of equipment in that period.[26]

The small cuboid incense burners inform us about a wider use of
incense than the sculptures and texts from the higher levels of society.
These objects are commonly found in private houses, rather than
shrines or temples, and so may better be explained in secular, rather
than religious, terms. That is to say, they were ancient air-fresheners,
without any necessary cultic connotation. They may have functioned in
antiquity as in modern times to perfume clothing, resulting in the
queen's "robes ... fragrant with myrrh and aloes and cassia" as
Ps 45:9[8] describes. That queen and other wealthy people would have
had superior quality incense burners, perhaps of silver or gold. Anyone
who has wandered down the side streets of an old town in the Near
East, especially after heavy rain, will have experienced how strong the
odours can be!

A remarkably high number of stone "incense altars," many with a
"horn" at each corner, has been found inside the olive oil processing
buildings at Ekron, near doorways (nine out of the seventeen found at
the site). In discussing them, one of the excavators, Gitin, has assumed
they all had a religious purpose because six examples came from
"Temple auxiliary buildings and at other sites such altars lay in cultic
areas (the Arad shrine, the Dan altar room, the Megiddo cult room)."[27]
However, as we have argued, the presence of an incense burner need
not imply a religious function, so we might suppose the stone altars in
the workshops at Ekron served for burning incense to counter the pun-
gent smells of the oil-pressing process. That they were larger, and more
weighty than the "small cuboid" ones, would prevent workers moving

---

26   A. R. Millard, "King Og's Bed and other Ancient Ironmongery," in *Ascribe to the
      Lord: Biblical and Other Studies in Memory of Peter C. Craigie* (ed. L. Eslinger and G.
      Taylor; JSOTSup 67; Sheffield: Sheffield Academic Press, 1988), 481–92.
27   Seymour Gitin, "Incense Altars from Ekron, Israel and Judah: Context and Typol-
      ogy," *ErIsr* 20 (1989): 52*–67*; idem, "New Incense Altars from Ekron: Context,
      Typology and Function," *ErIsr* 23 (1992): 43*–49*; idem, "Seventh Century B.C.E.
      Cultic Elements at Ekron," in *Biblical Archaeology Today 1990: Proceedings of the Second
      International Congress on Biblical Archaeology* (ed. A. Biran and J. Aviram; Jerusalem:
      Israel Exploration Society, 1993), 248–58; idem, "Israelite and Philistine Cult, and the
      Archaeological Record in Iron Age II: The 'Smoking Gun' Phenomenon," in *Symbio-
      sis, Symbolism and the Power of the Past: Canaan, Ancient Israel, and Their Neighbours
      from the Late Bronze Age through Roman Palaestina: Proceedings of the Albright/ASOR
      Centennial Symposium, Jerusalem, May 29–31, 2000* (ed. William G. Dever and Sey-
      mour Gitin; Winona Lake, Ind.: Eisenbrauns, 2003), 279–95.

in and out of the rooms with baskets of olives or jars of oil from accidentally overturning them.

Daniel 2:46

The purpose of this essay is to show how the previous discussion of texts and objects from the ancient Near East may aid the exegesis of a biblical passage.

Daniel 2:46 reports how the Babylonian king gave great honours to Daniel for telling him his dream and interpreting it: "Then king Nebuchadnezzar fell prostrate before Daniel and paid him honour and ordered that an offering and incense be presented to him" (באדין מלכא נבוכדנצר נפל על־אנפוהי ולדניאל סגד ומנחה וניחחין אמר לנסכה לה). Of the king's action, one writer has said, "In a chapter filled with superlatives and extreme situations, this is perhaps the most overwrought of all."[28] It is almost universally assumed that the king was treating Daniel as a god. Josephus already said that in the first century (*Ant.* 10.211) and, Jerome reported, the sceptical Porphyry assumed it in the third century.[29] Commentators have followed him, Collins, for example, writing, "The specifically religious character of the veneration is underlined by the mention of sacrifice and incense,"[30] and Porteous, Nebuchadnezzar's "payment of homage to Daniel might merely have meant the reversal of the homage a subject was expected to pay to the king. The use, however, of the terms sacrifice and incense shows that more is implied."[31] Alternatively, the passage in Daniel has been seen as an example of the Hellenistic "Benefactor Cult" in which altars were erected and sacrifices made in honour of someone who had done a noble deed for a person or a city not only after death, but even during his lifetime.[32] Others have suspected an ironic, even a humorous note in the description of a Babylonian potentate revering the exiled Jew and his God, prefiguring the prophecy of the dream itself (so Porteous). Embarrassed by the contradiction of a human being, a devout, monotheistic

---

28 S. Kirkpatrick, *Competing for Honor: A Social-Scientific Reading of Daniel 1–6* (BIS 74; Leiden: Brill, 2005), 89.

29 Jerome, *Expl. Dan.* (CCSL 75A, 795), I ii 46.

30 John J. Collins, *Daniel: A Commentary on the Book of Daniel* (Hermeneia; Minneapolis, Minn.: Fortress, 1993), 171.

31 N. W. Porteous, *Daniel: A Commentary* (OTL; London: SCM, 1965), 51.

32 B. A. Mastin expounded this explanation in "Daniel 2 46 and the Hellenistic World," *ZAW* 85 (1973): 80–93, from which much of the information and many of the references given here are drawn.

Jew, being treated as a divinity, Jerome himself and others since have supposed that the honours were offered to the Deity Daniel represented, rather than to the man himself.[33] Thus Delcor wrote, "Nabuchodonosor . . . se prosterne devant lui comme devant un dieu. . . . Il ordonne même qu'on lui offre des sacrifices. Il pense sans doute qu'une telle science ne peut qu'être d'origine divine. Chose curieuse Daniel ne refuse pas ces honneurs. . . ."[34] Hartman and Di Lella commented, "One cannot evade the difficulty by supposing that the 'worship' ($s^e\bar{g}id$) was merely civic homage; the words 'sacrifice' ($minh\bar{a}h$) and 'incense' ($n\hat{i}h\bar{o}h\hat{i}n$, literally, 'pleasant-smelling offerings') are strictly religious terms, borrowed in fact from the Hebrew ritual vocabulary." Daniel accepted worship for his God.[35]

In more recent decades the view has been gaining ground that the narratives in the first six chapters have a strong Babylonian background.[36] If Nebuchadnezzar's action is seen in that context, the difficulty it seems to present may disappear. The vocabulary and material remains combined suggest a man might receive such honour without any religious nuances.

According to biblical Hebrew texts, falling prostrate before someone (נפל על פנים) was a gesture of respect that was paid to a prophet, a king, and a benefactor (1 Kgs 18:7; 2 Sam 9:6; Ruth 2:10) as well as to heavenly beings. In Aramaic fragments of the Book of Giants and of the Book of Enoch the phrase also occurs in a context of respect or fear for heavenly beings or spheres.[37] The verb for "paid him honour" (סגיד) is widely used with regard to deities, but it occurs in the Aramaic papyrus of Ahiqar of the fifth century BC at Elephantine, where the royal

---

33 Jerome, *Expl. Dan.* (CCSL 75A, 796), I ii 47, cf. *Jerome's Commentary on Daniel*, trans. Gleason L. Archer (Grand Rapids, Mich.: Baker, 1958), 33.

34 M. Delcor, *Le Livre de Daniel* (SB; Paris: Lecoffre, 1971), 83. Cf. Edward J. Young, *A Commentary on Daniel* (London: Banner of Truth Trust, 1949), 81; J. G. Baldwin, *Daniel* (TOTC; Leicester: Inter-Varsity, 1978), 94–95; J. E. Goldingay, *Daniel* (WBC 30; Dallas, Tex.: Word Books, 1989), 52; E. Lucas, *Daniel* (AOTC 20; Leicester: Inter-Varsity, 2002), 77.

35 L. F. Hartman and A. A. Di Lella, *The Book of Daniel* (AB 23; Garden City, N.Y.: Doubleday, 1978), 150–51 (the words quoted are from p. 150).

36 John J. Collins, "Daniel, Book of," *ABD* 2:30–31.

37 4Q531 14 3, in É. Puech, *Qumrân Grotte 4.XXII: Textes Araméens, première partie* (DJD XXXI; Oxford: Oxford University Press, 2001), 66 and, earlier, in K. Beyer, *Die aramäischen Texte vom Toten Meer*, Ergänzungsband (Göttingen: Vandenhoeck & Ruprecht, 1994), 122; 4Q204 VI 27 is restored in J. T. Milik, *The Books of Enoch: Aramaic Fragments of Qumrân Cave 4* (Oxford: Oxford University Press, 1976), 194, 196, followed by F. García Martínez, *The Dead Sea Scrolls Translated: The Qumran Texts in English* (trans. W. G. E. Watson; Leiden: Brill, 1994), 252, but not by K. Beyer, *Die aramäischen Texte vom Toten Meer* (Göttingen: Vandenhoeck & Ruprecht, 1984), 239. I am indebted to Brian Mastin for bringing these passages to my attention.

official, Ahiqar, relates, "I bowed and prostrated myself" before king Esarhaddon (גהנת וסגדת, 1.13). Porten and Yardeni now read the word long read סגדוהי in line 10 as נגדוהי, "his chiefs."[38] It should be noted that the narrative part of Ahiqar is set in the context of the Assyrian court and is written in a style of Aramaic which is more "eastern" than the language of the proverbs, which has a "western" flavour.[39] In the fifth century BC, the Greek historian Herodotus reported that, when Persians met in the streets, "when a man of inferior rank meets one of superior rank, the inferior prostrates himself (προσκυνέω) upon the ground and does reverence to the other" (1.134), while the adventurer Xenophon reported that all prostrated themselves before the Persian pretender Cyrus (Cyr. 8.3.14).[40] Frye, discussing the status of the Persian kings, wrote "it would seem that for the Achaemenids even proskynesis did not signify the abject humility before a god, but rather the sign of respect towards royalty, for the nobility a bow with the kissing of one's hands as depicted on reliefs at Persepolis, or with knee bending, or even, in the case of supplications or requests, full prostration on the ground, especially for menials. In neither case was god worship intended."[41]

The "offering" made to Daniel was a מנחה which, in Hebrew, does not have an exclusively religious connotation, for it can denote both a sacrifice in a cultic setting and also, perhaps originally, a gift presented by an inferior to a superior (as in Gen 43:11). It occurs in Aramaic only in texts describing temple offerings, associated with incense and sacrifice (לבונה ועלוה) at Elephantine, with animals and libations in Ezra 7:17, and with sacrifice in the Genesis Apocryphon.[42] In themselves, therefore, the "honour" and the "offering" do not demand a cultic interpretation for Nebuchadnezzar's action.

Nebuchadnezzar's order that "an offering and incense be presented" to Daniel uses a verb that in biblical Hebrew commonly means "to pour a libation" (נסך), which Lacocque stressed implies a cultic purpose: "The terms used are those of the sacerdotal vocabulary as, for example, in Lev. 1–7. The verb נסך properly signifies the pouring out of libations."[43] In extant Old Aramaic texts the term occurs three times, in

38 TADAE 3:26–27.
39 James M. Lindenberger, The Aramaic Proverbs of Ahiqar (Baltimore: Johns Hopkins University Press, 1983), 288–92.
40 References given by Pierre Briant, From Cyrus to Alexander: A History of the Persian Empire (Winona Lake, Ind.: Eisenbrauns, 2002), 190, 222–23, with the comment, "the rite did not imply that the king was considered a god."
41 R. N. Frye, The Heritage of Persia (London: Weidenfeld and Nicolson, 1962), 96.
42 TADAE 1. A4.7.21; A4.8.21; A4.9.9; A4.10.11; 1QapGen X 16; XXI 2, 20.
43 A. Lacocque, The Book of Daniel (London: SPCK, 1979), 54.

the Sefire Stelae. In I A 26 it is the action of the god Hadad in sending hail upon Arpad, but in I B 38 and III 7 (and restored in III 5) it refers to providing food for people (III 5, 7, ותסך להם לחם).[44] Without other early Aramaic examples, a possible similar secular application in Dan 2:46 cannot be treated as certain, yet neither can an exclusively cultic application.

The question of the incense (ניחחין) presented to him demands more attention, for this last honour has been a stumbling-stone to commentators, incense being considered to belong to religious cult, burnt before a divine presence, usually in the form of a statue. The word, which is found also in Ezra 6:10, may be a loan from Hebrew in Aramaic, and all its other occurrences are in cultic passages. However, the evidence of the lexicon does not stand alone; other ancient material may expand it.

There are two well-known ancient sculptures which, it is submitted, illustrate Nebuchadnezzar's intention. The first is the well-known Assyrian relief of the mid-seventh century BC from the palace of Ashurbanipal in Nineveh, which represents a victory celebration. The king reclines on a couch with his queen sitting beside him, while in a tree hangs the head of the defeated rebel Elamite king Te-umman. As the king and queen drink, they are soothed by the aroma arising from incense burners placed beside them, one at the head of the king's couch, one behind the queen's throne.[45] We may deduce that there were others on the other, hidden, side of the king and queen. The identification of these objects is not in doubt, they share the same form as those used in the rituals already described, and it is likely they were made of gold.[46]

The second scene is the pair of reliefs from the Achaemenid palace at Persepolis which have long been believed to show Darius I enthroned with his crown prince Xerxes beside him, although nowadays there is some debate over the identity of the royal figures.[47] Before

---

44   J. A. Fitzmyer, *The Aramaic Inscriptions of Sefire* (rev. ed.; BibOr 19a; Rome: Pontifical Biblical Institute, 1995), 114, who compares Dan 2:46; J. C. Greenfield, "Two Proverbs of Ahiqar," in *Lingering over Words: Studies in Ancient Near Eastern Literature in Honor of William L. Moran* (ed. T. Abusch, J. Huehnergard, and P. Steinkeller; Atlanta, Ga.: Scholars Press, 1990), 194–201 (199–201). A. Dupont-Sommer, *Les Inscriptions araméennes de Sfiré (Stèles I et II)* (Paris: Imprimerie Nationale, 1958), 146, simply rendered the verb by "verser"; H. Donner and W. Röllig, *KAI* 2:257, 267, rendered the verb "giessen" at I B 38, but "ausgiessen, ausschütten, versorgen" at III 5, 7.

45   Barnett, *Sculptures from the North Palace of Ashurbanipal*, pls. 63, 64.

46   References to gold and silver for incense burners are given in *CAD* N/2, 216, s.v. *nignakku*.

47   E. F. Schmidt, *Persepolis I: Structures, Reliefs, Inscriptions* (Chicago: The Oriental Institute, 1953), 162–69. For the debate about the figures, see E. M. Yamauchi, *Persia and the Bible* (Grand Rapids, Mich.: Baker Book House, 1990), 360–62.

the king stand two incense burners, perfuming the air between him and those receiving an audience. Each is a tall stand, tapering upward from a flared base to a bowl set above down-curving leaf mouldings. The bowl is covered by a conical lid, stepped like a ziggurat, with arrow-shaped piercings to allow the smoke to escape. The shape of the burners is all but identical to examples in silver unearthed in a Persian period tomb at Uşak in Turkey. Those are 28 cm (11 inches) high, with silver chains attaching the covers to the stands.[48] Very similar incense burners are depicted on Achaemenid seals.[49] Somewhat similar bronze incense burners have been found in tombs near Shechem and in Jordan.[50] The presence of incense burners in tombs indicates that they were part of the normal furniture of people of importance in this life, left to accompany them for use in the next life, like the other, clearly secular utensils placed in those tombs.

In his authoritative *History of the Persian Empire*, Olmstead deduced from the Persepolis sculpture that "[t]he use of frankincense . . . before the king's presence is one more hint that in Persia the monarch was reverenced as something more than human,"[51] assuming it was a divine prerogative, as in many Achaemenid seal designs which show incense burners in cultic scenes.[52] (Olmstead's use of the term "frankincense" is unsupported.) Now neither in Assyria nor in Babylonia is there any indication that the king was treated as divine or that individuals were deified in their lifetimes, nor was it the case in Persia, as the citations given above make clear. Such concepts would have been alien to the thought of those times. Therefore, the extravagant honour Nebuchadnezzar paid to Daniel should be treated as the natural reaction of a relieved and satisfied despot; in reality it "might merely have meant the reversal of the homage a subject was expected to pay to the king," as Porteous expressed it (see above). Verse 48 makes that clear: "Then the king gave Daniel high honours. . . ." His action should not be interpreted as directed to Daniel's deity, nor as offering Daniel divine status, but as exalting him to a quasi-royal position, in the style that would be recognized and which was not so very different from the

---

48 İ. Özgen and J. Öztürk, *Heritage Recovered: The Lydian Treasure* (Ankara: Ministry of Culture, General Directorate of Monuments and Museums, 1996), 114–17.

49 P. H. Merrillees, *Catalogue of the Western Asiatic Seals in the British Museum: Cylinder Seals VI: Pre-Achaemenid and Achaemenid Periods* (London: British Museum, 2005), 121.

50 E. Stern, "Achaemenian Tombs from Shechem," *Levant* 12 (1980): 90–111, esp. 94–98; L. A. Khalil, "A Bronze Caryatid Censer from Amman," *Levant* 18 (1986): 103–10.

51 A. T. Olmstead, *History of the Persian Empire* (Chicago: University of Chicago Press, 1948), 217.

52 Merrillees, *Cylinder Seals VI*, 121.

position Belshazzar offered and gave to him, on the night when Babylon fell to the forces of Persia.[53]

Throughout his career, Graham Davies has been concerned to use material remains and ancient texts in biblical exegesis, so this essay attempts to do the same, an offering (מנחה) to mark his retirement from teaching, and appreciation of a long friendship.

---

53 Thus the incense-burners which Sennacherib's reliefs depict two Assyrian soldiers carrying from Lachish need not have furnished a temple or shrine, *pace* N. Naʾaman, "The debated History of Hezekiah's Reform in the Light of Historical and Archaeological Research," *ZAW* 107 (1995): 179–95 (191–93). See also I. Finkelstein and N. A. Silberman's statement that the Lachish relief "depicts what seem to be cult items removed by Assyrian troops . . . possibly indicating the continuing existence of a cult place there until late in the days of Hezekiah" (*The Bible Unearthed* [New York: Free Press, 2001], 250n). The incense-burners could rather have perfumed the governor's palace, as D. Ussishkin has now observed ("Symbols of Conquest in Sennacherib's reliefs of Lachish," in *Culture through Objects: Ancient Near Eastern Studies in Honour of P. R. S. Moorey* [ed. T. Potts, M. Roaf, and D. Stein; Oxford: Griffith Institute Publications, 2003], 207–17 [215]).

Between Scroll and Codex?

Reconsidering the Qumran Opisthographs

GEORGE J. BROOKE

I. Introduction

Generations of scholars have wondered about the move from scroll to codex, especially amongst early Christians.[1] Many questions remain unanswered. Roman notebooks and strings of writing tablets are commonly seen as influential steps along the way.[2] Did items with writing on both sides, opisthographs, play a part in this change? Amongst other purposes these can satisfy the criteria of comprehensiveness and convenience that are often noted as key factors in the gradual move to the use of the codex.[3] In addition, it is likely that opisthographs reflect personal use of written materials, a significant factor in the early Christian adoption of the format.[4] This short study concerns the opisthographs from Qumran from the late Second Temple period; their striking diversity might yet conceal some matters that could contribute to the discussion of the development of writing materials in the Eastern

---

1   See, e.g., Colin H. Roberts and Theodore C. Skeat, *The Birth of the Codex* (Oxford: Oxford University Press, 1983); amongst others Roberts and Skeat acknowledge Theodor Birt's *Das antike Buchwesen in seinem Verhältniss zur Litteratur* (Berlin: W. Hertz, 1882).

2   Note also the "concertina" format of writing tablets from Vindolanda, a possible intermediate stage between roll and codex: Alan K. Bowman, "Roman Military Records from Vindolanda," *Britannia* 5 (1974): 360–73; Robin Birley, *Vindolanda: A Roman Frontier Post on Hadrian's Wall* (London: Thames and Hudson, 1977), 154–55.

3   E.g., Roberts and Skeat, *The Birth of the Codex*, 73.

4   On other aspects of Christian codices, see the informative essays in William E. Klingshirn and Linda Safran, eds., *The Early Christian Book* (Washington: Catholic University of America Press, 2007).

Mediterranean in antiquity, where opisthographs had long been known.[5]

Several items found in the Qumran caves contain writing on both sides. A relatively high proportion of these are papyrus sheets.[6] Wise reviewed sixteen possible Qumran opisthographs in a study concerned with Hebrew and Aramaic book culture.[7] He argued that the majority of scrolls written on papyrus and all the opisthographs were probably personal copies.[8] He asserted that since "opisthographs never circulated by purchase, they are virtually certain indicators of private copies."[9] In particular, he proposed that the unusual features of 4Q201 (*Enoch*[a]) can be explained by classifying it as a personal copy, a possibility made all the more likely because it is an opisthograph.[10] Since Wise's work the most comprehensive study of the Qumran opisthographs has been undertaken by Tov.[11] In an appendix to his study[12] Tov lists thirty-five opisthographs from the Judean desert: nine from Wadi Daliyeh, twenty-one from the Qumran caves, one from Naḥal Ḥever/ Wadi Seiyal, and four from Masada.

---

5   See, e.g., Emanuel Tov, *Scribal Practices and Approaches Reflected in the Texts Found in the Judean Desert* (STDJ 54; Leiden: Brill, 2004), 69.

6   This raises questions about the relative cost of papyrus and its uses, often for documentary texts. For the late Second Temple period see Karel van der Toorn, *Scribal Culture and the Making of the Hebrew Bible* (Cambridge, Mass.: Harvard University Press, 2007), 19–22, and esp. 274 n. 43 (papyrus was not cheap). On papyrus at Qumran, see Philip S. Alexander, "Literacy among Jews in Second Temple Palestine: Reflections on the Evidence from Qumran," in *Hamlet on a Hill: Semitic and Greek Studies Presented to Professor T. Muraoka on the Occasion of his Sixty-Fifth Birthday* (ed. M. F. J. Baasten and W. T. van Peursen; OLA 118; Leuven: Peeters, 2003), 3–24, esp. 7–8 (papyrus relatively expensive for the community). Stephen J. Pfann, "Reassessing the Judean Desert Caves: Libraries, Archives, Genizas and Hiding Places," *BAIAS* 25 (2007): 147–70, has proposed that use of papyrus was a lay practice; priests preferred leather.

7   Michael O. Wise, *Thunder in Gemini and Other Essays on the History, Language and Literature of Second Temple Palestine* (JSPSup 15; Sheffield: JSOT Press, 1994), 130, 132–37. Wise's list contains some errors, notably the inclusion of 4Q259 and 4Q377.

8   Wise does not consider the absence of paleo-Hebrew divine names in the opisthographs; perhaps these manuscripts were not used in public reading.

9   Wise, *Thunder in Gemini*, 130.

10   Note also that no opisthographs found at Qumran are written on the verso of authoritative scriptures, except for 4Q201, if indeed *Enoch* was deemed to be authoritative.

11   Tov, *Scribal Practices*, 68–73.

12   Tov, "Appendix 3: Opisthographs from the Judean Desert," in idem, *Scribal Practices*, 295–97.

Of the twenty-one itemized opisthographs from Qumran six are on leather and fifteen on papyrus.[13] But formulating statistics like these is problematic. First, what might actually form each item? For example, on Tov's list the nature of the eight papyrus opisthographs written with cryptic script is very uncertain. These "manuscripts" consist of just a few fragments each, sometimes only one small fragment: should these papyrus fragments be differentiated as proposed? Their cryptic script might suggest they belong together, since the script does not seem to be widely used in the Qumran corpus; but such script on papyrus sheets might rather suggest some common practice in sectarian communication and thus indicate that more rather than fewer examples of such practice might have survived. Some of the other groupings of papyrus fragments, such as for 1Q70/1Q70a and 4Q518/4Q519, are almost certainly from more than one manuscript.

Another problem with Tov's list is that he has excluded a legal text where signatures occur on the verso[14] and the Qumran *tefillin*. Including these increases the number of opisthographs considerably. Furthermore, since the Qumran *tefillin* are all on leather, the proportion of opisthographs from Qumran on leather also increases. Since in particular the *tefillin* reflect specialist scribal conventions, it is important to include them. Such conventions possibly influenced decisions in other cases for presenting texts on both recto and verso.[15]

There are several different ways of describing the data and expounding the significance of the opisthographs. Should the modern interpreter of the evidence give priority to the more circumstantial

---

13 Although fragments make counting difficult, of the 850–900 Qumran manuscripts approximately 140 (ca. 13%) are on papyrus; of the 140, 18 are documentary texts, the rest non-documentary; see Emanuel Tov, "The Papyrus Fragments Found in the Judean Desert," in *Lectures et relectures de la Bible: Festschrift P.-M. Bogaert* (ed. J.-M. Auwers and A. Wénin; BETL 144; Leuven: Peeters, 1999), 247–55. For opisthographs Tov's list (*Scribal Practices*, 295–97) yields for Qumran 71.4% on papyrus and only 28.6% on leather; if the tefillin are included, the proportions change, even if the tefillin are counted in groups.

14 The legal text is 4Q345: see Ada Yardeni, "345. 4QDeed A ar or heb," in Hannah Cotton and Ada Yardeni, *Aramaic, Hebrew and Greek Documentary Texts from Naḥal Ḥever and Other Sites with an Appendix Containing Alleged Qumran Texts (The Seiyâl Collection II)* (DJD XXVII; Oxford: Clarendon, 1997), 292–95 (292–93). Like Tov, I omit this from detailed consideration below; it almost certainly does not come from Cave 4. Two signatures appear on the verso.

15 Manuscripts with titles on the verso should also be mentioned, though these titles serve no independent literary purpose. See 1QS; 4Q8c (*Gen*ʰ), 4Q249 (*pap cryptA Midrash Sefer Moshe*), 4Q257 (*papSerekh ha-Yahad*ᶜ), and 4Q504 (*Words of the Luminaries*). On 4Q257 see Philip S. Alexander and Geza Vermes, *Qumran Cave 4.XIX: Serekh ha-Yaḥad and Two Related Texts* (DJD XXVI; Oxford: Clarendon, 1998), 66, and pl. VI: "This writing might be the remains of a title, but it is hard to make any sense of it."

aspects of the data, such as the possible scarcity of writing materials, or emphasize some of its more intentional qualities, such as the possible literary relationship between the texts on both sides? It is perhaps most appropriate to begin with the physical aspects of the opisthographs, moving towards the closer description of the texts that they contain.

II. Classifying the Data

A. Material

Reckoning with the material remains of the opisthographs is of prime importance for their better understanding. It is worth listing those manuscripts or collections of fragments that are on papyrus[16] and those that are on leather.[17]

On papyrus there are the following twelve items: 4Q250a (cryptA Text Concerning Cultic Service B?), 4Q250b (cryptA Text Related to Isa 11), 4Q250c/4Q250d (cryptA Unidentified I/J), 4Q250e/4Q250f (cryptA Unidentified K/L) 4Q250g (cryptA Unidentified M), 4Q250h (cryptA Unidentified N), 4Q250i (cryptA Unidentified O), 4Q250j (cryptA Miscellaneous Texts B), 4Q433a/4Q255 (Hodayot-like Text B/Serekh ha-Yahad[a]), 4Q499/4Q497 (Hymns and Prayers/War Rule-like Text A), 4Q503/4Q512 (Daily Prayers/Ritual of Purification B), and 4Q509/4Q496+4Q506 (Festival Prayers[c]/War Rule[f]+Words of the Luminaries[c]).[18] In addition 1Q70/1Q70a (Unclassified Fragments), a group of thirty-one fragments, and 4Q518/4Q519 (Unclassified Fragments), a group of sixty-eight small fragments, remain unclassified; some of the fragments of 4Q518/4Q519 may well belong to the other three papyrus

---

16   On papyrus manufacture and distribution see Sydney Aufrère, "La fabrication du papyrus égyptien et son exportation," in *Encyclopédie religieuse de l'univers végétal de l'Égypte ancienne* 3 (ed. S. Aufrère; Orientalia monspeliensia 15; Montpellier: Université Paul Valéry, 2005), 103–17.

17   The reader should return to these lists for the manuscripts' names. The first named item is on the recto, the second on the verso.

18   Tov, *Scribal Practices*, 296, lists these fragments as two items; actually there is just one manuscript with one composition on the recto and two on the verso. See Daniel K. Falk, *Daily, Sabbath, and Festival Prayers in the Dead Sea Scrolls* (STDJ 27; Leiden: Brill, 1998), 59–61.

opisthographs edited by Maurice Baillet.[19] All these compositions are apparently consistently in Hebrew.[20]

On leather there are the following sixteen *tefillin* slips: 4Q128 (*Phyl A*), 4Q129 (*Phyl B*), 4Q134 (*Phyl G*), 4Q135 (*Phyl H*), 4Q136 (*Phyl I*), 4Q137 (*Phyl J*), 4Q138 (*Phyl K*), 4Q139 (*Phyl L*), 4Q140 (*Phyl M*), 4Q141 (*Phyl N*), 4Q142 (*Phyl O*), 4Q143 (*Phyl P*), 4Q144 (*Phyl Q*), 4Q145 (*Phyl R*), 4Q148 (*Phyl U*), and XQPhyl slip 4. There are also the following five manuscripts: 4Q201/4Q338 (*Enoch*[a] *ar/Genealogical List?*), 4Q324/4Q355 (*Mishmarot C/Account C ar or heb*), 4Q343 (*Letter nab*), 4Q415/4Q414 (*Instruction*[a]*/Ritual of Purification A*), and 4Q460 frg. 9/4Q350 (*Narrative Work and Prayer/Account gr*).[21] Of these 4Q343 is of uncertain provenance, most probably not coming from Qumran at all. Only one of these five opisthographs is clearly in Hebrew on both sides. On these leather manuscripts there are commonly combinations of languages on the recto and verso: Aramaic + Hebrew, Hebrew + Aramaic, Hebrew + Greek. 4Q343 is in Nabatean.

B. Size

A second matter of description is to determine, where possible, the size of the material, notably whether the items contained single columns or were much longer scrolls.

In several instances nothing can be said about this, because the remains are so small and fragmentary.[22] This is the case for 1Q70/1Q70a frgs. 1–12. It is also the case for the eight Cave 4 manuscripts written in cryptic script; although papyrus fibres can help in the association of fragments, whatever is the case with the editor's preference for differentiating the one, two or three fragments into separate manuscripts, all the eight proposed manuscripts survive in only small scraps.[23]

---

19 4Q518/4Q519 are presented in Maurice Baillet, *Qumrân Grotte 4.III: (4Q482–4Q520)* (DJD VII; Oxford: Clarendon, 1982), 304–9; some of their fragments may belong to 4Q499/4Q497, 4Q503/4Q512, or 4Q509/4Q496+4Q506.

20 The absence of opisthographs amongst the Cave 7 fragments argues against them containing early Christian works. On this point, and its particular refutation, see Carsten P. Thiede, *The Earliest Gospel Manuscript? The Qumran Fragment 7Q5 and Its Significance for New Testament Studies* (Carlisle: Paternoster, 1992), 3.

21 Tov, *Scribal Practices*, 296, lists 4Q342 as an opisthograph, but Ada Yardeni, "342. 4QLetter? Ar," in Cotton and Yardeni, *Aramaic, Hebrew and Greek Documentary Texts*, 285, states clearly that "there are no remains of script on the verso." The provenance of 4Q342 is uncertain.

22 This also applies to the unclassified small fragments of 4Q518/4Q519.

23 See Stephen J. Pfann, "250a. 4Qpap cryptA Text Concerning Cultic Service B?", "250b. 4Qpap cryptA Text Related to Isa 11," in S. J. Pfann et al., *Qumran Cave*

In other instances it is obviously appropriate that the opisthograph occurs on a small single sheet: this is the case for the Cave 4 phylacteries, for which small pieces of leather were used. It is also likely that 4Q343, a letter, was written on a single sheet.[24] In these cases the genre of the composition has played a determining role in the selection of the size of the writing material.

In yet other cases it is difficult to know whether an original sheet of leather was whole or in pieces when the verso was inscribed. For example, 4Q201 only has writing on its verso (4Q338) in the fragments that contains cols. II and III. Or again, only frg. 9 of 4Q460 has writing on the verso, suggesting that just a small part of the manuscript was reused, in this case to record a list of cereals in Greek; Larson has noted that the manuscript might have been rolled up with the end of the composition on the outside, since the part that was reused was presumably readily available.[25]

Two small fragments have been assigned to 4Q324, *Mishmarot C*. From the remains of seven lines of text that survive Talmon and Ben-Dov suggest that 4Q324 is the "remnant of a scroll which presumably contained a register of the dates of the Saturday afternoons on which the different priestly courses entered the Temple prior to the onset of their week of service on the following Sunday morning."[26] On the verso of both fragments there is writing.[27] While it is possible to calculate roughly how long *Mishmarot C* might have been, it is impossible to say how long the text on the verso was.

Much more extensive are the remains of 4Q499/4Q497. Fifty-four small fragments have been assigned to this papyrus manuscript. Some of the fragments preserve edges of columns of writing in 4Q497, so the manuscript had several columns. On the recto 4Q499 preserves no clear indications of column structure. Even more extensively preserved are 4Q503/4Q512: there are 232 fragments.[28] Several of them probably need

---

4.XXVI: Cryptic Texts and Miscellanea, *Part 1* (DJD XXXVI; Oxford: Clarendon, 2000), 680–681. The published plate provides only the recto; on PAM 40.637 the verso of frg. 2 of the manuscript has possible traces of ink; and on PAM 43.414 the verso of all three fragments shows possible traces of ink but no legible text.

24 See Ada Yardeni, "343. 4QLetter nab," in Cotton and Yardeni, *Aramaic, Hebrew and Greek Documentary Texts*, 286.

25 Erik Larson, "460. 4QNarrative Work and Prayer," in *Qumran Cave 4.XXVI: Cryptic Texts and* Miscellanea, *Part 1*, 369, 371.

26 Shemaryahu Talmon with Jonathan Ben-Dov, "324. 4QMishmarot C," in Shemaryahu Talmon, Jonathan Ben-Dov and Uwe Glessmer, *Qumran Cave 4.XVI: Calendrical Texts* (DJD XXI; Oxford: Clarendon, 2001), 103–6 (103).

27 Ada Yardeni, "355. 4QAccount C ar or heb," in *Qumran Cave 4.XXVI: Cryptic Texts and* Miscellanea, *Part 1*, 296.

28 Baillet, *Qumrân Grotte 4.III: (4Q482–4Q520)*, 105–36.

to be reordered from the presentation in the principal edition, as has been suggested, for example, by Falk;[29] this scroll was at least a dozen columns long with writing on both sides for its entirety. However, the most fragments, over 300, have been assigned to a scroll whose recto contains one liturgical composition of *Festival Prayers* (4Q509) and whose verso contains two compositions, a copy of the *War Rule* (4Q496) and a copy of the *Words of the Luminaries* (4Q506), though these texts were added at different times.[30]

Also more extensive are the remains of 4Q415/4Q414. Its 32 fragments nearly all have writing on both recto and verso, but determining how extensive the text on the verso was is impossible. The editors of 4Q415 declare that "one cannot tell if a complete manuscript was reutilised or only several of its sheets. If the latter is the case, no more of the original manuscript with its verso uninscribed seems to have survived elsewhere. Furthermore, from the condition of these fragments, which seem fairly well preserved by the standards of others from cave 4, one cannot tell what it was that provoked the rejection of these sheets and their subsequent re-use by a second scribe."[31] The editor of 4Q414 describes its verso surface as "poorly preserved."[32]

Something similar may be the case with 4Q255/4Q433a. The first fragment of 4Q255 contains text that has some correspondence with 1QS I, 1–5, while fragment 2 has parallels with 1QS III, 7–12;[33] the texts of the remaining two fragments cannot be identified, but the implication overall is that 4Q255 was a sheet with several columns of writing on it.[34] However, determining the length of the text on the verso is impossible.

---

29 Falk, *Daily, Sabbath, and Festival Prayers*, 21–57.

30 See Baillet, *Qumrân Grotte 4.III: (4Q482–4Q520)*, 56–58; various revisions have been proposed: see Falk, *Daily, Sabbath, and Festival Prayers*, 59–94 and 155–215.

31 John Strugnell and Daniel J. Harrington, "415. 4QInstruction (*mûsār lĕmēvînᵃ*)," in J. Strugnell, D. J. Harrington, and T. Elgvin, *Qumran Cave 4.XXIV: Sapiential Texts, Part 2. 4QInstruction (Mûsār lĕ Mēvîn): 4Q415 ff.* (DJD XXXIV; Oxford: Clarendon, 1999), 41–71 (41).

32 Esther Eshel, "414. 4QRitual of Purification A," in. Joseph Baumgarten et al., *Qumran Cave 4.XXV: Halakhic Texts* (DJD XXXV; Oxford: Clarendon, 1999), 135–54 (135).

33 Alexander and Vermes, *Qumran Cave 4.XIX: Serekh ha-Yaḥad*, 27–38.

34 Alexander, "Literacy among Jews in Second Temple Palestine," 7, suggests that papyrus was used for the earliest copy of the *Rule of the Community* because local skin production was not yet under way.

C. Layout

Having considered the sizes of the surviving opisthographs, we can move to a third perspective, namely the layout of the texts.[35] As Tov suitably has observed, there are three systems in use.

First, Tov himself has suggested that in leather documents, apart from the *tefillin* and for the inscription of titles, the usual system was for the verso to be inscribed upside-down in relation to the recto.[36] This layout is the case for 4Q201/4Q338 (leather) in which it is possible that some kind of genealogical list is inscribed on the verso of a manuscript carrying the opening chapters of *1 Enoch*. This layout is also the case in the relationship of recto to verso in 4Q324/4Q355 (leather), in 4Q343 (leather), in 4Q415/4Q414 (leather), and in 4Q460/4Q350 (leather). There are also papyrus manuscripts from Qumran arranged like this: fragments 1–12 of 1Q70/1Q70a,[37] the unclassified 4Q518/4Q519 frgs. 21–30, and 4Q509/4Q496+4Q506.

The same is also the case for 4Q255/4Q433a (papyrus), though there is disagreement about which side is the recto and which the verso. Alexander and Vermes claim that 4Q255 is on the verso with the vertical papyrus fibres uppermost,[38] whereas Milik considered 4Q255 to be on the recto. For 4Q433a Schuller has proposed that since either side of a papyrus scroll might be inscribed first, the identification of recto and verso is not altogether significant. She has considered, however, that, because 4Q433a is paleographically later than 4Q255, 4Q433a represents the scroll's re-use.[39] Whatever the case, the writing on one side is upside-down compared with that on the other.

The second way is for the writing on the verso to lie perpendicularly, at 90°, in relation to the text on the recto. For papyrus manuscripts this can be readily explained by the lay of the papyrus strands.[40]

---

35 For 4Q250a and 4Q250b only small traces of ink are visible on the verso.

36 Tov, *Scribal Practices*, 70. On p. 70 Tov erroneously lists 1Q70 and 1Q70a as a leather manuscript.

37 Józef T. Milik, "Textes non bibliques," in D. Barthélemy, J. T. Milik et al., *Qumran Cave I* (DJD I; Oxford: Clarendon Press, 1955), 77–149 (149). Milik divided these fragments into three groups: frgs. 1–6; 7–10; 11–12.

38 Alexander and Vermes, *Qumran Cave 4.XIX: Serekh ha-Yahad*, 28. A comparison of the plates of 4Q255 (DJD XXVI, Plate I) and 4Q433a (DJD XXIX, Plate XV) strongly suggests that 4Q255 is on the recto.

39 Eileen Schuller, "433a. 4QpapHodayot-like Text B," in *Qumran Cave 4.XX: Poetical and Liturgical Texts, Part 2* (ed. Esther Chazon et al.; DJD XXIX; Oxford: Clarendon, 1999), 237–45 (237). Schuller cites Milik's annotation in *A Preliminary Concordance to the Hebrew and Aramaic Fragments from Qumrân Caves II–X*, printed from a card index prepared by R. E. Brown et al. (5 vols.; Göttingen; privately printed, 1988).

40 This orientation is on the unclassified 4Q518/4Q519 frgs. 66–68; and probably others.

The majority of the Cave 4 *tefillin* are also written in this way: "en général, on tournait le morceau de 90° pour écrire sur le verso." As Milik rightly noted: "Cette coutume est plus naturelle pour les papyrus que pour les parchemins, pour les actes et documents (en particulier 'contrats doubles') que pour les textes littéraires."[41] Milik's observation might be taken one step further: perhaps the scribal convention for copying *tefillin* was based on some papyrus exemplars that were written precisely in the standard fashion for papyrus opisthographs.[42] The 90° presentation of opisthographic texts in the *tefillin* applies to 4QPhyl A, B, G, H, I, J, K, M, O, P, Q, R, U and XQPhyl slip 4.

The third way of describing the layout is as for a page of a codex, the writing on both recto and verso being laid out in the same way. This was probably the case for the two small papyrus fragments assigned to 4Q250c/4Q250d and also for 4Q250e/4Q250f.[43] In the much more extensive remains of 4Q499/4Q497, the writing on the verso is in the same position as on the recto; the scroll has simply been turned over and the writing on the verso has begun at the end of the scroll, running for several columns in the reverse direction. This might indicate something about the length of the scroll: perhaps it was shorter, rather than longer. The relationship of 4Q503/4Q512 is the same with the writing on both sides the same way up.[44] Several of the unclassified fragments of 4Q518/4Q519, such as frgs. 1–19, some of which might belong to either of the two more extensive manuscripts just described, also were written in this way.

D. Scribal Hands

A fourth descriptive aspect concerns the style of hand on each side of the manuscript. Difference in hand, especially a difference that might be datable, might incline one to suppose that the texts were written by

---

41   J. T. Milik, "Tefillin, Mezuzot, Targums," in R. de Vaux and J. T. Milik, with contributions by J. W. B. Barns and J. Carswell, *Qumrân Grotte 4.II* (DJD VI; Oxford: Clarendon, 1977), 31–90 (36).

42   Though inscribed on one side only, the Nash Papyrus could have been an exemplar from which scribes copied tefillin.

43   As these are laid out in *Qumran Cave 4. XXXVI: Cryptic Texts and* Miscellanea, *Part 1,* on Plate XLVII.

44   The two sides are neatly laid out in alternating plates in Baillet, *Qumrân Grotte 4.III: (4Q482 – 4Q520),* Plates XXXV–XLVIII; for frgs. 1–3 in detail, see Falk, *Daily, Sabbath, and Festival Prayers,* Plates I–III.

different scribes at different times, possibly implying that the text on the recto had gone into disuse and that the verso was current.[45]

For 1Q70/1Q70a the two hands are distinct. Milik proposed that on the recto of frgs. 1–6 the writing is "calligraphique (texte littéraire sans doute)," whereas on the verso the writing is "une cursive assez évoluée (texte non littéraire probablement),"[46] with the text on the verso forming the reuse of the papyrus. Something similar can be said for 4Q201/4Q338: although few letters remain on the verso they are markedly different from the hand on the recto, but this does not necessarily mean that the texts on the two sides are unrelated. For 4Q324/4Q355 the hand on the recto is identified as "late Hasmonean or early Herodian bookhand"[47] whereas on the verso Yardeni has identified "a cursive script."[48] For 4Q415/4Q414 the hand of 4Q415 on the recto is an early "formal Herodian hand,"[49] with some late Hasmonean features; the hand of 4Q414 is clearly different from that of 4Q415, "the script can be defined as Herodian, written in a thick *ductus*."[50] For 4Q255/4Q433a, 4Q255, in a "crude, early cursive . . . in places, virtually indecipherable," is dated to the second half of the second century BCE,[51] whereas 4Q433a is in a "Hasmonaean semiformal hand . . . dated c. 75 BCE."[52] For 4Q460/4Q350 the Hebrew composition on the recto is written in a semi-formal script "from the late Hasmonean or early-Herodian period (75 BCE to the turn of the era),"[53] whereas the recto carries an account in Greek written later.[54] Baillet has also argued that the hand of the recto of 4Q499/4Q497 is a little earlier than that of the verso, "des environs de 75 avant J.-C.,"[55] while that on the verso (4Q497) "pourrait dater des environs de 50 avant J.-C."[56] For 4Q503/4Q512 Baillet has observed that the hands for the two sides, though different, share many features and probably both come from the early first century BCE.[57]

---

45 For some manuscripts, e.g., 4Q250a, not enough evidence remains for any valid comment.
46 Milik, "Textes non bibliques," 149.
47 Talmon with Ben-Dov, "324. 4QMishmarot C," 104.
48 Yardeni, "355. 4QAccount C ar or heb," 296.
49 Strugnell and Harrington, "A. Instruction," 42.
50 Eshel, "414. 4QRitual of Purification A," 135.
51 Alexander and Vermes, *Qumran Cave 4.XIX: Serekh ha-Yaḥad*, 29.
52 Schuller, "433a. 4QpapHodayot-like Text B," 238.
53 Larson, "460. 4QNarrative Work and Prayer," 370.
54 Cotton, "350. 4QAccountgr," in *Qumran Cave 4.XXVI: Cryptic Texts and* Miscellanea, Part 1, 294.
55 Baillet, *Qumrân Grotte 4.III: (4Q482–4Q520)*, 74.
56 Baillet, *Qumrân Grotte 4.III: (4Q482–4Q520)*, 69.
57 Baillet, *Qumrân Grotte 4.III: (4Q482–4Q520)*, 105, 262.

For 4Q509/4Q496+4Q506 the situation is intriguingly different: on the recto the *Festival Prayers* were written in a "[c]alligraphie de la fin de la période asmonéenne, environ 70–60 avant J.-C.,"[58] whereas 4Q496 "est d'une main pré-hérodienne difficile à dater, mais qui doit être peu antérieure à 50 avant J.-C."[59] and 4Q506 has a "calligraphie très évoluée, dont certaines formes se rapprochent de celles attestées dans les ossuaires post-hérodiens. Elle peut dater des environs du milieu du Ier siècle après J.-C."[60] The two texts on the verso were written by two different scribes, seemingly a generation or more apart.[61]

Several opisthographs have the same hand on recto and verso. For none of the *tefillin* from Cave 4 does Milik hint that the hands on the recto and verso are different. For 4Q343, the Nabatean letter, the hand of both sides is the same. In the case of the small fragments in cryptic script assigned to 4Q250c/4Q250d the editor has identified the style on each side as "semi-formal hand with some semi-cursive traits; second century BCE."[62] For the slender evidence of 4Q250e/4Q250f he declares the hand of the first to be "semi-formal hand with some semi-cursive traits; second century BCE," and of the second to be simply a "semi-formal hand of the second century BCE."[63] So in the former case both sides might just be by the same scribe, in the latter the two sides are probably by two different scribes.

E. Contents

Mention of the scribal hands leads to a fifth way of describing the data: the texts themselves. Here there are several issues: whether or not the composition on each side is recognizable, whether or not it has sectarian associations, what its language is, and whether its scribal tradition can be determined.

To begin with it is the case that some texts are not possible to read beyond a few letters or words: for 1Q70/1Q70a Milik proposed on the

---

58 Baillet, *Qumrân Grotte 4.III: (4Q482–4Q520)*, 184.

59 Baillet, *Qumrân Grotte 4.III: (4Q482–4Q520)*, 58.

60 Baillet, *Qumrân Grotte 4.III: (4Q482–4Q520)*, 170.

61 Several unclassified fragments in 4Q518/4Q519, such as 1 and 24, clearly have different hands on recto and verso. More often, however, not enough survives to enable a secure judgement.

62 Stephen J. Pfann, "250c. 4Qpap cryptA Unidentified Text I," in *Qumran Cave 4.XXVI: Cryptic Texts and Miscellanea, Part 1*, 683; repeated on 684 ("250d. 4Qpap cryptA Unidentified Text J," in *Qumran Cave 4.XXVI: Cryptic Texts and Miscellanea, Part 1*).

63 Pfann, "250e. 4Qpap cryptA Unidentified Text K," "250f. 4Qpap cryptA Unidentified Text L," in *Qumran Cave 4.XXVI: Cryptic Texts and Miscellanea, Part 1*, 686–687.

basis of the style of the handwriting that on the recto there was a literary text and on the verso something non-literary; he implied that there
was no relationship between the compositions on the two sides—at
least for one of the possible manuscripts involved. 4Q250a may contain
some kind of cultic text on the recto, because of the survival of the three
letters]*mnh*[;[64] all suggestions about the verso text are mere speculation. All the other papyrus manuscripts inscribed in cryptic script have
no identifiable text on either one or both sides, so nothing can be said
about the textual relationship between their two sides.

For the Cave 4 phylacteries the texts on both sides are clearly related, but intriguingly not in an entirely uniform manner. The groups of
G–I[65] and L–N[66] have text that runs continuously on the recto from one
piece of leather to another with the same happening on the verso,[67]
whereas the group of J–K[68] has the text continue on the verso directly
from the recto, as is apparently usual according to the other single phylactery slips that have been preserved. As the phylacteries have the
same hand at work on both sides, so with 4Q343, the Nabatean letter,
the text on both sides should be closely related.

For 4Q201/4Q338 Milik thought about a century lapsed between the
writing of the two sides, with the verso possibly being a school exercise, "as the surface of the verso is badly blotted with ink."[69] Milik considered the text on the verso to be a genealogical list, possibly of the
patriarchs, since the word *hwlyd* occurs several times.[70] Tov has endor-
sed Milik's readings on the verso, though without attempting to present any kind of line-by-line text; he has wondered whether the two
texts might be related indirectly, since a genealogical list of patriarchs
would correspond well with the section of Genesis upon which the
opening chapters of *1 Enoch* seem to be based.[71]

---

64   Pfann, "250a. 4Qpap cryptA Text Concerning Cultic Service B?", 680.
65   4Q134 (Phylactery G): recto Deut 5:1–21; verso Exod 13:11–12; 4Q135 (Phylactery H):
     recto Deut 5:22–6:5; verso Exod 13:14–16; 4Q136 (Phylactery I): recto Deut 11:13–21;
     Exod 12:43–13:10; verso Deut 6:6–7?
66   4Q139 (Phylactery L): recto Deut 5:7–24; verso uninscribed; 4Q140 (Phylactery M):
     verso Deut 5:33–6:5; recto Exod 12:44–13:10; 4Q141 (Phylactery N): recto Deut 32:14–
     20, 32–33.
67   Milik, "Tefillin, Mezuzot, Targums," 72, suggests that 4QPhyl M has the text of Deut
     5:33–6:5 on the verso.
68   4Q137 (Phylactery J): recto Deut 5:1–24; verso Deut 5:24–32; 6:2–3; 4Q138 (Phylactery
     K): recto Deut 10:12–11:7; verso Deut 11:7–12.
69   Józef T. Milik, *The Books of Enoch: Aramaic Fragments of Qumrân Cave 4* (Oxford: Clar-
     endon, 1976), 139.
70   Milik, *The Books of Enoch*, 139.
71   Emanuel Tov, "338. 4QGenealogical List?" in *Qumran Cave 4.XXVI: Cryptic Texts and
     Miscellanea, Part 1*, 290.

In a similar fashion the two compositions in 4Q499/4Q497 both contain some hymnic or prayer language. Baillet has associated the fragments of 4Q497 with a composition like the *War Rule*, even though the match to the *War Rule* is difficult, whereas for 4Q499 he supposes that it contains just hymns and prayers.[72] Thus it might be that this manuscript had collections of hymns on both sides, one of which was resonant of the *War Rule*. Whatever the case, the relationship between the compositions on the two sides remains very uncertain. Both compositions are presented in the full orthography of the Qumran scribal school, and so the manuscript was in the same context for the two stages of its writing. Something similar seems to have happened with 4Q509/4Q496+4Q506: a copy of a liturgical text on the recto, in this case *Festival Prayers*, has received a copy of the *War Rule* on its verso not long after the recto has been penned, but in addition a further liturgical text, the *Words of the Luminaries*, has also been added somewhat later on the verso. Again, all three compositions are inscribed in the so-called Qumran scribal practice.

For 4Q324/4Q355 the composition on the recto has some features of full orthography and is part of a *Mishmarot* register of dates concerning Temple service from the fifth to the seventh months (frg. 1) and the eighth month (frg. 2) of the fifth year of the six-year cycle. The composition on the verso is some kind of account; only a few letters and numerical marks are legible in Hebrew or Aramaic. There is no clear relationship between the compositions on the two sides, unless one envisages a priest making a calculation on the reverse of his rota. The same can be said for 4Q415 with a copy of *Instruction* on the recto, written with the limited use of vowel-letters, and a copy of some kind of *Ritual of Purification* on the verso, written in full orthography; there seems to be no direct relationship between the texts on the two sides—a manuscript from outside the so-called Qumran scribal tradition, but probably of wide educational interest,[73] has been reused within it. Perhaps it is significant that the closely related 4Q512 was also copied on the verso of a manuscript. Different compositions are also found on 4Q255/4Q433a, the recto containing a copy of at least part of the *Rule of the Community*, in which full spelling predominates, and the verso, 4Q433a, a *Hodayot-like Text*, some kind of poetry presented in full orthography; there is no direct relationship between the two compositions, though both were probably addressed to the Maskil (1QS III, 13; 4Q433a 2 2).

---

72   Baillet, *Qumrân Grotte 4.III: (4Q482–4Q520)*, 69, 74.
73   See, e.g., Leo G. Perdue, *The Sword and the Stylus: An Introduction to Wisdom in the Age of Empires* (Grand Rapids, Mich.: Eerdmans, 2008), 376–78.

Even more clearly unrelated are the compositions on 4Q460/4Q350: 4Q460 consists of a narrative with some poetry; 4Q350 is an account in Greek. The editors of both texts have observed that the reuse disrespects the text on the recto: Larson has noted the divine address in the prayer on the recto (4Q460) and so has wondered "whether the Qumran sectarians would reuse a scroll that contained the tetragrammaton (frg. 9 i 10) for such a profane use as recording a list of cereals,"[74] whereas Cotton has talked of 4Q350 as evidence that the caves were tampered with in antiquity, implying that the re-use might have been by the Roman army.[75]

What can be said overall? Some genres of text are more likely to be represented on opisthographs as continuous text from one side to the other. This applies to 4Q343, a letter in Nabatean, as also to the *tefillin*. Some opisthographs are simply the re-use for documentary purposes of pieces of manuscripts containing literary compositions. Some opisthographs seem to fall under the broad category of collections of texts, a widespread literary phenomenon in antiquity,[76] that may reflect systems of education.[77] In particular such collections seem to have a cultic or liturgical dimension; if opisthographs are indeed an indication of personal manuscript use, then such collections might be a further indication of the Jewish move to private prayer in late Second Temple times. Privacy seems also to characterize the opisthographs written in cryptic script; perhaps these were sheets with just one or two columns of writing on each side that could be easily transported from one sectarian location to another.

III. Concluding Remarks

In this study we have considered the range of opisthographs found in the Qumran caves. The wide scope of the material is perhaps surpris-

---

74 Larson, "460. 4QNarrative Work and Prayer," 369.

75 Cotton, "350. 4QAccountgr," 294.

76 See Wise, *Thunder in Gemini*, 132, 139. An example close to Qumran is the papyrus opisthograph from Masada (Mas 721 r, v): Aeneid 4.9 (recto); three words from another poet (verso). (Hannah M. Cotton and Joseph Geiger, *Masada II: The Yigael Yadin Excavations 1963–1965, Final Reports: The Latin and Greek Documents* [Jerusalem: Israel Exploration Society and the Hebrew University of Jerusalem, 1989], 31–35.)

77 On the caution needed in reconstructing school systems, see Graham I. Davies, "Were There Schools in Ancient Israel?" in *Wisdom in Ancient Israel: Essays in Honour of J. A. Emerton* (ed. John Day, Robert P. Gordon, and H. G. M. Williamson; Cambridge: Cambridge University, 1995), 199–211. Nevertheless, some opisthographs might have had some educational function.

ing. My interest in the opisthographs arose as a question. In what ways should these Jewish manuscripts from the late Second Temple period be viewed in light of the gradual introduction of the codex form that seems to have been beginning approximately contemporaneously? Do they contribute anything to the debates about the origin of the codex? For the most part it seems that these Qumran opisthographs have nothing to offer, but three matters are worth considering.

First, papyrus is the dominant material in the group of manuscripts that are opisthographs. Whether leather or papyrus was used in the initial construction of book pages, it remains clear that papyrus was the preferred material of the early Christian codices, from the second century CE onwards, and possibly even earlier.

Second, in this collection from the Qumran caves there are individual sheets that have continuous writing on both sides. Chief amongst these are the *tefillin*. For the most part the layout of the texts on the recto and verso in each case are at 90° to one another. Perhaps this reflects some kind of convention based on papyrus exemplars. This suggests that the copying practice for the Qumran *tefillin*, if not also the contents of such leather slips, needs to be considered in a broad cultural context. In addition, if the use of opisthographs is a reflection of personal use, then the Qumran *tefillin*, though hidden in cases, are artefacts that correspond with developments in private prayer. Indeed, several of the continuous Qumran opisthographs carry cultic texts and may be personal copies of extracts of prayers, hymns, and cultic instructions.

Third, amongst all the diversity noted in this study, a small group of scrolls was written as opisthographs with the writing the same way up on both the recto and the verso. Some of these scrolls were of considerable length. If such a scroll was rolled so that the composition on the recto could be read on opening, then should readers actually require the text on the verso, they would need to go all the way to the end to find the start of the composition. Though this might not have been a major inhibiting factor,[78] I wonder whether, as at Vindolanda, a concertina folding of the papyrus was ever considered, so that the compositions on both sides of the scroll could remain accessible simultaneously. For those compositions with one or two columns on a single sheet with the writing the same way up on both sides, as was possibly the case with a couple of manuscripts in cryptic script, then the text

---

78 Roberts and Skeat, *The Birth of the Codex*, 49–50, suggest that these perceived problems are anachronistic retrojections from modern book culture.

would be presented very much as later pages in a bound volume were to be.[79]

The suggestion of this small contribution is that opisthographs from the period when the codex was gradually beginning to emerge need to be considered as part of the data that might have prompted, influenced or encouraged the move from scroll to codex. The opistho-graphs from the Qumran caves probably did not exert any such influ-ence on their own, but as part of long historical and geographically widespread scribal practices, they provide primary data which may offer hints for the better understanding of broader cultural phenomena.

---

79 More widely the assumption is that preparation preceded writing, that is, papyrus rolls were cut up first into rectangles to provide sheets to be folded and interleaved. The suggestion here is that that might have been prompted by the handling of an already inscribed papyrus scroll.

Liberty in the Coin Legends of the Jewish Revolts

WILLIAM HORBURY

The Hebrew phrases "liberty of Jerusalem" and "liberty of Israel" were current in Judea during the years of unrest from 66 to 135 CE. Coins of the First Revolt against Rome bear Hebrew legends in palaeo-Hebrew script, including "liberty of Zion," and "of the redemption of Zion," and Bar-Kokhba coin-legends in the same script include "of the redemption of Israel," "of the liberty of Israel," and "Jerusalem."[1] Hebrew and Aramaic documents which have been re-dated to the First Revolt present the Hebrew phrases "of the liberty of Jerusalem," "of the redemption of Israel," and "of the redemption of Israel in Jerusalem"; and Bar-Kokhba documents follow suit with years "of the liberty of Israel" and "of the redemption of Israel."[2] In all these cases "liberty" and "redemption" render the Hebrew nouns ḥērût and gĕʾullâ, respectively.

This body of catchwords and dating formulae has engaged historians as evidence for the self-definition of two independent Jewish

---

1   E. Schürer, *The History of the Jewish People in the Age of Jesus Christ*, ET rev. and ed. by G. Vermes, F. Millar, M. Goodman, M. Black, and P. Vermes (4 vols.; Edinburgh: T&T Clark, 1973–1987), 1:544–45, 605–6; more fully, Y. Meshorer, *A Treasury of Jewish Coins from the Persian Period to Bar-Kochba* (in Hebrew; Jerusalem: Yad Ben-Zvi, 1997), 105–44; idem, "The Coins of Masada," in Y. Yadin, J. Naveh and Y. Meshorer, *Masada I: The Yigael Yadin Excavations 1963–5, Final Reports* (Jerusalem: Israel Exploration Society, 1989), 69–132 (107, 114, 118); L. Mildenberg, *The Coinage of the Bar Kokhba War* (Typos 4; Aarau: Sauerländer, 1984), 365–68.

2   H. Eshel, "Documents of the First Jewish Revolt from the Judean Desert," in *The First Jewish Revolt: Archaeology, History, and Ideology* (ed. A. M. Berlin and J. A. Overman; London: Routledge, 2002), 157 63 on Mur22 (gĕʾullâ), 25 (ḥērût), 29 and 30 (gĕʾullâ), all formerly dated in Bar-Kokhba's era; D. Goodblatt, *Elements of Ancient Jewish Nationalism* (Cambridge: Cambridge University Press, 2006), 127–29, reviews and accepts the redatings; for Bar-Kokhba texts see J. T. Milik in A. Benoit, J. T. Milik, and R. de Vaux, *Les grottes de Murabbaʿât* (DJD II; Oxford: Clarendon, 1961), 121–34, on Mur23 (ḥērût), 24 (gĕʾullâ); H. Cotton and A. Yardeni, *Aramaic, Greek and Hebrew Documentary Texts from Naḥal Ḥever and other Sites* (DJD XXVII; Oxford: Clarendon, 1997), 19–37, 65–70, 121–22, on XḤev/Se 7, 8, 8a, 13 (ḥērût), 49 (gĕʾullâ); A. Yardeni in J. Charlesworth et al., *Miscellaneous Texts from the Judaean Desert* (DJD XXXVIII; Oxford: Clarendon, 2000), 125–29, on Sdeir 2 (gĕʾullâ); Y. Yadin, J. C. Greenfield, A. Yardeni, and B. A. Levine, eds., *The Documents from the Bar Kokhba Period in the Cave of Letters* (JDS 3; Jerusalem: Israel Exploration Society, 2002), 142–49, on P.Yadin 42 (gĕʾullâ).

states.[3] *Ḥērût*, "liberty," stands out as the single non-biblical word, being otherwise first attested in the Mishnah and the Passover Haggadah. At the same time it recalls the contemporary popularity of *libertas* and ἐλευθερία as political slogans.[4] Here the antecedents of the catchword *ḥērût* are reviewed again, with attention both to Hebrew prayer and to Greek and Latin political vocabulary, the two poles between which interpretation oscillates.

Thus *ḥērût* on bronze coins of years 2 and 3 (and perhaps year 1) of the First Revolt has been taken to indicate humanly-won independence, in accord with the confidence of these earlier years, whereas "redemption" on bronze coins of year 4 would reflect critical times and signify divine deliverance (cf. Josephus, *B.J.* 4.575, 6.312–13).[5] First Revolt coins allow such readings, for year-dates appear on the obverse, the phrases with catchwords on the reverse, and it is not clear that the years noted are years of "liberty" or "redemption."[6]

Yet, as against this contrast, in documents the "years of redemption" are interchangeable with the "years of liberty."[7] Thus in deeds dated during the First Revolt, year 2 (Mur29) as well as year 4 (P. Mur. 30) is a year "of the redemption of Israel." On Bar-Kokhba coins, "redemption" appears in year 1, "liberty" in years 2 and 3; but "redemption" as well as "liberty" appear in documents of years 2–3 (Mur24, XḤev/Se 49, year 2; Sdeir 2, year 3). "Redemption" in these sources is then humanly-achieved rather than, or as well as, God-given, and the catchwords can now seem consistently political.

Emphasis was soon laid, however, on the God-given character of liberty as well as redemption. Hengel, adducing Josephus and rabbinic

---

3   C. Roth, "The Historical Implications of the Jewish Coinage of the First Revolt," *IEJ* 12 (1962): 33–46; M. Goodman, "Coinage and Identity: The Jewish Evidence," in *Coinage and Identity in the Roman Provinces* (ed. C. Howgego, V. Heuchert and A. Burnett; Oxford: Oxford University Press, 2005), 163–66; Goodblatt, *Elements of Ancient Jewish Nationalism*, 123–39, 167–203; M. Hengel and A.-M. Schwemer, *Jesus und das Judentum* (Tübingen: Mohr Siebeck, 2007), 117.

4   R. Syme, *The Roman Revolution* (Oxford: Clarendon, 1939), 154–55 ("*Libertas* is . . . a convenient term of political fraud").

5   B. Kanael, "The Historical Background of the Coins 'Year Four . . . of the Redemption of Zion,'" *BASOR* 129 (1953): 18–20; Meshorer, *A Treasury of Jewish Coins*, 108, 114; with qualifications, Roth, "The Historical Implications of the Jewish Coinage of the First Revolt," 43; J. J. Price, *Jerusalem under Siege: The Collapse of the Jewish State 66–70 C.E.* (Brill Series in Jewish Studies 3; Leiden: Brill, 1992), 113.

6   Goodblatt, *Elements of Ancient Jewish Nationalism*, 124.

7   Milik, in Benoit, Milik, and de Vaux, *Les Grottes de Murabbaʿât*, 120, 135; similarly, D. R. Schwartz, "Freiheit III. Antikes Judentum," in *RGG* (4th ed.; 1998–2007), vol. 4, cols. 308–9 (the sense of the two words on the coins seems to be more or less the same).

texts, linked the pair not only with one another, but also with interpretation of the Exodus.[8] Thus a Passover thanksgiving preserved in the Mishnah (*Pesaḥ*. 10:5) and in the Passover Haggadah mentions that "He brought us forth from bondage to liberty (*lĕ-ḥērût*)," and in longer texts goes on to add, as one of a series of comparable phrases, "and from servitude to redemption (*li-gĕʾullâ*)."[9] This further series is probably secondary, but its attestation of a similar formula with "redemption" suggests, as the coins do, that "liberty" and "redemption" were readily linked. In the Eighteen Benedictions, somewhat comparably, the Seventh has the petition "redeem us," and the Tenth begins "Blow the great horn for our liberty (*ḥērût*)," going on to pray for the ingathering.[10] Against any view of the rebels as simply political nationalists, Hengel then urged that their "liberty" was to be understood, like "redemption," from the biblical tradition, as part of an essentially religious ideology of revolt stemming from Judas the Galilaean.[11]

One reaction to this religious interpretation was to reaffirm the political (as well as religious) import of both "liberty" and "redemption."[12] Political emphasis is further represented in views which, moving towards the other interpretative pole, envisage a Jewish share in the

---

8   M. Hengel, *The Zealots* (Edinburgh: T&T Clark, 1989), 110–22; trans. of *Die Zeloten* (2d rev. ed.; Leiden: Brill, 1976). He is followed on the coinage by S. Vollenweider, *Freiheit als neue Schöpfung: Eine Untersuchung zur Eleutheria bei Paulus und in seiner Umwelt* (FRLANT 147; Göttingen: Vandenhoeck and Ruprecht, 1989), 138–45 (also stressing the influence of Greek and Roman ideals); Price, *Jerusalem under Siege*, 26–27 (the same slogans covered differing outlooks); Goodblatt, *Elements of Ancient Jewish Nationalism*, 168–69 n. 3.

9   *Pesaḥ*. 10:5 in C. Albeck, *Shishah Sidre Mishnah, Seder Moʿed* (Jerusalem: Mosad Bialik, 1954), 178 (the longer text); G. Beer, ed., *Faksimile-Ausgabe des Mischnacodex Kaufmann A 50* (The Hague: Nijhoff, 1929; repr. in 2 vols., Jerusalem, without publisher's name, 1968), 1:122 ("from bondage to liberty," only); Passover Haggadah, thanksgiving *lephikhakh*, in S. and Z. Safrai, *Haggadat Ḥazal* (Jerusalem: Karta, 1998), 228 (the form with "from bondage to liberty," only, is more original in both the Mishnah and the Haggadah).

10   C. W. Dugmore, *The Influence of the Synagogue on the Divine Office* (2d ed., Westminster: Faith Press, 1964), 117–18 (Hebrew and English); Schürer, *The History of the Jewish People in the Age of Jesus Christ*, 2:457, 460. That the Eighteen Benedictions show the religio-political character of liberty and redemption in Bar-Kokhba coin-legends was underlined by K.-G. Kuhn, "Israel in der nachalttestamentlichen jüdischen Literatur," *TWNT* 3:360–70 (362); idem, *Achtzehngebet und Vaterunser und der Reim* (WUNT 1; Tübingen: Mohr Siebeck, 1950), 17.

11   Hengel, *The Zealots*, 142, refers to J. Klausner, *Jesus of Nazareth* (London: Allen & Unwin, 1925; repr. 1952), 162; trans of *Yeshu Ha-Noṣri* (Jerusalem: Shṭibl, 1921 or 1922): "the more extreme nationalists"; G. F. Moore, *Judaism* (3 vols.; Cambridge, Mass.: Harvard University Press, 1927–1930), 3:22, "fanatical nationalists."

12   T. Rajak, *Josephus* (London: Duckworth, 1983), 139–43; eadem, "Jewish Millenarian Expectations," in Berlin and Overman, *The First Jewish Revolt*, 164–88 (177).

liberty-focused Greek and Roman invective against tyranny.[13] An understanding of the revolts as wars of religion does not, however, in principle rule out political interpretations of the catchwords. This had emerged from Roth's presentation, slightly earlier, of a closely similar view.[14] More recently, Hengel and Schwemer have correlated the "liberty" of First Revolt coins not only with the Exodus but also with the existence for four years of Jerusalem and part of Judea as a "free state."[15]

A second and overlapping phase of inquiry asks what national sensibility is implied by "Jerusalem," "Zion," and "Israel"—the names with which "liberty" is linked—and stresses the distinctiveness of the coinage.[16] So Goodman notes that the images on First Revolt coins differ from those on Roman coinage—although, it might be added, the *legends* with "liberty" recall contemporary Roman legends with LIBERTAS.[17] These legends also contrast, however, as Goodman stresses, with Hasmonean coin-legends, which were likewise presented in palaeo-Hebrew script. The revolt coinage uses Hebrew only, but Hebrew,

---

13   J. Giblet, "Un mouvement de résistance armée au temps de Jésus?" *RTL* 5 (1974): 409–26 (Judas the Galilaean taught Greek ideals of political liberty); S. Pines, "Al gilgulim shel ha-munah herut," *Iyyun* 33 [= *Sepher ha-yovel* for N. Rotenstreich] (Jerusalem, 1984–85), 244–59 (256) (Greek and Roman influence on a distinctive Jewish ideology of liberty); D. Flusser, "*Harughe Metsada be'eynehem u-ve'eyne vene doram,*" reprinted from *Jews and Judaism in the Second Temple, Mishna and Talmud Period: Studies in honour of S. Safrai* (in Hebrew; ed. A. Oppenheimer, Y. Gafni, and M. Stern; Jerusalem: Yad Ben-Zvi, 1993), 116–46, in D. Flusser, *Judaism of the Second Temple Period: Sages and Literature* (ed. S. Ruzer; Jerusalem: Yad Ben-Zvi, 2002), 68–98 (69–86, on contact between Greek and Jewish concepts of liberty; I owe these two references to Professor M. Kister); Flusser, "The Roman Empire in Hasmonean and Essene Eyes," in his *Judaism of the Second Temple Period* (2 vols.; Grand Rapids. Mich.: Eerdmans, 2007–2009), 1:175–206 (Pesher Habbakuk exemplifies the critique of Roman imperialism reflected in Roman authors); Vollenweider, *Freiheit als neue Schöpfung,* 145 (the eschatological "liberty" of the rebels also owes something to Greek thought).

14   C. Roth, *The Historical Background of the Dead Sea Scrolls* (Oxford: Blackwell, 1958), 5–6, criticizing both Josephus and Joseph Klausner: "[The revolutionaries'] concern was not merely to triumph over the Romans, but also, as a preliminary or concomitant, to establish the Kingdom of Heaven on earth"; idem, "The Zealots in the War of 66–73," *JSS* 4 (1959): 332–55 (337–38).

15   Hengel and Schwemer, *Jesus und das Judentum,* 117.

16   Goodblatt, *Elements of Ancient Jewish Nationalism,* 121–36; Goodman, "Coinage and Identity: The Jewish Evidence"; idem, *Rome and Jerusalem: The Clash of Ancient Civilizations* (London: Allen Lane, 2007), 18–19.

17   Goodman, "Coinage and Identity: The Jewish Evidence"; Ch. Wirszubski, *Libertas as a Political Idea at Rome during the Late Republic and Early Principate* (Cambridge: Cambridge University Press, 1950), 159 (LIBERTAS PUBLICA on coins from Galba onwards); Vollenweider, *Freiheit als neue Schöpfung,* 138, n.163 (Roman libertas-legends the exemplars for the Jewish coins).

Aramaic, and Greek all appear on Hasmonean coins (although one might add that Hebrew was the main language used); and the names Jerusalem, Zion, and Israel denote the political entity, but Hasmonean coins name Judah or the "association of the Jews," *ḥeber ha-yĕhûdîm*.[18]

Without ignoring the distinctiveness of the coin-legends, I should like to reconsider their links with their surroundings through a focus on the catchword *ḥērût*, "liberty," taking for granted its simultaneous attraction of political and religious associations, but following in particular the traces of its incorporation into prayer-language.

The Early Currency of *ḥērût*

The Mishnah has often been used as a help towards envisaging types of Hebrew spoken or written, alongside Aramaic, in Hasmonean and Herodian Judea.[19] This help will be circumscribed if the Hebrew of the Qumran texts is taken, as Qimron holds, to represent Hebrew spoken in Jerusalem, while Mishnaic Hebrew derives from Hebrew used elsewhere and becomes widespread only after the fall of Jerusalem.[20] Nevertheless, as far as vocabulary is concerned, some non-biblical words in Mishnaic Hebrew are indeed attested in pre-Mishnaic inscriptions and documents, including the Qumran texts (notably 4QMMT). Many of these sources are used in the Sheffield *Dictionary of Classical Hebrew*, which covers all kinds of Hebrew earlier than the period of the Mishnah. The noun *ḥērût* was not registered, however, among words beginning with *ḥêt* in this dictionary, even though some revolt coins and documents were among the sources.[21] It is then worth noting specifically that the legends of the revolt coinage attest this Mishnaic word in Hebrew contexts in Jerusalem before the capture of the city by Titus.

---

18 Goodman, "Coinage and Identity: The Jewish Evidence"; Hasmonean coin-legends in S. Ostermann, *Die Münzen der Hasmonäer* (NTOA 55; Fribourg, Switzerland: Academic Press; Göttingen: Vandenhoeck & Ruprecht, 2005), 54–59.

19 H. Graetz, *Geschichte der Juden* (9 vols.; 2d ed.; Leipzig: Leiner, 1863), 70 (*Neuhebräisch* under John Hyrcanus); M. H. Segal, *A Grammar of Mishnaic Hebrew* (Oxford: Clarendon, 1927; repr. 1958), paras. 19–20; A. Sáenz-Badillos, *A History of the Hebrew Language* (Cambridge: Cambridge University Press, 1993), 162–63, 168–71; trans of *Historia de la lengua hebrea* (Sabadell: AUSA, 1988); E. Qimron and J. Strugnell, *Qumran Cave 4, V: Miqsat Maʿase ha-Torah* (DJD X; Oxford: Clarendon, 1994), 107–8.

20 E. Qimron, "Ha-lashon veha-reqaʿ ha-leshoni shel kitbe Qumran," in *The Qumran Scrolls and their World* (in Hebrew; ed. M. Kister; 2 vols.; Jerusalem: Yad Ben-Zvi, 2009), 2:551–60 (553–54).

21 *DCH* 1:55–56 (sources); vol. 3 (including words beginning with *ḥêt*).

In documents it can appear in Hebrew phrases quoted in Aramaic texts, and in these contexts has been indexed as an Aramaic word.[22] In the light of the coins, however, it seems that in all these cases *ḥērût* is part of a Hebrew formula quoted in the Aramaic text, as happens with *gĕʾullâ* formulae and the Hebrew phrase *ha-nāśî ʿal yiśrāʾēl* in Aramaic Bar-Kokhba documents.[23] Correspondingly, *ḥērût yiśrāʾēl* appears in the Hebrew lower text of the double deed P. XḤev/Se 8.[24]

The immediate setting of *ḥērût* in the coin-legends receives some light from the prominence of ἐλευθερία in Josephus and Paul. These Jewish authors span a period in which discussion of liberty in the Roman empire, ongoing since the Augustan age, was intensified in connection with Nero and Domitian.[25] Josephus indeed rivals the coins in presenting liberty as an Israelite motto. He makes the Greek ἐλευθερία the leitmotiv of speeches not only by anti-Roman rebels, but also, later on, by Moses and the Maccabees.[26] Moses assures himself of the people's love of liberty, and the disciples of Judas the Galilaean have an unshakable love of liberty (Josephus, *Ant.* 2.281; 18.23). Joshua camps at a place called Galgala (Gilgal), signifying "liberty" from Egypt and the misery of the wilderness (Josh 5:9, paraphrased in Josephus, *Ant.* 5.34).[27] In a speech by Samuel the condition of Israel without an earthly king is "liberty" (*Ant.* 6.60).[28]

---

22 See the indices of Aramaic words, s.v. *hrw*, in Benoit, Milik, and de Vaux, *Les grottes de Murabbaʿât*, 295, and Cotton and Yardeni, *Aramaic, Greek and Hebrew Documentary Texts from Naḥal Ḥever and other Sites*, 353.

23 Yardeni in Charlesworth et al., *Miscellaneous Texts from the Judaean Desert*, 125–29 (Sdeir 2, perhaps a promissory note, of the third year of Israel's *gĕʾullâ*); Yadin, Greenfield, Yardeni, and Levine, *The Documents from the Bar Kokhba Period in the Cave of Letters*, 144 (P.Yadin 42, lease of the first year of Israel's *gĕʾullâ*), 308 (P.Yadin 54, letter with the formula *ha-nāśî ʿal yiśrāʾēl*).

24 Cotton and Yardeni, *Aramaic, Greek and Hebrew Documentary Texts from Naḥal Ḥever and Other Sites*, 28; restored in the lacunose Hebrew text of the double deed P. XḤev/Se 7, p. 21.

25 A. Momigliano, review of Ch. Wirszubski, *Libertas as a Political Idea at Rome during the Late Republic and Early Principate*, JRS 41 (1951): 146–53 (148–49, 152), urging inter alia that the imaginary tale of Vespasian's discussion of the ideal constitution with philosophers in Alexandria in 70 (Philostratus, *Vit. Apoll.*, 5:27–36) truly reflects the type of debate current after Nero's death. Imperial claims to bring *libertas* are exemplified in Virgil, *Ecl.* 1.27 (Octavian); Statius, *Silvae* 1.6, 42–44 (Domitian).

26 Josephus, *B.J.* 2.348 (advocates of war against Rome praise liberty); 4.228 (the Zealots Eleazar and Zacharias); 7.334, 344 (Eleazar son of Jairus); *Ant.* 3.44 (Moses); 12.281 (Mattathias), 302–4 (Judas Maccabaeus); 13.198 (Simon).

27 The reproach of Egypt now removed (Josh 5:9) is taken as servitude to Egypt; Josephus's understanding of the Hebrew is discussed by E. Nodet, *Flavius Josèphe: Les Antiquités juives* (4 vols., in progress; Paris: Cerf, 1990–), 2:123 n. 4 on *Ant.* 5.34.

28 Here, as in *Ant.* 4.146 (autonomy "belongs to freemen who have no master"), Josephus touches the Roman commonplace that *libertas* means a polity without a

In all these cases Josephus is in touch with nuances of ἐλευθερία and *libertas* as used by Greek and Roman contemporaries (nn. 17, 25 and 28, above). He probably also, however, reflects the importance of ἐλευθερία and its Aramaic and Hebrew counterparts in Judea. Thus when in Josephus God-given "signs of liberty" are deceptively forecast by prophet-like figures under Felix (*B.J.* 2.259), as they had once been granted genuinely to Moses (*Ant.* 2.327), the Greek may reflect a Hebrew phrase like ʾōtôt (lĕ-)ḥērût, or an Aramaic counterpart. To return to the coins, their Hebrew slogans "liberty of Zion" and "liberty of Jerusalem" seem to be echoed in Josephus when the Idumaeans, urged by Zealots from Jerusalem, seize weapons "as for the liberty of the mother-city" (Josephus, *B.J.* 4.234, cf. 245).

In Paul, Jewish political overtones of liberty emerge in Romans, where Egyptian slavery and exodus liberation stand behind "the bond-age of corruption" and "the liberty of the glory of the children of God" (Rom 8:21, cf. Exod 4:22–23); and in Galatians, where the biblical theme of Jerusalem as bondwoman and freewoman (Lam 1:1; Isa 52:2–3; 1 Macc 2:11) introduces emphasis on the current bondage of the city (Gal 4:25), and the claim that "the Jerusalem that is above is free" (Gal 4:26). Contact with a strand of Jewish piety in which obedience to God is liberty is suggested by 2 Cor 3:17, "but where the spirit of the Lord is, there is liberty." Here, in accord with the general likelihood that Paul understood Aramaic and Hebrew, there is a case for his knowledge of Hebrew ḥērût in particular; for an early form of the rabbinic reading of "the writing of God engraved [ḥārût] on the tablets" (Exod 32:16) in the sense of ḥērût, "liberty," seems likely to underlie the passage from "engraved on stones" (2 Cor 3:7) to ἐλευθερία (3:17).[29] Delitzsch, who shared the view that Hebrew remained in use alongside Aramaic, will not then have been anachronistic when he used ḥērût to render ἐλευθερία in Pauline epistles written probably from the late forties onwards.[30]

Some vogue for the Hebrew word might then be guessed from Paul as well as Josephus, and also from John 8:33 (the seed of Abraham are

king; see Wirszubski, *Libertas as a Political Idea at Rome*, 5 on Livy 2.15, 3 "*non in regno populum Romanum sed in libertate esse.*"

29   *Tanḥuma Buber*, Exodus, *Ki Thissa*, 12, f. 56b (views of this 'liberty' ascribed to R. Judah b. Ilai, R. Nehemiah, and others); *m.* ʾ*Abot* 6.2, considered with 2 Corinthians 3 by Vollenweider, *Freiheit als neue Schöpfung*, 142–43, 268, 398 (without raising the question of Paul's knowledge of the Hebrew word).

30   Franz Delitzsch, trans., *Siprê ha-Bĕrît ha-Ḥădāšâ* (1899, repr.; *Foreign Bible Society: A Contribution to Hebrew Philology* (Leipzig: Dörffling & Franke, London: British and Foreign Bible Society, 1927), at Rom 8:21; 1 Cor 10:29; 2 Cor 3:17; Gal 2:4; 5:1, 13; on Hebrew after the Exile, idem, *The Hebrew New Testament of the British and* 1883), 30–32.

free) and Jas 1:25; 2:12 (the law of liberty). The attestations of the Hebrew word from the late sixties onwards can thus be aligned with the prominence of ἐλευθερία in Greek Jewish and Christian texts to suggest the currency of Hebrew ḥērût not only from the sixties, but probably already in the forties and fifties.

Two passages from Hasmonean literature, over a hundred years earlier, offer only uncertain glimpses of ḥērût, but in any case throw further light on the antecedents of the coin-legends. In 1 Maccabees, translated from a Semitic language, probably Hebrew, the encomium of Simon Maccabeus and his sons in 1 Macc 14:26 ends "and by war he drove the enemies of Israel from them, and they confirmed liberty (ἐλευθερία) to him [Israel]." Simon and his sons are probably the subject throughout, despite the change of number.[31] In verse 26 it is possible that ἐλευθερία renders an original ḥērût.[32] However this may be, as patriotic publicity probably issued in Hebrew, and in the sense "liberty of Israel," the passage foreshadows the revolt coin-legends.

The Qumran texts likewise treat liberty through biblical phraseology. They seem not to attest ḥērût. An allusion to it in the Community Rule in the sense of the liberty of willing law-observance has been suggested, however, in three references in the Maskil's Hymn to praise or repentance as "an engraved ordinance," ḥôq ḥārût; cf. Exod. 32:16, cited above (1QS X, 6, 8, 10, with parallels in 4QS^d=4Q258 IX, 1–12 and, less fully, in 4QS^b=4Q256, 4QS^f=4Q260).[33] Here the interpretative reading of ḥērût noted above may already be presupposed.[34]

This understanding suits the Pentateuchal connection of law-giving with liberation, and the covenantal character of Qumran piety.[35] It might also gain support from the second reference to ḥôq ḥārût (1QS X, 8). The Maskil duly prays at daily, annual, and septennial times.[36] His

---

31 F.-M. Abel, *Les livres des Maccabées* (Paris: Gabalda, 1949), 255, followed by U. Rappaport, *The First Book of Maccabees* (Jerusalem: Yad Ben-Zvi, 2004), 311.

32 *Hophesh* (Sir 7:21) is also possible. Rappaport, *The First Book of Maccabees*, 311, renders by ḥērût, but (p. 3) he is not attempting a retroversion. Pines, "*Al gilgulim shel hamunah herut*," 247 holds that ḥērût did not appear in the original of 1 Maccabees, but does not discuss this passage.

33 F. M. Cross et al., eds., *Scrolls from Qumrân Cave 1 . . . from Photographs by John C. Trever* (Jerusalem: Albright Institute and Shrine of the Book, 1972), 144–45 (1QS X); P. S. Alexander and G. Vermes, *Qumran Cave 4, XIX: Serekh ha-Yaḥad and Two Related Texts* (DJD XXVI; Oxford: Clarendon, 1998), 120–24.

34 The possibility of this dual sense in 1QS X was allowed by G. R. Driver, *The Judaean Scrolls* (Oxford: Blackwell, 1965), 543–44; R. Fabris, *Legge della libertà in Giacomo* (Supplementi alla Rivista Biblica 8; Brescia: Paideia, 1977), 103–13.

35 Fabris, *Legge della libertà in Giacomo*, 91–103 (on Lev 26:3-13), 111–13.

36 Alexander and Vermes, *Qumran Cave 4, XIX*, 120 tabulate the references to times of prayer.

septennial prayer will take place at the beginning of the weeks of years, "at the appointed times of liberty (*dĕrôr*), with all my being, as an engraved ordinance" (1QS X, 8). Here *dĕrôr* is the liberty of the Sabbatical-year slave-release, for which the word is used in Jer 34:8, 15, 17, but this sense will include the liberty of the Jubilee in the fiftieth year, with which alone *dĕrôr* is linked in the Pentateuch (Lev 25:10 *dĕrôr*, Targums *ḥêrûtâ*).[37] At the Jubilee this "liberty" or slave-liberation is part of the general "redemption" (*gĕʾullah*, Lev 25:24, 29) of property.

Here then in Leviticus a link between "redemption" and the theme of liberty appears, but the point of interest now is the link between the Jubilee and liberty. This aspect of the Jubilee is already singled out in Isa 61:1, on coming deliverance, and probably also in Isa 27:13, where the blowing of a great horn "in that day" signals the return of exiles to worship in Jerusalem.[38] It is developed in 11QMelchizedek, in which the returning Melchizedek proclaims liberty to the captives (Isa 61:1) in the tenth jubilee, the end of days (11Q13 II, 4–6); for the understanding of future deliverance as a Jubilee compare *Pss. Sol.* 11:1–2. In the reference to *ḥôq ḥārût* in 1QS X, 8 the interpretation *ḥērût* would then fit the context well.

In all, an allusion to *ḥērût* in the Maskil's Hymn is certainly possible, but more would be needed to make it firmly probable at this relatively early date. What does emerge clearly from these Qumran texts is the importance of Hebrew *dĕrôr*, the "liberty" especially of the Jubilee, a word rendered in this context by the Targums with *ḥêrûtâ*, and of its link with future liberation.

To summarize, in the background of the coins the importance of ἐλευθερία in Josephus, Paul, and other texts suggests some vogue for the Hebrew *ḥērût* before as well as during the First Revolt, and shows that the coin-legends form part of a widespread discourse on liberty; Josephus indicates the respectability as well as the danger of the catchword.

In the Hasmonean age, glimpses of *ḥērût* are uncertain; but 1 Macc 14:26 on Israel's liberty anticipates the liberty-formulae of the revolts against Rome, and attests patriotic publicity on this subject in Hebrew. Qumran texts highlight Jubilee "liberty," *dĕrôr*, and its link with future liberation. The later rôle of ἐλευθερία and *ḥērût* in this Jubilee context is now considered.

---

37 *Targums Onkelos, Neofiti,* and *Ps.-Jonathan* on Lev 25:10; *Targum Jonathan* on Isa 61:1.

38 Possible allusion to the Jubilee law of Lev 25:9–10 is noted in both these passages by R. J. Coggins, "Isaiah," in *The Oxford Bible Commentary* (ed. J. Barton and J. Muddiman; Oxford: Oxford University Press, 2001), 433–86 (457, 481).

The Liberty of the Jubilee

The importance of the Jubilee "liberty" (děrôr) is signalled not only by 11QMelchizedek, and (implicitly) Pss. Sol. 11:1–2, but also by Greek biblical versions. Here its association with ἐλευθερία begins to emerge. Thus the LXX rendering ἄφεσις (Lev 25:10; Isa 61:1; Jer 34 [41]:8, 15, 17; Ezek 46:17) links it with the septennial year of "release" (Deut 15:1, LXX ἄφεσις), for which děrôr is used in Jeremiah, as noted above, but seems not wholly to have satisfied the public; for ἄφεσις was matched by the transliteration δαρώρ (Lev 25:10) or δερώρ (Ezek 46:17), which Jerome on Ezekiel ascribes to Theodotion.[39] This presentation was in turn rivalled, however, by the translation ἐλευθερία, recorded as an alternative in Septuagintal manuscripts at Lev 25:10 and, with ascription to Aquila, in the Syro-Hexaplar version of Jer 34(41):15.[40] In the Old Latin likewise libertas appears beside remissio in quotation of Isa 61:1.[41]

The currency of this translation ἐλευθερία well before the time to which Aquila is usually assigned is suggested, however, by Philo and Josephus. Both use the word when they expound the Jubilee law of Lev 25:10. Philo can simply add it epexegetically to ἄφεσις: the number fifty proclaims release (ἄφεσις) from slavery and entire liberty (ἐλευθερία) (Sacr. 122; Det. 63), or signifies "entire release to liberty" (Mut. 228); God proclaims "release and liberty" to suppliant souls (Her. 273), and "the release, the entire liberty of the soul" is announced (Congr. 108). Here the philosophico-theological stress on "entire" liberty may match a legal sense, for one rabbinic explanation of děrôr is that it means ḥērût to live and trade wherever you wish.[42] Josephus simply and boldly says that ἰώβηλος, "Jubilee," means ἐλευθερία (Ant. 3.283). The Hebrew yôbēl, which he gives in a declinable Greek transliteration, occurs in Lev 25:10–55, 27:17–24; Num 36:4 (contrast děrôr, found in this sense in the Pentateuch only at Lev 25:10). From Lev 25:28 onwards yôbēl is rendered in LXX by ἄφεσις.[43] Josephus perhaps recalls this translation, but

---

39 F. Field, Origenis Hexaplorum quae supersunt (2 vols.; Oxford: Clarendon, 1875), 1:211a; 2:894a.

40 Field, Origenis Hexaplorum quae supersunt, 2:674a.

41 Quodvultdeus, Liber promissionum, 2:31, 68 (libertas); 3:10, 11 (remissio); see Petrus Sabatier, Bibliorum Sacrorum Latinae Versiones Antiquae (3 vols.; Rheims: R. Florentain, 1743), 2:625; R. Braun, ed., Quodvultdeus: Livre des promesses et des prédictions de Dieu (2 vols.; SC 101–2; Paris: Cerf, 1964), 1:448; 2:516.

42 Babylonian Talmud, Roš Haš. 9b, in discussion of m. Roš Haš. 1:1 "on 1st Tishri is the New Year for Years of Release and Jubilee years"; an etymology ascribed to R. Judah b. Ilai links děrôr with dûr, "to dwell."

43 P. Harlé and D. Pralon, Le Lévitique (La Bible d'Alexandrie 3; Paris: Cerf, 1988), 198.

then gives what had become a regular alternative, when he renders by ἐλευθερία.

Greek-language sources thus link ἐλευθερία with the Jubilee law, and through Philo and Josephus suggest an emphasis on Jubilee liberty in the later Herodian age. This liberty had then long been associated with future deliverance, as seen in 11QMelchizedek and *Pss. Sol.* 11:1, and as suggested already by Isa 27:13; 61:1. Both these elements in interpretation of Lev 25:10 probably lie behind the Tenth Benediction (n. 10, above), which at first follows Isa 27:13, with its own echo of the Jubilee, and then redoubles the echo with the word "liberty:" "Blow the great horn (Isa 27:13, cf. Lev 25:9) for our *ḥērût* (Lev 25:10, Targums *ḥêrûtâ*, Greek interpretations with ἐλευθερία), and raise a banner (Isa 11:12) for the gathering of our exiles."[44] The Jubilee liberty is probably also already presupposed in part of a prayer from the Maccabean age which forms one of the antecedents of the Eighteen Benedictions, 2 Macc 1:27: "Gather our dispersion, free those enslaved among the nations."

Interpretation of the Jubilee liberty as the preliminary to the future return can also be perceived in Philo's celebrated sketch of the ingathering (*Praem.* 164–65). Here he broadly follows the Pentateuchal prediction that confession of sins by the exiles will lead to their return (Lev 26:40–41, cf. Deut 30:1–3); turning to virtue at its highest, they will shame their masters into releasing them. Before saying this, however, Philo inserts the statement that "all shall be set free as by one signal on one day" (*Praem.* 164), and after it he goes on "when they have gained this unexpected ἐλευθερία" they will journey by one impulse from scattered spots world-wide to the one appointed place (*Praem.* 165). The quoted passages seem to reflect not Leviticus 26, but Lev 25:9–10, on the sound of the horn on the day of atonement and the proclamation of liberty, and Isa 27:13, on the sound of the horn "on that day" followed by return to Jerusalem; and this is not unexpected given Philo's own concern with Jubilee liberty, and the existing presentation of the Jubilee as the time of future deliverance in later parts of Isaiah, 11QMelchizedek, and the Psalms of Solomon. Within the context of *De praemiis*, the association of the Jubilee with the day of atonement unites the insertion felicitously with the theme of confession and amendment which marks Lev 26:40–41 and Deut 30:1–3. Despite emphasis on travel

---

44   In some forms of the Benediction a further echo of Lev 25:10 appears in the continuation "and proclaim liberty (*děrôr*) to gather us together"; so MSS of *Siddur Rab Amram*, cited by I. Elbogen, *Der jüdische Gottesdienst in seiner geschichtlichen Entwicklung* (3d ed., Frankfurt-am-Main, 1931; repr. Hildesheim: Olms, 1962), 50; ET, with ET of supplements in the Hebrew version edited by J. Heinemann, *Jewish Liturgy: A Comprehensive History* (Philadelphia: Jewish Publication Society, 1993), 44–45.

from all over the world, the overall stress of the passage falls, in accord with the tenor of Leviticus 25–26, not on the diaspora separately but on the restoration of Israel as a whole.[45]

These interpretations of coming deliverance as Jubilee liberty match those of the past exodus as a slave-liberation, expressed in the Mishnah and the Passover Haggadah with the use of *ḥērût*, as noted above. The exodus is already a liberation in the Pentateuch, as variously indicated in such passages as Exod 3:20; 6:6; Lev 26:13; Deut 7:8; but this is not yet expressed with a noun which can be rendered "liberty," as happens later in Josephus (*Ant.* 2.281, 327; 3.44, all cited above) and also implicitly in Paul (Rom 8:21, cited above; cf. Exod 4:22–23). The Jubilee law, however, did include the noun *dĕrôr*, which could be interpreted by *ḥērûtâ*, *ḥērût* or ἐλευθερία. This development coincided with interpretation of the exodus as liberty, helped to focus the hope for a new exodus on liberty, and forms part of the background of *ḥērût* in the coin-legends. In the Jubilee context, the word had entered the vocabulary associated with the sacred books.

The Coin-Legends and Prayer-Tradition

Prayer built on this interpretation of past and future exodus as liberty, as seen above in Passover thanksgiving, the Eighteen Benedictions, and the prayer-text 2 Macc 1:27. In daily prayer in Josephus's time the exodus was already mentioned morning and night, as later prescribed in the Mishnah (*Ber.* 1:5; Josephus, *Ant.* 4.212). Now it should be noted that exodus-based interpretation and prayer can, like the coin-legends, link liberty and redemption together, and link both of them with Israel, Zion, and Jerusalem.

This double linkage has biblical antecedents which were developed in interpretation of the exodus. Liberty and redemption come together, as seen already, in Lev 25:10, 24, and, without the nouns, in the exodus narratives, as in Exod 6:6, "I will recover you from their bondage, and redeem you."[46] Correspondingly, Philo reads Abraham's movement from fifty to ten in prayer for Sodom as movement from ἄφεσις (connected with the Jubilee and just interpreted by Philo with ἐλευθερία) to ἀπολύτρωσις, "redemption" (*Congr.* 109). Similarly, a Pauline passage

---

45   P. Volz, *Die Eschatologie der jüdischen Gemeinde im neutestamentlichen Zeitalter* (2d ed. of idem, *Jüdische Eschatologie von Daniel bis Akiba*; Tübingen, 1934, repr. Hildesheim: Olms, 1966), 345.

46   Here and below "redemption," in translation or summary of Hebrew texts, is used only when *gĕʾullah* or a part of the verb *gāʾal* appear in the Hebrew.

with an exodus background noted above uses first ἐλευθερία and then ἀπολύτρωσις (Rom 8:21, 23).[47]

The second link, between liberty and/or redemption and Jerusalem, appears in the Song of Moses, on the planting of the redeemed people in the sanctuary (Exod 15:13; 17); this event will come again, as intimated in Deutero-Isaiah on the "redemption" and "liberty" (of the people and Zion/Jerusalem in a new exodus (Isa 52:9; 59:20; 61:1; 62:12; 63:4). This link emerges in later interpretation and prayer at 2 Macc. 1:27–29, "free those in bondage . . . plant thy people in thy holy place, as Moses said," and, in close approximation to the coins, Luke 2:38, where the devout await "the redemption (λύτρωσις) of Jerusalem"; a similar understanding of the past exodus emerges at Acts 7:35, on Moses as a redeemer (λυτρωτής).

Against this background of exodus interpretation the Eighteen Benedictions as a whole unite the catchwords of the coinage: redemption, liberty, Jerusalem, and Israel. In the Seventh, cited above (n. 9), "Look upon our affliction, and plead our cause, and redeem us for thy Name's sake," the wording echoes Ps 119:153–54, but also recalls Exod 3:17, "I have surely looked upon the affliction of my people"; and 6:6 "I will redeem you." Then liberty is the theme of the Tenth, "Blow the great horn . . . ," discussed above. Then in the Fourteenth mercy is asked for Jerusalem or for Israel, Jerusalem, and Zion.[48]

This sequence of petitions for redemption, liberty, Israel, Zion, and Jerusalem matches the catchwords of the coin-legends, and its set of prayer-themes probably goes back to their period; for this central petitionary section of the Eighteen Benedictions, from the Fourth to the Sixteenth (Seventeenth), is anticipated in outline long before the time of the coins in the prayers of Sir 36:6–14 (prayer for new signs and wonders—on the old exodus lines, as promised in Micah 7:15—and then for ingathering, Israel, Jerusalem, Zion); 2 Macc 1:25–29 (gather the dispersion, free the enslaved, plant the people in the holy place); and *Pss. Sol.* 11:1–9 (Jubilee horn in Zion, ingathering, Israel, Jerusalem). Liberty was

---

47   The Jubilee association of liberty and redemption is noted by R. W. Wall, "'The Perfect Law of Liberty' (James 1:25)," in *The Quest for Context and Meaning: Studies in Biblical Intertextuality in Honor of James A. Sanders* (ed. C. A. Evans and S. Talmon; Biblical Interpretation Series 28; Leiden: Brill, 1997), 475–97 (490–91), with reference to links of λύτρον with ἄφεσις in Leviticus 25 (as at verses 26–28) and sabbatical-year legislation.

48   This series of three appears in the Palestinian text translated in Schürer, *The History of the Jewish People in the Age of Jesus Christ*, 2:461, and in the similar benediction forming part of the *Birkath ha-Mazon*, asking for mercy upon Israel, Jerusalem, and Zion, in S. Singer, *The Authorized Daily Prayer Book* (2d ed., London: Eyre and Spottiswoode, 1962), 379.

already implied (2 Macc 1:27), but its express mention in this context became more common, especially through the Jubilee vocabulary, as noted above, and "redemption" was likewise favoured by this context, with Isa 61:1, as Luke-Acts indicates.

Liberty in the Coin-Legends

Discussion of the early currency of *ḥērût* suggested its importance before the First Revolt in the discourse on liberty reflected in Josephus and Paul, and its thematic if not verbal connection with Hasmonean publicity and Qumran texts on the Jubilee. It was then urged, with appeal to Greek Jewish biblical interpretation, that the Jubilee law formed an important context for the entry of *ḥērût* and ἐλευθερία into the biblical vocabulary of the exodus and the hoped-for new exodus. Exodus-Jubilee "liberty" and "redemption" figured in prayer, including the Eighteen Benedictions, and this prayer-usage influenced the coin-legends. It did not, however, exclude influence from the wider currency of "liberty" as a political catchword. *Ḥērût* could evoke the connotations of ἐλευθερία and *libertas*, words used to express Jewish, Greek, and Roman aspirations in the Roman empire, and mottoes needed by all claimants to power.

May they on this occasion carry warm greetings and good wishes to a friend and colleague of long standing.

"... wie es eigentlich gewesen"

Historical "Facts" and the Reconstruction of the History of "Ancient Israel"*

JOACHIM SCHAPER

"[A] particular truth known by actual observation or authentic testi-mony, as opposed to what is merely inferred, or to a conjecture or fic-tion"—that is how the Oxford English Dictionary defines the term "fact." This study is concerned with the concept of historical "facts" and how that concept is used in writing the history of ancient Israel. It will therefore not present exegeses of biblical texts. Instead, it will deal with a fundamental concept of historiography, but will do so from an Old Testament scholar's perspective.

Unlike Gaul, the present article will be divided into four parts. In the first one, called "Facts: A Prelude," I shall start with a discussion of the concept of facts, especially historical facts. In the second part, "'Facts' and (Biblical and Other) Sources," I shall sketch what some Old Testament scholars think about historical facts. This will be followed by a discussion of some concepts of "facts" held from the late nineteenth century onwards, and a section entitled "'Ancient History' and the 'History of Ancient Israel,'" addressing the conceptualization of facts in the works of historians of (classical) antiquity. Special attention will be paid to the contributions made by Finley. In the fourth part, called "Methodology: Texts and Material Remains," I shall delineate the rela-tion between textual and archaeological sources. Conclusions and sug-gestions concerning future work in the reconstruction of the history of ancient Israel and Judah will be presented in the last section.

---

* The present essay goes back to a paper presented at the University of Sheffield in February 2008.

I. "Facts": A Prelude

Leopold von Ranke, the star historian of Prussia in the early nineteenth century, famously stated that it is the historian's task to say "wie es eigentlich gewesen"—what things had actually been like, how things had in fact happened.[1] Another star historian, this time a twentieth-century Englishman, had the following to say about Ranke's statement:

> When Ranke in the 1830s, in legitimate protest against moralizing history, remarked that the task of the historian was 'simply to show how it really was (*wie es eigentlich gewesen*)', this not very profound aphorism had an astonishing success. Three generations of German, British, and even French historians marched into battle intoning the magic words '*Wie es eigentlich gewesen*' like an incantation—designed, like most incantations, to save them from the tiresome obligation to think for themselves. The Positivists, anxious to stake out their claim for history as a science, contributed the weight of their influence to this cult of facts. First ascertain the facts, said the Positivists, then draw your conclusions from them. In Great Britain, this view of history fitted in perfectly with the empiricist tradition which was the dominant strain in British philosophy from Locke to Bertrand Russell. The empirical theory of knowledge presupposes a complete separation between subject and object. Facts, like sense-impressions, impinge on the observer from outside and are independent of his consciousness. The process of reception is passive: having received the data, he then acts on them.[2]

Although the jury is still out on whether or not this was a fair evaluation of the meaning of Ranke's statement,[3] Carr's remarks about facts indeed deserve to be taken very seriously. What Carr is doing here is to question the notion of "facts speaking for themselves." However, he

---

1   His famous words are found in L. (von) Ranke, *Geschichten der romanischen und germanischen Völker von 1494 bis 1535*, vol. 1 (Leipzig: G. Reimer, 1824), vi.

2   E. H. Carr, *What is History? The George Macaulay Trevelyan Lectures delivered in the University of Cambridge January–March 1961* (ed. R. W. Davies; 2d ed.; Harmondsworth: Penguin Books, 1987), 8–9. Carr, like virtually everybody else quoting the most famous line ever written by von Ranke, fails to put it in context. Here it is: "Man hat der Historie das Amt, die Vergangenheit zu richten, die Mitwelt zum Nutzen zukünftiger Jahre zu belehren, beygemessen: so hoher Aemter unterwindet sich gegenwärtiger Versuch nicht: er will bloß sagen, wie es eigentlich gewesen" (Ranke, *Geschichten der romanischen und germanischen Völker*, v–vi). Ranke thus states—seemingly modestly, but in fact very assertively—that he regards his research as being free from the diktat of paedagogical and ethical objectives and as being characterized by true, *wissenschaftliche* objectivity. On this important point, cf. Alexandre Escudier, "Theory and Methodology of History from Chladenius to Droysen: A Historiographical Essay," in *History of Scholarship: A Selection of Papers from the Seminar on the History of Scholarship Held Annually at the Warburg Institute* (ed. C. R. Ligota and J.-L. Quantin; Oxford–Warburg Studies; Oxford: Oxford University Press, 2006), 437–85 (465–66).

3   Cf. the actual context of Ranke's remark; see above, n. 2.

questions even more than that, undermining the concept of "facts" altogether when he states that "[t]he belief in a hard core of historical facts existing objectively and independently of the historian is a preposterous fallacy."[4] As he rightly puts it,

> It used to be said that the facts speak for themselves. This is, of course, untrue. The facts speak only when the historian calls on them: it is he who decides to which facts to give the floor, and in what order or context.[5]

In what follows, I would like to explore the notion of "historical facts," with special regard to its significance in the current debate on the history of ancient Israel/Palestine. It will become obvious that the said "belief in a hard core of historical facts existing objectively and independently" is indeed "very hard to eradicate,"[6] and I hope to demonstrate what a detrimental effect that belief is still having on the reconstruction of the history of ancient Israel.

I also intend to show how the notion of facts is often related, in the current debate, to concepts of the hierarchy of sources that are, in some cases, implicit in the arguments put forward or, in other cases, explicitly and often aggressively stated. From that will follow a few remarks about historical methodology, remarks which will attempt to resolve some of the impasses in the current debate.

II. "Facts" and (Biblical and Other) Sources

We have just heard about "the preposterous fallacy" that is "[t]he belief in a hard core of historical facts." Contrast with that the following statement by Niels Peter Lemche, made in the context of a discussion of the relative merits of the "genres" of Old Testament Theology and History of Israelite Religion:

> Wir wollen Beweise haben, wir begnügen uns nicht mit Vermutungen und grundlosen Theorien. Wir anerkennen nicht weiter Sprachfiguren oder rhetorische Aussagen anstelle von Tatsachen und logischer und wissenschaftlicher Akribie.[7]

---

4   Carr, *What is History?*, 12.
5   Carr, *What is History?*, 11.
6   Carr, *What is History?*, 12.
7   N. P. Lemche, "Warum die Theologie des Alten Testaments einen Irrweg darstellt," *Jahrbuch für biblische Theologie* 10 (1995): 79–92 (83). This reminds one of the argument put forward by B. J. Diebner, "'Es läßt sich nicht beweisen, Tatsache aber ist' — Sprachfigur statt Methode in der kritischen Erforschung des Alten Testaments," *DBAT* 18 (1984): 138–46.

One should be absolutely clear about the nature of the conclusions Lemche and others are drawing: since the "proof" and the "facts" as desired by Lemche—i.e., proof and facts that could *conclusively prove* that the Old Testament traditions are historically reliable sources and a firm basis for historical reconstruction—cannot be adduced, all these traditions are by definition regarded as literary products which are useless for the purpose of historical reconstruction. Only where there is "external evidence"—i.e. non-biblical material (for this is Lemche's interpretation of the concept of external evidence)—can we begin to speak of "proof." Where there is none, we are wasting our time with "rhetorical statements."[8]

This brings us to the second aspect of the approach chosen by Lemche and others, that is, the hierarchy of sources implicit in their statements. If the claims about historical events and developments found in a biblical text cannot be corroborated by external evidence—and as we have seen, that means, on Lemche's terms, by non-biblical evidence— any reconstruction of the history which that text purports to narrate cannot but fail—indeed, it is "pure guess-work" and an "intellectual pastime." Thus, Lemche in fact claims that biblical texts are, by definition, secondary sources. In P. R. Davies' *In Search of 'Ancient Israel,'* we find the same underlying assumption when we read the following passage about scholarly works on the Babylonian Exile:

> Biblical scholarship, true to the procedure which characterizes it, has taken the biblical 'exile' as an historical description, preservation and all, and then developed its own historical construct, a period during which many prophetic books were redacted, the Deuteronomistic history was edited, the Priestly writings encoded, the poems of 'Second Isaiah' composed, and often much else. Of this period we *actually* know next to nothing. We have preserved for us a note of rations for Jehoiachin of Judah, we have the Murashu archives, showing (perhaps) many prosperous Jews later running businesses in Babylonia. We know that centuries later there is a Babylonian Jewish community. But the idea that the authentic 'Israel' was preserved by deportees and replanted in Palestine several decades later by their grandchildren is a fairly suspicious piece of ideology on the part of the biblical writers and even more dubious speculation on the part of biblical scholars.[9]

---

8   Cf. N. P. Lemche, "Theologie," 83: "Was ohne 'external evidence' vorgestellt wird, ist nur Mutmaßung und intellektueller Zeitvertreib. Darum [!] datieren wir das Alte Testament spät."

9   P. R. Davies, *In Search of 'Ancient Israel'* (JSOTSup 148; Sheffield: JSOT Press, 1992), 40–41.

Let us have a closer look at two assumptions made by Davies. We shall then proceed to show what his assumptions teach us about the state of the current debate.

The first of Davies's assumptions is: we know next to nothing about the period called the "exile" because we have very little non-biblical evidence. What this means is that only non-biblical sources are reliable sources.

Davies's second assumption is that the concept of the "authentic 'Israel' [that] was preserved by deportees and replanted in Palestine several decades later by their grandchildren is a fairly suspicious piece of ideology." Therefore, it is of no use to a scholar trying to come up with a historical reconstruction of the period in question.

Let us start with the first assumption. First, there is *no reason to assume* right from the start that the textual sources found in the Hebrew Bible are any less reliable than the textual sources we have inherited from other ancient Near Eastern cultures. Also, no other discipline in the humanities sets out with the assumption that its main corpus of inherited texts is by definition historically less valuable than all other extant sources. Second, there is *no reason to assume* that textual sources are by definition less helpful in the process of historical reconstruction than archaeological artefacts. Indeed, it is important to realize—and I shall discuss this in the fourth part of this paper—that the biblical texts with which we work are, in a precise, meaningful sense, artefacts. I am not making this statement in a metaphorical manner, as I shall demonstrate soon.

I would like to move on to Davies's second assumption. In a manner similar to my answers to the first one, let me start by pointing out that there is *no prima facie reason to assume* that the concept of an "authentic 'Israel' . . . preserved by deportees and replanted in Palestine several decades later . . . is a fairly suspicious piece of ideology." If it is—which might well be the case—there is *no reason to assume* that it is any more or any less "ideological" than comparable texts generated by other ancient Near Eastern cultures. As any Assyriologist or classicist will happily admit, the texts they deal with on a daily basis are full of ideological concepts of types similar to the ones we find expressed in the Deuteronomistic History, Ezra-Nehemiah, Chronicles, or other such texts. The point is not that they are "ideological" but how we deal with them as historians. Also, let me note in passing that Davies uses the term "ideology" in a pejorative manner, whereas it is normally used—quite simply, technically, and precisely—to refer to systems of thought, belief, or doctrine, and so on, that are operative in a given cultural and social context. I wonder what lies behind Davies's use of the term in the passage I quoted. It is strangely reminiscent of the use conservative and fundamentalist circles tend to make of it: theology = good; ideology = bad.

Views similar to those of Davies have been put forward by, among others, H. Niehr. Niehr, one of the rather few German "minimalists," classifies the evidence along the lines of primary and secondary sources, but has a non-traditional view of the relative merits of texts and archaeological finds. He follows Knauf's definition, classifying as primary sources those "that were produced in the course of the events as they were happening," and as secondary sources those "that were produced after the events in an attempt to clarify for future generations how things were thought to have happened."[10] He then says:

> Wendet man diese Grundsatzunterscheidung auf das Arbeiten mit alttestamentlichen Texten an, so muß man sehen, daß das AT für die Geschichte und Religionsgeschichte Israels und Judas der vorexilischen Zeit nur ‚secondary evidence‘ liefert. ‚Primary evidence‘ für die Geschichte Israels und Judas liegt hingegen vor mit aller Art von archäologisch erhaltenem Material (Gebäude, Kunstobjekte, Tontafeln, Ostraka, Papyri, Siegel und Bullen etc.).[11]

This kind of classification simply reverses the traditional way of applying the distinction between primary and secondary sources, of which more below.[12]

Let me summarize: the assumption shared by Davies, Lemche, Thompson, and Niehr is that the biblical textual sources are by definition secondary, if not tertiary, sources. Another shared assumption is that non-biblical, and especially non-textual, sources are, by definition, more reliable with regard to the task of historical reconstruction. If attempts at historical reconstructions of events and developments narrated in the Hebrew Bible cannot be corroborated by external—i.e., non-biblical—evidence (preferably of an archaeological nature), then such attempts are, according to Lemche, "assumptions" and "intellectual pastimes." He wants "facts." So does Davies. He does not say so explicitly, but the dichotomies he constructs—like that between "ideology" and something else—betray the same desire finally to arrive, in a manner of speaking, at a bedrock of truth. The underlying concept of

---

10 Cf. H. Niehr, "Die Reform des Joschija: Methodische, historische und religionswissenschaftliche Aspekte," in *Jeremia und die 'deuteronomistische Bewegung'* (ed. W. Groß; BBB 98; Weinheim: Beltz Athenäum, 1995), 33–57 (34), taking up E. A. Knauf, "From History to Interpretation," in *The Fabric of History: Text, Artifact and Israel's Past* (ed. D. Edelman; JSOTSup 127; Sheffield: JSOT Press, 1991), 26–64 (46).

11 H. Niehr, "Die Reform," 34.

12 Cf. the section below on "Methodology: Texts and Material Remains."

"historical reliability" is something they share with conservatives and fundamentalists.[13]

It is interesting to see that, in that sense, Lemche, Thompson, Davies, and their fellow-combatants are not postmodern at all, as some have claimed, but intensely "high modern" — in the manner of the first half of the nineteenth century, emulating Ranke (not very successfully, though), to be precise. Why? Because of their concept of "facts." But what is a (historical) "fact?" It is remarkable that none of the writers mentioned explores this foundational problem.[14]

Contrary to such rather naïve twenty-first century statements about facts, we find, in some of the best nineteenth century historians, a much richer and more adequate understanding of the problem arising from the concept of "facts." It was J. G. Droysen who wrote in 1857 (!),

> daß nicht die Vergangenheiten, nicht das unabsehbare Durcheinander von ‚Tatsachen', das sie erfüllte, uns als Material der Forschung vorliegen, daß diese Tatsachen vielmehr mit dem Moment, dem sie angehörten, für immer vergangen sind, daß wir menschlicherweise ja nur die Gegenwart, das Hier und Jetzt haben.[15]

Droysen turns against the "eunuchian objectivity"[16] of Ranke's type of historicism and "emphasizes the contextual character of all knowledge, and the transcendental conditions of the constitution of all historical knowledge."[17] Droysen's *Historik* marks a new departure in the development of historicism; many of the problems to which he draws attention, and the new problems and questions to which his work gave rise, are still unsolved.[18] And those who demand, like Lemche, "facts" instead of "figures of speech" and "proof" instead of "conjectures and groundless theories," have not engaged with the problems which were identified very clearly by Droysen and others — like Rickert and

---

13 Cf. K. A. Kitchen, *On the Reliability of the Old Testament* (Grand Rapids, Mich.: Eerdmans, 2003).

14 This is unfortunately also true of the most systematic refutation of the "minimalist" position which has been published so far: J. B. Kofoed, *Text and History: Historiography and the Study of the Biblical Text* (Winona Lake, Ind.: Eisenbrauns, 2005).

15 Cf. J. G. Droysen, *Historik: Rekonstruktion der ersten vollständigen Fassung der Vorlesungen (1857); Grundriß der Historik in der ersten handschriftlichen (1857/1858) und in der letzten gedruckten Fassung; Textausgabe von Peter Leyh* (Stuttgart-Bad Cannstatt: Frommann-Holzboog, 1977), 457–58.

16 Cf. Droysen, *Historik*, 236. The passage is quoted by Escudier, "From Chladenius to Droysen," 479.

17 Escudier, "From Chladenius to Droysen," 479–80. The term "transcendental" is of course used in the Kantian sense.

18 On the effects of historicism on theology, cf. M. Murrmann-Kahl, *Entzauberte Heilsgeschichte: Der Historismus erobert die Theologie 1880–1920* (Gütersloh: Gütersloher Verlagshaus Gerd Mohn, 1992).

Weber[19]—who, in the nineteenth and early twentieth centuries, were under the influence of Kantian epistemology. They arrived at the central epistemological insights that help us to establish a sufficient degree of objectivity in historical research, insights that neither the "minimalists" nor the "maximalists" seem to be aware of.[20]

III. "Ancient History" and the "History of Ancient Israel"

What could be the consequences for current work on ancient Israelite history? In order to find that out let us first have a look at the way scholars in disciplines cognate to Old Testament Studies go about their business. Ancient History is particularly interesting in this regard. Hornblower writes that,

> though there are fairy-tale elements in Herodotus, particularly the early stretches, it is not likely, nor has it been demonstrated, that Herodotus is merely an ingenious teller of lies and fairy-tales—a view which surely makes too little allowance for the difficulty of using oral tradition. There is another objection. We sell the pass too cheaply if we allow that literary or other rather rhetorical stylization of presentation are somehow incompatible with truthful reporting.[21]

Ancient historians tend, on the whole, to be considerably more balanced in their views of the significance and reliability of ancient sources. I have just provided a practical example, so to speak, from the ancient historian's workshop. If we look at what ancient historians have to say about this from a more theoretical perspective, it is helpful to consult Finley's works, since he probably was, amongst those dominating the debate in the latter half of the twentieth century, the one who was most acutely aware of the methodological problems involved in the critical reconstruction of events and processes in ancient history.

Finley states that ancient historians have always been unusual, compared to other historians, because of their being

---

19   Cf. H. Rickert, *Kulturwissenschaft und Naturwissenschaft* (6th and 7th ed.; Tübingen: Mohr Siebeck, 1926); M. Weber, "Die 'Objektivität' sozialwissenschaftlicher und sozialpolitischer Erkenntnis," in idem, *Gesammelte Aufsätze zur Wissenschaftslehre* (7th ed.; ed. J. Winckelmann; Tübingen: Mohr Siebeck, 1988), 146–214.

20   For a detailed discussion of new ways of writing the history of ancient Israel based on the insights of the neo-Kantian tradition and in the context of *historische Kulturwissenschaften*, cf. J. Schaper, "Auf der Suche nach dem alten Israel? Text, Artefakt und »Geschichte Israels« in der alttestamentlichen Wissenschaft vor dem Hintergrund der Methodendiskussion in den Historischen Kulturwissenschaften," *ZAW* 118 (2006): 1–21, 181–96.

21   S. Hornblower, "Introduction," in Greek Historiography (ed. S. Hornblower; Oxford: Clarendon, 1994), 1–72 (18).

not in the first instance historians but men trained in language and literature who call themselves classicists (or Hellenists) and classical philologists, epigraphists and papyrologists. . . . [F]or many classicists, history is
in effect another discipline.[22]

Similarly, historians of ancient Israel have virtually without exception
been philologists: that is really what Old Testament scholars raised in
the context of Western academe effectively are. Finley's work is a good
example of what we need in Old Testament Studies. Just as he
strengthened the interaction between classical philologists/ancient historians and the mainstream of the study of history, present-day Old
Testament/Hebrew Bible scholarship needs to re-establish contact with
that mainstream. Finley's situation in his own subject was strangely
similar to that of Old Testament scholars who try to address the problems posed by writing the history of ancient Israel. The remedies he
offers could help us, too, and we shall discuss some of them in the next
section. Suffice it for the moment to say that Finley's position in the
discipline of Ancient History has been summed up rather well by
Elizabeth A. Clark, who rightly states that

> Finley faulted classicists' ignorance of larger debates occurring within the
> historical profession. They naively accept the explanations proffered by
> ancient writers, he charged, instead of posing questions that the texts
> themselves do *not* ask, exploring that which past societies *fail* to divulge.
> Such procedures, Finley proposed, would generate new hypotheses and
> explanatory models for the field.[23]

What we can conclude from all of the above is that, indeed, biblical
scholarship, if it is "true to the procedure which characterizes it," to use
Davies's words, is true not to a procedure that characterizes *it alone*, but
to one that characterizes *a number of other disciplines* as well, disciplines
which deal with textual and archaeological evidence. Actually, this is
not very surprising, since the said procedures were developed concur-
rently, in the eighteenth and nineteenth centuries, by a number of historical disciplines, often in close cooperation with each other: Classics,
Ancient History, Biblical Studies—many of them informed by the
evolving study of hermeneutics, as exemplified in Schleiermacher's
famous treatise which established a common ground for all of the
above-mentioned areas of study.[24] The point is, however, that it is time

---

22 M. I. Finley, *The Use and Abuse of History* (London: Chatto & Windus, 1975), 71–72.

23 E. A. Clark, *History, Theory, Text: Historians and the Linguistic Turn* (Cambridge,
Mass.: Harvard University Press, 2004), 166.

24 F. Schleiermacher, *Hermeneutik und Kritik: Mit besonderer Beziehung auf das Neue Testament, aus Schleiermachers handschriftlichem Nachlasse und nachgeschriebenen Vorlesungen herausgegeben von Friedrich Lücke* (Berlin: Reimer, 1838). The *Kritische Gesamtaus-
gabe* does not yet include this work.

for scholars exploring the history of ancient Israel systematically to review their hermeneutics of history and their methodology. While ancient history has made some progress towards a more self-reflective approach to the source-material, Old Testament Studies are still lagging behind. The reason for this is, in my view, that the parallels between the problems faced by historians of ancient Israel and those encountered by historians of Greece or Rome are commonly ignored. Even the most recent publications[25] do not address the remarkable parallels between the situation of historians of ancient Israel, who are in fact Old Testament scholars and/or Hebraists and/or Semitists, and that of ancient historians, who are really classical philologists. Addressing this issue systematically and using the resulting observations as tools for the task of reviewing the way in which we reconstruct the history of ancient Israel would be immensely helpful.

IV. Methodology: Texts and Material Remains

The preliminary exploration of the notion of facts and of a presumed hierarchy of sources which I have presented and which has, I think, made obvious the need for a hermeneutical and methodological review brings me to a very important point. That point was made by C. Hardmeier and the present author in recent publications concerning the relation between textual and archaeological sources.[26] That archaeologists and textual scholars are indeed confronted with what is structurally the same problem becomes obvious from the area where we have an overlap, so to speak, between archaeology and exegesis, that is, in epigraphy.

The same observation has been made by an archaeologist, who sums it up as follows:

> Both texts and artifacts symbolically represent a particular perception of reality; both are "encoded messages" that must be decoded, using rational,

---

25 Cf., for instance, L. L. Grabbe, *Ancient Israel: What Do We Know and How Do We Know It?* (London: T&T Clark, 2007). On "historiography" in *antiquity*, cf. The *Past in the Past: Concepts of Past Reality in Ancient Near Eastern and Early Greek Thought* (ed. H. M. Barstad and P. Briant; Oslo: The Institute for Comparative Research in Human Culture/Novus, 2009).

26 Cf. C. Hardmeier, "Zur Quellenevidenz biblischer Texte und archäologischer Befunde: Falsche Fronten und ein neues Gespräch zwischen alttestamentlicher Literaturwissenschaft und Archäologie," in *Steine—Bilder—Texte: Historische Evidenz außerbiblischer und biblischer Quellen* (ed. C. Hardmeier; Arbeiten zur Bibel und ihrer Geschichte 5; Leipzig: Evangelische Verlagsanstalt, 2001), 11–24, and J. Schaper, "Auf der Suche nach dem Alten Israel?"

critical methods as well as empathy; both remain somewhat enigmatic, however skillful and persistent the attempts to penetrate their full meaning. Finally, I would argue simply that both objects and texts are artifacts, that is, thought and action frozen in the form of matter, the "material correlates of human behavior." Even the Bible is an artifact, in this case what I have called a "curated artifact," or an item that originally functioned in one social context but has subsequently been reused in other ways and settings.[27]

Textual scholars are thus in a position that can be compared to that of archaeologists, and *vice versa*. However, with regard to their methodology textual scholars are prone to a temptation which archaeologists cannot fall victim to in quite the same way, that is, the temptation of going straight to what is perceived as "the content" of a given text. Instead of following the "irreversible linearity of the recorded text" and trying to understand the "correlation between text surface and narrative function(s),"[28] exegetes are all too often tempted to go straight for what they perceive as the "content" and the "message" of the text. Exegetes are prone to this particular kind of mistake because the primary material objects carrying their texts have disappeared, whereas, in the case of archaeology, they are present, and their materiality cannot be ignored.

What is called for, therefore, is not a facile sarcasm with regard to the endeavour of scholars employing established historical-critical methods, but a continuous refinement of those methods. As Hardmeier puts it in a paper on methodology,

> important impulses in this central field are to be expected above all from linguistic research efforts which illuminate generalizable correlations between the surface structure (*Oberflächengestalt*) of narrative texts and the narrative strategies and structuring devices (*Gestaltungsmittel*) that are effective in the process of text production and that the narrator employs in realizing a specific communicative effecting purpose (*Wirkabsicht*). Such research efforts move objectively in the framework of a text concept which defines surface texts in the sense of a language sign sequence as components or action substrata of communicative actions respectively.[29]

---

27 W. G. Dever, *What Did the Biblical Writers Know and When Did They Know it? What Archaeology Can Tell us about the Reality of Ancient Israel* (Grand Rapids, Mich.: Eerdmans, 2001), 71. Cf. idem, "The Silence of the Text: An Archaeological Commentary on 2 Kings 23," in *Scripture and Other Artifacts: Essays on the Bible and Archaeology in Honor of Philip J. King* (ed. M. D. Coogan, J. C. Exum, and L. E. Stager; Louisville, Ky.: Westminster John Knox, 1994), 143–68 (144–46).

28 C. Hardmeier, "Old Testament Exegesis and Linguistic Narrative Research," in idem, *Erzähldiskurs und Redepragmatik im Alten Testament: Unterwegs zu einer performativen Theologie der Bibel* (FAT 46; Tübingen: Mohr Siebeck, 2005), 57–76 (60).

29 Hardmeier, "Old Testament Exegesis," 60.

One might say: what is called for is, in the precise sense of the term, an "archaeology" of the texts and their production.[30]

At the deepest level, it is therefore not possible to uphold the methodological barrier between textual sources and material remains since the textual sources themselves are artefacts in need of interpretation, like any archaeological remains, and, conversely, the use of archaeological remains for historical reconstruction is in need of a hermeneutics, just as texts are.[31]

Finley, when he was considering the respective characteristics of history and archaeology, made the following statement about the relation between archaeology and history:

> At issue are not two qualitatively distinct disciplines but two kinds of evidence about the past, two kinds of historical evidence. There can thus be no question of the priority in general or of the superiority of one type of evidence over the other; it all depends in each case on the evidence available and on the particular questions to be answered.[32]

It will by now have become obvious that Finley was right when he said that. Indeed, textual scholars and archaeologists have much to learn from each other, and maybe the exegetes can, at the moment at least, learn more from the archaeologists than *vice versa*.

---

30 This view was, of course, first propagated by the members of the group *Archäologie der literarischen Kommunikation*, whose work resulted in a number of inspiring volumes on the methodology of literary and related studies.

31 The growing awareness of the need for such a hermeneutics becomes obvious from the fact that the practice of archaeology and its (conscious and unconscious) presuppositions have in recent years been scrutinised in considerable detail; cf., to name just two major examples, I. Hodder and S. Hutson, *Reading the Past: Current Approaches to Interpretation in Archaeology* (3d ed.; Cambridge: Cambridge University Press, 2003) and B. G. Trigger, *A History of Archaeological Thought* (2d ed.; Cambridge: Cambridge University Press, 2006).

32 M. I. Finley, *Ancient History: Evidence and Models* (London: Chatto & Windus, 1985), 20. Cf., with regard to biblical interpretation, G. I. Davies, "An Archaeological Commentary on Ezekiel 13," in Coogan, Exum and Stager, *Scripture and Other Artifacts*, 108–109, where Davies says about the "modern archaeological commentary" that "its aim is still 'to explain' and 'to make clear in plain language what has been written obscurely.' It is not, primarily at least, to prove (or disprove) the historicity of the Bible. As such, to speak of an archaeological commentary corresponds well with the aim of those biblical scholars who continue to see the findings of archaeology and Near Eastern studies as having an important contribution to make to the understanding of the Bible alongside such disciplines as linguistic study, text-critical research, literary criticism in its varied senses, and theological reflection. An archaeological commentary in this sense will certainly not see itself as a rival to other kinds of commentary, but it will seek to identify those features in the biblical text (especially obscure ones) for which archaeological evidence can offer some clarification." Although, unlike Finley, Davies assumes (at least) a (*de facto*) priority of the text, he seems to be as opposed as Finley is to the notion of "the priority in general or of the superiority of one type of evidence over the other."

There are, indeed, questions we ask the sources which require attention to both archaeological and non-archaeological source materials in such a way as to make them both indispensable. Finley describes that kind of situation when he states that "[t]here are contexts in which the two types of evidence have to be deployed together so closely that in a sense neither is of much use without the other."[33] It follows from this that the notion of a hierarchy of sources is erroneous. True, it is a notion that has a long and dignified history in the practice of history-writing, but it is nevertheless ultimately misleading.

Let us explore why. Historians have been differentiating between primary, secondary, and other sources since the very first beginnings of modern European history-writing in the seventeenth century. It is in that tradition that literary sources are often classified as primary sources, whereas archaeological ones are seen as secondary. Here again Moses Finley's analysis is helpful. He describes two traditional scholarly attitudes which, by the way, ancient historians characteristically have in common with Old Testament scholars working on the history of ancient Israel:

> The first is that statements in the literary or documentary sources are to be accepted unless they can be disproved (to the satisfaction of the individual historian). This proposition derives from the privileged position of Greek and Latin, and it is especially unacceptable for the early periods of both Greek and Roman history, where the archaeological evidence bulks so large (and daily grows proportionally still larger) and where the quantitatively far from inconsiderable literary tradition is particularly suspect. The second proposition is that the most insistent historical question one can put to an archaeological find is, Does it support or falsify the literary tradition? That approach gives automatic priority to literary evidence, and, in the history of early Rome, for example, has led to optimistic claims of archaeological support for the literary tradition, resting on highly selective tests.[34]

However, as we have seen, the distinction itself is misleading and should indeed be abolished. Rather, the evidence must be weighed anew in every single case. No kind of artefact, textual or non-textual, must be privileged over the other.

This works both ways, of course. *Both* the conservative "Biblical History of Israel"-type of approach promoted by Provan, Long, and Longman[35] *and* the Copenhagen variety of the "hermeneutics of suspicion" fail to take this insight on board.

---

33 Finley, *Ancient History*, 20.
34 Finley, *Ancient History*, 21.
35 Cf. I. Provan, V. Philips Long, and T. Longman III, *A Biblical History of Israel* (Louisville, Ky.: Westminster John Knox, 2003).

Conclusion

What does all of the above mean with regard to future work on the history of ancient Israel and Judah? We have looked at three of the problems involved: the concept of "fact," the relation between facts and sources, and the hierarchy of sources.

Future studies of methodology and future attempts at writing histories of ancient Israel should take into account that, as we saw earlier, "[t]he facts speak only when the historian calls on them: it is he who decides to which facts to give the floor, and in what order or context."[36] But what is the criterion that determines whether or not the historian's decisions are sound? We can find that criterion if we develop further Weber's insight in his essay on the "objectivity" of understanding and enquiry in the social sciences. He states in that essay that it is not the supposedly "factual" relations between so-called "things," but the "noetic relations between problems which form the basis for the fields of scientific research."[37] In the same manner, it is the historian who establishes the so-called "facts." The test these facts have to undergo is whether they make sense in the context of the overall construct established by the historian's work. It is here that Hardmeier's *lock and key* test comes in: if "facts" relating to the same problem have been established independently of each other in different areas of research and tie in with each other—that is, if they fit like a key into its lock—then these "facts" can be assumed to be "true" because they provide the basis for a coherent, non-contradictory explanation of the evidence.[38]

What the considerations which I have presented here show with great clarity, I hope, is that the impasse in the current debate can only be resolved by tackling the problem at the most fundamental level, that is, epistemologically. The nature of the writing of history has to be understood by all participants in the debate. It is the Kantian tradition that provides us with the key to understanding the nature of the enterprise of historiography. In Carr's *What is History?*, Kant and Droysen are not even mentioned. In the notes Carr wrote in preparation for a second edition—which never saw the light of day because Carr died before he could finish it—Kant plays a much greater role. Carr made a note of the following passage from the *Critique of Pure Reason*:

---

36 Carr, *What is History?*, 11.
37 Cf. Weber, "Die 'Objektivität,'" 166: "Nicht die 'sachlichen' Zusammenhänge der 'Dinge,' sondern die gedanklichen Zusammenhänge der Probleme liegen den Arbeitsgebieten der Wissenschaften zugrunde."
38 Cf. Hardmeier, "Quellenevidenz," 22–23.

Not until we have for a long time unsystematically collected observations to serve as building materials, following the guidance of an idea concealed in our mind, and indeed only after we have spent much time in the technical disposition of these materials, do we first become capable of viewing the idea in a clearer light, and of outlining it architectonically as a whole.[39]

This is how the historian works. The truth of this statement should be taken seriously by all those participating in the debate, and especially by the "minimalists" and the "maximalists" — both sides are not *radical* enough to do justice to the evidence.

It is my great pleasure to be able to contribute my thoughts on the matter to the Festschrift for Graham Davies and dedicate them to him on the occasion of his retirement from office, thus expressing my thanks to a great scholar and teacher to whom I am very grateful.

---

39 Quoted according to E. H. Carr's notes towards a second edition of *What is History?* The notes were published by R. W. Davies in an appendix entitled "From E. H. Carr's Files: Notes towards a Second Edition of What is History?" in E. H. Carr, *What is History?*, 157–83; the quotation from the *Critique of Pure Reason*, referred to as "Kant, Critique of Pure Reason (1781), p. 835" is on pp. 163–64.

The "Way of the Wilderness" on Sixteenth-Century Maps

JOHN R. BARTLETT

In 1979 Graham Davies published his study *The Way of the Wilderness*.[1] This study, based on a doctoral dissertation submitted to the University of Cambridge in 1975, is particularly concerned with the development of Jewish, Christian, and Arabic interpretation of the biblical "wilderness itineraries," and remains an indispensable resource for research into this area of Old Testament topography. This present article, in tribute to Graham Davies's work, explores the presentation of the wilderness itineraries in western cartography in the sixteenth century.

Davies examines the evidence from the Jewish Targums, the Midrashim, and Rashi, from Christian scholars like Eusebius and Jerome, and from medieval Arab geographers like Mukaddasi and Yakut. The story could be continued by examination of a mass of material, including the medieval *Mappae Mundi* tradition or the twelfth- and thirteenth-century descriptions of the Holy Land such as those of John of Wurzburg (ca. 1160), Theoderich (ca. 1171–1173), and Burchard (Brocardus) (ca. 1280), but for our purposes we shall begin with a late fifteenth-century picture-map drawn by Erhard Reuwich to illustrate Bernhard von Breitenbach's *Sanctarum peregrinationum in montem Syon . . . atque in montem Synai . . . opusculum* (1486).[2] Reuwich presents his map (map 1) as a panorama of the Holy Land, seen from the west, with Jerusalem in the middle, Damascus to the left (north), and Cairo to the right (south). Towards the right the viewer sees the head of the Gulf of Suez, with the Israelites' path across it ("via per quam filii Israelitorum sicco pede transiverunt mare rubrum") towards desertum Helym ("ubi xii fontes & lxx palmae," Exod 15:27), Mons Oreb ("ubi data fuit decaloga"), and Mons Synay ("sepulchrum Sanctae Katherinae").

1   G. I. Davies, *The Way of the Wilderness: A Geographical Study of the Wilderness Itineraries in the Old Testament* (SOTSMS 5; Cambridge: Cambridge University Press, 1979).

2   Bernhard von Breitenbach, *Sanctarum peregrinationum in montem Syon ad venerandum Christi sepulchrum in Jerusalem, atque in montem Synai ad divam virginem et matirem Katherinam opusculum* (Mainz: E. Reuwich, 1486). For a bibliography, see H. W. Davis, *Bernhard von Breydenbach and his Journey to the Holy Land, 1483–4: A Bibliography* (London: J&J Leighton, 1911).

Map 1. Section of E. Reuwich's map showing the Sinai peninsula and Red Sea,
from B. von Breitenbach's *Sanctarum peregrinationum . . . opusculum* (Mainz, 1486)
(Board of Trinity College, Dublin)

Reuwich does not illustrate the whole Israelite route across the wilderness, but locates certain places, for example, the water-bearing rock which Moses struck in the desert and the mountain on which Moses was buried. Of particular interest is that the eastern arm of the Red Sea can be seen reappearing northwards from behind Mount Sinai. Reuwich understood clearly the topographical relationship of Sinai to the two gulfs at the head of the Red Sea.

Sometime between 1522 and 1525,[3] Lukas Cranach published his map (map 2) of the Holy Land.[4] Cranach's map was used in 1525 in an edition including parts of Luther's translation of the Old Testament published by Christoph Froschauer of Zurich, and in 1526 in a Dutch Bible published by J. Liesveldt in Antwerp.[5] The main feature of Cranach's map, taking up the whole of the lower left foreground, is the route of the Israelites' march through the wilderness marked "Seir" and "Edom." Cranach constructs this map not from Numbers 33, as later map-makers do, but mostly from the story as recounted in the books of Exodus and Numbers, illustrating the more important events with small vignettes.[6] He begins with Sochot (Succoth, Exod 12:37), shows

---

3   Armin Kunz, "Cranach as Cartographer: The Rediscovered *Map of the Holy Land*," *Print Quarterly* 12 (1995): 123–44.

4   For the reconstruction of this map, see Kunz, "Cranach as Cartographer," 123–25.

5   C. Delano Smith, "Maps in Bibles in the Sixteenth Century," *The Map Collector* 39 (1987): 2–14 (4–5).

6   See Kunz, "Cranach as Cartographer," 132–34.

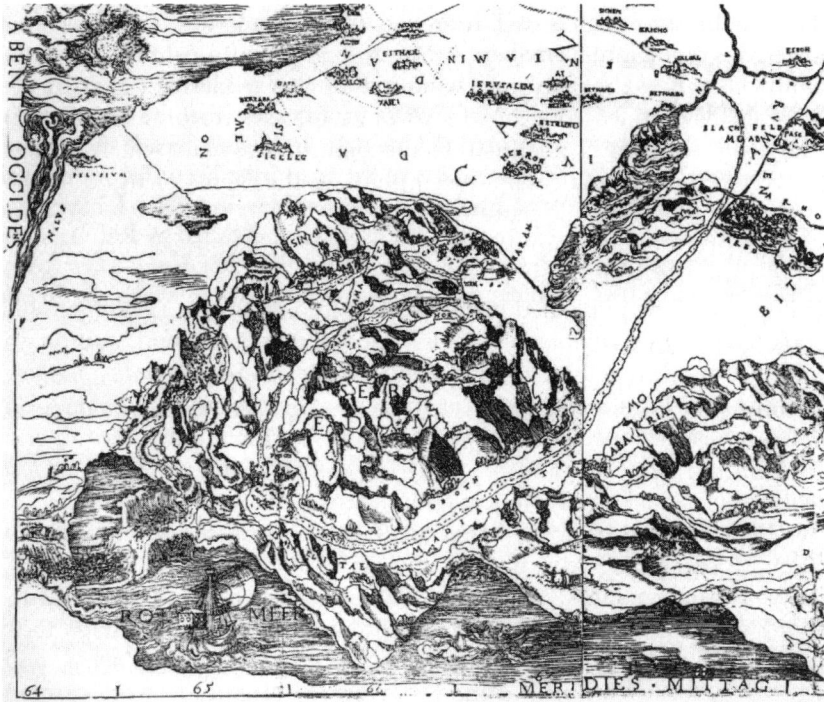

Map 2. L. Cranach the Elder, section of "Map of the Holy Land," ca. 1522–1525 (Kunz 1995)
(Armin Kunz and *Print Quarterly* 12 [1995], 124)

the Israelites crossing the Sea pursued by the Egyptian chariotry, and
then locates Ethan (Etham, Exod 13:20); Marath (Marah, Exod 15:23);
Elim (Exod 15:27); Sur (wilderness of Shur, Exod 15:22); Sin (wilderness
of Sin, Exod 16:1), with an illustration of the manna from heaven on the
ground; Rephedim (Rephidim, Exod 17:1), with an illustration of Moses
striking the rock; Sinai (Exod 19:1), with an illustration of Moses on top,
and the golden calf being worshipped below; Cades (Kadesh) Barnea
and the wilderness of Pharan (Paran, Num 13:26), with an illustration
of the result of Korah's rebellion (?); Zin (and Hebron, Num 13:21);
(Mount) Hor (Num 20:22); Salmona (Zalmonah, Num 33:41); Punon
(Num 33:42), with an illustration of the serpents from Num 21:6–9;
Oboth (Num 21:10; 33:43); Abarim (Iye-abarim, Num 21:11; 33:44); (the
river) Sared (Zered, Num 21:12); (the river) Arnon (Num 21:13); (the
river) Iaboc (Jabbok, Num 21:24); and the Blachfeld Moab (plains of
Moab, Num 22:1). Cranach also locates Mount Pisga (Pisgah,
Num 21:20) and the city of Ar (Num 21:28). This reconstruction of the
Israelite route through the wilderness, presented as a winding curve

through the mountains of Edom, set a precedent that would be followed by biblical map-makers through the sixteenth century. (Delano
Smith classifies Cranach's presentation of the wilderness route as a
"zigzag" as distinct from the "loop" of Ziegler, Mercator, and others.[7])
Cranach's concern is to illustrate the biblical story, to which he has
converted the Ptolemaic map; he emphasizes the events pictured by the
vignettes rather than the place-names.[8]

Perhaps the most important and scholarly sixteenth-century cartographer for the Holy Land was Jacob Ziegler (born ca. 1470, died in
1549). In 1532 he published his researches into biblical geography in his
book *Quae intus continentur.*[9] This appeared in a second edition in
1536,[10] bound together with *Terrae Sanctae altera descriptio, authore
Vuolffgango Vueissenburgio pridem Academiae Basiliensis Mathematico*, an
Index, totius operas locupletissimus, qui in priore editione desiderabatur, and
an *Elenchus, quo libro et capita Bibliorum et quoties singuli Palestinae loci
continentur*, which gives biblical references for Ziegler's place-names.

Ziegler notes[11] that for his sources he drew on the sacred history
from Moses to the Maccabees, from Hieronymus, Strabo, Josephus,
Pliny, Ptolemaeus, and Antoninus. He also used the accounts of Burchard of Mt Zion, and Bernard von Breitenbach. Ziegler's maps took
their form and orientation from Ptolemy's *Quarta Asiae Tabula*, and
were oriented with north at the top. Degrees of latitude were printed
on the left and right margins, and of longitude along the top and
bottom, of the maps. Ziegler's text gives coordinates for many of the
biblical place-names.

Ziegler uses the *mansiones* of Numbers 33 (see the table below) to
supply a large proportion of the toponyms for his section headed *Mar-
marica* (i.e., Egypt) (pp. lviiii–lxxv) and *Arabia Petraea* (pp. lxxvi–lxxxiv).

Num	Vulgate	Luther	Ziegler Text	Coordinates			Tabula
1	Ramesse	Raemses	Rahamesses (Arsenoitis)	63	30	5	Septima
2	Soccoth	Suchoth	Sucho	63	15	29 55	Septima

---

7   Delano Smith, "Maps in Bibles in the Sixteenth Century," 5.

8   E. M. Ingram, "Maps as Readers' Aids: Maps and Plans in the Geneva Bibles," *Imago
     Mundi* 45 (1993): 29–44 (30).

9   J. Ziegler, *Quae intus continentur: Syria ad Ptolomaici operis rationem . . . Palestina . . .
     Arabia Petraea . . . Aegyptus . . . Schondia . . . Holmiae . . . ; Regionum superiorum singulae
     tabulae geographicae* (Strassburg: Petrus Opilio, 1532).

10   J. Ziegler, *Terrae Sanctae, quam Palestinam nominant, Syriae, Arabiae, Aegypti et
     Schondiae doctissima descriptio* (Strassburg: Wendelin Rihel, 1536).

11   Ziegler, *Quae intus continentur*, xv.

Num	Vulgate	Luther	Ziegler Text	Coordinates	Tabula
3	Aetham	Etham	Ethan Deserti	-	Septima (Ethan)
3a	Phiahiroth	Hahiroth	Pichachiroth	62 50 29 40	Septima (Eicha-chiroth)
3b	Beelsephon	Baal Zephon	Bahal Sephon	63 25 29 45	Septima
4	Magdolum	Migdol	Magdolum	63 20 31 5	Septima
5	Mara	Marah	Marah castra	63 30 29 50	Septima (Marath)
6	Helim	Elim	Elim	63 45 29 50	Septima
7	Super mare rubrum	An das Schiff-meer	Campus super mare	66 10 29	Septima (= castra super mari)
8	Desertum Sin	In der Wüsten Sin		65 21 31 26	Septima (Sin)
9	Dephka	Daphka	Daphchah	64 14 29 46	Septima
10	Alus	Alus	Alus	64 30 29 46	Septima
11	Raphidim	Raphidim	Rephidim	64 44 29 46	Septima
12	Desertum Sinai	In der Wüsten Sinai	Sina	-	
13	Sepulchrum concupiscentiae	Die Lüstgraber	Chibroth Hat-tahavah	-	
14	Aseroth	Hazeroth	Chaseroth	64 50 30 14	Septima
15	Rethma	Rithma	Rithma	-	
16	Remmonphares	Rimon Parez	Rimmon peres	-	
17	Lebna	Libna	Libna	-	
18	Ressa	Rissa	Rissah	-	
19	Ceelatha	Kehalatha	Cheleloth	-	
20	Mons Sepher	In Gebirge Sapher	Sepher mons	64 56 30 50	Septima
21	Arada	Harada	Cheradah	-	
22	Maceloth	Mekehaloth	Macheloth	-	
23	Thaath	Tahath	Tachath	-	
24	Thare		Tarach	-	
25	Methca	Mithka	Mithchah	-	
26	Esmona	Hasmona	Casmonah	-	Septima (Hasmo-nah)
27	Moseroth		Moseroth	64 38 31 4	Septima
28	Baneiacan	Bne Jaakon	Beeroth Bene iahachon	64 50 31 18	Septima
29	Gadgad	Horgidgad	Ghidghad mons	64 30 30 50	Septima
30	Hietebatha	Jathbatha	Iothbathah	64 45 30 50	Septima
31	Ebrona	Abrona	Habronah	65 1	Septima
32	Asiongaber	Ezeongaber	Hesionghaber	65 10 31 6	Septima

Num	Vulgate	Luther	Ziegler Text	Coordinates	Tabula
33	Desertum Sin/Cades	In der Wüsten Sin das ist Kades	Sin / Cades [map, Chades] Barnea	65 20 31 16/ 65 22 31 29	Septima
34	Mons Hor	An den Berg Hor	Hor mons	65 30 31 12	Septima
35	Salmona	Zalmona	Salmonah	65 46 31 12	Septima (Salmonai)
36	Phinon	Phunon	Punon	66 6 31 12	Septima
37	Oboth	Oboth	Oboth	66 20 31 12	Septima
38	Ieabarim	Igim am Gebirge Abarim	Hijm [map, Hiim] hahabarim	66 32 31 18	Septima
39	Dibongad	Dibon Gad	Dibon Ghad	66 48 31 32	Septima
40	Elmondeblathaim	Almon Diblathaim	Halmon Diblathaimah	66 48 31 44	Septima
41	Montes Abarim contra Nebo	Gebirge Abarim gegen Nebo	Habarim mons	66 5 31 25 [p. liiii, 66 29 31 58]	Quarta
42	Campestria Moab	Die Gefilde der Moabiter	Campestria Moab [p. liiii]	-	

The area of the wilderness journey is covered mainly by Ziegler's *Tabula Septima* (map 3). Ziegler has plotted these names on his map in an orderly route. After crossing the sea, the Israelites head east across the Desert of Sin to Rephidim (no. 11), and then head north along the Amoreus mons until they reach Hasmonah (no. 26), from which they double back in a south-westerly loop to take in Beeroth Ben Iahachon, Moseroth, Ghidghad, Iothbathah, and Habrona, before proceeding to Hesionghaber, Sin, Chades Barnea, Hor Mons, Salmonai, Punon, Oboth, Hiim Hahabarim, Dibon Ghad, and Halmon Diblathaimah. At this point the route leaves Ziegler's *Tabula Septima*, and the next point on the route of Numbers 33 — Montes Abarim — appears on *Tabula Quarta*. The campestria Moab are not named on Ziegler's maps. Ziegler's *Tabula Septima* does include, however, a number of places visited by the Israelites on their wilderness march drawn from the other biblical narratives. Thus Ziegler's map shows also a rock at Choreh (Choreb) near Rephidim (Exod 17:6), Madian (Midian, Exod 18:1), Paran (Num 13:3; Deut 1:1), Chebron (Hebron, Num 13:22), Arath (Arad, Num 21:1), *igniti serpentes* (cf. fiery serpents, Num 21:6), Zered, torrens, vallis (valley of Zered, Num 21:12), Puteus (Beer Putens [*sic*] in Ziegler's text = well, cf. Num 21:17), Mattanah solitudo (Mattanah, Num 21:18), Nachaliel (Nahaliel, Num 21:19), Bamoth (Num 21:19), Vallis (the valley lying in the region of Moab, Num 21:20),

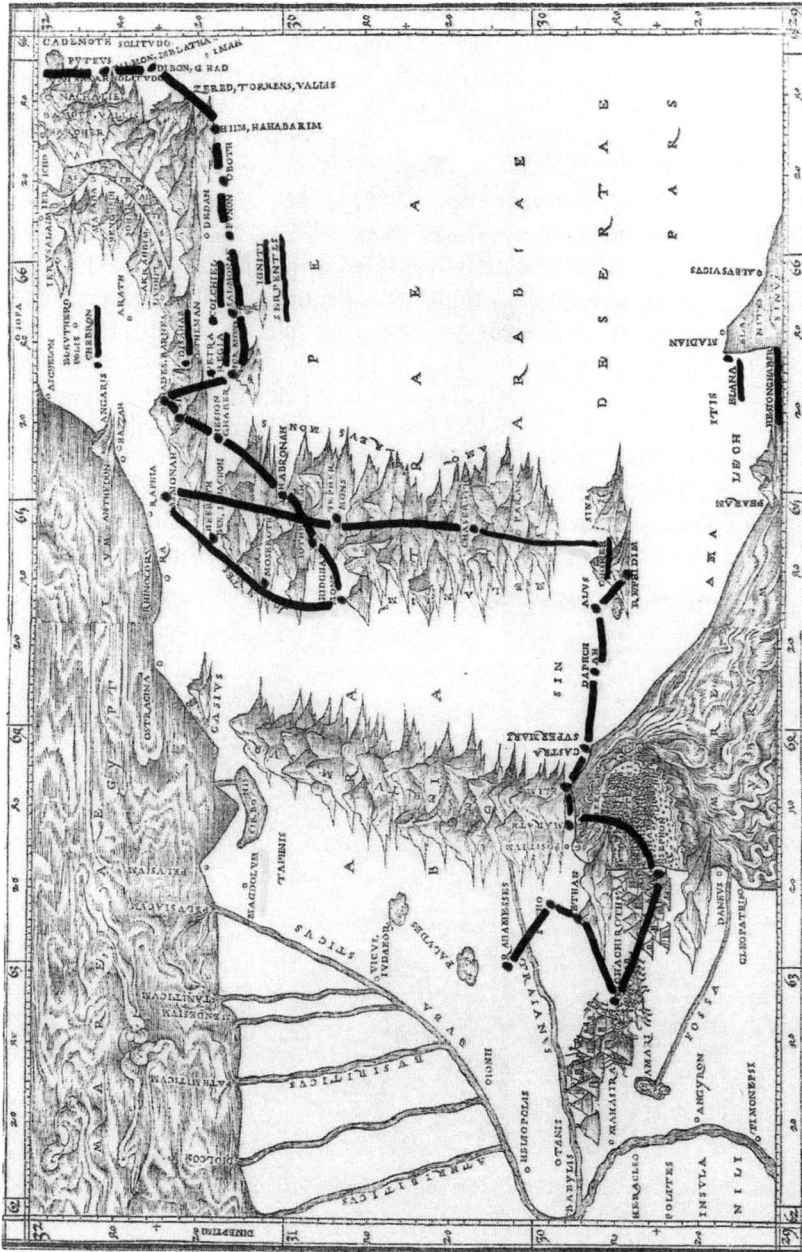

Map 3. J. Ziegler, "Tabula Septima," from *Quae intus continentur* (Strassburg, 1532) (Board of Trinity College, Dublin)

Hesion ghaber (Ezion-geber, Deut 2:8;Ziegler distinguished the Ezion-geber of Deut 2:8 from the place in Num 33:36, describing the former in his text as *portus*, cf. 1 Kgs 9:26 [p. 76], and giving the two places different coordinates), Disahab (Di-zahab, Deut 1:1), Cademoth solitudo (wilderness of Kedemoth, Deut 2:26), Haroher (Aroer, Deut 2:36); Ziegler's text (p. liiii) says "quae est iuxta ripam torrentis Arnon"; *Tabulae* 3, 4, 5, and 7 show a town in the *middle* of the Arnon, probably illustrating the following words of Ziegler's text, "& civitas quae est in medio vallis." Ziegler includes also Dedan (cf. Jer 25:23; Ezek 27:20), Luchit (Luhith, Isa 15:5), Albus vicus (from Strabo), Colchiel ("metallum, procul xi m. a Catachrysea sive Disahab," p. lxxxiii), Elana villa (which Ziegler identifies in his text [p. lxxvi] with Haila, Elat), and Petra regia (Arabum), which Ziegler identifies in his text (p. lxxxi) as "dicta Sela & Arachen, a Chaldaeis Recem, ab Hebraeis Iaktheel."

In 1535 Miles Coverdale (1488–1569), like Luther an Augustinian monk, published in Antwerp[12] his English translation (based mainly on Luther's German translation and the Vulgate) of the Bible, with both Old and New Testaments and the Apocrypha. This edition contained a

Map 4. Miles Coverdale, section of "Descripcio Terrae Promissionis" from the Coverdale Bible, 1535, facsimile edition (Folkestone, 1975) (Board of Trinity College, Dublin)

---

12   David Daniell, *The Bible in English* (New Haven, Conn.: Yale University Press, 2003), 179.

map entitled *Descripcio Terrae Promissionis, quae alias Palestina, Canaan, vel terra Sancta nuncupatur.*[13] In spite of its title, however, the map (map 4) is strongly focused on the Exodus and Wilderness story. This map is oriented with the Montana Foelicis Arabiae on the top left and Libanus on the bottom left; the mouths of the Nile appear centre right. The map focuses on the Exodus and the Israelites' route through the wilderness. Though upside down to Ziegler's map, it has important features in common with it—for example, the direction lines extending to Rome, Venice, Babylon, Regensburg, and other places, the mouths of the Nile, and the curved shape of the Dead Sea. The map omits those names on the list of Numbers 33 for which Ziegler could give no coordinates. Coverdale's map prints the names of deserts and mountains in upper case, the remainder in lower case. The draughtsmanship, even if Hans Holbein the Younger was involved,[14] makes the Israelite route on Coverdale's map much harder to follow than Ziegler's, which is a model of clarity; but Coverdale's map, like Ziegler's, has the Israelites proceed roughly east from the Red Sea as far as Raphidim, where the Israelites turn north through the mountains until they reach Hasmona; from here they make a circle to the southwest via Mosseroth, Bne Iaekon, Gadgad, Iatbatha, Abrona, Ezeongeber, and Elath, until they reach Cades Barnea, very close to Hasmona, whence they turn east towards Phunon and Oboth and the region east of the Dead Sea. This south-westerly loop clearly follows Ziegler's locations for these sites, though correcting Ziegler's apparent sequence (on his map; see Ziegler's text, p. lxxx) in which Beeroth ben Iahachan precedes Moseroth in the presumed line of march (*contra* Num 33:31). There is no question of the Israelites' returning to touch the Red Sea at Ezeongeber and Elath, which are located almost at the very centre of the map.

In 1537 Girardus Mercator (1512–1594) published his map *Amplissima Terrae Sanctae Descriptio ad Utriusque Testamenti Intelligentiam* at Louvain (map 5). The map was printed from six engraved copperplate sheets; the six sheets pasted together formed a wall-chart 98.4 x 43.4 cm. The only known complete copy survives in the Biblioteca Comunale Augusta in Perugia [I.C.94 (3)] and was published in 1927 by

---

13   See Miles Coverdale, *Biblia: The Byble: That is, the Holy Scrypture of the Olde and New Testament, Faythfully Translated in to Englyshe* (Antwerp: M. de Keyser, 1535); facsimile, *The Coverdale Bible 1535, with an introduction by S. L. Greenslade* (Folkestone: Dawson, 1975), 12–13, 26; C. Delano-Smith and E. M. Ingram, *Maps in Bibles 1500–1600: An Illustrated Catalogue* (Geneva: Librairie Droz, 1991), 39 (figure 16), 40–41 (figure 18), 144.

14   Delano Smith, "Maps in Bibles in the Sixteenth Century," 6.

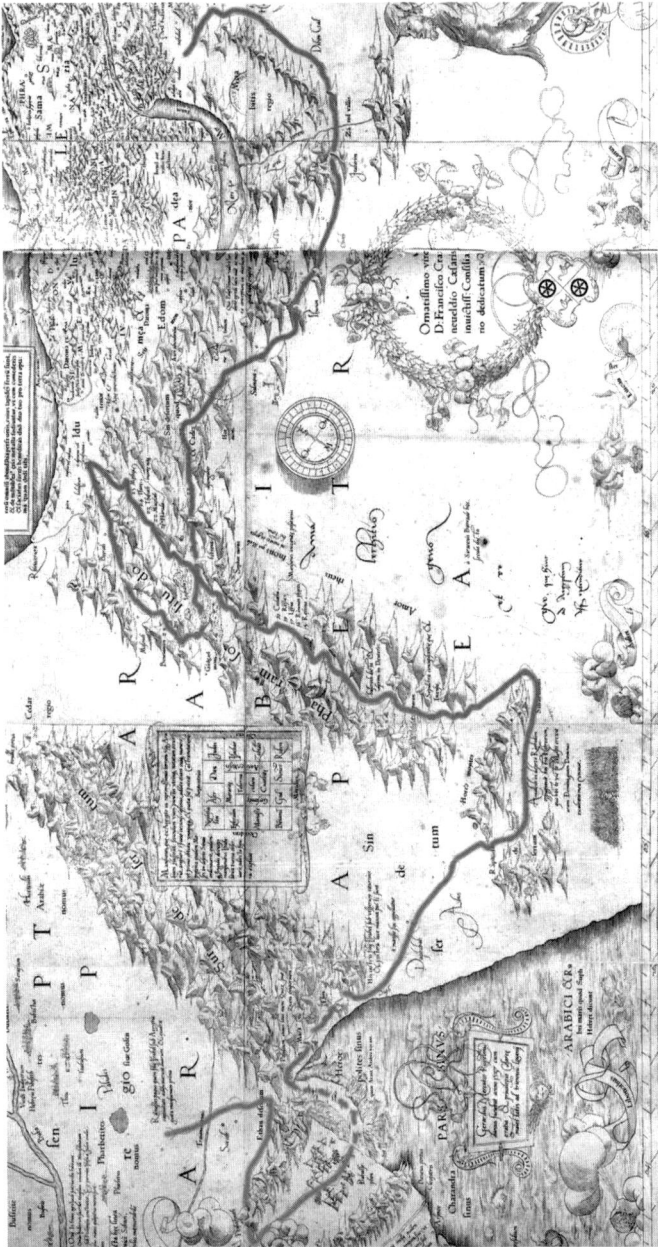

Map 5. G. Mercator, section of "Amplissima Terrae Sanctae Descriptio
ad Utriusque Testamenti Intelligentiam" (Louvain, 1537)
(Perugia, Biblioteca Comunale Augusta, I.C.94 [3])

R. Almagià.[15] In the early seventeenth century a new impression was made from the original plates by C. J. Visscher in Amsterdam.[16] Mercator presented the Holy Land from a viewpoint apparently high in the air to the south of Mt Sinai, looking north; the Mediterranean coast runs in a convex curve across the top of the map from the Nile delta on the left to Phoenicia on the right. In the centre foreground is the wilderness of Israel's wanderings. Mercator incorporates the list of Numbers 33, using Ziegler's coordinates for the *mansiones* as the basis for his own presentation of the way of the wilderness. Mercator is the first cartographer to number the *mansiones* on the map. Those places for which Ziegler gives no coordinates (Rithma, Remmon Phares, Lebna, Ressa, Ceelatha [nos. 15–19], Harada, Maceloth, Thahath, Thare, Methca [nos. 21–25]) are listed with the comment "mansiones incognitae positionis" (nos. 15–19) or "incertae notae" (nos. 21–25). Ziegler's location of *mansiones* nos. 27–30—Moseroth, Beneiaacan, Gadgad mons, Ietebatha—to the west resulted in Mercator's giving the Israelite route a westward loop (as Coverdale's map had), then circling back to cross the former line of march in an easterly direction towards the southern end of the Dead Sea; having rounded this, it turned north towards Moab. On this route Ziegler's Hesionghaber (= Mercator's Asiongaber, no. 30) is located between Hebrona (no. 31) and the desert of Sin and Cades (no. 33), in the middle of the wilderness. This had the advantage that Mercator's route did not have to double back south (as in most later maps) to Ezion-geber at its biblical location on the Gulf of ʿAqaba (cf. Deut 2:8; 1 Kgs 9:26). Ziegler solved this problem by presenting two Hesionghabers, one in the wilderness, and the other, identified as a *portus*, on the Gulf of ʿAqaba. In 1537 Mercator avoided the problem by leaving the Gulf of ʿAqaba off his map.

It is clear that in his preparation of the 1537 map Mercator was particularly interested in the route of the Israelites through the wilderness. He makes this clear in his address to the reader, presented in a cartouche on the lower right hand corner of the map:

> Candido lectori s[alus]. Palestinam hanc, & in eam per Arabicas petras ex Aegypto Hebreorum iter ex Zieglero fidissimo horum chorographo deprompsimus, nominibus illius ad veterem Bibliorum translationem, quantum potuim, variatis, quando huic ut usitatissime potius inserviendum videretur.

---

15   Roberto Almagià, *La carta della Palestina di Gerardo Mercatore (1537)* (Fondo Italiano per lo Studio della Palestina 1; Florence: Istituto Geografico Militare, 1927), 5–8.

16   Reproduced in K. Nebenzahl, *Maps of the Holy Land: Images of Terra Sancta through Two Millennia* (New York: Abbeville, 1986), 72–73; see also C. Delano Smith and E. M. Ingram, "La carte de la Palestine," in *Gerard Mercator cosmographe* (ed. M. Watelet; Antwerp: Fonds Mercator, 1994), part 4, 268–83.

> Fair reader, greeting! We have drawn this map of Palestine, and the Hebrews' route into it from Egypt through the stony regions of Arabia, from Ziegler, the most faithful cartographer of these things, his place-names being adjusted, as far as possible, to the old translation of the Bible, since this seemed most serviceable for our purpose.

Mercator states expressly that he has drawn his map of Palestine *and of the Israelites' route from Egypt.* He has placed the Israelites' route through the wilderness at the very centre of his six sheets, giving them maximum and indeed exaggerated space, making in consequence the land of Israel and Judah seem comparatively cramped. In this he is perhaps following the lead of Cranach, who also placed the wilderness route at the centre foreground of his map.[17] Mercator emphasizes his theme by including a number of vignettes—the Israelite camp round the Tabernacle in the desert (cf. Numbers 2), the battle of the Amale-kites and Israelites at Rephidim (Exodus 17), the serpent in the wilderness near Salmona (cf. Num 21:8)—and by setting quotations from Micah 6:3–4 ("I brought you up from the land of Egypt . . . ") and Deut 8:7–10 ("the Lord your God is bringing you into a good land . . . ") below the scene of Christ on the cross at the top centre of the map.

In 1538 Wolfgang Wissenburg (1496–1575) published a wall-map in 8 sheets, 105 x 74.5 cm, *Descriptio Palestinae Nova*, dedicated to the Archbishop of Canterbury, Thomas Cranmer, presumably in approval of Cranmer's reforming theology.[18] Wissenburg was a biblical scholar who had contributed a biblical gazetteer entitled *Terrae Sanctae Descrip-tio* to Ziegler's 1536 edition. Wissenburg's map (map 6), of which one copy survives in the Bibliothèque Nationale in Paris [GEDD 2987 (10.402)], is largely dependent on Ziegler's, presenting a similar coast-line, and incorporating a compass rose, and straight lines indicating distances from Rome and other important places. Wissenburg follows Numbers 33 for the route of the Israelites' march through the wilder-ness, listing and numbering the *mansiones* in sequence on a clearly defined zigzag path; he does not adopt the southwesterly loop on Mer-cator's 1537 map. Each halting place (*mansio*) is indicated by a tent encampment; between them Wissenburg shows a marching column of Israelites. Wissenburg inserts a number of vignettes illustrating the wilderness accounts: between Ethan and Pihachiroth Pharaoh's army; in the Red Sea the wreckage of Egyptian chariots; at Solitudo Sinai a plan of the Tabernacle; on top of Mt Horeb appears Moses, with horns ("faciem . . . cornutam," Exod 34:35, Vulg.), and on top of Sinai the

---

17 For this theme in sixteenth-century Bibles, see Delano-Smith and Ingram, *Maps in Bibles 1500–1600*, 25–52.

18 See Nebenzahl, *Maps of the Holy Land*, 74–75.

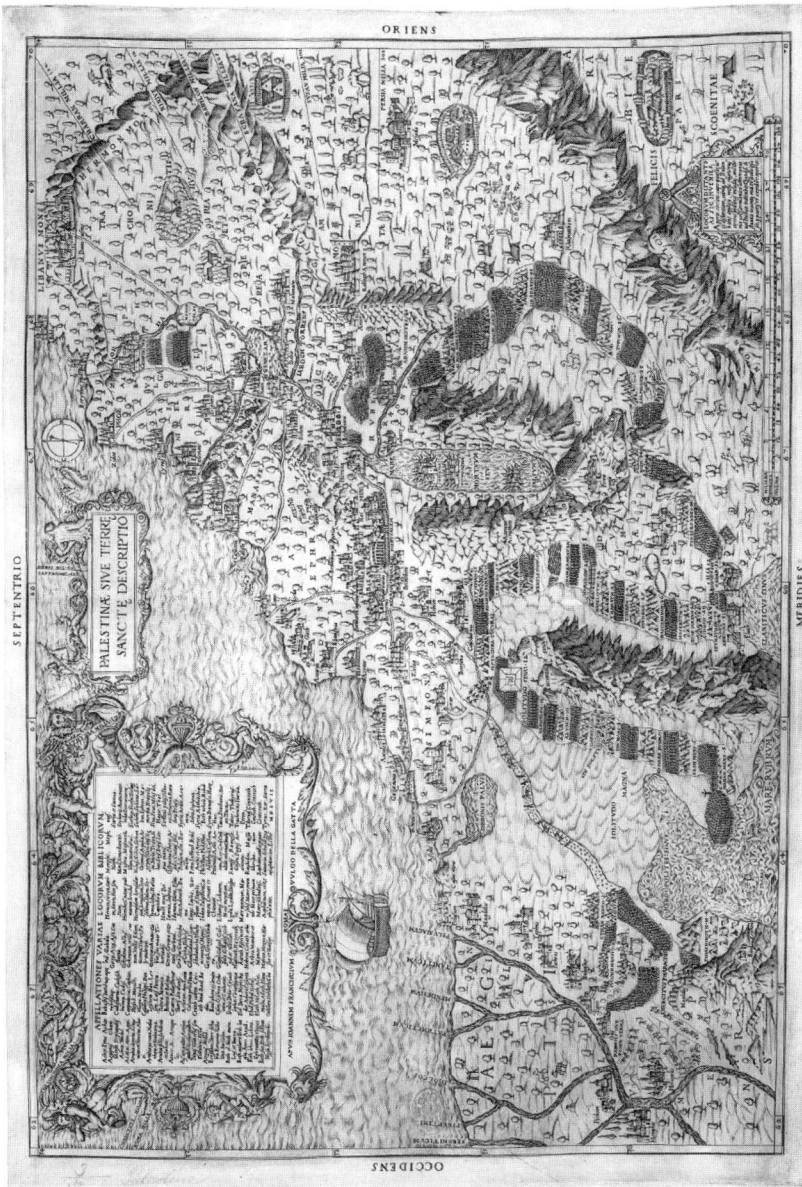

Map 6. G. F. della Gatta's reduced version (Rome, 1557) of W. Wissenburg, "Descriptio Palestinae Nova," 1538 (© The British Library Board, K.Top.3.50)

Lord; at Sepulchra Concupiscentiae the arrival of a flock of quails; near Sin quae Cades the grave of Miriam; near Salmonah the fiery serpents and the bronze serpent set on a pole. Like Cranach and Mercator, Wissenburg seems to focus the whole map on the route through the wilderness, which takes up the lower centre of the map, with Mount Sinai prominent in the middle. Unlike Ziegler and Mercator, however, Wissenburg locates the Ezion-geber of Num 33:35 alongside Elath at the head of the Elanitic Gulf of the Red Sea, and so has the Israelites, after crossing the Gulf of Suez, proceed north to march round Horeb/Sina, then turn south to Ezion-geber, and thence north-east round Moab towards the promised land across the Jordan near Jericho. Wissenburg thus accommodates the information from Deut 2:8, that the Israelites on their wilderness route visited Ezion-geber at the Red Sea. The route drawn by Wissenburg was to become in essence the route accepted by most cartographers. Mercator in his *Europae descriptio* of 1554 and *Europae descriptio emendata* of 1572 is influenced by it but does not take the Israelites as far south as the coast of the Red Sea.

However, in 1554 Mercator published a map of Europe (*Europae descriptio*) which included the Sinai peninsula and the Gulfs of Suez and ʿAqaba at its bottom right hand corner. A copy of this map survived at Breslau municipal library until 1945, but is now known only from a facsimile made in 1889, and from a later revised edition of it (*Europae descriptio emendata*) published in 1572.[19] A copy of this revised version exists at Perugia's Biblioteca Comunale Augusta [I.C.94 (2)]. This map (map 7) is on a much smaller scale than the 1537 map, and Mercator therefore does not include all the names of the Numbers 33 list, omitting those for which Ziegler gave no coordinates, together with Ethan desertum, Sin, Rephidim desertum, and sepulchra concupiscentiae. Mercator also sharply revised the route through the wilderness, removing the westward loop of Asemona, Moseroth, Beneiaacan, Gadgad mons, and Ietebatha, and steering the Israelites north to Asemona before making them turn sharply south past Beeroth to Moseroth, Gadgad mons, and Ietebatha, where they turn sharply north again to go past Hebrona, Asiongaber, Sin desertum, Hor mons and north to Moab. (On the southern tack from Asemona, Mercator, apparently following the sequence on Ziegler's map, has set Beeroth [located by Ziegler with Beneiaacan] before rather than after Moseroth in the list.) On this map, Mercator includes the Elanitic Gulf (Gulf of ʿAqaba), locating Elana at its northern end, and Hesiongaber south of Elana

---

19   For detailed references see A. Dürst, "The Map of Europe," in *The Mercator Atlas of Europe: Facsimile of the Maps by Gerardus Mercator Contained in the Atlas of Europe, circa 1570–1572* (ed. M. Watelet; Pleasant Hill, Oreg.: Walking Tree Press, 1998), 31–41.

Map 7. G. Mercator, section of "Europae descriptio emendata," 1572
(Perugia, Biblioteca Comunale Augusta, I.C.94 [2])

along the western coast of the Gulf, thus recognizing (as Ziegler does) another Hesiongaber; but he does not have the Israelites visit it. Thus Mercator still ignores the problem set by Deut 2:8.

Tilemann Stolz (in Latin, Tilemannus Stella) (1525–1589) was a student at Wittenberg, where he studied geography and mathematics. He published his first map of Palestine in 1552; the cartographer Ortelius reproduced a version of this in his *Parergon*, entitled *Typus chorographicus, celebrium locorum in regno Iudae et Israhel, arte factus a*

Tilemanno Stella Sigensi, in 1624.[20] In 1557 Stella published a second map, entitled *Itinera Israelitarum ex Aegypto loca et insignia miracula diversorum locorum et patefactionum divinarum descripta a Tilemanno Stella Sigenensi ut lectio librorum propheticorum sit illustrior* ("The journeys of the Israelites from Egypt, the places and famous miracles of different places and divine revelations described by Tilemann Stella of Siegen that the reading of the prophetic books might be made clearer"). This was a woodcut map, in nine sheets, of which only one copy is known to exist.[21] The same map was reprinted (complete with the 1557 date) on nine sheets by Bernard Puteanus in Antwerp in 1559.[22] Ortelius used this map in his *Theatrum Orbis Terrarum* (1570 and subsequently)[23] under the title *Palestinae sive totius Terrae Promissionis nova descriptio auctore Tilemanno Stella Sigenens.* (This was the immediate source for the English map of Canaan engraved by "Humfray Cole Goldsmith a English man born in ye north and pertaining to ye Mint in the Tower 1572."[24]) The 1570 map reappeared, printed from a recut plate, in the 1579 edition of Ortelius's *Theatrum* (a small cartouche above the main cartouche gives the date), and yet again printed from a newly engraved plate in Ortelius's *Parergon* (1624), with "Deut. 8" inscribed in the upper small cartouche, and the Latin text of Deut 8:7–9 in the larger cartouche below (map 8).

Like the earlier maps of Cranach, Coverdale, Mercator, and Wissenburg, Stella's map focuses on the wilderness journey of the Israelites. The direction of Stella's route follows Wissenburg's closely. Thus the trail leads from the coast of the Gulf of Suez north past Sinai, and then turns south back towards the coast of the Elanitic Gulf. However, there are differences. Wissenburg has the Israelites turn north after Marah, and start turning south again after Hazeroth. Stella has the Israelites turn north at Alusch, travel well past Mt Sinai, and turn south again at Hasmonah. Both Wissenburg and Stella locate Azion gaber just north of the northern end of the Sinus Elaniticus, close to Elana vel Elath. Stella's map, however, shows a second Asion gaber (as Wissen-

---

20   Abraham Ortelius, *Theatri Orbis Terrarum Parergon* (Antwerp: Balthasar Moretus, 1624).

21   R. W. Karrow, *Mapmakers of the Sixteenth Century and Their Maps* (Chicago: Speculum Orbis Press for the Newberry Library, 1993), 502.

22   Nebenzahl, *Maps of the Holy Land,* 76–77.

23   Abraham Ortelius, *Theatrum Orbis Terrarum* (Antwerp: Gielis Coppens van Diest, 1570).

24   P. Barber, "Humphrey Cole's Map of Palestine," in *Humphrey Cole: Mint, Measurement and Maps in Elizabethan England* (ed. S. Ackerman; London: British Museum Occasional Paper 126, 1998), 97–100; the quotation is from the cartouche on Cole's map, reproduced as figure 43 on p. 98.

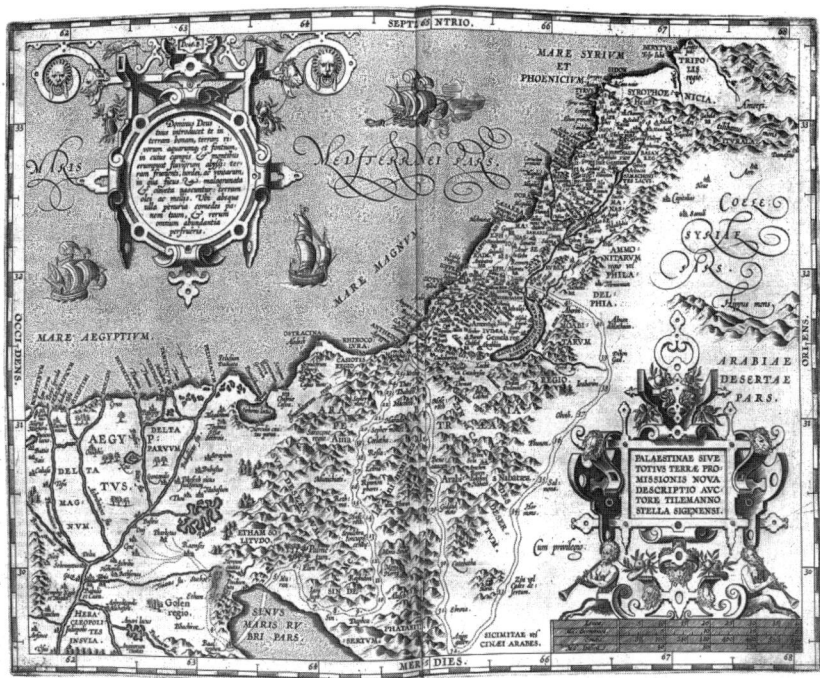

Map 8. A. Ortelius's version of Tilemann Stolz (Stella), "Itinera Israelitarum ex Aegypto . . . ," 1557, from *Parergon* (Antwerp, 1624) (Board of Trinity College, Dublin)

burg's does not) south of Elana on the west coast of the Sinus Elaniticus, so Stella presumably is not identifying the Ezion-geber of Num 33:35–36 with the Ezion-geber of 1 Kgs 9:26. For the toponyms from Numbers 33, Stella seems in some cases to follow Wissenburg, in others Mercator. His map is less pictorial than Wissenburg's, the route being marked by a stony track and the encampments by tents. An indistinct figure (?) and clouds (?) appear on the top of Sinai. In the Desert of Sin there is a plan of the encampment of the tribes around the Tabernacle. Aaron's grave appears near Hor, Maria's (Miriam's) near Zin vel Cades Desertum. There is no sign, however, of the quails or the serpents in the wilderness.

In 1556 a cartographer named Petrus Laicksteen (*fl.* ca. 1556–1570) travelled through the Holy Land observing and noting details of geography and topography. He later passed his notes to Christianus Sgrooten (ca. 1532–1608), a cartographer employed by Philip II of Spain. In 1570 Hieronymus Cocus (Cocq) of Antwerp published a map, printed from copper plates on nine sheets, based on the work of these two men. The text at the top of the main map reads *Nova descriptio amplissimae Sanctae Terrae quam M[agiste]r Petrus Laicksteen Astronomus perambulavit ac visitavit An[n]o rede[mp]tionis 1556 per Christianum Sgroothenum Reg[is] Ma[iesta]tis Hispan[iae] etc. Geographum collecta 1570* ("A new description of the Holy Land at its widest extent which Master Petrus Laicksteen, Astronomer, toured and visited in the year of redemption 1556, put together by Christian Sgrooten, Geographer of his Majesty the King of Spain, 1570").[25] In 1584 Ortelius published a map *Terra Sancta a Petro Laicstain perlustrata et ab eius ore et schedis a Christiano Schrot in tabulam redacta.*[26]

Cocq's nine-sheet spread contained two maps. The larger map, covering seven and a half of the nine sheets, showed the territories of the tribes of Israel. The smaller map (map 9), set into the top left hand corner of the whole, focused on the Exodus and the wilderness wanderings, showing the land both sides of the Jordan and the Dead Sea from Egypt and the Red Sea in the south to Mons Libanus in the north. The wilderness region between the Red Sea and the Dead Sea takes up over half of this map, whose main emphasis is clear. The *mansiones* are numbered, and printed in upper case letters. The Israelites' route through the wilderness on Laicksteen-Sgrooten's map, however, does not follow the line taken by Coverdale (1535), Mercator (1537), Wissenburg (1538), Mercator (1554), and Stella (1557). After leaving Sinai, the route on this map heads north-east to Asseroth, then west to Arada, then takes another easterly loop towards Esmona, then a westerly loop to Gadgad, and then crosses east again past Asion gaber and round the southern end of the Dead Sea before turning north through Moab. Laicksteen-Sgrooten make no attempt to bring the Israelites into contact with the Elanitic Gulf (whose existence is indicated by a northward turn of the coast of the Sinai promontory but no more). The vignettes of earlier maps are completely lacking from the Laicksteen-Sgrooten map, though the sepulchre of St Catherine is prominently displayed on Mt Sinai. A note explains that the wilderness route is that used by contemporary pilgrims travelling from Gaza to Sinai, Cairo, and Mecca. This map was dedicated by the publisher not to the new learning of the Reformers but to the Catholic Bishop Gerard of Groesbeck, and Sgrooten himself was in the pay of King Philip II of Spain.

In 1572 the Spanish linguist and theologian Benedictus Arias Montanus (1527–1598) produced the final volume of the Antwerp Polyglot Bible (*Phaleg, sive, De Gentium Sedibus primis, orbisque terrae situ,*

---

25   See Nebenzahl, *Maps of the Holy Land,* 82–83, pl. 29. One might have expected "amplissima" in the map's title, the adjective qualifying "descriptio," but the text clearly reads "amplissimae," qualifying "sanctae terrae."

26   A. Ortelius, *Additamentum III Theatri Orbis Terrarum* (Antwerp: C. Plantin, 1584).

Map 9. P. Laicksteen and C. Sgrooten, inset from "Nova descriptio amplissimae
Terrae Sanctae" (Antwerp, 1570) (© The British Library Board, Maps C.10.b.2)

liber).[27] The third of the four maps included was entitled *Terrae Israel omnis ante Canaan dictae in tribus undecim distributae accuratissime et ad sacras historias intelligendas oportuniss[ime], cum vicinarum gentium adscriptione tabula et exactissimo mansionum XLIII situ*. The outline of Arias Montanus's maps goes back to the fifteenth-century Ptolemaic *"tabulae modernae,"* with east at the top and the Palestinian coast at the bottom. Arias's presentation of the Red Sea and wilderness is quite different from that of Mercator and his followers. On Arias's map (map 10), the northern end of the Red Sea approaches close to the south-east corner of the Mediterranean, and the wilderness region is squashed into a narrow rectangle, bounded on the north by a river running east-west (the brook of Egypt?), and on the south by the more or less parallel coast of the Red Sea. The wilderness road takes a central route eastwards through the mountains via Sinai to Thahath (*mansio* no. 22), where it turns sharply west and returns along the shore of the Red Sea to Asiugaber and Desertum Sin (*mansiones* 32 and 33), where it turns sharply east again, crossing the original route between *mansiones* 18 and 19 (Zehelatha and Mons Sepher), before heading round the southern end of the Dead Sea and north through Moab. Arias's route appears to create difficulties for the sequence of *mansiones*. No. 7, the *castra ad mare* of other topographers, is unnamed on Arias's map. The *sepulchra concupiscentiae* have disappeared, their place at no. 12 being taken by Hasseroth, with consequential renumbering until an unnamed *mansio* 24 appears. Nos. 25–33 are given the usual place-names, but Arias separates out Desertum Sin and Cades into two places (nos. 33 and 34), perhaps in order to put at least one *mansio* into the long section on his map between Desertum Sin and Mons Hor. From Mons Hor to Abarim the usual numbers are thus advanced by one (nos. 35–42), a forty-third *mansio* appearing near Keriathaim in the territory of Reuben.

For this map, Arias has drawn entirely on biblical sources—the Edomite tribes of Genesis 36, the tribal lists for Reuben, Gad, and Half-Manasseh from the book of Joshua, and the *mansiones* of Numbers 33. "On ancient Palestine," the cartographer Ortelius had noted (in the text accompanying Stella's second map), "Jerome must be read, and also that which B. Arias Montanus has written in our time in his *Chaleb*."[28] Arias, however, was a student of the biblical text, not an observant traveller or professional cartographer, and his maps show regression

---

27 Benedictus Arias Montanus, *Phaleg, sive De Gentium Sedibus primis, orbisque terrae situ, liber* (Antwerp: C. Plantin, 1572).

28 Ortelius, *Theatrum Orbis Terrarum* (1570): "De veteri Palaestina legendi sunt quoque D. Hieronymus atque ea quae scripsit nostro tempore B. Arias Montanus in suo Chaleb."

Map 10. Benedictus Arias Montanus, section of "Terrae Israel omnis . . . tabula,"
Phaleg (Antwerp, 1572) (Board of Trinity College, Dublin)

rather than advance on the work of Mercator, Stella, and Laicksteen-Sgrooten.

The last important sixteenth-century contributor to our theme was Christian Adrichom (Adrichomius) (1533–1585). Adrichom's well-known map *Situs Terrae Promissionis SS Bibliorum intelligentiam experte aperiens*, first published at Cologne by J. Birckmann in 1593,[29] drew on the full range of earlier scholarship—Josephus, Jerome, Hegesippus, Pliny, Ptolemy, Strabo, Brocardus, Breidenbach, Saligniacus, and others—and quarried more deeply into the biblical sources than his

---

29 Christian Adrichom (Adrichomius), *Theatrum Terrae Sanctae et biblicarum historiarum cum tabulis geographicis aere expressis* (Cologne: J. Birckmann, 1593).

predecessors did. The outline of his map (map 11) goes back to the "modern" maps of the Ptolemaic corpus, and behind them to the Sanuto-Vesconte tradition, with east at the top and the Palestinian coast at the bottom. But Adrichom shows little first-hand knowledge of the topography. He misplaces the Transjordanian rivers, he gives the Dead Sea a western twist at its southern end, and gives the Red Sea one arm only, with no indication of its division into two gulfs. Adrichom has the Israelites cross the Red Sea, then head east as far as Alus (*mansio* 10) before travelling north to Rethma (*mansio* 15), where they turn south, zigzagging south again through the desert to Asiongaber (*mansio* 32) and Elath, where they turn north and traverse the desert of Zin (Cades) to reach Hor mons (*mansio* 34), where they turn east and pass via Phunon and Oboth (*mansiones* 36 and 37) round the south-east corner of the Dead Sea. The Israelites' path lies confined between chains of mountains running roughly north–south. The general topographical conception is not unlike that of Tilemann Stella a generation earlier, though the *mansiones* between Alus and Asiongaber are allocated differently. Adrichom provides many illustrations of the biblical story along the route—the camp by the sea, the battle at Raphidim with Aaron and Hur supporting Moses's arms on the mountain above, the tomb of St Catherine on Mt Sinai and the cloud and fire above it, Moses striking the rock at Petra, the tomb of Aaron, the serpents in the wilderness, and so on. Adrichom's map of the wilderness wanderings is a pictorial recreation of the biblical text. Adrichom, like Arias, was a biblical scholar rather than a scientific cartographer, and his map, though remaining popular and influential, offered no real advance on the work of Ziegler and Mercator.

The early sixteenth-century cartographers of the Holy Land had a particular interest in mapping the Exodus and the wilderness journey. Cranach's map exemplifies this interest, and appears in Luther's new translation of the Bible into German. Coverdale put one map, with the wilderness itinerary at the centre, into his translation of the Bible. (Delano Smith points out that it was Protestant, not Catholic bibles that illustrated the text with maps.[30]) There was probably a theological typology at work in these Reformation translations; Christians were to see themselves as fleeing their Roman captivity into the promised land of the reformed church. Ziegler's work, however, relates to the regions of Syria, Palestine, Arabia, and Egypt, or to the whole Terra Sancta, as the titles of his 1532 and 1536 editions show; his focus is not limited to

---

30   C. Delano Smith, "Maps as Art *and* Science: Maps in Sixteenth-Century Bibles," *Imago Mundi* 42 (1990): 65–83 (66, 79).

the wilderness itineraries. Mercator presents a wide screen, but the wilderness region takes the centre stage in his 1537 map, in which the land is viewed from the south, thus foreshortening the northern regions; the same is true of Wissenburg in 1538. Tilemann Stella's first map (1552) presents the kingdoms of Judah and Israel, but his second map (1557 and 1559) reverts to the Exodus and wilderness theme. Subsequent maps take the eye off the wilderness region, presenting the whole land on a consistent scale. The Laicksteen-Sgrooten maps refer the Exodus-wilderness material to a smaller inset map and reduce the pictorial content. Arias and Adrichom place no special emphasis on the Exodus-wilderness itineraries, seeing them as part of a much larger biblical history and geography. The concerns and emphases of cartographers continued to change through the seventeenth and eighteenth centuries. Interest in the route of the Exodus and wilderness wanderings was again raised by the archaeological and historical research and the exploration and cartographical surveys of the nineteenth and twentieth centuries, and maps marking the wilderness itineraries continue to be produced. The accuracy of their contents has been greatly improved by the work of modern biblical and historical scholarship, not least that of the scholar to whom this *Festschrift* is dedicated.

Map 11. C. Adrichom, section of "Situs Terrae Promissionis SS Bibliorum intelligentiam experte aperiens," 1593, from Mercator, *Atlas*, translated into English by H. Hexham, vol. 2 (Amsterdam, 1641) (Board of Trinity College, Dublin)

Part II

Biblical Texts

"Couch" or "Crouch"?

Genesis 4:7 and the Temptation of Cain*

ROBERT P. GORDON

Genesis 4:7 is crucial to the interpretation of the Cain story, but unfortunately the verse has a translational crux or two at its core. We shall not travel far in the secondary literature before encountering the claim, or a quotation to the same effect, that it is (one of) the most difficult verse(s) in Genesis. At the same time, the general sense and direction of the verse, as of the narrative that frames it, are reasonably clear. Cain, having had his offering rejected by YHWH, "was very angry, and his face fell" (v. 5). No explanation for the rejection is given, though there may be a clue in the fact that it is Cain and his offering, and in that order, that are said to have failed to satisfy YHWH.[1] YHWH asks the reason for Cain's anger, and then comes verse 7:

> If you do what is right, is there not acceptance? But if you do not do what is right, sin is lying at the door (*lpth ht't rbs*). Its desire (*těšûqātô*) is for you, but you must master it.

Discussion in this essay will revolve around the three words translated "sin is lying at the door" and their implication. I shall not address the other main crux in the verse, the meaning of *ś't*. What is proposed is, in any case, compatible with either of the main explanations of the word that have so far been advanced. *ś't* may, by ellipsis, indicate a lifting up (cf. BH *nś'*) of the face, answering to Cain's "fallen face" described in verses 5 and 6, and implying acceptance by YHWH, or it may be suggestive of the forgiveness (so also BH *nś'*) that will follow amendment of the behaviour that caused his rejection in the first place. More to the

---

* I am grateful to Ora Lipschitz and Simcha Friedman for providing me with bibliographical information (much more than I could use!) on Cain, Abel, and Genesis 4.

1 Contrast Amos 5:22; Mal 2:13. At the same time, M. G. Brett makes the point that in biblical narratives divine favour does not necessarily depend upon human performance (*Genesis: Procreation and the politics of identity* [Old Testament Readings; London: Routledge, 2000], 36).

point, the verse recounts God's warning to Cain about the consequences of letting his anger take control of him.

The most obvious problem with the translation "sin is lying at the door" is that of incongruence: the subject (*ḥṭʾt*) is feminine and the participle (*rbṣ*) masculine. This problem can be solved without difficulty, whether by treating "sin" as a personification, with an implied masculine referent, or by emendation on the assumption of haplography, restoring *ḥṭʾt trbṣ* for MT *ḥṭʾt rbṣ*, or by treating *rōbēṣ* as a substantive, as in "sin is at the door, a lurker."[2] Whichever of these is preferred, the meaning remains the same: "sin is lying at the door."[3]

The *rābiṣu*

Many writers, on the other hand, are attracted to the explanation that apparently was first proposed by H. Duhm in his *Die bösen Geister im Alten Testament*, published in 1904.[4] Duhm cited the Babylonian term *rābiṣu*, one of whose meanings is "demon" and which, being itself participial in form, supports the possibility that *rbṣ* is a participial noun. The resultant translation would run: "sin is a demon at the door." In fact, Duhm assumed that *ḥṭʾt* was an explanatory gloss and that the text originally said, "the demon is at the door."[5] I shall not argue the point with him, except to note the absence of any textual or versional indication of the secondariness of "sin" in the verse. Even the Septuagint, reading ἥμαρτες ("you have sinned") in the course of a notable disagreement with the MT, implies the consonantal reading found in the MT.

The support that has been expressed for the *rābiṣu* explanation since it was first proposed requires that it be taken seriously, even if there is sometimes a hint of *faute de mieux* when commentators commit to it. Its explanatory potential was in any case considered strong enough for Smit, in a short Festschrift article written in Latin and published in 1951, to cite Gen 4:7 in illustration of a point made in the papal encyclical "Divino afflante Spiritu" (1943) about the domestication of ancient

---

2   So GKC §145u ("a substantival participle").

3   *Genesis Rabbah* XXII:6 offers a different kind of solution: "At first sin is weak like a woman, then it grows strong like a man."

4   H. Duhm, *Die bösen Geister im Alten Testament* (Tübingen: J. C. B. Mohr, 1904), 7–10.

5   Duhm, *Die bösen Geister*, 9.

Near Eastern terms and concepts in the biblical tradition.[6] In this instance, says Smit, Moses or his editor corrects the pagan view of the *rābiṣu*: it is sin attacking humans (*hominem incautum* ["careless humans"]) that is the real *rābiṣu*.[7]

As the Akkadian lexicons make clear, the term *rābiṣu* had very distinct significances.[8] The bulk of the entries in *CAD* relate to officialdom, inspectors, commissioners—people "acting on higher authority"—and this usage is attested already in the Old Akkadian period, as well as in Old Assyrian and Old Babylonian texts. The term is also used for deities and kings as guardian figures, and then also for demons such as lurk about in order to attack humans. There are, indeed, references to *rābiṣu* demons in connection with doors or gates (cf. Gen 4:7),[9] but they are also associated with living quarters, roads, wells, and corners.

The *rābiṣu* explanation is represented in the occasional Bible translation, with NEB and REB "sin is a demon crouching at the door" and NAB "sin is a demon lurking at the door" clearly influenced by it. Waschke does not expressly commit himself to the *rābiṣu* explanation in the *ThWAT* entry on *rābaṣ*, but, in noting that most exegetes agree that there is some connection between *rōbēṣ* and the *rābiṣu*, surmises that "[d]emonic mythological notions originally associated with the realm of animals and gods among Israel's neighbors may account for the OT use of the root *rbṣ* in connection with the 'deep' (Gen 49:25; Deut 33:13), 'sin' (Gen 4:7), or a 'curse' (Deut 29:19[20])."[10] It will be prudent to deal with this excrescence on the original theme before proceeding further. Aside from Gen 4:7, Waschke is referring to "the deep that lies below" in Gen 49:25 and Deut 33:13, and to curses that overtake covenant-breakers in Deut 29:19[20]. These are, however, unconvincing as instances of vestigial demonic mythology in the Old Testament. Waschke might appear to have a better text in Isa 13:21, where it is envisaged that, following the overthrow of Babylon, "demons will lie down (*rbṣ*) there."[11] However, the translation of BH *ṣî* by "demon" is

---

6   Iohannes O. Smit, "Serpens aut daemonium? (Gen. 4, 7)," in *Miscellanea biblica et orientalia R. P. Athanasio Miller O.S.B., completis LXX annis, oblata* (ed. Adalbert Metzinger; Studia anselmiana: Philosophica theologica 27–28; Rome: Herder, 1951), 94–97.

7   Smit, "Serpens," 97. A similar emphasis on the theological reworking of the *rābiṣu* concept is already found in G. E. Closen, "Der ‹ Dämon Sünde › (Ein Deutungsversuch des massorethischen Textes von Gen 4, 7)," *Bib* 16 (1935): 431–42 (440–42).

8   See *CAD* R, 20–23.

9   See, for example, Closen, "Der ‹ Dämon Sünde ›," 436–40.

10   E.-J. Waschke, "רָבַץ *rābaṣ*, מַרְבֵּץ *marbeṣ*, רֶבֶץ *rebœṣ*," *ThWAT* 7, cols. 320–25 (322, 325) (= *TDOT* 13:298–303 [300, 303]). The quotation is from *ThWAT* 7, col. 322 = *TDOT* 13:300.

11   Waschke, *ThWAT* 7, cols. 324, 325 (=*TDOT* 13:301, 303).

not at all secure, and the association between demonology and the verb
rbṣ even at this point is highly disputable. There is no obvious reason
why *ṣî* in Isa 13:21 should differ from other occurrences of the word in
Isaiah (34:14; cf. 23:13) and Jeremiah (50:39), where also it is in the
company of desert creatures such as the jackal, hyena, and the ostrich,
and most probably itself denotes an animal.[12]

As I have already indicated, the *rābiṣu* has received only a qualified
welcome in Genesis study. Gunkel mentions Duhm's explanation, but
his main preoccupation is with the unmarked door in the verse: he is
not at all sure that wild animals normally "lurk" around doors. "And in
front of which door does sin lurk?" he asks.[13] G. R. Driver expresses
considerable doubt about the *rābiṣu* explanation in Gen 4:7. This is perhaps the more significant given the extent to which he used Akkadian
elsewhere in order to illuminate Hebrew lexicology. Driver notes that
not only would Gen 4:7 involve a *hapax legomenon*, it would provide a
rare instance of an Akkadian mythological term in Hebrew prose: foreign mythological elements are more apparent in *poetic* sections of the
Old Testament.[14] Westermann allows a connection with the *rābiṣu* but
doubts that a personification or "demonization" of sin in the way often
assumed by commentators is conceivable "in so early a text." He introduces his own complication by assuming an earlier form of text involving the shade of Abel.[15]

Barré, writing in the *Dictionary of Deities and Demons*, entertains the
rābiṣu explanation, but he notes problems.[16] First, if *rōbēṣ* actually represents *rābiṣu*, "one would expect the antecedent to be the tenor of the
metaphor (*ḥaṭṭāʾt*, 'sin') rather than the vehicle (*rōbēṣ*)."[17] Barré is referring to the suffix in *tĕšûqātô* ("its desire") and its proper antecedent. He
would expect to be able to paraphrase the MT along the following lines:
"sin is a croucher demon at the door, and *sin's* desire is for you"—
except that "sin" is feminine and the suffix in *tĕšûqātô* is masculine,

---

12   The essential point remains even if, with NRSV, reference to "goat-demons" and
     "Lilith" is allowed in Isa 34:14. NRSV itself finds mainly desert creatures in verses 13–
     15.

13   H. Gunkel, *Genesis übersetzt und erklärt* (6th ed.; HAT 1/1; Göttingen: Vandenhoeck &
     Ruprecht, 1964), 43–44. In the first edition (Göttingen: Vandenhoeck & Ruprecht,
     1901) there is, of course, no reference to the *rābiṣu* (39).

14   G. R. Driver, "Theological and Philological Problems in the Old Testament," *JTS* 47
     (1946): 156–66 (157–60).

15   C. Westermann, *Genesis*, I, *Genesis 1–11* (BKAT 1/1; Neukirchen-Vluyn: Neukirchener
     Verlag, 1974), 408.

16   M. L. Barré, "Rabiṣu רבץ," *DDD*², 682–83 (683).

17   The quotation is as in the second edition of *DDD*. The first edition (*DDD*¹, cols. 1287–
     90 [1289]) talks in terms of "subject" and "predicate nominative," rather than "tenor"
     and "vehicle."

which appears to favour *rōbēṣ* as antecedent. Barré also finds the position of *lpth* ("at the door, opening") strange if it denotes the door or opening of a tent. Perhaps even more significant for our further discussion is his observation that the *rābiṣu* attacks its victims, rather than tempting them to do wrong. *rābiṣu*, then, has attraction, but it poses problems and it would be unique in the Old Testament. There are various terms occurring elsewhere in the Old Testament that, rightly or wrongly, are associated with demonology, but *rābiṣu* is not one of them. Moreover, as Hendel notes, there is no evidence of a croucher demon in any of the West Semitic religions: "With the variety of West Semitic malevolent spirits and demons available, it is difficult to think that in this verse Yahweh casually alludes to a minor Mesopotamian demon."[18]

There is also the question of phonology. The Hebrew *rōbēṣ* appears to represent a participial form corresponding to the *pāris* participial noun-formation in *rābiṣu*. Does this suggest that *rōbēṣ* had achieved the status of a substantive equivalent of *rābiṣu* whose misfortune is to occur only once in Biblical Hebrew?[19] And should discussion be conducted in terms of cognate forms or loanword/*Fremdwort*? The respective vowel patterns are also represented in the Hebrew *nōqēd* and Akkadian *nāqidu*, meaning "sheepfarmer," words described by Mankowski as "independent survivals of an old Semitic root."[20] On the other hand, the analogy of Akkadian *(w)āšipu* and Hebrew *ʾaššāp*, both meaning "healer," with the latter displaying a vocalization associated with a number of terms for trades and occupations, might suggest that, if *rōbēṣ* is a loanword, we should expect it to be vocalized differently.[21] Of course, the Masoretic vocalization is late, and the imperative in the LXX ἡσύχασον, for example, implies a different pointing; nevertheless the question of vocalization deserves airing, if only to avoid oversimplifying discussion of the possible relationship between *rōbēṣ* and *rābiṣu*. And even though the Masoretic vocalization crystallized at a late stage in the transmission of the text, it is also recognized as preserving traditions of pronunciation that reach back centuries earlier. Its lateness

18   R. S. Hendel, *The Text of Genesis 1–11: Textual Studies and Critical Edition* (New York: Oxford University Press, 1998), 45–46 (46).

19   L. Ramaroson, "A propos de Gn 4,7," *Bib* 49 (1968): 233–37, notes the differing views on the part of proponents of the *rābiṣu* explanation as to whether the *rābiṣu* represents a borrowing from Babylonia or a common Semitic feature (234).

20   P. V. Mankowski, *Akkadian Loanwords in Biblical Hebrew* (HSS 47; Winona Lake, Ind.: Eisenbrauns, 2000), 103–4.

21   Mankowski, *Akkadian Loanwords*, 43–44, regards *ʾaššāp* as a definite loanword in Danielic Hebrew, since a root *wšp* in Akkadian would lead one to expect a West Semitic cognate based on a *yšp* form.

could be invoked against discussion of the vocalization of any word found in the Hebrew Bible, yet that would be a self-denying ordinance to no point or purpose.

Translations of *lptḥ ḥṭʾt rbṣ*

It will help discussion to pay closer attention to the translation of *rōbēṣ* in some Bible translations, mainly in English. A translational-cum-interpretative issue will be highlighted in the process.

Vulgate	(statim) in foribus peccatum aderit
Tyndale	(by and by) thy synne lyeth open in the dore
Luther	so ruht die Sünde vor der Tür
Geneva	sin lieth at the door
AV	sin lieth at the door
RV	sin **coucheth** at the door
ASV	sin **coucheth** at the door
[BDB	at the door sin makes its lair]
JPS	sin **coucheth** at the door
RSV	sin is **couching** at the door
NASB	sin is *crouching* at the door
NEB	sin is a demon *crouching* at the door
NIV	sin is *crouching* at your door
NJB	Sin is *crouching* at the door
NJPS	Sin **couches** at the door
NAB	sin is a demon lurking at the door
REB	sin is a demon *crouching* at the door
NRSV	sin is lurking at the door
ESV	sin is *crouching* at the door

This sample of mainline versions shows that there has been a tendency away from "lying" and "couching" to "crouching" and "lurking," as perhaps best illustrated in RSV "couching" and NRSV "lurking." The difference between "couch" and "crouch" may not be regarded as great, but there is a difference, and we may assume that "crouch" has gained ground partly because of the background presence of the *rābiṣu*, even where a version does not have a specific reference to a demon, and partly because the verb "crouch" is much more familiar in contemporary English than is "couch." This second observation points us in the direction of what has been called "banalization" in discussion of

Freudian psychoanalysis and textual analysis: the "substitution of one word by another whose meaning is actually or apparently the same, but whose usage is more familiar to the copyist."[22] "Couch" basically means "lie down," whereas "crouch" is more suggestive of squatting ("adopt a position where the knees are bent and the upper body is brought forward and down," *Concise Oxford Dictionary*) and, crucially, fits better with the idea of hostile intent. Of the more recent versions, only NJPS retains "couch," which was the word used in the 1917 JPS version. As we shall see, this more accurately represents BH *rbṣ*. BH *krᶜ* is the verb better rendered "crouch," and we have a useful juxtaposition of *rbṣ* and *krᶜ* in Gen 49:9 to illustrate their respective nuances: *krᶜ rbṣ kʾryh* ("He crouches down, he stretches out like a lion," NRSV). The use of *krᶜ* to describe action preparatory to lying down can also be illustrated from Num 24:9 and Judg 5:27.

The distinction between "couch" and "crouch" becomes the more important when discussion turns to the kind of creature indicated in Gen 4:7 as "couching" at the door. Gunkel, as we have noted, has a problem with the idea of a wild animal, "to which sin is compared here," lying in wait at doors.[23] He is, at any rate, thinking of a wild animal. For Spurrell sin is being compared to a "ravenous beast" and—with an eye on 1 Pet 5:8 and on the Arabic sobriquet "lier in wait" for "lion"—is possibly to be identified as a lion.[24] S. R. Driver assumed a wild animal in our verse, though he knew his Hebrew and English too well to think of the beast as other than "couching" at the door.[25] König thought of a predator lying in wait at a tent door.[26] Most recently, the *New Living Translation Study Bible* informs that sin "is pictured as a vicious animal lying in wait to pounce on Cain."[27] However, a survey of the occurrences of BH *rbṣ* will suggest that this assumes too much for the root.

The noun subjects used with *rbṣ* can be divided into several groups. The first category concerns domestic animals, namely flocks (Gen 29:2; Isa 17:2; Zeph 2:14; cf. Isa 13:20; Jer 33:12; Song 1:7), donkeys (Gen

---

22 See Sebastiano Timpanaro, *The Freudian Slip: Psychoanalysis and Textual Criticism* (London: Verso, 1976; repr., 1985), 21 (see also 30–40, 92–95); trans. of *Il lapsus freudiano: Psicanalisi e critica testuale* (Florence: La nuova Italia, 1974).

23 Gunkel, *Genesis*, 43.

24 G. J. Spurrell, *Notes on the Hebrew Text of the Book of Genesis* (Oxford: Clarendon, 1887), 50.

25 S. R. Driver, *The Book of Genesis, with Introduction and Notes* (3d ed.; London: Methuen, 1904), 65.

26 E. König, *Die Genesis eingeleitet, übersetzt und erklärt* (Gütersloh: Bertelsmann, 1919), 279.

27 *New Living Translation Study Bible* (Carol Stream, Ill.: Tyndale House, 2008), 28.

49:14; Exod 23:5; Num 22:27 ["lay down under Balaam"]), and calves
(Isa 27:10). *rbṣ* is also used of a bird sitting upon fledglings (Deut 22:6).
The second main group comprises wild animals: Judah crouching and
lying down like a lion that has returned from the prey (Gen 49:9), the
leopard that in the vegetarian future lies down with the young goat (Isa
11:6), lions settling down in their lairs at sunrise after a night's prowl-
ing (Ps 104:22), a lioness lying down among her cubs (Ezek 19:2), desert
animals, instead of flocks, resting among the ruins of Babylon (Isa
13:21; cf. v. 20), and Pharaoh *sub figura* a great monster lying among the
streams of the Nile (Ezek 29:3). In Isa 11:7 *rbṣ* describes the peaceful
"ecoexistence" of the young of animals both domesticated and wild. It
also describes the happy state of humans resting securely (Isa 14:30;
Ezek 34:14, 15 [Israel compared to a flock]; Zeph 2:7; 3:13 ["they shall
feed and lie down"]; Ps 23:2; Job 11:19). Other occurrences without
human or animal subject have already been noted: the great deep that
lies beneath (Gen 49:25; Deut 33:13), curses falling/resting upon someone (Deut 29:19[20]). Finally, *rbṣ* is used in the Hiphil for laying down
stones during construction work (Isa 54:11).

There is also a noun *rēbeṣ*, denoting the abode of the righteous
(Prov 24:15), and of jackals (?) (Isa 35:7), a resting-place for herds (Isa
65:10), and the fold ("resting-place") that Israel are said to have forgotten (Jer 50:6). There are also two occurrences of *marbēṣ*, in Ezek 25:5 (the
resting-place of a flock) and Zeph 2:15 (a lair for wild animals).

In addition, the etymologically related *rābaʿ* denotes lying down for
sexual purposes (see Lev 18:23; 19:19; 20:16), while in Ps 139:3 the sense
is simply "lying down," in contrast to "going about."

None of this requires a hostile sense for the action described by *rbṣ*;
in almost every case something opposite is indicated. Occasionally a
hint of aggression is found in Gen 49:9,[28] but there are clear contraindi-
cations in the verse: Judah as lion is said to have returned from the
prey, and in the final colon of the verse the question is asked, "Who
dare rouse him?" The Pharaonic "monster" in Ezek 29:3 is "lurking,"
according to REB, but NRSV's use of "sprawling" is at least as good (NIV
"lying"). Our survey shows that *rbṣ* invariably describes a restful state,
as much when referring to wild animals as domestic. If *rbṣ* were to be
rendered with emphasis on aggressive or ferocious intent in Gen 4:7, it
would be a unique occurrence of this particular sense or nuance.

It is interesting, at the same time, to find early evidence of the urge
to give the beast menace, if not actual teeth. "A lion lies in wait for

---

28   Cf. J. Azevedo, "At the Door of Paradise: A Contextual Interpretation of Gen 4:7,"
     BN 100 (1999): 45–59 (53).

prey, so does sin for evildoers," according to Sir 27:10, with possible recollection of sin's designs on Cain in Gen 4:7. As indicated above, Jerome translates our phrase by *statim in foribus peccatum aderit* ("*forthwith* sin will be present at the door"), paralleled in Tyndale's "*by and by* thy synne lyeth open in the dore," where "by and by" means "soon, presently." In talking about sin "being present," Jerome may have been influenced by the discussion of sin and temptation in the New Testament Letter to the Romans—see Rom 7:21[29]—but *statim* probably has another explanation. If we retrovert the word into Hebrew one of the most obvious candidates is *lptᶜ*. *ptᶜ* is listed as a substantive meaning "suddenness," and it is used adverbially, in this basic form, in three places (Hab 2:7; Prov 6:15; 29:1). It is also found with the preposition *beth* in Num 6:9; 35:22, in correspondence with its Akkadian interdialectal equivalent *ina pitti/ina pittimma* ("in suddenness," "suddenly"). There are also two occurrences of *lptᶜ* with the same meaning (Isa 29:5; 30:13). Moreover, there is a clear tendency for *ptᶜ*, with or without preposition, to be clause-initial (see Num 35:22; Isa 30:13; Hab 2:7; Prov 6:15; 29:1). All in all, it is probably too much of a coincidence that in translation of a phrase beginning with *lptḥ* Jerome inserts *statim*, which can equate with *lptᶜ*. But does this mean that there was a variant reading, with *lptᶜ* for *lptḥ*, which Jerome has incorporated in his translation, or was he simply aware of a midrashic equating of *lptḥ* and *lptᶜ*, perhaps with a side glance at such texts as Prov 6:12–15 and 29:1, which speak of the sudden (*ptᶜ* [6:15; 29:1]) ruin of those who plot evil and refuse warning?

As something of an antiquarian curiosity-cum-coincidence, we may note the view of Riessler that traces of an underlying Babylonian original (*Keilschriftvorlage*) are detectable in Genesis 2–11 (especially) and that several features of 4:7 are explicable on this basis. In particular, Riessler assumed that *ina pitti* ("suddenly") in this Babylonian original had been misread as *ina piti* ("at the door"), which in turn gave rise to MT *lptḥ*. His translation of the verse runs: "Ist es nicht so: wenn du gut handelst, kannst du fröhlich sein; wenn du aber nicht gut handelst, wird *plötzlich* [my italics] ein böser Geist, dessen Verlangen nach dir geht, daherkommen und du wirst ihm zu Beute fallen."[30] Riessler does not appeal to Jerome in support of his egregious theory.

---

29 N. T. Wright, *The Climax of the Covenant* (Minneapolis, Minn.: Fortress, 1992), 226–30, argues that the Cain story is echoed in Romans 7.

30 P. Riessler, "Das Alte Testament und die babylonische Keilschrift," *TQ* 93 (1911): 493–504 (500–501).

Reptilian revisited?

Jerome's expedient insertion of *statim* testifies in its own way to the inert associations of *rbṣ* in general, and in Gen 4:7 in particular. It would appear reasonable, therefore, to ask what kind of animal is implied in the verse, and part of the purpose of this study is to explore the possibility that the divine warning to Cain revisits the reptilian world of Genesis 3. Clearly, for this to be feasible we shall have to be persuaded that *rbṣ* is an appropriate verb for reptile (in)activity.

What, then, do snakes do in the Old Testament? Obviously they bite (*nšk*), as in Gen 49:17; Num 21:6, and eat dust, as in Isa 65:25; Mic 7:17 (cf. Gen 3:14). Locomotorily, they go (*hlk*) on their belly (Gen 3:14). They also crawl (*zḥl*): Deut 32:24 refers to the poison of "those that crawl in the dust," while there is a more explicit paralleling of "snake" and "crawl" in Mic 7:17 ("They will lick dust like a snake, like those that crawl on the ground"). *rbṣ*, on the other hand, does not occur with the more common words for snake—*nāḥāš* and *peten*—in the Old Testament, but then there are no references to snakes resting or nesting. However, there is Ezek 29:3, which compares Pharaoh to a *tannîm* (*sic*) that sprawls in the channels of the Nile. *tannîm* is widely recognized as either a variant or a mistake for *tannîn* (so many Hebrew manuscripts), variously translated "serpent," as in the story of the confrontation between Moses and the Egyptian magicians (Exod 7:9, 10, 12; see also Deut 32:33; Ps 91:13), or "sea monster," as in the general creation narrative in Gen 1:21 (see also Isa 27:1; 51:9). *tannîm* in Ezek 29:3 tends to be rendered by "great monster" (NIV, REB) or "great dragon" (NRSV); it is, at any rate, reptilian, as the general context suggests, and *rbṣ* is used to describe it at rest. We may note that *tannîn* (*sic*) occurs in parallel to *peten* in Deut 32:33; Ps 91:13, and in parallel to *nāḥāš* in Isa 27:1.

The evidence of the Akkadian verb *rabāṣu*, cognate with BH *rbṣ*, also calls for consideration. Not surprisingly, the much larger Mesopotamian literary corpus has many more references to snakes as compared with the Old Testament. Just like BH *rbṣ*, the Akkadian verb can be used of wild animals in quiescent mode, though occasionally it is perhaps more suggestive of menace than its biblical counterpart, as when two lions lie down at the beginning of the night in proximity to a city gate. The following citations taken from the Chicago *Assyrian Dictionary* show *rabāṣu* in association with *ṣīru* ("snake"):[31]

> *kî ša ṣīru šikkû ina libbi issêt ḫurrete la errabūni la i-ra-bi-ṣu-u-ni*
> just as snake and mongoose do not enter and bed down in the same hole

---

31   *CAD* R, 11–12.

šumma ṣīru ina muḫḫi erši amēli NÁ-iṣ
if a snake lies down on a man's bed

šumma ṣīru ana muḫḫi šerri lakî NÁ-iṣ
if a snake lies down on a small baby

minde ina libbi rīmi annê ṣēru ra-bi-iṣ
perhaps the snake is lying (*CAD* "lurking") inside this wild bull

On the slender basis of Ezek 29:3, therefore, and with some collateral from Akkadian *rabāṣu*, we may venture to extend the range of creatures potentially suggested by *rōbēṣ* in Gen 4:7 to include reptilians. The possibility of a closer relationship between Cain's temptation and that described in the preceding chapter begins to come into view.

The "opening," enticement, and Genesis 3

What, then, of the "opening" or "gate" of Gen 4:7? I have already noted the possibility that Jerome reflects another tradition of reading *lptḥ* as *lptʿ*, and I have reported Barré's problem with the positioning of *lptḥ* at the beginning rather than the end of the clause.[32] Doors or tent openings, of course, are not just of interest to animals—or demons for that matter—contemplating attack. Spurrell, who thinks in terms of a "ravenous beast," looks to Prov 9:14 for illumination.[33] Here "Woman Folly" sits at the door (*petaḥ*) of her house, "on a seat at the highest point of the city," inviting passers-by to enjoy her hospitality (vv. 15–18). But it is *her* brazen door—if one may indulge in a transferred epithet—that is in question, and almost instinctively we imagine that the unmarked opening or door of Gen 4:7 is more likely to be Cain's own "door." Cassuto comments relevantly: "The verse simply says *door (entrance)*, and the commentator is not called upon to determine what Scripture leaves undetermined. It means, apparently, *your door* in a general sense, that is, the place through which you are wont to go in and out constantly; in other words, it will always be found in your

---

32   However, in so-called "nominal clauses" the sequence adverb-subject-predicate appears to be unexceptionable, given the variability of word-order in such clauses (see P. Joüon and T. Muraoka, *A Grammar of Biblical Hebrew*, vol. 2, *Part Three: Syntax; Paradigms and Indices* [SubBi 14/2; Rome: Editrice Pontificio Istituto Biblico, 1991], 573 [§154h]; Joüon and Muraoka cite Gen 4:7 as an instance of "the fronting of the object or adverbial modifier" for the sake of emphasis).

33   Spurrell, *Notes on the Hebrew Text*, 50.

path."[34] That the opening or gate belongs to Cain may be implied in the Vulgate's *egrediamur foras* in verse 8, picking up *in foribus* in verse 7.

Spurrell's citing of Prov 9:14 at any rate brings us away from the idea of attack to that of enticement, and this is the direction in which, as the title of this article suggests, I wish to go. A text that associates enticement with the door of the victim is Job 31:9, where Job protests his innocence of adulterous thought or act:

> If my heart has been enticed by a woman or if I have lain in wait at my neighbour's door (*ptḥ*) . . .

Job does indeed speak of lying in wait (*'rb*), but this is inimical only in an indirect sense: he is thinking of seduction, not attack. *'rb* is in a kind of parallelism with *npth* ("has been enticed"). In fact, Castellino has already pointed to the possible relevance of Job 31:9 in a short piece published in 1960.[35] In his view, "at the door" is a proverbial expression in Gen 4:7 and Job 31:9. Unfortunately, Castellino (444) goes on to explain *těšûqātô* in the following clause in Gen 4:7 in terms of "'greed' in a hostile sense, of a beast eager to devour," which surrenders the potential advantage offered by the Job reference. More plausibly, with the encouragement of Job 31:9 we can interpret Gen 4:7 in terms of enticement or seduction, rather than feral attack. This again brings us close to the thought-world of Genesis 3 and the deception of Eve by the serpent.

The suggestion of a relationship between 4:7 and 3:1 is, of course, not new. An earlier generation of commentators was more inclined to cross-refer the two texts, without necessarily going into detail on how the relationship might work.[36] Since the intervention of the *rābiṣu*, less has been made of the possible connection, for obvious reasons. Such cross-referring to the previous chapter of Genesis makes good sense given their obviously close relationship. Documentary analysis attributes the two chapters to the "J" source, though the subject-verb-object sequence in 4:1 is recognized as marking the beginning of a new narrative segment within "J." There are, moreover, shared elements between the chapters that suggest their origin in a common source. Most quoted in this respect are the questions in 3:9 and 4:9 respectively: "Where are you?" and "Where is your brother Abel?" There are also complementary follow-up questions, "What is this you have done?" (3:13), and

---

34   U. Cassuto, *A Commentary on the Book of Genesis, Part One: From Adam to Noah* (Jerusalem: Magnes Press, 1961; repr., 1978), 211; trans. of *Mēʾādām ʿad nōaḥ* (Jerusalem: Magnes Press, 1944).

35   G. R. Castellino, "Genesis IV 7," *VT* 10 (1960): 442–45.

36   Paul Heinisch, *Das Buch Genesis* (HSAT 1/1; Bonn: Peter Hanstein, 1930), 145, describes the connection between 3:1 and 4:7 as "offenkundig."

"What have you done?" (4:10). Again, both stories involve expulsions of offending parties, whether from the garden in Eden or from the settled land outside Eden, and both use the verb grš for the acts of expulsion (3:24; 4:14). Most striking is the reprise and adaptation in 4:7 of the judgment pronounced on Eve in 3:16: "your desire will be toward your husband and he will rule over you" and "its desire is toward you, but you must rule over it."

The presence of this last sentence in 4:7 has been problematical for many writers, for whom generally the original statement is too contextually suited to the judgment on Eve to feature, even modified and redirected, in the warning to Cain. Box appealed to columnar considerations: 3:16 and 4:7 stood opposite each other in their respective manuscript columns, and 4:7b is attributable to accidental repetition of the corresponding words in 3:16.[37] Haupt thought of 4:7b as an ancient protest, initially inserted in a manuscript margin, against the judgment sentence on Eve in 3:16. It was inserted by a woman, or by "a man under the influence of a woman."[38] Westermann concluded that most of 4:6 and 4:7 is secondary, in view of the repetition of elements from 4:5b and 3:16.[39]

Certainly, if the near-repetition of 3:16b in 4:7b is not accidental, then it is a very deliberate adaptation of the earlier version, whether it is to be regarded as original or secondary. In its original setting it has to do with conjugal desire,[40] which is not at all in view in 4:7.[41] At the same time, we have noted that 3:16b//4:7b represents but one of several features shared between chapters 3 and 4. Moreover, if creative reworking of 3:16b accounts for 4:7b, this feature would belong with other

---

37   G. H. Box, "Genesis iv. 7 and iii. 16: A Suggestion," *ExpTim* 10 (1898–1899): 425–26.

38   P. Haupt, "An Ancient Protest against the Curse on Eve," *Proceedings of the American Philosophical Society* 50 (1911): 505–17 ("some one—possibly a woman, or a man under the influence of a woman, a species of the genus *Homo*, which is common— added to this statement in the margin: *His desire is unto thee, and thou wilt rule over him*" [508]).

39   Westermann, *Genesis 1–11*, 407.

40   The meaning of *tšwqh* is discussed by K. A. Deurloo, "תשוקה ›dependency‹, Gen 4,7," *ZAW* 99 (1987): 405–6; Deurloo, as his title indicates, favours a meaning such as "dependency."

41   The Septuagintal "his/its turning is toward you, and you will rule over him/it" may have in mind the relationship between Cain and Abel, especially since the Greek rendering in the first part of the verse provides no alternative antecedent for the third person references in "his/its" and "him/it." For this reading of the MT see M. Ben Yashar, "Zu Gen 4 7," *ZAW* 94 (1982): 635–37. Deurloo, "תשוקה," 405, agrees with Ben Yashar in interpreting the half-verse in terms of the social relationship between Cain and Abel. This is obviously suited by Deurloo's preference for the meaning "dependency" (see preceding footnote).

literary touches, at once skilful and playful, that are found in the same chapter. The story begins with play on Cain's name, "For," says Eve, using the Hebrew verb *qnh*, "I have 'gained' a man with the Lord." There is the possible play on the downcast face of Cain in verse 6, when the next verse offers the possibility of "lifting up," whatever the exact nuance intended. Cain's sarcastic riposte, "Am I my brother's keeper?" (v. 9), seems to jibe at his dead brother's vocation, meaning in effect, "Am I a shepherd's shepherd?" If it was Cain who built the first city (v. 17), then he is shown in bold disregard of his sentence to nomady (v. 12); if it was Enoch his son, then there is undeclared wordplay on *ʿîr* ("city") in Irad, the name of Enoch's son (v. 18). Finally, Williamson has argued that the use of two different infinitives from the same verb *nśʾ*, in verses 7 and 13, is a stylistic device to distinguish between the two different senses of the verb in the respective verses, and in particular to discourage the reader from attributing the sense of the first occurrence to the second.[42]

In all probability, then, 4:7b came about as a daring adaptation of 3:16b to the story of the struggle between Cain and his nemesis. But if 4:7a is not about feral attack so much as about sin "couching" at Cain's door hoping to entice him, then the repetition of the language of 3:16 in 4:7b ("its desire is for you") becomes more understandable, and what we read in the chapter is, in a somewhat stronger sense than is usually meant, the account of the temptation of Cain.

As to the identity of the "coucher" in Gen 4:7, it is, of course, impossible to prove that it is the serpent of chapter 3. But the possibility should not be ruled out. The serpent's reappearance would have relevance for the question of gender incongruence mentioned at the start of this study. For if sin (feminine) is couching (masculine participle) at Cain's door, and behind the reference there lies the serpent, then it is easier to tolerate the MT reading as it is. Moreover, the serpent's background presence would be perfectly compatible with the view that sin is personified here.[43] The serpent would be displaying its subtlety in waiting to take advantage of Cain, and a certain kind of consistency with the temptation scene in chapter 3 would be achieved. At the same

---

42   H. G. M. Williamson, "On Getting Carried Away with the Infinitive Construct of
      נשׂא," in *Shai le-Sara Japhet: Studies in the Bible, its Exegesis and its Language* (ed. M. Bar-
      Asher, D. Rom-Shiloni, E. Tov, and N. Wazana; Jerusalem: Bialik Institute, 2007),
      357*–67* (363*).

43   Driver, "Theological and Philological Problems," 158, comments on the absence of
      the definite article with *ḥṭʾt* as evidence that sin is "virtually personified" in Gen 4:7.
      He cites occurrences of anarthrous "sin" in Prov 13:6; 14:34; 21:4; 24:9 in support,
      though they are scarcely convincing as evidence. The view that sin is personified in
      Gen 4:7 is usually made independently of the argument about the definite article.

time, chapter 4 is in other respects a more violent chapter than chapter 3—*pace* the enmity announced in 3:15—and consistency with chapter 3 should not be the decisive factor in our characterizing of Cain's nemesis.

It gives me great pleasure to dedicate this essay to Graham Davies and to record my immense admiration of him as a scholar and as a colleague over many years.

The Flood and the Ten Antediluvian Figures in Berossus and in the Priestly Source in Genesis

John Day

It has long been recognized by modern scholars that there is a connection between the account of Noah's flood in Genesis 6–8 and the Mesopotamian flood tradition. Not so many scholars realize, however, that this was already recognized almost two thousand years ago by the Jewish historian Josephus, who knew the Mesopotamian story from the account written in Greek by the Babylonian priest Berossus, and who clearly implies that this and the Genesis account refer to the same event (*Ant.*, 1.93; *Ag. Ap.*, 1.130).[1] With the advent of archaeological discoveries in the Near East in the nineteenth century and subsequently and the discovery of the much earlier Mesopotamian version of the flood story in tablet 11 of the Gilgamesh epic,[2] as well as the even earlier accounts in the Atrahasis epic[3] and brief Sumerian version,[4] it is not surprising that the later version in Berossus has tended to be somewhat neglected by Old Testament scholars. It is, however, Berossus on whom I wish to focus in this article, and to draw attention to the fact that the Priestly version of the flood story in Genesis 6–8 stands closer to that found in Berossus in certain respects than it does to the earlier known Mesopotamian flood accounts. Similarly, the preceding list of ten antediluvian patriarchs in Genesis 5 stands closer to Berossus's version of the ten

---

1   Josephus, *Ant.* 1.94–95 then goes on to mention other historians of antiquity who had alluded to the flood: Hieronymus the Egyptian, Mnaseas, and Nicolaus of Damascus.

2   Many translations of Gilgamesh are available but see now the massive edition and commentary of Andrew R. George, *The Babylonian Gilgamesh Epic: Introduction, Critical Edition and Cuneiform Text* (2 vols.; Oxford: Clarendon, 2003), as well as his shorter volume, *The Epic of Gilgamesh: The Babylonian Epic Poem and Other Texts in Akkadian and Sumerian* (London: Allen Lane, 1999).

3   Wilfred G. Lambert and Alan R. Millard, *Atra-ḫasīs: The Babylonian Story of the Flood* (Oxford: Clarendon Press, 1969); S. Dalley, *Myths from Mesopotamia* (Oxford: Oxford University Press, 1989), 1–38; Benjamin R. Foster, *Before the Muses: An Anthology of Akkadian Literature* (3d ed.; Bethesda, Md.: CDL Press, 2005), 227–80.

4   Miguel Civil, in Lambert and Millard, *Atra-ḫasīs*, 138–45; Thorkild Jacobsen, *The Harps that Once . . . : Sumerian Poetry in Translation* (New Haven, Conn.: Yale University Press, 1987), 145–50. Cf. too Jacobsen's article, "The Eridu Genesis," *JBL* 100 (1981): 513–29.

antediluvian kings in certain respects than it does to earlier known versions of the Sumerian King List. That this should be the case ought not to surprise us, since P (ca. 500 BCE) and Berossus (ca. 280 BCE) are both late works, standing relatively close in time.[5]

The first distinctive point of connection between Berossus and P that I wish to draw attention to is that, unlike the earlier Mesopotamian flood accounts found in the Atrahasis and Gilgamesh epics, Berossus gives a precise date for the beginning of the deluge, just as P does, in contrast to the earlier J source. Remarkably, the Priestly flood account is the only event in Genesis that receives precise dates in terms of both days and months. Dalley has previously noted that Berossus and P have in common that they give a date for the start of the flood,[6] but so far as I am aware no one hitherto has pointed out that their dates are remarkably similar. For Berossus, the flood commenced on the fifteenth day of Daisios, Daisios being the second month in the Macedonian calendar corresponding precisely to Babylonian Ayyaru, Hebrew Iyyar (April/May).[7] Likewise, the Priestly source informs us in Gen 7:11 that Noah's flood began on the seventeenth day of the second month, which was similarly in April/May, i.e., Iyyar 17, only two days later than the date given in Berossus. (The Septuagint refers rather to the twenty-seventh day of the month, but Hendel argues convincingly that the MT's seventeenth day is original.[8]) This similarity would seem to be too great to be due to a chance coincidence, even granting that the period

---

5   For an English translation of Berossus's account of the flood and the antediluvian figures, which space prevents me from citing here, see Stanley M. Burstein, *The Babyloniaca of Berossus* (Sources and Monographs: Sources from the Ancient Near East 1/5; Malibu, Calif.: Undena, 1978), 20–21 or Gerald P. Verbrugghe and John M. Wickersham, *Berossos and Manetho, Introduced and Translated: Native Traditions in Ancient Mesopotamia and Egypt* (Ann Arbor, Mich.: University of Michigan Press, 1996), 46–51. The Greek text of Berossus, together with a German version of excerpts from the Armenian, is to be found in Paul Schnabel, *Berossos und die babylonisch-hellenistische Literatur* (Leipzig: B. G. Teubner, 1923), as well as in Felix Jacoby, *Die Fragmente der griechischen Historiker* 3C/1 (Leiden: Brill, 1958), 364–97 (no. 680).

6   Dalley, *Myths from Mesopotamia*, 6.

7   On Daisios see, e.g., Wilhelm Dittenberger, "Daisios," in *PW* 4, 2014–15. In the Seleucid period when Berossus wrote the Macedonian and Babylonian calendars were completely meshed together; see Alan E. Samuel, *Greek and Roman Chronology: Calendars and Years in Classical Antiquity* (Handbuch der Altertumswissenschaft 1/7; Munich: C. H. Beck, 1972), 139–44.

8   Ronald S. Hendel, *The Text of Genesis 1–11: Textual Studies and Critical Edition* (New York: Oxford University Press, 1998), 54–55 points out that not only does the Septuagint differ from all other ancient versions and ancillary sources (*Jubilees*; 4QCommGen A) in reading "twenty-seventh" rather than "seventeenth" but its reading may easily be explained as due to a simple misreading of עשר יום as עשרים (the Septuagint lacks a reference to "day" here).

from March to May is the general period for flooding in Mesopotamia. Berossus is hardly dependent on Genesis here, so it seems natural to suppose that Berossus was indebted to a late Babylonian tradition similar to that on which P also drew. That this parallel has gone unnoticed up till now is perhaps in part attributable to the fact alluded to above that less attention has been paid by Old Testament scholars to classical sources like Berossus since the advent of archaeological discoveries of more ancient Near Eastern texts.[9] But additionally, nineteenth- and early twentieth-century biblical scholars, who were doubtless more prone than subsequent scholars to read Berossus, often assumed that P's second month meant the second month of the autumnal rather than the spring calendar (e.g., Dillmann, Franz Delitzsch, Sayce, Samuel R. Driver;[10] similarly Josephus, *Ant.*, 1.80; *Tg.Ps.-J.*[11]), which thus obscured the parallel with Berossus. It is, however, clear that P employed the spring calendar throughout his work (e.g., Exod 12:2; Lev 16:29–30; 23:5, 6, 27, 34, 39; 25:9).

Another point on which the Priestly version of the flood narrative agrees with Berossus over against earlier Mesopotamian tradition is the landing place of the ark. According to the Gilgamesh epic 11.142–46, the ark landed at Mt Nimush (previously read Niṣir[12]). As a result of another reference to Mt Nimush in the annals of Ashurnaṣirpal II it is generally accepted that this is to be equated with the impressive mountain now known as Pir Omar Gudrun, located south of the lower Zab in southern (Iraqi) Kurdistan, near Suleimaniyah.[13] In another text Mt

9   Cf. my observations in John Day (ed.), *William Robertson Smith: Lectures on the Religion of the Semites, Second and Third Series* (JSOTSup 183; Sheffield: Sheffield Academic Press, 1995), 30, where I note the rich use of classical Greek and Latin sources made by the great nineteenth-century scholar William Robertson Smith and express the view that modern Old Testament scholars have much to gain by giving such sources renewed attention.

10   Cf. August Dillmann, *Die Genesis* (5th ed.; KEHAT 11; Leipzig: S. Hirzel, 1886), 130; Franz Delitzsch, *Neuer Commentar über die Genesis* (Leipzig: Dörffling & Franke, 1887), 176; Archibald H. Sayce, *The Early History of the Hebrews* (London: Rivingtons, 1897), 126; Samuel R. Driver, *The Book of Genesis* (WC; London: Methuen, 1904), 90.

11   The version of the flood story in *Tg. Neof. 1* is not clear in this regard, and support for seeing either the autumnal or the spring calendar here is found in later glossators. See Martin McNamara, *Targum Neofiti 1: Genesis Translated, with Apparatus and Notes* (ArBib 1A; Edinburgh: T&T Clark, 1992), 78 n. j (on Gen 8:13).

12   Cf. Wilfred G. Lambert, "Note brève, Niṣir or Nimuš?" *RA* 80 (1986): 185–86; Dalley, *Myths from Mesopotamia*, 133 n. 135; George, *The Babylonian Gilgamesh Epic*, 1:516 n. 252.

13   Cf. Ephraim A. Speiser, "Southern Kurdistan in the Annals of Ashurnasirpal and Today," *AASOR* 8 for 1926–1927 (1928): 1–41 (17–18); Mario Liverani, *Studies in the Annals of Ashurnasirpal II, 2: Topographical Analysis* (Quaderni di Geografia Storica 4;

Nimush is referred to as "the mountain of Gutium," which confirms its location in the Zagros range, as George has noted.[14] The Priestly source in Gen 8:4, however, locates the landing of the ark considerably further north-west on "the mountains of Ararat." Ararat is the name the Old Testament gives to Armenia, corresponding to the country known in Assyrian sources as Urartu (cf. 2 Kgs 19:37 = Isa 37:38; Jer 51:27). But in spite of Gen 8:4's reference to "the mountains of Ararat" in the plural, leaving the precise mountain undesignated, the singular term "Mt Ararat" later became used of the landing place of the ark and came to be identified with a particular impressive Armenian mountain otherwise known as Ağri Daği, situated in the east of modern Turkey. However, this equation is simply a medieval supposition arising no earlier than the eleventh or twelfth century CE,[15] but it has led to a widespread popular misconception that the mountain now known as Mt Ararat is where the ark is supposed to have landed (not to mention occasional misguided attempts to discover fragments of the ark there!). Earlier sources had located the landing place of the ark much further south in Armenia or in northern Kurdistan in an area variously known as Qardu (e.g., *Tg.Neof.* 1, *Tg.Onq.*, *Tg.Ps.-J.*, and Peshitta) or the mountains of the Korduaians of Armenia (Berossus).[16] Now it is interesting to observe that Berossus mentions both Armenia and the mountains of the Korduaians (Gordyene) in connection with the landing of the ark—indeed he clearly regards the latter as included within the former—thus indicating that he had the most southerly part of Armenia in mind. He states that "[i]t is also said that the land in which they found themselves was Armenia. . . . A portion of the ship which came to rest in Armenia still remains in the mountains of the Korduaians of Armenia."[17] Since Berossus is hardly dependent on Genesis it seems that, as in the case of the dating of the onset of the deluge noted above, both the Priestly writer and Berossus depended on a variant Babylonian tradition locating the landing place of the ark in Armenia rather than much further to the south-east at Mt Nimush. Interestingly, the first-century BCE historian Nicolaus of Damascus, whose account, reported in

---

Rome: Università di Roma "La Sapienza," Dipartimento di Scienze storiche, archeologiche e antropologiche dell'Antichità, 1992), 48.

14   George, *The Babylonian Gilgamesh Epic*, 1:516 n. 252, referring to the text published by Erica Reiner, "*Lipšur* Litanies," *JNES* 15 (1956): 129–49 (134–35, no. 41).

15   See the evidence from the sources usefully collated by Lloyd R. Bailey, *Noah: The Person and the Story in History and Tradition* (Columbia: University of South Carolina Press, 1989), 68–79, 81.

16   Cf. Bailey, *Noah*, 65–68.

17   Cf. Burstein, *The* Babyloniaca *of Berossus*, 20–21.

Josephus, *Ant.* 1.94–95, appears to be independent of both Berossus and Genesis, also implies that the ark landed in Armenia.[18]

A further point that Berossus and P have in common over against the earlier Mesopotamian flood accounts, unnoticed hitherto so far as I am aware, is that they both reject the depiction of the ark in the Gilgamesh epic (11.30) and apparently the Atrahasis epic (see the fragmentary passage in 3.1.26) as a perfect cube and envisage it rather as analogous to a more normal boat in shape, with the length much greater than the breadth. Thus, in the Gilgamesh epic (11.28–30, 58–59), Ea informs the flood hero, Utnapishtim, "The boat that you are going to build, her dimensions should all correspond: her breadth and length should be the same . . . one 'acre' was her area, 10 rods (= 60 yards) each her sides stood high, 10 rods (= 60 yards) each, the edges of her top were equal." However, in contrast Berossus claims that the boat was 5 stades (= 1,000 yards) long and 2 stades (= 400 yards) wide,[19] and P states (Gen 6:15) that the ark was 300 cubits (= 150 yards) long, 50 cubits (= 25 yards) wide and 30 cubits (= 15 yards) high. Although the precise figures in P and Berossus are quite different, these authors agree in envisaging the ark as having longer and shorter sides, over against earlier known Mesopotamian sources.

Yet another parallel between the Priestly account and Berossus is that in both (prior to the flood narrative) the flood hero is cited as the tenth in a series of ten remarkably long-lived antediluvian figures, and this has its background in the earlier Sumerian King List.[20] Most

---

18 According to Nicolaus the ark landed on "a great mountain in Armenia, over Minyas, called Baris." Minyas must be identical with Minni in Jer 51:27, mentioned there adjacent to Ararat (Urartu), and attested also in Assyrian inscriptions as Mannai; it denotes an area south of Lake Urmia. George L. Huxley, "Nikolaos of Damascus on Urartu," *GRBS* 9 (1968): 319–20 is wrong in equating Baris with the mountain now known as Mt Ararat, following Heinrich Kiepert, *Formae Orbis Antiqui* (Berlin: D. Reimer, 1902), v, and Hans Treidler, "Βάρις ὄρος," in *KlPauly* 1:825–26. Further, the name Baris may be related to that of Mt Lubar, attested in *Jub.* 5:28; 7:1 (cf. 7:17; 10:15) as the landing place of the ark, as originally suggested by Archibald H. Sayce, "The Cuneiform Inscriptions of Van, Deciphered and Translated," *JRAS* 14 (1882): 377–732 (389 n. 1).

19 Cf. Burstein, *The Babyloniaca of Berossus*, 20.

20 For the antediluvian rulers in the Sumerian King List see Thorkild Jacobsen, *The Sumerian King List* (AS 11; Chicago, Ill.: University of Chicago Press, 1939), 70–77; Jacob J. Finkelstein, "The Antediluvian Kings: A University of California Tablet," *JCS* 17 (1963): 39–54 (45–46); Jean-Jacques Glassner, *Mesopotamian Chronicles* (SBLWAW; Leiden: Brill, 2004), 57–59. There is also a most helpful chart in James C. VanderKam, *Enoch and the Growth of an Apocalyptic Tradition* (CBQMS 16; Washington, D.C.: Catholic Biblical Association, 1984), 36–37. Cf. too Helge S. Kvanvig, *Roots of Apocalyptic: The Mesopotamian Background of the Enoch Figure and of the Son of Man*

modern scholars accept that Genesis 5 is ultimately dependent on some version of this list.[21] However, Hasel and Westermann are amongst the few who have rejected such a connection, both emphasizing that the precise number of antediluvian figures varies in different texts.[22] Earlier versions of the Sumerian King List vary between seven/eight, eight, nine, and ten kings: UCBC 9-1819 has seven or eight, WB 444 has eight, K 12054 has nine, while only WB 62 has ten[23] (a later version, W 20030, 7 has seven). It is mistaken and illogical of Westermann[24] to reject the notion that Genesis 5 is dependent on the King List on the grounds that most earlier lists have eight rather than ten figures, since not only do earlier versions of the King List vary between seven/eight, eight, nine or ten names, but it is precisely the fact that P is late that would lead one to expect that it would follow a late version of the King List tradition such as that attested in Berossus, which has ten figures.[25] Hasel's main argument is to emphasize the differences between the Mesopotamian and biblical lists (for example, the former has Sumerian names, the latter Semitic, the former lists kings but the latter has figures who are not kings, the former has lengths of life and the latter lengths of reign), but this is no problem, since the Priestly writer was clearly free

(WMANT 61; Neukirchen-Vluyn: Neukirchener Verlag, 1988), 160–72 for valuable comparative material relating to the different versions of the King List.

21   Cf. Heinrich Zimmern, "Urkönige und Uroffenbarung," in *Die Keilinschriften und das Alte Testament* (ed. Eberhard Schrader; 3d ed.; Giessen: Reuther & Reichard, 1902–1903), 530–43, who originally proposed the idea. A selection of the many who followed include Gerhard von Rad, *Das erste Buch Mose: Genesis* (5th ed.; ATD 2/4; Göttingen: Vandenhoeck & Ruprecht, 1958), 56, ET *Genesis* (2d ed.; OTL; London: SCM Press, 1963), 69; Wilfred G. Lambert, "A New Look at the Babylonian Background of Genesis," *JTS* 16 (1965): 287–300 (292–93); VanderKam, *Enoch and the Growth of an Apocalyptic Tradition*, 23–51; Dalley, *Myths from Mesopotamia*, 6.

22   Gerhard F. Hasel, "The Genealogies of Gen 5 and 11 and their Alleged Babylonian Background," *AUSS* 16 (1978): 361–74; Claus Westermann, *Genesis 1–11* (BKAT 1/1; Neukirchen-Vluyn: Neukirchener Verlag, 1974), 471–77, 485–86, ET *Genesis 1–11* (London: SPCK, 1984), 348–52, 358.

23   In a letter dated December 2, 2001, Wilfred G. Lambert informed me that an Old Babylonian version of the Sumerian King List which had been on the market also has ten names, though he did not know where it was to be found. As of 2009, when I contacted him again about this, he still did not know.

24   Westermann, *Genesis 1–11*, 475, ET *Genesis 1–11*, 350.

25   Curiously, in addition to Berossus, the earliest King List of all (WB 62), which dates from ca. 2000 BCE, also has ten names. However, Kvanvig, *Roots of Apocalyptic*, 170–71 interestingly notes that the names of the antediluvian kings in Berossus correspond most closely by far to those found in K 12054, and K 12054 is also the only cuneiform version of the King List which relates directly to the flood story, like Berossus. K 12054 dates from ca. 650 BCE and is the latest attested version of the King List prior to the time of Berossus (and P). Of the remaining King Lists, W 20030,7 is even later than Berossus (ca. 165 BCE), whilst two others date from the Old Babylonian period (WB 444 from ca. 1817 BCE and UCBC 9-1819 from ca. 1700 BCE).

to transform the tradition, just as J and P were able to do with the Mesopotamian flood story.

Continuing our discussion of the antediluvian figures, we should note that the special character Enoch, seventh in the list of the ten antediluvian patriarchs in Genesis 5,[26] has his origin in Enmeduranki,[27] who is listed seventh out of the ten antediluvian kings in Berossus, whom he calls Euedorankhos. Enmeduranki is listed seventh in two other versions of the King List (WB 444; W 20030, 7) but only in Berossus is he seventh out of ten, making the parallel with Genesis 5 particularly striking. This again strongly supports the view that P and Berossus shared some common traditions. (In UCBC 9-1819 Enmeduranki is sixth out of seven or eight, in K 12054 he is sixth out of nine, in WB 444 he is seventh out of eight, in W 20030, 7 he is seventh out of seven, and in WB 62 he is eighth out of ten.) It is also striking that Enoch is said to have lived for 365 years, 365 being the number of days in a solar year. Enoch's solar connection is further highlighted later in the so-called Astronomical Book of Enoch, 1 Enoch 72–82, where he appears as an advocate of the solar calendar. As has often been noted, this finds a ready explanation in the fact that Enmeduranki was specifically associated with Sippar, the city of the sun god Shamash, and is also said to have entered the presence of Shamash as well as of Adad.[28] The alternative explanation of the 365 years of Enoch's life sometimes offered, that it implies that he lived a full life, is unconvincing,[29] since his earthly lifespan is actually much less than that of all the other figures in Genesis 5. Again, Enmeduranki's intimacy with the gods referred to above doubtless lies behind the statement in Gen 5:22, 24 that "Enoch walked with God."[30] Further, these gods are said to have taught Enmeduranki

---

26 In J's genealogy in Genesis 4 a figure called Enoch is of the third generation of humanity, and it seems clear that his transferral to seventh place in P's genealogy in Genesis 5 (involving the reversal of Enoch and Mehujael/Mahalalel) highlights his significance. On the importance of the seventh place in certain biblical genealogies, see Jack M. Sasson, "A Genealogical »Convention« in Biblical Chronography?" ZAW 90 (1978): 171–85; idem, "Generation, Seventh," in IDBSup, 354–56.

27 See VanderKam, Enoch and the Growth of an Apocalyptic Tradition, 33–45; Kvanvig, Roots of Apocalyptic, 214–342.

28 Wilfred G. Lambert, "Enmeduranki and Related Matters," JCS 21 (1967): 126–38 (130, 132).

29 Contra Westermann, Genesis 1–11, 485, ET Genesis 1–11, 358.

30 Bearing in mind this polytheistic background, VanderKam, Enoch and the Growth of an Apocalyptic Tradition, 31, 44 has argued that this should rather be rendered "Enoch walked with the angels." However, the more usual translation "walked with God" should be retained here. This is supported by the fact that the identical phrase is also used by P of Noah in Gen 6:9 (including speaking of האלהים, as in Gen 5:22, 24, rather than אלהים), where it is indubitable that the meaning is "walked with God" rather

various kinds of divination, knowledge of which he subsequently passed on to other humans, something which fits in with the fact that in the later Enochic literature Enoch became regarded as an apocalyptic visionary and seer (similarly *Jub.* 4:17–26). The reference to Enoch's being taken up to heaven at the end of his life is admittedly not paralleled in what is said anywhere about Enmeduranki, though, as noted above, it is reported that he was privileged to have access to the divine assembly during his lifetime. Rather, it is plausible to suppose that the motif of Enoch's being taken up at the end of his life was appropriated from the comparable taking up of the Mesopotamian flood hero, which is attested in the Sumerian flood story, Gilgamesh, Atrahasis (preserved in the fragment from Ugarit), and Berossus, but specifically rejected for Noah in Genesis, unlike many other aspects of the Mesopotamian flood story which are appropriated.[31] (Incidentally, both Noah and Enoch are described by P as having "walked with God" [Gen 5:22, 24; 6:9], a phrase used of nobody else in the book of Genesis; this indicates that P saw a resemblance between the two.)   Nevertheless, although the figure of Enoch is certainly modelled in many ways on Enmeduranki, and though these figures are uniquely the seventh out of ten antediluvian figures only in P and Berossus, the specifically solar connections of Enmeduranki are absent from Berossus, where he is associated with the city of Pautibiblon (= Badtibira) rather than Sippar, the city of the sun god. Here, therefore, P must have been indebted to the more usual tradition associating Enmeduranki with Sippar and the sun rather than that which is attested in Berossus.

It has also occasionally been claimed that there is a precise mathematical relationship between the length of time attributed to these ten long-lived figures in P and in Berossus. This was first argued by Jules

---

than "walked with the angels"; cf. Gen 6:11, which just afterwards similarly uses האלהים of the deity, and the fact that Noah is nowhere else associated with angels.

31   Cf. VanderKam, *Enoch and the Growth of an Apocalyptic Tradition*, 49–50. This seems more likely than the theory of Riekele Borger, "Die Beschwörungsserie *bīt mēseri* und die Himmelfahrt Henochs," *JNES* 33 (1974): 183–96, according to which Enoch's ascension derives from that of Utu-abzu, Enmeduranki's apkallu (sage). However, this seems less likely than derivation from the Mesopotamian flood hero. First, traditions pertaining to the Mesopotamian flood hero would have been much better known in Israel than those concerning Utu-abzu. Secondly, the same verb "take" (Hebrew לקח, Akkadian *leqû*) is used in connection with the disappearance of both Enoch and the Mesopotamian flood hero; compare Gen 5:24, "Enoch . . . was no more, because God took him," with Gilgamesh epic 11.206, where Utnapishtim states, "So they took me and caused me to dwell in the distance, at the mouth of the rivers." Contrast Utu-abzu, of whom it is simply stated that "he ascended to heaven." Interestingly, the parallel with the flood hero in Gilgamesh is even closer in *Jub.* 4:23, where we read, "He [Enoch] was taken from human society, and we led him to the Garden of Eden," for the Garden of Eden similarly lay at the mouth of the rivers; cf. Gen 2:10–14.

Oppert in the nineteenth century, who noted that in Berossus the ten antediluvian kings reigned for 432,000 (= 86,400 x 5) years, whereas the ten antediluvian figures in P lived for 1,656 years, which he claimed was equivalent to 86,400 weeks.[32] On this view one must assume that in order to reduce the Babylonian figures P divided the Babylonian numbers underlying Berossus by five, and then converted the resulting number into weeks, thus yielding 1,656 years instead of 432,000 years. If Oppert is correct, this would support the originality of the Masoretic figures over against those found in the Septuagint and Samaritan Pentateuch, which instead of 1,656 years report the length of the period as 2,242 and 1,307 years respectively, as well as over various modern scholarly estimates as to what the original length of the antediluvian period in P was intended to be. However, there are two reasons why we should reject Oppert's view. First, although Berossus's 432,000 years are indeed the equivalent of 86,400 x 5 years, it is only possible to make the Masoretic text's 1,656 years equivalent to exactly 86,400 weeks by presuming that a very precise length of the solar year was in view, just a fraction above 365.217 days, but no independent grounds are given for believing that P had this precise length in mind. Oppert would appear to have decided on the particular length that he did in order to make it fit his theory! Secondly, as a result of a comparison of the Masoretic figures with those given in the Septuagint and the Samaritan Pentateuch, it is generally accepted nowadays that the Masoretic figures for the antediluvian period do not always represent the original ones, but have in certain places been deliberately modified in order to avoid a number of anomalies in the original chronology in which certain of the antediluvian patriarchs had inappropriately outlived the flood.[33] Overall, therefore, Oppert's claim that there is a precise mathematical relationship between the numbers in Berossus and Genesis 5 must be rejected.

---

32   Jules Oppert, "Die Daten der Genesis," *Nachrichten von der Königlichen Gesellschaft der Wissenschaften in Göttingen* 10 (1877): 201–23 (205–9); also later more briefly in idem, "Chronology (I)," *JE* 4:64–68 (66–67). Although noted in some older Genesis commentaries, it appears to have been overlooked since the commentary of John Skinner, *A Critical and Exegetical Commentary on Genesis* (ICC; Edinburgh: T&T Clark, 1912), 135, who sits on the fence regarding its veracity, but cf. more recently Dalley, *Myths from Mesopotamia*, 6, who supports Oppert.

33   See, for example, the discussions in Ralph W. Klein, "Archaic Chronologies and the Textual History of the Old Testament," *HTR* 67 (1974): 255–63; Hendel, *The Text of Genesis 1–11*, 61–71.

Similarly, older attempts to find precise correlations between some
of the names of the ten antediluvian figures in Genesis 5 and Berossus[34]
have long been abandoned. Thus, Berossus's third name, Amelon, was
connected with Akkadian *amēlu*, "man," and compared with the third
name in Genesis 5, Enosh, "man," Berossus's fourth name, Ammenon,
understood to be related to Akkadian *ummānu*, "workman," was connected with the fourth name in Genesis 5, Kenan, supposedly meaning
"smith," and Berossus's eighth name, Amempsinos, taken to represent
Akkadian Amēl-Sin ("man of Sin"), was held to underlie the name
Methuselah ("man of Shelah" [allegedly a god's name]), the eighth
figure in Genesis 5. However, all these attempts were based on the misconception that the names of the antediluvian Mesopotamian kings in
Berossus were Akkadian, whereas earlier forms of the Sumerian King
List have shown that they are Sumerian. Thus, Amelon actually represents the name Ammeluanna, Amempsinos derives from Ensipazianna,
and Ammenon perhaps represents Enmenunna.[35]

Several times above I have mentioned that it is scarcely possible
that the parallels between Berossus and the P flood and antediluvian
figures to which I have drawn attention were due to Berossus's
dependence on Genesis. Berossus was a Babylonian priest of Bel (Marduk) writing an account of Mesopotamian history for the benefit of a
Greek-speaking audience, and throughout his work he was clearly
dependent on earlier Mesopotamian sources. This is supported by the
fact that ancient cuneiform texts provide numerous parallels to points
in his narratives, both in general and with specific reference to the flood
and the antediluvian figures. Nowhere is there any obvious dependence on the Old Testament in his work. The particular parallels to
which I have drawn attention above are therefore most naturally similarly to be attributed to dependence on earlier Mesopotamian sources,
even if we do not now have access to them. Again, when we consider
the nature of these particular parallels, they are not so blatant as to
suggest the direct dependence of Berossus on Genesis. Thus, whilst
Genesis and Berossus give very similar dates for the beginning of the

34 E.g., Zimmern, "Urkönige und Uroffenbarung," 531–32, 539–40; Hermann Gunkel,
    Genesis (3d ed.; HAT 1/1; Göttingen: Vandenhoeck & Ruprecht, 1910), 132, ET *Genesis*
    (Macon, Ga.: Mercer University Press, 1997), 134; Skinner, *A Critical and Exegetical
    Commentary on Genesis*, 137.

35 Cf. Jacobsen, *The Sumerian King List*, 73 n. 18, 74 n. 25, though he prefers to see Amm-
    enon as a doublet of Amelon; VanderKam, *Enoch and the Growth of an Apocalyptic
    Tradition*, 27–28. Already H. Zimmern, who first proposed identifying some of the
    names as Akkadian (see previous footnote), came to reject this view in "Die altbaby-
    lonischen vor- (und nach-)sintflutlichen Könige nach neuen Quellen," *ZDMG* 78 (NF
    3, 1924), 19–35 (24).

flood, they are not identical, and whilst they both present an ark that is longer than it is broad, the figures again do not correspond precisely. Further, although the landing place of the ark in both P and Berossus is in Armenia, P uses the Hebrew name Ararat and Berossus the Greek name Armenia, and Berossus also goes on to specify the Korduaian mountains of Armenia (i.e., Gordyene), something unheard of in P. Again, although Berossus has ten antediluvian figures like P, the names and years of the figures in Berossus tend to follow various older Mesopotamian versions of the King List and do not agree with P at all (for which latter, of course, the figures were not even kings). Moreover, whilst we know that P's seventh figure, Enoch, derives from the Mesopotamian Enmeduranki, known as Euedorankhos in Berossus, where he also appears in seventh place, the seventh placing is not unique in Mesopotamian sources (only his placing in Berossus as seventh out of ten names, comparable to P's placing of Enoch, is unique), and nothing actually said about Euedorankhos in Berossus suggests dependence on P. As we have already seen, the solar connections of this seventh figure, still visible in P, are absent from Berossus. Berossus's dependence on Genesis is thus extremely unlikely.

Finally, we should mention the recent book by Gmirkin, which puts forward a new and audacious thesis about the relationship of Berossus to Genesis.[36] He argues at great length, but totally unconvincingly, that the Hebrew Pentateuch was not compiled until about 273–272 BCE in Alexandria, not long before the Greek Septuagint translation was undertaken there, with Genesis 1–11 being dependent on Berossus's *Babyloniaca* (dated to 278 BCE) and Exodus on Manetho's *Aegyptiaca* (ca. 285–280 BCE). Gmirkin's position thus represents the ultimate in terms of a minimalist late dating of the Old Testament, fully accepting the Copenhagen school's view that it is a Hellenistic book. By focusing so narrowly on Genesis 1–11 and the story of the exodus and their alleged dependence on Berossus and Manetho, however, Gmirkin overlooks many important matters relevant to the dating of the Pentateuch, including pointers to a far more extended process of composition. Just to cite one important point, Van Seters, in a critical review, notes that for Gmirkin "[a]ll references to the stories of Genesis or Exodus in the rest of the Hebrew Bible, such as the numerous allusions in Second Isaiah to creation, to the flood story, to the patriarchs, to the exodus and

---

36   Russell E. Gmirkin, *Berossus and Genesis, Manetho and Exodus: Hellenistic Histories and the Date of the Pentateuch* (LHBOTS 433; Copenhagen International Series 15; London: T&T Clark, 2006).

sea crossing, to the wilderness journey, are disqualified as unreliable for dating the Pentateuch and are therefore not even considered."[37]

With regard to the specifics of the accounts of the flood and the antediluvian figures, Gmirkin is guilty of both omissions and inaccuracies. Although striving to find all possible parallels between Berossus and Genesis 1–11 so as to support dependency, he fails to note most of the parallels pointed out above. Thus he is unaware that Berossus and P have very similar dates for the beginning of the flood. Again he fails to note that Berossus and P are distinctive in depicting the ark as more like a normally shaped boat, greater in length than breadth, in contrast to earlier known Mesopotamian flood accounts in which it was a perfect cube. He further fails to note that Berossus and P are distinctive in locating the landing of the ark in Armenia, wrongly claiming that the Gilgamesh epic likewise situated it there,[38] whereas the latter rather placed it further south-east in southern Kurdistan, as we noted earlier. Moreover, even by concentrating on the flood narrative and the preceding genealogy of ten long-lived figures alone it is easy to see serious problems with Gmirkin's daring thesis that Genesis was dependent on Berossus. For example, Berossus's account of the sending out of the birds envisages a threefold sending out of birds in the plural, unlike Genesis, which has rather a threefold sending out of one bird at a time (Gen 8:8–12, J), comparable (though not identical) to the Gilgamesh epic, in addition to the initial sending out of another bird (Gen 8:7, probably P).[39] Moreover, the account of Noah's sacrifice following the flood (Gen 8:20–21, J), in which Yahweh smells the sweet savour of the sacrifice, clearly echoes what we read in the Atrahasis and Gilgamesh epics, where the gods gather round like flies and smell the sweet savour of the sacrifice. However, Berossus's account, whilst mentioning the sacrifice, makes no reference to the deities smelling it. Again, Enoch's life of 365 years finds its explanation, as we have seen above, in Enmeduranki's association with Sippar, the city of the sun god. However, Berossus's version of the King List does not even associate Enmeduranki with Sippar, but rather with Pautibiblon (= Badtibira), so P must have been dependent on the more usual Mesopotamian tradition associating Enmeduranki with Sippar and the sun god for his attribu-

---

37 John Van Seters, review of Russell E. Gmirkin, *Berossus and Genesis, Manetho and Exodus, JTS* 59 (2008): 212–14 (212). Other critical reviews include Lester L. Grabbe in the *Society for Old Testament Study Book List 2007* (London: Sage, 2007), 117, and Joyce R. Wood in the online *Journal of Hebrew Scriptures* 8 (2008).

38 Gmirkin, *Berossus and Genesis, Manetho and Exodus*, 111.

39 Gmirkin, *Berossus and Genesis, Manetho and Exodus*, 112 curiously reverses the consensus as to the source attribution without discussion, attributing Gen 8:8–12 to P and Gen 8:7 to J, though this latter view does have supporters.

tion of 365 years to Enoch, not on Berossus. Overall, therefore, it is inconceivable that Genesis was dependent on Berossus,[40] and the parallels between Berossus and Genesis are rather to be attributed to the sharing of certain common traditions.

In conclusion, Berossus and the Priestly source in Genesis have a number of distinctive points in common which are not found in earlier known Mesopotamian accounts of the flood and the antediluvian figures. These are most naturally to be explained on the supposition that P and Berossus shared a common knowledge of certain late Babylonian traditions.[41]

It is a great pleasure to dedicate this essay to my good friend, Graham Davies, a scholar who has made a highly distinguished contribution to the study of the Old Testament and its background over many years. An important strand of his work has been the study of the Pentateuch and he also has a particular interest in the light shed on the Old Testament by ancient Near Eastern sources, and, most unusually for an Old Testament scholar nowadays, he holds a degree in Classics. It is therefore hoped that this essay, which brings together the study of the Pentateuch, ancient Near Eastern material, and classical sources, will provide a fitting tribute in his honour.

---

40   Gmirkin attempts to get round the problem that closer parallels to Genesis 1–11 can sometimes be found in earlier Mesopotamian sources than in Berossus by proposing that our current text of Berossus represents an abbreviation of an earlier, fuller version of Berossus, which would have had the material in question. This, however, smacks of special pleading. In addition, it fails to explain cases noted above in which Berossus has a version contradictory to what we find in Genesis, whilst at the same time earlier Mesopotamian sources are more in agreement with Genesis.

41   It has been suggested to me that the details in Berossus might have been deliberately corrupted in the course of Christian transmission so as to bring them into line with Genesis. However, this is extremely unlikely. First, the correspondences are not so blatant as to lead one to such a conclusion. Secondly, of the two Christian transmitters of Berossus's account of the flood (via Alexander Polyhistor), Eusebius and George Synkellos, the second actually goes out of his way to emphasize the differences between the account in Berossus and in Genesis, so may hardly be suspected of bringing the texts closer together. See Verbrugghe and Wickersham, *Berossos and Manetho*, 51.

"P" as Editor: The Case of Exodus 4:18–26*

WILLIAM JOHNSTONE

This article is prompted by a response which Graham Davies made to me in an exchange of emails in August 1998. At that time, I was engaged in preparing for publication a collection of essays drawing an analogy in method of composition between Chronicles and Exodus.[1] The final form of both Chronicles and Exodus, I was arguing, represents a radically revised edition of an earlier version attested in the Deuteronomic corpus: the Deuteronomistic History in the former; the version implied by the reminiscences, and to some extent the laws, in Deuteronomy in the latter. In the introductory chapter, I had found it useful to comment on Graham Davies's influential works on the wilderness itinerary of the Israelites, but before publishing these comments I had thought it better to verify with him that I was not guilty of distorting his views. He replied with characteristic courtesy and preciseness. But his very first response was: "I am surprised that you don't feel it necessary to debate with my 'Composition' article,[2] because if there is an analogy between Exodus and Chronicles (as distinct from their sources), then I (and quite a few others) have to be wrong in maintaining that P was originally an independent source." I did not then engage directly with Davies's arguments,[3] nor shall I here, because it

---

1   W. Johnstone, *Chronicles and Exodus: An Analogy and its Application* (JSOTSup 275; Sheffield: Sheffield Academic Press, 1998).

2   I.e., G. I. Davies, "The Composition of the Book of Exodus: Reflections on the Theses of Erhard Blum," in *Texts, Temples, and Traditions: A Tribute to Menahem Haran* (ed. M. V. Fox, V. A. Hurowitz, A. Hurvitz, M. L. Klein, B. J. Schwartz, and N. Shupak; Winona Lake, Ind.: Eisenbrauns, 1996), 71–85. See also, idem, "K^D in Exodus: An Assessment of E. Blum's Proposal," in *Deuteronomy and Deuteronomic Literature: Festschrift C. H. W. Brekelmans* (ed. M. Vervenne and J. Lust; BETL 133; Leuven: Leuven University Press, 1997), 407–20.

3   E.g., that the P material in (Genesis and) Exodus evinces sufficient continuity, coherence, and comprehensibility in itself, as well as contradiction and duplication of the parallel narrative(s), to be identified as, in origin, a separate written composition (Davies, "Composition," 74–84). An unwillingness hastily to depart from the traditional J, E, D, and P hypothesis of the origins of the Pentateuch is evident in Davies's later works, e.g., "'God' in Old Testament Theology," in *Congress Volume Leiden 2004* (ed. A. Lemaire; VTSup 109; Leiden: Brill, 2006), 175–94 (especially 184–85); idem,

seemed to me, and still does, that a further consideration has to be taken into account. The freedom and authority with which the present "final form" of Exodus (and Numbers[4]) reuses the underlying material attested in the reminiscences in Deuteronomy, above all the way in which it breaks up and transposes that material, suggests that the writer responsible for that final form was more than a "redactor." However much independent material he introduced that might justify his work being termed a "source," he was also reproducing in part that earlier material and handling it with such purposeful vigour in the service of a clear ideology that he merits the title "editor." The present article proposes another case in point of this free and authoritative editing: Exod 4:18–26.

This passage is notorious for the problems of interpretation that it presents.[5] The following account attempts to locate it within the threads of the biblical argument.

The starting-point of the discussion is the question of the affiliation of v. 23b: "you refused [מאן] . . . behold, I am about to [הנה + first singular pronoun + inceptive participle]. . . ." It seems clear, as the following table suggests, that this formulation belongs to a pattern that is about to be repeated, with variations, in six of the Plague narratives that follow in Exod 7:14–11:10:

Plague	verb מאן in conditional threat	הנה + first singular pronoun in suffixed or independent form + inceptive participle announcing impending plague
II	if you refuse,	behold, I am about to strike (7:27)
VIII	if you refuse,	behold, I am about to bring (10:4)

So similarly, with slight modification of expression:

"The Exegesis of the Divine Name in Exodus," in *The God of Israel* (ed. R. P. Gordon; UCOP 64; Cambridge: Cambridge University Press, 2007), 139–56 (152).

4   An extension of my argument into Numbers (and Genesis) will be found in W. Johnstone, "The Use of the Reminiscences in Deuteronomy in Recovering the Two Main Literary Phases in the Production of the Pentateuch," in *Abschied vom Jahwisten: Die Komposition des Hexateuch in der jüngsten Diskussion* (ed. J. C. Gertz, K. Schmid, and M. Witte; BZAW 315; Berlin: De Gruyter, 2002), 247–73; idem, "Recounting the Tetrateuch," in *Covenant as Context: Essays in Honour of E. W. Nicholson* (ed. A. D. H. Mayes and R. B. Salters; Oxford: Oxford University Press, 2003), 209–34.

5   See, e.g., A. E. Gorospe, *Narrative and Identity: An Ethical Reading of Exodus 4* (Biblical Interpretation Series 86; Leiden: Brill, 2007), 224. The book by John T. Willis (*Yahweh and Moses in Conflict: The Role of Exodus 4:24–26 in the Book of Exodus* [Bible in History 8; Bern: Peter Lang, 2010]) appeared too late to be considered here.

| IV | if you do not, | behold, I am about to unleash (8:17) |
| V | if you refuse, | behold, the hand of Yhwh is about to be (9:2–3) |

Or, מאן or similar verb in accusation:

| I | Pharaoh has refused; | behold, I am about to strike (7:14, 17) |
| VII | you are still acting high-handedly; | behold, I am about to rain down (9:17–18) |

This group of six Plague narratives, I, II, IV, V, VII, and VIII, may thus be distinguished from a second group of three, III, VI, and IX, where this pattern does not occur.

Demarcation between these two sets of Plague narratives is confirmed by other features. In the group of six, a prior confrontation between Moses and Pharaoh is envisaged. The plagues are announced before the event; they are conditional; Pharaoh has a choice to comply or not; he remains a free moral agent. These plagues are designed to force Pharaoh to release Israel from Egypt; in conveniently neat terminology, they are "*Erzwingungswunder* [compulsion wonders]."[6]

By contrast, in the group of three, the plague falls without warning. Pharaoh is offered no choice; Yhwh has foreknowledge of Pharaoh's reaction and predetermines the outcome. These plagues are naked displays of Yhwh's power even in Egypt; they are "*Schau-/Demonstrationswunder* [demonstration wonders]".

The distinctiveness of the two series is confirmed by the distinctiveness of the main verbs used to express the hardness of Pharaoh's heart:

כבד occurs in the refrains in Plagues II, IV, V, and VII, where Pharaoh hardens his own heart (Exod 8:11, 28; 9:7, 34; in Plague I a variation occurs: "he did not apply his heart to this either" [7:23]);

חזק in the refrains in Plagues III, VI, and IX, where, essentially, Yhwh hardens the heart of Pharaoh (Exod 8:15; 9:12; 10:27; see also Exod 7:3–5, 13).[7]

---

6   I borrow the terminology from L. Schmidt, *Beobachtungen zu der Plagenerzählung in Exodus vii 14–xi 10* (StudBib 4; Leiden: Brill, 1990).

7   One may suspect, then, that the use of the verb חזק at the end of Plague VIII (Exod 10:20) is an editorial adjustment (by P, as the discussion below suggests; there are many such others; see my analysis in n. 23). I here revise my earlier opinion (Johnstone, *Chronicles and Exodus*, 226 n. 24).

These two groups of Plague narratives do not stand in isolation but belong to much wider contexts. Their affiliation seems clear. The group of three links with what may for convenience be called "the commissioning of Aaron narrative" in 6:2–7:13 (for example, the confrontation with Pharaoh's magicians in Plagues III and VI is prepared for in 7:8–13). That passage has, in turn, distinctive views on the history of covenant and of the revelation of the name "Yhwh": the covenant was concluded long ago with the Patriarchs, to whom the Deity made himself known as "God Almighty," not as "Yhwh," the name reserved for revelation to Moses (Exod 6:2–5). These distinctive views link with preceding passages not only in Exodus, especially 2:23–25, but also in the Patriarchal narratives in Genesis, especially, for present purposes, Genesis 17. The association with Aaron, father-to-be of the Priesthood, makes the conventional attribution of these and related texts to "P" prima facie likely.

By contrast then, the remaining materials, the distinctive group of six Plague narratives and its preface in what may for convenience be termed "the commissioning of Moses narrative" in Exod 3:1–6:1 (with its parallel discussion of, for example, the significance of the Name, "Yhwh," in 3:14–15), should be attributed to "non-P."[8]

If all these observations are sound, then it seems plausible to identify Exod 4:18–26 as non-P. Other considerations appear to support this attribution: the "staff of God" in v. 20b picks up the reference in v. 17; Exod 4:18–26 would provide a non-P aetiology for circumcision that is alternative to P's in Genesis 17; the primitiveness of the use of a flint for circumcision suggests ancient practice (cf. Jos 5:2 [DtrH]).[9]

---

8   For the now widely current non-committal terminology, "P" and "non-P," which signalizes perhaps the minimal critical consensus, see, e.g., W. Oswald, *Israel am Gottesberg: Eine Untersuchung zur Literaturgeschichte der vorderen Sinaiperikope Ex 19–24 und deren historischen Hintergrund* (OBO 159; Fribourg, Switzerland: Universitätsverlag; Göttingen: Vandenhoeck & Ruprecht, 1998), 8–16, 226, who offers a review of major exponents (from Albertz to Zenger). He provides another conveniently neat set of terminology for the general problematic: when and how in the presumed centuries-long process of *Fortschreibung* did the *Neben-* and *Gegeneinander* of separate and possibly competing P and non-P change to the *Mit-* and *Ineinander* of associated and combined P and non-P in the present Pentateuch or Hexateuch? Subsequent discussions do not seem materially to have altered the issues; e.g., T. B. Dozeman and K. Schmid, eds., *A Farewell to the Yahwist? The Composition of the Pentateuch in Recent European Interpretation* (SBL Symposium, Series 34; Atlanta, Ga.: SBL, 2006); see my review in *JSS* 54 (2009): 276–78; E. Otto, *Die Tora: Studien zum Pentateuch: Gesammelte Aufsätze* (BZAR 9; Wiesbaden: Otto Harrassowitz, 2009); see my review in *BO* 67 (2010), cols. 374–85.

9   Reaching back to the Stone Age, suggests W. H. Schmidt, *Exodus* (BKAT 2/3; Neukirchen-Vluyn: Neukirchener Verlag, 1983), 227. But how misleading it can be to step from antiquity of institution to presumed antiquity of literary source is illus-

Nonetheless, there are problems with this attribution of Exod 4:18–26, at least en bloc, to non-P. It seems clear that Exod 4:18–26 is intrusive in its non-P context: the immediately preceding verse, 4:17, is set at the Mountain of God; the immediately succeeding verse, 4:27, picks up the same setting (cf. the paragraph markers in MT). Exodus 4:18 should perhaps be tolerated as a brief excursion back to Midian (it somewhat conflicts with 4:19 which in terms of temporal sequence it should follow; and with 4:20, since it could imply that Moses returns to Egypt without his family). But 4:19–26, at all events, are difficult to accommodate within the narrative of the meeting of Moses and Aaron at the Mountain of God (4:14–17, 27–31). Furthermore, vv. 21–23 seem intrusive within their own immediate context: v. 24 picks up from v. 20. They also repeat, oddly if they are from the same non-P narrative, the commissioning of Moses in Exod 3:18–20 of what to say and do in Pharaoh's presence before he has had a chance to carry out that commission. For such reasons (the intrusion within an intrusion), W. H. Schmidt, for example, standing in the tradition of Wellhausen, proposes a multiplicity of hands: J, vv.19–20a, 24–26; E, vv. 18, 20b; the post-P Redactor, vv. 21–23.[10]

I wish to propose another explanation. Exod 4:22–23 is indeed, in origin, non-P. But it no longer stands in its original non-P context. On the evidence of the above table on the structure of six non-P Plague narratives, Exodus 4:22–23 fits perfectly before Exod 11:4 within the structure of Plague X, which has so far in the discussion been conspicuous by its absence. Verse 22, "Israel is my firstborn son," gives the rationale for the accusation in v. 23, "you have refused to let [my firstborn son] go," which, in turn, provides the reason for the announcement, "behold, I am about to slay your firstborn son." The ensuing verses, Exod 11:4–8 describe how the slaughter of the firstborn will happen (as indicated below, there are, however, I believe, some P

---

trated by Leonard Woolley's anecdote of his encounter with a sheepshearer at Carchemish in the 1920s who "picked up a couple of large flints, knocked them together and chipped out for himself in a minute a perfectly good long flint knife. . . . He said, 'Of course we used to use iron scissors, but they are no good compared to a flint.' One was really back living for a moment in the Stone Age" (*As I Seem to Remember* [London: George Allen and Unwin, 1962], 70–71).

10 Schmidt, *Exodus*, 211. The list of commentators holding similar views could be extended vastly. Using the terminology "P" and "Non-P," J. C. Gertz, for instance, *Tradition und Redaktion in der Exoduserzählung: Untersuchungen zur Endredaktion des Pentateuch* (FRLANT 186; Göttingen: Vandenhoeck & Ruprecht, 2000), 328–33, proposes: non-P, vv. 18–20a, 24–26; post-P final Redactor, vv. 20b?, 21–23; post-redactional expansion, v. 20b?. T. B. Dozeman, *Exodus* (Eerdmans Critical Commentary, Grand Rapids, Mich.: Eerdmans, 2009), also espousing "Non-P" and "P," was not available to me at the time of writing.

adjustments also in 11:4–8, not to mention the P summary in 11:9–10). The non-P narrative continues in Exod 12:29–36 with the carrying out of that slaughter.

That Exod 4:22–23 originally belonged to the context of 11:3/4 is confirmed by two features. (1) There is now no accusation before 11:4 to motivate Plague X, as would be expected according to the pattern of the non-P Plague narratives. (2) The past tense of the verbs in the accusation in Exod 4:23 is wrong for their present context: "I have said . . . but you have refused" suits the context of 11:4, which presupposes the long set of previous encounters between Moses and Pharaoh, but not the commissioning of Moses in Exodus 4, where Pharaoh has yet to be confronted. If it were original in its context, 4:23 should run in some such manner as: "I say to you . . . If you refuse."[11]

To my mind, such a transposition of Exod 4:22–23 from 11:3/4 should come as no surprise. If these observations are sound, this transposition simply takes its place as one of many such transpositions in Exodus (and Numbers) of non-P material. More contentious, perhaps, is the identification of the editor responsible for this transposition as P.[12]

A brief outline of the argument that I have pursued in other locations,[13] that P is the final editor who is responsible for the transposition of already existing non-P materials into new contexts, is appropriate here, for Exod 4:22–23 is, I now believe, to be added to the list.

---

11   The observation that 4:22–23 fits appropriately before 11:4 goes back to the Samaritan Pentateuch, which repeats the substance of 4:22–23 at 11:3/4 (A. von Gall, *Der hebräische Pentateuch der Samaritaner* [Berlin: Töpelmann, 1966 (1918)], 136). See also B. Lemmelijn, "The So-Called 'Major Expansions' in SamP, 4QpaleoExod^m and 4QExod^j of Ex 7:14–11:10: On the Edge between Textual Criticism and Literary Criticism," in *X Congress of the International Organization for Septuagint and Cognate Studies: Oslo, 1998* (ed. B. A. Taylor; SBLSCS 51; Atlanta, Ga.: SBL, 2001), 429–39; her conclusion seems essentially to be that the Samaritan repetition does not support the restoration of a Pre-P text in Exod 11:3/4 but represents a harmonization.
     The "fit" of 4:22–23 with 11:4 has been noted by modern commentators (e.g., J. P. Hyatt, *Exodus* [NCB; Edinburgh: Oliphants, 1972], 85), but is not generally espoused; e.g., W. H. C. Propp, *Exodus 1–18: A New Translation with Introduction and Commentary* (AB 2; New York: Doubleday, 1999), 218, resists such a "violent editorial transposition"; he attributes the material to "J." I do not advocate the retransposition of 4:22–23; I merely observe that 11:3/4 is its original location in pre-P.

12   In that case, non-P is pre-P; and *Nacheinander* is to be added to Oswald's list of options for the relationship between P and non-P in n. 8 above.
     My identification of the passage as P is not, in the event, so far removed from the positions of, say, W. H. Schmidt and Gertz: they both argue for post-P redaction on the grounds that the redactor knew both P and non-P. My argument is simply that P himself is the editor involved.

13   In, e.g., my works cited above.

The instrument for separating P from non-P in Exodus (and Numbers) is provided by the reminiscences in Deuteronomy. These reminiscences show marked differences on concrete details (Realien) about, especially, itinerary, chronology, and festivals (these differences supply much "harder" criteria than, say, use of language or ideology). Because of the instrumentality of Deuteronomy in the establishment of "non-P," I feel that "non-P" should be dignified by a positive title, the "D-version."[14]

Itinerary: Deuteronomy is innocent of most of the place-names in the pre-Sinai narrative in Exod 15:22–19:2: Marah, Elim, Wilderness of Sin, Rephidim, even Sinai, for which D uses "Horeb"; for good measure, Rameses and Succoth (Exod 12:37), Etham (Exod 13:20), and Pi-hahiroth (Exod 14:1) can be added. These places are to be found, however, in the final summary of the wilderness itinerary in Numbers 33 (the same phenomenon of general innocence occurs in D's reminiscence of the itinerary in the post-Horeb narrative in Numbers; the location of Kadesh is especially instructive—in year 1 in Deut 1:19; in year 40 in Num 33:36–38; contrast the narrative in Num 13:1–22:1). Such incidents as Deuteronomy does recall that presently occur in Exod 15:22–19:2 it places after departure from Horeb: Massah-Meribah (Deut 9:22; in the matching narrative in Exodus-Numbers it would occur at Num 11:3/4). In Deut 1:6–19, the appointment of judges takes place not, as presently recounted in Exodus 18, on the eve of arrival at Sinai but on the eve of departure from Horeb. Narratives in the present pre-Sinai narrative in Exod 15:22–19:2 (manna and quails, water from the rock, hostility of the native population) have parallels in the post-Horeb D-narrative in Numbers 11–21. I have therefore concluded that Exod 15:22b–19:2a is a new composition by P, including and transposing materials already available in other contexts in the underlying version as attested by the reminiscences in Deuteronomy. That reuse by P accounts for the presence of recognizably D material in 15:22b–19:2a, for example, 15:25b–26; 17:2, 4–7, that has, however, been transposed from its former D-context in Num 11:3/4, as, I am arguing, Exod 4:22–23 has been transposed from Exod 11:3/4.

---

14 Indeed, since the establishment of P is precisely the point at issue, and since it is D that enables P to be identified, I should prefer to speak of "D" and "non-D"; for example, the tabernacle is missing in D but not the tent of meeting (Deut 31:14), thus enabling Exodus 25:1–31:18*; 34:29*–40:38 to be identified as non-D (*alias* P).

Chronology: In the D-version, Israel reaches Horeb on the third day (Exod 3:18; 5:3; 8:23; cf. "eagles' wings", 19:4). The present final form/P-edition has Israel arrive at Sinai in the third month (19:1).

Festivals: The seven-day Passover of Deut 16:1–8 is matched by a seven-day Passover narrative in the D-version of Exod 12:29–24:8*: three days' pilgrimage to Horeb; three days' preparation at Horeb (19:11, 15); sealing of the covenant on the basis of the Book of the Covenant (20:22–23:33) on the seventh day (24:4). For P, the covenant was made long before Sinai, with the Patriarchs (Exod 6:2–5; 2:24; Genesis 17). What happened at Sinai was the revelation of Law. Hence, P detaches Passover as a one-night observance (12:1–13) and associates Weeks/"Pentecost" with the revelation of Torah. Thus P radically re-edits the climactic Plague of the D-cycle (11:1–8*; 12:29–36), dismembers it and redistributes its elements, including the material now in 4:22–23.

But, I believe, Exod 4:19–26, the wider context of 4:22–23, should as a whole be regarded as a P-insertion into the D-version. The reason given in 4:19 for it now being safe for Moses to return to Egypt matches 2:23 (identified as P above). There is reason to believe that Zipporah has been secondarily introduced into this context: in Exod 18:2–3, she and her sons are brought back to Moses by her father Jethro. But, if she is brought back then, why is she brought back here now? The two incidents are harmonized by the lame, unexplained phrase in 18:2b: "after he [Moses] had sent her away." In any case, in the D-version, if Jethro is associated with the appointing of judges (Deut 1:6–19), his coming to Moses is on the eve of departure from Horeb which in the matching D-version in Exodus-Numbers falls at the junction Exod 34:29a*/Num 10:29. If Zipporah figured in the D-version at all, she would appear at that juncture in the entourage of Jethro along with her brother(?), Hobab. I suggest, therefore, that Zipporah provides the P envelope in Exod 4:19–20, 24–26 for vv. 21–23. The non-mention of Zipporah and her sons in 4:18 suggests that that verse is indeed to be ascribed to the D-version. Exodus 4:21 is to be assigned to P: God hardens [חזק] the heart of Pharaoh, as in the group of three P Plague narratives; the later shortened form of the first singular personal pronoun, "I," אני, is used in contrast to אנכי in the D-material, for example, v. 23.[15]

If the above argument is sound, one has now to ask what the function of Exod 4:22–23 was in its original location at 11:3/4 and why the P-edition felt it necessary to move it from that location.

---

15   This is the preponderant usage. In crude statistical terms, the shorter form occurs only seven times in Deuteronomy as against fifty-six times for the longer form.

The function of Exod 4:22–23 as part of the theological programme of the original D-version is surely not far to seek: the climactic Plague of the D-narrative, 11:1–8*; 12:29–36, to which 4:22–23 was integral, provided the aetiology for the dedication of the firstborn. As Israel, the Lord's firstborn, had been rescued from Egypt at the cost of the Egyptian firstborn, so it was incumbent upon Israel for ever after to dedicate to the Lord their firstborn in commemoration and gratitude. The association of dedication of firstborn with release of Hebrew slaves and seven-day Passover is confirmed by the legislation in Deut 15:12–16:8, where the sequence of the release of Hebrew slaves (15:12–18), the dedication of animal firstborn (15:19–23), and celebration of Passover (16:1–8) strikingly corresponds to the sequence of the narrative of the D-version of Exod 1:1–24:8, the freeing of the Hebrew slaves (1:1–12:36*), the dedication of firstborn, human and animal (13:1–16*, intercalated with eating of unleavened bread for seven days), and Passover as seven-day pilgrimage festival (13:17–24:8*). The connection of the climactic Plague with Passover night in 12:1–28, 43–51, rather than with the dedication of firstborn, comes only with the P-editor. The D-version's is the more logical account: Israel lives apart in Goshen, safe from the plagues (Exod 8:18; 9:26). How could the Israelites be threatened by an intervention by God designed for their own rescue and safety and need to daub their doorposts and lintels with the protective blood of the Passover victim? According to Exod 12:22 [P], Israel are not to leave their houses until the morning, yet in 12:29–31 [D] the exodus takes place at midnight. The Passover victim in Exod 12:3, 5 [P] is not specified as firstborn.[16]

The P-editor has instituted a full-scale revision of this D-version. In line with P's revision of festivals,[17] not least the separation of Passover from Covenant, Exodus 12 now provides the aetiology for the observance of Passover as a one-night festival, not for the dedication of the firstborn. There are, therefore, two parts to P's revision:

(1) Revision of the means of dedication of the firstborn.

In the D corpus, there is, in fact, a perplexing vagueness about the means and the occasion of the dedication of the human firstborn. In

---

16   On my earlier assumption that Exod 4:23–24 was in its original context in 4:18–26, which belonged to the D-version, I proposed that the function of 4:18–26 was to state that, as all Israel had to dedicate their firstborn in commemoration of their liberation, so it was necessary that, in the preface to the whole Plague narrative, Moses, as the leader of that liberation, had himself to be redeemed at the cost of the redemption of his own firstborn by circumcision (*Exodus* [OTG; Sheffield: JSOT Press, 1990], 109).

17   W. Johnstone, "The Revision of Festivals in Exodus 1–24," in *Yahwism after the Exile: Perspectives on Israelite Religion in the Persian Period*, (ed. R. Albertz and B. Becking STAR 5; Assen: Royal Van Gorcum, 2003), 99–114.

DtrH and DtrJer there is a strong polemic against child sacrifice, which was apparently rife in the immediately pre-exilic period (e.g., 2 Kgs 16:3; 17:17; 21:6; Jer 32:35); the practice is explicitly forbidden in Deuteronomy itself, Deut 18:10. The assumption must be that the sacrifice of the firstborn of appropriate domestic animals was deemed sufficient substitute. Other legislation in Deuteronomy (Deut 12:6, 17–18; 14:22–28), however, associates the offering of the firstborn of domestic animals not with Passover (as Deut 15:19–23 seems to suggest) but with the offering of first fruits and tithes and thus with the other pilgrimage festivals, Weeks and Tabernacles (Deut 16:9–17; 26:1–15). Whenever the occasion was, there must be doubt about its practicability: the keeping alive of the firstborn of every cow, sheep, and goat, unworked, for up to a year (Deut 15:19), and the driving of these en masse to the central sanctuary for slaughter, even granted the possible concessions in Deut 14:24–27.

Given the realities of the Jewish community in the post-exilic period (to which P, if post-D, belongs), scattered in Diaspora as well as gathered in Return, the Deuteronomic model of sacrificial worship by the one people at the one central sanctuary three times per year remains an unrealizable ideal. For P, the whole tribe of Levi now fulfils the role of firstborn vicariously on behalf of Israel (Numbers 3). The reason for the dedication of the firstborn remains the same: commemoration of the redemption of Israel at the cost of the Egyptian firstborn (Num 3:13). The firstborn of animals become part of the emoluments of the priests (Num 18:17–18). The timing of the sacrifice of the firstborn "on the eighth day" (Exod 22: 29b)[18] is confirmed in Lev 22:27. As far as the human firstborn male is concerned, the "eighth day" must refer to circumcision as the primary rite of dedication (Gen 21:4; Lev 12:3).

By the transposition of Exod 4:22–23 into its new context in Exod 4:19–26, P disconnects it from D's rites of dedication of the human firstborn associated with Passover and reinterprets it in terms of circumcision, a rite that can be practised on the eighth day by any family anywhere, including the Diaspora. But circumcision, as the sign of the covenant with the Patriarchs (Genesis 17), applies to every Israelite male. The switch to the plural, "sons", in Exod 4:20, despite the fact that so far in the Exodus narrative only one son of Moses has been mentioned (2:22), is therefore significant: both of Moses' sons are available

---

18   The legislation in Exod 22:27–29 requiring the offering of firstborn on the eighth day is clearly non-D. Features suggest, however, that it is post-D, i.e., P. The rare word מלאה "fullness" (?), in the preceding verse, recurs in Num 18:21 [P] precisely in the context of the emoluments of the priests. The נשיא may refer to the leader in, e.g., Num 7:2, 11–78 [P].

for circumcision. Exodus 4:25, "her son," does not make clear which son is circumcised. The hapax legomenon מולת in v. 26 may be a genuine plural, "circumcisions [of both sons]," rather than abstract plural, "circumcision." In Exod 12:43–50, P reconnects circumcision with Passover as the essential precondition for participation by any male.

Exod 4:19–26 thus does not provide an aetiology for circumcision that is alternative to Genesis 17. Rather, it is an emphatic statement that Moses, the mediator of the covenant at Horeb on the non-P scenario, is bound by, is forcibly subordinated to, P's prior covenant with Abraham, its terms and its sign. The attack on Moses by Yhwh in Exod 4:25 is explained by Genesis 17:14: "Any uncircumcised male who is not circumcised in the flesh of his foreskin shall be cut off from his people; he has broken my covenant." The phrase, "[that person] shall be cut off from his people," which confirms the identity of Genesis 17 as P (see, e.g., Lev 7:20–27; the phrase does not occur in Deuteronomy), expresses the instrumentality of Yhwh himself in imposing the death penalty (see Lev 17:10; 20:6). The presumption must be that Moses, in exile from his people, married to the daughter of a foreign priest, had neglected to ensure the circumcision of his own son(s). Zipporah accuses Moses, "You are a bridegroom of blood to me;" like any Jewish male, he fathers her son(s) only in association with the practice of circumcision, and the shedding of blood that that rite necessarily involves. The plural form of "blood" in Exod 4:25, 26, however, may mean "blood-guilt," "guilt of an offence that incurs the death penalty" (see, e.g., Lev 20:9–27). Zipporah, in an act of scrupulous religious observance, circumcised her son, and touched Moses's foot (a euphemism for genitals?; see, e.g., Isa 7:20) with the foreskin, thus involving him in the act and preserving his life by this rite of incorporation into the covenant community. As has often been observed,[19] there is a similar use of the verb "to touch" in Exod 12:22 [P] of the protective sign of the blood of the Passover victim. Both are apotropaic signs.

(2) Elevation of the significance of Passover.

P makes further adjustments to D's final plague narrative. A concluding summary is introduced in 11:9–10, thus drawing a line between the Plague-cycle and the Passover night. The remnant of Plague X in Exod 11:1–8 is conjoined with 10:21–29 [P] to make a new final plague narrative (there is thus no contradiction between 10:28–29, Pharaoh's warning to Moses never to see his face again, and the continuation of

---

19   E.g., B. M. Levinson, *Deuteronomy and the Hermeneutics of Legal Innovation* (New York: Oxford University Press, 1997), 59 n. 17. For circumcision, see David A. Bernat, *Sign of the Covenant: Circumcision in the Priestly Tradition* (SBLAIL 3; Atlanta, Ga.: SBL, 2009).

the dialogue between Moses and Pharaoh in 11:4–8). The number ten is maintained by prefacing the whole by the new "portent" worked by Aaron in Exod 7:8–13 [P]. These adjustments ensure that the P Plague cycle begins and ends with cosmic portents. In Exod 10:21–23, the darkness in the households of the Egyptians is contrasted with light in the dwellings of the Israelites. The creation ordinance, "let there be light" (Gen 1:3 [P]), is confirmed for Israel while Egypt is returned to primordial chaos. Aaron's first portent in Exod 7:8–13 also portends primordial chaos: his stick turns into a תנין, which swallows the Egyptian magicians' תנינים (cf. Gen 1:21, Isa 27:1; Ps 74:13).

By the separation of Plague cycle and Passover narrative, P introduces a qualitative difference between two: the plagues are מפתים, portents of a culminating disaster; the Passover is the culminating disaster itself. It is the eventuation of the cosmic demonstration, the consummation of the *Schauwunder*. This is made explicit in Exod 12:12. Whereas in Exod 6:6; 7:4 "great acts of judgment" are vaguely talked about, in Exod 12:12 these acts of judgment are specifically "on all the gods of Egypt." The compulsion of D's cycle of *Erzwingungswunder* is overtaken by theomachy. In that cosmic conflict, Israel are protected by the apotropaic sign of blood.

If radical reinterpretation, even polemical correction, seems too strong a term to use of P's revision of the D-version, I adduce, finally, the complementary case of Exod 3:18–20, the parallel narrative of the commissioning of Moses, where similar issues arise. In the light of the above argument, verses 18 and 20 belong to the D-version's *Erzwingungswunder* narrative (the three days' chronology, v. 18; the pilgrimage festival and sacrifice are features of the Passover in Deut 16:1–8; in v. 20, the "wonders" are designed to compel Pharaoh; the verb, "let go," שלח, intensive stem, links with the legislation in Deut 15:12, 13 [bis], 18 on the release of Hebrew slaves; so Jer 34:9–10). Verse 19, by contrast, is a comment by P (the theme of the foreknowledge of God; the use of the shorter form of the first singular personal pronoun, אני). The note in NRSV correctly renders the Hebrew of the last phrase: the exodus is not worked "by a strong hand". This is a polemical refutation of how, according to the D-version, the exodus is accomplished (e.g., Exod 6:1; 12:33; 13:9).[20] One of the fixed phrases in Deuteronomy about the action of Yhwh in the exodus is that Israel is redeemed precisely

---

20   J.-L. Ska, "Note sur la traduction de *wᵉloʾ* en Exode III 19b," *VT* 44 (1994), 60–65, defends the translation of MT as "unless with a strong hand" without emendation, though acknowledging that no exact parallel to the construction can be found. His motive is to avoid contradiction with such texts as Exod 3:20; 6:1; 13:9. In my view, contradiction is precisely the point.

"by a strong hand and an outstretched arm" (Deut 4:34; 5:15; 7:19; 11:2; 26:8; "strong hand" alone in Deut 6:21; 7:8; 9:26; "strong hand" may in these Deuteronomic passages refer specifically to the climactic Plague, the slaying of the firstborn, and "outstretched arm" to the crossing of the Red Sea). It is striking that the P-editor reuses but alters that expression in Exod 6:6: the deliverance of Israel remains "by an outstretched arm" but "by a strong hand" has been replaced by "by judgements." To describe Plague X, the climactic act of the slaying of the Egyptian firstborn, merely as a manifestation of Yhwh's "strong hand," the compulsion of Pharaoh, does not go far enough for the P-editor; for him it represents nothing less than "judgements on all the gods of Egypt" (Exod 12:12). The culminating act is a cosmic battle in which the Egyptian gods are exposed as powerless.[21] For P, deliverance is not simply from a condition, the state of slavery, as in D, but from a realm, "the land of Egypt."[22] The D-version no doubt originally read Exod 3:19 more pallidly as a conditional threat: "If Pharaoh refuses to listen to you and will not release you, then (v. 20) I shall stretch out my hand and strike Egypt . . ."

What, then, is the character of P on the evidence of Exod 4:18–26: "source" or "edition"? One might justly term P a "source" if it merely contributed the huge distinctive bodies of material that run, for example, from Exodus 25–31*; 34:29–Numbers 10:28*, amounting to almost 30% of the Pentateuch. These distinctive materials he may well himself have had a considerable hand in composing or at least in transmitting from a school, class, or profession of which he was a member. They do not, however, constitute a continuous narrative source, but blocks, represented as revealed in the course of a single year (as contrasted with the preceding 2,666 years of P's chronology to date), readily detachable from their contexts. One might equally justly term P a "source" if in other parts of the Pentateuch one were faced merely with the interweaving and integration of two separable accounts, each continuous and independent, with the harmonizing of inconsistent features. In that case, the combination of P with non-P might be regarded as the work of a redactor. The above discussion suggests a more elaborate and sophis-

---

21   It is possible, then, that P has polemically demoted the root חזק from D's estimate of the climactic act of the slaying of the Egyptian firstborn to the refrains of Plagues III, VI, and IX in his series of ten "wonders" designed for the necessary hardening of Pharaoh's heart in preparation for the final cosmic showdown. In Jos 4:24, in what appears to be a P-edited passage (e.g., in Jos 4:16 the "priests" bear the "ark of the testimony" in contrast to the "Levites" who bear the "ark of the covenant" in, e.g., Deut 10:8), the "strong hand" is related to the crossing of the Red Sea/Jordan.

22   In Exodus 1–12, the phrase, "the land of Egypt," occurs some forty times, overwhelmingly in P material.

ticated process. The sovereignty, freedom, and authority with which these intricate modifications are carried out can only be attributed, I believe, to the deliberate design of a single powerful theological mind, to P, fully aware of that earlier version, acting as his own editor.[23] P's edition cannot be intended to be a replacement, for much of the original version is retained unrevised, most strikingly, Deuteronomy itself, for the most part unedited by P, despite the fact that it preserves many contrasts with the P-edition. The preservation of distinctive D suggests that harmonization is not the point. Dialogue, debate, and dialectic are intrinsic to the Pentateuch in its "final form."

---

23 On the one hand, P's separable Plagues, III, VI, and IX, hardly amount to an independent cycle worthy of the name. On the other, the intricacy with which the separable D-cycle of seven plagues has been modified in detail and the sheer volume of these modifications are evidence that P not only knew the D-cycle (as Davies concedes, "Composition," 80) but actively engaged with it. My full analysis, in contrast to that offered in *Chronicles and Exodus*, 241, would now be as follows (main differences highlighted):

```
D     7:14–16a      17b–18      20aβ–21a      23-25; 26–27  29
P 7:8–13;    16b–17a      19–20aα     21b–22              28

D     4–6bα     8–11aγ          16–18a      20a   21–28; 9:1–7;
P 8:1–3   6bβγ–7    11aδb; 12–15;   18b–19   20b                8–12;

D 9:13    17–18a      23aαβ    23b    26–27aγi    28–29bβ      33–34aβi
P      14–16    18b–22    23aγ   24–25      27aγiib    29bγ–32

D     34b    35aβ    10:1a    3–4    6b–11   13–14aα    14aγ–bα      16abα
P 9:34aβii  35aα    35b;    1b–2    5–6a    12      14aβ      14bβ–15

D                   17aγ*–19    20b;    11:1–3   4:22–23
P 10:16bβ–17aαβ (+ "and" of 17aγ)      20a    21–29;            11:4

D 11:5-6a (except "all the land of")  7aαβ         12:29–36.
P                 6b    7aγ–8; 9–10
```

As I have said in other contexts, such analysis is artificial. The identification of P does not recreate P as an original, independent document but evidences the production of a new combined document, the D-version received and reconceived by P, as DtrH is in Chronicles. See B. Lemmelijn, "The So-Called 'Priestly' Layer in Exod 7,14–11,10: 'Source' and/or/nor 'Redaction'?" *RB* 109 (2002): 481–511: "P . . . at least in the 'Plague Narrative' of Exod 7,14–11,10, is not to be seen as a separate, self-reliant narrative, or 'source,' but rather as a 'redaction' that in addition to its own material, also reworked, complemented and integrated the existing material at hand" (which, however, she regards as "J," 507–8). Her general analysis of P is less complex in detail than mine but her conclusion about the nature of P applies then *a fortiori* to my position. I prefer the weightier term "edition" to "redaction." Her monograph, *A Plague of Texts?: A Text-Critical Study of the So-Called 'Plagues Narrative' in Exodus 7:14–11:10* (OtSt 56; Leiden: Brill, 2009), was not available to me at the time of writing.

"Kingdom of Priests"

What is Priestly in Exodus 19:6?

PHILIP JENSON

Introduction

The threefold affirmation in Exod 19:5–6 that the Israelites were to be a treasured possession (*sĕgullâ*), a kingdom of priests (*mamleket kōhănîm*) and a holy nation (*gôy qādôš*) comes at a climactic point in the Exodus narrative. The Israelites have been delivered from the Egyptians and sustained through the wilderness, as on eagles's wings (v. 4). They now come to the immediate goal of the Exodus, an encounter with Yhwh at Mount Sinai (vv. 1–2). There Moses ascends to God, who delivers a foundational speech that sums up what has gone before (19:4), sets out the present charge on those assembled (v. 5), and looks to the ongoing future of the newly formed covenant people (vv. 5–6).[1]

> 3　Then Moses went up to God; the LORD called to him from the mountain, saying,
>
> > "Thus you shall say to the house of Jacob, and tell the Israelites:
>
> 4　　　You have seen what I did to the Egyptians,
> 　　　and how I bore you on eagles' wings
> 　　　and brought you to myself.
>
> 5　and now
>
> > 　if you obey my voice and keep my covenant
> > 　　you shall be to me
> > 　　　　a treasured possession (*sĕgullâ*)

1　For a discussion of the syntax see Jo Bailey Wells, *God's Holy People: A Theme in Biblical Theology* (JSOTSup 305; Sheffield: Sheffield Academic Press, 2000), 39–45; Rudolf Mosis, "Ex 19, 5b, 6a: Syntaktischer Aufbau und lexikalische Semantik," *BZ* 22 (1978): 1–25.

out of all the peoples
indeed/for (*kî*) the whole earth is mine

6 and you shall be to me
a priestly kingdom (*mamleket kōhănîm*)
and a holy nation (*gôy qādôš*).

These are the words that you shall speak to the Israelites."

The three significant terms have had an incalculable influence on how Jews and Christians have understood themselves. Yet their precise meaning continues to elude definitive exposition, despite numerous studies and a recent extensive monograph.[2] My approach to the question will be to focus on the meaning of "kingdom of priests." While "holy nation" is distinctive, a number of other texts assume that the people can be holy (Lev 11:44; 19:2; Deut 7:6). It is far rarer to find the whole people described in priestly terms (with the eschatological exception of Isa 61:6). In almost all the texts priesthood is restricted to a particular group within Israel, the sons of Aaron or members of the tribe of Levi.

As a doctoral student my exploration of the concepts of holiness and priesthood was encouraged, with humility and incisive questioning, by Graham Davies. This is presented to him as a thank-offering for his exemplary scholarship and continuing personal friendship.

Evaluating the Proposals

A number of criteria have been applied to the evaluation of the various meanings offered for "kingdom of priests:"

(1) Grammar. A good number of possible relationships between the two nouns "kingdom" and "priests" are possible, some of them less likely than others. However, the uniqueness of this particular combination of terms makes the force of this criterion uncertain.

(2) Syntax. "Kingdom of priests" is parallel to "treasured possession" and "holy nation," but this does not mean that they are synonymous. The first is separated from the others by intervening phrases. The second and third might be complementary, describing two parts of a whole, or there could be some progression of meaning or emphasis.

---

2   John A. Davies, *A Royal Priesthood: Literary and Intertextual Perspectives on an Image of Israel in Exodus 19.6* (JSOTSup 395; London: T&T Clark, 2004). This includes a full bibliography.

(3) Election. There is a twofold emphasis on Israel's distinctiveness, first as those chosen "out of all the peoples." The following phrase declares that "the whole earth is mine" before elucidating Israel's identity in the second and third terms. Election is a corporate concept, rather than an individual one (as is usually implied by the "priesthood of all believers"), but how Israel relates to the other peoples may be given a minimal or maximal interpretation.[3] Christian interpreters often highlight a positive mediating or missionary relationship between Israel and the nations,[4] whereas exacting exegetes tend to minimise this aspect of the election motif since it is not prominent in the immediate context.[5]

(4) Narrative context. The speech is part of a longer discourse that can be defined as the chapter (19), the section (19–24), or indeed the entire Sinai revelation (Exodus 19–Numbers 11). A particular challenge is relating the priesthood of the whole people in Exodus 19 to the specific Aaronic priesthood that will be described in detail in the description of Israel's worship.

(5) Social-historical setting. The previous criterion highlights the narrative or canonical setting of the text. This criterion highlights diachronic questions about source, redaction, and transmission. What social and historical setting is reflected in the decisive redaction of the text?

The diversity of interpretations reflects in part the varying weights that different scholars put on these different criteria.

A Kingdom Ruled by Priests

We begin with a relatively recent approach that highlights a specific approach to the grammar and history of the phrase. In this view the phrase does not describe the whole people, but is to be understood on the analogy of phrases such as the "kingdom of Og" (Num 32:33).[6] "Kingdom" in the construct state can have the nuance of active rule,

---

3   Cornelis Houtman, *Exodus* (4 vols.; Historical Commentary on the Old Testament; vols. 1–2, Kampen: Kok, 1993–96; vols. 3–4, Leuven: Peeters, 2000–2002), 2:446; vols. 1–3 trans. of *Exodus* (3 vols.; COut; Kampen: Kok, 1986–1996).

4   Christopher J. H. Wright, *The Mission of God: Unlocking the Bible's Grand Narrative* (Downers Grove, Ill.: IVP Academic, 2006), 329–33.

5   Mosis, "Syntaktischer Aufbau," 25.

6   R. B. Y. Scott, "A Kingdom of Priests (Exodus xix 6)," in *Papers Read at the International Meeting of Old Testament Scholars, Leiden, 1950* (ed. P. A. H. de Boer; OtSt 8; Leiden: Brill, 1950): 213–19 (217–18).

such as "the beginning of the rule (*mamleket*) of Zedekiah" (Jer 28:1). The genitive is subjective, indicating that the priests are the subject of the action indicated by the construct. It can also be described as a possessive genitive, since the genitive owns or possesses the noun in the construct state.[7] The phrase thus refers to a priestly class that exercises the equivalent of a royal office over Israel.

There are a number of texts that associate priesthood with rule. Melchizedek is both priest and king (Gen 14:18–20) and even Abram acknowledges his authority. One of the main functions of a ruler is to administer law and justice (2 Sam 8:15; Ps 72:1), and in the previous chapter we have seen Jethro the priest of Midian giving Moses advice about these matters (Exod 18:13–23). The identification of a priestly élite has been linked to a complementary understanding of the next phrase, so that "holy nation" describes the rest of the people.[8] The priestly elite are to rule in a way that ensures the non-priestly majority becomes a holy nation.

What might be a fitting historical and social setting for this interpretation? A ruling priestly élite implies a time of writing or final redaction when there was no monarchy, perhaps before its institution or after the fall of Jerusalem in 587 BCE, when the monarchy ceased to be an effective power.[9] These rather different datings reflect a general difficulty in identifying the source and redaction history of the speech, or indeed the chapter. Its language and style does not match any of the traditional sources. For example, Deuteronomy makes use of "treasured possession," but uses "holy people" ('*am qādôš*), not "holy nation" (Deut 7:6; 14:2). This highlights rather the distinctiveness of the Exodus formulation. The uniqueness of "kingdom of priests" further undermines any definitive attribution to a known source. It is not surprising that there are many different analyses of the redaction of the passage. While there are plenty of unevennesses and puzzles in Exodus 19, it is possible to make a good case for the overall coherence and unity of the text.[10]

---

7 GKC §128g (p. 416); *IBHS* §9.5.1g (p. 145); J. C. L. Gibson, *Davidson's Introductory Hebrew Grammar: Syntax* (4th ed.; Edinburgh: T&T Clark, 1994), 30.

8 William L. Moran, "A Kingdom of Priests," in *The Bible in Current Catholic Thought* (ed. John L. McKenzie; Saint Mary's Theology Studies; New York: Herder, 1962), 7–20. He is followed by Adrian Schenker, "Besonderes und allgemeines Priestertum im Alten Testament: Ex 19,6 und Jes 61,6 im Vergleich," in *Pfarrei in der Postmoderne? Gemeindebildung in nachchristlicher Zeit: Für Leo Karrer* (ed. Alois Schifferle; Freiburg: Herder, 1997), 111–16.

9 Moran, "Kingdom of Priests," 18–20.

10 T. Desmond Alexander, "The Composition of the Sinai Narrative in Exodus xix 1–xxiv 11," *VT* 49 (1999): 2–20.

The notion of priestly rule faces other difficulties. Melchizedek and Jethro appear not so much as typical priests as the specific high priest of a city or nation. Rule is thus not a priestly as much as a high priestly possibility. It is also uncertain whether political rule was ever regarded as a central feature of the priestly office for Israel. The sons of Aaron have authority in the area of the sanctuary, but Moses effectively rules the nation, and it is he who appoints officials who exercise civil authority (Exod 18:25–26). Joshua becomes the leader of Israel, not a son of Aaron (Num 20:15–23). In the historical books the high priest was the occasional channel of divine guidance, and was no doubt influential because of the importance of the religious sphere and the closeness of the temple to the palace (2 Kgs 11:19). But this is not the same as possessing direct political power. After the exile a variety of leaders appear to have arisen. Ezra was a priest, but he was also a scribe, and his legal authority derives from a commission of the Persian king rather than his priestly status. Zechariah 6:11 portrays a crowning of the high priest Joshua, but this is unlikely to be an usurpation of royal authority (cf. v. 13).[11]

Most significant of all is that the immediate context of the phrase in Exodus focuses on the entire people without distinction. Moses addresses the house of Jacob and the children of Israel (Exod 19:3), two parallel terms encompassing the whole nation. The probability is that the following three phrases are also describing the people. It is only later in the chapter that we come across Israelite priests (19:22, 24). For various reasons, then, "kingdom ruled by priests" is an unlikely meaning.

A Priestly Kingdom

The other main proposals are that the phrase indicates a royal priesthood or a priestly kingdom. "Royal priesthood," βασίλειον ἱεράτευμα, is the translation of the LXX and 1 Pet 2:9, where the construct is taken to be the equivalent of an adjective (cf. Ps 2:6; Prov 21:20). The more common construction though is the adjectival genitive.[12] On the analogy of constructions such as *malkê ḥesed* (kings of mercy = merciful kings; 1 Kgs 20:31) the phrase would mean "priestly kingdom" (NRSV; Vulg. *regnum sacerdotale*; Aquila βασιλεία ἱερέων). But the difference

---

11 C. L. Meyers and E. M. Meyers, *Haggai, Zechariah 1–8: A New Translation with Introduction and Commentary* (AB 25B; Garden City, New York: Doubleday, 1987), 349–54.

12 *IBHS* §9.5.3c (p. 151); Gibson, *Hebrew Grammar*, 33.

between royal priesthood and priestly kingdom may not be great, since the interpretation depends more on the wider context of its occurrence than any grammatical parallel. Indeed some take *mamleket* as an absolute rather than a construct.[13] The Targums simply juxtapose the two nouns, as in "kingdoms priests" (*Tg. Onq. mlkyn khnyn*) or "kingdoms and priests" (*Tg. Neof. mlkyn wkhnyn*).

The idea of kingdom probably reflects the correlative notion of Yhwh as king, although this is not emphasized in the context (Exod 15:18 is an exception) and the parallel with *gôy* nation suggests that the focus of interest is on the priestly character of the kingdom. What, though, is the conception of priesthood that informs its use in this phrase? Priests are a particular group of specialists within a nation, but here the reference is to the whole people. The previous narrative context is of relatively little help. Jethro the priest of Midian is a significant figure (Exod 2:16; 3:1; 18:1), but nothing specific is stated about the nature of his priesthood. On the other hand Exodus 19, whenever it was written, was written from a later Israelite point of view and so can draw on the wide range of knowledge that its author or redactor would have had about priesthood. There are therefore a number of possible analogies that have been made in the interpretation of the phrase.[14] The following suggestions about the central character of priesthood may be analysed:

1. Priests Serve God

The fundamental metaphor for a temple is that it is God's house, with the priests being his attendants or servants.[15] Ibn Ezra and Nahmanides gloss the phrase as "those who serve me" (*měšārětay*), a widespread title for priests (Exod 29:30; Jer 33:21; Ezek 45:4; Joel 1:9). GNB paraphrases the phrase as "you will serve me as priests." Priestly service is largely concerned with the care of the temple/Tabernacle and the performance of cultic rituals (Exod 28:35; 35:19). Sacrifice in particular was the central act of worship (cf. Exod 10:26) and the characteristic ritual carried out by priests (Jer 33:18). Its proper performance required specialist

---

13 J. B. Bauer, "Könige und Priester, ein heiliges Volk (Ex. 19, 6)," *BZ* NF 2 (1958): 283–86.

14 See the summaries of priestly roles in Wells, *God's Holy People*, 102–24; Siegbert Riecker, *Ein Priestervolk für alle Völker: der Segensauftrag Israels für alle Nationen in der Tora und den vorderen Propheten* (SBB 59; Stuttgart: Katholisches Bibelwerk, 2007), 248–51.

15 Menahem Haran, "Temple and Community in Ancient Israel," in *Temple in Society* (ed. Michael V. Fox; Winona Lake, Ind.: Eisenbrauns, 1988), 17–25.

priestly expertise that the people as a whole did not possess, or need to possess, since the detail was delegated to priests. Before the formal institution of priesthood Exodus describes the role of the young men in undertaking sacrifices on behalf of the whole people (24:5).

There is little point, then, in regarding the whole people as simply serving Yhwh in this way. Childs takes an active view of this service: "Israel as a people is also dedicated to God's service among the nations as priests function within society."[16] But there remains a significant difference between the specific service of the priests in the sanctuary and the service that might be expected of the entire people. It is unlikely that the people are expected to offer sacrifices on behalf of the nations. The attractiveness of this view may be that "service" has a wide range of meanings, and can easily take on a more ethical or theo-logical character rather than the ritual emphasis that is a specifically priestly service.

The related verb "to serve" is also used to translate the verb ʿbd. The goal of the Exodus is stated in several places (Exod 3:12; 7:16) as being to "serve" (RSV) or "worship" (NRSV) Yhwh. But the normal meaning of ʿbd is work (5:18), particularly the toil demanded of slaves (1:13–14). Its frequent appearance in Exodus is probably intended to highlight the contrast between the oppressive slavery of Pharaoh and the liberating slavery of Yhwh. It is often associated (20:5; 23:24) with "bow down" (hištaḥăwâ), the verb for honouring a higher person or a god. The elec-tion of Israel is so that they serve and honour Yhwh and no other gods. This is the central demand on Israel's obedience and the first com-mandment (Exod 20:5; Deut 5:9). But this kind of service has no essen-tial priestly dimension. While priests can be called slaves/servants of Yhwh (ʿabdê yhwh, Ps 135:1), this is not a distinctive title. There is work associated with the Tabernacle, but this is its construction by skilled workers (Exod 36:1) or its transport by the non-priestly Levites (Num 4:19).

Working out this analogy, then, requires a generalization from the rather specific cultic service of the priests to a more general calling that is not associated specifically with priesthood.

2. Priests Are Holy

Since "priestly kingdom" and "holy nation" are parallel phrases and "kingdom" is often synonymous with "nation" (1 Kgs 18:10; Jer 1:10),

---

16 Brevard S. Childs, *Exodus* (OTL; London: SCM, 1974), 367.

this implies that "priests" is parallel to "holy." In the priestly writings Aaron and his sons are consecrated as priests and attain a holiness that enables them to serve in the holy Tabernacle in ways impossible for ordinary Israelites (Exod 29:44; Lev 8:30). In Exodus 19:22 the priests who approach the Lord must consecrate themselves (*hitpaᶜel* of *qdš*). In the context of chapters 19–24 these are likely to be the male firstborn sons, who belong to the Lord in a special way (13:2) and who are called upon to offer burnt offerings and peace offerings (24:5). This too reflects a close link between priesthood and holiness.

For Scott the people are a "kingdom set apart like a priesthood," and "the whole phrase . . . simply designates Israel as worshippers of Yahweh, a positive counterpart of the idea of separation from the worship of other gods expressed in גוי קדוש."[17] Scott highlights a contrast, but it is more likely that the terms are aligned, for holiness is primarily a positive concept.[18] The special priestly status of the people enables them to worship Yhwh in ways impossible for the nations who do not share their holy status. The analogy of priesthood implies a qualitative difference between Israel and the nations, not merely a geographical or social distinctiveness.[19] The passive view of holiness would see this as simply referring to Israel's status. A more active view would be that Israel's calling is to reveal that holiness to the nations.

Yet to what extent is holy a distinctively priestly quality? For holy can be used to describe the people without any priestly nuance. In my view holiness is a contextual term, describing a special belonging to God whose content varies according to situation.[20] Israel possesses a general holiness, a status of belonging to God that distinguishes it from the nations on account of its election. But when the context is internal to Israel, then it is priests that have a special belonging to God. There is resistance to these two being confused (Numbers 16). The particular holiness of the priests distinguishes them from the rest of the people and even the other clans of Levi in the priestly writings. The emphasis on general rather than particular holiness is associated with the Holiness Code of Leviticus 17–26 (along with other passages such as 11:44–45), whereas the priestly writings emphasize the particular holiness of priests. How these perspectives are related historically and redaction-

---

17   Scott, "Kingdom of Priests," 218–19.

18   Philip P. Jenson, *Graded Holiness: A Key to the Priestly Conception of the World* (JSOTSup 106; Sheffield: JSOT Press, 1992), 48.

19   Thomas B. Dozeman, *Commentary on Exodus* (The Eerdmans Critical Commentary; Grand Rapids, Mich.: Eerdmans, 2009), 446.

20   Philip P. Jenson, "Holiness in the Priestly Writings of the Old Testament," in *Holiness: Past and Present* (ed. Stephen C. Barton; Edinburgh: T&T Clark, 2003), 93–121.

ally remains a lively discussion, but their contextual character implies that there may be no essential clash.[21] In Exodus 19 the context is that of the general distinctiveness of Israel in relation to the nations, making it less likely that a particular priestly understanding of the holy priesthood is being activated in the other phrase.

Another difficulty is what practical implications this priestly holiness might mean for the people. The early Jewish commentary *Mekilta* is informative in refusing a retreat to generalities. Priestly holiness and service of Yhwh brought great responsibilities, but there were compensations, including the right to take certain portions of a sacrifice (Lev 6:26; 1 Sam 2:12–17). *Mekilta* suggests that the whole nation attained a priestly ritual status at Sinai, so that it could eat of the holy things (the classification of a wide range of offerings and sacrifices). Unfortunately Israel's sinfulness meant a restriction of this privilege to the priests.

> It says, however: "And priests." But "priests" might mean nonfunctioning priests, as when it says: "And David's sons were priests (*kohanim*)" (2 Sam 8:18)? Therefore Scripture says: "And a holy nation." Hence, the sages said: The Israelites before they made the Golden Calf were eligible to eat of the holy things. But after they made the Golden Calf these holy things were taken from them and given to the priests exclusively.[22]

Propp also pursues this line of thought: "kingdom of priests" and "holy nation" "cumulatively express the extreme sanctity of *all* Israel." All Israel possesses a priestly quality that required "observing special restrictions in diet, marriage, sexuality, mourning, hygiene, etc."[23] A rather specific cultic definition of priesthood is here being used to understand the nature of both holiness and priesthood. Priests are governed by more rigorous laws than other Israelites, but is this the essence of their priesthood, or the consequence of one of the other proposals suggested in this analysis? In enjoining Israelites to be holy, Leviticus 19 does not refer explicitly to priestly behaviour. Requirements are related to the general character of Yhwh and his will for all, not what is demanded of priests.

---

21 The priestly emphasis is challenged by the later Holiness School, according to Israel Knohl, *The Sanctuary of Silence: The Priestly Torah and the Holiness School* (Minneapolis, Minn.: Fortress, 1995), 180–86. See the review of the complex historical-critical discussion in Christophe Nihan, *From Priestly Torah to Pentateuch: A Study in the Composition of the Book of Leviticus* (FAT 2/25; Reihe; Tübingen: Mohr Siebeck, 2007), 1–19.

22 Jacob Zallel Lauterbach, *Mekilta de-Rabbi Ishmael: A Critical Edition on the Basis of the Manuscripts and Early Editions* (3 vols.; The Schiff Library of Jewish Classics; Philadelphia, Pa.: Jewish Publication Society of America, 1933–1935), 2:205.

23 William H. C. Propp, *Exodus 19–40: A New Translation with Introduction and Commentary* (AB 2A; New York: Doubleday, 2006), 158.

3. Priests Teach

The teaching role of the tribe of Levi is reflected in Deut 33:10. The levitical priests have charge of the law that is kept in the ark of the covenant (Deut 17:18; 31:9). In the priestly writings the priests are responsible for knowing and performing the various laws of sacrifices and other rituals (Lev 6:2; 15:32; Num 5:29). The importance of the priestly discernment of what is holy or profane, impure and pure is emphasized in Lev 10:10, although the next verse may imply a broader scope in requiring the priests to "teach the people of Israel all the statutes that the LORD has spoken to them through Moses" (10:11).

Working out this feature for the whole people usually reflects an active understanding of election. The people are called to communicate the law of God to the nations, just as priests teach the law to the people. The context of Exod 19:5–6 is precisely that of hearing and obeying what God has spoken (v. 8). The law is the great gift of Sinai, which Israel is now called upon to pass on in turn to the nations.

Once again we must take care that "teaching" does not become too generic a term, for priestly teaching is primarily about ritual matters. A more general teaching, such as summed up by the Ten Commandments, would be more relevant for the kind of knowledge of God that would benefit other nations.[24] But the Decalogue is addressed to and received by the whole people, not the priests. Instruction of the nations is found in the oracle of Isa 2:3, where there is a further emphasis on the specific presence of Yhwh on the temple mountain. But elsewhere the presence of God on Mount Zion is seen as the inheritance of all the people, rather than a priestly privilege.

4. Priests Are Moral and Religious Examples

In the priestly writing the laws governing the behaviour of priests are stricter than those for other Israelites (Leviticus 21). Their obedience has to be precise, and the closeness of Yhwh magnifies the danger of any infringement. Holiness is not primarily an ethical category, but the call to holiness cannot be divorced from ethical obligations (Lev 19:2). The sin of Aaron's sons, Nadab and Abihu, is notoriously difficult to specify (10:1–2), but a comparison with Numbers 16–17 invites a reading that includes not merely ritual impropriety but in addition a wilful element

---

24   Peter Enns, *Exodus* (The NIV Application Commentary; Grand Rapids, Mich.: Zondervan, 2000), 389.

of rebellion. The general principle is that those who teach the law are particularly required to live by those laws (Rom 2:21; Ja 3:1). The prophets hold the priests accountable for their ethical and religious failures (Hos 6:9; 10:5; Mal 3:11), and later writers give the phrase an ethical interpretation (*Jub.* 33:20).

By analogy, then, the people are to lead exemplary lives of obedience and faith in comparison to the nations.[25] The question is whether irreproachable behaviour is a distinctively priestly attribute. The key ethical and religious demands are made on the entire people, amongst whom the priests are included. It is an interpretation that is attractive to those who see holiness as having an important ethical component, but this is unlikely to be a primary meaning of holiness in the Old Testament.

5. Priests Draw Near to the Lord

In Exod 19:22 the priests are characterized as those who approach (*ngš*) Yhwh. "The essence of the priestly prerogative consisted in access to the presence of God."[26] In the priestly Pentateuchal accounts the tabernacle is the place where God graciously deigns to dwell (Exod 25:8). Any Israelite is able to come "before the Lord" and draw near to him (Lev 1:2; 9:5), but this is only up to a certain point. They are restricted to the court of the tabernacle. Only the sons of Aaron are allowed to enter the holy place, offer incense, and perform the blood rituals. Only the high priest is able to enter the innermost sanctum, the holy of holies, where the Lord dwells in dangerous intensity (Lev 10:1–3; 16). Even the Levites do not have the level of holiness that is required to enter the holy places (Num 1:51; 3:10).

The other themes can be closely related to this emphasis. Their holy status allows priests to draw especially near to the holy God, who dwells in his house or palace/temple or holy place. The service of the priests is to maintain the integrity of the place of presence. Teaching about purity and impurity ensures that impurity endangers the holiness of the dwelling place of God as little as possible. A central feature of the sacrificial system was to deal with various kinds of impurity. Access to the divine presence allowed the mediation of God's power to

---

25 J. G. Janzen, *Exodus* (Westminster Bible Companion; Louisville, Ky.: Westminster John Knox, 1997), 134. Similarly Christoph Dohmen, *Exodus 19–40* (HTKAT; Freiburg: Herder, 2004), 63.

26 Davies, *Royal Priesthood*, 162.

bless (Num 6:22–27). A number of commentators emphasize the "special intimate relationship" between priest and God.[27]

On the other hand, the Sinai narrative highlights that all the people encounter the presence of Yhwh. While Moses ascends the mountain itself and speaks to him face to face (Exod 19:3; 33:11), Yhwh comes down before the eyes of all the people (19:11; cf. Num 14:14) and they tremble at his theophanic presence (Exod 19:16–19). Just as impurity prevents priests entering the tabernacle, so the people are commanded to wash their clothes and avoid any sexual encounter that will bring impurity (vv. 14–15; Lev 15:16–18). The coming of Yhwh at Sinai is a unique event, but the privilege of access to the divine presence for all will be continued through the institution of the tabernacle and later the temple.

An early Jewish exegetical tradition suggested that this privileged access to Yhwh was in mind here without any specific priestly character (cf. the citation from *Mekilta* above). Rashi glosses the phrase as "princes (*śārîm*)" and compares it to when David's sons are called priests (2 Sam 8:18). The suggestion is that it can be a term for court officials, those who are intimate with the king and have access to his presence.[28]

The theme can be related to the election of Israel: "Just as the priests stand nearer to God than the people, so the Israelites stand nearer to Yhwh than the other nations."[29] Only Israelites can come before the true God, whereas the gods of the other nations are idols and illusions.[30] It is this unique access to the presence of God that makes them a holy nation. When other texts refer to the divine presence on Zion, it is not regarded as the exceptional privilege of the priests or even the inhabitants of Jerusalem, but as a gift to the whole people. While experienced in intense ways at the temple or during great festivals, it is significant for Israelite prayer and orientation at other times and in other places (1 Kgs 8). The proposal leaves open, as the book of Exodus itself does, the question whether and how the people might mediate this presence to the nations.

---

27   John Hall Elliott, *The Elect and the Holy: An Exegetical Examination of I Peter 2:4–10 and the Phrase "Basileion Ierateuma"* (NovTSup 12; Leiden: Brill, 1966), 54–55.

28   Hans Wildberger, *Jahwes Eigentumsvolk: Eine Studie zur Traditionsgeschichte und Theologie des Erwählungsgedankens* (ATANT 37; Zürich: Zwingli Verlag, 1960), 81–82.

29   Paul Heinisch, *Das Buch Exodus* (HSAT 2; Bonn: Peter Hanstein, 1936), 146 (my translation).

30   J. B. Bauer, "Könige und Priester," 286.

6. Priests Mediate

Finally we may note how priests are go-betweens or mediators, representing the people to Yhwh, and Yhwh to the people. Priests sacrifice
an animal on behalf of its offerer. They take its blood into the sanctuary, but it is the offerer who primarily benefits (Lev 4:20; 10:17). When
the high priest comes before Yhwh in the sanctuary he wears a breast-
plate with twelve precious stones that represent the twelve tribes of
Israel (Exod 28:21; 39:14). On the other hand priests communicate the
will of God to the people. They declare on his behalf what is pure or
impure (Lev 10:10), teach the people (see above) and bless them (Gen
14:19–20; Num 6:22–27; Deut 10:8). "As the one who moves between
heaven and earth, the priest is ideally placed to be a mediator of divine
blessing and an imparter of divine truth."[31]

An active interpretation of Israel's election suggests on this view
that Israel is similarly called to mediate between the true God and the
nations, for which being a "holy nation" is a requirement.[32] But what
precisely is mediated? It could include the aspects already mentioned
(service, holiness, knowledge, presence). Many refer to the theme of
blessing to the nations that goes back to the Abrahamic covenant (Gen
12:3). Yet this is a reading of the text in the frame of a wider biblical
theology, rather than a proposal with a firm exegetical basis.

Conclusion

Despite its recent popularity, "a kingdom ruled by priests" appears to
be an unlikely interpretation of "kingdom of priests." While grammati-
cally attractive, the immediate context strongly suggests that the three
key terms, "treasured possession," "kingdom of priests," and "holy
nation," all refer to the whole people.

The more likely translation is "priestly kingdom," where, however,
several proposals have been made about the nature of the "priestly"
character attributed to the people. Many of these are closely related.
Priests are consecrated in order to draw close to Yhwh in his holy sanctuary, where they serve him through offering sacrifices on behalf of the
people and mediating his blessing. Their responsibilities and closeness
to Yhwh's presence require them to be exemplary in their ritual and

---

31   Davies, *Royal Priesthood*, 168.
32   Frank Michaeli, *Le livre de l'Exode* (CAT 2; Neuchâtel: Delachaux & Niestlé, 1974),
      165–66.

moral behaviour, while their specialist expertise fits them to teach the people. Interpreters tend to select one or more of these features depending on a wider understanding of the theology of Exodus and the Bible, and their own interests.

The main difficulty in extending a particular priestly feature to the whole people is that there are important differences between the specific status and role of the priests and those of the rest of the people. However, the explicit analogy between priests and people invites such a generalization. The difference between priest and people then becomes a difference of degree rather than of kind, although this sits awkwardly with the detail of the priestly office. The extent of this hermeneutical move is often disguised by the ambiguity of the key terms (e.g., service, holiness, teaching, nearness), which tend to have a specific ritual focus for priests but can take on a general meaning when used of the whole people. Furthermore, the non-cultic ethical and religious qualities that would appropriately distinguish Israel from the nations are precisely commandments given to all, not the priests.

Even if this paper has taken us no nearer to solving the puzzle of the meaning of "kingdom of priests," it may encourage interpreters to become more aware of how they move from what characterizes priests to how this might apply to the whole nation. The uniqueness and ambiguity of the text, combined with its rich narrative and theological setting, suggest that there is no simple or easy answer, but an invitation to reflect on its potential significance for readers and hearers down to the present day.

The Fifth Commandment in Context

DAVID L. BAKER

Honour your father and your mother; so that you may live long on the land which the LORD your God is giving to you. (Exod 20:12)

Honour your father and your mother, as the LORD your God has commanded you; so that you may live long and so that it may go well with you on the land which the LORD your God is giving to you. (Deut 5:16)[1]

The fifth commandment[2] has been considered by some rabbis to be the most important of all,[3] and there is little doubt it has moulded Jewish traditions of family life over the centuries and continues to do so today. It has been seen as an exhortation to filial piety, comparable to the teaching of Confucius;[4] and in the New Testament it is described as "the first commandment with a promise" (Eph 6:2). Some have treated it as a rule addressed to children, instructing them to respect and obey their parents.[5] Others have questioned its relevance to those with absent or abusive parents. In order to obtain a better understanding of its meaning, this article will examine the fifth commandment in context, specifically the cultural context of the ancient Near East and the canonical context in which Jews and Christians have read it throughout the centuries.

---

1 I have made my own translation of Old Testament texts cited in this article. Nash Papyrus and LXX add "it may go well with you and so that" in Exodus, probably because of the presence of this phrase in the Deuteronomic parallel. The order of the clauses "so that you may live long" and "so that it may go well with you" is reversed in LXX Deuteronomy.

2 I follow the Jewish numbering of the commandments, used in Eastern Orthodox and Reformed churches, which goes back to Philo and Josephus and is arguably the oldest. The numbering used in Roman Catholic and Lutheran churches follows a tradition which goes back to the Peshitta and several church fathers. Honouring parents counts as the fifth commandment in the former numbering, and fourth in the latter.

3 Solomon Goldman, *The Ten Commandments* (ed. Maurice Samuel; Chicago, Ill.: University of Chicago Press, 1956), 177.

4 Song Nai Rhee, "Fear God and Honor your Father and Mother: Two Injunctions in the Book of Proverbs and the Confucian Classics," *Enc* 26 (1965): 207–14.

5 J. Alec Motyer, *The Message of Exodus: The Days of Our Pilgrimage* (Leicester: Inter-Varsity, 2005), 227. This point is made in several texts (e.g., Prov 1:8; Eph 6:1; Col 3:20), but whether it is also the purpose of the fifth commandment is less certain.

Cultural Context

In the space of a short article it is not feasible to make a detailed study of attitudes towards parents and older people in the ancient Near East, so I focus on a selection of legal and wisdom texts concerned with the matter. Three main concepts are apparent: dignity, worship, and care.

Dignity

Literary and royal inscriptions from the Old Babylonian period show that children were expected to honour (*kbd/kabātu*) and revere (*yrh/palāḥu*) their parents.[6] One of the prime concerns of care for the elderly in the ancient Near East was their dignity, according to Westbrook.[7] Younger people were expected to maintain the older person's status in society. An Egyptian example is the administrative arrangement called "the staff of old age" by which an elderly person who could not continue to work effectively retained his position but had a younger assistant to carry out the work. Westbrook compares this with the respect for senior citizens in Lev 19:32, in contrast to the compulsory retirement and preference for younger workers that is common in modern societies.

A similar concern is apparent in the Assyrian story of Ahiqar, an elderly sage who has no son of his own and passes his wisdom on to his nephew Nadin instead.[8] However, Nadin is treacherous and plots against his uncle, almost causing his death. In one version of the story he justifies his behaviour on the basis of his uncle's senility:

> My father Ahiqar is grown old, and stands at the door of his grave; and his intelligence has withdrawn and his understanding is diminished.[9]

Several pieces of wisdom from the *Words of Ahiqar* relate to maintaining the dignity of parents and elders:

---

6   Marten Stol, "Care of the Elderly in Mesopotamia in the Old Babylonian Period," in *The Care of the Elderly in the Ancient Near East* (ed. Marten Stol and S. P. Vleeming; Leiden: Brill, 1998): 59–118 (60, 62).

7   Raymond Westbrook, "Legal Aspects of Care of the Elderly in the Ancient Near East: Introduction," in *The Care of the Elderly*, 1–22 (12–13).

8   The oldest extant version is an Aramaic papyrus of the fifth century BC from Elephantine. The text is incomplete, and fuller but later versions have survived in Syriac, Armenian, and other languages. For a detailed introduction, plus translation and notes on the Aramaic text, see J. M. Lindenberger, "Ahiqar," *OTP* 2:479–507. For a synopsis of several different versions, see "The Story of Aḥiḳar," translated by J. Rendell Harris, Agnes Smith Lewis and F. C. Conybeare (*APOT* 2:715–84).

9   Syriac version, §3.1 (*APOT* 2:740).

My son, when thou seest a man who is older than thee, rise up before him.[10]

Whoever takes no pride in his father's and mother's name may Shama[sh] not shine [on him], for he is an evil man.[11]

Son, love the father who begat thee, and earn not the curses of thy father and mother; to the end that thou mayst rejoice in the prosperity of thy own sons.[12]

Very similar sentiments are expressed in Lev 19:32 and Prov 20:20; 23:22.

Worship

Clearly parents, and elderly people in general, were considered worthy of special honour and respect in the ancient Near East. There is also evidence that the duty of honour continued after the death of the one who was honoured. This was not simply a matter of providing an appropriate burial, though that was certainly included.[13] Ancestor worship was apparently common in Egypt, Ugarit, and Mesopotamia, probably with a view to obtaining blessings from the deceased. This seems to be implied by a passage in the Aqhat Legend which records the duties of a son:

> Someone to raise up the stela of his father's god,
>   in the sanctuary the votive emblem of his clan;
> To send up from the earth his incense,
>   from the dust the song of his place[14]

There is also an Ugaritic accession liturgy in which departed kings are summoned to bestow blessings on the new king.[15]

---

10 Syriac version, §22 ("The Words of Ahikar," translated by A. E. Goodman [*DOTT*, 270–75 (273)]); cf. Armenian version, §2.80 (*APOT* 2:739).

11 Aramaic version, §49 (*OTP* 2:504); cf. "The Words of Ahiqar," translated by H. L. Ginsberg (*ANET*, 427–30 [429]).

12 Armenian version, §2.18 (*APOT* 2:732). §2.78 is almost identical (*APOT* 2:738).

13 E.g., a second-millennium contract from Nuzi states: "as long as A. lives, B. shall give him food and clothing and honour him. When he dies, he shall mourn him and bury him" (Westbrook, "Legal Aspects," 13).

14 "The ꜣAqhatu Legend," translated by Dennis Pardee, *COS* 1.103:343–56 (344), trans. from *CTA* 17 i 27–34. Lines 3 and 4 may be referring to ancestor worship at the family vault, which was located under the house in Ugaritic custom, according to Pardee (344, n. 8). Cf. John F. Healey, "The *pietas* of an Ideal Son in Ugarit," *UF* 11 (1979): 353–56.

15 "The Patrons of the Ugaritic Dynasty (KTU 1.161)," translated by Baruch A. Levine, Jean-Michel de Tarragon, and Anne Robertson, *COS* 1.105, 357–58. This is the majority interpretation of the text (e.g., Baruch A. Levine and Jean-Michel de Tarragon,

Several scholars argue for the existence of similar practices in ancient Israel,[16] while others deny it.[17] It is notable that tombs are of relatively little importance in biblical Israel compared with many other cultures, ancient and modern. Jacob marks Rachel's tomb with a pillar (Gen 35:20), while Absalom and Shebna make advance preparations for their own memorials (2 Sam 18:18; Isa 22:15–16), but there is no record of pilgrimages or worship in connection with ancestral tombs. The dead are lamented (e.g. 2 Sam 1:17–27; 1 Kgs 13:30; Jer 34:5; Amos 5:16–17; 8:10), but the biblical laments do not include any religious element. Laceration and shaving the forehead in mourning, though common elsewhere, are not acceptable for Israelites (Lev 19: 27–28; Deut 14:1; cf. Jer 47:5).[18] Israelites who offer the triennial tithe make a formal declaration that none of it has been offered to the dead (Deut 26:14), implying that some people do make offerings to the dead but certainly not authorising it (cf. Ps 106:28; Sir 30:18). Consultation of the dead is strictly forbidden (Lev 19:31; 20:6, 27; Deut 18:10–14; cf. 2 Kgs 21:6; 23:24), and the one recorded attempt to do this ends in disaster (1 Samuel 28). It seems to me that Israel differed significantly with its neighbours in relation to the dead, at least in principle. While it is possible that ancestor worship occurred from time to time in ancient Israel, there is no doubt that the practice would have been contrary to normative Yahwism.[19]

"Dead Kings and Rephaim: The Patrons of the Ugaritic Dynasty," *JAOS* 104 (1984): 649–59), though Brian B. Schmidt, *Israel's Beneficent Dead: Ancestor Cult and Necromancy in Ancient Israelite Religion and Tradition* (Tübingen: Mohr Siebeck, 1994; repr. Winona Lake, Ind.: Eisenbrauns, 1996), 100–20 sees it as a coronation ritual, incorporating mourning rites for the deceased king, without any implication of an ancestor cult.

16 E.g., Klaas Spronk, *Beatific Afterlife in Ancient Israel and in the Ancient Near East* (Kevelaer: Butzon & Bercker, 1986); Theodore J. Lewis, *Cults of the Dead in Ancient Israel and Ugarit* (Atlanta, Ga.: Scholars Press, 1989); "The Ancestral Estate (נַחֲלַת אֱלֹהִים) in 2 Samuel 14:16," *JBL* 110 (1991): 597–612; Elizabeth Bloch-Smith, *Judahite Burial Practices and Beliefs About the Dead* (Sheffield: Sheffield Academic Press, 1992); cf. Herbert Chanan Brichto, "Kin, Cult, Land and Afterlife: A Biblical Complex," *HUCA* 44 (1973): 1–54; Bill T. Arnold, "Religion in Ancient Israel," in *The Face of Old Testament Studies: A Survey of Contemporary Approaches* (ed. David W. Baker and Bill T. Arnold; Grand Rapids, Mich.: Baker, 1999), 391–420 (414–15).

17 E.g., Roland de Vaux, *Ancient Israel: Its Life and Institutions* (London: Darton, Longman & Todd, 1961), 56–61; rev. trans. of *Les institutions de l'Ancien Testament* (2 vols.; Paris: Cerf, 1958–60); Schmidt, *Beneficent Dead*; Philip S. Johnston, *Shades of Sheol: Death and Afterlife in the Old Testament* (Leicester: Apollos, 2002), 167–95.

18 These practices are also mentioned in Jer 16:6 (cf. Isa 22:12). The former is associated with worship of other gods in 1 Kgs 18:28 and Hos 7:14.

19 For Christian reflections on ancestor practices in Asia today, see Bong Rin Ro, ed., *Christian Alternatives to Ancestor Practices* (Taichung, Taiwan: Asia Theological Association, 1985).

Care

Another major concern of ancient Near Eastern laws and wisdom concerning family relationships is practical care and support for ageing parents.

King Lipit-Ishtar of Isin, in the prologue to his twentieth-century BC laws, records:

> With a . . . decree (?) I made the father support his children, I made the child support his father. I made the father stand by his children, I made the child stand by his father.[20]

Legal texts from the Old Babylonian period refer to the obligation to support parents economically and stipulate how much was expected from children.[21]

The Egyptian Instruction of Any gives advice about proper treatment of one's mother:

> Double the food your mother gave you,
> Support her as she supported you;
> She had a heavy load in you,
> But she did not abandon you.
> When you were born after your months
> She was yet yoked [to you],
> Her breast in your mouth for three years.
> As you grew and your excrement disgusted,
> She was not disgusted, saying: "What shall I do!"
> When she sent you to school,
> And you were taught to write,
> She kept watching over you daily,
> With bread and beer in her house.[22]

The duties of a son in the Ugaritic Aqhat Legend, already mentioned in connection with ancestor worship, are also concerned with practical care for a father:

> To shut up the jaws of his detractors,
>   to drive out anyone who would do him in;
> To take his hand[23] when [he is] drunk,
>   to bear him up [when he is] full of wine;
> To eat his grain[-offering] in the temple of Baʿlu,
>   his portion in the temple of ʾIlu;[24]

---

20 Lines ii.16–24 ("The Laws of Lipit-Ishtar," translated by Martha Roth [*COS*, 2.154:410–14 (411)]).

21 Stol, "Care," 60, 62.

22 §7 ("Instruction of Any," translated by Miriam Lichtheim, *COS*, 1.46:110–15[113]); cf. Sir 7:27–28; Tob 4:4.

23 Cf. Isa 51:18.

24 Cf. 1 Sam 1:4.

To resurface his roof when rain softens it up,
    to wash his outfit on a muddy day.[25]

As well as these specific laws and instructions, various other documents provide information about the care of the elderly in the ancient
Near East.[26] This care includes provision of basic needs (especially
grain, oil, and clothing), plus practical help with daily living when required.[27]

Canonical Context

The Decalogue is often divided into two groups of commandments, one
of four and the other of six, respectively dealing with relationships to
God and to one's neighbour.[28] This was suggested by Augustine and
has been the traditional division in the Catholic and Lutheran churches
(though in their numbering the division is actually between the first
three and last seven commandments). One attraction of this division is
that it matches the two great commandments of loving God and loving
one's neighbour (Deut 6:5; Lev 19:18; cf. Mic 6:8; Matt 22:36–40). However, it is not quite so simple as this, because the sabbath commandment is not only concerned with relating to God but also with the need
of vulnerable members of the community to enjoy a weekly holiday.

Others see two groups of five commandments, the first distinctively
Israelite and the second reflecting a more universal social morality.[29]
Each commandment in the first group includes the phrase "The LORD
your God" and has one or more motive clauses (if the introduction can
be taken to supply these for the first commandment, as it does according to the punctuation of NRSV). The second group prohibits actual and
intended mistreatment of other human beings. These commandments
are mostly brief in form, though the last is somewhat extended.
According to Jewish tradition, each tablet contained five commandments, which would accord with this division of the Decalogue (cf.
Philo, *Decalogue* 50; Josephus, *Ant.* 3.101). However, it does not account

---

25   *COS* 1.103:344; trans. from *CTA* 17 i 27–34. On this text, see also Oswald Loretz, "Das
     biblische Elterngebot und die Sohnespflichten in der ugaritischen Aqht-Legende,"
     BN 8 (1979): 14–17.

26   Stol and Vleeming, eds., *The Care of the Elderly.*

27   Westbrook, "Legal Aspects," 10–14.

28   E.g., Eduard Nielsen, *The Ten Commandments in New Perspective: A Traditio-Historical
     Approach* (SBT 2d ser. 7; London: SCM, 1968), 33–34; trans. of *Die zehn Gebote: Eine
     traditionsgeschichtliche Skizze* (ATD 8; Copenhagen: Munksgaard, 1965); John I.
     Durham, *Exodus* (WBC 3; Waco, Tex.: Word Books, 1987), 290.

29   E.g., Moshe Weinfeld, *Deuteronomy 1–11* (AB 5; New York: Doubleday, 1991).

for the fact that the first group of five commandments is almost six times as long as the second group, unless it was thought to be only a brief form of the commandments that was engraved in stone.[30]

Each of these divisions has its merits. The first seems to fit the content better, since one group is concerned with relating to God and the other with relating to human beings. The second is preferable from the perspective of form, distinguishing between long and short commandments. There are also other possible divisions, which will not be discussed here.[31]

A key factor is the interpretation of the fifth commandment. Philo (*Decalogue* 106–07) believed that it was placed on the borderline between the two groups because parents stand on the borderline between the mortal and the immortal. On the one hand, parents are human and might be included in the category of people who are to be loved and respected (as in the following five commandments); on the other hand, they are partners with the Creator in bringing children into the world and therefore to be honoured as the Creator himself is honoured.[32]

According to this view, to honour one's mother and father is not merely a matter of social relationships, but part of one's respect for God. It is not concerned with preventing harm to other people (as in the last five commandments), but advocates a fundamental virtue (expressed positively, like the fourth commandment on honouring the sabbath). The reward for keeping the fifth commandment is long life "on the land which the LORD your God is giving to you," complementing the introduction to the first commandment (Exod 20:2//Deut 5:6) and so making an *inclusio* to round off the first half of the Decalogue.

---

30 According to Heinrich Ewald, *The History of Israel* (8 vols.; London: Longmans, Green & Co., vols. 1–2, 3d ed., 1876; vols. 3–8, 2d ed., 1878–1886), 2:160–62; trans. of *Geschichte des Volkes Israel* (7 vols. in 8; 3d ed; Göttingen: Dieterich, 1864–1868), the first group specifies the duty owed by the inferior and dependent to the superior, while the second group treats the mutual duties between human beings. Anthony Phillips, *Ancient Israel's Criminal Law: A New Approach to the Decalogue* (Oxford: Blackwell, 1970), who also divides the commandments into two groups of five, believes that the second group is designed to protect the person (not property), but this depends on the doubtful assumption that the eighth commandment refers to kidnapping rather than stealing.

31 For other suggested divisions, see Reinhard Gregor Kratz, "Der Dekalog im Exodusbuch," *VT* 44 (1994): 205–38; Matthias Millard, "Das Elterngebot im Dekalog: Zum Problem der Gliederung des Dekalogs," in *Mincha* (ed. Erhard Blum; Rendtorff Festschrift; Neukirchen-Vluyn: Neukirchener, 2000): 193–215; Motyer, *Exodus*, 215–20.

32 Cf. Gerald Blidstein, *Honor Thy Father and Mother: Filial Responsibility in Jewish Law and Ethics* (New York: Ktav, 1975), 1–8; Oded Yisraeli, "Honoring Father and Mother in Early Kabbalah: From Ethos to Mythos," *JQR* 99 (2009): 396–415, esp. 403–9.

The rationale of the commandment and its position in the Decalogue may be related to the concept of parents as God's image-bearers
and therefore his representatives in bringing their children into the
world (Gen 1:26–28; 5:1–3). In any case, in the Decalogue, honouring
parents is a virtue which follows naturally from honouring God, his
Name, and his Day. In Leviticus 19, honouring parents is closely integrated with honouring God and keeping the sabbath, and the word
"revere" (ירא) is used, a term often used for reverence of God:[33]

> Each of you shall revere your mother and your father, and keep my sab-
> baths; I am the LORD your God. (Lev 19:3)

> You shall stand up in the presence of the aged, and show respect for the
> elderly; and you shall revere your God—I am the LORD. (Lev 19:32)

It may be concluded, therefore, that the Decalogue consists of two
groups of five commandments, the first concerned with respect for God
and the second with respect for other human beings. Honouring
mother and father forms the conclusion to the first group rather than
the introduction to the second. There is a descending sequence in each
of the two groups, beginning with the most serious matter and ending
with something slightly unexpected (from apostasy to honouring parents; from killing to coveting).

The Fifth Commandment

The fifth commandment may be seen as the fundamental principle for
family and social life in the Old Testament.[34] Like the rest of the commandments, it is addressed primarily to adults rather than young people, though the latter are included as well.[35] It is universal in application, since all have or have had parents, and those who have been
separated from their birth parents generally have others who have
effectively fulfilled that role in their lives.

---

33 Most of the first group of commandments are alluded to in Lev 19:3–4, and two of
    the second group in vv. 11–12.

34 Harry Jungbauer, *"Ehre Vater und Mutter": Der Weg des Elterngebots in der biblischen
    Tradition* (Tübingen: Mohr Siebeck, 2002), 130–35; cf. Johann Gamberoni, "Das
    Elterngebot im Alten Testament," *BZ* 8 (1964): 161–90. On the family in ancient
    Israel, see Leo G. Perdue et al., *Families in Ancient Israel* (Louisville, Ky.: Westminster
    John Knox, 1997); James A. Sanders, "The Family in the Bible," *BTB* 32 (2002): 117–
    28; Richard S. Hess and M. Daniel Carroll Rodas, eds., *Family in the Bible: Exploring
    Customs, Culture, and Context* (Grand Rapids, Mich.: Baker Academic, 2003).

35 Rainer Albertz, "Hintergrund und Bedeutung des Elterngebots im Dekalog," *ZAW*
    90 (1978): 348–74; Walter J. Harrelson, *The Ten Commandments and Human Rights* (rev.
    ed.; Macon, Ga.: Mercer University Press, 1997), 78–88.

The commandment is expressed positively,[36] like the preceding commandment on honouring the sabbath, though prohibition of the negative is certainly included (cf. Deut 27:16). To harm, curse, or persistently disobey a parent is treated as a particularly serious crime in Old Testament law, leading to capital punishment (Exod 21:15, 17; Lev 20:9; Deut 21:18–21).[37] However, the positive formulation of the commandment makes it broader than simply a prohibition of parent abuse. It is assumed that to honour parents is natural and proper (cf. Deut 32:5–6, 18–19), and to treat them in any other way is unacceptable behaviour in the covenant community.

Keeping the fifth commandment has its own reward—long life in the land given by God. This expression can refer to both individual (Deut 6:2; 22:7) and corporate (11:8–9; 30:16–20) longevity, in the latter case focusing on the length of time Israel is granted to live in the promised land. Both may be in view here.[38] Israelites who honour those who have given them life will receive an appropriate blessing—extension of their life on earth (cf. Prov 4:10). The Deuteronomic version of the commandment expands the promise of longevity with the characteristic words "and so that it may go well with you" (cf. 4:40; 5:29; 6:3, 18;

---

36 Some scholars suppose that the "original" form of the commandment was negative (e.g., Ernst Sellin, *Geschichte des Israelitisch-Jüdischen Volkes* [2 vols.; Leipzig: Quelle & Meyer, 1924–1932], 1:83–84; Harrelson, *Ten Commandments*, 34), but this supposition is without evidence and it is unnecessary to insist that the original author must have expressed all ten sentences in a uniform way (cf. Phillips, *Criminal Law*, 66, 80; Brevard S. Childs, *Exodus: A Commentary* [London: SCM, 1974]; Durham, *Exodus*). Erhard S. Gerstenberger, *Wesen und Herkunft des "Apodiktischen Rechts"* (Neukirchen-Vluyn: Neukirchener, 1965), 43–50 also argues for the originality of the positive form, suggesting that it arose in clan instruction. Whether or not they are to be seen as the place of *origin* of this commandment, there is certainly no doubt that its sentiments would be at home in wisdom circles (cf. Prov 1:8; 15:5; 19:26; etc.). On the "original" form of the Decalogue, see David L. Baker, "The Finger of God and the Forming of a Nation: The Origin and Purpose of the Decalogue," *TynBul* 56 (2005): 1–24 (11–14).

37 Cf. Laws of Hammurabi §195: "If a child should strike his father, they shall cut off his hand" ("Laws of Hammurabi," translated by Martin Roth [*COS*, 2.131:335–53(348)]). In Exod 21:15, capital punishment is stipulated for this offence. In Philo's discussion of the Exodus law, he criticises those who reduce the penalty to cutting off the hand (*Spec. Laws* 2.243–48).

38 Cf. Cornelis Houtman, *Exodus* (4 vols.; Historical Commentary on the Old Testament; vols. 1–2, Kampen: Kok, 1993–1996; vols. 3–4, Leuven: Peeters, 2000–2002), 3:57–58; vols. 1–3 trans. of *Exodus* (3 vols.; COut; Kampen: Kok, 1986–1996); Patrick D. Miller, "'That It May Go Well With You': The Commandments and the Common Good," in *The Way of the Lord: Essays in Old Testament Theology* (FAT 39; Tübingen: Mohr Siebeck, 2004), 136–63 (140–43).

12:25, 28; 22:7), and adds a further motive clause: "as the LORD your God has commanded you" (cf. 4:23; 5:12; 13:6; 20:17).[39]

Two of the ancient Near Eastern concepts discussed above are also important in Old Testament teaching on attitudes towards parents and elders, namely dignity and care; while ancestor worship is mentioned only rarely and always as something to be avoided. There is also a distinctive feature which emerges from a study of the fifth commandment in its canonical context—respect for tradition.

Dignity

The first concern of the commandment is respect for parents and maintenance of their dignity. The word "honour" (כבד) elsewhere denotes an attitude of worship towards God (Ps 86:9; Prov 3:9; Isa 24:15), and also God's attitude of care towards human beings (Ps 91:15). This two-way honouring is explicit in the word of God to Eli: "those who honour me I will honour" (1 Sam 2:30). The same word is used of submission to human authority (1 Sam 15:30). In Barth's words, "to honour some one really means to ascribe to him the dignity which is his due."[40]

At this point it is important to distinguish between dignity and authority. Some interpreters discuss the purpose of the commandment in terms of parental authority.[41] However, the biblical emphasis is on filial responsibility, focusing on the duty of children to honour rather than the right of parents to exercise authority.[42] Unlike modern laws which tend to focus on rights and freedoms, biblical law is more concerned with obligations and responsibilities.[43]

It is notable that Israelite mothers and fathers are due equal honour from their children. Perhaps to emphasize this point in a patriarchal society, the version of the commandment in Lev 19:3 puts the mother

---

39   I am assuming that the Deuteronomic version is later than that in Exodus, as I have argued elsewhere (David L. Baker, "Ten Commandments, Two Tablets: The Shape of the Decalogue," *Them* 30.3 (2005): 6–22 (14–16).

40   Karl Barth, *Church Dogmatics* (4 vols in 14; Edinburgh: T&T Clark, 1936–1977), 3/4: 243; trans. of *Die kirchliche Dogmatik* (4 vols. in 14; vol. 1/1 Munich: Kaiser, 1932; vols. 1/2 onwards Zürich: Evangelisches Buchhandlung Zollikon, 1938–1970).

41   Jungbauer, "*Ehre*," 82–84; cf. Albertz, "Hintergrund," 348–49.

42   Blidstein, *Honor*, xi–xii, 20. Barth, *Church Dogmatics*, 3/4: 242 comments: "The authority of parents proclaimed in the fifth commandment is not that of a power posited and exercised as a right, but that of a spiritual power."

43   Miller, "That It May Go Well," 141–43; Mona DeKoven Fishbane, "'Honor Your Father and Your Mother': Intergenerational Values and Jewish Tradition," in *Spiritual Resources in Family Therapy* (ed. Froma Walsh; 2d ed.; New York: Guilford, 2009), 174–93 (182–83).

before the father.[44] In virtually every biblical reference to attitudes towards parents, whether in law or wisdom or prophecy, both mother and father are mentioned. This is distinctive compared with other parts of the ancient Near East, where the status of women was generally lower, and most extant texts are concerned with respectful attitudes towards one's father or older men in general. The main exception is the Egyptian Instruction of Any (quoted above), which advises support for one's mother.

Honouring mother and father is emphasised repeatedly in Proverbs.[45] This includes obeying their teaching (1:8–9; 6:20; 15:5; 23:22; 30:17), bringing them joy by becoming wise (10:1; 15:20; 23:23–25; cf. 17:21, 25; 28:4), and not hurting or cursing them (19:26; 20:20; 28:24; 30:11). The point is expanded further in Deuterocanonical wisdom literature (Sir 3:1–11; 7:27–28), including duties of giving practical help in old age (Sir 3:12–16) and conducting a proper burial (Tob 4:3–4; 6:15; cf. 14:11–13; Gen 47:29–30). The prophets say relatively little about honouring parents, though it is assumed as a fundamental virtue (Isa 1:2; 3:5; Ezek 22:7; Mic 7:6; Mal 1:6; cf. 4:6).[46]

Care

As elsewhere in the ancient Near East, for Israelites to honour their parents would no doubt have included practical care. In his detailed study of the fifth commandment, and its development throughout the Bible, Jungbauer argues that responsibility for care of elderly parents is one of its most basic concerns.[47] Examples of care for parents are recorded in the Old Testament narratives (Gen 45:9–11; 47:12; 1 Sam 22:3–4), as well as examples of disrespect (Gen 9:22; 27:18–27; 35:22). A New Testament reference to honouring widows is concerned with providing for them (1 Tim 5:3–8; cf. Acts 6:1). This is presumably motivated, at least in part, by gratitude for the care which parents give to children in their early years.[48]

Sometimes it will seem a burden to care for elderly parents; though it is probably rare that children have to do *more* for their parents in

---

44   Though LXX, Peshitta, and Vulgate reverse the order.
45   Barth, *Church Dogmatics*, 3/4:249 describes the book of Proverbs as "a large-scale commentary on the fifth commandment."
46   Deuteronomy makes the same assumption (32:5–6, 18–20).
47   Jungbauer, *"Ehre,"* 80–82.
48   Blidstein, *Honor*, 8–19.

their latter years than was done for them in their childhood. In one of the rabbinic writings we read:

> A man who can afford it and does not support his aged parents is a murderer. God is bitterly disappointed in such a man. "I made respect of them of equal importance with respect of Me," He thunders against him. "If I had lived with this man, he would have treated Me as he did them. It is good that I did not come near him." (*S. Eli. Rab.*)[49]

Tradition

A further matter addressed by the fifth commandment is respect for tradition, especially for the religious education given by one's parents.[50] Barth expresses it as follows: "The honouring of parents required of children does not mean the outward and formal subjection of the will of the younger to that of the older generation, but the respecting of the latter as the bearer and mediator of the promise given to the people with regard to its existence."[51] This fits with the conclusion reached above that the fifth commandment belongs to the first group, which is primarily concerned with respect for God. As Phillips points out, it should help to ensure that children would maintain the faith of their parents.[52] That religious education was primarily the responsibility of parents in ancient Israel is certainly clear in Deut 6:6–7; 11:18–19; 32:7; and Proverbs 1–7.

Medieval rabbis refer to the significance of the fifth commandment for the preservation of religious tradition, so that each new generation accepts the teachings of their elders and passes it on to the next.[53] Honouring of parents leads to respect for ancestral tradition, and so has a stabilising effect on society. This is evident in the theological questions that young Israelites ask their parents about the past (Exod 12:24–27; 13:14–15; Deut 6:20–25; Josh 4:6–7). Another biblical example is that of the Rechabites and their faithfulness to the principles of their ancestor (Jer 35).

This may be compared with the idea of filial piety, considered the root of all virtue in Confucian ethics.[54] Honouring parents is fundamental, and includes respect for their authority and obedience to their

---

49   Quoted by Goldman, *Ten Commandments*, 178.
50   Jungbauer, "*Ehre*," 84–87.
51   Barth, *Church Dogmatics*, 3/4:242, expounded in 243–49.
52   Phillips, *Criminal Law*, 81.
53   Blidstein, *Honor*, 19–24.
54   Rhee, "Fear God," 212–13.

instruction. However, this does not mean absolute obedience to one's immediate father, especially when it comes to moral matters, but can also be understood more generally as respect for tradition.[55] The father is not an independent authority figure, because he also defers to his own father, and so to the ongoing tradition of knowledge and wisdom. It is therefore assumed that parents who stand within the tradition are able to guide their children in the Way. But if a father should be out of line with his ancestors, filial piety may require the child *not* to follow him, but to seek a better path in accordance with the ancestral tradition.

Honouring parents includes acknowledging their maturity and wisdom. Younger people often prefer their own way of doing things, but should be careful not to act as though it is easy to do better than one's forebears, or assume that new ideas are automatically an improvement on old ones. No one starts life in a vacuum. Everyone belongs to a historical and cultural context, and has much to learn from the experience of others, even when choosing to differ.[56]

Concluding Reflections

According to the biblical and extra-biblical texts discussed in this article, relationships between the generations are foundational to human society. Those who build a society which honours the old may expect to enjoy such honour themselves in due course, as is the case in many traditional societies. Modern Western society, in contrast, tends to glorify youth and dread old age. Young energetic people are appointed to jobs in preference to older people with experience and maturity. People do their best to stay young—or at least look young—as long as possible, looking on time as an enemy. Tradition is outmoded; innovation is the watchword.

Of course, there are enormous cultural differences in the way human beings relate across the generations. For example, to put ageing parents in a nursing home rather than accommodating them in one's own home would be a scandalous idea in some cultures. In another culture, however, provision of professional nursing care may be a way of honouring parents, so long as it is done for their genuine good and

---

55   A. T. Nuyen, "The Contemporary Relevance of the Confucian Idea of Filial Piety," *Journal of Chinese Philosophy* 31 (2004): 433–50.

56   Cf. Jan Milič Lochman, *Signposts to Freedom: The Ten Commandments and Christian Ethics* (Minneapolis, Minn.: Augsburg, 1982), 81–82; trans. of *Wegweisung der Freiheit: Abriss der Ethik in der Perspektive des Dekalogs* (Gütersloh: Gerd Mohn, 1979); Fishbane, "Honor," 175–78.

not a relinquishing of responsibility. Today's world is very different from that of the ancient Hebrews, and it is not realistic for us simply to model our family life on theirs.

Some see the fifth commandment as easy to keep, others as the most difficult of all, no doubt depending to some extent on their own experiences of family life. In this broken world, some parents have done little that is positive for their children apart from bringing them into the world, and children from such homes inevitably have greater difficulty in honouring their parents than those blessed with happy homes. For example, victims of child abuse may struggle with the fifth commandment. Other biblical resources may help them recover from their pain and find strength in the divine parent who demonstrates true love towards them, expressed in terms that are both fatherly (Deut 1:30–31; Ps 103:13) and motherly (Isa 49:15; 66:12–13).[57] In such a situation, disturbed parental behaviour has to be resisted and blind obedience is clearly not required. Nevertheless, to honour one's parent may mean to avoid shaming them, choosing instead to rebuke them gently and firmly, and take appropriate action to deal with the issues. Intergenerational family therapy can be helpful here in bringing together the values of honouring parents and the need for personal authenticity, enabling clients to respect their parents while still respecting themselves.[58]

The validity of the fifth commandment is not dependent on having perfect parents, but on the role of parents as God's representatives in giving life.[59] Like other commandments—such as those prohibiting murder, adultery, and theft—it applies to all, whether or not they are good to us or deserve our respect. It is natural to treat well those who treat us well (cf. Matt 5:46–47), but the Decalogue challenges members of the covenant community to go further than that. We may find the fifth commandment easy or hard or almost impossible to keep. Nevertheless, it reminds us of our origins, while encouraging us to look to the future, and reminds us to show the greatest respect for the family, as the core of human society.[60]

---

57   Marshall S. Scott, "Honor thy Father and Mother: Scriptural Resources for Victims of Incest and Parental Abuse," *Journal of Pastoral Care* 42 (1988): 139–48.

58   Fishbane, "Honor," esp. 180–91.

59   Barth, *Church Dogmatics*, 3/4:251–57.

60   Two significant works on the fifth commandment came to hand after this article was completed, both of which have valuable insights: Byron L. Sherwin, "The Fifth Word: Honoring Parents," in *The Ten Commandments for Jews, Christians, and Others* (ed. Roger E. Van Harn, Richard John Neuhaus, and Peter W. Ochs; Grand Rapids, Mich.: Eerdmans, 2007; with response by Anathea E. Portier-Young), 87–111; Patrick

I am grateful for the privilege of writing this article in honour of Professor Graham Davies. Apart from his teaching and writing, which is well known and widely appreciated, I have benefited personally from Graham's advice and encouragement in my own teaching and writing. I take this opportunity of wishing him a long and fruitful retirement.

D. Miller, *The Ten Commandments* (Louisville, Ky.: Westminster John Knox, 2009), 167–220.

Deuteronomy and the Babylonian Diaspora

ERNEST NICHOLSON

I

It is history that the exiles deported to Babylonia in the early sixth century were destined to live out their lives there, like Jehoiachin and the members of his family deported with him (2 Kgs 25:27–30), to be succeeded by a generation which had never lived in or even put foot in the homeland. Further, although under Persian rule in the late sixth century some of their descendants returned to the homeland, numerous others did not but remained in the towns where they had been born, grew up, worked and pursued their livelihood, married and raised their families, and buried their grandparents and parents.[1] In this they were no different from immigrants generally throughout history for whom, after the first generation or two, the land to which they had emigrated becomes their home, whatever affection they may retain for the ancestral homeland.

The letter in Jeremiah 29 (esp. vv. 4–7) offering advice to those recently exiled to Babylonia is a vignette of the social reality which before long the Judean deportees faced: that the might of Babylonia was in no imminent danger of being overthrown, that there was thus no realistic alternative to settling down where they had been transported and securing as best they could their community, and providing for their families. The letter assumes a prolonged sojourn, long enough for population increase of the exiled communities and the development of means of livelihood in their new environment, long enough, it envisages, for second and third generations to be born; the letter implies also the opportunity of living peacefully and thriving economically alongside the native citizenry, and of benefiting from the prosperity of the indigenous population for which they are exhorted to

---

1 See the discussion of this by B. Becking, "'We All Returned as One!': Critical Notes on the Myth of the Mass Return," in *Judah and the Judeans in the Persian Period* (ed. O. Lipschits and M. Oeming; Winona Lake, Ind.: Eisenbrauns, 2006), 3–18.

pray. The letter thus considers the community to which it is addressed to be sufficiently permanent in its new location as to take on, over time, a new life of its own.

The prospects for, and opportunities open to, the Judean exiles as briefly stated in this text are confirmed by the evidence of cuneiform sources from the Neo-Babylonian and Achaemenid periods. That many exiles of Judean descent remained in Babylonia and were still there in the Achaemenid period, as for example Ezra–Nehemiah records, is attested in texts of the Murašû archive from Nippur and other towns in its vicinity and extending over the second half of the fifth century BCE, that contain western Semitic names, numbers of them compounded with the theophoric element Yhwh. In addition, recent research has yielded new information about the Judean exiles in the Neo-Babylonian period itself, including some that sheds light upon the earlier years of the sixth century BCE. This information also comes from a substantial archive[2] from two locations, one of which, the town āl-Našar, has been known for some time, the other a city in the same vicinity near Nippur and bearing the hitherto unattested place-name āl-Yāḫūdu, "Judah city," which some suggest was "Babylonian Jerusalem."[3] According to Pearce, the name in one of its earliest appearances, which she dates to 572 BCE, is written with a gentilic ending -a-a (URUšá LÚia-a-ḫu-du-a-a)[4] indicating that the city was so named after groups who came from Judah and thus was at first known as "the city of the Judeans." Pearce also finds that before long this ending is dropped and the city is known simply by the toponym "the city Judah" (URUia-a-ḫu-du), thus suggesting that "the Judean deportees and their descendants were sufficiently established in the social and economic life of Babylonia for their town to be referred to simply as 'Judah-ville' or the like." She believes that this may have already been how the town's name was newly signified as early as the third decade of the sixth century BCE.[5]

---

2   For this archive and a preliminary description of the information it yields see L. E. Pearce, "New Evidence for Judeans in Babylonia," in Lipschits and Oeming, *Judah and the Judeans,* 399–411.

3   For the texts and their translation see F. Joannès and A. Lemaire, "Trois tablettes cunéiformes à l'onomastique ouest-sémitique," *Transeu* 17 (1999): 17–33. On the appropriateness of the name "Jerusalem" see W. G. Lambert, "A Document from a Community of Exiles in Babylonia," in *New Seals and Inscriptions, Hebrew, Idumean, and Cuneiform* (ed. Meir Lubetski; Sheffield: Sheffield Phoenix Press, 2007), 201–5 (205). Lambert's observations are in support of the suggestion originally made by M. Weippert, "Israel und Juda," *RlA* 5:200–208 (200).

4   Pearce, "New Evidence for Judeans," 401 n. 7 lists nine orthographies of the city, including this, which is the final one in her list.

5   Pearce, "New Evidence for Judeans," 402.

Našar town and Yāḫūdu and other places mentioned in association with them in this archive were, like Nippur, located in central Mesopotamia where, it has been estimated, there were altogether twenty-eight such settlements for Judeans, out of a total of two hundred, distributed over the whole region of Nippur.[6] The texts indicate the participation of the Judean exiles in legal and commercial matters as well as agriculture and fishing from as early as 572 BCE, that is, a mere fifteen years after the destruction of Jerusalem. The activity is evidenced in receipts for payments, debt notes for commodities owed, sales of livestock, leasing of houses, etc. It seems also that Judeans were officially entrusted with a measure of fiscal administration relating to their community, and there is some evidence of an officially organized Babylonian administrative district of a mainly Judean population, a ḫaṭru.[7] In short, there is sufficient evidence "to show that the Judean exiles . . . were not isolated from the world of their Babylonian masters, indeed could have been exposed to a variety of its facets, social, economic, political, and cultural."[8] It shows also that the Judean immigrant population of Našar and Yāḫūdu and other places in their vicinity associated with them were not sitting upon their hands waiting for news of an imminent return home!

We know too of other minority ethnic groups who had been uprooted by the Babylonians from their native lands and cities, mostly in the west of the region, and settled in areas of Babylonia. Legal and economic documents from the Murašû archive record toponyms in the vicinity of Nippur, all of which are of western origin: there is reference to a canal (nār Milidu) near which people deported from Milid in Asia Minor were settled, and of communities from Phoenicia, Syria, Philistia (including Ashkelon and Gaza), deportees from towns in Syria, and mention of Arab exiles; another canal is referred to as "the Egyptians' Canal" (nāru ša ᴸᵁMiṣiraia), reminiscent of the Judean community among whom Ezekiel lived in the town "Tell Aviv" by the nār Kabāru-canal which ran through or close by Nippur. Another toponym refers

---

6   See E. J. Bickerman, "The Babylonian Captivity," in CHJ 1:342–58 (346).

7   Pearce, "New Evidence for Judeans," 405–6.

8   For a cautious sketch see P. Machinist, "Mesopotamian Imperialism and Israelite Religion: A Case Study from the Second Isaiah," in *Symbiosis, Symbolism, and the Power of the Past: Canaan, Ancient Israel, and their Neighbors from the Late Bronze Age through Roman Palestina* (ed. W. G. Dever and S. Gitin; Winona Lake, Ind.: Eisenbrauns, 2003), 237–64 (255–56; the quotation is on p. 256).

simply to ᵁᴿᵁ*Galutu* = "exile city," thus signalling, as in the case of
Yāḫūdu, the origin of its inhabitants and how they came to be there.[9]

II

What may we deduce from such evidence concerning the conditions in
which the Judean exiles lived in their different settlements in Babylonia
where they were caught up in the legal, commercial, and economic
affairs of everyday life? The settlements named after the different
population groups mentioned above indicate that the Babylonian
authorities did not seek to assimilate these groups of deportees into
their own native population or to intermingle them with each other.
There was, that is, a degree of segregation, but there is no evidence that
the settlements were ghetto-like, and no reason to believe that access to
each other or communication between them was in any way restricted;
neither is there any evidence of persecution by the state authorities. The
settlements, which were on crown lands, were especially in rural areas,
but some were also close to cities such as Borsippa and Uruk or in cities
such as Nippur and Babylon itself, where Jehoiachin and his family and
entourage were brought and maintained by the Babylonian court.
These various ethnic population groups were free to manage their lives
and livelihood and to worship their national gods.

That there was a process of acculturation is in no doubt, however,
including the adoption of the worship of Babylonian gods. Thus among
the Babylonian personal names of Judeans evidenced in the Murašû
texts were some containing theophoric elements of the names of Babylonian gods. The evidence suggests that Judean fathers with Babylonian
religious names could give their sons names containing the theophoric
element of their ancestral God Yhwh, whilst in other cases the patro-
nyms of sons bearing Babylonian names were Judean and comprised
the theophoric element Yhwh.[10] It seems, on this evidence, that some

---

9   See I. Eph'al, "On the Political and Social Organization of the Jews in Babylonian
     Exile," in *XXI. Deutscher Orientalistentag vom 24. bis 29. März 1980 in Berlin: Vorträge*
     (ed. F. Steppat; ZDMGSup 5; Wiesbaden: Franz Steiner, 1983), 106–12.

10   Some Judean leaders who bore Babylonian names (e.g., Zerubbabel), including
     names with theophoric elements of Babylonian deities (e.g., Sheshbazzar, Shenazzar)
     were most likely assigned them by the Babylonian authorities. See Machinist,
     "Mesopotamian Imperialism," 256, following R. Zadok, *The Earliest Diaspora: Israel-
     ites and Judeans in Pre-Hellenistic Mesopotamia* (Publications of the Diaspora Research
     Institute 151; Tel Aviv: Tel Aviv University Press, 2002), 57. The names containing
     such theophoric elements identified in the Akkadian texts referred to above were of
     course freely chosen and not imposed externally.

Judean exiles worshipped Babylonian deities as well as continuing the worship of Yhwh.[11] This much, indeed, can already be inferred from various texts in the Hebrew Bible. Thus Deut 4:28 "foretells" the worship by Israelite exiles of gods "of wood and stone that neither see, nor hear, nor eat nor smell"; Jeremiah, as narrated in Jer 5:19; 16:13, prophesies that the exiles of Judah will "serve other gods day and night" in a foreign land; evidently some elders among the deportees of 597 BCE, who had decided to follow "the nations and tribes of other lands" and "worship wood and stone," came to consult the prophet Ezekiel (20:32; cf. 14:1–3), the inference being that such worship would be in addition to their own ancestral worship of Yhwh; Deutero-Isaiah (48:5) declared in advance to fellow-Judeans what Yhwh was about to do for his people lest when it happens they should boast that it was the work of their "idols." The "spectrum" of worship among the exiles would thus have included those who worshipped Yhwh alone, some who lost faith in Yhwh (cf., e.g., Isa 40:27) and adapted to the local culture and religion,[12] and others for whom encroachment of the indigenous culture would have yielded, not a systematized theology, and probably not participation in the official imperial cult, but a form of, as it were, "home spun" syncretism which would have included devotion to Babylonian deities alongside their ancestral God Yhwh.[13]

The threat and the challenge that would have confronted the Judean exiles are self-evident: how in this culturally and religiously multiplex society, which, in addition to its ruling, native population, was home to many other minority ethnic communities, each with its own religious and cultural heritage, were they to retain and sustain their own national, cultural, and religious identity? We know that a

---

11 For a fuller discussion see Bickerman, "The Babylonian Captivity," 352–54, and idem, "The Generation of Ezra and Nehemiah," first published in *PAAJR* 45 (1978): 1–28, reprinted in idem, *Studies in Jewish and Christian History* (2 vols.; Ancient Judaism and Early Christianity 68/1–2; Leiden: Brill, 2007), 2:975–99 (989–93).

12 R. Albertz writes of "the temptingly easy possibility" of Judeans "immersing themselves in the ethnic mosaic of the Babylonian Empire. Undoubtedly, not a few chose this path" (*Israel in Exile: The History and Literature of the Sixth Century B.C.E.* [Atlanta, Ga.: Society of Biblical Literature, 2003], 105; trans. of *Die Exilszeit* [Stuttgart: W. Kohlhammer, 2001]).

13 Cf. W. G. Lambert: "The city cults were the preserve of the official priesthood, of the ruler, and perhaps the upper classes. Ordinary people might share in the spirit of the more important annual festivals, but the city temple was not a place of their devotions. For them the niche at home or the street corner shrine was the place of religion" ("The Historical Development of the Mesopotamian Pantheon: A Study in Sophisticated Polytheism," in *Unity and Diversity: Essays in the History, Literature, and Religion of the Ancient Near East* [ed. H. Goedicke and J. J. M. Roberts; Baltimore: Johns Hopkins University Press, 1975], 191–200 [191]).

substantial body of them succeeded: the return by some to the homeland in the late sixth century and by others subsequently under Ezra
and Nehemiah, and not least of all the Judean/Jewish diaspora community that continued to reside in Mesopotamia throughout the
Achaemenid period and beyond evidence this.[14] It is the case also that
the other ethnic minorities mentioned above maintained their national
identity throughout decades in exile in Babylonia; this was not therefore a phenomenon peculiar to the Judean communities. The fact is,
however, that apart from those who returned under Persian rule to
their homelands, all of these other ethnic groups eventually disappeared from Babylonian society, that is, were assimilated. Drawing
attention to this, Eph‘al has pertinently observed: "The outstanding
survival of the Jews in Babylon as an entity-in-exile in the subsequent
period . . . remains, however, a problem demanding further explanation."[15] By what means, religious and social, therefore, were the Judean
exiles enabled to maintain their ethnic, communal, and religious
identity?

The inference is warranted that an agenda would have emerged,
directed at the conditions and challenges of exile in Babylonia, one that
focused upon present realities, acknowledging that exile would not be
a brief sojourn—in which case probably for many their settlement in
Babylonia would be permanent—and that hopes for a future return
home that became increasingly far off could not substitute for new
thinking and initiatives to defend and sustain the community against
ethnic, cultural, and religious extinction.

My contention is that the authors and redactors to whom we owe
the book of Deuteronomy addressed themselves to just such needs of
the exiles, and that in such a way they gave thought and wrote, not for
an interim situation requiring "survival strategies," but for a new age
in the history of their people, who were now no longer identified
simply as the resident population of the ancestral homeland, but
embraced also what we have come to describe as the diaspora, in this
instance specifically the Babylonian diaspora.

It might immediately be objected that the Israel to which Deuteronomy is addressed is the state—historically the Judean state—rather
than a community of stateless exiles, or that the book's authors had in

---

14   Bickerman, "The Generation of Ezra and Nehemiah," 17 [1978] = 988 [2007], finds
     evidence of a heightened use of names compounded of Yhwh among the Babylonian
     Judean community in the second half of the fifth century BCE, suggesting perhaps a
     fresh interest and pride in their ancestral Judean and religious roots.
15   See I. Eph‘al, "The Western Minorities in Babylonia in the 6th–5th Centuries B.C.:
     Maintenance and Cohesion," *Or* 47 (1978): 74–90 (88).

mind a newly constituted state in the wake of the destruction of the kingdom of Judah.[16] No state with a monarch, even a titular one, is seriously provided for in the book, however, and there is an absence of the nature and essence of "kingship" (מלוכה) or "kingdom," "sovereignty" (ממלכה); neither is any other temporal head of state mentioned.[17] Instead, the clear impression is of a decentralized society with locally appointed leaders—"wise, understanding, and experienced men" chosen by their local community according to an arrangement set in place by Moses (Deut 1:13). The characterization of Israel as a community of "brothers" further strengthens this impression. More importantly, however, the distinctive depiction of Israel in Deuteronomy is "the people of Yhwh." That is, a theology of "election" pervades Deuteronomy's understanding of Israel and determines the distinguishing "self-awareness" which those to whom we owe the book sought to inculcate (see below).

Such a society with a focus upon local communities and led by local leaders is wholly conceivable among the scattered settlements of Judeans in Babylonia. There is good evidence in postexilic texts (Ezra 2:3–20, 39–62; Neh 7:5–72[73]) of the formation among the exiles of tightly knit kinship groups bearing the title בית אבות, "fathers' house," that probably replaced the earlier and more ancient "clan" structure of the preexilic era.[18]

Was such a society of Judeans in exile, living in a number of different towns and cities in Babylonia, a focus of some of the main concerns of the authors of the book of Deuteronomy? There is space here for only an outline of the case for such a suggestion.

---

16 See, for example, R. E. Clements, "The Origins of Deuteronomy: What Are the Clues?", pp. 508–16 in R. E. Clements, R. W. L. Moberly, and G. J. McConville, "A dialogue with Gordon McConville on Deuteronomy," *SJT* 56 (2003): 508–31, who suggests that Deuteronomy was intended as "a written book of polity for a state" offering a "new social and juridical order" to replace "the failed monarchic order" in Judah following the catastrophe of 587 BCE. The quotations are from pp. 511, 514.

17 See especially the observations of L. Perlitt, "Der Staatsgedanke im Deuteronomium," in *Language, Theology, and the Bible: Essays in Honour of James Barr* (ed. S. E. Ballentine and J. Barton; Oxford: Oxford University Press, 1994), 182–98. Cf. also E. W. Nicholson, "*Traditum* and *Traditio*: The Case of Deuteronomy 17:14–20," in *Scriptural Exegesis: The Shapes of Culture and the Religious Imagination: Essays in Honour of Michael Fishbane* (ed. D. A. Green and L. S. Lieber; Oxford: Oxford University Press, 2009), 46–61.

18 See Albertz, *Israel in Exile*, 106.

III

It has long been observed by commentators that one of the most acute concerns of the book of Deuteronomy is the religious threat that other nations pose for Israel. Thus S. R. Driver wrote of the encroachment of other religions as "the pressing danger of the age" which "the author strove to resist by every means in his power. Not only does he repeatedly declare, in solemn terms, that if allowed to prevail, they will ultimately involve Israel in national ruin; but a large number of provisions—much larger than in the Book of the Covenant—are aimed directly against them."[19] We can speak of an "ethos of encroachment" pervading the book, of an "in-group-out-group" culture born of an anxiety for group survival.[20] It is not simply ethnic foreigners who pose a threat to Israel's wellbeing and threaten its religious and moral boundaries, however: "the most profound threat to Israel's survival . . . is posed not by enemies who live far away but by 'indigenous outsiders,'" that is, "bad insiders."[21]

Stulman analyses a number of texts in Deuteronomy dealing with capital crimes against the community. The crimes are various, including enticement to apostasy, a prophet speaking falsely in Yhwh's name, premeditated murder, a rebellious son, harlotry, adultery, rape, and abducting and selling a brother Israelite into slavery. Of these, enticement to apostasy is my main interest here. Stulman draws attention to four texts: Deut 13:2–6; 13:7–12; 13:13–19; 17:2–7. Of these, the first two relate to enticement by a prophet or "dreamer of dreams" and to one's own kin or an intimate friend, the third to "miscreant" co-citizens ("sons of Belial"), the fourth, in 17:2–7, to any apostate individual, man or woman. Capital punishment is prescribed with the object of "purging the evil from [Israel's] midst." Stulman's study shows that the percentage of statutes pertaining to apostasy is much higher than in the Book of the Covenant and, indeed, than in other ancient Near Eastern legal codes.

From his analysis of such texts, Stulman concludes that these ordinances carrying the death penalty in Deuteronomy reflect "a great deal of *internal* anxiety and a marked sense of vulnerability. The world of D[euteronomy] is fragile and fraught with danger, and Israel's survival

---

19   S. R. Driver, *A Critical and Exegetical Commentary on Deuteronomy* (ICC; Edinburgh: T&T Clark, 1895), xxxi–xxxii.

20   See L. Stulman, "Encroachment in Deuteronomy: An Analysis of the Social World of the D Code," *JBL* 109 (1990): 613–32.

21   Stulman, "Encroachment in Deuteronomy," 615.

is perceived to be in jeopardy."[22] The danger comes not from outsiders but from individuals or deviant groups within the community itself. It is they who are the source of the marked apprehension of encroachment which is so characteristic of Deuteronomy and which also comes through in the pronounced parenetic style of the book with its incessant, earnest call to faithfulness. By "reinforcing its social and religious constraints, D[euteronomy] intends to produce a strong internal coherence and stability and to protect insiders and existing structures from dangerous indigenous outsiders."[23]

Commentators who have examined this feature of Deuteronomy have usually understood the source of such encroachment to be the religious and cultic institutions of immemorial Canaanite culture of the preexilic period, as, indeed, Deuteronomy and its related corpus generally narrates or implies. In addition there is evidence of cults devoted to east Semitic deities in Jerusalem in the late preexilic period, perhaps an outcome of a process of acculturation through more than a century of Assyrian imperial dominion—the "Queen of Heaven" (Jer 7:18; 44:17–19, 25), Tammuz (east Semitic Dumuzi, Ezek 8:14), the worship of "the host of heaven" (2 Kgs 17:16; 21:3, 5; Zeph 1:5; Jer 8:2; 19:3), the presence in the Temple of "horses dedicated to Shamash" (2 Kgs 23:11), the worship of the sun in the inner court of the Temple (Ezek 8:16).

It is not throwing caution to the wind, however, to claim that, to a more intense degree than in the homeland, encroachment would have been a forceful threat among the Judean communities exiled to live amidst Babylonian religious, cultic, and festal institutions, divinely validated, as it would have seemed, by a triumphant imperial state. That Deuteronomy dwells so anxiously upon encroachment, providing no less than four separate formulations of the danger it poses, where one would have been sufficient, and stressing that it comes not only from leaders in the community (prophets and "dreamers of dreams") and deviant groups but also from one's nearest and dearest—brother, son, daughter, beloved wife, cherished friend—makes good sense against such a social and religious background. These formulations show no dependence upon earlier statutory ordinances, and are aptly described as "legal homilies,"[24] which are unmistakably Deuteronomic compositions.

---

22 Stulman, "Encroachment in Deuteronomy," 626.
23 Stulman, "Encroachment in Deuteronomy," 632.
24 There is an obvious air of unreality in these texts, strikingly so in Deut 13:12–18, which envisages the razing of whole cities and the annihilation of their populations and livestock, though without any indication of the authority under which such action, which would have had to be national, would be implemented (establishing

IV

These texts do not stand alone, however, and here I draw attention to a further text which shares a similar concern with encroachment and which unquestionably presupposes an exilic background for its composition. It is usually regarded as deriving from a secondary hand. As such, however, it offers further evidence that recognizably secondary texts in Deuteronomy were by no means all directed towards serving its incorporation into the Deuteronomistic History corpus (DtrH), but that an equal driving force in the *Fortschreibung* of the book was the development of Deuteronomy as "the book of the torah," a designation to which I shall return below.

This text is Deut 4:1–40, which was probably a still later addition to Deuteronomy than the Decalogue pericope which follows in 5:1–27[25] and of which it may be described as a sort of prefatory extrapolation. It dwells upon various leading motifs and themes of the Decalogue pericope (see below), but pride of place is given to solemn and repeated warnings against the making of any image (vv. 15–31), combined with a scornful polemic against idols described as "wood and stone, the work of men's hands, that neither see, nor hear, nor eat, nor smell" (v. 28), a depiction that is strikingly reminiscent of the ridicule of the idols of the Babylonian cult by Deutero-Isaiah (Isa 40:18–20; 44:9–20; 46:5–7). Such a strong echo of the polemic of Deutero-Isaiah suggests an exilic background for the composition of Deut 4:1–40. This is confirmed by the equally striking similarities in thought between v. 32, with its allusion to creation—only here in Deuteronomy—and such passages as Isa 45:18–21; 46:9–10, and by the declarations in vv. 35 and 39 ("know therefore this day, and lay it to your heart, that the LORD is God in heaven above and on the earth beneath; there is no other") and the affirmations in such passages as Isa 43:10–13; 44:6–8; 45:6–7, 22.[26]

Though it places on Moses's lips a grave threat of exile (vv. 26–28), this text is not primarily intended as having been an "early warning" justifying God's present judgment upon his people and composed with

---

guilt and marshalling a task force to mount an assault on the city and carry out the mass executions, followed by the destruction of the city, reducing it to a desolate tell for ever). It is no objection to a Babylonian setting for the composition of these texts, therefore, to say that such actions could not have been sanctioned under Babylonian law, since they would have been equally unrealistic measures in the homeland, whether during the monarchical or exilic periods. In short, the texts have much more to do with the rhetoric of persuasion than with legal reality.

25   See A. D. H. Mayes, *Deuteronomy* (NCB; London: Marshall, Morgan & Scott, 1979), 161.

26   Mayes, *Deuteronomy*, 153–57.

this broad theme of the Deuteronomistic History in mind. Rather, its author intended it much more as part of Deuteronomy as torah. Its marked hortatory, "sermonic" nature holds the key to its primary purpose as exhortation and instruction. Thus its solemn warnings virtually run into each other: "take heed . . . take good heed to yourselves . . . beware lest you act corruptly by making an image . . . lest you lift up your eyes to . . . the sun and the moon and the stars, all the host of heaven (cf. 17:2–3) . . . take heed to yourselves, lest you forget the covenant . . . and make an image . . . if you act corruptly by making an image . . . I call heaven and earth to witness against you this day, that you will soon utterly perish from the land." In short, in tone, the passage is shot through with an anxious and urgent need to meet a present danger that threatens the future of the community to whom it was addressed in the later exilic period or the early postexilic, surely most probably the community of the Babylonian exiles. And no less than in the case of the "legal homilies" of Deuteronomy 13 such unremitting warning and exhortation was directed at a community whose survival is threatened, not by foreign, cultural enemies, but by members within that community, that is, by "indigenous outsiders."

V

The Decalogue (Deut 5:6–21) calls for attention here also, since there are good reasons for viewing it as having been introduced secondarily to the book of Deuteronomy by a deuteronomistic redactor,[27] and good grounds also for believing that it was composed in the exilic period though drawing upon earlier custom and tradition.[28]

There is no mistaking the primal significance that Deuteronomy attaches to the Decalogue, the "ten words" (5:6–21), which are said to have been spoken directly by Yhwh to Israel, crowning the theophany at the primordial assembly of the people at Horeb/Sinai. These commandments inscribed on two tables of stone by God's own hand and placed in "the ark of the covenant" (10:1–5) are thereby designated the quintessential terms of the covenant and normative for the ordering of Israel's life before God. They are headed by a declaration of Yhwh's

---

27 See, for example, Mayes, *Deuteronomy*, 161–62.

28 For details see F.-L. Hossfeld, *Der Dekalog: Seine späten Fassungen, die originale Komposition und seine Vorstufen* (OBO 45; Göttingen: Vandenhoeck & Ruprecht, 1982), especially his discussion of the prohibition on the making of images (258–62), the misuse of the name of Yhwh (243–47), the Sabbath commandment (247–52), and the command to honour parents (252–59).

intimate relationship with Israel wrought in the deliverance from bondage (v. 6)—"election"—and by two commandments, the one (v. 7) outlawing the worship of other gods, the other (v. 8) forbidding the making of any divine image, including any image of Yhwh. The positioning of vv. 9–10, which refer back to "other gods" in v. 7, has the effect of bracketing the two commandments together, and, indeed, together they are of the essence of "Yahwism."[29]

Among indications of the background to Deut 5:6–21, the commandment for the observance of the Sabbath day (vv. 12–15), upon which Deuteronomy's presentation of the Decalogue places special emphasis,[30] has every appearance of having been conceived among the exiles as a distinctive way of expressing and conserving the community's religious and cultural identity, and there is much agreement among commentators about this.[31] A range of texts, all of them deriving from the exilic or early postexilic period (Leviticus 23; Isa 56:2, 4, 6; 58:13; 66:23; Jer 17:19–27; Ezek 20:12–13, 16, 20, 21, 24; 22:8, 26; 23:38; 44:24; 46:1, 3, 4, 12), lends support to this view. There has been growing agreement also that the conception of the weekly Sabbath drew upon an ancient new moon Sabbath festival mentioned in such texts as 2 Kgs 4:23; Isa 1:13; Hos 2:13; Amos 8:5, as well as upon customary law reflected in Exod 23:12; 34:21 commanding rest from labour on the seventh day of the week (in each of these texts the verb "to rest" (šābat) but not the noun "Sabbath" is employed).

That the ordinance is "to hallow" (lĕqaddēš) the Sabbath, which is "the LORD's Sabbath," may indicate not only desisting from work but also some form of religious or liturgical act, though any suggestion that it marked the beginning of synagogue worship is conjectural. It is striking, however, that the Decalogue, though an ostensibly foundational declaration of Yhwh's will for his people at Horeb/Sinai, contains not the merest mention of altar or sacrifice,[32] and the surmise is prompted

---

29   Hossfeld, *Der Dekalog,* 282, writes of the framework of vv. 6–16 as offering "eine Kurz-Theologie von Jahwe in Tat und Wesen."

30   See N. Lohfink, "Zur Dekalogfassung von Dt 5," *BZ* 9 (1965): 17–32, who argues that the structure of the Decalogue in Deuteronomy 5 has the effect of presenting the Sabbath command as central to the Decalogue and not simply as its fourth commandment. Cf. also Mayes, *Deuteronomy,* 164–65.

31   For a discussion of its origin and its relation to earlier cultic and social institutions see Hossfeld, *Der Dekalog,* 247–52. For a summary of the issues see R. Albertz, *A History of Israelite Religion in the Old Testament Period* (2 vols.; London: SCM Press, 1994), 2:408–11; trans. of *Religionsgeschichte Israels in alttestamentlicher Zeit* (Göttingen: Vanderhoeck & Ruprecht, 1992).

32   The Book of the Covenant, by contrast, contains the altar law in Exod 20:24; the provision for sacrifice and cultic festivals in Exod 34:17–25 provides a further contrast.

(a) that this arose from a tenacious adherence among the exiles to the confinement of all sacrificial worship to the Jerusalem Temple, and (b) that the newly conceived weekly Sabbath consecrated to Yhwh was marked by some kind of family or possibly communal act of worship.

The commandment honouring parents (v. 16) has no earlier formulation or "proto-text" in the Hebrew Bible which might have been a source for the author of this clause, though respect and submission to parental authority is a familiar topic in the wisdom literature (Prov 1:8; 13:1; 19:26; etc.). Since the combination of a prescription with the promise of blessing is familiar in Deuteronomy (e.g., Deut 4:40; 5:33; 6:2; 11:9; 22:7; 30:18; 32:47), there is no need to question the unity of this clause and its deuteronomic authorship. The importance attached to honouring parents is of a piece with the emphasis among the exiles upon family and family associations ("fathers' house") as the main social entity, as noted above. Commentators also draw a close association between the inclusion of such a clause in the Decalogue and the injunction, which occurs a number of times in Deuteronomy (4:9–10; 6:7–10, 20–21; 11:18–21; 31:13; 33:46), requiring parents to instruct their children in the torah,[33] and they consider the primary intention of the commandment to be that of maintaining and fortifying the role of parents in the transmission and teaching of the law, which is probably a development of the exilic period. The easy-to-learn nature of the Decalogue with its mnemonic number ten may thus not have been the least consideration among the intentions of those who drafted this text.

The Decalogue's emphasis upon the quintessentially distinctive features of "Yahwism" and its requirement of Israel's monolatrous faithfulness, its accent upon the family as the primary entity in its society and the font of social control as well as the context in which the torah is taught and learned (see below), the injunction "hallowing" the seventh day as "Yhwh's Sabbath"—such contents and emphases would surely have had conspicuous pertinence to a community uprooted and exiled from its ancient religious and cultic, social, and cultural moorings and transplanted into an environment of ever-present encroachment.

VI

The injunction in Deuteronomy requiring parents to teach their children the commandments leads immediately to consideration of a

---

33 See Mayes, *Deuteronomy*, 161–62, and for fuller discussion Hossfeld, *Der Dekalog,* 254–59.

further significant feature of the book. This is the description of Deuteronomy as "the/this torah" or "this book of the torah" (Deut 1:5; 4:8,
44; 17:18, 19; 27:3, 8, 26; 28:58, 61; 29:20[21], 28[29]; 30:10; 31:9, 11, 12, 24,
26; 32:46). In such a description of "the words that Moses spoke to all
Israel beyond the Jordan" (Deut 1:1, cf. v. 5) is reflected for the first
time the concept of an authoritative "scripture" in prescribing and
guiding Israel's relationship with Yhwh. It is authoritative for the king,
who is to meditate upon it day and night as commanded in Deut 17:14–
20, where its deuteronomistic author has placed on Moses's lips the
measure whereby in the Deuteronomistic History the monarchy is
judged and found wanting,[34] and it is the torah that was declared by
Yhwh's "servants the prophets" and the neglect and abrogation of
which, in the face of the warnings of these prophets, brought judgment
upon Israel and Judah (e.g., 2 Kgs 17:13–14, 23; 21:10; 24:2).

Yet the significance attached to the torah in the broader
theologically apologetic context of the Deuteronomistic History is
surely surpassed by the remarkable conjoining of the "book of the
torah" with the conduct of family life in which the torah is to be both
learned by parents and also taught by them to their children as commanded by Moses (Deut 4:9–10; 6:7–10, 20–21; 11:18–21; 31:13; 33:46).
This marks a shift in religious action from temple, altar, and sacrifice
and the offices that went with these to family life as the institution
which, it seems, is now charged with conserving and inculcating the
commandments in obedience to which lies blessing. And the conviction
and, indeed, the passion with which these authors lodge and impel this
teaching of the torah within the family and so throughout the community is manifest: "You shall therefore lay up these words of mine in
your heart and in your soul; and you shall bind them as a sign upon
your hand, and they shall be as frontlets between your eyes. And you
shall teach them to your children, talking of them when you are sitting
in your house, and when you are walking by the way, and when you
lie down, and when you rise. And you shall write them upon the doorposts of your house and upon your gates" (Deut 11:18–20).

Such a shift in religious action focusing upon the torah presupposes
a new social reality which is most plausibly identified with the conditions to which the Judean exiles in Babylonia had to adapt, and which
called for new forms of religious expression and piety that would
maintain their ancestral worship of, and faith in, Yhwh in the changed
world in which they now lived. It is further evidence that the thinkers
and authors to whom we owe Deuteronomy were writing, not for an

---

34   For this assessment of Deut 17:14–20 see Nicholson, "*Traditum* and *Traditio.*"

interim situation requiring "survival strategies," but for a new age in the history of their people, who were now no longer identified simply as the resident population of the ancestral homeland, but embraced also what we have come to describe as diaspora communities.

This wider embrace may also be reflected in, or at least was facilitated by, a further prominent feature of Deuteronomy. As the Deuteronomist's "prayer of Solomon" indicates (1 Kgs 8:29, 30, 35, etc.; cf. Dan 6:11–12[10–11]), for the exiles the Jerusalem Temple determined the direction in which one prays (the "kibla"), and this is clearly related to Deuteronomy's claim for Jerusalem as the place which Yhwh chose "to place his name there." In such a way Jerusalem and the Temple remained a bond between those who lived in the homeland and the Judean communities in Babylonia. Later, members of these exilic communities would provide financial support for the rebuilding of the Temple though they themselves remained where their ancestors had been deported (Zech 6:10–11; Ezra 1:6; 2:68–69; 7:15–16; 8:33). Deuteronomy's "name theology," reflected in this prayer, itself marks an advance upon any notion that Yhwh is "localized" in the Temple—"heaven and the highest heaven cannot contain thee" (1 Kgs 8:27)—and is expressive of a break with older, cruder notions of divine dwelling in favour of a universalist understanding of God's presence with his people. Thus "from heaven" God spoke to Israel at Horeb (Deut 4:36, 39), "from heaven" he blesses his people and the land (Deut 26:15), and "from heaven" his "dwelling place" he hears the prayers of his people in exile no less than in the homeland.

VII

Deuteronomy has been aptly epitomized as expressing "a reflective universalism which attempts to transform and revitalize traditional Israelite belief for an age which presented a serious threat to that belief."[35] There is of course a longer background to the emergence of this universalist perspective which Deuteronomy presupposes than the destruction of the Judean state and the Babylonian exile. The dominance of Assyria for over a century in the latter part of the preexilic period, and not least of all the fate of the Northern Israelite state, will themselves have induced fresh thinking in the face of what appeared to

---

35   A. D. H. Mayes, "Deuteronomy 14 and the Deuteronomic World View," in *Studies in Deuteronomy in Honour of C. J. Labuschagne on the Occasion of his 65th Birthday* (ed. F. García Martínez, A. Hilhorst, J. T. A. G. M. van Ruiten, and A. S. van der Woude; VTSup 53; Leiden: Brill, 1994), 165–81 (175).

be a permanent new world order that upturned local world views. The preaching of the eighth-century prophets and their message of judgment would also have generated a theological transformation in Israel's perception of itself, and of the nature of its relation to Yhwh, and ultimately of how Israelites were to conceive of God as the world of great empires and their high gods bore down upon them. Certainly the thinking that has found expression in Deuteronomy did not spring from a historical or theological vacuum; it echoes earlier as well as contemporary voices, and mediates concepts of diverse origins including prophetic, wisdom, and priestly milieus.

Among the theologically central features of Deuteronomy preeminence surely goes to its depiction of Israel as "the people of Yhwh." All else amounts to ways in which this is realized, confirmed, and protected. The Israel that at one time was a community of tribes and subsequently two monarchical states has been eclipsed, and it seems that there is no thought of an envisaged re-institution of either of these two forms of society. It seems, indeed, that the designation of Israel as "the people of Yhwh" is designed to supplant such alternatives.[36] As we have also seen, however, Deuteronomy presupposes a jarring disjuncture between its vision of "the people of Yhwh" and the social reality that is "Israel." The "people of Yhwh" are called in the book to be a distinct and separate people, but we are left in no doubt of a serious threat to the realization of this. This threat comes, again as we have seen, not from foreigners and "outsiders," but from within the community itself, from "indigenous outsiders" whose deviant ways undermine the society's norms and authority and who, if left unchecked, would bring about internal disintegration. Hence the injunction that such groups or individuals are to be "purged from the midst" of Israel.

It follows that in such a society status is "achieved" rather than "ascribed," [37] that is, does not depend solely on genealogical descent, gender, tribal or clan affiliation, etc., but is achieved by commitment and the fulfilling of prescribed norms and goals, which are enshrined in "the book of the torah." Such a society is the vision of Deuteronomy, whose authors strove in the face of a social reality that included forces corrosive of such a vision and subversive of their endeavour to

---

36   See Mayes, "Deuteronomy 14 and the Deuteronomic World View," 176.

37   This terminology is employed by H. Eilberg-Schwartz, *The Savage in Judaism: An Anthropology of Israelite Religion in Ancient Judaism* (Bloomington, Ind.: Indiana University Press, 1990), to characterize the essential difference between the priestly community and the early Christian community. For its applicability to Deuteronomy, see Mayes, "Deuteronomy 14 and the Deuteronomic World View," 179–80.

conserve and revitalize their inherited religious tradition and institutions and its moral ethos so as to create a new self-understanding that would bind together and sustain into the future this now scattered people as one people who are called by the title "the people of Yhwh."

This is the central task which the authors and redactors who composed "the book of the torah" set themselves, and it accounts for pre-eminent features of the book such as its zealously persistent demand for the exclusive worship of Yhwh, its pressing concern with encroachment, its earnest teaching/preaching style that exhorts, threatens, warns, and promises, itself thus signalling a background fraught with danger for the community, and its distinctive call to Israel to choose life and blessing rather than curse and death—features that are hallmarks of Deuteronomy.

My proposition is therefore that we have underestimated the degree to which Deuteronomy as torah was shaped and developed to meet the challenge that life in exile posed for the survival of the cultural and religious heritage of the Judean communities there, that, indeed, the essential nature of the book—what makes Deuteronomy Deuteronomy—is more plausibly understood against this background than that of the long domination of Judah by the Assyrians. What the authors and redactors of Deuteronomy may owe to that earlier period, especially to the reign of Josiah, so celebrated in the Deuteronomistic History, requires fresh investigation.

It is a pleasure to contribute to this volume honouring Graham Davies, whose learning and scholarship I salute, and whose friendship across the years I deem a privilege.

The Dead Sea Scrolls and the Date of the Final Stage of the Pentateuch

Armin Lange

Since I met Graham Davies at the University of Tübingen, he has been a friend and colleague for many years. I have fond recollections of my visits to Cambridge and his home. Although Graham's interests are in pre-exilic times and range from archaeology via epigraphy to the pre-exilic parts of the Hebrew Bible, he has always impressed me with his wide-ranging scholarly curiosity, even for my work on the Dead Sea Scrolls, some 500 years removed from Graham's own passions. Since one of Graham's major works is his commentary on the Book of Exodus, I hope it is a fitting contribution to his Festschrift to ask how the Dead Sea Scrolls help to determine when the final redaction of the Pentateuch was complete.

In recent decades there has been renewed interest in the question of how the present shape of the Pentateuch developed and when it was finished. Since even a brief review of this discussion would exceed the limits of this article, the reader is referred to existing surveys and edited collections documenting the various positions.[1] Rather, my focus will be on the question of how to determine by relative chronology when the Pentateuch was finished.

Considering the relative chronology of textual witnesses to the Pentateuch, the first question to be addressed is, what is the final stage of the Pentateuch? Furthermore, how do the other early versions of the Pentateuch relate to this final stage? Do the quotations of Pentateuchal texts and adaptations by ancient Jewish paratextual literature provide evidence of when the various texts of the Pentateuch developed? If all these questions can be answered, do the Dead Sea Scrolls establish a *terminus ante quem* for the final redaction of the Pentateuch?

---

1   Cf. C. Houtman, *Der Pentateuch: Die Geschichte seiner Erforschung neben einer Auswertung* (CBET 9; Kampen: Kok Pharos, 1994); J. C. Geertz, K. Schmid, and M. Witten, eds., *Abschied vom Jahwisten: Die Komposition des Hexateuch in der jüngsten Diskussion* (BZAW 315; Berlin: de Gruyter, 2002); T. Römer, J.-D. Macchi, and C. Nihan, eds., *Introduction à l'Ancien Testament* (Geneva: Labor et fides, 2004), 67–113; G. N. Knoppers and B. M. Levinson, eds., *The Pentateuch as Torah: New Models for Understanding Its Promulgation and Acceptance* (Winona Lake, Ind.: Eisenbrauns, 2007).

1. What is the Final Stage of the Pentateuch?

In Judaism a standardised text of the Pentateuch is evident by the middle of the first century CE or soon after. Beginning with the finds from Masada, the text of all Pentateuch scrolls is virtually identical to the consonantal text of Codex Leningradiensis (CL). Textual deviation from the consonantal text of this Codex is 2% or less.[2] Even the orthography of these manuscripts is almost identical to CL.

30–1 BCE	MasLev[a] (Mas1a), MasDeut (Mas1c)
10 BCE–30 CE	MasLev[b] (Mas1b)
50–100 CE	4QGen[b] (4Q2; not from Qumran), XLev[c] (MS Schøyen 4611), XHev/SeNum[b] (XHev/Se 2), SdeirGen (Sdeir 1)
100–135 CE	MurGen-Exod.Num[a] (Mur 1)

Table: Hebrew Manuscripts of Genesis–Deuteronomy from Masada, Qumran Nahal Hever, Wadi Sdeir, and Wadi Murabbaʿat arranged by Paleographic Dates.[3]

The table above shows that, already before the first Jewish war, the consonantal text of the Masoretic Pentateuch was widely accepted in Judaism. It was this consonantal text that became the canonical text of the TanaK in Rabbinic Judaism.

In my opinion, the recensional history of the Septuagint, the chronological distribution of the proto-Masoretic manuscripts from Qumran and the other sites at the Dead Sea, as well as Rabbinic evidence, demonstrate that this proto-Masoretic text was created as the standard text of the Hebrew Bible in the second half of the first century BCE.[4] Semi-Masoretic manuscripts from Qumran point even further back. They deviate more than 2% from the consonantal text of CL but do not attest to any of the major textual deviations of, for example, the Samaritan and pre-Samaritan texts. A good example is 4QGen-Exod[a]

---

2   For a history of research on the textual standardization of the Hebrew Bible and its proto-Masoretic text, see A. Lange, "'They Confirmed the Reading' (y. Taʿan. 4:68a): The Textual Standardization of Jewish Scriptures in the Second Temple Period," in *From Qumran to Aleppo: A Discussion with Emanuel Tov about the Textual History of Jewish Scriptures in Honor of his 65th Birthday* (ed. A. Lange, M. Weigold, and J. Zsengellér; FRLANT 230; Göttingen: Vandenhoeck & Ruprecht, 2009), 29–80.

3   MasGen (Mas1); Mur(?)Gen[b] (Mur[?]); ArugLev; 5/6HevNum[a] (5/6Hev 1a); 34SeNum (34Se 2); XHev/SeDtn (XHev/Se 3); MurDtn (Mur 2); MurJes (Mur 3) are not included in the list below, because they are too damaged for textual and/or orthographic classification.

4   See Lange, "They Confirmed the Reading," passim.

(4Q1) which is dated paleographically to the years 125–100 BCE.[5] This means the creation of the proto-Masoretic standard text of the Pentateuch was no more than a text-critical fine-tuning of an existing text.

Do the semi-Masoretic manuscripts thus represent the final stage of the Pentateuch, and, if so, when was this text created? Traditionally experts of both lower and higher criticism argue that the final stage of the Pentateuch is represented by its final redaction, that is by a text located before the various textual versions had arisen owing to scribal corruption of the Pentateuch's manuscript tradition. The Qumran Dead Sea Scrolls have shown though that there is no clear line between redaction and scribal corruption.[6] Several versions of the Pentateuch in particular attest to late Pentateuchal redactions or translations of them. Examples include the Reworked Pentateuch manuscripts 4Q364 and 4Q365, the pre-Samaritan and Samaritan texts, and the OG textual tradition of, for example, the Book of Exodus. Do the Qumran manuscripts or the Septuagint and Samaritan textual traditions attest to earlier versions, that is redactions, of the Pentateuch?

2. The Textual History of the Pentateuch in the Light of the Samaritan Pentateuch and the Septuagint

For both the Samaritan Pentateuch and the Old Greek translation this question has been answered in the affirmative. As early as 1628, Morinus[7] and Cappelus[8] viewed the Samaritan Pentateuch as a text of the Pentateuch more original than MT. Almost 200 years later, Gesenius demonstrated convincingly that MT preserves the more original text of

---

5   For the paleographic date of 4QGen-Exod[a], see J. R. Davila, "1. 4QGen-Exod[a]," in E. Ulrich and F. M. Cross, *Qumran Cave 4.VII: Genesis to Numbers* (DJD XII; Oxford: Clarendon, 1994), 7–30 (8).

6   Cf., for example, E. Ulrich, *The Dead Sea Scrolls and the Origins of the Bible* (Studies in the Dead Sea Scrolls and Related Literature; Grand Rapids, Mich.: Eerdmans, 1999), 99–120.

7   Joannes Morinus, *Vetus Testamentum secundum LXX et ex auctoritate Sixti V. pontif. max. editum. Cum scholiis romanae editionis in singula capita distributis. Nunc primum e regione textus graeci opposita est Latina translatio . . . His ut corpus Bibliorum integrum lectori constaret auctarium accessit Novum Testamentum graece latinique ad fidem probatorum Codd. [et] versionis vulgatae* (Paris: Sonnius, 1628).

8   Louis Cappelus, *Diatriba de veris et antiquis ebraeorum literis: Opposita D. Joh. Buxtorfii de eodem argumento, Dissertationi. Item Jos. Scaligeri, adversus ejusdem reprehensiones, Defensio et ad obscurum Zoharis locum illustrandum brevis exercitatio* (Amsterdam: Ludovicum Elzevirium, 1645).

the Pentateuch.[9] Most of the 6000 variants between SP and MT (1900 of which correspond to the LXX as well) go back to a pre-Samaritan text which is known today from the Qumran library (4QpaleoExod^m [4Q22] and 4QNum^b [4Q27]). Only those variants of SP that focus on Mount Gerizim and the Samaritans were inserted into this pre-Samaritan text as part of a Samaritan reworking. A paleographic comparison between the paleo-Hebrew script of SP and ancient paleo-Hebrew scripts points to the reign of John Hyrcanus I as the time when the Samaritan Pentateuch was produced—most probably after John Hyrcanus I destroyed Samaria in 128 BCE.[10] A date of SP some time after 128 BCE implies in turn that the final (semi-Masoretic) stage of the Pentateuch predates the reign of John Hyrcanus I since the underlying pre-Samaritan base-text of SP is a reworking of a semi-Masoretic text. The 1900 shared readings between LXX and (pre-)SP show that this pre-Samaritan text either developed out of the Hebrew *Vorlagen* of the LXX or was influenced by them.

Not only (pre-)SP, but also the Hebrew *Vorlagen* of the Pentateuch-LXX have been understood as earlier versions of the Pentateuch predating MT. Since the work of Frankel[11] it has been a common opinion in LXX research that each book of the Pentateuch was translated separately into Greek. These translations were produced subsequently by different translators most probably in the third century BCE.[12] The OG texts of the Pentateuch hence raise the question whether each book of the Pentateuch had its own independent textual history.

---

9   W. Gesenius, *De pentateuchi samaritani origine, indole et auctoritate commentatio philologico-critica* (Halle: Renger, 1815).

10 Cf. W. F. Albright, *From the Stone Age to Christianity: Monotheism and the Historical Process* (Baltimore, Md.: John Hopkins University Press, 1946), 336 n. 12; F. M. Cross, *The Ancient Library of Qumran and Modern Biblical Studies* (New York: Doubleday, 1958), 127–28; J.-D. Purvis, *The Samaritan Pentateuch and the Origin of the Samaritan Sect* (HSM 2; Cambridge, Mass.: Harvard University Press, 1968), 98–118; B. K. Waltke, "Prolegomena to the Samaritan Pentateuch" (Ph.D. diss., Harvard University, 1965), 225–26.

11 Z. Frankel, *Historisch-kritische Studien zu der Septuaginta: Nebst Beiträgen zu den Targumim*, vol. 1.1: *Vorstudien zu der Septuaginta* (Leipzig: Vogel, 1841); idem, *Über den Einfluss der palästinischen Exegese auf die alexandrinische Hermeneutik* (Leipzig: Barth, 1851).

12 For the dates of the Old Greek versions of Genesis, Exodus, Leviticus, Numbers, and Deuteronomy, see, e.g., G. Dorival, "Les origines de la Septante: la traduction en grec des cinq livres de la Torah," in M. Harl, G. Dorival, and O. Munnich, *La Bible grecque des Septante: du judaïsme hellénistique au christianisme ancient* (Initiations au christianisme ancien; Paris: Cerf, 1994), 39–82.

Excursus: The Pentateuch – One Text of Many

The Dead Sea Scrolls help to answer this question. For some of the manuscripts from Qumran and the other sites it is highly unlikely that they ever contained more than one book of the Pentateuch. Although only fragments survive for almost all manuscripts of the books Genesis–Deuteronomy, their original height can be reconstructed. The height of a scroll allows in turn conclusions about how much text an individual manuscript could have contained. When the diameter of a scroll became wider than its height, it became increasingly difficult to roll. As a rule of thumb, scrolls were not wider in diameter than they were high.[13] Examples of scrolls which did not contain more than one book of the Pentateuch include 4QLev[d] (4Q26), 11QLev[b] (11Q2); MasLev[b] (Mas1b); 4QDtn[b–e] (4Q29–32). This means individual books of the Pentateuch were copied separately and were hence affected individually by scribal corruption. But several scrolls were found at the various sites around the Dead Sea that even in their preserved text contain several books of the Pentateuch: 4QRP[b.c.d] (4Q364–366),[14] 4QGen-Exod[a] (4Q1); 4QpaleoGen-Exod[l] (4Q11); MurGen-Exod.Num[a] (Mur 1); 4QExod-Lev[f] (4Q17); 1QpaleoLev-Num[a] (1Q3 1–11, 12?, 15?); and 4QLev-Num[a] (4Q23). A material reconstruction of 4QRP[c] (4Q365) makes it likely that this manuscript once contained the whole Pentateuch. It is further remarkable that 55% of those Qumran manuscripts which can still be identified as copies of the Pentateuch or copies of books of the Pentateuch exceed 30 lines per column in height: 4QRP[b] (4Q364; 39 lines); 4QRP[c] (4Q365; 43 lines); 1QGen (1Q1; 35 lines); 2QGen (2Q1, 44 lines); 4QGen-Exod[a] (4Q1; 36 lines); 4QGen[b] (4Q2; 40 lines); 4QGen[e] (4Q5; 50 lines); 4QpaleoGen-Exod[l] (4Q11; 55–60 lines); 1QExod (1Q2; 30 lines); 4QExod[b] (4Q13; 50 lines); 4QExod[c] (4Q14; 41–42 lines); 4QExod-Lev[f] (4Q17; 60 lines); 4QpaleoExod[m] (4Q22; 32–33 lines); 1QpaleoLev-Num[a] (1Q3 1–11.12?.15?; 44 lines); 4QLev-Num[a] (4Q23; 43 lines); 4QLev[b] (4Q24; 41 lines); 11QpaleoLev[a] (11Q1; 42 lines); 4QNum[b] (4Q27 30–32 lines); 4QLXXNum (4Q121; 34 lines); 1QDtn[a] (1Q4; 47 lines); 1QDtn[b] (1Q5; 40 lines); 4QDtn[i] (4Q36; 39–40 lines); 4QpaleoDeut[r] (4Q45; 32 lines). Similarly six out of the seven Pentateuchal manuscripts found at the other sites around the Dead Sea exceed 30 lines in height: MurGen-Exod.Num[a] (Mur 1; 50 lines); SdeirGen (Sdeir 1; 40 lines); XHev/SeNumb (XHev/Se2; 44 lines); MasDtn (Mas1c; 42 lines); MurDtn (Mur 2; 30–31 lines); XHev/SeDtn (XHev/Se3; 39 lines).

This means that the majority of the Pentateuchal manuscripts among the Dead Sea Scrolls are high enough to have once contained either all five or at least several books of the Pentateuch. One of the earliest manuscripts from the Qumran library, 4QExod-Lev[f] (4Q17; middle of the third century BCE) not only contains parts of both

---

13   Cf. H. Stegemann, "Methods for the Reconstruction of Scrolls from Scattered Fragments," in *Archaeology and History in the Dead Sea Scrolls: The New York University Conference in Memory of Yigael Yadin* (ed. L. H. Schiffman; JSPSup 8; Sheffield: Sheffield Academic Press, 1990), 189–220.

14   That 4QRP[b–e] are copies of different texts of the Pentateuch and not manuscripts of a rewritten composition has been shown by M. Segal, "4QReworked Pentateuch or 4QPentateuch?" in *The Dead Sea Scrolls Fifty Years after their Discovery: Proceedings of the Jerusalem Congress, July 20–25, 1997* (ed. L. H. Schiffman, E. Tov, J. C. VanderKam, and G. Marquis; Jerusalem: Israel Exploration Society and The Shrine of the Book, 2000), 391–99.

Exodus and Leviticus but is also among the tallest scrolls in the Qumran library (60 lines). It once contained most probably the whole Pentateuch. It seems likely, therefore, that already in Second Temple times the Pentateuch was transmitted as one textual unit with one textual history. The Old Greek translations of Genesis, Exodus, Leviticus, Numbers, and Deuteronomy are the exception to this rule. They were translated individually because one person was not able to translate the whole Pentateuch or because the needs of Egyptian Judaism did not require Greek translations of all books of the Pentateuch at the same time.

We return to the question whether the various Old Greek translations of Genesis–Deuteronomy attest to an earlier text of the Pentateuch than MT: the differences from MT in the OG texts of Genesis–Deuteronomy cannot be attributed exclusively to their translators. The Qumran manuscripts 4QLev^d (4Q26) and 4QDeut^q (4Q44) are not identical to the Hebrew *Vorlagen* of these Old Greek translations but are so close to them that to a significant extent their disagreements with MT go back to (a) variant text(s) of the Pentateuch. OG-Exodus provides a good example of how far the Old Greek translations of Genesis–Deuteronomy reflect earlier textual versions. In general, the OG text of Exodus harmonizes its Hebrew *Vorlage*.[15] "But the dominant characteristic of Exod as a translation document is its expansionist character. On the whole Exod expands far more than contracts. Where the Hebrew is abrupt, the Greek tends to smoothen out the text."[16]

The expansionist character of OG-Exodus notwithstanding, the significant differences between MT and LXX in Exodus 35–40 go back to the Hebrew *Vorlage* of OG-Exodus. In MT the description of how the tabernacle was built (Exodus 35–40) corresponds to the ordinances for the tabernacle in Exodus 25–31. In the OG text Exodus 35–40 differs significantly from the ordinances in Exodus 25–31. Compared to the report of the building of the tabernacle in MT-Exodus 35–40, OG-Exodus 35–40 attests to a shorter text with a different sequence. OG-Exodus 35–40 summarizes the building report and has a text sequence which is technically more plausible. Hence MT-Exodus 35–40 harmonized the shorter version with the ordinances of Exodus 25–31.[17] That the text of OG-

---

15   See J. W. Wevers, "Translation and Canonicity: A Study in the Narrative Portions of the Greek Exodus," in *Scripta Signa Vocis: Studies about Scripts, Scriptures, Scribes, and Languages presented to J. H. Hospers* (ed. H. L. J. Vanstiphout; Groningen: John Benjamin, 1986), 295–303.

16   J. W. Wevers, *Text History of the Greek Exodus* (MSU 21; Göttingen: Vandenhoeck & Ruprecht, 1992), 148.

17   Cf. A. Aejmelaeus, "Septuagintal Translation Techniques: A Solution to the Problem of the Tabernacle Account," in *Septuagint, Scrolls and Cognate Writings: Papers Presented to the International Symposium on the Septuagint and Its Relations to the Dead Sea Scrolls and Other Writings* (ed. G. J. Brooke and B. Lindars; SBLSCS 33; Atlanta, Ga.:

Exodus 35–40 goes back to a *Hebrew Vorlage* is also demonstrated by 4QExod-Lev[f] (4Q17) since this manuscript agrees with LXX against MT in Exod 40:17, 20, 22.

So far I have shown: The Hebrew text of the Pentateuch has one shared textual history. The semi-Masoretic text of the Pentateuch predates the second half of the first century BCE and was reworked by both pre-SP and SP. The OG-translations of Genesis–Deuteronomy go back to Hebrew *Vorlagen* which differ from MT. What remains unclear is when the Hebrew *Vorlage* of the OG and the semi-Masoretic text developed.

3. The Textual History of the Pentateuch in the Light of the Dead Sea Scrolls

In addition to semi-Masoretic, pre-Samaritan manuscripts and manuscripts which are close to the Hebrew *Vorlagen* of OG Genesis–Deuteronomy, the Qumran library attests to non-aligned Pentateuchal manuscripts which predate the second half of the first century BCE. The table overleaf lists the Pentateuch manuscripts from Qumran according to text-type and paleographic date.

The character and textual groupings especially of the non-aligned manuscripts from Qumran have not as yet been studied in detail. For many of them nothing more than their classification as non-aligned is known. Nevertheless, the table shows that the various non-aligned Pentateuchal manuscripts from Qumran go back to at least the third or second century BCE. Non-aligned texts of the Pentateuch are hence not always late deviations from the Pentateuch's semi- and proto-Masoretic texts but occur early in the textual history of the Pentateuch, too. For the question of the date of the final redaction of the Pentateuch two non-aligned manuscripts are especially important: 4QRP[c] (4Q365) and 4QDeut[q] (4Q44).

Scholars Press, 1992), 381–402; A. Y. Kim, "The Textual Alignment of the Tabernacle Section of 4Q365 (Fragments 8a–b, 9a–b i, 9b ii, 12a i, 12b iii)," *Textus* 21 (2002): 45–69.

	Semi-MT	Proto-MT	Semi-MT or pre-SP	Pre-SP	Vorlage of LXX	Non-aligned
ca. 250 BCE						4QExod–Lev[f]
200–150 BCE			5QDeut			
150–100 BCE						4QLev–Num[a], 4QDeut[b], 4QDeut[c]
125–75 BCE			4QDeut[d]			
125–100 BCE	4QGen–Exod[a]					
100–25 BCE	4QpaleoGen–Exod[l]			4QpaleoExod[m]		4QRP[e], 4QpaleoDeut[r]
100–50 BCE			4QDeut[i]			
75–50 BCE			4QDeut[f], 4QDeut[o]			4QRP[b], 4QRP[c], 4QRP[d]
ca. 50 BCE			4QGen[g]			4QGen[f] 4QLev[b]
50–1 BCE						4QDeut[h]
50–25 BCE		4QDeut[e]	4QGen[e], 4QGen[j]			4QExod[c]
30 BCE –20 CE				4QNum[b]	4QLev[d]	4QExod[b]
30–1 BCE			4QLev[e]			4QDeut[k1], 4QDeut[k2], 4QDeut[n]
1–50 CE		4QDeut[g]			4QDeut[q]	11QpaleoLev[a]
20–68 CE			4QGen[c]			1QDeut[b]
ca. 50 CE						4QDeut[j]
50–68 CE			4QLev[c]			2QExod[a]

4QRP^c (4Q365)

Originally the manuscripts 4Q158 and 4Q364–67 were regarded as five copies of one rewritten Pentateuchal composition.[18] Contrary to this earlier understanding, Segal has demonstrated that 4Q158 and 4Q364–67 do not belong to one composition. Only 4Q158 copies a rewritten Pentateuchal composition, while 4Q364–67 attest to four different texts of the Pentateuch.[19] Therefore, 4QRP^c (4Q365) needs to be treated separately from the other manuscripts which were designated as "Reworked Pentateuch" in the DJD series.

One of the most important issues discussed in connection with 4QRP^c (4Q365) is its relation to the *Temple Scroll*. Tov and White identified five fragments to be distinguished from the rest of the manuscript, and designated them as 4QT? (4Q365a).[20] All five fragments were copied by the same scribe as the rest of 4QRP^c (4Q365) and use the same orthography as 4QRP^c (4Q365), but attest to a text unknown from the Pentateuch.

> Frg. 1 contains material concerning the Festival of Unleavened Bread. Frg. 2 i discusses the Day of Firstfruits and other sacrificial ordinances, and then contains the beginning of the description of the middle court of the temple. Col. ii gives the names of the gates of the outer court. Finally, frgs. 3, 4 and 5 i contain the specifications of certain buildings and objects probably associated with the temple.[21]

Furthermore, 4Q365a 2 recalls the text of 11QT^a (11Q19) XXXVIII; XLI–XLII. For this phenomenon four explanations are possible. 4Q365a could be

- a copy of the *Temple Scroll*;[22]
- a copy of one of the *Temple Scroll's* source texts;[23]
- a modified version of the *Temple Scroll*;[24]

---

18 See, e.g., E. Tov and S. A. White, "Reworked Pentateuch," in H. W. Attridge, T. Elgvin, J. Milik, S. Olyan, J. Strugnell, E. Tov, J. C. VanderKam, and S. White, in consultation with J. C. VanderKam, *Qumran Cave 4.VIII: Parabiblical Texts, Part 1* (DJD XIII; Oxford: Clarendon, 1994), 187–351 (187–96).

19 M. Segal, "Reworked Pentateuch," passim; cf. idem, "Biblical Exegesis in 4Q158: Techniques and Genre," *Textus* 19 (1998): 45–62.

20 Tov and White, "Reworked Pentateuch," 319–20.

21 Tov and White, "Reworked Pentateuch," 319.

22 Thus first Y. Yadin, *The Temple Scroll*, vol. 1: *Introduction* (Jerusalem: Israel Exploration Society, 1983), 8–9.

23 Thus first M. Wise, *A Critical Study of the Temple Scroll from Qumran Cave 11* (SAOC 49; Chicago, Ill.: The Oriental Institute of the University of Chicago, 1990), 58–59.

24 Thus B. Z. Wacholder, "The Fragmentary Remains of the 11QTorah (Temple Scroll): 11QTorah^b and 11QTorah^c plus 4QparaTorah Integrated with 11QTorah^a," *HUCA* 62 (1991): 1–116 (4).

- a part of 4QRP^c (4Q365). In this case 4QRP^c (4Q365) would have
  preserved one of the *Temple Scroll*'s sources.[25]

Decisive is the observation made by Stegemann in an unpublished lecture in 1994 at the University of Tübingen. According to Stegemann the
damage patterns of 4Q365a 2 and 4QRP^c (4Q365) 6 are so similar that
both fragments must come from subsequent layers of the same scroll.
In other words, 4Q365a and 4Q365 are not two manuscripts but one
manuscript. The five fragments labelled 4Q365a preserve additional
long texts of 4Q365. Hence 4QRP^c (4Q365) is hence one of the Pentateuchal source texts for the *Temple Scroll* as indicated by the overlaps
between 4Q365a 2 and 11QT^a (11Q19) XXXVIII; XLI–XLII.

Incorporating the five fragments of 4Q365a, there are a total of 67
damaged fragments of 4QRP^c (4Q365). The text of fragments A–X remains unidentified. Of the Pentateuch, fragments 1–38 preserve parts
of Gen 21:9–10; Exod 8:13–19; 9:9–12; 10:19?, 20; 14:10, 12–17, 19–21;
15:16–20, X, 22–26; 17:3–5; 18:13–15; 26:34–36; 28:16–17, 19–20; 29:20–22;
30:37–38; 31:1–3; 35:3–5; 36:32–38; 37:29; 38:1–7; 39:1–5, 8–19; Lev 11:1–2,
17, 21–24, 32, 40–42, 44–45; 13:6–8, 15, 17–18, 51–52; 16:11–12, ?; 18:26–
28; 23:42–44; 24:1–2, X; 25:7–9; 26:17–28, 30–32; 27,34?; Num 1:1–5; 3:26–
30; 4:47–49; 7:1, 78–80; 8:11–12; 9:15, 17–19, 22–23; 10:2–3; 13:12, 14–15,
13, 16–25, 29–30; 15:26–28; 17:20–24; 27:11; 36,1–2; Deut 19:20–21; 20:1.
Fragment 37 preserves parts of either Deut 2:24 or 2:36. That passages
from all the books of the Pentateuch are still extant implies 4QRP^c
(4Q365) once contained the whole Pentateuch, and measured between
22 and 27 metres long.[26] Paleographically, 4QRP^c (4Q365) can be dated
to the years 75–50 BCE.[27] In addition to the extrabiblical text of the five
fragments from 4Q365a, 204 textual variants between 4QRP^c (4Q365),
MT, SP, and LXX can still be identified in the 1204 identifiable, if sometimes only partially-preserved, words of 4QRP^c (4Q365). 4QRP^c (4Q365)
reads 58 times with and 146 times against MT, 69 times with and 135
times against SP, 36 times with and 127 times against LXX, and attests to
98 non-aligned readings. 7 variant readings of 4QRP^c (4Q365) are
extensive in size (once with and six times against MT, seven times
against SP, once with and six times against LXX; six non-aligned read-

---

25 Thus first J. Strugnell in a letter to B. Z. Wacholder (quoted in: *The Dawn of Qumran:
    The Sectarian Torah and the Teacher of Righteousness* [HUCM 8, Cincinnati, Ohio: Heb-
    rew Union College Press, 1983], 205–6) and H. Stegemann, "The Origins of the Tem-
    ple Scroll," in *Congress Volume: Jerusalem 1986* (ed. J. A. Emerton; VTSup 40; Leiden:
    Brill, 1988), 235–56 (237).

26 Cf. Tov and White, "Reworked Pentateuch," 192.

27 See White, "Preliminary Report," 271; Tov and White, "Reworked Pentateuch," 260–
    61.

ings). Examples include a longer Song of Miriam in Exod 15:22 and the lack of Exod 39:6.

The statistics show that 4QRP^c (4Q365) can best be described as a non-aligned text of the Pentateuch which developed out of a pre-Samaritan text tradition.[28] Tov describes the relationship between 4QRP^c (4Q365) and pre-SP as follows.

> 1. In minutiae, 4Q365 is closer to ᴍ than to the other sources. 2. No evidence, positive or negative, has been preserved with regard to harmonizing additions. 3. In the layout of the Song at the Sea, the spacing resembles that of ᴍ, and not that of 𝔐. 4. 4Q365 does not reflect two cases of editorial manipulation of ᴍ (sequence: Exod 26:35; 30:1–10; 26,36ff. [frg.~8a–b]; transposition of Exod 29:21 after v 28 [frg. 9b ii]). 5. 4Q365 often differs from ᴍ in 'non-aligned readings' which should be ascribed to 4QRP's rewriting of the biblical text. Among these are omissions of 4Q365 of the following verses: Exod 14:18; 39:6–7; Lev 11:19; and the different internal sequence of Num 13:12–16.

That the text attested by 4QRP^c (4Q365) rewrites a pre-Samaritan text of the Pentateuch is corroborated by its closeness to 4QNum^b (4Q27).[29]

4QExod-Lev^f (4Q17)

Of 4QExod-Lev^f (4Q17) five damaged fragments are preserved. Fragments 1–4 contain remnants of Exod 38:18–22; 39:4–7, 9–11, 13–24; 40:8–27; Lev 1:13–15, 17; 2:1. Fragment 5 remains unidentified. With 60 lines, 4QExod-Lev^f (4Q17) is among the tallest scrolls from the Qumran library[30] and it is possible that 4QExod-Lev^f (4Q17) once contained the whole Pentateuch. This observation is all the more important as 4QExod-Lev^f (4Q17) dates paleographically to the middle of the third century BCE.[31] 4QExod-Lev^f (4Q17) is hence the earliest known manuscript of the Pentateuch.

Twenty-nine textual variants between 4QExod-Lev^f (4Q17), MT, SP, and LXX can still be identified in the 259 (sometimes only partially) preserved words of 4QExod-Lev^f (4Q17). The manuscript reads two times with and 27 times against MT, six times with and 23 times against SP, five times with and 13 times against LXX, and attests to 21 non-aligned readings.

---

28 Cf. Tov, "Textual Status," 65–73; Tov and White, "Reworked Pentateuch," 194–95.

29 Tov and White, "Reworked Pentateuch," 194.

30 Cf. F. M. Cross, "17. 4QExod-Lev^f," in Ulrich and Cross, *Qumran Cave 4.VII* (DJD XII), 133–50 (134).

31 See Cross, "4QExod-Lev^f," 134; cf. idem, "Development," 153–58.

The order of the text of 4QExod-Lev[f] is significant in determining its textual affiliations. Chap. 39:3–24 preserved in this manuscript immediately precedes chap. 40 in agreement with the order of the Massoretic and the Samaritan traditions. On the contrary, in the Septuagint, chap. 39:10–32 is found at 36:10–32 in a radically different ordering of the tradition.[32]

Because of its six readings conforming to SP, 4QExod-Lev[f] (4Q17) has often been characterized as a forerunner of the pre-Samaritan text,[33] but, since the majority of its readings are non-aligned, 4QExod-Lev[f] (4Q17) can best be described as a non-aligned textual witness.[34] Constraints of space do not allow for a comprehensive study of the variant readings of 4QExod-Lev[f] (4Q17). The examples of Exod 39:21 and 40:17 show that the manuscript is expansionistic in character.[35] 4QExod-Lev[f] (4Q17) therefore attests to an expansionistic recension of an earlier Pentateuchal text. That 4QExod-Lev[f] (4Q17) is not the autograph of this recension is demonstrated by two haplographies in Exod 40:18.[36]

To conclude: 4QExod-Lev[f] (4Q17) expands a text which already knows some pre-Samaritan variant readings. This means that the base text of 4QExod-Lev[f] (4Q17) is not semi-Masoretic in character but is already a somewhat altered semi-Masoretic text. Because 4QExod-Lev[f] (4Q17) was copied in the middle of the third century BCE, the altered semi-Masoretic base text of its recension must go back at least to the early third century BCE, but might be significantly earlier.

4QDeut[q] (4Q44)

Five heavily damaged fragments of 4QDeut[q] (4Q44) are preserved, which attest to parts of Deut 32:9–10.?.37–43. Fragments 2–5 belong to two columns of the original scroll. The second column is followed by a handle-sheet. The last verse before the handle-sheet is Deut 32:43 which also constitutes the end of this scroll. The relatively small height of 4QDeut[q] (4Q44) (11.4 cm; 11 lines) renders it improbable that it once

---

32   Cross, "4QExod-Lev[f]," 135–36.

33   Cf., e.g., Cross, "4QExod-Lev[f]," 136.

34   Cf. E. Tov, "The Biblical Texts from the Judaean Desert—An Overview and Analysis of the Published Texts," in *The Bible as Book—The Hebrew Bible and the Judaean Desert Discoveries* (ed. E. D. Herbert and E. Tov; London: British Library, 2002), 139–66 (156).

35   For the expansionistic character of the variants in question, see Cross, "4QExod-Lev[f]," 139.

36   For the two haplographies, see Cross, "4QExod-Lev[f]," 142.

contained the whole Book of Deuteronomy. Most likely 4QDeutᑫ (4Q44) covered only the song of Moses from Deut 32:1–43.[37]

Among the 56 (partly) preserved words of 4QDeutᑫ (4Q44), 13 variant readings between MT, LXX, SP, and 4QDeutᑫ (4Q44) are extant. 4QDeutᑫ (4Q44) reads once with and 12 times against MT, two times with and 11 times against SP, seven times with and six times against LXX. Two variants are non-aligned readings.

> 4QDeutᑫ and the Massoretic textus receptus display distinctly variant forms of the text – more than one variant for every pair of the scroll's short lines. 4QDeutᑫ, or its Vorlage, however, should not be naïvely dismissed as a so-called 'vulgar text' for a number of reasons. Virtually all of its readings are documented in other biblical manuscripts; some readings (שמים 32:43) are more ancient than those preserved in 𝔐 which revised polytheistic terms secondarily for theological purposes; and other readings (אדמת 32:43) appear superior to unusual forms in 𝔐.

> Though not identical to 𝔊, 4QDeutᑫ shares several unique readings with the Septuagint version of Deuteronomy and bears witness to the existence of the variant Hebrew Vorlage used by the Septuagint translator, at least for this section of Deuteronomy. . . . 4QDeutᑫ and 𝔊 agree in seven readings against 𝔐 including all of the significant readings.[38]

Either 4QDeutᑫ (4Q44) attests to the Hebrew *Vorlage* of OG-Deut or more likely to a shared ancestor of both the Hebrew *Vorlage* of OG-Deut and a semi-Masoretic text. In either case, 4QDeutᑫ (4Q44) attests to a text of the Pentateuch which was later reworked in line with a semi- or proto-Masoretic text. This would mean the few words of 4QDeutᑫ (4Q44) preserve all that is left of the earliest text of Deuteronomy and most likely of the whole Pentateuch.

To summarize: The Qumran library points to a textual plurality of the Pentateuch in the Second Temple period, unknown before the Dead Sea Scrolls were found. Both non-aligned Pentateuch-texts and the Hebrew *Vorlagen* of the OG-translations sometimes developed from the Pentateuch's semi-Masoretic text(s) (for example, 4QRPᶜ [4Q365]; 4QExod-Levᶠ [4Q17]), but in rare cases also preceded it (4QDeutᑫ [4Q44]). The example of 4QExod-Levᶠ (4Q17) shows that the Pentateuch's non-aligned texts go back to at least the third century BCE.

---

37 Thus first H. Stegemann, "Weitere Stücke von 4 Q p Psalm 37, von 4 Q Patriarchal Blessings und Hinweis auf eine unedierte Handschrift aus Höhle 4 Q mit Exzerpten aus dem Deuteronomium," *RevQ* 6 (1967–1969): 193–227 (220).

38 Skehan and Ulrich, "4QDeutᑫ," 138; cf. also P. W. Skehan, "A Fragment of the 'Song of Moses' (Deut. 32) from Qumran," *BASOR* 136 (1954): 12–15.

4. The *Temple Scroll* and the Book of Ezra/Nehemiah

Of key importance for the question of the date of the final stage of the Pentateuch is how the Book of Ezra/Nehemiah, the *Temple Scroll* from Qumran, and 4QRPᶜ (4Q365) are related to each other. It has already been shown above that the Pentateuch recension which is attested in 4QRPᶜ (4Q365) is one of the sources for the *Temple Scroll*.

Nehemiah 10:35 relates that priests, Levites, and the people, should use the oracle of the lot to determine the sequence in which they should bring the wood offering to the house of God (cf. Neh 13:31).[39] The precise phrase used to describe the sequence is לבית אבתינו ("according to the house of our fathers"). Neh 10:35 claims that this is a prescription written in the Torah (ככתוב בתורה "as it is written in the Torah"). Although Neh 10:35 states explicitly that this procedure is commanded in the Torah, such a prescription is attested neither in the Masoretic Pentateuch, nor in any other of its versions. The lack of such a command in the Pentateuch has elicited various explanations. Clines speaks, for example, of the "creation of facilitating law."[40] Blenkinsopp argues that Neh 10:35 "is implicit in the requirement that the priests keep the fire for the morning and evening sacrifice burning continuously, for which fuel was required (Lev. 6:2, 5–6 [9, 12–13])."[41]

Against such interpretative remedies it needs to be stated that the sequence in which the wood offering is to be brought to the temple is regulated in a passage of 4QRPᶜ (4Q365) which follows Lev 24:2, that is in 4QRPᶜ (4Q365) 23 9–11.[42]

(9)] the [fe]stival of fresh oil, they shall bring wood two [
(10)] the ones who bring on the fir[st] day, Levi [
(11) Reu]ben and Simon [and on t]he forth day [

Differing from Nehemiah 10:35, 4QRPᶜ (4Q365) 23 9–11 mentions neither the oracle of the lot nor families. Instead, a sequence is given for the tribes of Israel in which they should provide wood for the wood offering. Although this is not an exact parallel, in my opinion, Nehe-

---

39 For my ideas concerning Neh 10:35, see also "From Literature to Scripture: The Unity and Plurality of the Hebrew Scriptures in Light of the Qumran Library," in *One Scripture or Many? Canon from Biblical, Theological, and Philosophical Perspectives* (ed. C. Helmer and C. Landmesser; Oxford: Oxford University Press, 2004), 51–107, 77–80.

40 D. J. A. Clines, "Nehemiah 10 As an Example of Early Jewish Biblical Exegesis," *JSOT* 21 (1981): 111–17 (112); see also H. G. M. Williamson, *Ezra, Nehemiah* (WBC 16; Waco, Tex.: Word Books, 1985), 336.

41 J. Blenkinsopp, *Ezra-Nehemiah: A Commentary* (OTL; Philadelphia, Pa.: Westminster, 1988), 317.

42 Translation according to Tov and White, "Reworked Pentateuch," 293.

miah 10:35 attests to an interpretative use of the prescription of 4QRP^c (4Q365).[43]

A close parallel to 4QRP^c (4Q365) 23 9–11 can be found in the *Temple Scroll* (11QT^b VI, 11–15 [lines 16–17 overlap with 11QT^a XXIII, 3–4]):[44]

> (11) [And after the festival of fresh oil, they shall bring,] (12) to the alta[r the woo]d, [namely the twelve tribes of the people of Israel, and they shall offer: on the first day] (13) the tribes[of Levi]and Judah, on the [second]d[ay Benjamin and the sons of Joseph, on the third day, Reuben and Simon] (14) on the fourth day Issachar [and Ze]bulon, [on the fifth day Gad and Asher, on the sixth day Dan] (15) and Naphtali.

It has been argued that in their passages on the feast of the wood offering, both the text of 4QRP^c (4Q365) and the *Temple Scroll* echo Nehemiah 10:35.[45] But in light of the *Temple Scroll*'s dependence on other passages attested in the manuscript 4Q365, it seems more likely that the *Temple Scroll* depends on the text copied in 4QRP^c (4Q365). This means both the *Temple Scroll* and the Book of Ezra/Nehemiah use the 4QRP^c-text of the Pentateuch independently from each other.

That both the *Temple Scroll* and the Book of Ezra/Nehemiah use the 4QRP^c-text of the Pentateuch provides a fixed point in the relative chronology of the Pentateuch's various texts and recensions. Both the *Temple Scroll* and the Book of Ezra/Nehemiah are qualified to provide a *terminus ante quem* for one of the later recensions of the Pentateuch's text, that is the 4QRP^c-text of the Pentateuch. The question of when the *Temple Scroll* and the Book of Ezra/Nehemiah were written becomes crucial then for establishing a *terminus ante quem* of the final stage of the Pentateuch.

For the *Temple Scroll*, the *terminus ante quem* is set by its oldest preserved manuscript, 4QT^b (4Q524), dated paleographically to around 150 BCE.[46] The *terminus post quem* can be derived from relative chronology and the history of architecture. Swanson argues that the *Temple Scroll* depends on 1–2 Chronicles, written in late Persian or early Hellenistic times.[47] As Broshi has shown, in Palestine the spiral staircase described

---

43 Against Tov and White, "Reworked Pentateuch," 295.

44 For the reconstruction and translation of 11QT^b VI:11–15, see F. García Martínez, E. J. C. Tigchelaar, and A. S. van der Woude, "20. 11QTemple^b," in *Qumran Cave 11.II* (11Q2–18, 11Q20–31) (DJD XXIII; Oxford: Clarendon, 1998), 357–409 (381–83). The reconstruction is based on 11QT^a and 4QRP^c.

45 Yadin, *Temple Scroll*, 1:123–24 (128).

46 See É. Puech, *Qumrân grotte 4 XVIII: Textes hébreux (4Q521–4Q528, 4Q576–4Q579)* (DJD XXV; Oxford: Clarendon, 1998), 87–88.

47 D. D. Swanson, *The Temple Scroll and the Bible: The Methodology of 11QT* (STDJ 14; Leiden: Brill, 1995), 237–39.

by the *Temple Scroll* for the north-western tower of the sanctuary (11QT^a XXX:3–XXXI:9) and the peristyles situated in the middle and the outer courtyards are attested only from Hellenistic times onwards.[48] Both observations argue for a *terminus post quem* in the third century BCE. In my opinion, the extremely free approach taken to the *Temple Scroll's* Pentateuchal base text and the *Temple Scroll's* own claim to be a legal text, which supersedes the Torah in authority, suggest a date in the third century BCE.

As for the Book of Ezra/Nehemiah, I cannot provide here a detailed reconstruction of its redaction history owing to constraints of space. It might suffice to say that for a long time, 1–2 Chronicles and Ezra/Nehemiah have been regarded as one literary work, which underwent (several) redactions, and was called the Chronistic history.[49] More recently, attempts have been made to understand 1–2 Chronicles and Ezra-Nehemiah as two separate literary works which were written subsequently.[50] This approach I will follow below. The name of the last high priest mentioned in the lists of Neh 12:11, 22, Jaddua,[51] suggests a setting of the final stage of the book of Ezra/Nehemiah in early Hellenistic times.[52] The evidence of Josephus shows that this Jaddua was still in office during the reign of Alexander the Great (*Ant.* 11.302).[53]

---

48   M. Broshi, "Visionary Architecture and Town Planning in the Dead Sea Scrolls," in *Time to Prepare the Way in the Wilderness: Papers on the Qumran Scrolls* (ed. D. Dimant and L. H. Schiffman; STDJ 16; Leiden: Brill, 1995), 9–22 (19).

49   L. Zunz, *Die gottesdienstlichen Vorträge der Juden, historisch entwickelt: Ein Beitrag zur Alterthumskunde und biblischen Kritik, zur Literatur- und Religionsgeschichte* (Berlin: Asher, 1832), esp. 22; M. Noth, *Überlieferungsgeschichtliche Studien* (Halle: Niemeyer, 1943), 110–80, esp. 110.

50   Thus first S. Japhet, "The Supposed Common Authorship of Chronicles and Ezra-Nehemiah Investigated Anew," *VT* 18 (1968): 332–72.

51   For the high priest Jaddua, see J. C. VanderKam, *From Joshua to Caiaphas: High Priests after the Exile* (Minneapolis, Minn.: Fortress, 2004), 63–85.

52   Cf., for example, O. Kaiser, *Grundriß der Einleitung in die kanonischen und deuterokanonischen Schriften des Alten Testaments,* vol. 1, *Die erzählenden Werke* (Gütersloh: Gütersloher Verlagshaus, 1992), 147–48.

53   F. M. Cross doubted the historicity of the lists in Neh 12:11, 22 and wanted to add at least two more names which in his opinion would have been lost from haplography (see, e.g., "A Reconstruction of the Judean Restoration," *JBL* 94 [1975]: 4–18). But based on a reevaluation of the evidence from the Wadi ed-Daliyeh papyri and Samarian coins, J. Dušek has proven the historicity of the lists in Neh 12:11, 22 (see *Les manuscrits araméens du Wadi Daliyeh et la Samarie vers 450–332 av. J.-C.* [Culture and History of the Ancient Near East 25; Leiden: Brill, 2007], 549–98).

5. Conclusions

To come back to the question of the *terminus ante quem* of the Pentateuch's final stage, the *Temple Scroll* and the Book of Ezra/Nehemiah
employ the 4QRP^c-text of the Pentateuch already in the third century
BCE. That they do so independently from each other points to a high
degree of authority that the 4QRP^c-text of the Pentateuch must have
acquired in the third century BCE. Such an acquisition of authority
would normally require a few decades. The dates of the *Temple Scroll*
and the Book of Ezra/Nehemiah in the third and the early third century
BCE respectively, push the date of the 4QRP^c-text of the Pentateuch into
the early third century BCE at the latest. But the 4QRP^c-text of the Pentateuch is only a reworking of a pre-Samaritan text, which in one or more
stages[54] rewrites and expands in turn a semi-Masoretic text, which is
based on a text with close ties to the Hebrew *Vorlagen* of the Old Greek
translations. 4QDeut^q (4Q44) is a Qumran manuscript which is at least
relatively close to if not identical with such a *Vorlage*. 4QDeut^q (4Q44)
points, furthermore, to the existence of a Pentateuch-text which precedes both the *Vorlagen* of the OG translations of the books of the Pentateuch as well as its semi-Masoretic text, and which was theologically
reworked by the latter text.

Taking the possibility into consideration of a pre-semi-MT text for
the Pentateuch as attested by 4QDeut^q (4Q44), two or three more
reworkings took place between the final stage of the Pentateuch and its
4QRP^c-text. These two or three reworkings between the final stage of
the Pentateuch and its 4QRP^c-text exclude a third century BCE date for
the final stage of the Pentateuch and point towards the fourth century
BCE instead. Relative chronology thus shows that the text of the Pentateuch as we presuppose it for its final stage goes back to late Persian
times if not earlier. 4QDeut^q (4Q44) alerts us to the possibility that,
except for the few fragments of this manuscript, the text of the final
stage of the Pentateuch might be lost behind its semi-Masoretic recension.

A date of the final stage of the Pentateuch in the fourth century BCE
or earlier is corroborated by 4QExod-Lev^f (4Q17). 4QExod-Lev^f (4Q17)
expands a Pentateuch text that includes some pre-Samaritan readings.
The base text of 4QExod-Lev^f (4Q17) is hence not semi-Masoretic in
character but is a reworked semi-Masoretic text. Because 4QExod-Lev^f
(4Q17) was copied in the middle of the third century BCE, the semi-

---

54   That the pre-Samaritan text of the Pentateuch evolved in several stages could be
     implied by the few pre-Samaritan readings of 4QExod-Lev^f (4Q17).

Masoretic base text of its recension must go back at least to the early third century BCE, but is most probably significantly earlier.

Furthermore, relative chronology points towards the existence of multiple different reworkings of a semi-Masoretic text already in the third century BCE (e.g., the 4QRP^c-text, the pre-Samaritan text(s), the 4QExod-Lev^f-text). Only the text attested by 4QDeut^q (4Q44) seems to precede the Pentateuch's semi-Masoretic text. This makes it plausible if not probable that the final stage of the Pentateuch predates these third-century BCE reworkings by several decades if not a century.

Relative chronology thus establishes a *terminus ante quem* for the final stage of the Pentateuch in the fourth century BCE under Persian rule and even raises the question whether it might not go back to the early fourth or even to the late fifth century BCE.

Reading Joshua after Samuel

GRAEME AULD

Graham Davies and I share many academic interests. We co-operated for a period in the management of the affairs of the then British School of Archaeology in Jerusalem (now the Kenyon Institute); and I have observed his career with great admiration. He has kindly agreed to release me from my commitment to prepare a commentary on Joshua under his editorship. But it gives me considerable pleasure to offer in his honour some observations and suggestions which I should have enjoyed developing further. After proposing a common origin for 1 Samuel–2 Kings and for 1–2 Chronicles,[1] I noted some first implications for re-reading Joshua.[2] The present essay develops this quest, which has also widened more recently to embrace Genesis.[3] Preparing a commentary on the books of Samuel[4] has reinforced my earlier hunches that much of what Genesis and Joshua had to say was strongly influenced by the developing account in Samuel of Israel's royal beginnings.

The books of Samuel look forwards—over and beyond the whole story of kingship in Israel and Jerusalem. There may be some minor differences of emphasis between Samuel and Kings, yet essentially these books belong together as a single history of monarchy. But it is to a much more limited degree that the books of Samuel look backwards in time. There are a few brief references to what we know as the Exodus traditions, both the deliverance from Egypt (1 Sam 2:27; 10:18; 12:6, 8) and the associated plagues on Pharaoh and his people (1 Sam 4:8;

---

1   A. Graeme Auld, *Kings without Privilege: David and Moses in the Story of the Bible's Kings* (Edinburgh: T&T Clark, 1994).

2   A. Graeme Auld, "Reading Joshua after Kings," in *Words Remembered, Texts Renewed: Essays in Honour of John F. A. Sawyer* (ed. J. Davies, G. Harvey, and W. G. E. Watson; JSOTSup 195; Sheffield: Sheffield Academic, 1995), 167–81; repr. in idem, *Joshua Retold: Synoptic Perspectives* (Old Testament Studies; Edinburgh: T&T Clark, 1998), 102–12.

3   A. Graeme Auld, "Reading Genesis after Samuel," in *The Pentateuch: International Perspectives on Current Research* (ed. T. Dozeman, K. Schmid, and B. Schwartz; Tübingen: Mohr Siebeck, forthcoming 2011).

4   A. Graeme Auld, *1–2 Samuel* (OTL; Louisville, Ky.: Westminster John Knox, forthcoming 2011).

6:6). The oldest such reference (2 Sam 7:6–7, BTH)[5] talks first about
Yahweh bringing Israel out, and then an intervening period during
which Yahweh and his ark moved about, residing in temporary
accommodation. This past is always reported, not by the narrator, but
by characters in the story. Nathan (2 Sam 7:6–7), Samuel (1 Sam 10:18;
12:6, 8), and an unnamed "man of God" (1 Sam 2:27) transmit on Yahweh's behalf the memory of the deliverance; and the Philistine enemy
is fully aware of how Israel's God had plagued Egypt (1 Sam 4:8; 6:6).

It is only in the most detailed of these few backward references
(1 Sam 12:8–11) that Samuel talks of Israel being settled "in this place"
after their fathers were brought out of Egypt. But Samuel surprisingly
credits Moses and Aaron with leadership under Yahweh during the
settlement, and not just during the liberation from Egypt. Some characters we know from the book of Judges are mentioned next (12:9–11),
though in a different order from that book. But there is complete silence
in the books of Samuel about the leadership of Joshua. And yet, and to
a very much greater degree than Samuel in his book, Joshua is integral
to every part of the book which bears his name. How then should the
many links between the books of Samuel and Joshua, including some
clusters of links, be assessed?

In this article, I want to follow up some proposals offered in a previous article, where I noted some features shared by the story (as found
in both Kings and Chronicles) of Solomon, successor to David, and the
story of Joshua, successor to Moses.[6] Both moved the ark onwards,
Solomon into the temple in Jerusalem and Joshua into the promised
land west of the Jordan. A religious festival followed each move, and
then each leader had a visionary experience. Female foreigners (the
Queen of Sheba and Rahab) were both left without *rûaḥ*, when they
became aware of their achievements; and other foreigners, both Tyrians
and Gibeonites, came to work for Israel's national shrine. In each detail,
I was suggesting that the story of Solomon had influenced the story of
Joshua.

I suggested in the same article that 1 Samuel was already a freshly
drafted preface to this older history of King David and his successors,
shared by 2 Samuel–2 Kings and 1–2 Chronicles. Given the absence of
Joshua from the brief retrospects in Samuel, should we reckon that the

---

5   For a brief account of what I call the Book of Two Houses, abbreviated in this article
     as BTH, see Graeme Auld, *Samuel at the Threshold* (SOTS Study Series; Aldershot:
     Ashgate, 2004), 5–6.

6   Graeme Auld, "Deuteronomists between History and Theology," in *Congress Volume:
     Oslo 1998* (ed. A. Lemaire and M. Sæbø; VTSup 80; Leiden: Brill, 2000), 353–67; repr.
     in *Samuel at the Threshold*, 193–203.

book of Joshua (and Judges too?) was a still more recent account of a still earlier stage in the nation's story? Although the books of Samuel make no reference to Joshua, and in fact credit others with leadership in the period of settlement in the land, there are many links of theme and language with the narratives in the book of Joshua. Did the authors of Samuel know these stories of an earlier period without Joshua? Or had they some reason for passing over Joshua without mention? Or did the authors of Joshua draw on the books of Samuel?

I

There is quite a dense set of links between Joshua 7 and 1 Samuel 13–15, which may be best approached by means of a detour into the book of Judges. It can be sensibly argued that the stories about both Jephthah and his daughter (Judg 11:29–40) and Micah's mother and her son (Judg 17:1–4) are narrative explorations of the situation in 1 Samuel 14 in which Jonathan is trapped by a double curse uttered by his father. More immediately, of course, Micah's mother is offering in the epilogue a sceptical account of Judge Jephthah in the central portion of the book of Judges. She had cursed the unknown thief who had stolen from her two hundred pieces of silver; but, when her son confessed to having taken the silver, she immediately called down a blessing on him. Had she met Jephthah, we might well believe that she would have told him forcefully: You don't kill your child just because she or he falls within the ambit of an oath or curse you have uttered. Words are just words, and oaths are just words; and a curse can be turned into a blessing by the person who uttered it. Of course, given the mistakes which Micah's mother goes on to make, we may not take her to be a very reliable critic of Jephthah. The prior story of Jephthah's vow (to "offer up whoever comes out of the doors of my house to meet me," Judg 11:31) may in part be challenging readers of Samuel to focus on Saul's words ("cursed be whoever eats food before it is evening and I have been avenged on my enemies," 1 Sam 14:24), the recklessness of which they have not had time to savour as they read them—in part because the king is so quickly saved by his people from the consequences of his curse.

When Jonathan hears of Saul's curse, he comments rather darkly (in MT at least) that his father "has deeply troubled (ʿkr) the land" (1 Sam 14:29); and he goes on to blame lesser Philistine casualties than might have been expected on the curse-strengthened fast imposed on his people. By contrast with this blow struck on the Philistines, which was not large, the blow struck by Jephthah on the Ammonites was very large. And the terms of the oath were kept; and his daughter, like Jonathan, signified to her father that she accepted the action he was bound to take (Judg 11:36; 1 Sam 14:43): a vow was a vow, and it had brought him success. Unlike Saul and Jonathan, who both speak explicitly of death, Jephthah speaks indirectly: his daughter, he tells her, has come to be among those who bring him "deep trouble" (ʿkr): he has opened his mouth to Yahweh and cannot turn back. She replies equally indirectly that, if he has done so, he must do to her what has gone forth from his mouth (Judg 11:35–36).

II

The book of Judges invites us twice to ponder the issue of a child impaled on the consequences of a (possibly) rash parental curse. However, Joshua 7 has a much more extensive relationship with the books of Samuel, and with 1 Samuel 13–14 in particular.

1. The similar numbers of forces involved in each campaign immediately catch the attention. Saul chooses a force of three thousand, two thousand under his own command and one under Jonathan. Joshua's spies advise him that an assault on Ai will require only two or three thousand. And it is only in these two biblical verses that two and three thousand are juxtaposed.

2. The geographical location of both stories is also similar, even if the double presence of byt ʾwn in MT is misleading: it is almost certainly secondary (part of a plus) in Josh 7:2; and in 1 Sam 13:5, LXX reads not Βαιθών, but Βαιθωρών.

3. It is hardly surprising that "flight" (nws) is part of both stories (Josh 7:4; 1 Sam 14:22).

4. But it is more remarkable that "sin" (ḥṭʾ) features in both (Josh 7:11, 20; 1 Sam 14:33, 34)—sin is mentioned only once more in the text of Joshua (24:19), but is much more at home in Samuel (26 times).

5. Formal "approach" (qrb) to the deity (Josh 7:14; 1 Sam 14:36) closely follows the (first mention of) sin.

6. And that in turn is followed by parties being "taken" (nlkd) through exercise of the sacred lot (Josh 7:15–18; 1 Sam 14:41–42).

7. There must be some doubt whether the use of ʿkr ("trouble deeply") attested by MT in 1 Sam 14:29 is original. ἀπήλλαχεν ("changed") is rare and unusual, but is attested in both LXXᴮ and LXXᴸ. If original, we should note that ʿkr is the only one of these distinctive terms which occurs in a different order in Joshua (7:25). The relative fixity

of these narrative elements shared by Joshua 7 and 1 Samuel 13–14 is all the more striking in that the cast of 1 Samuel 14 is larger, and there are more semi-independent scenes.

Other possibly significant links exist between wording in Joshua 7 and in chapters neighbouring 1 Samuel 13–14.

1. "Taken" by lot (6. above) is found also in 1 Sam 10:20–21, where we also meet "tribe" by its "families" (Josh 7:14, 16–17).
2. The "ban" (*ḥrm*) is mentioned 8 times in Joshua 7 and 8 times also in 1 Samuel 15.
3. Joshua "tore" (*qrʿ*) his clothes (7:6), and Samuel's robe is torn in 1 Sam 15:27–28.
4. *Piʿel* and *hitpaʿel* of *qdš* ("sanctify") are used together in Josh 7:13 and 1 Sam 16:5.

And other less usual words and phrases found in Joshua 7 have parallels more widely in 1–2 Samuel:

1. *nblh* ("pernicious folly," v. 15) in 1 Sam 25:25; 2 Sam 13:12;
2. "don't conceal it from me" (v. 19) in 1 Sam 3:17–18; 2 Sam 14:18;
3. "ascribe glory" (v. 19) in 1 Sam 6:5;
4. "like this and like this" (v. 20) in 1 Sam 4:7; 2 Sam 14:13; 17:15;
5. "stone" (*sql*, v. 25) in 1 Sam 30:6; 2 Sam 16:6, 13;
6. "great heap of stones" (v. 26) in 2 Sam 18:17;
7. "the heat of his anger" (v. 26) in 1 Sam 28:18 (see below).

III

Although links between Joshua and 1 Samuel 13–14 are concentrated most densely in Joshua 7, there are several elsewhere. Joshua 11:4 describes the massing of the Canaanites, and other indigenous peoples, for battle against Joshua and his people, in terms very similar to 1 Sam 13:5, on the Philistines massing against Saul: "a people like the sand which is on the lip of the sea in multitude." Other variations of this comparator are found in Judg 7:12 (camels of the easterners); 2 Sam 17:11 (recommendation for Absalom's army); 1 Kgs 4:20 (Israel and Judah happy and contented); 1 Kgs 5:9 (Solomon's wisdom).

One key feature of Joshua 7 is the divine covenant (7:11, 15), which forms a bracket round Yahweh's explanation to Joshua why the Ai campaign has failed. *bryt yhwh* is never used in the text of the much longer books of Samuel; but it is repeated from Josh 7:11, 15 in the climactic verse (16) of Joshua's first farewell speech (Joshua 23), which also repeats the rare *ʾp yhwh* from 7:1 (N.B. also 2 Sam 6:7; 24:1 for "Yahweh's anger"). *bryt yhwh* may be understood as the key diagnostic expression towards a conclusion that Joshua 7 is broadly later than 1 Samuel 14. If Yahweh's covenant forms a bracket round his key speech at the heart of the narrative, Yahweh's anger is no less structurally important to the narrator's framing of this material. It brackets the whole chapter (vv. 1, 26) and is also resumed in 23:16, along with *bryt yhwh*. These several observations appear to justify two conclusions: that Joshua 7 is integral to one of the main structures of the book of Joshua; and that it has drawn much of its language from the books of Samuel.

But it is worth considering also whether influence flowed back from Joshua 7 to Samuel, whether it operated first from Samuel to Joshua, and then back again to Samuel.[7] 1 Samuel 28 reports Samuel's *post mortem* scolding of Saul at Endor: he cannot help Saul, but simply reiterates the fateful consequences of not carrying out on the battlefield the divine instruction to put the Amalekites under a total ban. 1 Samuel 28:18 unusually makes *ḥrwn ʾpw* ("the heat of his anger") the object of the very common verb *ʿśh* ("do" or "make"). Hosea 11:9 provides the only other example of this usage in the Hebrew Bible: "I will not practise the heat of my anger, I will not again destroy Ephraim." The assonant *ḥrwn ʾpw* recapitulates very suggestively the expected term *ḥrm* ("ban"), which had been used so repeatedly in the report in 1 Samuel 15 of their "final" encounter, when Samuel had informed the king of his rejection for failing to carry out divine orders to the letter. 1 Samuel 15 is the only narrative in all of the books of Samuel which uses *ḥrm*; but it appears much more widely in Joshua (2; 6; 7; 8; 10; 11). Neatly, in addition to this back-reference, *ḥrwn ʾpw* in 1 Samuel 28 also offers a cross-reference to the related Joshua 7.

Several further links between Joshua and Samuel can be sketched and assessed more briefly.

1. It is only in these two books of the Hebrew Bible that the location of a corpse is marked by "a great heap of stones." Each of these informal "burials" is of an enemy, whether from within the people of Israel (Absalom, 2 Sam 18:17, and Achar,[8] Josh 7:26), or without (the king of Ai, Josh 8:29). Again, and partly overlapping, it is only in Joshua and Samuel that the bodies of enemies are first exposed by hanging on a

---

7   In a short contribution to the Colloquium Biblicum Lovaniense 59 (July 2010) Hartmut N. Rösel reported on the PhD thesis of Haim Hamiel: "The Conquest Narrative (*sic*) in the Book of Joshua: Their Creation and Editing" (Hebrew), University of Haifa, 2009. Quite independently, this dissertation clearly included some overlapping arguments and proposals.

8   Though he is named Achan in the MT of Joshua 7 (5 times) and 22:10, Joshua LXX and 1 Chr 2:7 know him as Achar. Because of his other links with Chronicles noted below, it is important to remember the alternate tradition of his name.

tree[9] and then thrown down (into a pit, or by the gate): Absalom (2 Sam 18:10), the king of Ai (Josh 8:29), and the five kings from cities in Judah (Josh 10:26). Absalom and the king of Ai provide the only complete parallels. Achan/r is stoned to death, and not hanged; and the five kings are hanged, but thrown into a cave. Viewed without reference to other considerations, the influence could have moved in either direction.

2. The route used by the census-takers shares several distinctive expressions with Joshua 13 and 19, from "the city that is in the midst of the wadi" (Josh 13:9, 16; 2 Sam 24:5), east of the Dead Sea, onwards.[10] In principle, this example is also neutral. As an indication of Joshua-priority, we can note that in the books of Samuel it is only in 2 Sam 24:5 that we meet the term "Canaanite." On the other hand, if the use of *hthlk* in 1 Chr 21:4, to denote the census-takers "traversing" the land, were deemed to be the original reading of BTH rather than *šwṭ* in 2 Sam 24:8,[11] we would be dealing with a counter-indication. We might conclude that the shorter introduction to the census story in 1 Chr 21:1–5 (with *hthlk*, but without the details of the route taken) had served as the inspiration for Joshua and his seven tribal representatives charged with writing a description of the land (18:4), before being expansively redrafted as 2 Sam 24:1–9.

3. The links in the formal exchanges in Joshua 24 and 1 Samuel 12 between the old leaders, Joshua or Samuel, and their people are even more interesting and diverse.

a. On both occasions (Josh 24:1; 1 Sam 12:7), the people "take their stand" (*htyṣb*) before the deity, and the leader then rehearses key elements of what the deity has done for them (Josh 24:2–13; 1 Sam 12:8–11).

b. Joshua and Samuel both cite formal witnesses: Joshua nominates the people themselves (Josh 24:22) and a stone (Josh 24:27); and Samuel, Yahweh and his anointed (1 Sam 12:5).

---

9   In the case of Absalom, the hanging is involuntary. David also has the mutilated bodies of the assassins of Saul's son hanged by the pool at Hebron (2 Sam 4:12). The only other hangings in the Hebrew Bible belong to the Joseph story in Genesis and the tale of Esther.

10 Further links can be noted in 2 Sam 24:5 // Josh 13:9+16, 23; 2 Sam 24:6 // Josh 13:11, 25, 31; 2 Sam 24:6–7 // Josh 19:28–29; 2 Sam 24:7 // Josh 19:2.

11 For further examples, see Graeme Auld, "Imag[in]ing Editions of Samuel: the Chronicler's Contribution," in *Archaeology of the Books of Samuel: The Entangling of the Textual and Literary History* (ed. Ph. Hugo and A. Schenker; VTSup 132; Leiden: Brill, 2010), 119–31; idem, "Synoptic David: the View from Chronicles," in *Raising Up a Faithful Exegete: Essays in Honor of Richard D. Nelson* (ed. K. L. Noll and Brooks Schramm; Winona Lake, Ind.: Eisenbrauns, 2010), 115–26.

c. When he reports that Joshua "laid down a statute and a ruling" (śîm ḥōq ûmišpāṭ) for his people (Josh 24:25), the narrator is echoing exactly a report about David (1 Sam 30:25), though in this case these words are found once more in the Hebrew Bible (Exod 15:25).

d. At the heart of each dialogue, we find the same pair of otherwise unique expressions. Samuel says "far be it from me to sin against Yahweh" and instructs the people "to serve [Yahweh] truly" (1 Sam 12:23–24). Joshua on his side follows his review of the past with the instruction "to serve [Yahweh] truly" (Josh 24:14), to which the people respond (v. 16), "far be it from us to forsake Yahweh." If the people cannot contemplate forsaking Yahweh (Josh 24:16), this is precisely the content of the sin which they confess before Samuel (1 Sam 12:10). It is only in these two passages in the Hebrew Bible that the abjuration ḥlylh is followed by l- introducing the person(s) involved, then mn- with an infinitive stating the action being refused or abhorred, with Yahweh as the object of that infinitive (it has been drawn to my attention by Chris Thomson that the construction itself is also found in Gen 44:7, 17).

e. It is a further double surprise that "serve" (ʿbd) and "truly" (bʾmt) are linked only twice in the Hebrew Bible, and in exactly these same two passages. Most of these links are neutral. However, the solemn ḥlylh is much more at home in Samuel (10 times) than in Joshua (only in 22:29, apart from 24:16). Then the two Joshua passages are probably among the latest components of that book; by contrast, one of the ten instances in Samuel (2 Sam 23:17) is shared with 1 Chr 11:19, and hence is derived from the older BTH.

4. The complexity is even more intricate when we review the Gibeonites in both books.

a. They come to David and claim an oath taken in their favour by Israel (2 Sam 21:2); and this "swearing" is reported in Joshua 9 (4 times in vv. 15–20)—vv. 6–16 had spoken (5 times) in terms of making a treaty.

b. The Gibeonites had been concerned to avoid the implications of a divine command that all the inhabitants of the land be "destroyed" (Josh 9:26); and they now complained to David that such destroying (hišmîd) was exactly what Saul had undertaken against them (2 Sam 21:5).

c. But apparently significant links with Joshua 9 are not confined to 2 Samuel 21. Only two curses in the Hebrew Bible are uttered using the plural ʾărûrîm: one by Joshua (Josh 9:23) and the other by David (1 Sam 26:19); and the broad context of each is similar, for both the Gibeonites and David are at the time protesting their right to remain in their land.

d. Then the expression *l' ykrt l-* or *mn-* ("there shall not be cut off of . . ."), stated in an implied double negative, is normally promissory— as, perhaps originally, in 1 Kgs 8:25; 9:5 (BTH). But, just twice in the Hebrew Bible, these words are intended as a threat: in Joshua's words immediately following his curse just cited (Josh 9:23) and in David's curse on Joab for killing Abner (2 Sam 3:29).

e. The next element in the link is that David (although on different occasions) echoes both parts of Joshua's double curse. And the immediately following verse (2 Sam 3:30) suggests that this link is a strong one: Abner fell by Joab's hand because he had killed Joab's brother— and precisely at Gibeon. Then again, it is to Saul that David is speaking (1 Sam 26:19) when he curses any humans who may have driven him from "Yahweh's heritage" (he can hardly curse the king by name to his face); and, when David hears the Gibeonites' complaint against Saul, he seeks a means whereby they may come to bless "Yahweh's heritage" (2 Sam 21:3), that same rare expression he had used to Saul.

Readers of the books of Samuel are justifiably surprised, when they come to the Gibeonites' complaint against Saul (2 Sam 21:4–6), that they have received no inkling in any of the narratives about Saul in 1 Samuel as to his behaviour towards Gibeon. In fact Saul is dead (1 Samuel 31) before Gibeon is first mentioned (2 Samuel 2); and the only (barely) plausible evidence of a recent atrocity there is the absence of any local inhabitants from the report on the contest between Abner and the men of Saul's house and Joab and the servants of David. By contrast, Joshua 9 does provide a full version of the earlier relationship between Gibeon and Israel, mentioned in 2 Sam 21:2. That might suggest that a later author of Joshua was free to fill out the background to 2 Samuel 21, even though authors of 1 Samuel, working earlier, had left untold the story of Saul's persecution of the Gibeonites. When we read Joshua and Samuel together, as parts of the same connected history of Israel in its land, the absence of any report of the intervening action by Saul against Gibeon is all the more surprising.

5. There is a further cluster of links towards the end of 2 Samuel 15, as David prepares to abandon Jerusalem. Just as re-crossing the Jordan would be symbolic of leaving the land, so too crossing the Kidron is symbolic of leaving the city. The memory of the entry into the land as reported in Joshua is triggered not so much by *'br* ("cross," vv. 23–24), one of the most common of verbs, nor even by "towards the desert" (v. 23), as by *'d-tm* ("till the completing of," v. 24). The use here of this phrase is unique in Samuel, but much more familiar in Joshua. Reinforced by *'d 'šr-tmw* (3:17) and *k'šr-tmw* (4:1), it is well anchored in the actual report of crossing the Jordan into the land (4:10). For good

measure, it is also used in the immediately following episode (5:6), reinforced by k'šr-tmw (5:8), and also lightly varied ('d-tmm) in 8:24; 10:20. One further relevant link is provided by the collective noun ṭp ("children"): it is used only this once in Samuel, where we learn that the youngsters of Ittai the Gittite (2 Sam 15:22) stay with him as he accompanies David—a contrast with the young of the Transjordanian two-and-a-half tribes, who stay east of the Jordan as their fathers accompany Joshua and the rest of their people in crossing to the west (Josh 1:14). This portion of the introductory chapter is probably a late element in Joshua; and the only other instance of ṭp in the book (8:35) is certainly late. [12]

IV

The spirit of this article requires a question at its end—but first some interim conclusions. It seems clear from our last example that the report of David's departure from Jerusalem across Kidron was secondarily enhanced to recall Israel crossing the Jordan into the land of promise. And the route taken by Joab and his party of census-takers could be based on information drawn from the book of Joshua. Yet here the relationship between the two books is probably more complex: I hold that 1 Chr 21:1–5 preserves an earlier version of the beginning of the census story, which may have influenced the drafting of Josh 18:2–10 before it was in turn expanded into 2 Sam 24:1–9. Granted these exceptions, the dominant direction of influence was from Samuel to Joshua, at least in the above samples. In some cases this is more straightforward: from 1 Samuel 13–14 to Joshua 7; and from 1 Samuel 12 to Joshua 24. However, just as Joshua 7 is heavily indebted to 1 Samuel 13–14 but also draws more widely from the books of Samuel, so too Joshua 9 draws together several strands: not just 2 Samuel 2–3 and 21, which mention Gibeon explicitly, but also David's protests about being uprooted from his own land by Saul (1 Samuel 26).

Where does the theme of the ban (ḥrm) belong in this pattern of links between Samuel and Joshua? My commentary on the books of Samuel[13] argues on other grounds that the core of 1 Samuel should be looked for within 1 Sam 9:1–25:1—from the emergence of Saul (9–10) to

---

12   The term is found predominantly in later books and parts of books: Gen 34:29; 43–50
     (7 times); Exod 10:10, 24; 12:37; Num (10 times); Deut 1:39; 2:34; 3:6, 19; 20:14; 29:10;
     31:12; Judg 18:21; 21:10; Jer 40:7; 41:16; 43:6; Ezek 9:6; Esth 3:13; 8:11; Ezra 8:21;
     2 Chr 20:13; 31:18.

13   See n. 4 above.

Saul in David's power (24) and the death of Samuel (25:1). 1 Samuel 1–8 is a fresh prologue; and 1 Samuel 25–30 includes several episodes retold from the first draft: Saul again in David's power (26); David again a refugee in Gath (27); and the death of Samuel (28:3a). The central core of the book had not only been supplemented at beginning and end, but was also rewritten expansively. Some of these expansions, Saul for a second time in the power of prophetic spirit (19:18–24), and the second announcement by Samuel of Saul's rejection by Yahweh (15), are of a piece with the supplements at the end (25–30): most obviously the second rejection (15) and Samuel's *post mortem* repetition of it (28). Were these revisions of 1 Samuel influenced by the widespread *ḥrm* theme in Joshua? Or was the author of Joshua 7 in debt to 1 Samuel 15 no less than to 1 Samuel 13–14? Samuel's "farewell" speech in 1 Samuel 12 is often taken to be one of the later elements in 1 Samuel; and, as noted at the beginning of these remarks, it has Samuel report Israel's settlement in the land without mention of Joshua. Was 1 Samuel 15 written still later than 1 Samuel 12, and under influence from Joshua? Or were the books of Samuel substantially complete before the book of Joshua was drafted?

Why Did Jael Kill Sisera?

A Canonical Perspective

PAUL NOBLE

It has long been recognized that the theological pattern of sin-punishment-deliverance first outlined in Judg 2:11–19 is then instantiated in each of the stories of the "major judges" in chapters 3–16.[1] More recently, however, literary studies of Judges have extended this insight in two important ways. First, it has been shown that the basic pattern contains many more elements than have hitherto been recognized; and second, it has been demonstrated that the pattern shows a progressive degeneration as the narrative moves from one story to the next. In particular, a number of scholars have persuasively argued that, from Gideon onwards, the judges increasingly act from motives of self-interest and personal gain.[2]

In the present article I shall try to argue, first, that Deborah and Barak also fit within this pattern; and second, that Jael's killing of Sisera is also motivated, in part, by considerations quite different from those officially ascribed to her in Judges 5.

I

To see how self-interest enters the motivations of Deborah and Barak, it is helpful first to look at the ideal portrayed by the two judges who precede them, Othniel and Ehud.

---

1   So, for example, George F. Moore describes the content of Judg 2:6–3:6 as "[t]he religious interpretation and judgement of the whole period as a recurring cycle of defection from Yahweh, subjugation, and deliverance" (*A Critical and Exegetical Commentary on Judges* [ICC; Edinburgh: T&T Clark, 1895], xiv). Cf. C. F. Burney, *The Book of Judges* (London: Rivingtons, 1918), xxxv–xxxvi.

2   For a thorough recent discussion, with extensive references to previous work, see Gregory T. K. Wong, *Compositional Strategy of the Book of Judges: An Inductive, Rhetorical Study* (VTSup 111; Leiden: Brill, 2006), 165–76.

The depiction of Othniel in Judg 3:7–11 is almost wholly imper-
sonal. As numerous commentators have pointed out, the narrative
consists almost entirely of formulaic terminology that has either been
introduced already in the theological preamble (2:11–19), or will recur
in subsequent episodes.[3] Apart from the briefest details of Othniel's
name and family relations (3:9), and of the oppressor whom he
defeated (3:8), there is nothing that is specific to Othniel and his particular situation. Thus the very form of the narrative precludes questions about Othniel's personal motives: he is simply an abstract
embodiment of the ideal of judgeship.

The story of Ehud (3:12–30) is thus the first in which a deliverer is
portrayed as an individualised character. He emerges, in fact, as a
leader of considerable daring and resourcefulness, displaying great
coolness and courage in assassinating the enemy king in the latter's
private quarters (with his attendants, though absent from the room, in
close proximity), and quickwittedness in exploiting the unexpected
twists of fortune that come his way.[4] With the Moabite king thus
removed, Ehud immediately leads the Israelites into battle with the
rallying-cry, "Follow after me; for Yahweh has given your enemies,
Moab, into your hand" (v. 28)—unambiguously crediting Yahweh
alone with the anticipated victory. As with Othniel, then, Ehud's only
motive is the service of God.[5]

With these two deliverers, then, having established the ideal, we
can now recognize the first small departure from it in Judges 4. In
response to Deborah's prophetic command to prepare his troops for
battle, Barak says he will do so only if Deborah accompanies him
(4:6–8). Deborah accedes, but adds that "your glory will not be upon

---

3   For a comprehensive analysis see Robert H. O'Connell, *The Rhetoric of the Book of
     Judges* (VTSup 63; Leiden: Brill, 1996), 82, and Yairah Amit, *The Book of Judges: The Art
     of Editing* (Biblical Interpretation Series 38; Leiden: Brill, 1999), 161–63.

4   See Amit, *The Book of Judges*, 171–98.

5   *Pace* O'Connell, who tentatively suggests that Ehud's summoning the Israelites to
     follow him was "a means to attain leadership among them," thus showing himself to
     be an "opportunist" who was "self-promoting" (*Rhetoric of the Book of Judges*, 97–98,
     cf. 84). O'Connell appears to concede, however, that there is nothing in the Ehud
     narrative itself to suggest such a motivation, since his argument for this interpreta-
     tion is that it would make the depiction of Ehud parallel that of other deliverers,
     such as Gideon and Jephtha. It seems to me methodologically unsound, however, to
     suppose that Ehud "must" resemble Gideon and Jephtha in this respect when
     Judges 3 affords no basis for such an assumption. Moreover, the fact that, when
     Ehud blew the trumpet in "the hill-country of Ephraim" sufficient "sons of Israel"—
     i.e., men drawn from all the tribes—to cut off ten thousand retreating Moabites came
     down from the hills and immediately placed themselves under Ehud's command
     (3:27–29), strongly suggests that this was a pre-planned action, of which Ehud was
     already the recognized leader.

the path you are travelling" (v. 9). Since this is clearly intended to penalise Barak for having made his obedience conditional, it strongly suggests that the personal kudos that might accrue to a successful military leader has become a matter of some importance for him (and perhaps for Deborah too).

Nothing further is made of this in Judges 4. The celebratory song in chapter 5, however, includes the following lines:[6]

> The peasantry prospered in Israel,
>   they grew fat on plunder,
> because you arose, Deborah,
>   arose as a mother in Israel. (v. 7)

> My heart goes out to the commanders of Israel
>   who offered themselves willingly among the people. (v. 9)

> Awake, awake, Deborah!
>   Awake, awake, utter a song!
> Arise, Barak, lead away your captives,
>   O son of Abinoam. (v. 12)

> [T]he chiefs of Issachar came with Deborah,
>   and Issachar faithful to Barak;
>   into the valley they rushed out at his heels. (v. 15)

Since these lines are sung by Deborah and Barak themselves (v. 1), there is a strong element of self-promotion here.[7] Clearly it is important to them that their heroism be publicly acclaimed.

The song also, of course, praises Yahweh for delivering his people. I have no wish to minimise this, or to suggest that Deborah and Barak's honouring of God is merely formal or less than sincere. On the contrary: Deborah and Barak first and foremost give glory to God. Yet they are also careful to ensure that they too share the limelight.

As I indicated above, the increasing role of personal motives for the deliverers who followed Deborah and Barak has been recognized by a number of previous studies;[8] so I will confine myself here to a brief summary:

---

6   Judges 5 is notorious for the number and the difficulty of its philological problems. Since, however, the point I wish to make comes through clearly enough in all the major English versions and scholarly translations of which I am aware, I shall circumvent these complications by simply quoting here the NRSV—without implying that I would necessarily endorse all of the translators' decisions.

7   Cf. Danna Nolan Fewell and David M. Gunn, "Controlling Perspectives: Women, Men, and the Authority of Violence in Judges 4 & 5," *JAAR* 58 (1990): 389–411 (401). Fewell and Gunn do not, however, relate this to the wider pattern of increasingly personal motives.

8   See n. 2.

1. Despite Gideon's diffidence throughout both his commissioning and the preparations for war (6:11–7:15), when the moment comes for him to lead his troops into battle he suddenly displays a remarkable sense of his own importance. Although his initial instruction—"*Me* you shall watch, and thus you shall do" (7:17)—while giving his own actions some prominence, is perhaps not unreasonable in the circumstances, he immediately proceeds first to an unnecessary repetition ("And it shall be: as I shall do, thus you shall do," v. 17), and then to a description of what he will do (v. 18). One gets the impression that Gideon likes the idea of all eyes being upon him. Moreover, he then instructs his men to go into battle with the war-cry, "For Yahweh and for Gideon" (v. 18)—as though the two of them were essentially co-leaders of the army. In both respects, this is in marked contrast to the self-effacing manner in which Ehud led his troops into battle (Judg 3:28, quoted above).

With the initial battle having broken the Midianites' strength, Gideon next set off in savage pursuit of their kings (8:4–21). When he has caught them, however, it emerges that he had a very personal motive for hunting them down: they had killed his brothers; therefore, he will not spare their lives (vv. 18–21).

2. When the elders of Gilead seek Jephtha's aid in their war against the Ammonites, they first invite him to become their military commander (*qāṣîn*, 11:6). Jephtha rebuffs them; but when they offer him the more elevated position of head (*rōʾš*) over all the Gileadites, he accepts (vv. 8–10). Jephtha is fully aware of the Gileadites' desperate plight, and exploits it for his own political advantage.

3. Samson shows no interest at all in trying to save his people from their oppressors; his battles with the Philistines are motivated solely by a desire to gain revenge for the wrongs he perceives them to have committed against him personally. He kills thirty men in Ashkelon to settle a wager that the Philistines had won unfairly (14:15–19); he sets their crops on fire in vengeance for the woman he considered to be his wife having been given to someone else (15:1–5); and so on. When he finally pulls down the Philistines' house upon them it is in revenge for their having blinded him (16:28).

Having, then, outlined how personal motives become increasingly important as the story moves from one deliverer/judge to the next, I shall now look more closely at Jael's place within this pattern. What were her motives for killing Sisera?

II

The fateful encounter between Sisera, the commander of King Jabin's army, and Jael, the wife of Heber the Kenite, is precipitated by Sisera's unexpected defeat before Barak. His forces routed, Sisera descends from his chariot and flees on foot to the tent of Jael, "for" (the narrator immediately explains) "there was peace between Jabin king of Hazor and the house of Heber the Kenite" (4:17). Yet despite the narrator's apparent helpfulness, this conspicuously fails to explain the most salient feature of Sisera's flight. It would serve perfectly well as an explanation of why he had fled to the house of Heber (or to Heber's encampment, or the like), but not why it was specifically to "the tent of Jael" that Sisera directed his steps.

Having reached the vicinity of his chosen destination, however, Sisera hesitates to proceed further. Only after Jael has come out to meet him, exhorted him to "turn aside, my lord, turn aside *to me*" (emphasis added), and further reassured him ("have no fear") does Sisera "turn aside *to her*, into the tent" (v. 18, emphasis added). Despite the narrator's general remarks, then, about the relationship between Jabin and the house of Heber, it is more specifically towards Jael that Sisera's intentions are directed; moreover, Jael herself echoes this in her invitation to him.

After Jael has tended to his immediate needs, Sisera enlarges upon the stratagem by which he hopes to escape. While Sisera takes a (no doubt, much-needed) rest, Jael is to stand at the entrance of the tent and tell anyone who might enquire that there is no man within (v. 20). Although few commentators have remarked on it, Sisera displays here a quite extraordinary level of confidence in Jael, with regard both to her willingness to help him, and to her ability to do so. Sisera, it will be recalled, is a defeated general fleeing for his life; as his instructing of Jael shows, he is well aware that the victorious Israelites may well be close behind him. If Jael were to be caught harbouring him in her tent, or it should come to light subsequently that she had done so, then her own life (and perhaps the lives of her family too) would likely be in great danger. Yet Sisera appears to have complete confidence in her willingness to help him, and in her resolve not wavering—even if she were confronted by armed pursuers on her threshold. Nor does Sisera doubt her ability to act out his lie convincingly. Hesitation on Jael's part, or ill-concealed nervousness in a situation fraught with danger for them both, could well arouse the Israelites' suspicions; yet Sisera appears to have no fears on that score.

That Sisera's plan makes great demands upon Jael is so evident that both must have recognized it, and each been aware that the other also recognized it. Now as it turns out, Jael does not prove to be a willing accomplice. On the contrary: once Sisera is soundly asleep, she kills him. Nonetheless, the fact that Sisera quite literally staked his life upon this strategem strongly implies that there must have been something about their situation—something about the relationship between them—that made Sisera quite certain that Jael would risk extremes of danger for him. And such a conviction is not reached easily, or quickly. That Sisera felt able to make such extreme demands of Jael, then, and that he took her apparent acceptance of them as perfectly natural, strongly suggests that, prior to this encounter, Sisera and Jael had already got to know each other very well indeed.

III

Judges 4 contains a number of further pointers to the nature of the relationship between Jael and Sisera, which I shall consider presently. The most pertinent clue, however, comes in Judges 5.

The relationship between Judges 4 and Judges 5 has been much discussed. For our present purposes, however, the most significant point is that Judges 5 sometimes sets an event from chapter 4 in a broader context, through adding details that enlarge upon the event's contemporary or antecedent circumstances. For example:

1. The depiction in Judg 4:15 of Yahweh's overthrow of Sisera's army is somewhat cryptic and lacking in detail. In chapter 5, however, this is given a broader, cosmic dimension as the stars fight against Sisera and the Kishon is inundated with torrential floods—thus indicating how the chariots were neutralised (5:20–21). Moreover, this water imagery recalls the depiction of Yahweh as a storm-God in 5:4–5, thereby tying in the battle against Sisera with traditions of divine theophany (cf. Deut 33:2; Pss 68:9–10[8–9]; 77:17–20[16–19]; etc.), and "suggest[ing] that in the victory [over Sisera] Yahweh has repeated his prowess of old."[9]

2. Judges 4 considers the consequences of Sisera's defeat primarily from a military perspective. All of his troops—including the feared chariot corps—are destroyed, and this is the first significant step towards the eventual demise of Jabin (4:15–16, 23–24). In chapter 5,

---

9 Barnabas Lindars, *Judges 1–5: A New Translation and Commentary* (Edinburgh: T&T Clark, 1995), 229; cf. Susan Niditch, *Judges: A Commentary* (OTL; Louisville, Ky.: Westminster John Knox, 2008), 78.

however, the defeat is set against the social background of the Canaanite women losing their menfolk (5:28–30)—yet with a reminder of the cruel fate that would have befallen the Israelite women if the Canaanites had won the battle ("Are they not finding and dividing the plunder? A wench, two wenches, for each man . . . ," v. 30).

With this in mind, let us consider the poetic description of Sisera's death in Judges 5:

> Between her legs[10] he bent down, he fell, he lay;
> Between her legs he bent down, he fell.
> Where he bent down, there he fell—destroyed!　　　　　　　　(5:27)

Especially since the publication of Alter's influential study, the sexual imagery in these lines has been widely recognized.[11] However, the function of this imagery has not, in my view, been satisfactorily explained. Alter's suggestion is that "[this] image of the Canaanite general felled by the hand of a woman, lying shattered between her legs, [is] a hideous parody of soldierly sexual assault on the women of a defeated foe"; "an ironic glance at the time-honored martial custom of rape."[12] However, there is no suggestion in these lines (or elsewhere) of sexual *aggression* or *coercion* by Sisera; moreover, Sisera seems a dubious choice, in this context, to represent martial prowess (he has just suffered a devastating defeat), and Jael an even less likely symbol of "the women of a defeated foe" (she is a member of a Kenite clan with whom the Canaanites are at peace). Nor does Niditch's suggestion of rape, but with genders reversed,[13] do justice to the text. Although Jael is the perpetrator of the violence, it is Sisera who is portrayed as making the sexual advances: *he* bends down between *her* legs.

10　Literally, "between her feet (*raglêhā*)," and similarly in the next line. But, as Susan Niditch has argued, "between her legs" better conveys "the visceral sexual quality of the imagery" ("Eroticism and Death in the Tale of Jael," in *Gender and Difference in Ancient Israel* [ed. Peggy L. Day; Minneapolis, Minn.: Fortress, 1989], 43–57 [47]).

11　Robert Alter, *The Art of Biblical Poetry* (Edinburgh: T&T Clark, 1985), 43–50; cf. Niditch, "Eroticism and Death," 46–48; idem, *Judges*, 81; Lindars, *Judges 1–5*, 279–80; and many other recent authors. Alter also finds sexual imagery in the corresponding section of Judges 4 (and again he has been followed by many others): Jael's "coming to" Sisera (*wattābô' 'ēlāyw*, 4:21) is similar to a phrase that elsewhere has a sexual meaning; her driving the tent-peg through him is an act of phallic aggression; etc. (Alter, *Art of Biblical Poetry*, 48–49). In my view, the case for finding sexual imagery in Judges 4 is not convincing, although it would take me too far afield to discuss it here. If it were accepted, however, it would make little difference to the argument I am developing.

12　Alter, *Art of Biblical Poetry*, 46, 49.

13　Niditch, *Judges*, 81: "The defeated enemy becomes the woman who is raped, the victor her rapist. Here, ironically, it is a woman who is in the position of rapist, the enemy male general her victim."

A better understanding of the sexual imagery in Judg 5:27 emerges, I think, if we view it as hinting at the antecedents that led to Sisera's death. Jael was able to kill him because he voluntarily put himself completely within her power. We have already seen that Sisera's trust in her implies that they knew each other very well; and the sexual imagery of 5:27 hints (I would suggest) at the nature of their relationship. Sisera trusted Jael completely because he loved her, and believed that she loved him. He asked her to take great risks on his behalf, and was confident that she would do so, because he believed that she was devoted to him. Their sexual relationship led to a closeness which convinced him that he could trust her with his life; but she exploited that trust to kill him. "Between her legs he bent down, he fell. . . . Where he bent down, there he fell—destroyed!"

IV

But why, then, *did* Jael kill Sisera? According to Fewell and Gunn, Jael's motives were primarily political. Her husband, Heber, was in league with Israel's enemies, the Canaanites; so with the Canaanites now defeated, Heber and his family were in grave danger of Israelite reprisals. Realising this, Jael killed Sisera to demonstrate her personal allegiance to the victorious Israelites.[14]

In my view, this reconstruction is open to a number of objections. Fewell and Gunn offer two reasons why Heber and his family would be odious to the Israelites. First, there was a state of "peace between Jabin . . . and the house of Heber" (Judg 4:17).[15] The expression šālôm bên . . . ûbên, however, can cover a wide range of political circumstances. In some cases it is used when there is a treaty between two parties that commits them to aiding and assisting each other in various ways (as there was, for example, between Solomon and Hiram, 1 Kgs 5:26[12]). In some cases, however, it means no more than that there was an absence (or cessation) of hostilities between the parties: "There was peace between Israel and the Amorites" (1 Sam 7:14) simply means that they were not at war with each other.[16] But if the peace between Jabin

---

14   Fewell and Gunn, "Controlling Perspectives," 395–96, 404.

15   At least, this is what Fewell and Gunn appear to be alluding to when they describe Heber as being "in league with their [sc. Israel's] enemies, the Canaanites," and showing "allegiance" to them ("Controlling Perspectives," 395, 404).

16   For other examples of šālôm meaning simply the absence of warfare see 1 Kgs 2:5; 20:18; 2 Kgs 20:19. Another relevant parallel is the pact of mutual non-aggression between Isaac and Abimelech. After they had exchanged oaths, Isaac set Abimelech

and Heber was no more than a treaty of mutual non-aggression then it is hard to see why this would turn the Israelites against Heber. For Fewell and Gunn's argument to be convincing the "peace" would have to commit Heber to giving the Canaanites substantial aid; but there is nothing in the phrase itself to support this.

Fewell and Gunn's main argument, however, turns on their reconstruction of Heber's alleged employment by the Canaanites:

> What is it that has brought Heber so far from home? What is it that has brought this Kenite, this smith—"Joiner Smith"—to a king whose power lies in his force of iron chariots? The reader does not have to guess very hard to see those iron chariots as Heber's livelihood.[17] ... No wonder Heber was not at home that day as the chariot force was readied for battle.[18]

In my view, this is completely unconvincing. Whatever merits Gray's thesis may have as a quest for the historical Kenites, it is the wrong kind of argument to appeal to in this context. To understand the motivations of Jael *as a character in this story* we must consider how she and the other characters are presented in the story. Neither in Judges nor elsewhere are the Kenites presented as itinerant smiths, and there seems no reason to suppose that the author of Judges 4 would assume that his readers knew that they were smiths (if, indeed, they were). As for the rest of Fewell and Gunn's diverting tale, its connection with Judges 4 appears to be tenuous at best. I can see nothing in the text to support the idea that Heber was "bound" to Jabin (any more than the Amorites were bound to Israel by the peace between them, or than Isaac was bound to Abimelech), or that Heber was away from home when Sisera called (rather than, say, being in his own tent, carousing with friends); or if he were absent, that it was on a business trip (whether for Jabin or for some other client), rather than on a family visit, or a religious pilgrimage. Moreover, even if Heber's encampment *was* fortuitously close to this particular battle, if he made his living through manufacturing and/or maintaining Jabin's chariots, then it would make far more sense for him to be located at Harosheth-ha-goiim (or wherever it was that the chariot corps was based).

Another point: if the political situation *was* as Fewell and Gunn suppose, then it would have been just as evident to Sisera that Jael and

---

and his party on their way and they departed "in peace" (*běšālôm*, Gen 26:31). Cf. Claus Westermann, *Genesis 12–36: A Commentary* (London: SPCK, 1985), 429.

17 Fewell and Gunn, "Controlling Perspectives," 395 n. 19: "On the Kenites as itinerant smiths doing business with the Canaanite cities and being appropriately located in 'proximity to the combatants,' see [John] Gray, [*Joshua, Judges and Ruth* (London: Nelson, 1967)], 271–73."

18 Fewell and Gunn, "Controlling Perspectives," 395–96.

her family were liable to Israelite reprisals as it was to Jael herself. But in that case, it would also be evident to Sisera that Jael would be very reluctant to assist him, since that would only deepen her guilt in the Israelites' eyes. So even if he felt able to compel her to help him, it should have been clear to him that he would need to be on his guard. Yet far from needing to compel her, Jael shows herself to be entirely willing to help him—even though this is contrary to her own best interests. And far from her difficult situation and suspicious cooperativeness making Sisera cautious, he trusts her completely—even to the extent of believing that she will hide him from the Israelites (while he sleeps), when it is quite evidently to her advantage (in the circumstances Fewell and Gunn are postulating) to hand him over to them. In other words, if it were in Jael's best interests (as Fewell and Gunn claim) to betray Sisera, then this would be just as evident to him as it was to her; and his entrusting her with his life would therefore be foolish in the extreme. Fewell and Gunn's reconstruction, then, makes Sisera's actions incomprehensible.

There is, nonetheless, one facet of the story that is illuminated by political considerations. Quite apart from any supposed "bond" between Heber and Jabin, the simple fact that Sisera was a Canaanite general would endanger Jael if she were to help him; and this explains why, despite Sisera's flight from the battle being directed specifically towards Jael's tent, by the time he reached it his resolve seemed to have almost deserted him. Jael's coming out from her tent and exhorting him to "turn aside (*sûrâ*), my lord, turn aside (*sûrâ*) to me" (4:18) strongly suggests that he was on the point of going straight past.[19] Sisera was experiencing conflicting emotions. On the one hand, he was hopeful that her love for him would impel her to help him; on the other hand, he was aware that the danger he brought could make her reluctant to do so. Her coming out to greet him, however, reassured him of her continuing loyalty to him; and thus she was able to lead him into the tent without him having the slightest presentiment of the great danger that now hung over him.

So why (once more) *did* she kill him? Clearly, her feelings for him were no longer as he believed them to be; and Judges 4 hints at why that was. There are two preliminary points to consider:

---

19 This also shows that Fewell and Gunn's remark ("Controlling Perspectives," 396) that "As a woman alone [Jael] can hardly risk turning away the defeated general and provoking his retaliation" is on completely the wrong track. If Jael thought that Sisera's presence in her tent would be undesirable she only had to stay inside and let him pass on.

1. Another aspect of Alter's study that has been deservedly influential is his recognition of Jael's "maternal role" *vis à vis* Sisera.[20] As soon as she sees him approaching she calms his fears, encourages him to come in, and settles him down to rest; when he asks for some water she fetches him milk, and then settles him down again.

2. Sisera begins his instructions to Jael (concerning how she is to safeguard him while he sleeps) with the *masculine* imperative ʿămōd, "Stand!" (4:20). Although this has often been emended (to a feminine imperative, or to an infinitive absolute construed as a strong imperative), Murray has suggested that the masculine imperative portrays Sisera as "commanding [Jael] as though she were one of his own troops."[21] This seems to me highly plausible. The speech which this imperative introduces, in which Sisera concisely anticipates a problem that might arise while he is resting and instructs Jael in how to deal with it, could indeed be that of a military officer stationing a sentry.

The relationship between Jael and Sisera is thus illuminated by portraying them in two pairs of complementary roles: of Jael's mother to Sisera's child (in which Jael anticipates and ministers to Sisera's basic physical and emotional needs); and of Jael's foot-soldier to Sisera's commanding officer (in which Jael mutely accepts whatever onerous tasks Sisera sees fit to impose upon her). One strongly suspects that both of these scenarios would have been deeply unsatisfactory to Jael. Both of them confine her to helping Sisera to satisfy *his* needs and implement *his* plans; neither of them provides for the satisfaction of her plans and needs and desires. Yet the narrative clearly portrays her as a strong-willed and independently-minded woman, who certainly did have plans and desires of her own. Her unilateral decision to kill Sisera, and the cool calculation with which she carried it through, is itself sufficient proof of that.

V

Another explanation of Jael's motives for killing Sisera that has found some advocates is that she acted out of "zeal for YHWH."[22] This does

---

20 Alter, *Art of Biblical Poetry*, 48.

21 D. F. Murray, "Narrative Structure and Technique in the Deborah-Barak Story (Judges IV 4–22)," in *Studies in the Historical Books of the Old Testament* (ed. J. A. Emerton; VTSup 30; Leiden: Brill, 1979), 154–89 (183 n. 49).

22 O'Connell, *Rhetoric of the Book of Judges*, 110, 125, 126; cf. Robert G. Boling, *Judges: Introduction, Translation, and Commentary* (AB 6A; Garden City, N.Y.: Doubleday, 1975), 97, 100, 119.

indeed seem to be implied by the praise she receives in Judges 5. It is unlikely that Deborah and Barak would have hailed her as "Most blessed of women . . . of tent-dwelling women most blessed" (v. 24) if her primary reason for killing Sisera had been to sort out her (now) unwelcome extra-marital entanglements (or to save herself and/or her family from Israelite reprisals). Again, I have no wish to play this down. A perenniel pitfall for studies of this nature is that concentrating upon a minor aspect of a text can appear to give it greater importance than a balanced exposition of the story would warrant. In truth, Jael's private motives (and Sisera's too) are hinted at rather than overtly explicated; clues are given, but they remain in the narrative's background.

First and foremost, then, Jael killed Sisera out of a desire to glorify God and to help his people; yet the text also suggests that she saw Sisera's flight to her tent as an opportunity to resolve some more personal issues. And in this she is an appropriate companion to Deborah and Barak, at this particular point in the literary structure of Judges 3–16.

It is my pleasure to wish Professor Davies a long, happy, and productive retirement.

By Stone and Sling

1 Samuel 17:50 and the Problem of Misreading David's Victory over Goliath

WALTER MOBERLY

It is a delight for me to write in honour of Graham Davies. I learned from him many of the disciplines necessary for good scholarly work on the Old Testament, and have greatly valued his continuing friendship since my doctoral days. I hope that an essay that looks at an issue not dissimilar to those raised in pentateuchal criticism on which Graham has worked extensively, and that also slightly touches on Graham's concern with biblical theology, will be a suitable contribution to a volume of essays that reflects and engages with his interests.

Introduction

The encounter of David and Goliath (1 Samuel 17) is one of the best-known of all biblical stories, whose meaning is apparently straightforward, at least if the story's regular appearance in Sunday School lessons for children is any guide. Nonetheless it is a story such that, the more one studies it, the more complex it becomes on almost every level—from text-critical issues, through questions of narrative sequence and coherence, to its overall nature, purpose, and meaning.

I want to suggest that what is true of the whole is also true of some of its parts, not least the one verse upon which I want to focus, 1 Sam 17:50. This reads (in the NRSV):

> So David prevailed over the Philistine with a sling and a stone, striking down the Philistine and killing him; there was no sword in David's hand.

At first sight this is entirely straightforward, a simple spelling out of the story's climactic moment and its significance. Nonetheless, the verse raises (at least) three problems, two of which are well-known, the third, however, unnoticed (as far as I can see from my dipping into the literature). I will propose that a recognition of the three problems together can lead one to see that a good reading of the verse may be a somewhat more complex undertaking than is initially apparent.

First Problem: The Death of Goliath[1]

The first problem posed by our text is the most obvious: how does what it says about the precise moment and manner of Goliath's death relate to what is said in the immediately following narrative sequence?[2] For 1 Sam 17:51a says:

> Then David ran and stood over the Philistine; he grasped his sword, drew it out of its sheath, and killed him; then he cut off his head with it.

Was Goliath killed by the stone (v. 50)? Or by his own sword (v. 51)? Was the moment of death when the stone hit him in the forehead?[3] Or was it when David used the sword—either first running him through and then cutting off his head, or killing him by cutting off his head?[4]

This tension can be handled in different ways. On the one hand, one can insist that there is a real discrepancy—if the words mean what they say, then there is a problem. So, for example, Campbell comments:

> David is twice reported killing the Philistine. In 17:50, he kills him and there was no sword in David's hand; with sling and stone he struck the Philistine and killed him. In 17:51, he kills him and the Philistine's sword was in David's hand; he drew the Philistine's sword, killed him, and cut off his head. The Hebrew verb "to strike" here can be ambiguous, involving either a blow or a killing; the Hebrew verb "to kill" here is unambiguous, unmistakably involving death.[5]

On the other hand, one can say that the problem only arises on a rather wooden handling of the narrative, which is perhaps insensitive to narrative conventions: say, either an initial statement receives subsequent detailed specification and qualification (i.e., v. 51 is epexegetic of v. 50),

---

1   I will follow the common practice of using "Goliath," even though 1 Samuel 17 uses it only twice (vv. 4, 23) and prefers "the Philistine."

2   Occasionally v. 50 is seen as problematic in relation to v. 49 rather than v. 51. H. Gressmann, for example, sees the presence of v. 50 after v. 49 as constituting "unnecessary repetition," part of the evidence for the collation of two originally separate accounts (*Die älteste Geschichtsschreibung und Prophetie Israels* [2d ed.; SAT 2/1; Göttingen: Vandenhoeck & Ruprecht, 1921], 70).

3   I retain the traditional understanding that the stone struck Goliath's forehead (*mēṣaḥ*) and not his greave (*miṣḥâ*).

4   The Hebrew can be read either way. Either "he killed" and "he cut off" depict two consecutive actions (so NRSV), or the second verb is epexegetic of the first.

5   Antony F. Campbell, *1 Samuel* (FOTL 7; Grand Rapids, Mich.: Eerdmans, 2003), 173.

or one is looking at a process with several parts to it, initiation and completion. So, for example, Fokkelman tackles the tension between v. 50 and v. 51 by saying:

> [V]erse 50 is not a link in the chain of actions, but an aside! This realization makes it unnecessary to see any contradictions with v. 51 and, for example, play off 50c [there was no sword in David's hand] against 51b [then he cut off his head with it]. . . .
>
> The three narrative forms [in v. 50] *wayyeḥĕzaq* . . *wayyak* . . *wayĕmîtēhû* ["prevail . . . strike . . . kill"] are the exact successor to the trio of wqtl-forms in v. 35c and hence the exact fulfilment of the pastoral scenario. For that reason *wayĕmîtēhû* already occurs in v. 50b; it is an advance taken by the narrator on 51c, and not a contradiction, for the elimination with the stone is the whole work and already implies the irrevocable defeat of the Philistine. The finishing off (the polel of 51c) is just what it is (finishing off): the self-evident completion of the job. And it is for that reason that the narrator considered it justified to intervene this early.[6]

However, Fokkelman also makes clear that he is thinking specifically in terms of narrative logic, when he allows that the placement of v. 50 prior to v. 51 is crucial:

> David has overcome the beast of prey like a real shepherd with the means of a shepherd [i.e., the parallelism of the verbs of v. 50 with those of v. 35c]. That must be established *now*, the narrator thinks, and he is right: if he had put his explanation *after* the dénouement of v. 51, he would really have had a problem and could not have escaped the reproach of contradiction.[7]

We will return to this issue later. For the present I would simply note that this difficulty of the means and moment of Goliath's death, when taken on its own, is open to diverse evaluation. Verse 50 can be read both as a smooth part of the narrative flow, anticipating v. 51, and as awkward within the narrative flow, contradicting v. 51. As far as I can see, neither evaluation has established itself over the other in the literature of commentary.

The Second Problem: Absence in the Septuagint

The second problem is that v. 50 is absent in the original LXX, but was added in the hexaplaric recension. However, one can hardly address this issue without noting the larger problem of the relationship between MT and LXX for the whole story of David and Goliath—for in

---

6   J. P. Fokkelman, *Narrative Art and Poetry in the Books of Samuel* (4 vols.; SSN 20, 23, 27, 31; Assen: Van Gorcum, 1981–93), 2:186–87.

7   Fokkelman, *Narrative Art and Poetry*, 2:187.

these two textual traditions the story exists in two substantially divergent versions. Or, to be more precise, although the version of the story in the Codex Alexandrinus (LXX^A) is much the same as in MT, within Codex Vaticanus (LXX^B) there is a significantly shorter account, which lacks 17:12–31, 41, 48b, 50, 55–58.[8] Unsurprisingly, enormous scholarly discussion has been devoted to this shorter account, which can be seen either as a secondary abridgment of MT or, perhaps more commonly, as an earlier original of which MT (and LXX^A) is an expansion.

Nonetheless, rather than enter into this discussion and perhaps try to account for v. 50 within a comprehensive thesis about MT and LXX in 1 Samuel 17, I propose a simple alternative, based on the absence of v. 50 from the original LXX: there is value in treating v. 50 on its own, as an independent gloss. The reasons for this will emerge in what follows.

The Third Problem: Poor Narrative Practice

The third problem posed by v. 50 has hardly been noticed, but is not for that reason insignificant. It concerns a major narrative convention. Why on earth should the narrator spell out the moral or point of the story?

It is a fundamental principle of good story-telling, like good joke-telling, that the material should contain its own meaning. To be sure, hearers and readers may not always get the point; but the point should be there for them to get, and they should get it by grasping the content that is presented to them. The story-teller or joke-teller who has to explain has thereby failed. Moreover, if the explanation comes in the middle of the climactic dramatic action, rather than at its end, and reiterates a point already made by the key character—David (v. 47)—then v. 50 is surely an exception to good narrative practice.

The principle is well exemplified in the discernible narrative conventions of the OT. Where there are narratives that contain a strong moral and/or theological "point"—which tend to be narratives that can be read in a relatively freestanding way, such as makes them useful for elementary pedagogy—then *it is the characters within the stories who make the point*. The general rule is that the major characters, at dramatically

---

8   This shorter account may conveniently be read in Albert Pietersma and Benjamin Wright, eds., *A New English Translation of the Septuagint* (New York: Oxford University Press, 2007), 260–61, or P. Kyle McCarter, Jr., *1 Samuel* (AB 8; Garden City, N.Y.: Doubleday, 1980), 284–86, 299–301. One needs to read the whole narrative from 1 Samuel 16 to chapter 18 in order to appreciate the coherence of the differing forms of the textual tradition.

critical moments, make speeches which contain the key words and concepts which convey what the story is about. Thus, for example, it is Joseph, not the narrator, who speaks of God's purposes for good that have undergirded family feuds and famine (Gen 45:4–8; 50:20); or Shadrach, Meshach, and Abednego speak only once, when their life is in the balance, to convey their trust in God's power to deliver and their loyalty to God come what may (Dan 3:16–18), and Nebuchadnezzar eventually acknowledges the rightness of this (Dan 3:28).

Prior to v. 50 the narrative in 1 Samuel 17 conforms to this principle. David has persuaded Saul to let him be Israel's champion and has confidently stated his faith in YHWH's power to deliver (v. 37). The narrator has refrained from any comment on David's first trying out Saul's armour and then rejecting it in favour of a handful of stones for his sling. When David and Goliath confront each other on the battlefield, Goliath speaks first with scorn and threats (vv. 43–44), but David then makes a relatively lengthy speech (vv. 45–47), which highlights the concerns of the narrative, summed up in: "YHWH does not save by sword or spear."

Why then the comment in v. 50? In part it repeats what David has already said, that the victory does not come by sword; and in part it spells out what any hearer/reader should gather anyway, that David's sling and stone brought him victory. Why then should a narrator spell out the obvious, and repeat in his own voice what has already been clearly articulated by his lead character?

Surprisingly, the modern scholar who perhaps more than any other has helped sensitize readers to the conventions, the poetics, of Hebrew story-telling—Alter—passes over this breach of good practice in silence. He draws no attention to it either in his discussion of the episode in his *Art of Biblical Narrative*,[9] or in his translation of, and commentary on, the books of Samuel.[10] Bar-Efrat at this point in his commentary simply offers a paraphrase.[11] Polzin does not except v. 50 from his remark on vv. 48–54 that "the narrator narrates as quickly as David runs in verses 48 and 51, or as the ranks flee and pursue in verses 51

---

9   See Robert Alter, *The Art of Biblical Narrative* (London: George Allen & Unwin, 1981), esp. 151, where Alter discusses "the narrative climax of Chapter 17, verses 45–51."

10   Robert Alter, *The David Story: A Translation with Commentary of 1 and 2 Samuel* (New York: W. W. Norton, 1999), 109.

11   Shimon Bar-Efrat, *Das erste Buch Samuel: Ein narratologisch-philologischer Kommentar* (BWANT 176; Stuttgart: Kohlhammer, 2007), 249–50. He also comments briefly on the interpretative significance of the similarity of wording between v. 50 and v. 35.

and 52."[12] For most commentators v. 50 apparently does not stand out from the surrounding narrative.

By contrast, Fokkelman indeed sees something of the unusual nature of v. 50, but quickly solves the problem:

> The narrator's decision to place v. 50 where it stands is bold and far-reaching. He has had the courage to stop the most sensational part of the narrative chain and demand attention for his commentary right in the middle of the dénouement. This shows that the narrator felt an urgent need, at the dramatic climax, to guide our interpretation by means of an authoritative explanation on his part. In v. 50 we have the most direct contact with the ideological source of the story.[13]

Apparently the interrupting of a dénouement to do something that breaches good narrative practice is remarkable only for its courage, not for its heavy-handedness. The narrator's "urgent need to guide our interpretation"—which is strange when it repeats an interpretation just given by the lead character a couple of sentences previously—is simply asserted to be explicable as an expression of ideological passion.

Interestingly, Fokkelman feels it appropriate to cite a parallel, and appeals to 2 Sam 13:15 as "a comparable intervention, a commentary in the middle of a dramatic action."[14] Here, after Amnon's rape of Tamar, we are told: "Then Amnon was seized with a very great loathing for her; indeed, his loathing was even greater than the lust he had felt for her." However, this differs from 1 Sam 17:50 in at least two ways. First, although it is indeed a comment in the middle of a dramatic narrative, it does not interrupt the narrative action, still less interrupt a dénouement, but comes at a hinge point, where the story moves on from the rape to its aftermath. Secondly, the narrator here is not repeating a point already made, or saying something self-evident. Rather, he provides psychological insight into a transformation within Amnon that explains his subsequent course of action; a transformation which, although indeed well-known to those acquainted with the psychology of undisciplined sexual passion,[15] is by no means self-evident to every hearer/reader of the story. Without such a comment, the story would be

---

12 Robert Polzin, *Samuel and the Deuteronomist: A Literary Study of the Deuteronomistic History: Part Two: 1 Samuel* (Bloomington, Ind.: Indiana University Press, 1993), 171. The peculiarity of v. 50 may have failed to register because Polzin's interest is so focussed on making sense of the famously problematic vv. 55–58 (171–76).

13 Fokkelman, *Narrative Art and Poetry*, 2:187–88.

14 Fokkelman, *Narrative Art and Poetry*, 2:188.

15 Most famous and memorable is Shakespeare's Sonnet 129: "The expense of spirit in a waste of shame / Is lust in action . . . Enjoy'd no sooner but despiséd straight; / Past reason hunted; and no sooner had, / Past reason hated . . ."

less intelligible. Thus Fokkelman's attempt to locate 1 Sam 17:50 within recognized narrative convention in the OT surely fails.[16]

Towards a Solution

As with many problems within the biblical text, a fruitful way of making progress can be to identify something within the context of the text's formation that could account for what stands in the text; that is, to identify the question to which v. 50 could be the answer. Of course, the exercise is necessarily conjectural, as we have no evidence other than the text itself, and the procedure is necessarily circular—one infers a situation from the text, and then explains the text in the light of that inferred situation. Nonetheless, there remains a difference between conjectures that are arbitrary or fanciful, and those that offer an illuminating scenario. Even if one lays weight, as I do, on the general importance (for Christian theology) of working with the biblical text in its received form, it is important to remain alert to possible factors behind the text which can in one way or other enrich one's reading. In other words, if one's synchronic reading is not to become flat or forced, one must always remain open to allowing possible diachronic factors to inform that synchronic reading. Anyway, I will propose a scenario which I hope will be found at least plausible, and perhaps even persuasive.

Initially I note how smoothly the battle narrative reads if one takes vv. 49, 51 as a continuous sequence without v. 50, as in the Old Greek. David strikes Goliath with a stone from his sling, and he falls forward on the ground; David runs up, stands over Goliath, and uses Goliath's own sword to kill him and cut off his head; at which point the Philistines see that their champion is dead and flee. The reader naturally envisages Goliath as stunned/wounded but not killed by the stone. Although David's bringing Goliath to the ground with his slingshot is the decisive action, David still has to finish him off (lest in a little while Goliath perhaps recover), which he does with fine chutzpah, adding

---

16   As a possible parallel to v. 50 David Firth (in correspondence) helpfully suggests 1 Sam 18:25b, where the narrator says in his own voice, in the third person, what he has already twice ascribed to Saul's thoughts, where Saul speaks in the first person (1 Sam 18:17b, 21a). This is indeed more intriguing for our purposes than 2 Sam 13:15. Although repetitive, it serves to underline that Saul's words have a hidden agenda; but it does not spell out a narrative "point" in the mode of 1 Sam 17:50. There is clearly, however, a fuller study to be done about the nature of narratorial comments and asides.

insult to injury[17] by using his victim's own sword.[18] So I suggest that the narrative originally existed without v. 50, as in the Old Greek.

But why then v. 50? If the recognition of v. 50 as a likely gloss is unremarkable, its presence is still unexplained. This is where the nature of one's conjecture about contextual origin is all-important. One approach is simply to appeal to general considerations about the ways in which piety may elaborate a narrative that is seen to be suitable. So, for example, Stoebe comments on v. 50:

> Because now in various places and independently of one another in both editions [sc. MT and LXX] *the traces of ornamenting elaborations* [Erweiterungen] *are found which wish to bring out more strongly the miraculousness of the event*,[19] nothing prevents one from assuming such also here. It must only be emphasized once again that the original report which is thus made prominent does not tell of a mere heroic deed, but rather of a victory in the power of God which goes beyond human capacity, thus already has kerygmatic character.[20]

But although indeed "nothing prevents" such an assumption of pious enhancement—although "miraculousness" is surely not the best category for the nature of the event—I suggest that this is still too general an assumption to give real purchase on the specific form of v. 50 and the problems it raises.

Moreover, it is important to consider exactly what v. 50 does, and does not, say. Ackroyd, for example, assumes, like Stoebe, that the comment is designed to highlight the divine dimension of David's victory: "Here is a comment on the implications of the contest. Against such odds, David could have been victorious only with God's help."[21] Yet this overlooks that v. 50 in fact makes no mention whatever of God. Ackroyd is conflating v. 50 with the words of David in vv. 45–47, where

---

17   "This Philistine is decapitated with his own sword because killing someone with his own weapon was deemed to be a particular disgrace for the killed person; cf. [1 Sam] 26,8; 2 Sam 23,21, and Ezra 6,11" (A. B. Ehrlich, *Randglossen zur Hebräischen Bibel* [7 vols.; Hildesheim: Georg Olms, 1968; repr. of Leipzig ed. (J. C. Hinrichs, 1908–1918)], 3:230 [Moberly translation]).

18   There is a puzzle in that Goliath's sword is not included in the initial depiction of Goliath's weaponry (1 Sam 17:5–7), although his sword is subsequently preserved as a sacred object and deemed to be incomparable (1 Sam 21:8–9). Indeed, the first sword to receive mention is that of Saul (1 Sam 17:39)! Nonetheless a sword is rhetorically included in Goliath's weaponry by David (1 Sam 17:45, 47). For discussion, see Stanley Isser, *The Sword of Goliath: David in Heroic Literature* (SBLStBl 6; Atlanta, Ga.: Society of Biblical Literature, 2003), 34–37.

19   My italics.

20   Hans Joachim Stoebe, *Das erste Buch Samuelis* (KAT 8/1; Gütersloh: Gerd Mohn, 1973), 339 (Moberly translation).

21   Peter R. Ackroyd, *The First Book of Samuel* (CBC; Cambridge: Cambridge University Press, 1971), 145.

indeed the victory is ascribed to God. Yet v. 50 focusses not on God but on the nature of the weaponry—positively David triumphed with sling and stone, negatively he had no sword. Why this particular focus?

I suggest a concrete scenario. Verse 50 is, I propose, a pedagogic response to a specific misreading of the David and Goliath story, a misreading particularly characteristic of an eager but immature and unsubtle mind—the sort of mindset one regularly encounters among children. Given the frequency with which the David and Goliath narrative is used among children today, it is not unreasonable to conjecture some comparable pedagogic context for the use of the story in antiquity.

If the story stands without v. 50, its concern is made specific by David in v. 47 in a way narratively adumbrated by Goliath's massive weaponry and Saul's offer of his own conventional armour, which David has already declined: "Not by sword or spear does YHWH save." However, there is one obvious difficulty that an eager but wooden mind can find in the text, as an infant essay in deconstruction: "David says that YHWH does not deliver by sword or spear. But in fact David kills Goliath with a sword. So doesn't the text contradict itself?!" This of course misses the decisive action being carried out by David's sling and stone. But it is the kind of reading that has its own logic, albeit of an abstracted, decontextualized nature: "not by sword; but David uses a sword." Thus it could seem appealing especially to a child who wanted to point out an adult's failure to see the obvious, and to proclaim that the emperor has no clothes.

How might a teacher who is telling the story respond to such a misreading, not only to correct it but also perhaps to prevent its recurrence? He could do three related things.[22] First, he could spell out in his own voice the point about the nature of David's victory that is already contained within the story but that the child has missed: "And so David prevailed over the Philistine with a sling and with a stone." Secondly, he could highlight the key point that David's victory came prior to his getting hold of Goliath's sword: "And he struck down the Philistine; there was no sword in David's hand." Thirdly, he could insert such wording into the narrative in the only place it could go, subsequent to David's action with the sling, and prior to David's action with Goliath's sword. That is, he must interrupt the narrative drama in mid-flow; he cannot leave it till the end of the narrative, for by then David has utilized the sword, and the objection could still be voiced.

---

22 I use the masculine pronoun out of a sense of general historical likelihood.

With those moves, which emphasize weapons (the point at issue) rather than God, we have v. 50.

Or rather, we almost have v. 50. For I have omitted one word, that is *wayĕmîtēhû*, where the verbal form is the *hip'il* of *mût*, "kill." Why this element, when the text would read smoothly without it? One could perhaps hypothesize a childish misreader of the text who had been particularly persistent ("But whatever the sling achieved, David still needed a sword to kill Goliath and so God's deliverance *did* include a sword as its means"), and who was rebutted by a claim that the stone delivered not just the winning, but also the fatal, blow—though this would constitute a real shift of meaning within the story, and invite a different question about the relation between this "clarification" and v. 51. In place of hypothesizing, however, it would be better at this point to look more closely at the verb *wayĕmîtēhû*.

We have already noted Campbell's claim that "the Hebrew verb 'to kill' here is unambiguous, unmistakably involving death." But is it in fact quite so simple? About a hundred years ago Ehrlich argued that there is a difference of meaning between the differing conjugations, *po'lel* and *hip'il*, of the verb *mût*; of which the former is used in v. 51 and the latter in v. 50. He says, when commenting on v. 51:

> Our verse [v. 51], however, coming after v. 50 is not at all too late. For there [v. 50] וימיתהו [*hip'il* of *mût*] expresses the fatal injury according to the exposition of Judg 9,54, while here וימתתהו [*po'lel* of *mût*] is so much as to say: and he did away with him.[23]

Ehrlich appeals to the narrative analogy of Judg 9:53–54 where Abimelech is fatally wounded by the millstone dropped by a woman but then asks his armour-bearer to finish him off with his sword, lest people say that he was killed by a woman. The precise word with which Abimelech instructs his armour-bearer to finish him off is *ûmôtĕtēnî* (*po'lel* of *mût*), on which Ehrlich's extensive note merits citation:

> According to the dictionaries מותת [*po'lel*] is synonymous with המית [*hip'il*]. It does not, however, require great acuity to see the falseness of this definition from our passage. For if it was the armour-bearer who killed Abimelech, that is if the latter had come away from the first injury with his life, how would one have been able to say of the hero left in injured condition that a woman had killed him? In fact, in the case of מות the *pi'lel*[24] is differentiated from the *hip'il*. In the former, one thinks of the immediate death as a consequence of the act; in the latter case, on the contrary, only about the causation of death, which, however, can follow even after a long time.

---

23   Ehrlich, *Randglossen zur Hebräischen Bibel*, 3:230 (Moberly translation).

24   Some older grammarians termed "*pi'lel*" the form that is now commonly called "*po'lel*" (for clarification regarding which I am indebted to Jon Levenson).

Therefore, המית can be used first and then מותת, with reference to the same object, as in 1 Sam 17,50 and 51; cf. also 1 Sam 14,13.[25]

Two further considerations may support Ehrlich's contention. The first is the simple question: how would one most naturally express in Hebrew the sense "X brought about/caused Y's death"? Would it not be by the *hipʿil* of *mût*, as is used in v. 50? This sense is also evident when the widow of Zarephath says reproachfully to Elijah, "You have come to me to bring my sin to remembrance, and to cause the death of [*lĕhāmît*] my son" (1 Kgs 17:18b NRSV).[26] The second is the observation that in the only other two narrative contexts in which the *poʿlel* of *mût* is used, it has the sense of "finish off/despatch."[27] Thus in the account of Jonathan and his armour-bearer at Michmash we read: "They [sc. the Philistines] fell (*wayyippĕlû*) before Jonathan, and his armour-bearer, coming behind, killed/despatched (*mĕmôtēt*) them" (1 Sam 14:13).[28] Alternatively, the young man who claims responsibility for Saul's death when bringing word to David of the battle on Mount Gilboa, says, as he recounts his interaction with Saul, that Saul said to him: "Come, stand over me and kill me (*ûmōtĕtēnî*); for convulsions have seized me, and yet my life still lingers" (2 Sam 1:9 NRSV).[29]

Thus there is a good case, in terms of the difference between the *hipʿil* and *poʿlel* of *mût*, for construing the sense of v. 50 as "he struck the Philistine and caused his death."[30] This not only emphasizes that the slingstone struck the decisive blow, and so underlines the concern of the explicatory intervention, but also does so without creating a conflict with the actual killing of Goliath in v. 51. The pedagogic interpolator chose his form of words carefully.

---

25 Ehrlich, *Randglossen zur Hebräischen Bibel*, 3:115 (Moberly translation).

26 This is not to deny that often the contextual sense of *hēmît* is simply "kill," as in David's words to Saul, 1 Sam 17:35.

27 Admittedly the poetic uses of *môtēt*, Jer 20:17; Pss 34:22[21]; 109:16 do not appear to convey any sense other than a straightforward "kill"; but this is not incompatible with its having distinctive idiomatic force in appropriate narrative contexts.

28 The text reads differently in LXX, but that does not affect the point of idiom within the Hebrew.

29 The further uses of *môtēt* in vv. 10, 16 simply repeat what is conveyed in v. 9.

30 Ehrlich's point is also occasionally made by other scholars, whether or not in dependence on Ehrlich. So McCarter comments on 1 Sam 14:13, "As in 17:51 the *Polel* of *mwt*, 'die,' refers to dispatching or 'finishing off' someone already wounded and near death. So also Judg 9:54; II Sam 1:9, 10, 16" (*1 Samuel*, 240).

Conclusion

If my proposal for 1 Sam 17:50 in any way commends itself, and we read the verse as a pedagogic riposte to a "clever" yet wooden misreading of David's victory, two issues may briefly be noted in conclusion.

First, we still need briefly to hypothesize the entry of v. 50 into the biblical text. Here the lack of the verse in the Old Greek could be a pointer towards, in all likelihood, a relatively late date for the addition of the verse. Once the story of David and Goliath was receiving sufficiently widespread circulation, an addition made its way into a Hebrew text, but did not also find its way into the earliest versions of the LXX. Perhaps this might be somewhere roughly around the turn of the era. It may also be that we should envisage the pedagogue as being himself, or as having ready access to, a scribe; and that the scribe should be located in Jerusalem, which would be an optimal context for making an addition to a recognized scroll of Samuel which would in due course become part of the standardized Hebrew text. Here, however, we can only guess, given the total absence of evidence—though the phenomenon of certain ancient interpretative comments being incorporated into the biblical text is well-recognized and not in principle controversial.[31]

Secondly, what difference might my proposal make to a good reading of the story overall? In one sense, the answer may be: very little. For, as the history of interpretation shows, readers have not found it difficult to make sense of the narrative sequence without my hypothesis. On any reckoning, however, the clarification about *wayĕmîtēhû* should be helpful.

Yet, in another sense, understanding the verse as I propose could help a reading in perhaps two ways. On the one hand, it should disincline us to take v. 50 as constituting a positive axiom in its own right—"YHWH saves by sling and stone"—as an apparent correlative of David's negative formulation "not by sword or by spear does YHWH save." That would unduly diminish the obvious potential of David's words to be open to a variety of surprising ways in which YHWH's deliverance may be realized—which regularly happens when scripture readers instinctively read the text analogically and metaphorically.

On the other hand, we can be alerted to the fact that it is easy to offer formulations of the "point" of the story which may have genuine pedagogic value and yet may risk reducing the richness of the text. It is

---

31 Some familiarity with ancient manuscripts and what is written in their margins can be illuminating.

notable, for example, that commentators often like to express their grasp of the story in terms of a single contrast, such as that between weakness and strength—a point which is obviously congenial to a Christian commentator in the light of the New Testament. McCarter, for example, comments:

> This is a struggle of the strong against the weak—but the weak fortified by the strength of Yahweh. So the fall of the Philistine, says David, will show the world that inferiority at arms is unimportant to Israel, which relies solely on its god for victory. . . . The theological implications are clear: it is Yahweh who gives victory, and he may give it to the weak (Israel) in order that his power might be known to all.[32]

Comparably Hertzberg sees the narrator in v. 50 as making the same one point that David makes in v. 47: "David's remark that this God needs neither sword nor spear to aid him, and that he uses what is weak to put the strong to shame reveals a basic law of the kingdom of God."[33] Nonetheless, despite the Christianly congenial nature of such a reading, the text's own content is surely richer than this and rather is suggestive of a number of related contrasts.

Thus a good reading should surely recognize that there is a contrast between trust in God (on David's lips) and complacent scorn (on Goliath's lips). There is a contrast between crude quantity (Goliath with his remarkable armour and weapons) and intelligent quality (David's insight and courage).[34] There is a contrast between an impressive-looking conventional approach (armour and swords in battle) and a strategy of daring and surprise (no armour, sling and stones the sole weapon,[35] and a staff, carried presumably to mislead as though it were David's weapon).[36] There is a contrast between the mundane but tried and trusted implement (David's sling) and the grand but awkward

---

32   McCarter, *1 Samuel*, 294, 297.

33   H. W. Hertzberg, *I and II Samuel: A Commentary* (OTL; London: SCM, 1964), 152, trans. of *Die Samuelbücher* (2d rev. ed.; ATD 10; Göttingen: Vandenhoeck & Ruprecht, 1960).

34   "Goliath moves into the action as a man of iron and bronze, an almost grotesquely quantitative embodiment of a hero, and this hulking monument to an obtusely mechanical conception of what constitutes power is marked to be felled by a clever shepherd boy with his slingshot" (Alter, *Art of Biblical Narrative*, 81).

35   It should not be forgotten that a sling was a recognized weapon of war (Judg 20:16; 2 Chr 26:14). However it could easily be underrated in comparison with swords and shields.

36   "David has the physical attributes and the weaponry to do the job; all he needs is the courage and the nerve. . . . [The story] is an example of how faith in God can enable people to do what in fact they can do but may be afraid to" (Campbell, *1 Samuel*, 181, 189).

because unfamiliar implement (Saul's armour).[37] And no doubt further contrasts could be formulated.

It is important, therefore, not to read v. 50 as in any way foreclosing these many dimensions of the text. My proposal is that if we see v. 50 as precluding a particular misreading, rather than establishing a right reading, then we may be slightly better placed to offer readings that do justice to the richness of the text.

---

[37]   "There is an exact indication of how God's miraculous deliverance and human dexterity meet in the use of sling and stone. . . . The extraordinary is quite ordinary, but above all: to the wise the ordinary is extraordinary" (Fokkelman, *Narrative Art and Poetry*, 2:188).

Why does the Deuteronomistic History Make no Mention of the Prophets to Whom Books are Attributed?

Joseph Blenkinsopp

I

The issue to be discussed in this paper, the so-called *Prophetenschweigen* problem, arises from the fact that, although prophecy plays a crucial role in Former Prophets, that is, the Deuteronomistic History (hereafter the History, also abbreviated as Dtr.), and the author names prophets at regular intervals throughout, the canonical or writing prophets, those in other words to whom books are attributed, are, with only two apparent exceptions, completely absent. Isaiah has a role in the account of Hezekiah's reign (2 Kgs 19–22), but this is a very different Isaiah from the prophet whose denunciations of Jerusalem and the civil and religious leadership are recorded in the canonical book. The Deuteronomistic Isaiah has more the profile of a "man of God," a kinder, gentler Elisha who heals, works miracles, chides occasionally, but in general plays a supportive role in contemporary politics. Where we might have expected a mention of Amos in the account of the reign of Jeroboam II (2 Kgs 14:23–29) we find instead a prophet, Jonah ben Amittai, who has nothing in common with the putative author of the canonical book apart from the name. Aside from these two anomalies, none of the fifteen book prophets is mentioned by the Historian. Jeremiah is especially conspicuous by his absence in view of the fact that the last chapter of the History (2 Kgs 24:18–25:30) serves as an appendix to the canonical book (Jeremiah 52). In short, this overall disconnect between Former and Latter Prophets is remarkable enough to call for an explanation.

Those canonical prophets who we might have thought merited mention in the History—Amos, Hosea, Isaiah, Micah, Nahum, Habbakuk, Zephaniah, Jeremiah, and possibly Ezekiel—are presented in their respective books as active between the eighth and the sixth century BC, corresponding to the last phase of the History beginning with 2 Kings 14. This last section is therefore the primary focus of our investigation, but any eventual explanation must take account of the Historian's understanding of the prophetic profile and role, and therefore take in the History as a whole. Noth's pioneering study postulated a self-contained historical work composed around the middle of the sixth century BC, before the division into canonical books, and comprising the bulk of Joshua, Judges, 1–2 Samuel, and 1–2 Kings.[1] The story of the wanderings in the wilderness narrated by Moses, together with the giving of the law and a brief account of the death of Moses (Deut 1:1–3:29; 31:1–13; part of 34:1–12), served as the introductory chapter of the History. The author (one individual, not a committee or school according to Noth) incorporated many sources into his narrative including the original Deuteronomic law book, etiological narratives in Joshua, tribal hero legends in Judges, and official annals and stories about prophets and men of God in 1–2 Samuel and 1–2 Kings. Noth resisted the idea, proposed or hinted at by Wilhelm Rudolph and Otto Eissfeldt, and later argued by Frank Moore Cross and others, of an earlier, pre-exilic version.[2] The author's hand can be identified throughout by characteristic vocabulary, phrasing, and themes, and a highly formalized style in general. Key ideas are expressed with particular clarity in connecting or summarizing passages (e.g., Joshua 12; Judg 2:11–23; 2 Kgs 17:7–20) and discourses at major junctures in the history (Josh 1:1–9; 23:1–16; 1 Sam 12:6–17; 1 Kgs 8:22–61). Following Noth, therefore, all this material from Deuteronomy to 2 Kings provides potential data for the understanding of the prophetic profile and the prophetic function in the History.

This is not the place to review and evaluate in detail the fate of the History in the hands of scholars since Noth's essay appeared at the height of the Second World War in 1943.[3] Cracks, fissures, and fault

---

1   Martin Noth, *Überlieferungsgeschichtliche Studien* (2d unaltered ed.; Tübingen: Max Niemeyer, 1957; first published 1943), 1–110; ET *The Deuteronomistic History* (JSOTSup 15; Sheffield: JSOT Press, 1981).

2   Wilhelm Rudolph, *Der "Elohist" von Exodus bis Josua* (BZAW 68; Berlin: Alfred Töpelmann, 1938), 240–44; Otto Eissfeldt, *Einleitung in das Alte Testament* (2d ed.; Tübingen: Mohr Siebeck, 1956), 289–98; ET *The Old Testament: An Introduction* (Oxford: Blackwell, 1966), 241–48; Frank Moore Cross, *Canaanite Myth and Hebrew Epic* (Cambridge, Mass.: Harvard University Press, 1973), 274–89. Cross's two-edition hypothesis is further defended and elaborated by R. D. Nelson, *The Double Redaction of the Deuteronomistic History* (JSOTSup 18; Sheffield: JSOT Press, 1981).

3   The reader will find a comprehensive and judicious account of scholarship on Noth's thesis in Thomas Römer and Albert de Pury, "Deuteronomistic Historiography (DH): History of Research and Debated Issues," in *Israel Constructs Its History: Deuteronomistic Historiography in Recent Research* (ed. A. de Pury, T. Römer and Jean-

lines have appeared, however. Some scholars have found Deuteronomy 1–3 when read as the opening chapter to be problematic. It is, after all, a discourse of Moses, as indicated by the title (1:1), not straightforward historical narrative. This literary observation raises the question of its relation to other Deuteronomy-type material elsewhere in the Pentateuch, especially in those passages in Exodus in which Moses speaks and acts.[4] The fact that the History concludes on an upbeat note, with the end of Jehoiachin's imprisonment (2 Kgs 25:27–30), is no less problematic in a history in which, according to Noth, the central theme is apostasy leading to total and definitive disaster—unless, of course, this final paragraph is taken to be a later addition. The same problem arises with Noth's anti-monarchic theme. In his interpretation of the story of Saul and David, Noth is obliged to concede that the Historian incorporated older narrative material favourable to the monarchy, but fails to explain what could have led him to do this, given the main thrust of the work. Equally unsatisfactory is his treatment of the Nathan oracle in 2 Samuel 7 which, since it proclaims an eternal Davidic dynasty, Noth was obliged to exclude from the History while postulating insertions designed to make its non-Deuteronomistic character less obvious.[5] It may well be that the least satisfactory element in Noth's evocative thesis is his failure to recognize that, in addition to the grim retrospective on the ethnic and national past, the Historian had his own prescription for the future of the survivors of the disaster—one which emphasized the necessity for a renewed turning to and seeking after Yahweh—with the verbs שוב and דרש used with reference to exile (Deut 4:29–30; 30:2).

In the course of more than half a century of critical scrutiny Noth's Deuteronomistic History has been sliced up into several editions or layers to the point where we may wonder, with van Seters, whether it

---

Daniel Macchi; JSOTSup 306; Sheffield: JSOT Press, 2000), 24–141; trans. of "L'historiographie deutéronomiste (HD): Histoire de la recherche et enjeux du débat," in *Israël construit son histoire: L'historiographie deutéronomiste à la lumière des recherches récentes* (MdB 34; Geneva: Labor et Fides, 1996), 9–120. See also Steven L. McKenzie, "The Books of Kings in the Deuteronomistic History," in *The History of Israel's Traditions: The Heritage of Martin Noth* (ed. S. L. McKenzie and M. Patrick Graham; JSOTSup 182; Sheffield: JSOT Press, 1994), 281–307.

4 See the section "Deuteronomic Traditions and the Pentateuch," in *Deuteronomy and Deuteronomic Literature: Festschrift C. H. W. Brekelmans* (ed. M. Vervenne and J. Lust Leuven: Leuven University Press, 1997), 301–498 and, with respect to Exod 19–34, my "Deuteronomic Contribution to the Narrative in Genesis-Numbers: A Test Case," in *Those Elusive Deuteronomists: The Phenomenon of Pan-Deuteronomism* (ed. Linda S. Schearing and Steven L. McKenzie; JSOTSup 268; Sheffield: Sheffield Academic Press, 1999), 84–115.

5 Noth, *The Deuteronomistic History*, 55.

can avoid death by redaction.[6] In addition to the first edition from the reign of Josiah, argued by Cross and his students, others have discovered an earlier Hezekiah version, and an even earlier one from the reign of Jehoshaphat.[7] Campbell also came up with a ninth century BC pre-Deuteronomistic record covering the entire period from Samuel to the death of Jehu (1 Samuel 1–2 Kgs 10). Taking up hints in McCarter's Anchor Bible commentaries on 1 and 2 Samuel, Campbell read this very extensive text as a self-contained history essentially about prophecy written from a prophetic perspective. He argued that it was incorporated into Dtr in its entirety as one single source.[8] These attempts to trim, expand or reconfigure the History certainly complicate the task of understanding the place of prophecy and the role of the prophet in it, since different (hypothetical) editions would presumably be products of different societies at different stages of development. But if we may accept, at a minimum, that the History in its final form was a product of the post-disaster period, whether from the mid-sixth century or somewhat later, whether in Judah or Babylon, we may take it that the final imprint was placed on the work at that time. The difficulty of the task will also be mitigated by the uniformity of language and style in Deuteronomy and associated writings, and our conclusions can in any case always be tested for consistency.

---

6   J. van Seters, "The Deuteronomistic History: Can it Avoid Death by Redaction?" in *The Future of the Deuteronomistic History* (ed. Thomas Römer; BETL 147; Leuven: Leuven University Press, 2000), 213–22.

7   André Lemaire, "Vers l'histoire de la rédaction des Livres des Rois," *ZAW* 98 (1986): 221–36, finds two stages of formation prior to the Josian redaction, from the ninth and eighth centuries respectively. Erik Eynikel, *The Reform of King Josiah and the Composition of the Deuteronomistic History* (OtSt 33; Leiden: Brill, 1996), divides Dtr into three stages: Hezekian, Josian, and Exilic. For the (extremely speculative) theory of successive layers (basic history, prophetic, nomistic) proposed by Walter Dietrich, a student of Rudolph Smend at Göttingen, see Römer and de Pury, "Deuteronomistic Historiography," 67–74; trans. of "L'Historiographie Deutéronomiste," 50–58.

8   Antony F. Campbell, *Of Prophets and Kings: A Late Ninth-Century Document (1 Samuel 1–2 Kings 10)* (CBQMS 17; Washington, D.C.: Catholic Biblical Association of America, 1986); idem, "Martin Noth and the Deuteronomistic History," in McKenzie and Graham, *The History of Israel's Traditions*, 31–62. The thesis is adopted by Campbell's student Mark A. O'Brien, *The Deuteronomistic History Hypothesis: A Reassessment* (OBO 92; Fribourg, Switzerland: Universitätsverlag Friburg Schweiz, 1989). A similar thesis is argued by Steven L. McKenzie, "The Prophetic History and the Redaction of Kings," *HAR* 9 (1985): 203–20. Prophecy-fulfilment, as dictating the basic structure of Dtr, is emphasized in Helga Weippert's "Geschichten und Geschichte: Verheissung und Erfüllung im deuteronomistischen Geschichtswerk," in *Congress Volume: Leuven 1989* (ed. J. A. Emerton; VTSup 43, Leiden: Brill, 1991), 116–31.

II

The Deuteronomistic theory of prophecy, as set out primarily in Deut 18:9–22 and secondarily in Deut 13:2–7; 34:9–12, can be summarized as follows. The *nābîʿ* must be a native Israelite ("from among your people") since prophecy is a uniquely Israelite phenomenon in contrast to forms of divinatory mediation practised among other peoples. (The author does not add that they were also practised in Israel). This first requirement is in keeping with the author's "nativism," tending towards xenophobia, for example in the stipulations concerning the monarchy (17:14–20). Prophets are charismatic individuals, "raised up" by the God of Israel (18:15, 18), and are therefore to be absolutely obeyed. Prophecy is to be understood as modelled on Moses as proto-prophet and paradigm for all those "raised up" by Yahweh after him, whether explicitly identified as נביאים or not.[9] Its origin is to be sought in the request for mediation at Horeb (Deut 18:16, cf. 5:23–29). This is the paradigmatic prophetic event. The people request Moses to act as their mediator, he approaches the deity, receives the revelation, and passes it on to the people gathered around the foot of the mountain. The communication has to do with the commandments, statutes, and ordinances which are to provide guidance for life in the land they are about to enter (Deut 5:29–31), and this is therefore to be the chief concern of the prophet. There is no mention of denunciations and comminations directed at civil authorities, priests, and other prophets which feature so prominently in the prophetic books. Prophecy has to do with expounding the law and inculcating its observance in the manner of Moses. There follow criteria for distinguishing between authentic and inauthentic prophecy (Deut 18:20–22), always the fundamental problem with the phenomenon of prophetic mediation. The prophet who speaks in the name of a deity other than Yahweh is false by definition and subject to the death penalty. This is so even when the prophet or dream-interpreter supports the message by signs and wonders, since in that case false prophecy is the means by which Yahweh is testing the faith of his devotees (Deut 13:2–6 [13:1–5]). The same judgement is

---

9   Hans Barstad, "The Understanding of the Prophets in Deuteronomy," *SJOT* 8 (1994): 252–56, identified "the prophet like Moses" with Joshua. Joshua was a charismatic once Moses anointed him as his successor, and as such was obeyed (34:9). He also qualifies in that the law was not to depart from his mouth (Josh 1:8), since Yahweh promises to put his words in the prophet's mouth (Deut 18:18). But the prescriptions about the prophet in Deuteronomy 18 are part of a section dealing with the author's ideal polity (judges, kings, priests, and prophets, 17:8–18:22). It therefore seems better to think of Joshua as the first of a series of charismatics, even though he is never identified as a נביא.

passed on the prophet who comes out with a message not authorized by Yahweh. Since this leaves unsolved the problem of verifying the source of the message, in the case of predictive announcements the simple falsification principle is applicable. Unfulfilled predictions may be disregarded.

The final paragraph of Deuteronomy, and therefore of the Pentateuch, distinguishes between the direct and unmediated face-to-face relationship with Yahweh proper to Moses and forms of mediation characteristic of the prophet (Deut 34:10–12).Since this statement occurs immediately after the commissioning of Joshua, and since Joshua is the first "prophet like Moses," duplicating in several respects the role of Moses,[10] the point may have been to affirm the superiority of Moses to his successor. However, similarity of vocabulary suggests that there is a deliberate reference to the "prophet like Moses" passage, and that this choice of language has the purpose of warning against reading Deut 18:15–19 as implying equal status between Moses and the prophets who followed him. Similarity does not entail equality.[11]

III

Turning from Deuteronomy to the History, the similarity of perspective on prophecy is easily detected. The prophet is patterned on Moses and his successor Joshua as "servant of Yahweh."[12] As with Joshua, whose primary concern is to be the study of the law (Josh 1:7–8), the principal task of the prophet is to urge obedience to the law and warn against the consequences of not observing it. The individual figures who stand out in the History—Samuel, Elijah, Huldah and others—all conform to this role. Since, whatever earlier versions may or may not have existed, the history of the kingdoms in its final form is viewed from the other side of disaster, the Historian's purpose in writing would have been to explain why, in spite of promise and covenant, the story could have

---

10   In later Jewish tradition Joshua is considered a prophetic figure; Sirach, for example, refers to him as "the successor of Moses in prophesying" (Sir 46:1).

11   See my *Prophecy and Canon: A Contribution to the Study of Jewish Origins* (Notre Dame: Notre Dame University Press, 1977), 80–95.

12   Moses as עבד יהוה in Deut 34:5; frequently throughout Joshua; in the probably Deuteronomistic Exod 14:31; and in 2 Kgs 18:12; 21:8. Joshua, a charismatic person (Deut 34:9, cf. Num 27:15–23), bears the same designation in Josh 24:29 and Judg 2:8. Prophets collectively are עבדיו הנביאים (2 Kgs 9:7; 17:13, 23; 21:10; 24:2) and the individual prophet is עבד יהוה (e.g., Ahijah, 1 Kgs 14:18; 15:29; Elijah, 1 Kgs 18:36; 2 Kgs 9:36; 10:10; Jonah ben Amittai, 2 Kgs 14:25). See Patrick D. Miller, Jr., "'Moses my servant': The Deuteronomic Portrait of Moses," *Int* 41 (1987): 245–55.

ended as it did. Viewed from this point of view, the History is an *apologia* for Israel's God. God is not to blame, since Israel and Judah were warned of the consequences of neglecting the law, and those who issued the warning were the prophets sent by God. So far, this is in keeping with the perspective of Deuteronomy which, in its final form, foresees the possibility of defeat and exile and proclaims the same message through Moses, the protoprophet (Deut 4:25–31; 28:62–68; 30:17–18). The one striking difference is that the History attributes the disaster exclusively to the adoption of non-Yahwistic cults. The emphasis on social injustice, the neglect of widows, orphans, and other disadvantaged and needy classes, one of the great leitmotifs of classical prophecy, is almost completely absent from the History and is never presented as a factor in the godforsakenness of defeat and exile.

Another characteristic of prophetic activity recorded in the History illustrates the principal criterion for authenticity in Deuteronomy, namely, the fulfilment of prophetic predictions. This prophecy-fulfilment pattern is so prominent as to suggest a reading of history as prophetically predetermined. It begins with Joshua's curse on whoever rebuilds Jericho which he has just destroyed, the working out of which long afterwards is explicitly noted (Josh 6:26; 1 Kgs 16:34). The ruin of the Shiloh priesthood announced by an anonymous man of God begins to be fulfilled with the banishment of the priest Abiathar (1 Sam 2:27–36; 1 Kgs 2:27). The prophet Ahijah, one of the prophetic kingmakers, predicts the fall of the Kingdom of Samaria long before it happened (1 Kgs 14:1–18; 15:29–30). A Judean man of God knows about Josiah and his desecration of the Bethel altar centuries before it happened (1 Kgs 13:2; 2 Kgs 23:16). There are also short-term predictions, the fulfilment of which is explicitly noted. Jehu ben Hanani foretells Baasha's downfall, and so it happened (1 Kgs 16:1–4, 7; 16:12–13). Elijah makes the gruesome predictions that dogs will lick Ahab's blood and feast on the dead Jezebel, and so, we are told, it happened (1 Kgs 21:19, cf. 22:38; 1 Kgs 21:23–24, cf. 2 Kgs 9:36–37).

A special instance of this prophetic criteriology is the story of the encounter of the Judean man of God with the old prophet of Bethel (1 Kings 13); special, because it appears to have been created ad hoc to demonstrate important requirements for authenticity.[13] The encounter

---

13   The incident seems to presuppose the extension of Josiah's territory to include Bethel, Josiah himself is named by the man of God, and the story has unmistakable echoes of Amos's encounter with the priest Amaziah in Bethel during the reign of a later Jeroboam. On this last point see the remarks of Peter R. Ackroyd, "A Judgment Narrative between Kings and Chronicles?" in *Canon and Authority* (ed. G. W. Coats and B. O. Long; Philadelphia, Pa.: Fortress, 1977), 71–87, with further references.

is set up with the prediction by the man of God of Josiah's desecration of the Bethel altar (13:1–2), the fulfilment of which will be duly noted (2 Kgs 23:15–18); a miraculous sign is given which is verified immediately (13:3); the man of God intercedes for the king whose hand he has just withered (13:4–6). All of this is consistent with the Deuteronomistic profile of the prophet as successful predictor of the future, sign-giver, and intercessor. We are then told about the prohibition to accept food and drink while at Bethel, essential for understanding the encounter with the local prophet which follows (13:7–10). Intercepted on his way back to Judah, the man of God allows himself to be persuaded by the mendacious revelation of the old Bethel prophet and accepts his hospitality (13:11–19); but while they were at table the Bethel prophet utters an authentic prophetic condemnation followed by a prediction of the man of God's death, and so it happened (13:20–26). In addition to providing a further example of fulfilment as indicative of authenticity, the story makes the point that an earlier oracle has precedence over a later one, especially when it entails a direct command from God. At the same time, it illustrates the Deuteronomistic view of false prophecy as a testing by God (Deut 13:4), though it is not made clear how the man of God was supposed to recognize the falsity of the Bethel prophet's report countermanding his original revelation.[14] In both this incident and the vision of Micaiah ben Imlah, in which an attendant in the heavenly court volunteers to be a lying spirit in the mouths of Ahab's prophets (1 Kgs 22:19–23), we cannot help noticing how thin the line is between testing and deceiving.

IV

The last section of the History, from the reigns of Jeroboam II in Israel and Uzziah in Judah to the final act, the paroling of the captive Jehoiachin (2 Kgs 14:23–25:30), has a notably different profile from the preceding narrative with respect to the part played by prophets in public

---

14　John Gray, *1 and 2 Kings: A Commentary* (2d ed.; Philadelphia: Westminster, 1970), 318–23; James L. Crenshaw, *Prophetic Conflict: Its Effect upon Israelite Religion* (Berlin: de Gruyter, 1971), 41–42; Robert R. Wilson, *Prophecy and Society in Ancient Israel* (BZAW 124; Philadelphia, Pa.: Fortress, 1980), 187–91; D. W. Van Winkle, "1 Kings xiii: True and False Prophecy," *VT* 39 (1989): 31–42; E. Eynikel, "Prophecy and Fulfillment in the Deuteronomistic History (1 Kgs 13; 2 Kgs 23,16–18) in *Pentateuchal and Deuteronomistic Studies: Papers Read at the XIIIth IOSOT Congress, Leuven 1989* (ed. C. Brekelmans and Johan Lust; Leuven: Leuven University Press; Peeters, 1990), 227–37; Joseph Blenkinsopp, *A History of Prophecy in Israel* (2d ed.; Louisville, Ky.: Westminster John Knox, 1996), 158–59.

affairs. For the most part they are alluded to only in general terms as Yahweh's servants (2 Kgs 17:13, 23; 21:10; 24:2), or the prophecy is referred directly to Yahweh with no named intermediary (15:12; 24:13). The only names occurring are Jonah ben Amittai, who has nothing in common with the author of the canonical book except the name; Isaiah, but not the radical critic of contemporary society and its institutions we encounter in the book (chapters 1–35); and Huldah consulted during Josiah's reign (22:14–20).[15] Since this is the time span during which, according to the superscriptions of the prophetic books, the canonical prophets were active, the question arises why they are conspicuous by their absence from the historical record of those years. We may allow that the prophetic books as such are products of the Second Temple period, and that they have been edited and expanded in the light of situations and exigencies during that time, but there seems to be no reason to doubt the existence of a significant body of material attached to specific individual prophetic individuals with which the Historian could have been, and indeed must have been, familiar.[16] So the problem of "the silence of the prophets" persists and invites speculation. Without taking up the issue in detail, I propose in the remainder of the essay to look at one or two case histories and draw some conclusions of a necessarily tentative nature.

2 Kings 14:23–29

The superscription to Amos places his activity during the roughly contemporary reigns of Jeroboam II of Israel and Uzziah (Azariah) of Judah. In the brief report on Jeroboam's reign in the History (2 Kgs 14:23–29), however, instead of Amos we encounter a prophet, Jonah ben Amittai, who supported Jeroboam's military activities in the name of the God of Israel and in response to the distress of Jeroboam's people. Jonah's oracle is therefore certainly considered to be a genuine prophetic utterance. But then, quite unexpectedly, the Historian adds the remark that "Yahweh had not said that he would wipe out Israel's name from under heaven, so he saved them by means of Jeroboam ben Joash" (14:27). The statement is clearly polemical, and the reference to

---

15   The inclusion of Huldah may appear to be somewhat surprising since her prediction of a peaceful end for Josiah was apparently not fulfilled (23:29), and therefore did not satisfy one of the principal criteria for authentic prophecy.

16   Noth, *Überlieferungsgeschichtliche Studien*, 97–98; ET *The Deuteronomistic History*, 86, held that the prophetic books were unknown to the Historian, but this opinion has not been widely shared.

Yahweh as the one speaking indicates polemic against a prophetic pronouncement of doom. The only prophet we know of who made such a statement at that time and in that place was Amos (8:2; 9:8a).[17] The one biographical passage in Amos, which interrupts the sequence of four visions (Amos 7:10–17) and was therefore probably inserted at a later time, predicts the violent death of Jeroboam and is preceded by a prediction of the end of the dynasty of Jehu ("the house of Jeroboam," 7:9). This too would have been unacceptable to the Historian, who approved of Jehu's anti-Baal activities, records the anointing of Jehu by a disciple of Elisha (2 Kgs 9:1–13), followed by the promise of a four-generation dynasty, the fulfilment of which is duly recorded after the assassination of Zechariah, fourth in succession (2 Kgs 10:30, cf. 15:12). The probability that Amos 7:10–17 was inserted into the book would suggest that at an earlier stage it represented an account of the reign of Jeroboam alternative to 2 Kgs 14:23–29. In that case Amos 7:10–17 would be an overwhelmingly negative version, featuring a politically confrontational prophet, while 2 Kgs 14:23–29 would be for the most part positive, featuring a supportive prophet, possibly attached to the Bethel cult.[18]

2 Kings 15:1–17:4

The next section of the History, from the accession of Zechariah, last in line of the Jehu dynasty, to Hoshea, last ruler in Samaria, more or less synchronic with Uzziah, Jotham, and Ahaz in Judah, corresponds to the time of the prophet Hosea's activity according to the inscription of the

---

17 Amos 9:8a, "Behold the eyes of the Lord Yahweh are on the sinful kingdom; I will destroy it from off the surface of the ground," is followed by what appears to be a later editorial modification, "except that I will not utterly destroy the house of Jacob" (9:8b). The Historian was therefore not the only one who found Amos's unconditional prediction of doom unacceptable.

18 Consult Frank Crüsemann, "Kritik an Amos im deuteronomistischen Geschichtswerk: Erwägungen zu 2. Könige 14:23," in *Probleme biblische Theologie: Gerhard von Rad zum 70. Geburtstag* (ed. H. W. Wolf; Munich: Kaiser, 1971), 57–63; Peter R. Ackroyd, "A Judgment Narrative between Kings and Chronicles?" 71–87; Klaus Koch, "Das Prophetenschweigen des deuteronomistischen Geschichtswerks," in *Die Botschaft und die Boten: Festschrift für Hans Walter Wolff zum 70. Geburtstag* (ed. J. Jeremias and L. Perlitt; Neukirchen-Vluyn: Neukirchener Verlag, 1981), 115–28; Christopher Begg, "The Non-Mention of Amos, Hosea and Micah in the Deuteronomistic History," *BN* 32 (1986): 41–53. Günther H. Wittenberg, "Amos and Hosea: A Contribution to the Problem of the 'Prophetenschweigen' in the Deuteronomistic History (Dtr)," *OTE* 6 (1993): 295–311, accepts that Amos's pronouncement of doom would have been unacceptable to the Historian, but places the latter during Josiah's reign.

book.[19] Assuming his familiarity with the prophecies of Hosea, we would expect the Historian to find much to applaud, especially the polemic against the Baal cults. On the other hand, Hosea, like Amos, predicted the end of the Jehu dynasty and condemned Jehu's bloody coup ("the blood of Jezreel," Hos 1:4), which was prophetically authorized and which the Historian recounts without disapproval (2 Kings 9–10). What the Historian would have made of Hosea's marriage with the אשת זנונים (Hos 1:2), if he knew of it, we do not know. A more significant point would be Hosea's radical rejection of the institution of monarchy,[20] far more than is contemplated in the History, which is in essence a history of the rulers of the two kingdoms, both good and bad.[21]

2 Kings 18–20

According to the inscription in the book, Micah's activity extended into the reign of Hezekiah. Here, too, there are features which we imagine would have appealed to the Historian, including Micah's prediction of the utter destruction of Jerusalem (Mic 3:12), of a kind repeated frequently during the last phase of the History.[22] The account of Jeremiah's trial in Jerermiah 26, in the course of which certain elders cited Micah's prediction (Jer 26:17–19) shows evidence of the same Deuteronomistic hand, the traces of which are evident throughout Jeremiah, as is widely acknowledged.[23] In this new context, the Micah

---

19   On the problems of this superscription—the lack of synchronism, the failure to mention rulers of Samaria after Jeroboam, the list of Judean rulers to establish the time of an Israelite prophet's activity—see the comments of A. A. Macintosh, *A Critical and Exegetical Commentary on Hosea* (ICC; Edinburgh: T&T Clark, 1997), 1–4.

20   Hos 8:4; 9:15; 10:3, 7. Both the institution and the liquidation of the monarchy were expressions of the divine anger (13:10–11).

21   On Hosea's absence from the History see Begg, "Non-Mention of Amos, Hosea and Micah."

22   2 Kgs 20:18; 21:10–15; 22:15–18; 23:26–27; 24:3–4.

23   Note, for example, the insistence on obeying "my servants the prophets" (v. 4), the threatened condemnation to death for what was thought to be a false prophecy (vv. 8–9, 11), and Jeremiah's counter-insistence that his threat that the Jerusalem temple would share the fate of the temple at Shiloh was authorized and authored by Yahweh (vv. 12, 15). Detailed demonstration in Ernest W. Nicholson, *Preaching to the Exiles* (Oxford: Basil Blackwell, 1970), 52–55; W. Thiel, *Die deuteronomistische Redaktion von Jeremia 1–25* (WMANT 41; Neukirchen-Vluyn: Neukirchener Verlag, 1973), 105–19; F. L. Hossfeld and I. Meyer, "Der Prophet vor dem Tribunal: Neuer Auslegungsversuch von Jer 26," *ZAW* 86 (1974): 30–50; Christof Hardmeier, "Die Propheten Micha und Jesaja im Spiegel von Jeremia xxvi und 2 Regum xviii–xx: Zur

text is no longer an absolute prediction of disaster but a call to repentance which Hezekiah heeded. While this source (Jer^D) has its own distinctive features, the commonality of ideology and language with the History increases the likelihood that the author of the History was familiar with Micah traditions in one form or another. In other respects, however, we can understand how several of the sayings of Micah generally accepted as authentic may not have made a good fit with the purposes and the general orientation of the History, even if the Historian would not have found them objectionable. Micah has much to say about social injustice[24] and shows little interest in denouncing alien cults. He not only launches a bitter attack on contemporary prophets (2:6–11; 3:5–8), but claims for himself a special source of inspiration outside of the normal channels ("I am filled with power, with the spirit of Yahweh, with justice and might," 3:8). This would not fit well into the contours of the ideal Deuteronomistic commonwealth in which the prophet has a carefully prescribed place alongside ruler, priest, and judge (Deuteronomy 17–18).

Several incidents connected with Sennacherib's punitive expedition following on Hezekiah's rebellion feature the prophet Isaiah: in reply to a delegation sent to him by the king he issues an optimistic oracle (2 Kgs 19:1–7 = Isa 37:1–7); after Hezekiah, threatened once again by the Assyrian generalissimo, goes to the temple to pray, Isaiah sends another and more explicit assurance that Jerusalem will survive the attack (2 Kgs 19:20–34 = Isa 37:21–35); during Hezekiah's serious illness he issues an oracle predicting his death, but then countermands it with another assuring him of fifteen more years of life, then prescribes a cure and provides a miraculous sign guaranteeing his prediction (20:1–11 = Isa 38:1–8, 21); finally, after the visit of the Babylonian envoys during Hezekiah's convalescence, Isaiah interrogates the king and predicts future ruin and destitution at the hands of the Babylonians (20:12–19 = Isa 39:1–8). It seems much more probable that the account as presented in 2 Kings has been copied into the book of Isaiah than that Isaiah 36–39 has served as a source for the Historian.[25] In much the same way, the last chapter of the History (2 Kgs 24:18–25:30) came to serve as historical appendix or epilogue for the book of Jeremiah (Jeremiah 52). We would assume that among the Historian's sources for his account of

---

Prophetie-Rezeption in der nach-joschijanischen Zeit," in *Congress Volume: Leuven, 1989* (ed. J. A. Emerton; VTSup 43; Leiden: Brill, 1991), 172–89.

24   Mic 2:1–5, 8–11; 3:1–3; 6:6–8, 9–12.

25   I presented arguments for the priority of the Kings version in "The Prophetic Biography of Isaiah," in *Mincha: Festgabe für Rolf Rendtorff zum 75. Geburtstag* (ed. Erhard Blum; Neukirchen-Vluyn: Neukirchener Verlag, 2000), 13–26 (20–21).

Hezekiah's reign were traditions in circulation at that time about a man of God called Isaiah who gave the ruler aid and support during the terrible crisis of 701 BC.[26]

Unlike the unsparing critic of people and institutions we encounter throughout the first part of the book, the Historian's Isaiah provides positive reinforcement to the ruler through oracular utterances, healing, miraculous signs and wonders, yet concludes with yet another prediction of disaster. All of this would have been entirely consistent with the point of view and aims of the History. The Isaiah who gives aid and comfort to Ahaz in the narrative core of the so-called *Denkschrift* (Isa 7:1–17) has a similar profile. The first sentence of this passage (Isa 7:1) is practically identical with the first sentence of the account of the Syro-Ephraimite crisis in 2 Kgs 16:5, which suggests a situation similar to the one about Amos and Jeroboam II commented on earlier. That is to say, an unfavourable account of the reign of Ahaz without Isaiah in 2 Kgs 16:1–20, and a much more favourable version with Isaiah in Isa 7:1–17.[27] The Historian's account of the Assyrian crisis in 2 Kgs 18:13–19:37 also seems to have incorporated two parallel versions. There are two intimidating addresses of the Rabshakeh (2 Kgs 18:19–25 continued in 28–35; 19:10–13), in both of which he boasts of the same cities conquered by the Assyrians (18:34; 19:13); Hezekiah visits the temple twice (19:1; 19:14); and Isaiah intervenes twice, providing basically the same assurance on each occasion (19:5–7; 19:20–34). We seem to be getting a glimpse of an early stage when the Historian, in putting together his account of the reigns of Jeroboam II, Ahaz, Hezekiah, and possibly other rulers, had access to more than one ver-

---

26   In addition to the article in the previous note see my "The Formation of the Hebrew Bible Canon: Isaiah as a Test Case," in *The Canon Debate* (ed. L. M. Macdonald and J. A. Sanders; Peabody, Mass.; Hendrickson, 2002), 53–67; idem, "Hezekiah and the Babylonian Delegation: A Critical Reading of Isaiah 39:1–8," in *Essays on Ancient Israel in Its Near Eastern Context. A Tribute to Nadav Naʾaman* (ed. Yairah Amit, Ehud Ben Zvi, Israel Finkelstein, and Oded Lipschitz; Winona Lake, Ind · Eisenbrauns, 2006), 107–22; Christopher Begg, "The Deuteronomistic Retouching of the Portrait of Hezekiah in 2 Kgs 20,12–19," *BN* 38/39 (1987): 7–13; idem, "Hezekiah's Display (2 Kings 20,12–19)," *BN* 38/39 (1987): 14–18; E. Ruprecht, "Die ursprüngliche Komposition der Hiskia–Jesaja Erzählungen und ihre Umstrukturierung durch den Verfasser des deuteronomistischen Geshcichtswerkes," *ZTK* 87 (1990): 33–66; A. H. Konkel, "The Sources of the Story of Hezekiah in the book of Isaiah," *VT* 43 (1993): 462–82.

27   See Peter R. Ackroyd, "The Biblical Interpretation of the Reigns of Ahaz and Hezekiah," in *In The Shelter of Elyon: Essays on Ancient Palestinian Life and Literature in Honor of G. W. Ahlström* (ed. W. Boyd Barrick and John R. Spencer; JSOTSup 31; Sheffield: JSOT Press, 1984), 247–59; repr. in idem, *Studies in the Religious Tradition of the Old Testament* (London: SCM, 1987), 181–92.

sion exhibiting different models of ruler-prophet relationship and of the prophetic profile in general.

We could no doubt scrutinize other prophetic writings which can be dated within the time frame of the History with a view to suggesting possible reasons for their non-mention in it.[28] All such reasons, as also the ones suggested above, will necessarily be speculative. We cannot even be sure in every case that the prophetic collections in question were known to the Historian. And, in general, we would suspect that institutionally unattached prophets like Amos, Micah, and Isaiah, whose attitude to the apparatus of state and its functionaries (ruler, officials, priests, prophets) was basically confrontational, could not be accommodated within either the ideal Deuteronomistic commonweal (Deut 17:8–18:22) or the Historians's view of the prophet-ruler relationship. They could not be subsumed under the criteria for authenticity either. The criterion of fulfilment or non-fulfilment (Deut 18:21–22), which dominates the History as we have seen, could not account for the appeal of these other prophets to a certain self-authenticating quality which they claimed to possess. The Historian may well have felt that such non-negotiable claims as that of Micah to be "filled with power, with the spirit of Yahweh, with justice and might" (Mic 3:8), or that of Jeremiah to utter words "like fire, like a hammer that breaks up rocks" (Jer 23:29) were inconsistent with the roles prophets were called on to play through the History and were therefore best left out of account.

---

28   Christopher T. Begg did this some time ago; in addition to articles mentioned earlier see the following: "The Non-Mention of Zephaniah, Nahum and Habakkuk in the Deuteronomistic History," *BN* 38/39 (1987): 19–25; "A Bible Mystery: The Absence of Jeremiah in the Deuteronomistic History," *IBS* 7 (1985): 139–66; "The Non-Mention of Ezekiel in the Deuteronomistic History, the Book of Jeremiah and the Chronistic History," in *Ezekiel and His Book: Textual and Literary Criticism and their Interrelation* (ed. J. Lust; BETL 74; Leuven: Leuven University Press, 1986), 340–43.

The Practicalities of Prophetic Writing in Isaiah 8:1

H. G. M. WILLIAMSON

In Isa 8:1 the prophet is told by God to "take thee a great tablet, and write upon it with the pen of a man" (RV). From the most ancient times for which we have evidence right down to the modern day there has been disagreement over the meaning of the word here rendered "tablet" as well as over what could be meant by the expression "the pen of a man." Since Graham Davies has made so many distinguished contributions to the study of both ancient Hebrew epigraphy and the prophetic literature, I hope that he will enjoy this reconsideration of the problem, offered in friendship and respect.

Attempts to render the words גליון גדול have varied remarkably. 1QIsaᵃ has the same consonants as MT, and all the ancient versions agree in rendering the second word as "big, large." Beyond that, however, they vary remarkably, as a simple listing will demonstrate: LXX has τόμον καινοῦ μεγάλου, "a piece of large new" (*NETS*: "a scroll of a new large one"), which makes no sense on its own, and it is likely that the additional dictionary entries for τόμος as "roll of papyrus; tome; volume" are simply attempts to make sense of this passage and others dependent upon it.[1] Some manuscripts add χάρτου, "of a (roll of) papyrus," which might be original, though since it appears at various places in the phrase in different manuscript traditions[2] it is probably rather a later insertion from a marginal explanation; it could well be, for instance, that it has been added in an explanatory manner on the basis of Jer 36:2 (and cf. v. 28), where MT has the same imperative introduction as our verse, but continues with a different and more readily intelligible object: קח־לך מגלת־ספר, which LXX (= 43:2) renders λαβὲ σεαυτῷ χαρτίον βιβλίου. The other versions have: Aquila: διφθέρωμα, "prepared hide, piece of leather," especially as material for writing; Symmachus: τεῦχος, "case for holding papyrus rolls; roll of writing material"; Theodotion: κεφαλίδα, "heading (?)," perhaps the space at the top of a column or section;[3] Peshitta: ܠܘܚܐ, "tablet" (though of course this is

---

1 LSJ, 1804.

2 See P. Katz, "Notes on the Septuagint," *JTS* 47 (1946): 30–33 (30–31).

3 At Ps 40:8 במגלת ספר is rendered ἐν κεφαλίδι βιβλίου (and so too Heb 10:7). According to W. L. Lane, *Hebrews 9–13* (WBC 47B; Dallas: Word Books, 1991), 255, "in the

really just a Syriac form of the Hebrew word); Vulgate: *librum*, "book"; and Targum: לוח, "tablet." Given that, as I will argue further below, the surface is to be written on with a stylus (חרט), it is clear that association with papyrus or scrolls is inappropriate;[4] the versions which take this line no doubt associated the word linguistically with מגלה, "scroll" (and again the possibility of comparison with Jer 36:2 might be considered).

This tradition is also attested in the medieval commentators, though with less certainty: Rashi מגילה or לוח, Kimchi אגרת, "letter," and Ibn Ezra either מגילה or, with an explicit cross-reference to Isa 3:23 (see below), בגד, a garment or piece of cloth on to which the letters should be embroidered.[5] We may also note what I take to be a play on words when he says that this is to prophesy the exile (גלות) of Samaria.

The proposal of Ibn Ezra to link to the only other occurrence of this word in the Hebrew Bible, namely at Isa 3:23, where it features as an item of uncertain meaning in the list of women's finery, has been taken further by a number of more recent commentators. If, as is frequently done, the word is linked to גלה, "reveal,"[6] then one possibility would be to consider that the word means a "mirror," which would have been of polished metal in antiquity. It could be in the list in Isaiah 3 and would also have been a possible surface on which to scratch a name.[7]

LXX . . . and in literature influenced by it, κεφαλίς denotes a 'scroll,' the form of the book that was customary prior to the time when the use of the codex became fashionable. If the qualifying term βιβλίου is understood as a gen[itive] of definition ('the book in a scroll form'), the phrase ἐν κεφαλίδι βιβλίου can be translated 'in the scroll'"; see more fully K. T. Schäfer, "ΚΕΦΑΛΙΣ ΒΙΒΛΙΟΥ," in *Wege zur Buchwissenschaft* (ed. O. Wenig; Bonner Beiträge zur Bibliotheks- und Bücherkunde 14; Bonn: Bouvier, 1966), 1–10.

4   A. Lemaire, "Vom Ostrakon zur Schriftrolle: Überlegungen zur Entstehung der Bibel," in *XXII. Deutscher Orientalistentag: Ausgewählte Vorträge* (ed. W. Röllig; ZDMGSup 6; Stuttgart: Franz Steiner Wiesbaden, 1985), 110–23, seems to assume that it is a sheet of papyrus, evidence for whose use in the biblical world he then proceeds to document (116–19). Surprisingly, however, he appears not to offer any evidence whatsoever for his surmise.

5   For a fuller survey of the rabbinic commentators, see H. Liss, *Die unerhörte Prophetie: Kommunikative Strukturen prophetischer Rede im Buch Yesha'yahu* (Arbeiten zur Bibel und ihrer Geschichte 14; Leipzig: Evangelische Verlagsanstalt, 2003), 190–91.

6   See W. Gesenius, *Philologisch-kritischer und historischer Commentar über den Jesaia* (Leipzig: Friedr. Christ. Wilh. Vogel, 1821), 324–25, and more recently, for example, J. Barthel, *Prophetenwort und Geschichte: Die Jesajaüberlieferung in Jes 6–8 und 28–31* (FAT 19; Tübingen: Mohr Siebeck, 1997), 184.

7   E.g., R. Lowth, *Isaiah: A New Translation; with a Preliminary Dissertation, and Notes, Critical, Philological, and Explanatory* (London: Thomas Tegg, 1824 [1st ed., London: J. Dodsley & T. Cadell, 1778]), 91; F. Delitzsch, *Commentar über das Buch Jesaia* (4th ed.; Leipzig: Dörffling & Franke, 1889), 151; ET *Biblical Commentary on the Prophecies of Isaiah* (Edinburgh: T&T Clark, 1894), 219.

Nevertheless, it seems unlikely, as there would not seem to be any particular reason for choosing this strange form of writing material.

An additional possibility which has been raised in more recent times is "waxed wooden tablet, such as has been found at Nineveh,"[8] though there does not seem to be any particular linguistic justification for this, and, indeed, Hicks has argued at length that the Hebrew word for a writing board was דלת (for which he suggests several examples from the West Semitic world).[9]

We thus find that modern translations and commentaries reflect as much variety as those from antiquity. Probably most popular is "tablet," but other renderings include "roll" (KJV), "seal,"[10] "scroll" (NIV), "placard,"[11] "piece of writing material" (GNB), "sheet" (JPS), "writing tablet" (REB), "signboard" (NLT), and so on.

There has been one significant attempt to solve the problem that includes emendation. Galling[12] (and cf. *BHS*) suggested that in order to keep the two occurrences of the word together גליון must refer to papyrus, a meaning which he finds suitable here and also in Isa 3:23 in view of some evidence which he adduces for the use of papyrus in the manufacture of some forms of clothing.[13] He then finds that the use of גדול is curious in this context for so short an inscription and so conjectures that it be emended to גורל, "lot," so that the whole phrase becomes something like "a public property deed (ein Allmende-Blatt)" on which is inscribed "For (ל) Maher-shalal-hash-baz"; this will have been a claim by way of a birth registration that at the next allocation his expected son should have a share in the communal land. There are several difficulties with this view, however. First, one would not normally expect the writing instrument for papyrus to be a חרט; second, the textual

---

8   G. R. Driver, "Isaiah i–xxxix: Textual and Linguistic Problems," *JSS* 13 (1968): 36–57 (40); cf. E. J. Young, *The Book of Isaiah*, vol. 1 (NICOT; Grand Rapids, Mich.: Eerdmans, 1965), 301. In the most recent edition of his *Semitic Writing from Pictograph to Alphabet* (ed. S. A. Hopkins; London: Oxford University Press, 1976), 80 and 239–40, however, Driver emphasized again that there is no certainty and he does not seem to have continued especially to have favoured his previous suggestion.

9   R. L. Hicks, "*Delet* and *mᵉgillāh*: A Fresh Approach to Jeremiah xxxvi," *VT* 33 (1983): 46–66.

10   P. Auvray and J. Steinmann, *Isaïe* (2d ed.; La Sainte Bible; Paris: Cerf, 1957), 50, though glossed in a footnote with "ou plutôt une tablette de bois ou de cuir."

11   J. A. Motyer, *The Prophecy of Isaiah* (Leicester: Inter-Varsity, 1993), 90.

12   K. Galling, "Ein Stück judäischen Bodenrechts in Jesaja 8," *ZDPV* 56 (1933): 209–18, the substance of which is repeated and updated in "Tafel, Buch und Blatt," in *Near Eastern Studies in Honor of William Foxwell Albright* (ed. H. Goedicke; Baltimore, Md.: Johns Hopkins University Press, 1971), 207–23 (221–22).

13   He cites in particular S. Krauss, *Talmudische Archäologie*, vol. 1 (Leipzig: Fock, 1910), 141, and in his later article he adds vol. 2 (1911), 262–63.

witness for גדול is unanimous, as we have seen,[14] so that even a slight conjectural emendation here should be contemplated only as a last resort; third, the proposed way of linking with Isa 3:23 is questionable (see further below) and the appeal to the use of papyrus in some items of clothing tenuous; and finally, Galling has to maintain that the initial writing in vv. 1–2 is simultaneous with the birth of the child so that, as some other commentators have independently argued, he proposes that ואקרב in v. 3 should be translated as a pluperfect—but the only evidence for this conjecture is the theory which it is seeking to support. The proposed emendation should therefore probably be rejected.

More recently a fresh approach has been advanced by Norin.[15] Recalling that in most current discussions the word has been explained as a *qiṭṭalôn* form from גלה, he notes that there are a number of examples of such roots which are also attested as, or which are very closely related to, double ʿayin roots. He cites כליון from כלל/כלה, בזיון from בזה, and cf. בזז, and שגיון from שגה/שגג. On this basis he proposes that גליון should not be associated with גלה but גלל (and here it may be noted in passing that we have already suggested that several of the renderings in the versions probably assumed this by linking the word with מגלה). From this he proposes that the word might have meant "cylinder seal"; as known from many ancient Near Eastern examples, names were often inscribed on these, and they could also have served as some form of amulet in the list of women's finery. He cites some examples from Collon's collection for their use in Palestine.[16]

Although, as we shall see, I have found Norin's linguistic comments valuable, his suggestion that גליון means "cylinder seal" seems improbable. The standard seal in Judah and Israel was the stamp seal, and there is no direct evidence whatsoever for the use of cylinder seals in this region by the local population.[17] Collon's discussion explicitly

---

14 In his second article, Galling draws attention to the brief discussion of Katz, "Notes on the Septuagint," 30–31. Katz observes that גדול is rendered in the LXX by two adjectives, καινοῦ μεγάλου. On the basis of Galling's first article, he therefore proposes that καινοῦ may represent an early corruption of κλήρου, a regular and wholly appropriate translation equivalent of גורל; this is favoured by *BHS*. As Katz readily acknowledges, however, this is wholly conjectural, and takes its starting point precisely from Galling's emendation. It cannot, therefore, be adduced as independent support.

15 S. Norin, "Was ist ein *gillajon*?" *VT* 56 (2006): 363–69.

16 D. Collon, *First Impressions: Cylinder Seals in the Ancient Near East* (rev. ed.; London: British Museum, 2005), 83–85.

17 Cf. N. Naʾaman and Y. Thareani-Sussely, "Dating the Appearance of Assyrian Ware in Southern Palestine," *TA* 33 (2006): 61–82, for a discussion that is completely separate from the present concern but which reaches this same conclusion. They conclude that such seals as have been found "made their way to Palestine along trade

states that nearly all the examples she cites are from Syria or of Syrian origin, and so "within the cuneiform sphere of influence." The occasional occurrence of some Egyptianizing motifs is hardly surprising, given both the extent of trade around the Fertile Crescent and Assyria's direct contacts with the region during Isaiah's own time. Occasional stray examples that have been found within Judah are clearly of foreign origin and cannot be cited to support local manufacture or use.[18] In addition to the absence of evidence for the use of such seals by native Judeans, it must also be asked why such an unusual choice of material should have been made here. The continuation of the passage suggests that the writing was intended to be some form of public statement, so that a cylinder seal, which is usually very small, would seem inappropriate; and the fact that it is here glossed as "large" only makes the implausibility greater.

While there are thus difficulties in accepting Norin's final proposal, his starting point allows us to suggest an alternative solution. There is a well-attested noun גלל in Aramaic[19] which is doubtless cognate with Akkadian galālu. In 1990 I undertook a brief study of this word in relation to its use in Ezra 5:8 and 6:4 (אבן גלל) in the light of its occurrence in an Aramaic gloss to one of the Elamite Fortification Tablets from Persepolis.[20] I sought there to demonstrate that the Aramaic meaning is close to the second attested meaning in Akkadian,[21] that contrary to Bowman's opinion it could not mean "stone" tout court,[22] but rather that, in view of the use of the Akkadian word with such fine objects as stelae, pillars, window frames, and dishes, and of the Aramaic word in significant building structures, it had rather to mean "stone treated in a spe-

---

routes and were most certainly purchased by wealthy individuals or institutions" (68).

18　For instance, the example Norin cites from Lachish is of Cypriote origin and in any case dates well before the Israelite period; see P. Beck, "A Cypriote Cylinder Seal from Lachish," TA 10 (1983): 178–81. An example from Beersheba cited by Collon is stated by P. Beck in her publication of it to have such mixed iconographical features as to suggest its provincial origin, and she tentatively suggests the mid-Euphrates area as its possible place of origin; "A Votive Cylinder Seal," in Y. Aharoni (ed.), Beer-Sheba I: Excavations at Tel Beer-Sheba, 1969–1971 Seasons (Tel Aviv: Institute of Archaeology, Tel Aviv University, 1973), 56–60. A. F. Rainey, "The Cuneiform Inscription on a Votive Cylinder from Beer-Sheba," in Aharoni, Beer-Sheba I, 61–70, also finds Aramaean features in the inscription.

19　DNWSI 1:224.

20　H. G. M. Williamson, "ʾeben gĕlāl (Ezra 5:8, 6:4) Again," BASOR 280 (1990): 83–88.

21　CAD G, 11.

22　R. A. Bowman, "אֶבֶן גְּלָל—aban galâlu (Ezra 5:8; 6:4)," in Dōrōn: Hebraic Studies: Essays in Honor of Professor Abraham I. Katsh (ed. I. T. Naamani and D. Rudavsky; New York: National Association of Professors of Hebrew, 1965), 64–74.

cial way"; "specially selected stone" seemed to me then to be the closest paraphrase available. I should now add in further support the fact that I had previously overlooked that *gll* also occurs in Palmyrene with the sense "stone slab, stele"; in the Tariff of Palmyra it occurs interestingly in the following context: *wktb ʿm nmwsʾ qdmyʾ bgllʾ dy lqbl hyklʾ*, "and be written with the former law on the stele which faces the temple."[23]

The possibility of its occurrence (modified morphologically in line with Norin's proposal) also in Hebrew had not occurred to me at that time, but Norin's proposal suggests that it might be extremely appropriate in the present context. While of course we must allow for some slight differences in nuance between the precise significance of cognate words in one language or another, the use of a specially prepared stone for a major public inscription seems entirely plausible, whether specifically as a stele, as some cognate uses might suggest, or more simply as a stone prepared by smoothing and the like for display purposes. Obviously many examples could be cited; I restrict myself to just one which has recently been published, and which furnishes a particularly striking parallel, namely an inscription from *Ḫirbet el-Mudēyine* in Jordan.[24] From the careful description of this Moabite inscription, we learn that the roughly triangular stone on which it was inscribed was prepared in advance as a writing surface "by scratching and smoothing with a sharp instrument" (cited from the English abstract). The inscription is complete, Weigl argues convincingly, with its final two letters on the reverse. It comprises three words (word dividers are used), and begins with a *lāmed*, so making it presumably some kind of dedicatory inscription. The meaning remains obscure, however, and the first word (*lḥnm*), which must be a name (preceded by ל), is unknown. The scribal quality is poor, though generally clear. While not wishing to overpress the parallels, it is clear that there are similarities with my suggested understanding of our Hebrew text in that I have argued that גליון is also a stone whose surface has been prepared, that it too was inscribed in a probably simple manner (see below on בחרט אנוש), and that it too begins with a *lāmed* (admittedly not quite dedicatory, however, though equally formulaic) followed by a peculiar name.

---

23   D. R. Hillers and E. Cussini, *Palmyrene Aramaic Texts* (Baltimore, Md.: Johns Hopkins University Press, 1996), 60 and 353; see previously *CIS* 2/3, §3913, 1 (lines 9–10) (p. 46).

24   M. Weigl, "Eine Inschrift aus Silo 4 in *Ḫirbet el-Mudēyine* (*Wādī eṭ-Ṭemed*, Jordanien)," *ZDPV* 122 (2006): 31–45 and pls. 10–11.

On this approach, the word should be distinguished from that which occurs in Isa 3:23. In my discussion of that verse elsewhere,[25] I proposed that it should be compared with Akkadian *gulēnu/gulīnu/gulānu*, "over-garment" of some kind.[26] Furthermore, noting the peculiarity that in both passages the word חרט also occurs in close proximity, I speculated that at 3:23 the Masoretes might possibly have been influenced to vocalize the word there in the same way as here, whereas a more likely original would have been גְּלִינִים. Even if this last suggestion goes one step too far, the fact remains that the two separate Akkadian cognates indicate that at worst we are dealing with homonyms here with meanings that would hardly allow for confusion.[27]

I turn secondly, then, to a consideration of the writing implement that Isaiah is told to use. בחרט אנוש, "with the stylus of a man," is an uncertain expression, though one for which no textual evidence suggests emendation. 1QIsaᵃ agrees with MT, though the ב was added above the line as a correction; LXX (γραφίδι ἀνθρώπου), Vulgate (*stilo hominis*) and Peshitta (ܟܬܒܐ ܕܐܢܫܐ) all follow MT exactly, and Targum (כתב מפרש), though paraphrasing, seems to have interpreted the phrase in the same way as many more recent commentators, as we shall see.

חרט, "stylus," is itself rare, though its meaning is not generally questioned. It occurs only once elsewhere in MT, at Exod 32:4, as the instrument with which Aaron fashioned gold into the golden calf. On this showing, some tool suitable for working with hard materials would clearly be intended. Some commentators, however, here emend the vocalization to חָרֶט, "bag/purse" (a suggestion evidently contemplated, even if understandably rejected, already by Rashi),[28] and this has been much discussed.[29] It is more likely, however, that even if this

---

25 H. G. M. Williamson, *A Critical and Exegetical Commentary on Isaiah 1–27*, vol. 1: *Commentary on Isaiah 1–5* (ICC; London: T&T Clark, 2006), 282–83.

26 *CAD* G, 127; *CDA* 96; cf. *BHS*.

27 Perhaps we should also note at this point the tentative suggestion of J. E. Hoch, *Semitic Words in Egyptian: Texts of the New Kingdom and Third Intermediate Period* (Princeton: Princeton University Press, 1994), 293–94, that Egyptian *gillā* might derive from גליון. It means "end of papyrus, blank margin," which has some parallels in post-Biblical Hebrew. However, this is too uncertain to use as the basis for an etymological argument that it derives from *glh* (as Hoch assumes in common with many others).

28 J. J. Petuchowski, "Nochmals 'Zur Anfertigung des "goldenen Kalbes,"'" *VT* 10 (1960): 74.

29 For a brief survey with bibliography, see J. I. Durham, *Exodus* (WBC 3; Waco: Word Books, 1987), 420; S. Schroer, *In Israel gab es Bilder: Nachrichten von darstellender Kunst*

approach is correct (something which need not be decided here), the vocalization need not be changed; as Gevirtz has shown, a plural חריטים could equally well have a singular חֶרֶט (compare פסילים/פסל, for instance). It appears, therefore, that the occurrence in Isa 8:1 on the one hand and those in 2 Kgs 5:23 and Isa 3:22 on the other hand are homonyms (and Gevirtz regards the one, with its plural in 2 Kgs 5:23 and Isa 3:22, as referring to a garment rather than a bag or purse).[30] Moreover, the sense at Exod 32:4 is disputed, as we have seen, so that there remains no other biblical evidence on which we can securely rely for determining the sense of our occurrence.

Early cognate evidence[31] provides little firm help (though note one attestation of *ḥrṭyt* in Phoenician which is usually thought to mean "sculptures" or the like),[32] but the reception tradition with regard to this word in Jewish sources seems so strong and unanimous as hardly to allow of doubt. As already noted, the versions give a consistent line of interpretation. In Hebrew we may note the occurrence of the word at 1QM XII, 3 (בחרט חיים),[33] while in 1QHᵃ I, 24 we find the expression חרת זכרון . . . חקוק. חרת here is usually identified with חרט, and given that it follows the root חקק, it can hardly mean anything other than "stylus" or the like;[34] Holm-Nielsen's "engraven . . . with the ink of remembrance"[35] makes no sense. It should further be noted that at Exod 32:16 we have חרות, "engraven." Older suggestions that this should be emended to חרוש have been subsequently discounted by the occurrence of this word in Sir 45:11,[36] where the reference is explicitly

im Alten Testament (OBO 74; Fribourg, Switzerland: Universitätsverlag Freiburg, Schweiz; Göttingen: Vandenhoeck & Ruprecht, 1987), 85–88.

30 S. Gevirtz, "חֶרֶט, in the Manufacture of the Golden Calf," Bib 65 (1984): 377–81, taking issue especially with the influential article of M. Noth, "Zur Anfertigung des 'Goldenen Kalbes,'" VT 9 (1959): 419–22. Gevirtz is followed in this respect by Schroer, In Israel gab es Bilder, 87.

31 For later evidence, see Tigre *haraṭäṭa*, "to scratch," according to W. Leslau, Ethiopic and South Arabic Contributions to the Hebrew Lexicon (University of California Publications in Semitic Philology 20; Berkeley, Calif.: University of California Press, 1958), 22.

32 Cf. DNWSI 1:404; KAI, §81.2.

33 On this, see the remarks by J. Carmignac, "Précisions apportées au vocabulaire de l'hébreu biblique par la guerre des fils de lumière contre les fils de ténèbres," VT 5 (1955): 345–65 (353).

34 For discussion, see M. Delcor, Les Hymnes de Qumran (Hodayot) (Paris: Letouzey & Ané, 1962), 87. He observes how this takes its natural place in developing ideas about heavenly records in late-biblical and post-biblical times.

35 S. Holm-Nielsen, Hodayot: Psalms from Qumran (ATDan 2; Aarhus: Universitetsforlaget, 1960), 18 and 25.

36 See P. C. Beentjes, The Book of Ben Sira in Hebrew (VTSup 68; Leiden: Brill, 1997), 80.

to engraving on stone, and quite frequently in the Dead Sea Scrolls.[37] It is more likely an earlier Aramaic form of the verb which evidently came to be accepted into Hebrew in its own right, and the evidence of 1QHᵃ suggests that the nominal form could then popularly be confused with the similar חרט.

It seems, then, that the sense of חרט as "stylus" was commonly accepted in antiquity. Quite how it is linked to עט is uncertain; the latter is usually rendered "pen,"[38] and this seems certainly to be the required meaning when it is associated with a scribe (Jer 8:8; Ps 45:2). In Jer 17:1 and Job 19:24 it is used metaphorically for a "pen of iron"; presumably the fact that this has to be spelt out, so to speak, implies that usually it was not such a hard object. So far as it goes, this all fits well with the conclusion that חרט refers to some sort of engraving tool. This, then, justifies the limiting of possibilities for the meaning of גליון, as argued above.

More uncertain is the use here of אנוש. While the context suggests that the aim is to say that the inscription will be clear and public, as in the case of the differently-worded Hab 2:2, it is not agreed how it could mean that. Many commentators compare אמת איש (Deut 3:11), which means "an ordinary cubit" as opposed to a giant's, and שבט אנשים (2 Sam 7:14), which means "a human, i.e., an ordinary, rod" as opposed to God's. From this Driver proposed that there is a contrast in our verse between a professional scribe, who would use a special stylus, and Isaiah, who would have used any common instrument with which one might scratch some letters.[39] Equally speculative was Lowth's observation, based on the fact that חריט occurs in Isa 3:22; he took this to mean "crisping pin" and so proposed that in our verse there was a concern to distinguish the ordinary workman's instrument from the pin used by women.[40]

More normally, though, following the Targum, the suggestion has been that the phrase is a metonymy whereby the instrument takes the place of the product so that an ordinary stylus refers to ordinary writing (cf. the English use of "hand"), perhaps (though not necessarily) with reference to the common alphabet as opposed to some form of more esoteric writing system; thus "in common characters," RSV; "in common writing," NEB.[41] The problem with this view is not only lack of

---

37 For references, see conveniently *DCH* 3:325.

38 Cf. Driver, *Semitic Writing*, 85–86 and 241.

39 Driver, *Semitic Writing*, 84–85.

40 Lowth, *Isaiah*, 91.

41 See, for instance, Gesenius, *Jesaia*, 325–26; F. Hitzig, *Der Prophet Jesaja* (Heidelberg: Winter, 1833), 95; A. Knobel, *Der Prophet Jesaia* (3d ed.; KEHAT 5; Leipzig: Hirzel,

evidence for such distinctions in either type of stylus or script in such a
context, but more particularly the failure to explain the choice of the
word אנוש as opposed to איש, as the parallels adduced would lead one
to suppose. Although this difficulty is often mentioned, I am not aware
of any attempt to explain it;[42] most commentators who support this line
do so with either an explicit or a tacit acknowledgment that it is *faute de
mieux*.

Before returning to the current vocalization, note should be taken of
a popular alternative.[43] So far as I can determine, it was Gressmann
who first proposed vocalizing אָנוּשׁ. This, however, was in a terse comment at the end of a footnote on some other topic: "Übrigens ist חרט
אָנוּשׁ *der 'härte' Griffel* zu lesen,"[44] and he offered no justification for his
rendering. Talmage guessed that "[a]pparently, he transferred the word
'hard' from the sense expressed in the phrase 'a hard (severe) illness
(*ānuš*)' to that expressed in the phrase 'a hard metal.'"[45] Galling followed him without further discussion, though with the suggestion that
it meant "unauslöschlich" (indelible).[46] While these proposals give
good sense in the context, there is no linguistic justification for the rendering. Talmage, therefore, proposed that, more in line with Akkadian
(*enēšu*) and Arabic (*ʾanuṯa*) cognates that mean "be weak," the word
here referred to "a broad nibbed [*sic*], flexible pen," capable of making
the expected broad strokes of the writing envisaged here, גליון being
papyrus, in his opinion. Unfortunately, גליון does not mean papyrus, as
we have seen, and חרט, which Talmage initially agrees means "stylus,"
cannot suddenly be transformed into a pen. What the justification is for
it being broad is nowhere explained.[47]

1861), 64; Delitzsch, *Commentar*, 151 = ET *Commentary*, 219; K. Marti, *Das Buch Jesaja*
(KHC 10; Tübingen: Mohr, 1900), 82; G. B. Gray, *A Critical and Exegetical Commentary
on the Book of Isaiah I–XXVII* (ICC; Edinburgh: T&T Clark, 1912), 142–43 (with hesitation).

42   A. B. Ehrlich's suggestion (*Randglossen zur Hebräischen Bibel* [7 vols.; Leipzig: J. C.
     Hinrichs, 1908–1918], 4:32), that it means that the individual letters that make up the
     inscription should be the size (height?) of a human being hardly deserves serious
     consideration.

43   I ignore as too remote to be plausible the brief suggestion that a differently vowelled
     form of the word was originally a cognate of Ugaritic *unṯ*, "obligation, servitude,
     tax," and that the present phrase therefore means "Griffel der Last (= ein Griffel der
     Lästiges aufschreibt)"; cf. O. Loretz, "Zu Ug. *unṯ* und He. *ʾn(w)š*," *UF* 8 (1976): 449.

44   H. Gressmann, *Der Messias* (FRLANT 43; Göttingen: Vandenhoeck & Ruprecht,
     1929), 239 n. 1.

45   F. Talmage, "חרט אנוש in Isaiah 8:1," *HTR* 60 (1967): 465–68 (467 n. 9).

46   Galling, "Ein Stück judäischen Bodenrechts," followed by H. Donner, *Israel unter den
     Völkern* (VTSup 11; Leiden: Brill, 1964), 20.

47   For a different approach that seems to come close to Talmage's solution, see K. van
     der Toorn, *Scribal Culture and the Making of the Hebrew Bible* (Cambridge, Mass.:

An alternative explanation of the emended vocalization has been put forward by Wildberger.[48] He draws attention to the phrase בחרט חיים in 1QM XII, 3, already noted above, and on the basis of the association of אנש with weakness/sickness, he suggests that the two phrases should be seen as opposites: as a חרט חיים is a "life-giving stylus," so a חרט אֱנוֹשׁ is a stylus that brings disaster. Despite the fact that this suggestion has been adopted by a number of commentators since,[49] it is implausible. אֱנוֹשׁ does not seem to be an appropriate antonym for חיים; מות might be expected, and in any case the shift from "sick" to "disaster" is not obvious. More significantly, however, the whole notion that the child's name is doom-bearing is rhetorically misplaced; the oracle was clearly intended, as the wider context shows, to be of encouragement to its audience, just as the inscription was to its readers, and although admittedly this would be to the severe loss of the invading coalition it would be inappropriate to focus on that in this introductory statement.[50]

It seems, therefore, that we should keep to the Masoretic vocalization and inquire if there is an alternative explanation. A suggestion that deserves further development was essentially advanced already by Kimchi. Observing that Isaiah received God's message in a vision, he was commanded to write it in reality, in this human world. The minority of more recent scholars who have adopted an approach which at any rate comes close to this have contrasted the phrase with מכתב אלהים (Exod 32:16). Of course, these cannot be directly contrasted, as otherwise we should expect מכתב in our verse as well, but there are perhaps

Harvard University Press, 2007), 336 n.13. Unfortunately, the logic of his argument at this point escapes me entirely: "The expression for 'brush' is ḥereṭ ʾĕnôš: ḥereṭ means 'stylus,' ʾĕnôš stands for 'weak, soft'; taken together, the expression refers to a brush of the type used on occasion by Egyptian scribes."

48 H. Wildberger, Jesaja, I, Jesaja 1–12 (BKAT 10/1; 2d ed.; Neukirchen-Vluyn: Neukirchener Verlag, 1980), 312 = ET Isaiah 1–12: A Commentary (CC; Minneapolis, Minn.: Fortress, 1991), 331–32.

49 E.g., O. Kaiser, Das Buch des Propheten Jesaja, Kapitel 1–12 (5th ed.; ATD 17; Göttingen: Vandenhoeck & Ruprecht, 1981), 174 = ET Isaiah 1–12: A Commentary (2d ed.; OTL; London: SCM, 1983), 178; W. Dietrich, Jesaja und die Politik (BEvT 74; Munich: Chr. Kaiser, 1976), 90–91.

50 J. Blenkinsopp, Isaiah 1–39: A New Translation with Introduction and Commentary (AB 19; New York: Doubleday, 2000), 237, goes so far as to comment that Wildberger's proposal "makes no sense in the context." The suggestion of J. Glück, "Paronomasia in Biblical Literature," Semitics 1 (1970): 50–78 (53), that this is an "equivocal pun" (a pun where "one or more of the multiple meanings conveyed or implied by a word in the phrase may suit or change the context") seems to rest mistakenly on a confusion of completely distinct lexemes as though they were a single lexeme with multiple meanings. He thus incorrectly states that אנוש has the following "common meanings": "usual, human, fatal."

other ways of supporting this general approach. Stade, for instance, proposed that there were pre-exilic notions of divine writing which were the predecessors of such later passages as God's secret writing in Daniel 5 and the notion which became popular later on of God having heavenly books.[51] What has not been previously brought into the discussion, however, is a study of the use of אנוש elsewhere, nor of the probable original literary context of the present passage. On the latter point, I take the view which is shared by a number of other recent studies that in what was probably Isaiah's own original composition, this paragraph followed immediately after 6:11.[52] It was therefore originally a direct continuation of the description of the scene in the divine council. Although already in v. 2 the setting moves away from that scene, so that we should probably envisage some sort of break before 8:1, the notion that Isaiah received his commission in such a visionary context is from a contextual point of view by no means so remote as Kimchi's initial proposal might appear.

In this context, I believe that the choice of the word אנוש also becomes more intelligible than has previously been realized. A survey of all its uses in the Hebrew Bible demonstrates that it has a far more restricted range of application than might initially be supposed.[53] With the exception of the unique בן־אנוש in Ps 144:3, it is always a collective, it never occurs in the plural or has the definite article, and it always occurs in poetry.[54] Furthermore, in the majority of occurrences the focus is on humanity's weakness, insignificance or mortality in comparison with the divine. The word's distribution is also distinctive, for it occurs 12 times in the Psalms, 18 times in Job, and 8 times in Isaiah; beyond that there are just single occurrences in Deuteronomy, Jeremiah, and Chronicles. Our present verse is the only occurrence in what is now certainly prose, and it may also be the only, or at least only one of a very few examples of, a pre-exilic occurrence.

---

51   B. Stade, "Zu Jes. 3,1.17.24. 5,1. 8,1f.12–14.16. 9,7–20. 10,26," *ZAW* 26 (1906): 129–41 (135–36).

52   See provisionally H. G. M. Williamson, *Variations on a Theme: King, Messiah and Servant in the Book of Isaiah* (Carlisle: Paternoster, 1998), 73–100. I hope to justify this more fully in the forthcoming second volume of my ICC commentary. Note especially that, as a third-person narrative, chapter 7 must have been added later to the original first-person narrative in chapters 6 and 8.

53   See the presentations by F. Maass, "אֱנוֹשׁ," *ThWAT* 1, cols. 373–75 (= *TDOT* 1:345–48), and especially by C. Westermann, *THAT*, "אָדָם *ʾādām* Mensch," 1, cols. 41–57 (= *TLOT* 1:31–42).

54   2 Chr 14:10 is only an apparent exception to this last point. The word occurs there in the course of a prayer by King Asa. The prayer has significant elements of parallelism within it, so that it is at the least imitative of liturgical poetry.

I suggest that these data strongly reinforce the proposal that the use of אנוש contrasts with God rather than with some other human, such as a professional specialist. Furthermore, if our passage originally followed 6:11, it is not impossible that in its earliest form it too was also poetic or at the least influenced by poetic convention. On that possibility it is of interest to note that it was preceded by a line in which humanity's frailty is very much in view, and indeed the occurrence there of אדם is noteworthy given the frequency with which אדם and אנוש occur in parallelism elsewhere. The occurrence of חרט rather than מכתב is, of course, determined entirely by the dictates of the context and so cannot be held against this line of interpretation. I conclude that, although the matter cannot be regarded as certain, the evidence for retaining MT is text-critically strongest and that sense can be made of it, and that its unusual choice of vocabulary can be understood once its earliest literary setting is taken into account. A rendering such as "with a human stylus" is not perfect, because it might be thought to contrast with the possibility that Isaiah could have used a "divine" stylus, but that is not the point. Rather, the divine command is concerned to stress that Isaiah should write the name in a very normal and visible manner. That emphasis continues in the following verses as well.

In this article I have tried to add further justification for the commonest, though not universally accepted, meaning of חרט, to explain the rather unusual use here of אנוש without the need for emendation, and to offer a new etymology and meaning of גליון. In a verse so full of difficulties, no solution can be regarded as certain, but I hope at least that the following rendering makes good sense in an eighth century BCE context and that it does linguistic and contextual justice to the text:[55] "And the Lord said to me, 'Take a large block of dressed stone and write on it with a human stylus, "Belonging to Maher-shalal-hash-baz."'"

55　Discussion of the meaning and significance of the words inscribed will have to be undertaken on another occasion.

"And he shall hear a rumour . . ."

(Isaiah 37:7; 2 Kings 19:7)

JAMES KINNIER WILSON

The concern of this article is to investigate what happened outside the gates of Jerusalem in the year 701 BC, that year, as so often recalled in the poetic legend that it inspired, when "the Assyrian came down like the wolf on the fold."[1] Ask any schoolboy, at least from earlier days, as to what happened at that time and the answer received will be quite definite: the Angel of the Lord went out at night and smote the Assyrian army in their thousands, "and when they rose up in the morning, behold, they were all dead men" (Isa 37:36; 2 Kgs 19:35).

From this point on, and necessarily so, the matter of our search will be serious. The truth of the event is at stake, and history if at all possible must be accurately served. Has this already happened with the translation of the NEB, "when morning dawned, they all lay dead"? The rendering, indeed, makes perfect sense, but one could question whether it is what the Hebrew text of 2 Kgs 19:35 is actually saying.

Let us turn for a moment to Assyria, where we have the other side of the picture. The Annals of Sennacherib are very complete and have been so for a long time. Is the year in question there represented? Yes, and we learn that the Assyrian army at that time invested, and received the booty of, 46 towns and villages in the area, and certain details of this are recorded. And Jerusalem? Well, in the familiar words, Sennacherib informs us that he enclosed Hezekiah (*Ha-za-qi-ia-ú*) in Jerusalem "like a bird in a cage" —but no battle details follow, we are not told why the siege was lifted, nor indeed are we given any other details (apart from a booty list) as to what eventually transpired. One might almost say that the silence is deafening.[2]

---

1   Lord Byron, "The Destruction of Sennacherib," in idem, *The Complete Works* (13 vols.; Newcastle-upon-Tyne: Cambridge Scholars Publishing, 2009), 3:315–16 (315).

2   Translations of the accounts of the whole campaign—the third in the king's reign, which, with the notice of Isa 36:1 and 2 Kgs 18:13, establishes the date—include A. Leo Oppenheim in *ANET*, 287–88; R. Borger in *TUAT*, 1/4, 388–91; and R. Borger in

Perhaps it should be mentioned that no account of the Siege of Jerusalem is found in Van De Mieroop's history of the Ancient Near East,[3] but this omission is most generously explained as lying outside the author's main interest, which concerns the movements and identities of the peoples studied. Amélie Kuhrt, however, carefully presents the two sides of the matter and accepts the traditional view that "a fatal plague" broke out among the Assyrian army during the siege.[4]

This last sentence is now my cue to enter the "plague" discussion. Indeed, I already joined the discussion when, at a biblical symposium some years ago, I was invited to read a paper on "Medicine in the Land and Times of the Old Testament."[5] The first conclusion that was reached suggested that, although opinion is not unanimous, there is nevertheless a strong case for taking the pestilence described in 1 Samuel 5 and 6 which struck the cities of Philistia about the year 1040 BC as indeed a pandemic of bubonic plague.

The case is essentially threefold. First, there is mention (1 Sam 5:6) of rats "ravaging the land" (LXX only), although their part in the outbreak seems not to have been understood.[6] Secondly, all five cities of the Philistines were involved in the plague (cf. 1 Sam 6:4, 17), so that its scale may be gauged accordingly. And, thirdly, the much featured ʿŏpālîm, not "tumours" and improbably "haemorrhoids,"[7] are taken to be those buboes, actually swollen lymphatic glands, which give the disease its distinctive name. The bubo does not of itself endanger life, so that the observation of 1 Sam 5:12, "Even those who did not die were plagued with the buboes," would be correct accordingly.

But it was considered, and I still consider, that it was not an outbreak of plague that forced Sennacherib and his army to leave the outskirts of Jerusalem in the year 701 BC. This explanation is not realistic and not medically sound. Even when the disease becomes pneumonic

---

TGI (2d ed., 1968; 3d ed., 1979), 67–69 (§39). At the time of writing, the contribution that will appear in the RIMA Project (that is, The Royal Inscriptions of Mesopotamia: Assyrian Periods), edited by Kirk Grayson and published by the University of Toronto Press, is still awaited.

3   M. Van De Mieroop, *A History of the Ancient Near East, ca. 3000–323 BC* (Blackwell History of the Ancient World; Oxford: Blackwell, 2004).

4   Amélie Kuhrt, *The Ancient Near East c. 3000–330 BC* (2 vols.; London: Routledge, 1995), 2:478, 512.

5   J. V. Kinnier Wilson, "Medicine in the Land and Times of the Old Testament," in *Studies in the Period of David and Solomon and Other Essays* (ed. Tomoo Ishida; Tokyo: Yamakawa-Shuppansha, 1982), 337–65.

6   Cf., interestingly, J. B. Geyer, "Mice and Rites in 1 Samuel V–VI," *VT* 31 (1981): 293–304.

7   For this earlier opinion see particularly G. R. Driver, "The Plague of the Philistines (1 Samuel v, 6–vi, 16)," *JRAS* 1950, 50–52.

and so spreads quickly by droplet infection, it cannot overtake a people in one night. I cite the following from an authoritative source, Sir Philip Manson-Bahr's *Synopsis of Tropical Medicine*, under "Pneumonic plague":

> Myriads of *P. pestis* expectorated in sputum; inhalation pneumonia; profuse, watery, blood-tinged sputum. Rigor, headache, malaise, intense prostration, cough, dyspnoea, delirium, stupor, râles, rhonchi. Death on 4th or 5th day.[8]

Believing, therefore, that we are on the wrong track, this paper takes a new direction altogether.

And I begin by saying that, in such ancient Semitic languages as I presume to know, there is not always a clear distinction between a statement of fact and a person's thought about that fact. To be sure, there are ways of expressing thought and, indeed, verbs "to think," but additionally such meaning may be expressed by the context alone.

Thus in the translation of the NEB Eccl 2:12b, transposed after v. 18, reads:

> "What sort of a man will he be who succeeds me,
> who inherits what others have acquired?"

The sentence, however, is not a statement of fact; it represents the writer's reflections about his future and requires an additional "(I thought)" before it.

In Song 5:3, there is, in the evening, a knocking at the door of our sleeping heroine, and amusingly (?) she "says to herself," or "thinks," (but the words are not in the text):

> "I have taken off my coat: must I put it on again?
> I have washed my feet: must I get them dirty again?"

In Akkadian, in the famous story of the Tale of the Poor Man of Nippur, lines 70–71 read in O. R. Gurney's translation:

> Gimil-Ninurta set his face towards the palace of the King, (thinking),
> "On the orders of the King, prince and governor give fair judgement."[9]

Similarly, in the Middle-Assyrian version of the legend of Etana, the King is wondering how he can feed the starving eagle cast so unceremoniously into the pit by the angry serpent. Line 6 of the text concerned reads:

---

8   Philip Manson-Bahr, *Synopsis of Tropical Medicine* (2d ed.; London: Cassell, 1952), 81. In the given description *"P."* stands for *Pasteurella*, so named after the French bacteriologist, Louis Pasteur (1822–1895).

9   O. R. Gurney, "The Sultantepe Tablets, 5: The Tale of the Poor Man of Nippur," *AnSt* 6 (1956): 145–64 (153).

[p]u-ut burti um-de-la-a uṭṭa[ta . . .]
(He thought): ["The fr]ont of the pit is covered with (wild) barl[ey grain]!"[10]

It is hoped that these, and other examples of which the reader will surely know, may be sufficient to make the point that, at least in literary writing, that which is believed or thought may not necessarily be indicated as such.

So why is this relevant to the presence of Sennacherib at the gates of Jerusalem? It is because in the light of it we may now translate 2 Kgs 19:35 (cf. Isa 37:36) as:

> And that night the Angel of the Lord went out and smote (or, struck) the 185,000 men of the Assyrian camp (into thinking, or, with the thought) that, should they [not] arise and go by the early morning, they would all be dead.

The following verse, if the probable time aspect may be inserted in parenthesis, would then read: "So (the same night) Sennacherib, king of Assyria, departed and returned to his residence at Nineveh."

Our reconstruction, however, is not quite ended, for both Isa 37:7 and 2 Kgs 19:7 carry a text which might seem to differ from the tradition as given above. It reads:

> (Be not afraid . . .) for, behold, I (the LORD) will send a spirit (?) (rûaḥ) unto him, and he shall hear a rumour, and return to his own land.

But, in fact, one could believe that these two verses bring everything together, that it was even by the means of a rumour, spreading like wildfire through the Assyrian camp, that the Angel of the Lord—as it was understood at the time—fulfilled his divine mission.

And what was the rumour, or what was it based on? It is tempting to supply this element of the night's alarm with reference to Herodotus. He writes of the sighting at the time of field mice (or rats?) gnawing the Assyrian bow-strings and shield straps,[11] and, whatever else may be said of this, it is well known that "ominous" happenings of all kinds formed a central part of Babylonian and Assyrian superstition.

May I say in conclusion, that it has been a privilege to write this brief paper in honour of a scholar whose Assyriological interests are widely known and which have at times been personally shared.

---

10   Cf. James Kinnier Wilson, *Studia Etanaica: New Texts and Discussions* (AOAT 338; Münster: Ugarit-Verlag, 2007), 21.

11   Herodotus, *Histories* 2.141.

About Third Isaiah . . .*

John Goldingay

Dear Graham,

I was enthusiastically grateful to you for recovering from someone's attic a copy of the hard-to-locate manuscript of the commentary
on Isaiah 40–55 for the ICC, as one of your early achievements as editor, and I was grateful again for the painstaking and careful way you
then worked through the manuscript, spotting errors and asking questions, yet keen (as you put it) not to try to turn it into the commentary
you yourself would have written. And now I am immersed in Isaiah
56–66 and wondering how you would write on these chapters. There
are a number of ways of approaching them, about which I have come
to some tentative positions. Of course some reflect predilections with
which I came to the work, but so far they have not been disconfirmed
by it.

I. Reading in Light of the Material's Redaction

First, Isaiah 56–66 is more profitably read as we have it than in light of
attempts to trace the process whereby it came into existence.

When Duhm definitively asserted the distinction between Isaiah
40–55 and 56–66, he located this "Third Isaiah" a century after the
Second, in the time of Ezra and Nehemiah.[1] Most subsequent commentators have agreed that chapters 56–66 are of separate origin from chapters 40–55, but some have located them in the early Persian period
rather than the time of Ezra and Nehemiah. Most have reckoned that
the material did not come from a single "Third Isaiah" but from a
number of authors, perhaps working in the early Persian period, perhaps over the century between that and the time of Ezra and Nehe-

---

* An earlier, longer version of the paper, read to the Old Testament Colloquium at
   Fuller Theological Seminary, is at http://documents.fuller.edu/sot/faculty/goldingay.
1 B. Duhm, *Das Buch Jesaia* (HKAT 3/1; Göttingen: Vandenhoeck & Ruprecht, 1892; 2d
   ed. 1902), e.g., v–xix, 379–80.

miah, perhaps some centuries going back into the monarchic period and/or on into the Greek period. But no consensus on their origin has emerged.

In a number of studies of the chapters, a motif recurs. One could call it a *Gattung* or form. In fact it is a subset of a salvation oracle. It has three elements:

(1) A lament: there is an impasse over dating these chapters.
(2) A prophetic testimony: but the key to understanding has now been revealed to me.
(3) An oracle: so here is the solution to the impasse.

The form appears in classic form in Hanson's *The Dawn of Apocalyptic*.[2] But Hanson's oracle has not generally been received with faith by subsequent scholars. Strawn thus takes up the form once more. He, too, notes that "the historical and linguistic arguments regarding Trito-Isaiah are at something of an impasse" and that "a way forward . . . does not seem to be forthcoming,"[3] as Hanson had said thirty years previously; his suggestion is to seek further external data. Blenkinsopp works with a broken version of the form, going straight from (1) to (3). He, too, notes that we lack the information on whose basis we can date the process of the chapters' composition, so that there are practically as many hypotheses regarding this process as there are commentators.[4] But then, surprisingly, he goes on to divide up and date the material, as if he has an oracle.

It is a plausible thesis that Isaiah 56–66 is a compilation of material issuing from a number of prophets and preachers that in various ways takes forward agenda and perspectives expressed in Isaiah 40–55 and elsewhere, and that accumulated gradually, at least over some decades at the beginning of the Persian period. But it is merely plausible; we do not know if it is true. Beyond seeing the chapters against the background of the Second Temple, we cannot relate them to particular periods. Whereas Childs's comment that Isaiah 40–55 have lost "their original historical particularity" is strange, given that they explicitly

---

2   P. D. Hanson, *The Dawn of Apocalyptic* (Philadelphia, Pa.: Fortress, 1975), e.g., 32–46; his commentary *Isaiah 40–66* (IBC; Louisville, Ky.: John Knox, 1995) continues to take the same positions, e.g., 191–92.

3   Brent A. Strawn, "'A World under Control,'" in *Approaching Yehud: New Approaches to the Study of the Persian Period* (ed. Jon L. Berquist; SemeiaSt 50; Atlanta, Ga.: Society of Biblical Literature, 2007), 85–116 (86, 87).

4   Joseph Blenkinsopp, *Isaiah 56–66* (AB 19B; New York: Doubleday, 2003), 42.

refer to Babylon and Cyrus, his comment does apply to Isaiah 56–66.[5] Seeking to set these prophecies in a more specific historical context involves working against the grain of the material, which declines to provide the information that would make this possible. The situation is similar to attempts to date psalms. This is not to say it is illegitimate to attempt to date the material. If we want to write the history of the Second Temple period, we will need a hypothesis regarding this. It does imply that in focusing on dating the material, we are not involved in interpreting Isaiah 56–66 itself. We are not seeking to read this text, but to read behind it, not to read with the text's grain, but against it. Smith observes that "the primary question concerning the majority of commentators" on Isaiah 56–66 "has been whether these chapters should be regarded as the work of one author or of a multiplicity of authors over a greater or lesser period of time."[6] Their primary focus? I cannot immediately think of a more saddening observation about Old Testament study.

If we cannot base an understanding of Isaiah 56–66 on a knowledge of when the material originated, we have to stop at the lament stage in that threefold form, and then ask how we live with the situation in which there is no revelation concerning the material's origin. The trouble is that "we do not know" is a phrase scholars have a hard time bringing to their lips. To utter it is an admission of defeat.

Barton argues that the aim of biblical criticism is to get at the plain meaning of the biblical text.[7] Why, then, is it called criticism? In advocating critical study with students, I usually begin by claiming that critical study originated as critique of the way the church had interpreted scripture, though it did eventually become criticism of scripture itself. Barton's argument helps me nuance that point. Criticism, he contends, takes an open-minded approach to the question what kind of text we are reading at any point. It is concerned with "the recognition of genre in texts and with what follows from this about their possible meaning."[8] But he also notes that criticism often begins from an awareness of difficulties in the text. And in the case of Isaiah 56–66, it is the presence of tensions that has been a stimulus to redaction-critical study: tensions over the relationship between Yhwh's commitment to the

---

5   Brevard S. Childs, *Introduction to the Old Testament as Scripture* (London: SCM; Philadelphia, Pa.: Fortress, 1979), 325–26; even more oddly, Childs suggests there are more historical references in Isaiah 56–66 than in Isaiah 40–55.

6   P. A. Smith, *Rhetoric and Redaction in Trito-Isaiah* (VTSup 62; Leiden: Brill, 1995), 1.

7   John Barton, *The Nature of Biblical Criticism* (Louisville, Ky.: Westminster John Knox, 2007), 3.

8   Barton, *The Nature of Biblical Criticism*, 5.

Jerusalem community and Yhwh's concern for the nations, between the future's dependence on Yhwh's promises being fulfilled and its dependence on the community's obedience, between the importance of religious observances such as the Sabbath and the importance of relieving the needy.

Redaction-critical study offers a form of explanation of such tensions. Except that it does not succeed. One reason is the fact that there are as many redaction-critical theories as there are redaction-critics, because by the same act of concealment whereby it hides its historical background, the material hides the evidence that would enable us to trace the process whereby it came into existence. It thereby invites us to read it as it stands with its tensions, not to reckon that we "solve" the "problem" of the tensions by locating them in different contexts or attributing them to different groups. It is sometimes said that reading the text without attending to the process whereby it reached the form that we have produces flat readings. But one can argue the opposite: "obvious tensions" in a document "can be easily solved by multiplying authors and life situations in which they wrote," but this generates a historical reconstruction "containing a string of flat positions. It is religiously and intellectually more profitable to explore the rich relief of the existent text."[9] Although redactional questions have been a major focus in study of Isaiah 56–66, this study has been confined to the *process* of redaction. It has not been so interested in the text that resulted from the process. Yet this text does have the virtue of existing, whereas all the redaction-critical hypotheses are simply that—hypotheses. In the case of Isaiah 56–66, the indications that the text has been neatly arranged (it is not merely an anthology) make it particularly natural to ask after the significance of this eventual text with its neat arrangement.

It also invites us to read the material in the order in which the text itself unfolds.[10] Smith (for instance) reads the material in light of the order in which it was (perhaps) composed rather than in the order in which the text presents itself. So 56:1–8 "takes up" terms and themes

---

9   Miroslav Volf, "Johannine Dualism and Contemporary Pluralism," in *The Gospel of John and Christian Theology* (ed. Richard Bauckham and Carl Mosser; Grand Rapids, Mich.: Eerdmans, 2008), 19–50 (21). Volf is referring to John's Gospel, but the point transfers to other works.

10   John D. W. Watts offers an interpretation that deals with the text sequentially, as he treats it as a drama, but his understanding seems arbitrary on both the macro- and the micro-scale. On his account, for instance, in much of Isaiah 56–58 the speaking alternates between "the heavens" and "the earth," and the addressee is the Persian king Darius I (*Isaiah 34–66* [rev. ed.; WBC 25; Nashville, Tenn.: Nelson, 2005], 811–46), but the text gives no indication that speakers alternate or that the heavens and the earth are the speakers or that Darius is the addressee.

from 60:1–63:6 "in order to clarify, or possibly correct" the statements there about the place of proselytes in the new community, while 58:1–59:20 "responds to a question or complaint raised by the people" concerning why Yhwh takes no notice of their fasting and "responds to the complaint by reinterpreting the preaching of TI [Trito-Isaiah] (60:1–63:6) in light of the criteria set out in 56:1–8."[11] As a whole, Isaiah 56–59 functions to prepare for the promises in 60:1–63:6, which come from the preceding two decades, the first years of the Persian period.

Now historically it may be the case that Isaiah 60–62 came first and that 56:1–8 is responding to it, and that 58:1–59:20 is reinterpreting those same chapters. But even if that is so, Isaiah 56–59 comes before Isaiah 60–62. When we reach Isaiah 60–62 we will appropriately consider the relationship of substance between them and what has preceded, but to begin by reading Isaiah 56 and 58–59 in light of Isaiah 60–62 is to put the cart before the horse. There are connections in which there is nothing illegitimate about doing that, but it does not count as reading Isaiah 56–66.

II. Reading in Light of a Sociological Theory

Second, the chapters need to be read in light of their own content rather than in light of a sociological theory.

Redaction-critical approaches characteristically read Isaiah 56–66 in light of conflicts within the Second Temple community. The books of Ezra and Nehemiah make clear that there certainly were such conflicts. Hanson's key for understanding them comes from the sociology of knowledge. He takes from Mannheim the insight that communities commonly include a ruling group who are happy with how things are, and a group who are alienated from power, dissatisfied with how things are, and looking for a future realization of how things should be. Hanson sees Isaiah 60–62 as the dreams of such visionaries, whereas Ezekiel 40–48 is "the blueprint of hierocratic realists or pragmatists."[12] Hanson's analysis also recalls that of Plöger.[13]

---

11 Smith, *Rhetoric and Redaction in Trito-Isaiah*, 59, 101.

12 Hanson, *The Dawn of Apocalyptic*, 71–72 (also 211–20), where he associates this distinction with Karl Mannheim's distinction between "ideology" and "utopia" in his *Ideologie und Utopie* (Bonn: Cohen, 1929); expanded ET, *Ideology and Utopia* (London: Routledge; New York: Harcourt, 1936).

13 Otto Plöger, *Theokratie und Eschatologie* (WMANT 2; Neukirchen-Vluyn: Neukirchener Verlag, 1959; 2d ed., 1962); ET *Theocracy and Eschatology* (Oxford: Blackwell, 1968; Richmond, Va.: John Knox, 1969). A difference is that Hanson works forwards from the exile and Isaiah 40–55, whereas Plöger works backwards from the Antio-

Hanson's contrast between Ezekiel 40–48 and Isaiah 56–66 raises questions; Ezekiel 40–48 is, after all, not exactly a realistic blueprint, and it is part of prophetic tradition. Indeed, any binary understanding of the community seems much too simple.[14] But Hanson is right that Isaiah 56–66 gives significant space to confronting other groups within the community and that this is a major characteristic of Isaiah 56–66 over against Isaiah 40–55. He then sees Isaiah 56–66 as giving a key role to a new form of prophetic address, the "salvation-judgment oracle." He describes this as warning some people of judgment coming on them, and promising deliverance to others;[15] it thus seems more natural to call it a judgment-salvation oracle.

In Hanson's view, chronologically 58:1–12 is the first example. Yet the oracle actually addresses not a group within the community but "my people . . . the household of Jacob." Far from implying a division of the people into wicked and righteous,[16] it implies that the wicked had better become the righteous, and that they can then enjoy Yhwh's deliverance. Hanson does grant that here the dichotomy between the two groups is incomplete;[17] actually, it is non-existent, as he implicitly allows in speaking of the prophecy "leaving the *possibility* of salvation open to the *whole* nation."[18]

The second judgment-salvation oracle, 59:1–20, similarly offers no indication that there are two groups in the community or that its polemic offers a basis for dividing it; the oracle relates to a whole community issue, as is the case when the chapters speak of the community's brokenness (57:14–21).

The third example, 65:1–25, also concerns itself with a "nation," a "people," but then contrasts this "nation" or "people" with "my servants" and sets contrasting destinies before them.[19] It is a plausible

---

chene crisis and Daniel. Plöger considers Isaiah 24–27, Zechariah 12–14, and Joel, though in a preface to the English translation (p. vi) he notes that it would be possible to incorporate Isaiah 56–66 into his account. While Plöger thus anticipates Hanson and recalls Mannheim, Hanson refers to Plöger only once in a footnote (relating to Chronicles and Daniel) and Plöger does not refer to Mannheim or the sociology of knowledge.

14 See, for example, the discussion in Rainer Albertz, *Religionsgeschichte Israels in alttestamentlicher Zeit* (2 vols.; Göttingen: Vandenhoeck & Ruprecht, 1992), esp. 2:461–68; ET *A History of Israelite Religion in the Old Testament Period* (2 vols.; London: SCM; Louisville, Ky.: Westminster John Knox, 1994), esp. 2:437–43.

15 For example, Hanson, *The Dawn of Apocalyptic*, 106–7.

16 Hanson, *The Dawn of Apocalyptic*, 108.

17 Hanson, *The Dawn of Apocalyptic*, 107.

18 Hanson, *The Dawn of Apocalyptic*, 108 (his emphasis).

19 "The servants of Yhwh" has been seen as a key motif in Isaiah 56–66 (cf. Blenkinsopp, *Isaiah 56–66*, 33, and his references), but if it were, it is odd that eight of the ten

view that "my servants" here and in the fourth example (66:1–16) refers to the faithful within the community. And this judgment-salvation oracle does promise judgment and salvation to different groups. But it is not clear that this phenomenon needs interpreting sociologically or positivistically rather than rhetorically. That is, it may still seek to challenge the community as a whole to become a faithful, servant community rather than an apostate one. This possibility may find support in the fact that the last of the judgment-salvation oracles (in Hanson's ordering), 56:9–57:13, includes no indication of the existence of an "alternative community" and mentions only the possibility that the individual who takes refuge with Yhwh "will own the land, will possess my holy mountain." The context here, too, suggests that the warnings to the wicked in 57:19–20 confront the community as a whole rather than presupposing a division within it.[20]

But let us suppose that a division within the community is indeed implicit in the judgment-salvation oracles. What is the nature of this division? According to Hanson's typology, the prophecy critiques the people who control the temple, whose own views appear in Ezekiel 40–48 and in the Torah itself. But the objects of critique in Isaiah 56–66 are people who sacrifice children, seek to make contact with dead family members, worship by means of images, and eat pork and other food forbidden by the Torah (57:5–13; 65:3–4; 66:17).[21] Such practices are attacked, not advocated, by Ezekiel, by the Torah, and earlier by prophets such as Isaiah and Jeremiah. Hanson thus sees the language of these passages as "symbolical" and "hyperbolical." It "*equate[s]* the cult of those attacked with Canaanizing sacrificial practices."[22] Now this is a possible interpretation of the allusive language in 66:3–4, whose point might be that God takes the same view of people who make proper offerings as of people who make forbidden ones.[23] But the openness of the elliptical language there contrasts with that in Isaiah 57 and 65, where there is nothing to point to a metaphorical understanding. Ironically, Hanson notes that Isaiah 56–66 "is ambiguous enough to be amenable to most any hypothesis, given an ample amount of eisegesis."[24]

---

occurrences of the expression occur in the last two chapters (seven in Isaiah 65). There is one in Isa 56:6, referring to foreigners, and one in 63:17, referring to the community as a whole.

20 As Hanson assumes, *The Dawn of Apocalyptic*, 78–79.

21 Much of the detailed interpretation of this critique is difficult, but there is no doubt regarding its central features.

22 Hanson, *The Dawn of Apocalyptic*, 147 (my emphasis).

23 1QIsaᵃ adds the preposition *kāp* to make this point; cf. LXX, Tg., Vulg., also NRSV, TNIV.

24 Hanson, *The Dawn of Apocalyptic*, 32.

Importing an interpretation into the text from his sociological model seems to be what Hanson does.[25]

But let us for a moment grant the possibility that the attacks in Isaiah 57 and 65 are expressed metaphorically. Are there passages where they are expressed literally? Hanson finds one in 66:1–2: "What is this house which you would build for me . . . ? All of these things my hand has made. . . . But upon this one I will look, the humble, who is broken in spirit and trembles at my word."[26] From this passage, he says, "it is clear that chapters 56–66 of Isaiah stem from a group that have no faith in the temple rebuilding program of the dominant priestly party, the Zadokites."[27] The problem with this understanding is its conflict with the relative enthusiasm for the temple running through the rest of Isaiah 56–66: see 56:7; 57:13; 60:7, 13; 64:11; 65:11.[28] But there is no need to infer that 66:1–2 clashes with passages that identify with the temple rebuilding project, since its comment on the relative insignificance of any building for God parallels the one put on Solomon's lips when he is in the very act of dedicating the First Temple. It thus by no means need imply opposition to temple building, only to overestimating it.

In taking conflict within the community as key to understanding Isaiah 56–66, Hanson's understanding parallels Duhm's, except that Duhm saw the conflict as one between the godly and the schismatics in the time of Ezra and Nehemiah.[29] It is an aspect of Duhm's extraordinarily wide and lasting influence on the study of the prophets—perhaps wider, longer-lasting, and less recognized than Julius Wellhausen's influence on the study of the Pentateuch.[30] It is routine and unexceptionable to emphasize that the Second Temple community was divided and that Isaiah 56–66 represents the stance of one of the groups within it. What is puzzling is the suggestion that there is something new in this situation, something new about conflict in the community. Even a cursory reading of 1 and 2 Kings, Isaiah 1–39, Jeremiah, Ezekiel, and other prophets makes clear that it had always been so. The community centered on Jerusalem had always been divided into groups with contrary faith positions that were battling for control of Jerusalem's temple and soul. While conflict is an important reality in the

---

25   Cf. Brooks Schramm, *The Opponents of Third Isaiah* (JSOTSup 193; Sheffield: Sheffield Academic Press, 1995), 88.

26   Hanson's translation, *The Dawn of Apocalyptic*, 164.

27   Hanson, *Isaiah 40–66*, 199.

28   Blenkinsopp, *Isaiah 56–66*, 294.

29   Duhm, *Das Buch Jesaia*, 379.

30   I owe this observation to my student Joseph Henderson.

Second Temple community, there is nothing distinctive about it in this respect.

In understanding Isaiah 56–66, sociological theory, and specifically a concern with conflicts between people identified with priestly thinking and with prophetic thinking, obscures rather than illumines.

III. Reading in Light of the Chapters' Own Form and Nature

Thirdly, and more specifically, the chapters need to be read theologically in light of their chiastic arrangement. Instead of taking redaction-critical or sociological theory as key to understanding Isaiah 56–66, it is appropriate to focus on the form and nature of the chapters themselves.

In what sense is Isaiah 56–66 a work? There is little basis for viewing it as resulting from the activity of a single author, though this does not exclude its exhibiting a coherence and unity (as well as tensions) issuing from a redactional process.[31] And that may be typical of the Old Testament, where there are rather few books that one could discuss in terms of authorial activity.

There is another framework within which one might raise questions about whether Isaiah 56–66 is a work. The scholarly world currently agrees that the development of Isaiah 56–66 should be understood in relation to the development of the book of Isaiah as a whole. Isaiah 56–66 never existed as a self-standing collection. So there is no such thing as "the book of Trito-Isaiah," as these chapters are sometimes called.[32] Even if all eleven chapters come from a single author, they present themselves not as a book but as part of a book. The formal nature of Isaiah 56–66 as part of a larger whole is complemented by the more substantial point that they often take up motifs, issues, and actual verses from Isaiah 1–55.

Yet it has come to be a common view that chapters 56–66 form a chiasm, along the following lines:[33]

---

31 Cf. Blenkinsopp, *Isaiah 56–66*, 37.

32 For example, Claus Westermann, *Das Buch Jesaja: Kapitel 40–66* (ATD 19; Göttingen: Vandenhoeck & Ruprecht, 1966), 245; ET *Isaiah 40–66* (London: SCM; Philadelphia, Pa.: Westminster, 1969), 306; Klaus Koenen, *Ethik und Eschatologie im Tritojesajabuch* (WMANT 62; Neukirchen-Vluyn: Neukirchener Verlag, 1990).

33 For example, P.-E. Bonnard, *Le Second Isaïe: Son disciple et leurs éditeurs: Isaïe 40–66* (EBib; Paris: Gabalda, 1972), 318–19; Rémi Lack, *La symbolique du livre d'Isaïe: Essai sur l'image littéraire comme élément de structuration* (AnBib 59; Rome: Biblical Institute Press, 1973), 125–34.

A. Preface and postscript: the place of foreigners in the service of Yhwh

    56:1–8   66:18–24

    B. Yhwh's challenges concerning the Jerusalem community's life

        56:9–59:8   65:1–66:17

        C. Prayers for Yhwh's forgiveness and restoration

            59:9–15a   63:7–64:11[12]

            D. Visions of Yhwh acting in judgment

                59:15b–21   63:1–6

                E. Visions of Jerusalem restored

                    60   62

                    F. The prophet's call

                        61

While there is room for debate about the details of this understanding, in outline it reflects concrete features of the text and it has been recognized by scholars of varying redaction-critical views. The outline helps illumine the nature of the chapters' message. An account of a prophetic call comes at the centre (F), as it might come at the beginning of a more linear structure. On either side (E) are visions of the restored Jerusalem that repeat in more glorious technicolour the kind of promises that appear in Isaiah 40–55. Outside these are concomitant promises of Yhwh's acting in judgment on the people's oppressors (D). Outside these are prayers that essentially plead with Yhwh to do what those visions portray (C). Outside these are two series of challenges about the community's life in both its social and worship aspects (B). Outside these is a pair of opening and closing brackets (A).

This intricate arrangement suggests that Isaiah 56–66 as a whole is a distinguishable unit that provides a particularly significant interpretive context for each chapter within it. In this respect it parallels other sections of the book such as chapters 1–12, 13–23, and 40–55, which are arranged (in varying ways); they do not comprise simply a series of anthologies.

Its distinctiveness over against those other sections is that only Isaiah 56–66 has a systematically concentric structure. Its rhetorical dynamic, then, contrasts in particular with that of Isaiah 40–55, which works in linear fashion, so that it is a little like a narrative with a plot. One cannot fully understand the significance of (for instance) 41:8–10

without considering 42:1–4, or that of 42:1–4 without considering 42:18–
25, and so on. Earlier passages raise questions that later passages
answer or at least take up again. I argued earlier for a linear reading of
Isaiah 56–66, for reading Isaiah 56 before Isaiah 60. But paradoxically, a
linear reading reveals to readers that while the chapters do first go
somewhere, they then come back again, and this uncovers a key aspect
of their burden. They are like Isaiah 40–55 in that any particular passage needs to be seen in light of the way the whole subsequently
unfolds; but the linear reading reveals that this unfolding is circular
rather than linear.

By its nature, a concentric structure has a different dynamic from a
linear one. It turns out to be doing something more ambiguous than
simply going somewhere. Its second half may indeed take the argument forward, as the second of two cola within a poetic line characteristically goes beyond the first. There will then be some linearity about a
chiasm; it is more like a spiral than a circle. But formally, at least, it
ends up coming back to where it started. And in Isaiah 56–66, this is a
telling indication of the thesis that emerges from the chapters. As their
opening verse announces, they expound two chief convictions, that
Jerusalem needs to face Yhwh's challenges about its life and that Yhwh
is committed to its glorious restoration. But like that opening verse,
they do not establish the relationship between these two convictions.
They simply juxtapose them. They do establish that it is an oversimpli-
fication to say that the vital thing is for Jerusalem to clean up its act,
and that its restoration will then follow. But neither is it the case that
Yhwh's act of restoration will take place irrespective of Jerusalem's
stance in relation to Yhwh.

Such significance in a chiasm emerges when one contrasts it with a
text such as Isaiah 40–55. There are texts that emphasize either divine
action or human action, and it is not then surprising if readers can see
the other emphasis lurking somewhere beneath their surface. Isaiah 40–
55 is such a text.[34] The genius of a chiasm (or is it the cowardice of a
chiasm?) is to avoid deconstruction by being upfront with the two
assertions that stand in tension with each other.

Now Childs opposes the view that the concentric structure of
Isaiah 56–66 is a key to its interpretation,[35] even though this structure is
an aspect of the canonical form of the text, to which Childs is committed to paying attention. Childs's opposition seems to stem from an

34 John Goldingay, "Isaiah xl–lv in the 1990s: Among Other Things, Deconstructing,
Mystifying, Intertextual, Socio-Critical, and Hearer-Involving," *BibInt* 5 (1997): 226–
46.

35 Brevard S. Childs, *Isaiah* (Louisville, Ky.: Westminster John Knox, 2001), 448–49.

ambiguity about the background of the identification of this concentric structure. As far as I have been able to tell, it was Westermann who first suggested the basic insights that led to the perception of it, but he did that in the course of his own attempt to trace the redaction history of the material. It is on account of this that for Childs, interpreting the material in light of its concentric structure yields too much to speculative historical-critical theories.

According to Westermann, chapters 60–62 comprise the *Kern*, the kernel or nucleus of the message of Isaiah 56–66.[36] There are at least three implications of the "nucleus" image, all of which Westermann accepts. The nucleus of something is the originating centre from which it develops. It is the object's control centre; nothing develops in the cell that is not determined by the nucleus.[37] And it is the object's structural centre.

The first implication is that Isaiah 56–66 gradually accumulated around Isaiah 60–62, and that may well be so. Roughly speaking, then, the chiasm reflects the chapters' historical origin. Isaiah 60–62 is the oldest material; 56:1–8 and 66:18–24 are the youngest; the intervening material comes from in between. The third implication, that a nucleus is the structural centre of something, is the one reflected in the concentric structure of the chapters.

But the second implication, that the nucleus or kernel is the control centre, does not hold. Westermann himself sees much of Isaiah 56–57 as preexilic in origin and much of Isaiah 63–64 as exilic, so here the so-called nucleus was attracting foreign material rather than generating material. Other sections see the community as divided into the faithful and the transgressors, and only the former will enjoy Yhwh's act of restoration; such a division does not appear in Isaiah 60–62, so that the so-called nucleus is not generating material but provoking what one might call hostile growth. Passages such as 58:1–12 correspond to Isaiah 60–62 in addressing the whole community but contrast with those chapters in making its restoration conditional on people's response to their challenge; this seems to involve some evolution in a direction that cannot be traced to the nucleus's DNA. Fourth, an oracle of judgment against a foreign nation such as 63:1–6 is "appended to the nucleus itself, chs. 60–62. The intention is perfectly plain; the attitude towards the nations expressed in chs. 60–62 is amended[38] by the addition of 'but thereafter God begins his great battle with them to destroy

---

36   Westermann, *Das Buch Jesaia: Kapitel 40–66*, 237; ET *Isaiah 40–66*, 296.

37   The kernel image has similar implications; a kernel or seed is or contains the embryo from which a plant grows.

38   Westermann's word is *korrigierend*, surely rather stronger.

them!'"[39] All the material that accumulates around chapters 60–62 thus raises questions about it rather than reinforcing the "message of salvation and nothing but salvation" that Westermann identifies there.[40]

All this points to another reason for surprise at Childs's reluctance to focus on the concentric shape of Isaiah 56–66, or at least to an irony in that reluctance. Reading the material as structurally embodying tensions over theological questions has theological implications that are congenial to Childs's emphasis on the way the chapters hold together theological perspectives that necessarily stand in tension: "often the retention of elements of tension within the canonical text has been judged to be essential to Israel's authoritative scriptures."[41] The similarity of the critique in 56:9–57:13, for instance, to that of preexilic prophecy suggests it confronts "the theological problem that turned on the continuing presence of the old along with the very real experience of the new." The relation between the two is "ontological, not just chronological, in essence." The new age is coming but the old will remain.[42] To put it another way, while Isaiah 40–55 is amenable to deconstruction without inviting it, Isaiah 56–66 wears its deconstruction on its sleeve. (Further, the fact that there are ontological questions here, that the chapters involve a complex substantial theological issue, suggests that the presence of theological tensions need not point to diversity of authorship. The chapters might reflect a wrestling with questions that a single prophet or theologian could recognize were complex.)

It is common to reckon that Isaiah 56–66 focuses on the problem that the wondrous promises of Isaiah 40–55 have failed to come true.[43] But this again seems to be read into the text rather than read out of it. While passages such as 59:1–2 may well respond to a protest that Yhwh is neither listening to the people nor delivering them, this is a protest that occurs elsewhere in the Old Testament without any implication that a promised deliverance has failed to arrive. The opening of chapter 56 indeed urges people to act in faithfulness and promises that Yhwh

---

39 Westermann, *Isaiah 40–66*, 304–5, trans. from idem, *Das Buch Jesaia: Kapitel 40–66*, 243.

40 Westermann, *Isaiah 40–66*, 296, trans. from idem, *Das Buch Jesaia: Kapitel 40–66*, 237 (*reine Heilsbotschaft*). Westermann sees this as a link with Isaiah 40–55, but this view of Isaiah 40–55 also means seeing elements in Isaiah 40–55 as later than the work of the main prophecy, and it is a sign that his understanding deconstructs; Isaiah 40–55 holds together the same two emphases as Isaiah 56–66, though not in such equal tension.

41 Childs, *Isaiah*, 441.

42 Childs, *Isaiah*, 463.

43 Cf. Hans-Joachim Kraus, "Die ausgebliebene Endtheophanie," in idem, *Biblisch-theologische Aufsätze* (Neukirchen-Vluyn: Neukirchener Verlag, 1972), 134–50 (143).

will act in faithfulness, but it does not give any indication that its exhortation and promise relate to disappointment with the non-fulfilment of Yhwh's promises. It does not give any indication of a psychological motivation: "the prophetic promise functions exclusively on the theological level" in holding together in necessary fashion God's promise and the need for the people's response.[44]

In handling such complex theological questions, Isaiah 56–66 shows itself to be a work of theology. Since the rise of biblical criticism, commentators have generally been wary of theological readings of texts, and have thereby risked leaving theological reading to people who will impose such readings from outside the text (for instance, from Christian theology) or will simply ignore its theological significance. But stating the text's own theology is part of exegesis. Indeed, since in biblical texts questions about God are at the centre of the agenda, explicating their theological significance is central to their exegesis. There is then a further irony about the way critical scholars often bring their apparently-unexamined theological preferences to texts and uncritically make what they take to be self-evident theological judgments about them (in these chapters, for instance, over questions such as "universalism" and "nationalism" or the relationship of concern for the needy and observing the Sabbath).

In seeking explicitly to handle theological questions, Childs is inclined to appeal to the chapters' "canonical" form. But the trouble with the word "canonical" is that it resembles the word "evolution" in being a hurrah word for some people and a boo word for others; that is, it is a word that carries either strong positive resonances or strong negative ones. It does not trigger people into cool-headed study. And it is regrettable if the impression gets conveyed that you have to believe in canonical interpretation in order to incorporate theological explication in your exegesis.

In *The Nature of Biblical Criticism*, Barton also argues that biblical criticism is practised by people who love their texts; otherwise they would not bother.[45] This is clear in the work of many critical scholars, but it is not always evident (sometimes they are explicit that they study the text because it is an influential cultural artifact some of whose convictions they dispute and want to critique; the innocent reader can easily miss this fact about the convictions that underlie their study). In light of their own nature, part of appreciating one's texts would be to

---

44   Childs, *Isaiah*, 456.
45   Barton, *The Nature of Biblical Criticism*, e.g., 89, where the point is made in italics.

explicate their theology, and in the case of Isaiah 56–66 its chiastic structure is key to doing so.

I wonder what you think?

Penitential Innovations within the Twelve

Mark J. Boda

It was while I was studying under Professor Davies that his commentary on the book of Hosea appeared in print.[1] This publication took me by surprise since at the moment I was benefiting from his expertise in Pentateuchal traditions and came to realize the breadth of his interests and knowledge in the Hebrew Bible. The present article is an attempt to follow in his footsteps by bringing together our common interests in the Torah and the Book of the Twelve and applying some of the discoveries I made under his tutelage to old problems and emerging hypotheses.

Tradition Echoes in Joel and Jonah

It has long been noted that, although radically different books in terms of genre, Joel and Jonah share common themes and key phraseology related to these themes.[2] The connections are largely confined to parts of each book: Joel 2:12–14 and Jonah 3:9–4:2. The shared theme is the call to repentance with the depiction of God's gracious response. At the heart of this is the call for the people to return (שׁוב, Joel 2:12–13; Jonah 3:8, 10) which, it is hoped, will prompt God to turn and relent (נחם ,שׁוב, Joel 2:14; Jonah 3:9–10). In the broader context the people's return in both cases is accompanied by fasting (צוֹם, Joel 1:14; 2:12; Jonah 3:5, 7) and the wearing of sackcloth (שׂק ,שַׂקִּים, Joel 1:8, 13; Jonah 3:5, 6, 8) and involves their animals (Joel 1:20; Jonah 3:7–8).[3] In both books the hope for God to turn and relent is rooted in the identical declaration of the

---

1 Graham I. Davies, *Hosea* (NCB; London: Marshall Pickering, 1992).

2 Jack M. Sasson, *Jonah* (AB; New York: Doubleday, 1990), 263; Thomas M. Bolin, *Freedom beyond Forgiveness: The Book of Jonah Re-examined* (JSOTSup 236; Sheffield: Sheffield Academic Press, 1997), 169–72; Hyun Chul Paul Kim, "Jonah Read Intertextually," *JBL* 126 (2007): 497–528 (513–15).

3 For this latter connection see Katharine J. Dell, "Reinventing the Wheel: The Shaping of the Book of Jonah," in *After the Exile: Essays in Honour of Rex Mason* (ed. J. Barton and D. J. Reimer; Macon, Ga.: Mercer University, 1996), 85–101 (88); T. Collins, *The Mantle of Elijah: The Redaction Criticism of the Prophetical Books* (The Biblical Seminar 20; Sheffield: JSOT Press, 1993), 72.

gracious character of Yhwh, unique in the Hebrew Bible (. . . חַנּוּן וְרַחוּם אֶרֶךְ אַפַּיִם וְרַב־חֶסֶד וְנִחָם עַל־הָרָעָה, Joel 2:13b; Jonah 4:2). In the broader context both books also focus attention on God's compassionate acts (חוּס, Joel 2:17; Jonah 4:10–11).[4] Furthermore, the hope for God to turn and relent is expressed in a phrase headed by the same rhetorical question (מִי יוֹדֵעַ יָשׁוּב וְנִחָם, Joel 2:14a; Jonah 3:9a).[5] Finally, both books provide a narrative description of God's response to the penitential act (Joel 2:18–27;[6] Jonah 3:10).[7]

There are points of discontinuity too. The message of repentance in Joel is directed at Judah and Jerusalem, while in Jonah at Nineveh. Joel is a poetic book dominated by prophetic speech with one brief narrative piece (Joel 2:18–19a), while Jonah is a narrative book with some poetry (ch. 2) and a brief prophetic speech (Jonah 3:4). And yet, at what many would consider to be the rhetorical turning point in each book, there appears common diction that forges the two books together.

---

4   James L. Crenshaw, *Joel* (New York: Doubleday, 1995), 137.

5   On the use of this expression in the Hebrew Bible see James L. Crenshaw, "The Expression *mî yôdēaʿ* in the Hebrew Bible," *VT* 36 (1986): 274–88.

6   Joel 2:18–19 contain a series of *wāw*-consecutives with imperfects, the foundation of Hebrew narrative. See the translation of Hans Walter Wolff, *Joel and Amos* (Hermeneia; Philadelphia, Pa.: Fortress Press, 1977), 54; trans. of *Dodekapropheton, 2: Joel und Amos* (2d ed.; Neukirchen-Vluyn: Neukirchener, 1975).

7   Some have tried to create disjunction between the repentance of the people and God's response, especially in Jonah: for example, Michael A. Fishbane, *Biblical Interpretation in Ancient Israel* (Oxford: Clarendon, 1985), 346–47; James L. Crenshaw, "Who Knows What YHWH Will Do?: The Character of God in the Book of Joel," in *Fortunate the Eyes that See: Essays in Honor of David Noel Freedman in Celebration of his Seventieth Birthday* (ed. Astrid Beck; Grand Rapids, Mich.: Eerdmans, 1995), 185–96; Alan Cooper, "In Praise of Divine Caprice: The Significance of the Book of Jonah," in *Among the Prophets: Language, Image and Structure in the Prophetic Writings* (ed. Philip R. Davies and David J. A. Clines; JSOTSup 144; Sheffield: JSOT Press, 1993), 144–63, but although the penitential expression is carefully nuanced (מִי־יוֹדֵעַ) to preserve God's sovereign freedom to forgive (as per Exod 33:19), the explicit statement of 3:10, the underlying allusion to the Jeremianic tradition (see below), and the play on words between the penitential expression (שׁוּב . . . רעה, Jonah 3:8, 10) and God's response (שׁוּב/נחם . . . רעה, Jonah 3:8, 10) clearly connect these acts (for this play see, for example, Graham I. Davies, "Uses of *rʿʿ* Qal and the Meaning of Jonah IV 1," *VT* 27 [1977]: 105–111). Some have argued that since Joel does not name specific violations by the people Joel 2:12–14 should not be treated as a call to repentance, but as a call to general trust: for example, G. Ogden, "Joel 4 and Prophetic Responses to National Laments," *JSOT* 26 (1983): 97–106; a treatise on innocent suffering: for example, Ogden, "Joel 4," 97–106; Crenshaw, "Who Knows," 186–89, 196; or a call to restore Yhwh's honour: for example, Ronald A. Simkins, "'Return to Yahweh': Honor and Shame in Joel," *Semeia* 68 (1994): 41–54. However, references to the people as "drunkards" in Joel 1:5, a negative term in the Hebrew Bible (e.g., 1 Sam 1:13; Isa 19:14; Jer 23:9), and the regular use of שׁוּב in reference to repentance in the prophetic literature suggest otherwise.

The many theories over the direction of dependence[8] are based on the assumption that these two books represent discrete literary units with distinct composition histories. It may also be considered that both books were shaped by the same people. The evidence above, however, suggests that to extract these sections from either of these books would be to remove their respective rhetorical hearts.[9]

External evidence may also suggest that Joel and Jonah are part of a common literary effort, since there is diversity in the placement of both books within the canonical traditions of the Book of the Twelve.[10] Thus, in the LXX Joel and Jonah are placed with Obadiah after the three prophets with explicit historical superscriptions in the eighth century BC (Hosea, Amos, Micah), while in the MT Joel, Jonah, and Obadiah are interspersed among Hosea, Amos, and Micah. In 4QXII[a] it appears that Jonah is placed in the final position of the collection. The uncertain placement of these three books within the Twelve may indicate that they are part of the latest phase of the development of the Book as a whole.

Exodus 32–34 in Joel and Jonah

Joel/Jonah and Exodus 32–34

Whatever the relationship between Joel and Jonah, the core of the common material most likely has been drawn from a source outside Joel and Jonah. It has often been argued that this material originated in ancient Israelite liturgical practices,[11] when the rites (sackcloth, fasting) and oral declarations regularly employed on days of fasting and penitence were incorporated. However, the appearance of lengthy material common only to these two passages suggests otherwise (esp. Joel 2:13b and Jonah 4:2b; Joel 2:14a and Jonah 3:9a). For instance, the list of

---

8   See R. B. Salters, *Jonah and Lamentations* (OTG; Sheffield: Sheffield Academic Press, 1994), 26, 55.

9   John Barton (*Joel and Obadiah* [OTL; Louisville, Ky.: Westminster John Knox, 2001], 35), calls Joel 2:12–14: "the book's heart;" while Duane A. Garrett ("The Structure of Joel," *JETS* 28 [1985]: 289–97), calls it the rhetorical hinge.

10   Aaron Schart, "Reconstructing the Redaction History of the Twelve Prophets: Problems and Models," in *Reading and Hearing the Book of the Twelve* (ed. J. D. Nogalski and M. A. Sweeney; SBLSymS 15; Atlanta, Ga.: Society of Biblical Literature, 2000), 36–38.

11   E.g., André Lacocque and Pierre-Emmanuel Lacocque, *The Jonah Complex* (foreword by Mircea Eliade; Atlanta, Ga.: John Knox Press, 1981), 11; Crenshaw, "Who Knows," 192–93; Barton, *Joel and Obadiah*, 25–26.

divine attributes found in both Joel 2:13b and Jonah 4:2b is clearly indicative of the long tradition of citing the formula from Exod 34:6–7, which is found many times throughout the Hebrew Bible (e.g., Num 14:18; Joel 2:13; Jonah 4:2; Nah 1:2–3; Pss 86:5, 15; 103:8; 111:4; 112:4; 145:8; Neh 1:5; 9:17, 19, 27, 28, 31).[12] However, no other citation uses the same form found in Joel and Jonah.

The first four attributes (חַנּוּן וְרַחוּם אֶרֶךְ אַפַּיִם וְרַב־חֶסֶד) are basically the same as the formula which appears elsewhere in the Hebrew Bible.[13] At the end of these four, however, Joel and Jonah both add a unique descriptor: וְנִחָם עַל־הָרָעָה, a phrase absent from Exod 34:6–7 or any of the other passages which employ the character creed. However, this collocation does occur in Exod 32:12 (וְהִנָּחֵם עַל־הָרָעָה) and 32:14 (וַיִּנָּחֶם יְהוָה עַל־הָרָעָה), the first in Moses' request for Yhwh to change his mind concerning judgement of the people, and the second in the narrator's description of Yhwh's response.[14] In addition, in Moses' request to Yhwh in 32:12 he employs both שׁוב and נחם, similar to Joel 2:14; Jonah 3:9.[15] The verbs נחם (nip'al) and שׁוב appear together in a few places in the Hebrew Bible. In three cases the people are the subject of both verbs (Exod 13:17; Jer 8:6; 31:19), in two cases God is the subject of נחם (nip'al) while humans are the subject of שׁוב (Jer 18:8; 26:3); and in five cases God is the subject of both verbs (Ps 90:13; Jer 4:28; Exod 32:12; Joel 2:13–14; Jonah 3:9–10). However, in all the passages in which these verbs appear together only in Exod 32:12; Joel 2:13–14; and Jonah 3:9–10 are both verbs used in succession with God as subject, with the verb נחם (nip'al) followed by עַל־הָרָעָה (Exod 32:12; Joel 2:13) and the verb שׁוב followed by מֵחֲרוֹן אַפֶּךָ (Exod 32:12; Jonah 3:9).

This strongly suggests that the source for this material in Joel and Jonah should not be restricted to Exod 34:6–7, but the broader context of Exodus 32–34.[16] Elements lying at the heart of these rhetorical turns in Joel and Jonah bracket this key narrative section in Exodus. It may also be that the employment of "who knows?" prior to the hopeful statement that God may turn and relent (Joel 2:14; Jonah 3:9) reflects the

---

12 See Gordon R. Clark, *The Word Hesed in the Hebrew Bible* (JSOTSup 157; Sheffield: JSOT Press, 1993), 247–52, on the distribution of components from Exod 34:6–7 in the Hebrew Bible.

13 For diversity in the order of the first two attributes, see below. Crenshaw, "Who Knows," 191 n. 32, suggests Exod 33:19 as the source of this switch in order.

14 Uriel Simon, *Jonah: The Traditional Hebrew Text with the New JPS Translation* (JPS Bible Commentary; Philadelphia, Pa.: Jewish Publication Society, 1999), xxxvii; trans. of *Jona: ein jüdischer Kommentar* (Stuttgart: Verlag Katholisches Bibelwerk, 1994).

15 Crenshaw, *Joel*, 137.

16 See esp. Dozeman, "Inner-Biblical Interpretation," 207–23.

functionally similar אוּלַי (perhaps) of Exod 32:30[17] as well as Yhwh's sovereign assertion in Exod 33:19b. Like intertextual bookends, the material in Joel and Jonah brings into the background the entire literary complex of Exodus 32–34.[18] It is that context to which we now turn.

Exodus 32–34 as Tradition

The latter half of the book of Exodus has been shaped by the programmatic statement of 25:8:

> Let them make for me a sanctuary, that I may reside in the midst of them (וְשָׁכַנְתִּי בְּתוֹכָם). According to all which I am about to show you, that is, the model of the tabernacle and the model of all its appurtenances, in the same manner you must construct it.

Chapters 25–31 provide the revelation (כְּכֹל אֲשֶׁר אֲנִי מַרְאֶה אוֹתְךָ) of this "model of the tabernacle," while chapters 35–40 the account of its construction (וְכֵן תַּעֲשׂוּ). Its completion in chapter 40 (40:33b, וַיְכַל מֹשֶׁה אֶת־הַמְּלָאכָה) prompts the fulfillment of the original purpose (וְשָׁכַנְתִּי בְּתוֹכָם) expressed in 25:8: "Then the cloud covered the tent of meeting and the glory of Yhwh filled the tabernacle" (40:34). Not explicitly anticipated at the outset of this new stage of revelation, however, are the events in Exodus 32–34 which are placed between these two literary complexes. And yet this intervening narrative highlights the necessity of the tabernacle structure isolating the holy deity from a people prone to sin.

According to Exodus 32 it is Yhwh who alerts Moses to the problems in the camp at the foot of Sinai (32:8–9). In what follows, Moses refuses God's offer to begin the nation anew through Israel's leader (32:10) and initiates a series of four mediatorial interventions (32:11–13, 31–32; 33:12–23; 34:9) to save the nation.

The first mediation is key for it is the one which successfully dissuades Yhwh from rejecting the nation as a whole (cf. 32:10 with 32:14). Leveraging Yhwh's concern for his fame among the nations (32:12a) and his promises to the patriarchs (32:13), Moses pleads with Yhwh to "turn (שׁוּב) from your fierce anger and change your mind (נחם *nipʿal*)

---

17 Cf. Crenshaw, "The expression *mî yôdēaʿ*," 274–88.

18 Other inner-biblical connections: cf. Joel 2:17 with Exod 32:12; Joel 2:11; 3:4 with Exod 34:10; Joel 2:14 with Exod 32:12, 14, 29; Joel 4:20 [3:20] with Exod 34:7; Jonah 3:7 with Exod 34:3; Jonah 3:4; 4:5 with Exod 34:28 (cf. Deut 9:18, 25); Jonah 4:2 with Exod 33:13; cf. Leslie C. Allen, *The Books of Joel, Obadiah, Jonah, and Micah* (Grand Rapids, Mich.: Eerdmans, 1976), 222; Wolff, *Obadiah and Jonah*, 149; Crenshaw, "Who Knows," 192, 194, 195; Bolin, *Freedom*, 165 n. 63; Simon, *Jonah*, xxxvii.

concerning the harm (עַל־הָרָעָה) intended for your people." The narrative report of Moses's success echoes the vocabulary in 32:14: "Yhwh changed his mind concerning the harm" (וַיִּנָּחֶם יְהוָה עַל־הָרָעָה). It is this depiction of the initial mediation that most likely underlies not only the hope for mercy in the wake of sin expressed in both Joel 2:14 and Jonah 3:9 (מִי יוֹדֵעַ יָשׁוּב וְנִחָם),[19] but also the expansion of the recitation of the classic character creed found in Joel 2:13 and Jonah 4:2 (וְנִחָם עַל־הָרָעָה).

At the narrative climax of the mediation process in chapters 32–34, prior to the renewal of covenant in 34:10–28, lies the self-revelation of Yhwh's name (Exod 34:6–7). While the second half of this self-revelation (34:7b) explains Yhwh's violent response to Israel's violation of the first commandment, the first half of the self-revelation (34:6b–7a) explains his willingness to renew covenant. A comparison with the form of this creedal recitation in Exod 20:5–6 (related there to the sin committed by Israel in Exodus 32), reveals the importance of the first half of this self-revelation at this juncture in the relationship between Yhwh and the people (see Table 1).

Exod 20:5–6	Exod 34:6–7
אָנֹכִי יְהוָה אֱלֹהֶיךָ	יְהוָה יְהוָה
אֵל קַנָּא פֹּקֵד עֲוֹן אָבֹת עַל־בָּנִים עַל־שִׁלֵּשִׁים וְעַל־רִבֵּעִים לְשֹׂנְאָי	אֵל רַחוּם וְחַנּוּן אֶרֶךְ אַפַּיִם וְרַב־חֶסֶד וֶאֱמֶת נֹצֵר חֶסֶד לָאֲלָפִים נֹשֵׂא עָוֹן וָפֶשַׁע וְחַטָּאָה
וְעֹשֶׂה חֶסֶד לַאֲלָפִים לְאֹהֲבַי וּלְשֹׁמְרֵי מִצְוֹתָי	וְנַקֵּה לֹא יְנַקֶּה פֹּקֵד עֲוֹן אָבוֹת עַל־בָּנִים וְעַל־בְּנֵי בָנִים עַל־שִׁלֵּשִׁים וְעַל־רִבֵּעִים

Table 1

Two differences highlight the shift from a context focused on warning (Exod 20:5–6) to one focused on forgiveness (Exod 34:6–7).[20] First, the phrase לְאֹהֲבַי וּלְשֹׁמְרֵי מִצְוֹתָי which followed חֶסֶד לַאֲלָפִים in Exod 20:6 is absent, taking the "emphasis off of Israel's ability to respond to God's covenant demands."[21] Second, the order in which Yhwh's attributes are presented is switched. In this, Widmer sees "a radical shift from an emphasis on divine jealousy to an emphasis on divine mercy, grace,

---

19 Compare also Jonah 3:10 and Exod 32:14.

20 See further Fishbane, *Biblical Interpretation*, 343–44.

21 R. W. L. Moberly, *At the Mountain of God: Story and Theology in Exodus 32–34* (JSOTSup 22; Sheffield: JSOT Press, 1983), 88.

and loyalty without denying justice."[22] This self-revelation at the end of the narrative complex of Exodus 32–34 explains Yhwh's response to the initial intercession of Moses in Exodus 32.

Contrasts between Exodus 32–34 and Joel/Jonah

The potential of the section on mercy in the character creed was not lost on those responsible for many other contributions to the Hebrew canon as it is this section that is nearly always recited at the expense of the rest of the self-revelation in Exod 34:6–7 (Pss 86:5, 15; 103:8; 145:8; Neh 9:17; Joel 2:13; Jonah 4:2). For those responsible for Joel and Jonah the employment of this part of the character creed is understandable since the contexts of each book reveal a community facing impending or present severe judgement for sin.[23]

There are significant disjunctions, however, between the two contexts (Exodus, the Twelve) into which this character creed has been incorporated. While Joel and Jonah incorporate the creedal statements from Exodus 32–34 into a context demanding a human penitential response as prerequisite for divine forgiveness, this is not true of Exodus 32–34. Human response is irrelevant to this forgiveness;[24] the focus is entirely on God's covenantal attributes and responsibilities,[25] and the mediatorial efforts of Moses both to enact justice (32:25–28) and seek mercy (32:11–13, 30–32; 33:12–23; 34:8–9).[26] There also is a careful nuancing of God's character through Yhwh's declaration in 33:19 that the proclamation is still subject to his sovereign will.

A second disjunction is seen in the narrative description of the treatment of the nation in the wake of the sin and forgiveness. While in Joel and Jonah the response is restricted to grace and mercy, Exodus 32–34 highlights serious consequences (capital punishment) for those at

---

22   Michael Widmer, *Moses, God, and the Dynamics of Intercessory Prayer: A Study of Exodus 32–34 and Numbers 13–14* (FAT 2/8; Tübingen: Mohr Siebeck, 2004), 185.

23   The people's sin is not delineated clearly in Joel or Jonah. In Jonah it is identified in general terms as הָרָעָה דַּרְכּוֹ and בְּכַפֵּיהֶם אֲשֶׁר הֶחָמָס (3:8, 10). For the sin in Joel see above n. 7.

24   There is one reference to the people's response (33:4–6), but this comes as a result of God's revelation that he will not personally accompany them. The term used here is אבל *hitpaʿel*, one that is not used for mourning over sin, but rather mourning over tragedy. See further Boda, *Severe Mercy*, 42 n. 24.

25   Identified by Widmer, *Moses, God*, 189, as Yhwh's *Wesenseigenschaften* and *Handlungsweisen*.

26   Contra *b. Yoma* 61a which assumes that penitence lies behind God's forgiveness here; cf. Nahum M. Sarna, *Exodus-Shemot* (JPS Torah commentary; Philadelphia, Pa.: Jewish Publication Society, 1991), 216.

the core of the rebellion (see Exod 32:25–28, 33–35), even after the promise of forgiveness (32:32).

These two characteristics of Exodus 32–34 (absence of repentance, depiction of forgiveness with punishment) can be discerned in the narrative description of Israel's refusal to enter the land in Numbers 14. There Yhwh threatens again to destroy the nation and fulfil his promises through Moses (14:12). As in Exodus 32 Moses appeals to Yhwh's international fame (Num 14:13–16) and patriarchal promises (14:16). Echoing Exodus 34 Moses recites elements from the character creed, before requesting forgiveness (cf. Num 14:19, סלח, נשׂא with Exod 32:32, נשׂא; 34:9, סלח). As in Exodus 32–34 Yhwh grants forgiveness (Num 14:20, סלח) based on Moses's intercession (כִּדְבָרֶךָ), but then announces capital punishment on that entire generation (Num 14:22–23). Again the people "mourn" (אבל hitpaʿel) over their predicament, admit their sin (חָטָאנוּ), and even seek now to demonstrate a change in behaviour (14:39–40). However, this is declared useless and is clearly ineffectual (14:41–45).

Although it appears that Joel and Jonah rely on the Torah (Exodus 32–34) for their theological foundation for the anticipated divine response, their agenda for dealing with sin and their response is different. In both Joel and Jonah the agenda is repentance, an issue absent from both Exodus 32–34 and Numbers 14. This shift suggests a development of tradition and it is to the sources of this development to which we now turn.

From Exodus 32–34 to Joel/Jonah

Exodus 32–34 and Jeremiah

The disjunction between Exodus and the Twelve prompts us to look to the book of Jeremiah as the catalyst for these innovations in Joel and Jonah. Jeremiah regularly argues for a reciprocal relationship between human repentance (שׁוב) and divine change (נחם), setting up what Wolff has called a threefold theological progression: from proclamation of judgement to repentance to retraction (Jer 18:7–8; 26:2–3; 36:2–3).[27] Identical collocations to those found in Jonah and Joel are found in Jeremiah.

---

27   Wolff, *Obadiah and Jonah*, 154.

Jeremianic Connections to Joel 2:13–14; Jonah 3:8–10, 4:2			
Jonah 3:8	וְיָשֻׁבוּ אִישׁ מִדַּרְכּוֹ הָרָעָה	שָׁבוּ מִדַּרְכָּם הָרָעָה	Jonah 3:10
Jer 18:11	שׁוּבוּ־נָא אִישׁ מִדַּרְכּוֹ הָרָעָה	שֻׁבוּ־נָא אִישׁ מִדַּרְכּוֹ הָרָעָה	Jer 35:15
Jer 23:22	וִישִׁבוּם מִדַּרְכָּם הָרָע	יָשֻׁבוּ אִישׁ מִדַּרְכּוֹ הָרָעָה	Jer 36:3
Jer 25:5	שֻׁבוּ־נָא אִישׁ מִדַּרְכּוֹ הָרָעָה	וְיָשֻׁבוּ אִישׁ מִדַּרְכּוֹ הָרָעָה	Jer 36:7
Jer 26:3	וְיָשֻׁבוּ אִישׁ מִדַּרְכּוֹ הָרָעָה		
Joel 2:12	שֻׁבוּ עָדַי בְּכָל־לְבַבְכֶם	וְשׁוּבוּ אֶל־יְהוָה אֱלֹהֵיכֶם	Joel 2:13
Jer 24:7	יָשֻׁבוּ אֵלַי בְּכָל־לִבָּם	לֹא־שָׁבָה אֵלַי . . . בְּכָל־לִבָּהּ	Jer 3:10
Jonah 3:9 / Jonah 4:2	וְנִחַם הָאֱלֹהִים / וְנִחָם עַל־הָרָעָה	וַיִּנָּחֶם הָאֱלֹהִים עַל־הָרָעָה אֲשֶׁר־דִּבֶּר לַעֲשׂוֹת־לָהֶם	Jonah 3:10
Joel 2:14	וְנִחָם	וְנִחָם עַל־הָרָעָה	Joel 2:13
Jer 18:8	וְנִחַמְתִּי עַל־הָרָעָה אֲשֶׁר חָשַׁבְתִּי לַעֲשׂוֹת לוֹ	וַיִּנָּחֶם יְהוָה אֶל־הָרָעָה אֲשֶׁר־דִּבֶּר עֲלֵיהֶם	Jer 26:19
Jer 26:3	וְנִחַמְתִּי אֶל־הָרָעָה אֲשֶׁר אָנֹכִי חֹשֵׁב לַעֲשׂוֹת לָהֶם	כָּל־הָרָעָה אֲשֶׁר אָנֹכִי חֹשֵׁב לַעֲשׂוֹת לָהֶם	Jer 36:3
Jer 26:13	וְיִנָּחֵם יְהוָה אֶל־הָרָעָה אֲשֶׁר דִּבֶּר עֲלֵיכֶם	נִחַמְתִּי אֶל־הָרָעָה אֲשֶׁר עָשִׂיתִי לָכֶם	Jer 42:10

Table 2

As seen in Table 2, Jeremiah shares with Jonah and Joel the collocation
נחם עַל־הָרָעָה, with Joel the collocation שׁוב . . . . בְּכָל־לֵב(ב) and with Jonah
שׁוב (אִישׁ) מִדַּרְכּוֹ הָרָעָה. Not only is the style and theology of Jeremiah
apparent in the penitential idiom of Jonah and Joel, but Jeremiah 36
appears to function as an "anti-model" for depicting the Ninevite repentance in ch. 3. Both include divine threat (Jer 36:7b; Jonah 3:4), publication of a fast using the unique phrase קרה צום (Jer 36:9; Jonah 3:5),
and awareness of king and court (Jer 36:12–20; Jonah 3:6).[28]

It appears then that the Jeremianic tradition if not corpus has influenced the reuse of the Exodus 32–34 tradition in Joel and Jonah.[29] While
in Exodus 32–34 the shift in divine orientation towards the nation is

---

28 Lacocque and Lacocque, *Jonah Complex*, 76–77; A. Feuillet, "Les sources du livre de
Jonas," *RB* 54 (1947): 161–86; A. Feuillet, *Études d'exégèse et de théologie biblique, Ancien
Testament* (Paris: Gabalda, 1975), 422; Simon, *Jonah*, xxxviii;

29 See the long list of connections between Jonah and Jeremiah in Feuillet, "Les
Sources," 153–54; Feuillet, *Études*, 421–23; Lacocque and Lacocque, *Jonah Complex*,
10–11, 75; Wolff, *Obadiah and Jonah*, 153; Salters, *Jonah and Lamentations*, 60; Dell,
"Reinventing the Wheel," 91; R. W. L. Moberly, "Preaching for a Response? Jonah's
Message to the Ninevites Reconsidered," *VT* 53 (2003): 156–68 (158).

based on the character of Yhwh and the intercession of Moses rather than repentance, the Jeremianic tradition reveals another perspective on the divine relenting tradition that emphasizes human repentance.

While some may see this as eliminating the need for Exodus 32 as a source for Joel/Jonah, these passages in Jeremiah, which focus on the impact of human repentance on the shift in divine orientation, only express the divine shift with the term נחם, while reserving the term שוב for human activity. In Exodus 32, as in Joel and Jonah, נחם and שוב are paired in the description of the divine shift.[30] This suggests that for those responsible for Joel and Jonah the Exodus 32–34 tradition "is mediated through the theological 'extension'" of Jeremiah.[31]

Exodus 32–34 and Penitential Prayer

While it appears that those responsible for Joel and Jonah have read Exodus 32–34 through the lens of the Jeremianic tradition, this latter tradition gives little attention to the character creed expressed in Exod 34:6–7.[32] Since the character creed is being used to encourage repentance in Joel and Jonah, what tradition justified such a reading of Exod 34:6–7? The first clue can be culled from close attention to the form of the character creed as it appears elsewhere in the Hebrew Bible:[33]

As can be seen in Table 3, one slight difference between the formula in Exod 34:6 and that found in Joel and Jonah is the reversal of the two initial adjectives רחום and חנון.[34] This version of the formula (חַנּוּן וְרַחוּם אֶרֶךְ אַפַּיִם וְרַב־חֶסֶד) is only found at one other place in the Hebrew Bible, in Neh 9:17 (cf. Neh 9:31). This penitential prayer also explicitly leverages Yhwh's gracious response to Israel during their rebellions in the wilderness, with specific focus on the Golden Calf rebellion (Neh 9:16–19), and uses this formula as the foundation for a

---

30 In one case in Jeremiah (4:28) these two verbs refer to a shift in God, but in that one case it is an absence of such a shift and it is not used in connection with human repentance. Elsewhere in the Hebrew Bible only Ps 90:13 employs these two verbs together (although the gloss there may be "comfort" rather than "change the mind").

31 Jonathan Magonet, *Form and Meaning: Studies in Literary Techniques in the Book of Jonah* (2d ed.; Bible and Literature Series 8; Sheffield: Almond, 1983), 74; cf. Walter Moberly, "Jonah, God's Objectionable Mercy, and the Way of Wisdom," in *Reading Texts, Seeking Wisdom: Scripture and Theology* (ed. Graham Stanton and David F. Ford; Grand Rapids, Mich.: Eerdmans, 2003), 158, who sees, in both Jonah and Joel, Exod 34:6–7 "conjoined" with an "axiom" reflected in Jer 18:7–10.

32 The only exception to this statement is the passing reference in Jer 32:18 to Exod 34:7 in a way that is typical of the Dtr tradition: Deut 5:9–10; 7:9–10; cf. Exod 20:6.

33 See the superb chart in Sasson, *Jonah*, 281–82.

34 See footnote 13 for how this switch may be related to the influence of Exod 32–34.

penitential expression. The rhetorical flow of this prayer first depicts Yhwh's earlier gracious orientation towards Israel before the conquest (Neh 9:7–23), then depicts Yhwh's later disciplinary orientation towards Israel while in the land (9:24–28), then, after intertwining the two (9:29–31), declares a communal penitential expression (9:32–37).[35]

Character Creed in the Hebrew Bible			
Exod 34:6–7			
יְהוָה יְהוָה אֵל **רַחוּם וְחַנּוּן אֶרֶךְ אַפַּיִם וְרַב־חֶסֶד** וֶאֱמֶת נֹצֵר חֶסֶד לָאֲלָפִים נֹשֵׂא עָוֹן וָפֶשַׁע וְחַטָּאָה וְנַקֵּה לֹא יְנַקֶּה פֹּקֵד עֲוֹן אָבוֹת עַל־בָּנִים וְעַל־בְּנֵי בָנִים עַל־שִׁלֵּשִׁים וְעַל־רִבֵּעִים			
חַנּוּן וְרַחוּם[36]		רַחוּם וְחַנּוּן	
אַתָּה אֵל־חַנּוּן וְרַחוּם אֶרֶךְ אַפַּיִם וְרַב־חֶסֶד וְנִחָם עַל־הָרָעָה	Jonah 4:2	רַחוּם וְחַנּוּן אֶרֶךְ אַפַּיִם וְרַב־חֶסֶד וֶאֱמֶת	Ps 86:15
חַנּוּן וְרַחוּם הוּא אֶרֶךְ אַפַּיִם וְרַב־חֶסֶד וְנִחָם עַל־הָרָעָה	Joel 2:13	רַחוּם וְחַנּוּן יְהוָה אֶרֶךְ אַפַּיִם וְרַב־חָסֶד	Ps 103:8
חַנּוּן וְרַחוּם אֶרֶךְ אַפַּיִם וְרַב־חֶסֶד וּבְרַחֲמֶיךָ הָרַבִּים	Neh 9:17	אֶרֶךְ אַפַּיִם . . . וְנַקֵּה לֹא יְנַקֶּה	
חַנּוּן וְרַחוּם יְהוָה אֶרֶךְ אַפַּיִם וּגְדָל־חָסֶד	Ps 145:8	יְהוָה אֶרֶךְ אַפַּיִם וְרַב־חֶסֶד נֹשֵׂא עָוֹן וָפֶשַׁע וְנַקֵּה לֹא יְנַקֶּה פֹּקֵד עֲוֹן אָבוֹת עַל־בָּנִים עַל־שִׁלֵּשִׁים וְעַל־רִבֵּעִים	Num 14:18
		יְהוָה אֶרֶךְ אַפַּיִם וּגְדָל־כֹּחַ[37] וְנַקֵּה לֹא יְנַקֶּה יְהוָה	Nah 1:3

Table 3

This penitential prayer provides a snapshot of the traditioning process by which the non-penitential tradition of Exodus 32–34 (and Num 14) could be leveraged to encourage repentance. This utilization of the

---

35 For this argument see Mark J. Boda, *Praying the Tradition: The Origin and Use of Tradition in Nehemiah 9* (BZAW 277; Berlin: Walter de Gruyter, 1999).

36 Cf. Pss 111:4; 112:4; 2 Chron 30:9; Neh 9:31, which all shorten the creedal statement to חַנּוּן וְרַחוּם. Neh 9:31 echoes Neh 9:17. Of these only the later 2 Chron 30:9 connects this creedal form to the penitential, probably a reflection of the influence of the Penitential Prayer tradition.

37 Cf. Num 14:17: יְגְדַּל־נָא כֹחַ.

character creed is not unique to Nehemiah 9, but characteristic of this entire tradition of penitential prayer.[38] Further connections between Joel/Jonah and this tradition of prayer are the ritual acts of contrition that accompany penitential prayers, including assembling (אסף, Joel 1:14; 2:10, 16; Neh 9:1; Ezra 9:4); fasting (צום, Joel 1:14; 2:12, 15; Jonah 3:5; Neh 9:1; Dan 9:3), and sackcloth (שׂק, שׂקים, Joel 1:8, 13; Jonah 3:5, 6, 8; Neh 9:1; Dan 9:3).[39] The penitential prayer tradition that arises in the Babylonian and Persian periods showcases an innovative use of the Exodus 32–34 tradition as a theological foundation for repentance in and after the exile.

Summary

It has been argued that there is substantial evidence that those responsible for Joel and Jonah are drawing on traditions regarding God's forgiveness of the nation found in Exodus 32–34. These traditions, however, have been mediated through the theological lens of both the Jeremianic and Penitential Prayer traditions of the Babylonian and Persian periods. Through this chain a tradition originally rooted in a non-penitential context is transformed into one that forms the foundation for repentance.

The Penitential Tradition of Joel and Jonah within the Book of the Twelve

It was noted at the outset that the origins of the books of Joel and Jonah as well as the book of Obadiah are often placed in a much later period than the other three books in the first half of the Book of the Twelve. While Joel, Jonah and Obadiah have consistently been dated to the exilic and post-exilic periods, Hosea, Amos and Micah explicitly link

---

38 Mark J. Boda, "Confession as Theological Expression: Ideological Origins of Penitential Prayer," in *Seeking the Favor of God, Volume 1: The Origin of Penitential Prayer in Second Temple Judaism* (ed. Mark J. Boda, Daniel K. Falk, and Rodney A. Werline; SBLEJL 21; Atlanta, Ga.: SBL, 2006), 21–50.

39 See Crenshaw, *Joel*, 134. See Henning Reventlow, *Liturgie und prophetisches Ich bei Jeremia* (Gütersloh: G. Mohn, 1963), 115–16, 154–155; G. W. Ahlström, *Joel and the Temple Cult of Jerusalem* (VTSup 21; Leiden: Brill, 1971), 136 for the use of Joel within a prophetic liturgy similar to Jer 14:1–15:9. This latter passage represents an early development in the Penitential Prayer tradition; cf. Mark J. Boda, "From Complaint to Contrition: Peering through the Liturgical Window of Jer 14,1–15,4," *ZAW* 113 (2001): 186–97.

themselves to the pre-exilic eighth century BC. Why have these three later books been intertwined with these three earlier books, either in between them as in the MT or at the end of them in the LXX? What role does the shared penitential tradition of Joel and Jonah play within the development and rhetoric of the Book of the Twelve?[40]

Haggai, Zechariah, Malachi, and Repentance

Evidence that the penitential traditions represented in Jeremiah and Penitential Prayer (esp. Nehemiah 9) influenced the presentation of repentance in Joel and Jonah lays the foundation for reflection on the development of the Book of the Twelve. Elsewhere I have argued for the influence of the Jeremianic tradition and Penitential Prayer on what I have come to call the Haggai–Malachi corpus which concludes the Book of the Twelve. This is seen in the prose sermon inclusion of Zech 1:1–6 and 7:1–8:23 which forms the core of the Haggai–Malachi corpus. There collocations unique to Penitential Prayer (again, esp. Nehemiah 9) and the Jeremianic corpus are found.[41] While there is more to the Haggai–Malachi corpus than the theme of repentance,[42] each section of the corpus provides exposure to the topic: from the call to and depiction of a change in behaviour (in relation to the temple) at the outset of Haggai (1:1–15), to the depiction of the future penitential scene in Zech 12:10–14, the echo in Mal 3:7 of the call to repentance in Zech 1:3, and expectation of a future penitential response at the close of the Haggai–Malachi corpus (Mal 3:24 [4:6]).[43]

The fact that Jonah and Joel share common sources to the Haggai–Malachi corpus for their penitential theology has implications for understanding the development of the Book of the Twelve. While many have seen Joel, Obadiah, and Jonah as related to a different stage in the development of the Book of the Twelve from that represented by Haggai–Malachi, those responsible for the Haggai–Malachi corpus may

---

40   For literature on this topic see Paul L. Redditt, "The Formation of the Book of the Twelve: A Review of Research," in *Thematic Threads in the Book of the Twelve* (ed. Aaron Schart and Paul Redditt; BZAW 325; Berlin: de Gruyter, 2003), 1–26.

41   Mark J. Boda, "Zechariah: Master Mason or Penitential Prophet?," in *Yahwism After the Exile* (ed. Bob Becking and Rainer Albertz; STAR 5; Assen: Van Gorcum, 2003), 49–69.

42   See further Mark J. Boda, "Messengers of Hope in Haggai–Malachi," *JSOT* 32 (2007): 113–31.

43   On this concluding emphasis on repentance, see Boda, *Severe Mercy*, 351–52; and on these verses as a canonical "seam" to the "Prophets," "Latter Prophets," or "Book of the Twelve," see Boda, "Messengers of Hope," 129 n. 46.

have been responsible for the inclusion and even creation of the books of Joel and Jonah (and possibly also Obadiah, if it is related to this stage as is most likely).[44] All of these books also share in common later provenance.[45]

This shared concern for the recovery of repentance in this latter phase of the development of the Book of the Twelve suggests that the Book of the Twelve was drawn together for the express purpose of promoting repentance in line with the vision of the book of Jeremiah and the Penitential Prayer tradition.[46] But why was this important?

Hosea, Amos, Micah, and Repentance

The issue of the role of repentance within the three 8th century prophets Hosea, Amos, Micah has been controversial. Although references to and calls for repentance appear regularly throughout the books (Hos 2:2–4, 7; 5:4; 6:1–3; 7:10, 16; 11:5; 12:6; 14:1, 2; Amos 4:6–11; 5:4–6, 14–15; Mic 6:6–8) most of these merely highlight the nations' inability to re-

---

44   E.g., Crenshaw, *Joel*, 148–49 (highlighting the similarity between Joel 2:18 and Zech 1:14; 8:2); cf. Boda, "Penitential Prophet," 49–69. Rex A. Mason, *Zephaniah, Habakkuk, Joel* (OTG; Sheffield: Sheffield Academic, 1994), 120 (Joel 2:19 and Hag 1:11), Nicholas Ho Fai Tai, "The End of the Book of the Twelve: Reading with Zechariah 12–14 and Joel 3," in *Schriftprophetie* (ed. Friedhelm Hartenstein, Jutta Krispenz, and Aaron Schart; Neukirchen-Vluyn: Neukirchener, 2004), 341–50; Barton, *Joel and Obadiah*, 26–27; Wolff, *Joel and Amos*, 48–49 (Mal 3:23 [4:5] and Joel 3:4; Mal 3:2 and Joel 2:11; Mal 3:10 and Joel 2:14). Wolff, *Obadiah and Jonah*, 18, 42–43, identifies Obadiah as a cult prophet within a setting akin to the fasts of Zech 7:3, 5; 8:19. This Jeremianic connection reveals another link to Joel, Jonah, and the Haggai–Malachi corpus, all of which have been influenced by Jeremiah.

45   Contrast those who see evidence of a "grace" redaction in those passages alluding to Exod 34:6-7 (Joel 2:12–14; Jonah 3:8–4:2; Mic 7:18–20; Nah 1:2–3a; Mal 1:9a): for example, Christopher R. Seitz, *Prophecy and Hermeneutics: Toward a New Introduction to the Prophets* (Studies in Theological Interpretation; Grand Rapids, Mich.: Baker Academic, 2007), 216; and Jakob Wöhrle, "A Prophetic Reflection on Divine Forgiveness: The Integration of the Book of Jonah into the Book of the Twelve," *Journal of Hebrew Scriptures* 9 (2009), Article 7. Such allusions are far too general; cf. Klaas Spronk, "Jonah, Nahum, and the Book of the Twelve: A Response to Jakob Wöhrle," *Journal of Hebrew Scriptures* 9 (2009), Article 8.

46   For the importance of repentance to the Book of the Twelve see Collins, *Mantle*, 65; James D. Nogalski, "Joel as 'Literary Anchor' for the Book of the Twelve," in *Reading and Hearing the Book of the Twelve* (ed. J. D. Nogalski and M. A. Sweeney; Symposium 15; Atlanta, Ga.: SBL, 2000), 91–109; Rolf Rendtorff, "How to Read the Book of the Twelve as a Theological Unity," in *Reading and Hearing The Book of the Twelve* (SBLSymS 15; Atlanta, Ga.: SBL, 2000), 75–87 (86); Paul R. House, "Endings as New Beginnings: Returning to the Lord, the Day of the Lord, and Renewal in the Book of the Twelve," in *Thematic Threads in the Book of the Twelve*, 313–38; Seitz, *Prophecy and Hermeneutics*, 234–38.

spond or insincerity in responding to such calls (Hos 2:7–8; 5:4; 6:1–4; 7:10, 14, 16; 8:1-3; 11:5, 7; 12:1–13:16; Amos 4:6-13; Mic 6:1–16). Alongside these are vivid descriptions of what appears to be certain judgement (Hos 2:9–13; 5:8–14; 11:5–6; 12:14; 13:16; Amos 1–2; 8:1–9:10; Mic 1-3; 7:1–10) and/or a future hope of God's unilateral initiative to restore his people (Hos 2:14–23; 3:1–3; 14:4–7; Amos 9:11–15; Mic 2:12–13; 4–5; 7:11–13), both of which at times are depicted as prompting repentance and confession (Hos 3:4–5; 5:15; 6:1–3; 14:1–7; Mic 7:16–20).

The diversity in the function of repentance in these books connected to eighth-century prophetic figures is what has prompted the diversity of conclusions over the role of repentance in these books. Regarding Hosea, Stuart treats repentance "as eschatological, not immediate," similar to the Deuteronomic expectations of Deut 4:30 and 30:6, 8.[47] In contrast, Davies considers the message of repentance as one of "two central demands of Hosea's message," while Sweeney sees the entire book (including ch. 14) as a penitential treatise with the hope that the community would avert judgement prior to its destruction.[48] Between these two views lies Wolff who distinguishes between exhortations having as their purpose the aversion of judgement (2:4–5; 4:15; 8:5a; cf. 10:12; 12:7) and those seen as realizable only after judgement (ch. 14).[49] Similar diversity of opinion can be seen for the interpretation of Amos. For example, Wolff does not take seriously the call for repentance in Amos because of the reigning mood of judgement, treating such penitential exhortations as only "a faint reminiscence of something nearly forgotten or otherwise hard to place" which are "swallowed up by the dark threats."[50] In contrast Paul argues that for the prophets "the decision of God is very often subject to change, but the change is dependent and contingent upon the people's return."[51] When interpreting Micah 1–5, Waltke speaks of Micah's "implicit call for repentance" and concludes that "all judicial sentences are in effect threats."[52] While Ben Zvi entertains the possibility that Micah's announcements of doom (in ch. 3) "might have carried an implicit call for repentance," he is clear that "this perspective is not advanced in the

---

47   Douglas K. Stuart, *Hosea–Jonah* (WBC 31; Waco, Tex.: Word Books, 1987), 7, 8, 19, 107, 192, 212.

48   Davies, *Hosea*, 150, cf. 299; Marvin A. Sweeney, *The Twelve Prophets* (2 vols; Berit Olam; Collegeville, Pa.: Liturgical Press, 2000), 26–27, 136–38.

49   Hans Walter Wolff, *Hosea* (Hermeneia; Philadelphia, Pa.: Fortress Press, 1974), 234–35.

50   Wolff, *Joel and Amos*, 251.

51   Shalom M. Paul, *Amos* (Hermeneia; Minneapolis, Minn.: Fortress Press, 1991), 162.

52   Bruce K. Waltke, *A Commentary on Micah* (Grand Rapids, Mich.: Eerdmans, 2006), 91, 186.

text."[53] For Wolff "dedication to a new life" (repentance) is not in view in the present for Micah, but is the intended outcome of the divine judgement.[54]

In all of these books one finds prophetic messages declaring what appears to be certain judgement, and yet also prophetic messages encouraging a penitential response. In the end all three books depict the frustration of these prophetic figures as the call for repentance is paid no attention and the warned judgement becomes a reality. While possibly fulfilling the purpose of theodicy, such a witness within the Book of the Twelve subtly undermines the efficacy of repentance as a solution for the sin of the community.

Such a trend can be discerned elsewhere in the prophetic corpus.[55] This is clear in the books of Jeremiah and Ezekiel which, although identifying the importance of repentance within the apparently normative prophetic process rehearsed in passages like Jeremiah 18, 25; Ezekiel 2–3, 20, 33, bear witness to the failure of the process, due to the unresponsiveness of the people, and announce judgement followed by a divine gracious and transformative initiative (Jer 24:6–7; 31:33–34; 32:37–40, 41–44; Ezek 11:19; 36:27–27; 37:14; 39:26). Additionally, this failure of the process is linked to the judgement of God in the prophetic commission of Isaiah in Isaiah 6, with the hope shifted to the creation of a holy seed through severe judgement.

The presentation of the eighth-century prophets in the first half of the Book of the Twelve (Hosea, Amos, Micah) as well as the literary works of Isaiah, Jeremiah, and Ezekiel (and the Deuteronomistic History) witness to the lack of efficacy in the penitential agenda. This lack would have challenged any attempt to return to the penitential agenda associated by those tradents of the earlier prophets with the pre-exilic age.

However, the inclusion of the later books Joel and Jonah among (or following as in LXX) these eighth-century BC prophets would have addressed any attempt to undermine the value of the prophetic penitential call as an appropriate solution for dealing with sin.[56] These two

---

53 Ehud Ben Zvi, *Micah* (FOTL 21b; Grand Rapids, Mich.: Eerdmans, 2000), 87.

54 Hans Walter Wolff, *Micah* (Minneapolis, Minn.: Augsburg, 1990), 222; see Wolff's struggle with the explicit call to repentance in Mic 6:6–8 (pp. 180, 183).

55 See Boda, *Severe Mercy*, 254–55.

56 Another option is to follow James D. Nogalski, *Redactional Processes in the Book of the Twelve* (BZAW 218; Berlin: de Gruyter, 1993), 1–57; Nogalski, "Joel as 'Literary Anchor,'" who sees this redaction as highlighting the qualities of the penitential community envisioned in such passages as Hosea 14; although see critique of R. J. Coggins, "Innerbiblical Quotations in Joel," in *After the Exile* (ed. J. Barton and D. J. Reimer; Macon: Mercer University, 1996), 75–84.

books provided two positive examples where repentance was effective.[57]

Conclusion

This paper has argued that those responsible for the literary units Joel and Jonah have drawn on the forgiveness traditions found in Exodus 32–34 through the dual penitential lenses of the Jeremianic and Penitential Prayer traditions of the Babylonian and Persian periods. This enabled those responsible for Joel and Jonah to employ a non-penitential forgiveness tradition for encouraging repentance. In this Joel and Jonah reflect a similar agenda to that found in the Haggai–Malachi corpus, especially its core section Zech 1:1–6; 7:1–8:23. One then could speak of a "penitential" redactional phase in the Book of the Twelve, one seeking to affirm the role of the penitential in the new restoration era. This phase involved the final shaping of the books of Joel and Jonah (and most likely Obadiah) and their placement into the Book of the Twelve along with the closely related Haggai–Malachi corpus. This suggests that the Book of the Twelve as a whole was designed, possibly among other things, to encourage repentance for a post-exilic audience who were to see themselves as that ideal community longed for by the eighth-century prophets.

These traditioning techniques reveal a balanced approach to tradition and innovation, one which, while celebrating tradition, strives for innovation, essential for keeping the tradition alive in each new generation. It is this approach that Professor Davies has encouraged in so many of us who have had the privilege of sitting under his tutelage, and for this I am deeply grateful.

---

57 See similarly Ronald E. Clements, "The Purpose of the Book of Jonah," in *Congress Volume: Edinburgh, 1974* (ed. J. A. Emerton; VTSup 28; Leiden: Brill, 1975), 16–28, who saw the book of Jonah bringing repentance to the forefront as typical of literature in the late 6th century bc; cf. Sandor Goodhart, "Prophecy, Sacrifice and Repentance in the Story of Jonah," *Semeia* 33 (1985): 43–73; Salters, *Jonah and Lamentations*, 60; and now Wöhrle, "Prophetic Reflection," contra John Day, "Problems in the Interpretation of the Book of Jonah," in *In Quest of the Past* (ed. A. S. van der Woude; OTS 26; Leiden: E.J. Brill, 1990), 32–47.

Hosea, Creation, and Wisdom

An Alternative Tradition

KATHARINE J. DELL

Despite Harper's somewhat overconfident statement that "Hosea is full of wisdom-thought,"[1] Hosea is not the first text to which one might turn for either creation ideas or a consideration of wisdom influence. However, both have been noted in the book.[2] In this article I wish to draw out these elements and look at them in a synthesis together. I have argued elsewhere that there is an important "alternative" tradition, which may have early roots in Israelite consciousness, that involves both creation ideas and interaction with the natural world and wisdom thought.[3] At times that is expressed in terms of covenant, which, in some of its formulations, contained an important creation element,[4] at others it is expressed through the use of certain forms, ideas, and motifs, associated with the wisdom literature.

---

1   W. R. Harper, *A Critical and Exegetical Commentary on Amos and Hosea* (ICC; Edinburgh: T&T Clark, 1905), 378.

2   E.g., Terence E. Fretheim, *God and World in the Old Testament: A Relational Theology of Creation* (Nashville, Tenn.: Abingdon, 2005), chapter 6 demonstrates the presence of creation texts in Hosea. H. W. Wolff (*Hosea* [Hermeneia; Philadelphia, Pa.: Fortress, 1974]; trans. of *Dodekapropheton 1: Hosea* [BKAT 14/1; rev. and enl. ed.; Neukirchen-Vluyn: Neukirchener Verlag, 1965]) is usually seen as the champion of wisdom influence in Hosea.

3   Katharine J. Dell, "On the Development of Wisdom in Israel," in *Congress Volume: Cambridge 1995* (ed. J. A. Emerton; VTSup 66; Leiden: Brill, 1997), 135–51. See also idem, "God, Creation and the Contribution of Wisdom," in *The God of Israel* (ed. R. P. Gordon; UCOP 64; Cambridge: Cambridge University Press, 2007), 60–72.

4   Katharine J. Dell, "Covenant and Creation in Relationship," in *Covenant as Context: Essays in Honour of E. W. Nicholson* (ed. A. D. H. Mayes and R. B. Salters; Oxford: Oxford University Press, 2003), 111–33.

Creation/Nature

Looking at the eighth-century prophets from the angle of ecological hermeneutics, Marlow[5] comments that Hosea is much more concerned than Amos or Isaiah with relationship with the people, but there is some interesting use of imagery of the natural world nonetheless. She notes that Hosea contains no cosmic language (unlike Amos and Isaiah), and mention of the natural world is largely in terms of land and produce. Hosea is particularly well known for his use of simile, and this is where he uses imagery of the natural world to describe both God and people.[6] Of course Hosea's marriage metaphor is his most famous image and yet interwoven with marriage imagery is the theme of the land and its fruitfulness (notably in Hos 1:2, 4–5; 2:18–20[16–18], 22–25[20–23]). Although Hosea seems to align land and people, land can be seen as a separate entity in Hosea's thought. In Hos 4:1–3, for example, there appears to be a direct correlation between the acts of the people and their consequences for the land. Marlow writes that here "the inextricable link between human behaviour towards God and other humans, and the well-being of the created order is clearly established."[7] This is in contrast to the more utilitarian approach of Hosea 2 where the land, and its fruitfulness, is at the centre of concern.

Wisdom Influence

Some of these same texts (Hos 1:2; 2:18[16]; 2:23–25[21–23]) have come into the discussion of wisdom influence upon Hosea. The hardest aspect is to find criteria for deciding what constitutes wisdom influence.[8] In Hosea any wisdom influence may simply be evidence of an integrated worldview in which any educated person would assimilate different genres from the surrounding world. All that can be found in Hosea is a smattering of wisdom forms and ideas, so that even the foremost proponent of wisdom influence on the eighth-century proph-

---

5   Hilary Marlow, *Biblical Prophets and Contemporary Environmental Ethics: Re-Reading Amos, Hosea, and First Isaiah* (Oxford: Oxford University Press, 2009).

6   Marlow, *Biblical Prophets*, 159–66.

7   Marlow, *Biblical Prophets*, 193.

8   James L. Crenshaw, *Old Testament Wisdom: An Introduction* (rev. and enl. ed.; Louisville, Ky.: Westminster John Knox, 1998) maintains that a narrow definition is essential, involving basically the mainstream wisdom books. At the other extreme of opinion is Donn F. Morgan, *Wisdom in the Old Testament Traditions* (Atlanta, Ga.: John Knox, 1981), who finds wisdom influence in texts of many genres.

ets, Wolff, isolated only a handful of passages showing such influence (i.e., Hos 2:24–25[22–23]; 5:1; 8:7; 13:13; 14:10[9]).[9] Nor is it likely that wisdom "groups" were in any way involved in the production of Hosea (except possibly at the final redactional stage—see discussion of Hos 14:10[9] below). Conversely, a small amount of prophetic influence can be found in Prov 1–9[10] (e.g., Prov 1:20–33), but it is not extensive enough to form conclusions about prophetic groups working in wisdom circles. Whilst actual "groups" may be hard to find, it does not detract from the attempt to find wisdom influence in Hosea or any other prophet, given that wisdom forms and ideas were part of the language of the educated of the time. Wisdom would seem to be best defined on both a narrow and a broader definition, the narrow confined largely to the mainstream wisdom books where they show strong evidence of wisdom form, content, and context, the broader being about a wisdom worldview or definition of reality permeating other texts. This might include wisdom forms, content, and context in smaller measure[11] or bring in characteristic wisdom theological ideas, including creation thought. That is not to say that all creation thought equals wisdom, but that creation does tend to be the theological thought-world of wisdom. As Zimmerli famously remarked, "Wisdom thinks resolutely within the framework of a theology of creation."[12] God is simply seen as creator/orderer/sustainer of the world in this literature, not redeemer or saviour of Israel *per se*. Perdue[13] has recently reaffirmed the primacy of creation in wisdom thought over scholars such as Schmid, who argued for the primacy of order as the fundamental assumption of wisdom—including creation but broader than it[14]—and Boström, who also subsumed creation under the order/natural law heading.[15] Perdue writes, "Creation theology in both its anthropological and cosmological expressions is . . . the basis for the entire sapiential

---

9   Wolff, *Hosea*, 53, 97, 142, 228, 239.

10   Katharine J. Dell, *The Book of Proverbs in Social and Theological Context* (Cambridge: Cambridge University Press, 2006).

11   See Katharine Dell, *Get Wisdom, Get Insight: An Introduction to Israel's Wisdom Literature* (London: Darton, Longman & Todd, 2000), chapter 6 on wider wisdom influence in the Old Testament.

12   Walter Zimmerli, "The Place and Limit of Wisdom in the Framework of the Old Testament Theology," *SJT* 17 (1964): 146–58 (146).

13   Leo G. Perdue, *Wisdom and Creation: The Theology of Wisdom Literature* (Nashville, Tenn.: Abingdon, 1994).

14   H. H. Schmid, *Wesen und Geschichte der Weisheit* (BZAW 101; Berlin: Walter de Gruyter, 1966).

15   L. Boström, *The God of the Sages: The Portrayal of God in the Book of Proverbs* (ConBOT 29; Stockholm: Almqvist & Wiksell International, 1990).

tradition. This means that the affirmation of the providence of God, the order of the cosmos, the divine gift of life, the nurturing of human beings throughout life, and the goal of living in harmony with creation are fundamental themes throughout the wisdom corpus."[16]

Once some wisdom influence is established as a possibility in relation to a text, there is the further question of whether it is a formative or a redactional influence. A recent tendency sees wisdom influence in terms of redaction—Hos 14:10[9] is the text that springs to mind, widely regarded as a wisdom addendum. Davies, whilst he concurs with this, remarks that Hosea is the only prophetic book to end with a wisdom sentence[17]—which begs the question in my mind why others of the Minor Prophets do not. This omission undermines the idea of a systematic wisdom redaction for the Minor Prophets.[18] Conversely, Macintosh[19] has argued for wisdom as an important formative influence on Hosea. He argues that what we have in Hosea is application of wisdom sayings to the present situation, which turns them into a prophetic concern. Macintosh writes, "In all this Hosea is his own man. If he knows the motifs of the wisdom tradition, he makes use of them, as he does of elements from other traditions, to forge a new theme, his own theme."[20] He calls wisdom "one element woven into the texture of his prophecy."[21] He argues that Hosea used wisdom motifs not as an authoritative source, but in order to modify and transform them in the service of his message.

The idea of a formative wisdom influence upon Hosea is a persuasive one. It is plausible, in my view, that Hosea would have known of wisdom both in its oral/family/tribal context—which would be part of the general milieu of society at large—and in its royal/educational

---

16   Perdue, *Wisdom and Creation*, 46.

17   Graham Davies, *Hosea* (NCB; London: Marshall Pickering; Grand Rapids, Mich.: Eerdmans, 1992), 309–10.

18   The theory of Ray van Leeuwen, "Scribal Wisdom and Theodicy in the Book of the Twelve," in *In Search of Wisdom* (ed. L. Perdue, B. Scott, and W. Wiseman; Louisville, Ky.: Westminster John Knox, 1993), 31–49, of a wisdom redaction across "the book of the twelve," based on Exodus 34 and apparent in Hos 14:10[9] should be mentioned. This idea is in my view improbable since the texts he selects are not otherwise linked, except by these thematic connections with the Exodus text.

19   A. A. Macintosh, "Hosea and the Wisdom Tradition: Dependence and Independence," in *Wisdom in Ancient Israel: Essays in Honour of J. A. Emerton* (ed. J. Day, R. P. Gordon, and H. G. M. Williamson; Cambridge: Cambridge University Press, 1995), 124–32. See also idem, *A Critical and Exegetical Commentary on Hosea* (ICC; Edinburgh: T&T Clark, 1997).

20   Macintosh, "Hosea and the Wisdom Tradition," 131.

21   Macintosh, "Hosea and the Wisdom Tradition," 132.

incarnation.[22] Fohrer concludes that the wisdom elements in Hosea indicate that "he was educated in a wisdom school, which served primarily for the training of royal officials."[23] This is probably overstated in that it is uncertain whether such a wisdom school existed or whether Hosea aligned himself with royal officials in any way, but it opens up an educational possibility. Although Hosea shows elements of hostility towards the establishment (e.g., Hos 5:1), he is clearly a sufficiently educated person to have come across a breadth of educational influences. The paucity of wisdom influence might suggest his relative lack of interest in wisdom compared to Amos and Isaiah.[24] This raises the wider issue of the dating of the wisdom enterprise, which, even if it did not have such a full flourishing at the time of Solomon as some older scholars maintained,[25] certainly was a formative influence in the preexilic period and not least on the eighth-century prophets. Although many references to "the wise" in the prophetic corpus have a polemical air (e.g., Jer 9:23–24), this opposition may have been overstressed, with a milder, formative influence also at work.

In this article I shall look at certain key passages, including those regarded as evidence of wisdom influence. However, rather than getting too involved in the wisdom definition debate, I would rather look at the passages along more thematic lines, linking up with creation/natural world ideas. Scholars such as Gemser[26] and Westermann[27] have argued for an important alternative theological tradition in the

---

22 See Dell, *The Book of Proverbs*, for a discussion of the different social contexts for the various parts of Proverbs and their origins in Israelite society.

23 Georg Fohrer, *Introduction to the Old Testament* (London: SPCK, 1970); trans. of E. Sellin, *Einleitung in das Alte Testament* (10th ed. rev. and rewritten by G. Fohrer; Heidelberg: Quelle & Meyer, 1965), 419.

24 As argued by J. W. Whedbee, *Isaiah and Wisdom* (Nashville, Tenn.: Abingdon, 1971).

25 E.g., G. von Rad, "The Beginnings of Historical Writing in Ancient Israel," in his *The Problem of the Hexateuch and Other Essays* (Edinburgh: Oliver & Boyd, 1966), 166–204; trans. of "Der Anfang der Geschichtsschreibung im alten Israel," *Archiv für Kulturgeschichte* 32 (1944): 1–12; repr. in his *Gesammelte Studien zum Alten Testament* (Munich: Chr. Kaiser, 1958), 148–88; E. W. Heaton, *Solomon's New Men* (London: Pica, 1974).

26 B. Gemser, "The spiritual structure of Biblical Aphoristic Wisdom," in *Adhuc loquitur: Collected Essays of Dr. B. Gemser* (ed. A. van Selms and A. S. van der Woude; Pretoria Oriental Series 7; Leiden: Brill, 1968), 138–49; repr. in *Studies in Ancient Israelite Wisdom* (ed. J. L. Crenshaw; New York, N.Y.: Ktav, 1976), 208–19.

27 C. Westermann (*Blessing in the Bible and the Life of the Church* [OBT; Philadelphia, Pa.: Fortress, 1978]; trans. of *Der Segen in der Bibel und im Handeln der Kirche* [Munich: Chr. Kaiser, 1968]), uses the language of "blessing" and makes a distinction between the saving acts of God in history and blessing from God as a constant action beyond the temporal realm. He finds the counter-theme of "blessing" in psalms, creation narratives, and wisdom.

Old Testament—what Gemser, following Rylaarsdam,[28] termed the
vertical axis rather than the horizontal. The horizontal represents the
action of God in history and in the story of Israel, the vertical represents
those texts that intersect that history and have a wider, universal, time-
less appeal. This is a helpful model in drawing out this alternative axis
in any text.[29] Whilst Hosea is in many ways grounded in the history of
a certain period as a context, with the prophet prophesying doom if the
people do not mend their cultic ways and advocating a vision of a right
relationship with God, the vertical axis cuts across his thought at certain points and it is that which I hope to draw out. This vertical axis
includes creation[30] and wisdom in both its cosmological and maxim-
making aspects. Far from seeing wisdom, along with creation, as a later
development in Israelite thought which linked up only at the Exile with
the horizontal axis of salvation history,[31] my contention is that it was
early and much more formative. This alternative tradition includes
covenant ideas in its remit, notably ones linked to creation thought and
the natural world, including the animal world.[32] In another article[33] I
suggest three possible stages in the linkage of covenant and creation
ideas. The first is a pre-prophetic, non-covenantal formulation of
"order" and right relationships that links up with wisdom ideas about
creation as the ground of order. The second is the use of the language
of covenant (ברית) in passages such as Genesis 9 and Hos 2:20[18] to
express the same ideas. The third are other covenant formulations with

---

28 J. C. Rylaarsdam, *Revelation in Jewish Wisdom Literature* (Chicago, Ill.: University of
    Chicago Press, 1946).

29 This kind of model has been taken up by Walter Brueggemann, "A Convergence in
    recent Old Testament Theologies," *JSOT* 18 (1980): 2–18, who suggests that across
    the Old Testament the dimension "blessing/aesthetic/cosmic" should be contrasted
    with that of "deliverance/ethical/ teleological."

30 H. H. Schmid argued against von Rad and saw creation as a central concept, along-
    side the concept of order, from early times. He wrote, "The controlling background
    of Old Testament thought and faith is the view of a comprehensive world order and,
    hence, a creation faith in the broad sense of the word—a creation faith that Israel in
    many respects shared with her environment" (*Wesen und Geschichte*, 110–11, my
    translation).

31 See Gerhard von Rad, "The Theological Problem of the Old Testament Doctrine of
    Creation," in *The Problem of the Hexateuch*, 131–43; trans. of "Das theologische Prob-
    lem des alttestamentlichen Schöpfungsglaubens," in *Werden und Wesen des Alten Tes-
    taments* (ed. P. Volz, F. Stummer, and J. Hempel; BZAW 66; Berlin: Alfred Töpel-
    mann, 1936), 138–47; repr. in his *Gesammelte Studien*, 136–47.

32 The animal world is a strong feature of wisdom, especially in Job 38–41, where
    God's delight in his creation of the animal world is apparent. See Katharine J. Dell,
    "The Use of Animal Imagery in the Psalms and Wisdom Literature," *SJT* 53 (2000):
    275–91.

33 Dell, "Covenant and Creation in Relationship."

close connections to the second group—notably the Sinaitic and Davidic. This alternative tradition probably linked up with cultic ideas[34] and it included wisdom forms, imagery, and theology. In fact such was the importance of creation for wisdom that the Wisdom figure herself (Proverbs 8) is involved in the creative process, alongside God.

Hosea 1:2; 2:3–15[1–13]. Indictment of People and Land

There appears to be a direct correlation in Hosea between the indictment of the house of Israel and that of the land itself. In Hos 1:2 "the land commits great whoredom by forsaking the LORD" and this link is carried through into chapter 2 with images of "a wilderness . . . parched land" (v. 5[3]); "thorns" (v. 8[6]); withdrawal of "the grain, the wine, and the oil" (v. 10[8]), "my grain in its time, and my wine in its season . . . my wool and my flax" (v. 11[9]); and desolation of "her vines and her fig trees" (v. 14[12]). Although presented as a part of the faithless wife metaphor, nonetheless a significant element of the drama involves the natural world. Indeed the interdependence of the human and natural world is made clear here.[35] Although this raises for the modern reader the problem that the natural world appears to suffer for the failings of human morality, that is how Hosea and other prophets saw the essential interaction between God, human morality, and the fate of the earth. The focus here is on the productivity of the land, which dries up. Another point is misunderstanding over God's provision. In Hos 2:7[5] the harlot mistakenly thinks that it is her lovers who give her "my bread and my water," forgetting that it is God who provides. The land and its fruits are entirely at his behest. This links up with the theme of the provision of land that is such an essential part of the salvation history (e.g., the patriarchal promise in Genesis 12). This in turn relates to God's role as creator and sustainer—the maintenance of creation is an important aspect that is often overlooked. God's constant giving of fertile and fruitful land is a source of praise. This is God's ongoing creative provision.

---

34 As propounded by H. H. Schmid, "Creation, Righteousness, and Salvation: 'Creation Theology' as the Broad Horizon of Biblical Theology," in *Creation in the Old Testament* (ed. B. W. Anderson; IRT 6; London: SPCK, 1984), 102–17; trans. of an abbreviated version of "Schöpfung, Gerechtigkeit und Heil," *ZTK* 70 (1973): 1–19.

35 Marlow, *Biblical Prophets*, 167, provides a helpful chart showing the correspondence between the indictment of the house of Israel and of the land.

Hosea 2:16–20[14–18]. A Turning Point

Following the indictment comes a change of tone in verse 16[14] in which God wishes to allure the faithless wife into the wilderness (a positive experience here, unlike in Hos 2:5[3]), longing for a re-establishment of the relationship. The desolation of vines in verse 14[12] is overturned in verse 17[15] and the Exodus recalled. This leads to the remaking of the covenant, first in verse 18[16] in relation to husband and wife, and then in verse 20[18] in reference to the animal world. Verse 20a[18a] is the chief expression of covenant in Hosea in relation to the natural world.[36] It is presented as God's initiative "for you" ("you" [Heb. "them"] probably referring to Israel). Here there is a picture of the restoration of harmony with animals: "I will make for you a covenant on that day with the wild animals, the birds of the air, and the creeping things of the ground." This can be seen as simply a reversal of Hos 2:14[12] where "the wild animals shall devour them."[37] Or it can be seen as an eschatological reversal of Gen 1:30 (the only verse that contains a list of the same three animals of Hos 2:20[18]). This sentiment is linked in verse 20b[18b] with removal of "the bow, the sword, and war," which may refer to human military activity alone, although all these arguably affect animals too. Fretheim notes that the covenant here—"of peace with the wild animal world"—does not include domestic animals.[38] The covenant rather is "a kind of truce that will characterize the relationship between Israel and this animal world in such a way that violence between them is excluded, but not that violence among the animals is."[39] There are echoes here both of the order of creation and of the covenant after the flood in Genesis 9. As Davies writes, "The origin of this form of covenant theology may well lie in creation-based motifs of the pre-exilic cult with a wider Near Eastern background."[40] This could therefore be an older view of a covenant with creation that is being brought into relationship by Hosea with ideas of a national covenant.[41] Connections have been posited with

---

36 This verse is often seen as a later addition on the premise that creation is a late doctrine in Israel. If that premise is taken away, then the argument collapses.

37 So J. L. Mays, *Hosea* (OTL; London: SCM, 1969), 49.

38 Fretheim, *God and World*, 87. Interestingly this distinction between types of animal is not made in the parallel in Gen 1:30.

39 Fretheim, *God and World*, 348 n. 14.

40 Davies, *Hosea*, 84.

41 Robert Murray, *The Cosmic Covenant* (London: Sheed & Ward, 1992), 29–30, argues for cosmic covenant ideas in this passage which are not solely reflective of the Sinai covenant, despite its mention in Hos 2:17[15].

the wisdom emphasis on world order and creation. The future orientation of this passage is then taken up in the verses that follow.

Hosea 2:21–25[19–23]. Restoration

In verses 21–22[19–20] there is a list of qualities attributed to Yahweh—
righteousness, justice, steadfast love, mercy. These reflect God's own
conduct and in turn what he expects from his "wife," i.e., his own people. Marlow points out that in other passages these attributes are a
reflection of a world order established by Yahweh, which includes the
natural world (e.g., Isa 11:3–9; 32:15–17).[42] There is a link here with the
wisdom sense of order in the world and in society. In verse 23[21] the
motif is that of a conversation between earth and heaven in terms of
"answer" (ענה). This is a dialogue or antiphonal response between God
and the heavens which will answer the earth, which in turn will answer
"the grain, the wine, and the oil" (i.e., the fruits of the earth) and in turn
shall answer "Jezreel" (a symbol for the house of Israel here). Fretheim
quotes Koch[43] on this "answer" theme and writes, "Hosea appears to be
thinking of a coherent chain in which God is the initiator, but an initiator who acts in interdependence with earth, man and nation . . .
nowhere does the Old Testament offer such a pregnant description of
natural process as in this sentence of Hosea."[44] "Heavens" (השמים)
encompasses in meaning both the dwelling place of God and the sky,
which gives rain for the crops. Earth is both the global earth and also
the land, which receives the rain and yields produce (v. 24[22]). Jezreel
means "God sows" and so is probably used as a deliberate wordplay.
As Marlow writes, "Hosea is deliberately alluding to the completion of
the cycle of nature, the sowing of seed which will yield the crops, but is
establishing it as YHWH's doing, rather than merely a human activity
(cf. Isa 28:23–29)."[45] Marlow also comments, "Marriage and agriculture
are . . . parallel metaphors for the mutual interdependence of people
and land and of their utter dependence upon YHWH."[46]

It is interesting that it is Hos 2:24–25[22–23] that is picked out by
those interested in wisdom influence upon Hosea. Wolff argues for the
influence here of "didactic motifs that derive from the sapiential study
of nature." He argues that it is the listing tendency (cf. onomastica from

---

42   Marlow, *Biblical Prophets*, 179.
43   Klaus Koch, "The Old Testament View of Nature," *Anticipation* 25 (1979): 47–52.
44   Fretheim, *God and World*, 262.
45   Marlow, *Biblical Prophets*, 181.
46   Marlow, *Biblical Prophets*, 181.

Egypt) that is the specific derivation from wisdom (e.g., Proverbs 30; Job 39–41). The aspect of relationship within nature is, in his view, Hosea's own synthesis.[47]

Hosea 4:1–3. The Land Mourns

The indictment against the people has a direct impact upon the land. In verse 1 "the inhabitants of the land" are mentioned, thus connecting people and land. Interestingly all people are the referent here, not just Israel. As Fretheim remarks, "Nations are held accountable to cre-ational law quite apart from their knowledge of the God who gave it."[48] This links up with a wider concept of "natural law" in the eighth-century prophets and beyond.[49] Macintosh comments that faithfulness (אמת) and loyalty (חסד) denote moral integrity and common decency respectively. They are then paired with "knowledge of God" (דעת־אלהים), cf. 4:6, a phrase that has led to much discussion in the con-text of Hosea and seems to have various overtones.[50] Davies argues that it includes legal and historical elements.[51] Morgan emphasizes the wider context of "knowledge of God" to include "all aspects of Israelite morality" and points to Hosea's frequent use of ידע "to know".[52] Mar-low comments that the phrase "encompasses relationship with God, as well as knowledge about him."[53] Hos 4:2 echoes the Decalogue, which seems to tie "knowledge of God" to the founding laws of Israel.[54] Dev-astation (v. 3) is the direct result of the indictment of the people, this time presented in legal, decalogic terms. "To mourn" (אבל) is used elsewhere in prophetic texts to describe the reaction of the natural world to the actions of Yahweh or human beings (cf. Amos 1:2). There is a hint of the act-consequence relationship here—evil acts lead to evil consequences for the land and all who live in it, wild animals, birds,

---

47   Wolff, *Hosea*, 53.
48   Fretheim, *God and World*, 138.
49   John Barton, "Natural Law and Poetic Justice in the Old Testament," *JTS* NS 30 (1979): 1–14.
50   Macintosh, *Hosea*, 127–29.
51   Davies, *Hosea*, 88.
52   Morgan, *Wisdom*, 74.
53   Marlow, *Biblical Prophets*, 187.
54   Marlow, *Biblical Prophets*, 189, draws out the link between the fifth commandment, "Honour your father and your mother, so that your days may be long in the land that the LORD your God is giving you" (Exod 20:12) and Hos 2:20[18], in which agri-cultural and pastoral fertility will accompany obedience to Yahweh's command-ments.

and fish included as well as human inhabitants, who "languish." This is another echo of the wisdom tradition, at least in Proverbs, in which good deeds are rewarded and the wicked punished. It is also an echo of creation and flood motifs from Genesis 1–9. Deroche argues for a reversal here of the order of creation, as expressed in Gen 1:20, 24, 28, as Israel's punishment. The same three groups of animals are mentioned—fish, birds, beasts—which represent for Deroche "the three spheres in which the animal kingdom lives" and hence the whole category.[55] Landy goes further to say that Hos 4:3 speaks of the breaking of the covenant with the creatures in Hos 2:20[18] and not just of the reversal of creation.[56] The land is not just "victim" but also "vehicle," to use Fretheim's language. He writes, "Simply using victim language for the land and its animals in these judgment texts insufficiently recognizes a vocation to which God calls them in the service of the divine purposes; at the least we could speak of the nonhuman as both victim and vehicle."[57]

Other Salient Verses in Hosea 4

Other verses from the remainder of Hosea 4 have been noted by scholars looking for wisdom influence in Hosea. I have already mentioned discussion of the phrase "knowledge of God" (Hos 4:1, cf. 4:6), which could have wisdom overtones. In Hos 4:11 we have a warning against wine that sounds very like a proverb (e.g., Prov 20:1). Hos 4:14 uses the verb בין "to understand," and "a people without understanding (עַם לֹא־יָבִין) comes to ruin" (NRSV) could well be a wisdom quotation. The verb translated "comes to ruin" (ילבט) is found twice in Proverbs (Prov 10:8, 10), but nowhere else in the Old Testament. Macintosh argues that here a general saying about an individual foolish talker is applied by Hosea to the whole people.[58] Hosea 4:16 uses similes taken from the natural world: "like a stubborn heifer . . . like a lamb in a broad pasture."[59] These phrases are used of Israel—God cannot control "stubborn" Israel or shepherd them, or indeed provide for them in his usual way.

---

55   M. Deroche, "The Reversal of Creation in Hosea," *VT* 31 (1981): 400–409 (403).
56   F. Landy, *Hosea* (Readings; Sheffield: Sheffield Academic Press, 1995), 54.
57   Fretheim, *God and World*, 279.
58   Macintosh, "Hosea and the Wisdom Tradition," 126.
59   The idea here is that Yahweh has to treat his people as an unshepherded sheep in a wide, open field.

Wisdom in Hosea 5–7

In Hosea 5–7 wisdom echoes are usually related to peoples' recurrent behaviour or to nature, although a couple of formal similarities to wisdom literature have been found. One such is in Hos 5:1, a summons in wisdom style. Wolff comments, "the wisdom teachers introduced their sayings with this summons (Prv 7:24 . . .). The form was then used to introduce instruction in the law (Prv 4:1; Job 13:6; 33:1, 31; 34:2, 16 . . .) and thus also became an introduction to the sayings of the prophets." Wolff sees it as a "summons to receive instruction," hence retaining its wisdom link.[60] In Hos 5:10 reference to removing landmarks is at home in the wisdom tradition (e.g., Prov 22:28; 23:10) as well as in deuteronomic tradition. In Hos 5:12 "like a moth" (RSV) introduces an image from the insect world[61] and Hos 5:14, more grandly, likens Yahweh to a lion or young lion, common in the Old Testament (e.g., Amos 1:2; 3:8), and in wisdom (Job 28:8). Another formal link is provided by Hos 6:2, in which there is a good example of numerical heightening: "after two days . . . on the third day . . . ," again common in the wisdom tradition, e.g., Prov 30:7–33. In Hos 6:4b "like a morning cloud . . . dew that goes away early" (cf. Hos 13:3) refers to the weather to describe Israel's short-lived love. In Hos 6:6 "knowledge of God" is once again featured, paired with "steadfast love" (חסד) as preferable to sacrifice and burnt offerings. In Hos 7:11 "like a dove—silly and without sense" takes up the quite common dove imagery of the Old Testament (e.g., Gen 8:8), used here in an unusually negative fashion. As Davies points out, the silly person or simpleton appears regularly in Proverbs (e.g., Prov 1:4) in conjunction with a lack of sense (Prov 7:7; 9:4, 16).[62] In Hos 7:14 lack of grain and wine leads people to self-harm, showing the fundamental interaction of the products of the land and fruitfulness and their effect upon the people, versus economic deprivation and hardship. Wolff sums this up well: "Thus Hosea's audience must have been struck by the great number of metaphors he employed. In principle, he omits no sphere of life; but the imagery drawn from the vegetable and animal world and from family life clearly predominates."[63]

---

60 Wolff, *Hosea*, 97.
61 I have chosen to use the RSV translation "moth" for עש, rather than NRSV "maggots." An alternative suggestion is "pus." The usual objection to "moth" is that it is more often a symbol of transience than of destruction. Davies, *Hosea*, 157, agrees with the translation "moth" and finds examples of destructive moths in Ps 39:11; Isa 50:9; 51:8; Job 13:28.
62 Davies, *Hosea*, 188.
63 Wolff, *Hosea*, xxiv.

Examples in Hosea 8–14

Hosea 8:7 uses the language of sowing and of "standing grain." Wolff finds two sapiential sayings here, the first with its emphasis on the connection between present action and its future consequences. He writes, "The order God has established in the world can be demonstrated to Israel's farmers by using the harvest as an example (v. 7a). The deed is the seed that sprouts up in abundance for harvest." He points out the use of רוח in wisdom literature, to denote a gentle breeze (Eccl 1:14, 17; Prov 11:29; Job 7:7), which then becomes a whirlwind—a destructive force "which, like the harvest, grows out of the seed of a gentle breeze." He continues, "The law of correspondence as well as the law of multiplication applies to sowing and harvest." He sees the wider context of the threat of the enemy's advance (vv. 1, 3) as having "partly helped determine Hosea's use of these sapiential sayings." The second saying "elucidates the objective side"—i.e., "a dry stalk of grain yields no meal"—standing grain in fields is undesirable and poor in quality. If it did yield a harvest the attacking enemy would devour it. Wolff suggests an analogy with Israel waiting for dead cultic objects to provide life. It is a difficult verse and so Wolff concludes that either "total crop failure or the enemy will rob the people of their food"—Hosea cannot be definite.[64]

In Hosea 9 there are images of grapes in the wilderness and figs as the first fruit in verse 10; of a young palm in verse 13 used as a historical retrospect to look back on better times; and of a dried-up root that will bear no fruit in verse 16. By contrast in Hos 10:1 the image of a luxuriant vine is used for Israel (a common image in the Old Testament—e.g., Isaiah 5). Hos 10:4 describes judgment springing up like "poisonous weeds," and "like a chip" (10:7) may indicate a twig, so that the point here is that the king will be routed by the Assyrians in the same way that a piece of wood is washed away by a flood. In Hos 10:10 "their double iniquity"(NRSV) is seen by Macintosh as a ploughing reference, and he cites ibn Janāḥ who translates "in their being harnessed to two ploughing beasts." Macintosh himself translates "because they have bound themselves to two wicked policies," leaving the explicit ploughing imagery aside.[65] However, he explains the connection thus: "The connection between ploughing, intention and thought can be illuminated by the verb ḥrš, which means not only 'plough' but also 'devise . . . usually evil but also good,'" (as also in Hos 10:12–13; cf.

---

64 Wolff, *Hosea*, 142.
65 Macintosh, "Hosea and the Wisdom Tradition," 129.

Prov 3:29; 6:14; 12:20; 14:22; Job 4:8).[66] Hos 10:11 goes on to speak of Israel positively as having been a "trained heifer" in the past and the ploughing imagery is continued up to verse 13. As Macintosh writes, "In his sustained use of the imagery of ploughing, Hosea has undoubtedly used concepts quarried from the field of wisdom sayings and, in particular, of those sayings which reflect the unity perceived between the moral order and the successful practice of technical agricultural expertise." Hosea is at pains to say here that the productivity of the land was exclusively under Yahweh's control (cf. Hos 2:23–25[21–23]), presumably to counter any claims to such a domain by the Canaanites and their gods.[67]

In chapter 13, Ephraim (Israel) in verse 3a is "like morning dew" that rapidly disappears (cf. Hos 6:4b). In verse 3b the images of chaff and smoke also suggest ephemerality. In Hos 13:7–8 we find images of Yahweh as both lion and leopard, who lurks menacingly. Yahweh is also a she-bear here, reminding one of Prov 17:12. Another passage extensively discussed by Macintosh is Hos 13:13. The link with wisdom seems to be the "unwise son" (cf. Prov 10:1; 13:1; 15:20, although in Proverbs it is usually the positive "wise son" that is featured). In Hos 13:13 the negative "unwise son" does not present himself for birth "at the proper time" (contrasting with the positive infant imagery in Hos 11:1–4). The idea of the proper time is a well-known wisdom theme (e.g., Ecclesiastes 3). Wolff writes on Hos 13:13, "Drawn from Wisdom (as 8:7), this imagery expresses the same ideas found in the sayings about Israel's refusal to return at the time of judgment."[68] Macintosh suggests an alternative translation here so that the verse refers not to the foetus who does not present himself, but to the male Ephraim who cannot give birth.[69] He translates, "When the time comes he will have no success in giving birth." His interpretation is that Ephraim will not endure "to the point when giving birth would normally afford relief . . . the persistent torment is a prelude . . . to doom and failure."[70] This is an unusual reading of this verse, which more traditionally would refer to the "proper time" for a baby to arrive, in this instance, unusually, the delay being blamed on the child itself.

---

66   Macintosh, "Hosea and the Wisdom Tradition," 130.

67   Macintosh, "Hosea and the Wisdom Tradition," 130–31. The quotation is from p. 130.

68   Wolff, *Hosea*, 228.

69   This is a surprising image to use, done perhaps for "shock" effect. Other passages where males are in situations comparable to that of a woman giving birth are Isa 37:3 and Jer 30:6.

70   Macintosh, "Hosea and the Wisdom Tradition," 127.

In Hos 14:3[2] we find a simple good/evil contrast that would be at home in the wisdom tradition. The reference to "lips" echoes the strong communication theme of the book of Proverbs (notably the emphasis on proper speech found in Prov 13:2; 15:26). In Hos 14:6–8[5–7] God is likened to dew; Israel will blossom like a lily, strike root, and spread out shoots. Israel is also likened to the olive tree, seen as flourishing as would a garden and a vine. This luxuriant picture fits in with the vision of hope in these verses. In Hos 14:9[8] Yahweh, similarly, is an evergreen cypress.

Hosea 14:10[9] has generated considerable discussion. It is widely regarded as a later addition to the main text.[71] However, Macintosh points out that, even if that is so, it still continues what went before in terms of vocabulary, e.g., the use of כשל "stumble" (cf. Hos 4:5; 5:5; 14:2[1]) and פשעים "transgressors" (7:13; 8:1) and of "wisdom" and "understanding" (Hos 13:13; 4:14).[72] Wolff argues that there is a double question here and a didactic sentence—a "tricolon, with the initial line followed by two lines in antithetic parallelism."[73] Asking questions is a technique widely found in the wisdom tradition (cf. Job 39; Eccl 8:1).

Conclusion

In conclusion, the overall picture here in Hosea is of a great familiarity with the natural world and a rich use of metaphor. One cannot necessarily say that all these metaphors are to be related to wisdom, but they are related to the broader overview of creation/nature/wisdom references. In reference to the definition of wisdom, there are some passages that use wisdom forms, more predominantly there are those with wisdom content and there may be some with a wisdom context, although context is hard to establish here. The wider context of creation/sustenance of land/fertility of land is certainly drawn out, with Yahweh at the head. There is an essential interrelationship Yahweh/the people; the people/the land; the land/Yahweh. This is spelt out strongly here. The "vertical axis" of Old Testament thought discussed above is an important aspect of Hosea's thought that I have tried to emphasize

---

71 Ehud Ben Zvi, *Hosea* (FOTL 21A/1; Grand Rapids, Mich.: Eerdmans, 2005), 314–16, argues that Hosea has a double conclusion, the first in 14:9[8] and the second in 14:10[9]. He states that the second conclusion is about "readers," i.e., how the book is going to be received.

72 Macintosh, "Hosea and the Wisdom Tradition," 124.

73 Wolff, *Hosea*, 239.

here. This emphasis is probably even more true of other eighth-century prophets . . . but that is for another day.

It is a great pleasure to dedicate this article to Professor Graham Davies, with whom I have had the honour of working in the Divinity Faculty in Cambridge over a number of years, who has been a wonderful colleague and continues to be a good friend. I hope that this article intersects not only with his interest in Hosea, but also with our shared interest in Old Testament theology.

Acrostics and Lamentations

ROBERT B. SALTERS

The purpose of this article is to set the phenomenon of the alphabetic acrostics of Lamentations in the context of acrostic and related phenomena in the ancient world and to draw conclusions as to purpose and significance.

The Phenomenon

While the earliest use of the term "acrostic" appears to be in its application to the prophecies of the Erythrean Sibyl (*Sib. Or.* 8.217–50) of about 300 CE, the phenomenon probably has its roots in the beginnings of writing itself, when poets/scribes would become absorbed/fascinated with what could be done with variable combinations of the signs in writing, quite apart from the grammar of their compositions; and this fascination has continued through the centuries[1] to the present day. R. A. Knox notes the passion for acrostics in the nineteenth and twentieth centuries in the English-speaking world, and the recent publication of *The Bible Code* bears witness to the continuing interest in the fascination with letters.[2] I referred to the beginnings of writing, not the beginnings of the alphabet, for the phenomenon pre-dates the development of the alphabet; and we begin our observations in those early days.

---

1   Acrostics were common among the Greeks of the Alexandrine period, as well as with Latin writers, Ennius and Plautus. Medieval monks were fond of them, as were the poets of Middle High German and the Italian Renaissance. Note also the "Acrostiteliostichon" of Joshua Sylvester (1563–1618) in J. Fuller, ed., *The Oxford Book of Sonnets* (Oxford: Oxford University Press, 2000), 36–37.

2   R. A. Knox, *A Book of Acrostics* (London: Methuen, 1924); M. Drosin, *The Bible Code* (London: Orion, 1997).

Acrostics in pre-alphabetic cultures

Babylonian[3]

The earliest example of the acrostics phenomenon in Babylonian literature is probably to be dated ca. 1000 BCE, viz. the so-called Babylonian
Theodicy; and there are several other compositions which date from
around the seventh century BCE. The fact that not much Babylonian
literature has come down to us and that a significant proportion of
what has is acrostic related, would lead us to suppose that the acrostic
phenomenon was well established in that culture. The Babylonian
Theodicy consists of twenty-seven 11-line stanzas. Within each stanza
each line begins with the same syllable, so that by the time the stanza
ends the phenomenon is well and truly communicated. The twenty-
seven stanzas produce the statement: "I, Saggil-kinam-ubbit, the incantation priest, am adorant of the god and the king." The poem consists of
a dialogue between a sceptic, who suffers injustice at the hands of the
gods, and a friend who tries to rationalize and who offers pious
rebukes. One could say that the debate about evil in the world and
unjust suffering is the substance and actual purpose of the work, but
that the author chose also to make a statement, identifying himself; and
he inserted that statement within the poem. The insertion was made in
such a way as to be clear and yet not obtrude. A Hymn to Nabu consists of four 10-line stanzas. Again, within each stanza the lines begin
with the same syllables. Here, the composition's purpose is to praise
the god Nabu, and the acrostic appears merely to confirm this in that
the syllabic construction states simply "God Nabu." The Hymn of
Ashurbanipal to Marduk consists of thirty 2- or 3-line stanzas, but only
the first syllable of each stanza is involved in the acrostic. Again, the
purpose is the praise of a god, Marduk, and the acrostic structure,
which reads "I am Ashurbanipal who prays to you; grant me life, O
Marduk, and I will sing your praise," identifies the author and appears
to give a slightly different slant to the composition, suggesting that it
could be a prayer.

---

3   J. F. Brug, "Biblical Acrostics and Their Relationship to Other Ancient Near Eastern
     Acrostics," in *The Bible in the Light of Cuneiform Literature* (ed. W. W. Hallo, B. W.
     Jones, and G. L. Mattingly; Scripture in Context 3; Ancient Near Eastern Texts and
     Studies 8; Lewiston, N.Y.: Edwin Mellen, 1990), 283–304 (293–96); W. M. Soll, "Baby-
     lonian and Biblical Acrostics," *Bib* 69 (1988): 305–23 (305–11).

Egyptian

In an anthology of Egyptian literature—stories, instructions, and poetry—edited by Simpson,[4] there are a number of ancient Egyptian compositions which exhibit features akin to acrostics. In "The Admonitions of an Egyptian Sage," possibly from the period of the 12th Dynasty, we have a long composition which divides into several sections. The lines of the first group (some sixty of them) all begin with the word "Indeed." This is followed by a group (about fifty) where the first word is "Behold"; and other beginning words are "Destroyed" and "Remember."[5] There is nothing esoteric about this poem. It is at once obvious that the author is consciously given to repetition. It is quite different from the aforementioned message acrostics, though the stress on the first words might suggest a relationship.[6] But in addition to this kind of composition, there are poems where *sequence*, as in the alphabetic acrostic, is to the fore. In the (incomplete) hymn to Amon (Leiden Papyrus I 350)[7] from the thirteenth century BCE, we have an example of numerical sequence, though in a rather sophisticated form, the poet also indulging in word-play. The units of the poem begin and end with the same word—a word which is *phonetically* equivalent (or nearly so) to the number of the unit. Brug puts it clearly: "A rough equivalent would be an English poem in which stanza 1 began and ended with 'won,' stanza 2 with 'to' or 'too,' stanza 4 with 'for,' stanza 8 with 'ate,' etc."[8] In a pre-alphabetic culture this type of (sequence) construction comes close to the alphabetic compositions of a later time.

Ugaritic

While admitting that Ugaritic has not provided us with any actual acrostics comparable to the Babylonian ones, Watson draws attention to passages where the poets have sought to repeat sounds and words at the beginning of poetic lines.[9] One example, where the word

---

4   W. K. Simpson, ed., *The Literature of Ancient Egypt* (New Haven: Yale University Press, 1972).

5   "The Admonitions of an Egyptian Sage," translated by R. O. Faulkner in Simpson, *The Literature of Ancient Egypt*, 210–29 (210–11).

6   Repetition is a common means of emphasis in both prose and poetry. It is the recurrence of the same word at the beginning of a poetic line which draws the eye and which reminds one of the acrostic.

7   A. H. Gardiner, "Hymns to Amon from a Leiden Papyrus," *ZÄS* 42 (1905): 12–42.

8   Brug, "Biblical Acrostics," 297.

9   W. G. E. Watson, *Classical Hebrew Poetry: A Guide to its Techniques* (JSOTSup 26; Sheffield: JSOT Press, 1984), 195.

"dwelling" heads six lines in a row, reminds one of "The Admonitions of an Egyptian Sage" (above).

Watson designates these "quasi-acrostics." They certainly reflect a poet's fascination with sounds and signs in writing and, although not much different from assonance and alliteration, are bordering on what we know as acrostics.

Chinese

The phenomenon has existed in China for many centuries. Here, in the absence of syllabic or alphabetic writing, poets, sophisticated and otherwise, are seen to have been fascinated by the possible multifaceted aspects of Chinese characters; and they indulged in most intricate handling of the various elements which comprise the many characters in the language. One simple example is a 4-line poem by Guan Han-qing (ca. 1210–1300 CE),[10] a major dramatist of the Yuan Dynasty (1271–1368 CE). In addition to the poem itself, which has to do with love, the author conveys a message via the initial character of each line. In this case the message is "I want to follow you, leaving here and going wherever you go."

Another, more sophisticated, example is a 6-line poem by Xie Ling-yun (385–433 CE),[11] a very important poet in the Eastern Jin Dynasty (316–420 CE).

1.　古人怨信次
2.　十日眇未央
3.　加我懷繾綣
4.　口脈情亦傷
5.　劇哉歸遊客
6.　處子勿相忘

In this poem about love and the agony of separation, the author disguises a further message in a very subtle manner. Taking the first two lines together and paying attention to the first character of each line, we notice that the first character of the first line is 古 and that of the second line is 十. The latter is also the upper element of 古. If we subtract 十 from 古 the remainder is another word: 口. Similarly, taking the first characters of the third and fourth lines and subtracting 口 from 加, the remainder is the word 力. Again, reading the fifth and sixth lines in the same way, we find that if we subtract 處 from 劇 the remainder is 刂. Adding all three remainders (口 + 力 + 刂 = 別), we get a word that

10　See Zhang Xue-hua and Zhao Mai-lu, eds., *Wang Jiangting* (Shanghai: Shanghai Literature and Arts Press, 1984), 18–19.
11　See Gu Shao-bo, ed., *Xie Lingyun Ji Jiaozhu* (Taipei: Li Ren Press, 2004), 240–41.

means "to depart/leave."[12] It would seem that, in this latter composition, the additional message might not be immediately obvious, but what may appear to a modern Western mind as hidden may not have seemed so to ancient Chinese literati who may have delighted in the challenge to sniff out the hidden words.

The features we have looked at in Babylonian, Egyptian, Ugaritic, and Chinese literature have all been in poetic material. They differ from one another in genre and function — hymn, prayer, signature, etc. — but what lies behind them all is a fascination with word/letter manipulation; and one gets the impression that the poets were displaying skills which enhanced their standing as poets.

Acrostics in Alphabetic Cultures

The development of the alphabet would eventually bring to an end the type of acrostic/composition which relied on signs, syllables, and words; but the fascination with writing signs continued, and the new mode of writing, in the letters of the alphabet, brought new and numerous possibilities.

Hebrew

The phenomenon of acrostics is to be seen in the Old Testament. Unlike the Babylonian and Chinese acrostics, there are no examples of "message" compositions; all are simply alphabetical—i.e., following the order of the alphabet. They occur at a number of points: Nah 1:2–8; Psalms 9–10, 25, 34, 37, 111, 112, 119, 145; Prov 31:10–31; Lamentations 1–4; and Sir 51:13–30. Some of these are alphabetically incomplete: in Psalms 9–10 ד, מ, נ, and ס are missing; in Psalm 25 ק is missing; in Psalm 34 ו is missing; in Psalm 145 נ is missing; while Nah 1:2–8 is a mutilated text[13] and ends at כ. While others are alphabetically complete,

---

12 I am indebted for these examples to Professor Leonard CHAN Kwok Kou, Dean of the Faculty of Languages, Hong Kong Institute of Education.

13 The question of incomplete alphabetic acrostics in the Hebrew Bible is interesting. It is difficult to imagine that a poet would begin the task of creating an acrostic only to abandon his attempt mid-stream, as it were, or fail to include all the letters. It is possible that the original compositions were alphabetically arranged and complete but that, in the course of transmission, they were unscrambled and altered to serve later purposes. It may well be that those responsible for the "damage" had not noticed that they were handling an alphabetically arranged piece. If we examine Codex Leningradensis B 19a, we might conclude that the Masoretes had scant regard for the acrostic phenomenon in that the only place where the alphabetic arrangement is noticed is at Psalm 119, and even there it is only that the blocks (of 8 ʾāleps, 8 bêts,

Psalm 119 is the outstanding example in the Hebrew Bible, for whereas most of the others have one line or verse which begins with a letter of the alphabet, continuing to the end of the alphabet, Psalm 119 has twenty-two sections, each containing eight verses which all begin with the same letter—8 x א, 8 x ב, etc. Lamentations 2–4 have a slightly different alphabetic order to the normal order.[14] In addition, there are several psalms which are composed of twenty-two verses—the number of letters in the Hebrew alphabet—though they are not themselves alphabetically arranged. Psalms 9–10 is a mixture of praise and prayer; Psalm 25 is a prayer; Psalms 34, 111, 112, 145, Nah 1:2–8 are hymns; Psalms 37, 119, Prov 31:10–31 are didactic poems; Lamentations 1–4 are songs of lament.

There are three alphabetic compositions among the Dead Sea Scrolls: the broken Hebrew text of Sir 51:13–20b(?), 30b (11QPs[a] Sirach), Apostrophe to Zion (11QPs[a] Zion), and an incomplete psalm, also known as Syriac Psalm 3 (11QPs[a] 155).[15] These are hymns of praise.

The Jewish commemoration of the destruction of Jerusalem and the Temple (586 BCE and 70 CE) takes place on the ninth of Ab. That it is a very ancient custom is confirmed by references to it in rabbinic writings, e.g., *Lev. Rab.* 15:4. Central to the service is the reading of the book of Lamentations, but afterwards there are many prayers which have accumulated over the centuries. These prayers take their inspiration from the book of Lamentations. The alphabetic structures seemed to appeal to author after author. We have one where a first line may begin with a letter of the alphabet, as in the book of Lamentations, and much more sophisticated ones where, for example, every stanza begins with the word *'êkâ*, the first strophe of the first stanza has five *'āleps*, the

---

etc.) are slightly separate from one another! The same is true of the Aleppo Codex, and one gets the impression that the scribes are unaware of the alphabetic composition and are more interested in the justified margins of the finished product. The translators of KJV, in placing the Hebrew letters above each block, are not following their Hebrew *Vorlage*: they are following the practice of some LXX and Vulg. manuscripts.

14   It would seem that the Hebrew order was not entirely rigid. Examples of the order *pê-'ayin* are seen in the *Vorlage* of the LXX of Proverbs 31, and are found also in abecedaries at Kuntillet 'Ajrud and in an ostracon at 'Izbet Ṣarṭah; cf. F. M. Cross, "Newly Found Inscriptions in Old Canaanite and Early Phoenician Scripts," *BASOR* 238 (1980): 1–20 (13); G. I. Davies, *Ancient Hebrew Inscriptions: Corpus and Concordance* (Cambridge: Cambridge University Press, 1991), 81, 113 (§§8.019.1; 8.020.1; 35.001.5).

15   J. A. Sanders, *The Psalms Scroll of Qumrân Cave 11* (DJD IV; Oxford: Clarendon, 1965), 79–89, 70–76.

second strophe six *bêts*; the first strophe of the second stanza has five *gîmel*s, the second strophe six *dālet*s, etc.[16]

Greek and Latin

While the Hebrew examples differ from the Babylonian, Egyptian, and Chinese examples, in that they are purely alphabetical, the Greek and Latin examples consist of a mixture of types.[17] The contact between Israel and the Classical world is usually thought to begin in earnest with Alexander the Great, but acrostics in the Greek and Latin cultures were popular. It is thought that Latin acrostics existed before Greek ones, although the fact that the Latin word for acrostics, "acrostichis," is merely a transliteration of the Greek might suggest otherwise. From the third century BCE, we have a Greek example where Nicander, a poet, cleverly inserts his name Nikandros using the initial letters of the lines.[18] Perhaps the most famous Greek example is the Christian one in *Sib. Or.* 8.217–50, dating from ca. 300 CE. There, while the text is a prophecy of doom and hardship for the world, the letters, read vertically, supply the statement "Jesus Christ, son of God, Saviour; Cross," the final words being: "This is our God, now proclaimed in acrostics; the king, the immortal saviour who suffered for us." The latter is akin to the Babylonian message acrostics. Closer, perhaps, to our alphabetic acrostics is the pagan hymn to the god Dionysus where, after an introductory line which encourages to praise, and which is repeated at the end of the hymn, there are twenty-four lines in an alphabetic arrangement. Not only does the first word begin with the relevant letter of the alphabet but also every word in that line! The wording (after the exordium) begins:

Ἀβροκόμην, ἀγοῖκον, ἀοίδιμον, ἀγλαόμορφον,
Βοιωτόν, βρόμιον, βακχεύτορα, βοτρυοχαίτην
Luxuriant, rustic, famous, of beautiful form,
Boeotian, boisterous, topped up with wine, of clustered hair.

A similar hymn exists to Apollo.[19]

A Latin example from the third century BCE is a short poem where the acrostic, using the initial letters of each line, reads: *Quae Q. Ennius fecit,* "Quintus Ennius wrote it."[20]

---

16 For further examples, see A. Rosenfeld, *Tisha B'Av Compendium* (New York: Judaica Press, 1986).
17 For a fuller survey, see R. Marcus, "Alphabetic Acrostics in the Hellenistic and Roman Periods," *JNES* 6 (1947): 109–15.
18 E. Courtney, "Greek and Latin Acrostichs," *Phil* 134 (1990): 3–13 (11–12).
19 Marcus, "Alphabetic Acrostics," 112.

There is an interesting alphabetic structure associated with a certain Publilius Syrus who came from Syria to Rome as a slave and who rose to prominence under Julius Caesar because of his wit and wisdom. He was famous for his proverbs/maxims and, after his death, these were gathered together and sorted into an alphabetic list: some fifty beginning with A, about forty beginning with B, etc. The result was some 730 lines (A to U).[21] It is thought that the arrangement of the lines alphabetically was an *aide-mémoire*. The compilers/admirers of Publilius do not exhibit any poetic skill, but the sayings are rhythmic in form.

The Hebrew and Classical acrostics are similar to those from the pre-alphabetic cultures in that they are all poetic in structure. They span various genres and they demonstrate great skill on the part of the authors. The difference between the Hebrew acrostics and the others is that the Hebrew acrostics do not include a "message" acrostic: they are simply alphabetic.

Acrostics and Lamentations

Looking at the book of Lamentations in the light of these very varied acrostics and related phenomena, the question arises as to the nature and function of the alphabetic acrostic in it.[22] Clearly, it must be seen in conjunction with the alphabetic arrangements in the Psalms and the Dead Sea Scrolls, but may it be related in any way to the phenomena in the Classical and in the pre-alphabetic cultures?

The book of Lamentations is unique in that there are four alphabetic acrostics in a collection of five poems. The fifth is "alphabetical" in that it has twenty-two verses—the number of letters in the Hebrew alphabet.[23] Chapter 3 echoes Psalm 119 in that, of the sixty-six lines, three are devoted to א, three to ב, etc. The book of Lamentations is unique in other ways, too, in that apart from the fifth poem, which is a straightforward communal lament much like those in the book of Psalms, the other four are a mixture of genres—communal lament, individual lament, dirge, prayer. But what seems to pervade all four poems is a sense of devastation at what happened to Jerusalem, an

---

20   This is quoted by Cicero (*Div.* 2.111); see W. A. Falconer, *Cicero: De senectute; De amicitia; De divinatione* (LCL; London: William Heinemann, 1923), 496.

21   For the list of maxims and translation, see J. W. Duff and A. M. Duff, *Minor Latin Poets* (LCL; London: William Heinemann, 1934), 14–111.

22   For a recent exploration of the meaning of the phenomenon, see E. Assis, "The Alphabetic Acrostic in the Book of Lamentations," *CBQ* 69 (2007): 710–24.

23   See note 35 below.

acknowledgement of guilt on the part of the people, a fear that it is the end of Yahweh's interest, and a faint hope that it is not.

Talmud and Midrash

In seeking for an explanation of the phenomenon of acrostics in the Hebrew Bible, one should ponder the work of the early exegetes, especially, though not exclusively, Jewish sources. But surely, if the purpose and significance of the biblical acrostics can be teased out, the comments of the rabbis in Talmud and Midrash will be of particular importance. It is in the Midrashic literature that meaning in scripture is given an airing, if not a thorough testing; and if there are homiletical points to be scored, that is where we shall find them. One would think that there would be plenty of suggestions in this literature as to the meaning of the acrostics in the Hebrew Bible, but there is precious little on the subject. One might be forgiven for coming to one of two conclusions—a) that the rabbis assumed that the meaning was obvious, or b) that they had not even noticed the phenomenon! That the latter conclusion is an unlikely position is seen from an examination of passages in Talmud and Midrash which allude to the alphabetic structure of some biblical passages. However, the references to these structures are done in a very detached manner. Thus, in a discussion, in *b. Ber. 4b*, of Psalm 145, where it is acknowledged that the psalm has an alphabetic arrangement, there is an allusion to Psalm 119 as having an eight-fold alphabetic arrangement. Nothing more is said. Indeed, in *Midr. Tehillim*, where one might expect that something might be made of the acrostic feature of Psalm 119, there is not a word about either the structure of the psalm or the meaning of the arrangement. It is not that they have not noticed the phenomenon: the casual allusions suggest that they are aware of the alphabetic arrangement.

The rabbis are more interested in the mileage which they can extract from esoteric and creative observations. Thus, on the superscription to Psalm 3, referring to David's escape from Absalom, reference is made in the Midrash to a passage (1 Kgs 2:8) apropos of this and where the term נמרצת occurs. How is נמרצת to be understood? As an acrostic (צרופה):

נ = נואף	adulterer
מ = מואבי	Moabite
ר = רוצח	murderer
צ = צורר	oppressor
ת = תועבה	abomination

On the question of Lamentations, there is little to go on; but we are not entirely bereft. In Proem 24 of Midrash Rabbah on Lamentations the question is asked (by Abraham): "'O Lord, why have you exiled my children and delivered them over to heathen nations who have put them to all kinds of unnatural death and destroyed the Temple . . . ?' The Holy One, Blessed be He, replied: 'Your children sinned and transgressed the whole of the Torah and the twenty-two letters of which it was composed'; and so it is stated 'All Israel have transgressed your law' (Dan 9:11)." Again, in the Midrash Rabbah on the first verse of Lamentations, the question is asked: "Why is the Book of Lamentations composed as an alphabetic acrostic?" The answer: "Because it is written 'All Israel have transgressed your law' (Dan 9:11), which is written from ʾālep to tāw; therefore this book is composed as an alphabetic acrostic, one corresponding to the other."

Medieval Jewish

The main medieval Jewish exegetes, Rashi, Ibn Ezra, David Kimchi, and Joseph Kara, are almost silent on the subject of acrostics; and this silence must correspond to the comparative silence in Midrash and Talmud. Even at Psalm 119 (which is surely the test case) little is said. Kimchi and Ibn Ezra note the alphabetic arrangement of the psalm but do not draw any significance from the fact, while Rashi is quite silent. Rashi does note in his commentary (on 1:1) on Lamentations that the book is composed of alphabetic acrostics but he makes nothing of it, while Ibn Ezra and Kara are silent. Now the silence of these commentators is remarkable, almost as remarkable as the absence of comment in Talmud and Midrash. The only snippet which borders on the realm of exegesis is found at Lam 2:16, regarding the order pê-ʿayin.[24] Rashi, leaning on b. Sanh. 104a, asks the question: "Why does פ precede ע here? Because they were saying with their mouths פה what their eyes עין had not seen." The Talmud passage is referring to the spies of the promised land.

---

24   On the question of the order pê-ʿayin, see note 14 above.

Modern

During the period of critical scholarship a number of theories have been put forward as to the significance of the acrostics in the Hebrew Bible and in the book of Lamentations in particular.

Didactic

It has been argued that the purpose of the alphabetic arrangement was to teach the order of the alphabet. Indeed, Luther called Psalm 119 "The golden ABC," and Munch argued that the acrostics were masterpieces of composition, devised to instruct schoolboys the alphabet,[25] in much the same way as our jingle: A is for apple, so rosy and red; B is for boy and also for bed. Now if the acrostics all derived from the Wisdom parts of the Bible we might give some credence to this suggestion, in that it may have been in the Wisdom circles that education took place; but while Proverbs 31, Sirach, and Psalm 119 may be classified in this way, the other examples fall outside the genre. That is to say, the categorizing of the instances points in another direction. Furthermore, the examples are quite sophisticated literature, not for the unschooled or uninitiated. Again, the device is something which is hardly recognizable by the ear: it needs to be seen; and if the alphabet is only discernible visually, then the person who could read these texts is already well acquainted with the alphabet. Besides, as Gottwald observes, the didactic view makes a mockery of the emotional dynamic in the composition.[26] I am not being entirely facetious when I raise the question: Which alphabetic order was it meant to instil in the schoolboy—the one in Lamentations 1, or that in Lamentations 2–4? Having said that, it may have been the case that the teaching of the alphabet was achieved by the listing of the letters; and abecedaries may have served in this connection.

Mnemonic

Some argue that the phenomenon arose as an aid to memory.[27] One might be better able to recall a poem or sequence if one had the crutch

---

25 P. A. Munch, "Die alphabetische Akrostichie in der jüdischen Psalmendichtung," *ZDMG* 90 (1936): 703–10.

26 N. K. Gottwald, *Studies in the Book of Lamentations* (SBT 14; London: SCM Press, 1954), 26.

27 This was a suggestion of Robert Lowth, *Lectures on the Sacred Poetry of the Hebrews* (Boston: J. T. Buckingham, 1829), 39, 318; cf. S. Bergler, "Threni V—Nur ein

of a fixed order. Now it is possible that the alphabetic acrostic *arose* in this connection, and one can see how in, say, a cultic situation the device could be very useful; but one must question whether this is what is at work in Lamentations. If the twenty-two letters of the Hebrew alphabet occurred only once in the book then we might envisage the reader being assisted in this way; but the fact is that we have twenty-two letters used in sequence four times in the book! It would seem, therefore, that the person reading or reciting the text is not helped much if they cannot remember which of the *bêts*, say, they are presently at![28] The context is not much of a help either, for the text of Lamentations is nowhere noted for its logical progression! But one must distinguish between the view that a certain poem has features which help to make it easily remembered and the view that the intention of these features is mnemonic.

Magic

One view interprets the use of the alphabetic arrangement as having magical qualities.[29] That the authors of the Hebrew acrostics believed that the use of the alphabet harnessed some supernatural power is *a priori* possible. Westermann dismisses this as an impossibility.[30] The Old Testament itself is inclined to come down heavily against magic of any kind, condemning Manasseh, for example, for his indulgence in magical practices. Magic as a whole is seen as an abomination in the Old Testament (Exod 22:17; Lev 20:27); and there are several scenes which depict a clash between pagan and true religion: Joseph and the Egyptian magicians (Genesis 41), Daniel and the Babylonian sorcerers (Daniel 2), Moses and Aaron and the magicians of Egypt (Exodus 7). These stories plus the denunciation of magic point to the fact that magic was seen as contradicting the belief in Yahweh as supreme and one who cannot be influenced by any human tricks or sleight of hand. The attacks on magic perhaps suggest that many Israelites had unofficially resorted to these practices, but the attack is so strong that it is unlikely that someone as pious and as orthodox as the authors of the

---

alphabetisierendes Lied? Versuch einer Deutung," *VT* 27 (1977): 304–20 (309–10); cf. also Assis, "The Alphabetic Acrostic," 712.

28   For further criticism of this interpretation, see Soll, "Babylonian and Biblical Acrostics," 320–22.

29   Cf. F. Dornseiff, *Das Alphabet in Mystik und Magie* (Leipzig: Teubner, 1922).

30   C. Westermann, *Lamentations: Issues and Interpretation* (Edinburgh: T&T Clark, 1994), 99; trans. of *Die Klagelieder: Forschungsgeschichte und Auslegung* (Neukirchen-Vluyn: Neukirchener Verlag, 1990).

Old Testament acrostics appear to be would have had magical notions in mind.

On the other hand, we may detect a growing interest in the letters of the Hebrew alphabet. There is the intensely alphabetical chapter 3— probably the latest of the five poems—and there is the very elaborate Psalm 119, usually thought to be a late composition. Subsequent to the translation of Lamentations into Greek (LXX), a hand other than the hand of the translator,[31] placed transliterated Hebrew letters (Ἄλεφ, Βήθ) above each verse (copied by the Vulgate); and this and the intensely alphabetic prayers of the ninth of Ab are probably not unconnected with the mystic interest in the alphabet which developed in medieval Judaism's Kabbalah.

Completeness

Early in the critical period, de Wette suggested that "the elegiac humour of the sufferer has here expressed itself with a certain completeness,"[32] and this view, which was followed by other scholars, has more recently been advanced and argued by Gottwald, who suggests that "[t]he function of the acrostic was to encourage completeness in the expression of grief, the confession of sin and the instilling of hope." The idea is that, in the utterance or writing of the entire alphabet, one may be attempting to embrace or exhaust some theme or emotion. "If the subject is to be exhausted, the alphabet alone can suffice to suggest and symbolize the totality striven after." Gottwald backs up his position with quotations from Talmud, (which speaks of "the people who fulfilled the Torah from ʾālep to tāw") and Midrash, which refers to Abraham keeping "the whole Torah from ʾālep to tāw." It is Gottwald's view that the author of Lamentations chose the acrostic form "to correspond to the internal spirit and intention of the work. He wished to play upon the collective grief of the community in its every aspect . . . so that the people might experience an emotional catharsis."[33] A num-

---

31 A different hand because the Ἀιν has been placed above the Φή verse and vice versa in chapters 2, 3, and 4.

32 W. M. L. de Wette, *A Critical and Historical Introduction to the Canonical Scriptures of the Old Testament* (2 vols.; Boston: Little & Brown, 1843), 2:532; enlarged trans., apart from material on the apocryphal books, of *Lehrbuch der historisch-kritischen Einleitung in die kanonischen und apokryphischen Bücher des Alten Testaments* (5th rev. ed.; Berlin: G. Reimer, 1840).

33 Gottwald, *Studies in the Book of Lamentations*, 28, 29, 30, citing *b. Šabb.* 55a (*The Babylonian Talmud, translated into English with notes, glossary and indices* [ed. I. Epstein; 35 vols.; London: Soncino, 1935–1952], *Moʿed* 1:254), and *Yal. Rubeni*, f. 48b, col. 2, quoted by J. Rendel Harris, *The Teaching of the Apostles* (Baltimore, Md.; Johns Hop-

ber of scholars are in sympathy with Gottwald, but, while there may be something in what he says, I feel that he goes too far in his interpretation. If the author of Lamentations had complete confession in mind, why did he not make an effort to list the sins that had been committed? It is true that the author confesses the guilt of the people and admits that the suffering is Yahweh's punishment for sin, but he does not itemize the sins. He does not use the full range of words for sin in Hebrew. He speaks only in general terms: 1:8, "Jerusalem has greatly sinned"; 1:18, "I have rebelled against his command"; 1:20, "I have been very rebellious"; 1:22, "all my sins"; 3:42, "we have sinned and rebelled"; 4:6, "the iniquity of the daughter of my people is greater than the sin of Sodom"; 4:13, "the sins of the prophets, the iniquities of our priests who shed the blood of the righteous"; 5:7, "our fathers sinned"; 5:16, "we have sinned." If what Gottwald claims is correct then we would have expected lists of transgressions and iniquities and sins but we do not get this. There is no evidence that the author is attempting this other than Gottwald's interpretation of the acrostic. We might have expected the author to mention specific acts of rebellion; but apart from the allusion to prophets and priests shedding the blood of the righteous (4:13), the very few references to sins are in such general terms that it might be deduced that the poet was not conscious of *specific* wrongdoing.

Order

In a recent article, taking a psychological approach to Lamentations, Joyce has put forward the view that the acrostic form and the generally disciplined handling of metre may reflect an attempt to establish some order in the immediate reaction in Israel to radical loss of meaning.[34] Without trying to minimize the effect of 586 BCE on the people of Jerusalem and Judah, one should note here that the alphabetic acrostic in the Old Testament is not confined to poems of disaster. This is not to say that the purpose of the acrostic is always the same, but one would also need to explain the reason for its existence in, say, Proverbs 31. One might point out, in this connection, that Lamentations 3, arguably the least intense of the poems, shows the strongest alphabetic structure.

---

kins University; London: Cambridge University Press, 1887), 83 n. 1 (correcting Gottwald).

34   P. M. Joyce, "Lamentations and the Grief Process: A Psychological Reading," *BibInt* 1 (1993): 304–20.

Artistic

The view that the alphabetic acrostics are the work of skilful poets is not new. It would be conceded by nearly all commentators on the Old Testament passages that we have mentioned. What would not be conceded is that we need look no further than this observation for the answer to our question. The fact that all the Old Testament passages are in verse—whether in Proverbs, Psalms, Lamentations, Nahum or Sirach—is something which should not go unnoticed. It should also be noted that the Babylonian, Egyptian, Chinese, and Classical examples of a similar or related phenomenon are also in verse. It may be that we miss the importance of this because we have not absorbed/cannot absorb the ancient culture, and the precise meaning of texts does not come over to us: it is not the kind of poetry that we are used to. Hebrew poetry is a difficult subject partly because we are so distant in time and culture from the minds that created it and partly because it does not give up its secrets easily. We do, however, recognize that one prominent feature is that of parallelism; and there are several forms of this— synonymous, antithetic, and staircase. Secondly, there is metre or rhythm, where there is a tendency, though not universal, to balance the stresses on each half-line. Hence we get 3:3, 4:4, and 3:2; and there are variations of this pattern. Thirdly, there is the question of poetic language—metaphor, assonance, play on words, double-duty verbs, etc., etc. None of the poetry of the Old Testament includes all of these features: staircase parallelism is rare, and the antithetic parallelism does not usually combine with 3:2 rhythm.

When learning Hebrew, I had to put English poetry into a Hebrew resembling that of the book of Psalms. It was challenging; in fact it was difficult! But I was never asked to create an alphabetic acrostic! One reason for this may have been that it was somehow felt that the alphabetic acrostic had nothing to do with Hebrew poetry. I think that that is a mistake. I think that the alphabetic acrostic arrangement in the Old Testament points to a feature of Hebrew poetry. Only some poets could achieve it, and that is, perhaps, why we have so little in the corpus. Some were better at it than others, and so we have the more intensified examples of Psalm 119 and Lamentations 3; and several passages, like Lamentations 5, which remain in the form of a twenty-two line poem.[35]

---

35 The existence of the 22-line chapter 5 and the 22-verse psalms raises the question of their relationship to the alphabetic acrostic and also the question of how the latter began their life. Did the author of the alphabetic acrostic begin to build his piece with an *ʾālep*, etc., or did he concentrate on the content of the poem and subsequently adjust to accommodate the alphabetic structure? Westermann (*Lamentations*, 100)

That this is the correct interpretation of the phenomenon is backed up by the fact that the Babylonian, Egyptian, Chinese, and Classical examples of a related phenomenon also occur in poetic form, never in prose. I think that it is also supported by the reluctance, on the part of the rabbis in Talmud and Midrash, to draw exegetical comment from the acrostic form. It is not that they are not interested in letters: there are many examples of this. Moreover, it cannot be a coincidence that the medieval Jewish commentators are also silent. In fact it is here that I draw my strongest evidence. As well as being a commentator on the Hebrew Bible, Ibn Ezra was a prominent Spanish poet, and, along with Solomon ibn Gabirol and Judah Halevi, wrote quite a lot of Hebrew poetry in his day, including alphabetic acrostics.[36] The fact that Ibn Ezra, the poet, does not draw any exegetical conclusions as to its use by the authors of the acrostics in the Hebrew Bible, suggests to me that Ibn Ezra, at least, and probably the others, regarded the phenomenon in the same light as the rhythm or the antithetical parallelism. The fact that Ibn Ezra wrote a second commentary on the book of Lamentations[37] and still remains silent on the matter, confirms this. I believe that he was admiring of the acrostic creators, and rightly so. I suggest that some poets who enjoyed writing poetry found in the alphabet an attractive container for their thoughts, and a challenge to their literary skills; and just as Shakespeare and others (and not every English poet!) used the sonnet form—although there is nothing hallowed about fourteen lines set out in the way a sonnet requires—so they thought that they had found a ready-made structure to convey their feelings and passions. They thought that the alphabetic arrangement raised the quality and tone of their work, making it worth the effort, and displayed an uncommon skill.

It is a pleasure to be associated with this volume in honour of my friend Graham Davies, who has illumined our path on many issues in Hebrew and Old Testament study and whose critical judgments in this field promise to be enduring.

---

seems to believe the latter. If he is right, then chapter 5 and the 22-verse psalms may have been "candidates" for alphabetizing.

36   Cf. Rosenfeld, *Tisha B'Av Compendium*, 178–79.

37   The authenticity of the commentary, which appears in *Mikraoth Gedoloth* as פי׳ הטעמים לראב״ע is disputed by some, cf. D. Shute, ed. and trans., *Commentary on the Lamentations of the Prophet Jeremiah/Peter Martyr Vermigli* (Sixteenth Century Essays and Studies 55; The Peter Martyr Library 6; Kirksville, Mo.: Truman State University Press, 2002), xxv.

"Slaves" in Biblical Narrative and in Translation

PETER J. WILLIAMS

Everyone with even a slight familiarity with the book of Exodus has heard that it tells of how the Hebrews were *slaves* in Egypt. Anyone more acquainted with the book may also be aware that it contains legal provisions discussing *slavery*. This article seeks to consider the term "slave" within translations of the Old Testament, paying particular attention to the book of Exodus and to some comparatively recent trends in Bible translation.[1]

Changes in Bible Translation

Since the translation of the King James Version (KJV), whose four hundredth anniversary coincides with the publication of this Festschrift, there has been a remarkable increase in the use of the term "slave" in Bible translations. In the KJV the term "slave" only occurs once in the whole Old Testament, namely in the exclamation "Is Israel a seruant? is he a home-borne *slaue?*" (Jer 2:14).[2] Here "slave" is not used to represent עֶבֶד but is in small print in the *editio princeps* (later to be replaced by italics), indicating that it does not represent a specific Hebrew word at all. Rather, the word complements "home-borne," which is used to render Hebrew יְלִיד בַּיִת. "Slave" has occurred because a synonym was required for the second clause, which was in parallelism to the first. The word "servant" had already been used, and so another term—one

---

1   This is in many ways a study of semantics and lexicography. My first serious encounter with these disciplines was while working for the Semantics of Ancient Hebrew Database Project under the supervision of Professor Davies.

2   It occurs a further six times in the KJV: Jdt 5:11; 14:13, 18; 1 Macc 3:41 (all plural); 1 Macc 2:11 ("bondslave" of a female); Rev 18:13 (translating σῶμα). By far the most common term in the KJV was "servant," but the translation also has a number of expressions—now archaic—for males and females in service: compounds with bond-included man, men, woman, women, servant (only Lev 25:39, never pl.), and maid(s). The KJV also had manservant, menservants, maidservant(s), handmaid(s), and handmaidens (not sg. in OT). Statistical searches for this article have been mainly performed using BibleWorks.

not particularly common in English at the time of the KJV—had to be pressed into service.

The Revised Version (RV) of 1885 retained this reference to "slave" in Jer 2:14 and added two further references in Deut 21:14 and 24:7.[3] Again, neither of these references represents the Hebrew word עֶבֶד. In fact, both are texts that talk specifically about "selling" people, and have in common that they are the only texts to contain the verb הִתְעַמֵּר, which the RV understands as to "deal with [someone] as a slave." The American Standard Version (ASV) of 1901 followed the RV in having only these three occurrences of the word "slave."

Subsequent Bible revisions, however, made significant changes. The Revised Standard Version (RSV) of 1952 had a total of 100 occurrences of the term "slave" in its Old Testament. The New Revised Standard Version (NRSV) of 1989 continued on the same trajectory, with a total of 142 occurrences of "slave" and 21 of "slavery."[4] Ironically, its translation of Jer 2:14 reads "Is Israel a slave? Is he a homeborn servant?", just like the KJV, but with reversal of the words "slave" and "servant," showing the extent to which by the time of translation "slave" had come to be associated with the word עֶבֶד. A completely separate revision of the KJV, namely the New King James Version (NKJV) in 1982, contained a total of 42 occurrences of the word "slave" and one of "slavery." While this is significantly fewer than the RSV and NRSV, it must be remembered that the NKJV was a translation that specifically sought to stay close to the KJV, and that the term "slave" was mainly used to replace archaic expressions in the KJV. The NIV (1984 edition) also fits the pattern of late twentieth-century translations, having the root "slave" 104 times and "slavery" 17 times in the Old Testament.

Nor is this merely a trend limited to Christian translations. The Jewish Publication Society (JPS) translation of 1917 follows the wording of the ASV closely, having the same three occurrences of "slave." In

---

3   In the following review we only consider the Old Testament section of translations. At the same time, translations with Apocrypha or New Testament show increased tendencies to use the word "slave," but these tendencies will not be analysed here. Likewise outside the remit of this article is the movement of the word "slave" to first definition in Hebrew dictionaries, to such an extent that the *DCH*, s.v. עֶבֶד, gives "slave, servant" and "slave" as its first two of nine definitions, even though the bulk of the entry deals with other sorts of occurrences which are more numerous.

4   For comparative purposes it is necessary to consider compounds of "slave," such as "slave-girl," as examples of the word "slave" since English translations often vary as to whether words graphically compounded or hyphenated. Thus the NIV has "slave girl," the NRSV "slave-girl," and the JPS (1985) translation has both "slave-girl" and "slavegirls."

contrast, the JPS revision of 1985 has 122 occurrences of the word "slave" and five of "slavery."

It is, of course, understandable that the appropriate word in any target language such as English would change over time, and it might at first glance be presumed that we have here a simple case of replacement of older terms by a newer one. However, often the word being replaced is not an archaism, but the word "servant," a word which these same translations acknowledge by numerical preponderance, is generally the most appropriate representative of עֶבֶד.

What we should not forget is that separating the KJV in 1611 and the RV in 1885 is a vast history. In 1619, only eight years after the KJV was published, Jamestown, Virginia, received the New World's first twenty slaves from Africa. Thereafter, the massive growth of the North Atlantic slave trade, large-scale slavery across parts of America, abolitionism and abolition, and the American Civil War were all to intervene before an authorized revision would come. It might therefore surprise some that, despite all of these events, when a revision was made, no one seems to have thought of introducing the word "slave" as a rendering of עֶבֶד. However, the RV was produced under rigid constraints and a desire to keep close to the language of the KJV wherever possible.

The mid-nineteenth century had, of course, seen a huge outpouring of publications concerning biblical texts relevant to slavery by abolitionists and anti-abolitionists.[5] These studies were often both technical and intended for widespread circulation. Amid all this heated, and sometimes sophisticated, debate, even those who opposed abolition were well aware that there might have been a significant distance between someone designated in Hebrew by the term עֶבֶד and the lot of a slave in the ante-bellum South. The surprising thing for us now reading these publications is the extent to which the belief in the inferiority of "Hamitic" (i.e., African) people was *central* to their arguments to

---

5   Relevant examples would be Josiah Priest, *Bible Defense of Slavery; and Origin, Fortunes, and History of the Negro Race* (Glasgow, Ky.: W. S. Brown, 1852); Charles Elliott, *The Bible and Slavery: in Which the Abrahamic and Mosaic Discipline Is Considered in Connection with the Most Ancient Forms of Slavery; and the Pauline Code on Slavery as Related to Roman Slavery and the Discipline of the Apostolic Churches* (Cincinnati, Ohio: L. Swormstedt & A. Poe, 1857); Isaac Allen, *Is Slavery Sanctioned by the Bible? A Premium Tract* (Boston, Mass.: American Tract Society, [1860]); Philip Schaff, *Slavery and the Bible: A Tract for the Times* (Chambersburg, Pa.: Kieffer & Co., 1861); Joseph P. Thompson, *Christianity and Emancipation: or, the Teachings and the Influence of the Bible against Slavery* (New York: Anson D. F. Randolph, 1863).

retain the institution of slavery,[6] although a range of biblical texts were regarded as giving legitimacy to that institution.[7]

In light of the extent to which relevant biblical texts were widely discussed in the nineteenth century it is noteworthy that it was not the nineteenth but the twentieth century that saw the large rise in the occurrences of the word "slave" in Bible translations. Nor is this merely a parochial observation about the use of the term "slave" in just one modern language, albeit one of the most significant languages in the world. The strange thing that we will see is that the same tendency can be observed in other languages.

In German, the Luther Bibel of 1912 has no occurrence of *Sklave*. The Revidierte Lutherbibel of 1984 has 39 of *Sklave* and 16 of *Sklavin*. A similar change can be seen between the Elberfelder translation of 1905 with five occurrences of *Sklave/in* and its revision in 1993 with 92. The Einheitsübersetzung of 1980 has 126.

Meanwhile, in Spanish, the Reina-Valera version of 1909 has three occurrences of *esclavo* or *esclava*, one of which is in Jer 2:14, and two of which occur in Deut 28:68; the 1960 revision has 13; the 1995 revision, 37. Though made prior to the 1995 revision, the Reina-Valera Actualizada aims for more contemporary Spanish and contains the words 83 times. La Nueva Versión International of 1979 has 177 occurrences.

The same development as shown in English, German, and Spanish also occurs in other languages such as Portuguese with *escravo/a* and Dutch with *slaaf/slavin* showing increased use in later or more contemporary translations.

---

6   The early exegetical developments giving rise to this view are traced meticulously in D. M. Goldenberg, *The Curse of Ham: Race and Slavery in Early Judaism, Christianity, and Islam* (Princeton: Princeton University Press, 2003).

7   Race was, of course, absolutely central to Priest's argument. Of considerably more sophistication was the lecture by Philip Schaff, one of the most scholarly opponents of political abolition. Schaff, famed for his productivity, including editing with others the thirty-eight volumes of the Ante-Nicene, Nicene, and Post-Nicene Fathers, opposed many aspects of American slavery, but held that it was wrong to intervene politically to abolish slavery. However, even for him, an argument from race was central and he thought this actually made American slavery superior to Roman: "Justice as well as due regard for our national honor and the influence of Christianity requires us also to place the Roman system of slavery far below the American, although the latter no doubt borrowed many obnoxious and revolting statutes from the Roman slave-code. Roman slavery extended over the whole empire and embraced more than one half of its subjects, American slavery is confined to the Southern States and to one eighth of our population; the former made no distinction between race and color, the latter is based on the inferiority of the African race; Rome legalized and protected the foreign slave trade, the United States long since prohibited it as piracy" (Schaff, *Slavery and the Bible*, 18).

Now the explanation for this phenomenon is probably in part the increasing commonness within the various languages of these words. However, the explanation is certainly not that the twentieth-century European and American culture, which produced these translations, was more sensitized to the issue of slavery than the nineteenth, which saw the question of slavery right at the forefront of political debate and the course of events. Nevertheless, the twentieth-century translations were not obliged to retain the KJV's wording as the RV had been, and thus the possibility of a significant shift in choice of lexeme was possible.

Divided Translations

There are, however, problems with the more recent Bible translations, and in particular the level of inconsistency that they display in the rendering of עֶבֶד and corresponding feminine terms such as שִׁפְחָה and אָמָה. Even the most contemporary translations still only render a fraction of the eight hundred or so Old Testament examples of עֶבֶד as "slave." Most references are still rendered "servant." Translations are, therefore, dividing between what they perceive as more negative and more neutral uses of the term. Thus, for instance, in Isa 52:13 translations are unanimous in using a more neutral term such as the English "servant," just as scholars speak of this as the beginning of the "Fourth Servant Song" and not the "Fourth Slave Song." This is the case, despite the fact that the figure in this passage, in the course of duty, is treated far worse than a typical slave. Likewise in a passage which speaks of an עֶבֶד יהוה, such as Josh 1:13, it is hard to find a translation which uses the word "slave." The movement towards using the word "slave" has been thus restricted to particular passages where the word is thought to denote someone with a particular societal status (e.g., Exod 21:2 or Deut 5:15). Meanwhile, secondary literature on עֶבֶד typically either focuses on the minority of occurrences that might reflect slavery as an institution or on the even smaller number of occurrences where the "Servant of the Lord" is a theological theme.[8]

---

8   Though "servants" are more common than "slaves" in modern Bible translations, anyone looking for an article on "Servants" in the *ABD* encounters merely a cross-reference to the article on "slavery." The majority of titles pertain to the so-called Servant Songs in the literature review in H. Ringgren, U. Rüterswörden, and H. Simian-Yofre, "עֶבֶד *ʿāḇaḏ*, עֶבֶד *ʿæḇæḏ*, עֲבֹדָה *ʿăḇoḏāh*," *ThWAT* 5, cols. 982–1012 (982–85). Studies of slavery typically distinguish "debt slavery" and "chattel slavery," though the terminological distinction in Hebrew is far from clear. See, for instance, G. C. Chirichigno, *Debt-Slavery in Israel and the Ancient Near East* (JSOTSup 141; Sheffield:

The procedure of dividing between more neutral and more negative uses of the word עֶבֶד does have historical precedent, going back to
early Greek renderings of the Old Testament. In the case of these renderings, there was, of course, no overarching editorial control, and it is
not therefore surprising that we should find differences of rendering
alongside different translation techniques. In the translation of the
Seventy in the Pentateuch, the most common rendering is παῖς (126
times) followed by θεράπων (38 times), and οἰκέτης (25 times). The scarcity of δοῦλος in the Pentateuch—it only occurs thrice—contrasts with
its presence elsewhere.[9] HALOT gives the numbers of LXX occurrences
representing עֶבֶד as 340 for παῖς, 310 for δοῦλος, and 42 for θεράπων. However, the δουλ- root does occur a total of 47 times in the Pentateuch, but
this is still few by contrast with the Greek Vamvas Bible of 1850 with
255 occurrences of the δουλ- root in the Pentateuch alone. Thus there
appears to be an increase in the use of δοῦλος through time.[10] Moreover,
in the Pentateuch, since the LORD himself has δοῦλοι (Deut 32:36), it is
hard to demonstrate that there is a strong contrast between more negative and more neutral terms.[11]

At the same time, there is probably some sort of contrast, as can be
seen from the book of Exodus. On the whole, the servants of Pharaoh

<hr />

JSOT Press, 1993), 82–84, and Bernard S. Jackson, *Wisdom-Laws: A Study of the Mish-
patim of Exodus 21:1–22:16* (Oxford: Oxford University Press, 2006), 83.

9   Benjamin G. Wright III refers to the "glaring absence of δοῦλος from the Greek Pentateuch" ("עבד/δοῦλος—Terms and Social Status in the Meeting of Hebrew Biblical and
Hellenistic-Roman Culture," in *Praise Israel for Wisdom and Instruction: Essays on Ben
Sira and Wisdom, the Letter of Aristeas and the Septuagint* (JSJSup 131; Leiden: Brill,
2008), 213–45 [244]; repr. from *Semeia* 83/84 [2001]). I am grateful to Myrto Theo-
charous for drawing my attention to this article.

10 It may be that the term also becomes more negative through time. Lewan Gordesiani, *Zur mykenischen Gesellschaftsordnung* (2d ed.; Tbilissi: Logos-Verlag, 2002), 30–
40, traces the term through its entire history, from its uncertain etymology, through
the Mycenaean stage in which it involved no semantic opposition to "free," its
absence from Homer, the development of its opposition to "free" in the context of
Athenian democracy, to some continuing problems of equating it with our term
"slave." I am most grateful to Dr Gordesiani for providing me access to this work. K.
Efkleidou, "Slavery and Dependent Personnel in the Linear B Archives of Mainland
Greece" (MA diss., University of Cincinnati, 2004, accessed 20 August 2009 from
http://www.ohiolink.edu/etd/), 212–18, likewise challenges the view that the *do-e-ro*
(> δοῦλος) of the Linear B tablets are necessarily slaves, providing evidence that a
number of them in Pylos were land owners.

11 Wright, "עבד/δοῦλος," 214, referring to use of δοῦλος in the Greek Old Testament,
states: "The term δοῦλος . . . quite simply communicated to the Greek reader in this
period something different from what the word עבד did earlier."

are described as his θεράποντες.[12] θεράπων is also the word that describes Moses' relationship with God (Exod 4:10; 14:31).

The switch between οἰκέτης and παῖς in Exod 5:15–16 in describing the relationship between the Israelites and their γραμματεῖς and Pharaoh suggests that the terms are being used as near synonyms for the sake of variety. Those who work for the Israelites themselves are described either as οἰκέτης (12:44; 21:26, 27) or παῖς (20:10, 17; 21:2, 5, 20, 32). On the basis of this distribution one might suppose that θεράπων is being used as the more neutral word, and παῖς and οἰκέτης as the more negative ones, but παῖδες is used once to describe Pharaoh's servants (11:8), and οἰκέται is even used in 32:13 to describe Abraham, Isaac, and Jacob in relation to God. Any suggestion, therefore, that one of these terms is inherently negative is problematic. Except in translating the phrase מִבֵּית עֲבָדִים, paraphrased as ἐξ οἴκου δουλείας (Exod 13:3, 14; 20:2), the term עֶבֶד is never rendered by a clearly negative term in the Old Greek of Exodus.

The view that the root עבד did not have negative associations is strengthened by the observation that the Exodus is not portrayed in the Hebrew as an escape from what is associated with that root. The stated aim of the Israelites' departure from Egypt is that they might "serve" (verb עָבַד) God (3:12; 4:23; 7:16, 26; 8:16; 9:1, 13; 10:3, 7, 8, 11, 24, 26 (bis). In fact, their remembrance of their escape from Egypt is described as their "service" (עֲבֹדָה, 12:25, 26; 13:5). The root עבד occurs *more* in the book of Exodus in association with the Israelites' service of God than it does of their service of the Egyptians. This, however, has been lost to most readers since the earliest translation, when the Old Greek translation of Exodus generally used positive terms such as λατρεύω and λατρεία for service of God. However, such inconsistency is not necessary for an ancient translation. Targum Onkelos used the same root (פלח) for the Israelites' service of both the Egyptians and of God. In fact, according to the *Comprehensive Aramaic Lexicon*, all but five examples of the verb עָבַד are represented by a formulation involving the root פלח.[13]

Moving outside the book of Exodus, we may consider a famously negative use of the term עֶבֶד and what might be seen as the first reference to slavery in the Bible.[14] In Gen 9:25 the term is used in the curse of Canaan, where the phrase עֶבֶד עֲבָדִים expresses the superlative status

---

12 Exod 5:21; 7:10, 20, 28, 29; 8:5, 7, 17, 20, 25, 27; 9:14, 20a, 30, 34; 10:1, 6, 7; 11:3; 12:30; 14:5. There are other occasions when the word is used in the same sense but without an equivalent in MT: 7:9, 10a; 9:8.

13 See the Targum Studies Module on http://cal1.cn.huc.edu/.

14 The root עבד has already been used extensively within the narrative, in both an Edenic and post-Edenic context (Gen 2:5, 15; 3:23; 4:2, 12).

given by the curse. Yet the Old Greek renders the phrase as παῖς οἰκέτης, both of which words are used in clearly positive contexts elsewhere. A text like Gen 9:25 means that it is not possible to make a division between biblical occurrences of particular Greek terms on the grounds that one is consistently neutral and another consistently negative. It is thus in the period between the earliest translation and the modern era that a number of languages have developed terms with consistently negative connotations and have used these at times to represent Hebrew עֶבֶד.

Nevertheless, the Hebrew term עֶבֶד is clearly not inherently negative. This is not merely obvious from within the Hebrew Bible, but also from the fact that it appears on seals and seal impressions where it manifestly provides evidence of the status of the signatory.[15] However, in each case the עֶבֶד is subject to a higher authority. עֶבֶד is also used when no genuine subjection to someone is implied, especially in forms with a second person possessive suffix (e.g., עַבְדְּךָ in Gen 18:3). Often, of course, when addressing the deity or a monarch the expression of subjection is real enough and in other cases subjection is at least feigned, even if this is understood as pure convention, without any deeper significance.

In addition to such occurrences, for which modern translations do not use the word "slave," there are legal contexts dealing with the acquisition of or control of persons, such as Exod 21:2; Lev 25:44–46, where the use of the rendering "slave" is more common today.

Our temptation to translate one set of occurrences by "servant" and another by "slave" has the disadvantage of driving a wedge between occurrences where Hebrew has used the same word. It also has the disadvantage of missing the point that in all cases, except where subjection is merely feigned for social convention, the subjection is equally real. In fact, in the case of an עֶבֶד יהוה the subjection and ownership are far more absolute than they are for any עֶבֶד of a human master. Nor is it legitimate to discount יהוה from being a "real" master and to argue that the real conditions of an עֶבֶד with a human master were rather different from an עֶבֶד with a divine one, since the translator cannot simply set aside the thought world of the ancient text and give meaning altogether separate from it. To make a strong distinction between one servitude and the other would require textual justification. However, Riesener concludes from her investigation of the term עֶבֶד that there is a fundamental unity to the different uses of the word. The reason it can desig-

---

15   E.g., G. I. Davies, *Ancient Hebrew Inscriptions: Corpus and Concordance* (Cambridge: Cambridge University Press, 1991), 161 (§100.321); or for עבד יהוה see 155 (§100.272).

nate anyone from a slave to a person of high honour or a person in relation to God is that it is fundamentally a relational term, which describes one person as dependent upon or subordinate to another.[16] Such a common feature to the occurrences of the term surely deserves to be brought out where possible.

The insight that we should not divide between occurrences of עֶבֶד helps us return to the book of Exodus and see that, though the narrative surely does involve escape from bondage and slavery, a contrast between "slave" and "free" does not form a lexical focus in the narratives.[17] It is not the root עבד which is, so to speak, made to do the work on its own of conveying the hardship endured by the Israelites. Rather, the root is brought into association with words such as קָשֶׁה "hard" or בְּפֶרֶךְ "with rigour," עִנָּה "afflict," מרר (pi'el) "make bitter," etc., and these terms in combination with the root עבד and expressions of the Israelites' own response convey the plight of the Israelites. The problem is not merely "service" in and of itself. All this can be missed when translations render the verb עָבַד and the noun עֶבֶד inconsistently.

What Possibilities Are There for Consistency?

Having considered the disadvantages of inconsistent translation, we now need to consider what possibilities exist for a consistent translation. This will obviously vary from language to language and this discussion will deal specifically with English. At the same time, we have seen earlier that a number of European languages have more or less moved together in the question of rendering עֶבֶד. Consequently, observations relevant to English are likely to have considerable relevance for those languages too.

Without considering archaic terms, the two main contenders to be considered as renderings of the term עֶבֶד are "servant" and "slave." Although these are the main terms in use today, we could consider other terms, such as "subject," focussing on subjection, which is involved in all occurrences, or "worker," focussing on the association of

---

16   Ingrid Riesener says that it is "ein *dynamischer Relationsbegriff* . . . Der so Bezeichnete wird damit als *abhängig* von seinem jeweiligen Bezugspartner charakterisiert" (*Der Stamm* עבד *im Alten Testament: eine Wortuntersuchung unter Berücksichtigung neuerer sprachwissenschaftlicher Methoden* [BZAW 149; Berlin: De Gruyter, 1979], 268–69).

17   Riesener, *Der Stamm*, 269, denies that the word עֶבֶד generally contrasts with "free," and states of the case of Hebrew slaves: "hier wird der Sklave nicht primär als Unfreier, als Besitz-'stuck' gesehen." A text like Exod 21:5 does provide some opposition between "slave" and "free," but even here arguably as much contrast is conveyed by the verb יָצָא as by the word חָפְשִׁי.

the root with "work," and especially the word עֲבֹדָה, often rendered "work." Many of the Slavic Bible translations retain precisely this strong association, as, for instance, the Russian Synodal Bible of 1917 which uses раб, a word strongly associated with "work," in such widely diverse texts as Gen 9:25; Lev 25:44; Josh 1:2; and Isa 52:13.

But it is still hard to believe that there is a credible alternative in English to "slave" or "servant." The problems with using the word "slave" consistently to represent all occurrences of עֶבֶד are reasonably obvious. So far English Bible translations have not even felt able to render 20% of the occurrences of עֶבֶד with the word "slave." The change of introducing "slave" everywhere would be significant and also feel entirely unjustified in most of the contexts. Those texts do not contain references to slaves, even allowing for a generous definition of the term "slave." Moreover, the connotations would be wrong. Nowadays the word "slave" is almost universally felt to have negative connotations (for good reasons, of course). To expand the use of the word "slave" to represent עֶבֶד in the Old Testament would mean more occasions when we translate a term that is not inherently negative with a term that is virtually always negative. The fact that there is a significant change of connotation when moving from Hebrew to English might in fact be a serious objection to rendering *any* of the occurrences of the word עֶבֶד by "slave."

In response, however, it might be said that such a change of connotation does not need to make a translation wrong. Changes of connotation are in fact an inevitable feature when we represent texts from a distant culture. The Old Testament allowed slavery and most civilized democracies claim that they do not. Therefore when we render Old Testament narratives about slavery into one of our languages we are bound to feel a conflict of values. This is what is felt in a modern context when passages about slaves are read in public.

However, the word "slave" is notoriously problematic when used to make cross-cultural observations, because systems of unfree labour vary so considerably from one culture to another. Just as one significant period of history intervened between the translation of the KJV and of the RV, so for much of Western consciousness *two* major slave societies intervene between the Old Testament and us today: those of the Roman Empire and of the New World. It is very hard for us to think of slavery without reference to these societies, and yet we must remember that the Old Testament was almost entirely written prior to or at least without reference to Classical culture, let alone the Roman Empire. We cannot, of course, altogether avoid using terms with false associations, but the stronger those associations are, the stronger the case is for avoiding the term.

The question of the extent of slavery (by a modern definition) in ancient Israel is one that we can separate from the question of the extent to which we are entitled to represent the word "slave" in translation of ancient texts. Whereas a strong case might be made that any actual people dealt with under the legislation found in Lev 25:44–46 would be slaves by one of our definitions, we need to distinguish between the actual status of persons, and the meaning of the word we are translating. Just as today there are very different conditions for those who are called "workers," and some of these amount to little more than slavery, the same could have been the case in the ancient world. That does not give warrant to a translator to render the same term in two different ways, because the term does not have radically different associations in the different contexts. Even if we conclude that the texts describe slavery, we must avoid confusing our nomenclature for such an institution with their nomenclature. In their nomenclature, non-Israelites who endured lifelong servitude were described by the same term as those who endured temporary servitude for debt, who were in turn described by the same term as those who served God. To render the term עֶבֶד sometimes as "slave" and at other times as "servant" fails to represent the fact that there really is no clear distinction between the various occurrences of the word.

Even in the cases of עַבְדְּךָ as a self-designation where translators appear to have no appetite to introduce the word "slave," the grounds for dividing between this and other cases are weak. In many cases the subjection expressed, for instance towards the deity, is quite real. The psalmist who used this expression thirteen times in Psalm 119 did not see himself as less subject to YHWH than anyone dealt with in an Israelite law code. The practice of rendering one as "servant" and the other as "slave" is therefore questionable. Of course, it would be even more questionable to distinguish between various uses of the term in self-designation and to translate some as "servant" and others as "slave."

The word "servant," on the other hand, has less definite associations, and a great deal of flexibility. It may pain modern consciences to use the word "servant" for any worker whom we regard as having in fact been in slavery, but such consciences may not in fact be the best guides to translation. The fact that someone who in sociological categories is a slave is denoted by a particular term does not imply that the term means "slave" any more than the word מֶלֶךְ means "puppet king" because it is sometimes used to denote one.

Aside from what we deduce from the biblical text, with its various safeguards to working conditions (for example, the Sabbath), we have very little which can tell us of actual working conditions for those in servitude in ancient Israel, which might justify the translation "slave" by reference to those conditions. If ownership be the decisive factor in justifying the translation "slave," we need to recognize that the term עֶבֶד does not itself convey the sense of being owned. Besides, there can be no ownership more absolute than ownership by YHWH. Occurrences of an עֶבֶד of the deity would therefore have to be first in line to be rendered "slave" if ownership were deemed a decisive factor in justifying the translation "slave."

Even comparative material from the ancient Near East may suggest that the word "slave" should be used only with caution. The Sumerograms ÌR and ARAD, which are equivalent of Akkadian *wardum*, are not necessarily negative either. As with the biblical term, they could be used for anything from a worker to a king, viewed in relation to the deity. They could be used of positions of privilege and favour.[18] Scholars often cannot even agree which strata of society should be called "slaves."[19]

"Servant" is a possible translation in all of these contexts. Its flexibility in English reflects the flexibility of the biblical term, as also of the ancient Near Eastern ones. It does not produce a false binary opposition between "slave" and "free," which is only occasionally part of the biblical language about an עֶבֶד.

To conclude, Bible translations have evidently struggled in rendering עֶבֶד and a number have chosen inconsistency, including selective uses of the word "slave." The choice of when to use "slave" has been, to some extent, arbitrary, and inconsistency about translating the root עבד can lead to a failure to appreciate elements common to all occurrences of the word, and some narrative dynamics, such as those of the book of Exodus. Use of the English rendering "servant" and its cognate terms still appears to have fewer disadvantages.

---

18 The biblical term עֶבֶד could be used in parallel with בָּחַר "choose" (Isa 41:8, 9; 43:10; 44:1, 2) and *בָּחִיר "chosen" (42:1; 45:4; 65:9, 15).

19 G. Galil, *The Lower Stratum Families in the Neo-Assyrian Period* (Culture and History of the Ancient Near East 27; Leiden: Brill, 2007), 7–13.

The Repentance of God

ANTHONY GELSTON

The title of this paper is at first sight shocking. For, especially in a religious context, the word "repentance" most commonly denotes a turning away from sin, from acts and words that a person has either said or done or failed to say or do. The implication is that the person who repents is actually guilty of moral evil. To predicate this of God is either inconceivable or blasphemous. Yet the King James version could say quite boldly, "the LORD repented him of the evil" (2 Sam 24:16).

To a considerable extent the apparent problem can be resolved by semantic considerations. Within the English language the word "repent" does not always or necessarily have moral connotations. The proverb "Marry in haste and repent at leisure" indicates an emphasis rather on regret at a past action, whose consequences have turned out to be less satisfactory than had been hoped or intended. What is regretted in this case is an act that was not inherently morally wrong, but one that with hindsight can be recognized to have been a mistake or a misjudgement, or even one whose consequences turned out to be unsatisfactory, although this could not have been foreseen. The word "evil" similarly, although often used of what is morally wrong, is also used not infrequently of something that may be morally neutral, but is regarded as "bad" in the effects it causes. Natural disasters are an obvious example of this use of the term. In the case of both "evil" and "repent" the moral sense falls within the semantic range of the word, but is not always or necessarily present. These distinctions are clearly illustrated in an important verse (Jer 18:8), to which we shall need to return: "if that nation repents of its evil . . . I will repent of the evil which I intended to do to them." The moral sense is clearly present in the conditional clause, but in the main clause it is more natural to see an indication of God's consequent change of mind, a decision not to inflict the punitive disaster he had previously intended. The inherent limitations and ambiguities of human language alert us to the necessity of reading statements about the repentance of God with close attention to the context in which they occur.

A convenient starting-point may be found in the narrative of Jonah 3–4. The relevant material begins in 3:9, where the king's proclamation of (moral) repentance in Nineveh ends with the question "Who knows whether God may relent and change his mind (ישוב ונחם), and turn (ושב) from his fierce anger, so that we shall not perish?" The next verse relates how God observed how the Ninevites "repented (שבו) from their evil (הרעה) ways," whereupon "God changed his mind (וינחם) about the evil (הרעה), which he had said he would do to them, and he did not do it." So far the picture is quite clear. The Ninevites repent from their (morally) evil ways, and God responds to this by a change of policy, and no longer inflicts on them the punitive disaster that he had previously intended, and announced through his prophet Jonah.

This change in God's policy, however, did not please Jonah. He offered a prayer (4:2), in the course of which he explained the reason why he had not carried out God's commission to proclaim his message to Nineveh when he first received it. It was that he was aware of the merciful character of God, and in particular how he is "ready to relent from punishing (ונחם על־הרעה)." The narrative does not specify the precise nature of Jonah's objection, whether it is in principle to any change of purpose on the part of God, or to any remission of penalty as inconsistent with the upholding of moral standards, or whether Jonah resents the prospect of the non-fulfilment of his earlier prediction as implying that he is a false prophet (cf. Deut 18:22), when he has actually carried out God's commission to the letter.

At this point Jonah takes up his station outside Nineveh to await events, and to see whether his divinely commissioned prediction would come true or not. When the plant God provides for his shelter from the sun withers (at God's instigation), Jonah once again protests, and in answer to God's challenge asserts that he is right to be angry. God then addresses Jonah: "You are concerned (חסת) about the plant, . . . and should I not be concerned (אחוס) about Nineveh . . . ?" (4:10–11).

This intriguing passage contains three verbs which are significant for our enquiry: שוב, נחם, and חוס. The word שוב is used frequently in a literal sense to denote a reverse change in direction, turning back towards or returning to some earlier position. In a religious sense it is used most frequently of people turning back to God in renunciation of either apostasy or some other sin; indeed, it is the normal word for "repent" in its common religious sense. Occasionally, however, it is used of the opposite change of direction, a turning away from God, as in Num 14:43. Moberly points out that usually, though not invariably, שוב is used of human repentance, and נחם of divine repentance.[1] In

---

1   R. W. L. Moberly, "'God Is Not a Human That He Should Repent' (Numbers 23:19 and 1 Samuel 15:29)," in *God in the Fray: A Tribute to Walter Brueggemann* (ed. Tod Linafelt and Timothy K. Beal; Minneapolis, Minn.: Fortress, 1998), 112–23 (115).

Jonah 3:9, however, both words are used together to express the possibility of a change of mind on God's part, and שוב is then used a second
time in the specific sense of God "turning back from his fierce anger,"
just as Moses prayed that God would "turn back from his fierce anger"
(Exod 32:12). It is probably true to say that the real distinction between
the two words is that שוב denotes an actual change in attitude, purpose,
or action, while נחם focuses rather on the emotional aspect, which may
often be the initial motivation for the change. We may compare Zech
1:3, where God summons the people to turn back to him, so that he
may reciprocally turn back to them, and 1:16, where God says that he
has turned back to Jerusalem in mercy.

The precise meaning of the word חוס is not easy to determine, but
in the majority of the passages where it occurs in the Hebrew Bible it
has the sense of sparing someone who is at one's mercy, whether as a
conqueror (e.g., Isa 13:18; Jer 21:7), a judge (e.g., Deut 19:21), or one
who enjoys a fortuitous advantage over an opponent (as in 1 Sam
24:11[10]). In Ps 72:13 it is used positively in a wider sense of the king's
responsibility for the protection and welfare of the poor among his
subjects. In Jonah 4:10 it is used in an unusual sense with respect to
Jonah's feeling of regret for the decay of the plant that had previously
afforded him shelter, to which the closest parallel is its use in Gen
45:20, where Pharaoh instructs Joseph to tell his brothers to migrate to
Egypt with their father and all their extended family, and not to "feel
any regret" over the property they have to leave behind. In Jonah 4:11,
despite the apparent parallel with v. 10, the word seems to be used
essentially in its more common sense of God sparing the guilty (in this
case the Ninevites) the penalty that had previously been announced as
quite properly due for their "evil ways" (3:10), of which they had in the
meantime repented. In view of the collocation of vv. 10 and 11, it is
perhaps appropriate to suggest that the word has additional overtones
in v. 11 of both regret and compassion, although in the context of the
narrative as a whole it surely denotes "spare" in the sense of remitting
a penalty due, and casts God in the role of a judge. In this respect it
may be compared to Ezek 20:17, where God had spared Israel during
the wilderness wanderings, and 24:14, where God announces that he
will not spare them now, as well as to Joel 2:17, where the priests are to
pray, "Spare your people, O LORD."

The verb נחם has quite a wide semantic range, which makes it difficult to be certain of its particular nuance in certain passages. For our
immediate purposes it is necessary to examine only a limited number
of passages. We may begin with two passages where God is said to
regret a previous action, because its consequences have not been in

accordance with his purpose. In Gen 6:6 God regrets having created the human race, because of the prevalence of human wickedness, and this regret leads to God's decision to destroy the human race by a flood, except for Noah and his family. In 1 Sam 15:11, 35 God regrets having made Saul king over Israel, because Saul has not carried out God's commands, and this leads to a decision to depose Saul and appoint David king in his place. Both of these passages suggest something very similar to human repentance. Yet in neither of them is there any suggestion that the original action which God now regrets was in itself morally wrong. It is the unintended consequences of God's action that lead him in each case to regret it, and to take subsequent action to change the resulting situation. Implicit in each case is God's allowing a measure of freedom to his creatures to decide for themselves whether or not to carry out his plans, so that the direct responsibility for things going wrong lies respectively with the human race and with Saul, and not with God. The verb נחם itself in these passages seems simply to denote God's regret at the outcome of his original action, and not the subsequent action he takes to remedy the resulting situation.

This prepares us for a number of passages in which the meaning of the verb, although including the element of regret, is focused more directly on the consequent action inspired by the regret, so that "relent" is perhaps a more appropriate translation. Very clear examples of this are to be found in Amos 7:1–3 and 4–6. Both of these passages begin with a vision of God initiating judgement, first by a plague of locusts and secondly by a devastating fire. In each case the prophet intervenes, interceding that God would forgive (סלח) or desist (חדל). In each case the incident closes with God relenting (נחם), and saying, "It shall not happen." In these passages there is no doubt that God is induced to regret his original intention, and to retract it before it has been implemented. In neither passage, however, is there any suggestion that God's initial intention had been morally wrong.

In fact the wider context of the book shows that it had been morally right. In the next two visions of the prophet (7:7–9 and 8:1–3) an explanation of the object seen is first required, but, before the prophet has time to intercede for the revocation of the threatened penalty, God announces that he will not pass by his people any more. The last of the five visions (9:1–4) concludes with the statement that God will set his eyes on them for evil and not for good, clearly in the sense of adversity/disaster instead of prosperity.

Running through all these visions, as indeed through the whole book, is the picture of God as judge of his people Israel, and the evil with which he threatens them is a penalty for their sin. When the prophet intercedes with God in the first two visions, it is not on the grounds that Israel had repented (as in the case of Nineveh in Jonah 3:10), but simply on the grounds that they would not be able to survive the penalty. The fact that God relents in these cases, where there is no moral ground for rescinding the penalty in repentance on the part of the people, suggests that the word נחם in 7:3, 6 expresses the concept not only of God relenting, but also that he shows compassion, in a way similar to his compassion for the Ninevites in Jonah 4:11, where it is expressed rather by the word חוס. We shall need to return to this aspect of the meaning of נחם.

In the meantime it is necessary to examine further the use of נחם in the sense of "relent" or "reverse" a decision. There are a number of passages in which the idea occurs of reversing a decision previously announced. This is particularly the case where it is a question of God relenting over some "evil" (רעה) in the sense of "adversity" or "disaster," in effect a penalty already pronounced. In Exod 32:12–13, for instance, Moses pleads with God to relent of the evil he had threatened against the Israelites. Like Amos, Moses is unable to plead any repentance on the part of Israel as a ground for God to relent. Rather he pleads God's earlier promise to the patriarchs, and the potential misinterpretation of God's judgement by the Egyptians, if it were to be carried out. Accordingly in v. 14 God relents. Similarly, although this time without human intercession, in 2 Sam 24:16 and the parallel passage 1 Chr 21:15 God relents of an already initiated plague before it reaches Jerusalem.

The classic passage, however, is Jer 18:7–10, where God likens his dealings with nations to a potter working with clay. There is a clear balance between vv. 8 and 10, where God reverses his previous decision to impose respectively evil or good in response to a change on the part of the nation. In v. 8 God says that if a nation, on whom he has already pronounced judgement, turns back (ושב) from their moral evil (מרעתו), then God will relent (ונחמתי) of the disaster (הרעה) that he had intended to inflict on them. On the other hand, in v. 10 God says that he will relent (ונחמתי) of the good he had intended to do to a nation if it does evil in his sight. In this passage it is clear that the disaster is conceived as a merited penalty for moral evil, and prosperity as a reward for moral good, but that neither is an irrevocable decision, for both may be reversed in the light of a change of attitude and behaviour on the part of the nation concerned. As Moberly expresses it, "human repentance can avert a threatened disaster, while human wrongdoing can forfeit a promised good," and again, "YHWH's sovereignty is not exercised arbitrarily, but responsibly and responsively, interacting with the moral, or immoral, actions of human beings."[2] It is also clear in this passage that this pattern of divine judgement, which can be revoked if the guilty nation repents, is presented as universal in the scope of its operation. It is not confined to God's relationship with Israel. This is entirely consistent with God revoking the threatened penalty against the Ninevites in Jonah 3:10. The pattern is, however, definitely applied to God's dealings with Israel in Jer 26:3, 13, 19 and 42:10.

At this point we need to take note of passages in which it is said that God will not go back on a decision. In Jer 15:6 God announces that he is weary of relenting (נלאיתי הנחם), and in 20:16 the prophet refers to the destruction of Sodom and Gomorrah, when God did not relent (ולא נחם). In Ezek 24:14 God announces that his judgement is irrevocable: he will neither spare (חוס) nor relent (נחם). Similarly in Zech 8:14 God did not relent (לא נחמתי). In Jer 4:28 there is a particularly strong statement: God has spoken (דברתי), resolved (זמתי), and will neither relent (ולא נחמתי) nor go back on his judgement (ולא־אשוב ממנה). All of these passages may be understood as referring to particular situations, in which God will not relent, without going against the general principle that he will relent in response to repentance on the part of the people. Moberly draws attention to another passage, Ps 110:4, where the statement that God will not relent (ולא ינחם) is attached, not to the threat of a penalty, but to God's oath that David is to be a priest for ever after the order of Melchizedek.[3] This too relates to a particular situation, and indicates that a settled purpose on God's part can be positive as well as negative.

There are, however, two passages which at first sight suggest a different general principle, namely that God is consistent, and does not change his mind. These are Num 23:19 and 1 Sam 15:29. In the first Balaam tells Balak that God is not a human being, subject to changing his mind (ויתנחם). God does not speak, and then fail to carry out what he has said. In the second Samuel similarly tells Saul that God does not relent (ולא ינחם), because he is not a human being, who might be expected to change his mind (להנחם).

These two passages have been discussed thoroughly by Moberly,[4] and his main conclusions may be conveniently summarized here. He begins by pointing out that in each of these passages the word "repent" is accompanied by another verb denoting lying, deceit, or speaking falsely (כזב in Num 23:19 and שקר in 1 Sam 15:29). In both passages this is connected with the statement that God is not a human being, the implication being that insincerity and faithlessness are characteristic of

---

2   Moberly, "God is Not a Human," 113, 114.

3   Moberly, "God is Not a Human," 116.

4   Moberly, "God is Not a Human," 116–21.

human beings but not of God. Moberly then goes on to show that in each of these passages the statement on which God is not prepared to go back is a specific divine purpose. In Num 23:19 God is not prepared to go back on his announced purpose to bless Israel by yielding to Balak's request for a curse on them. In 1 Sam 15:29 God has already deposed Saul and determined to appoint David king over Israel in his place, and he is not prepared to go back on this decision. These two passages, then, are seen to conform to the same pattern as those considered above, where God's commitment to a decision relates to particular situations, and they are not in conflict with the general principle of mutuality and responsiveness in God's relationship with humans as set out in Jer 18:7–10.

Another whole dimension to the semantic range of the root נחם is that of "comfort" and "compassion." The active sense of "comfort" is expressed chiefly in the *pi'el* stem, although it is not always easy to distinguish the *pi'el* from the *nip'al* (the forms can be identical in the perfect tense). Particularly significant for our purposes is God's summons to comfort his people in Isa 40:1, where the sequel makes it clear that the essential content of this comfort consists in the announcement that the period of penal servitude that they have undergone is now complete. Similarly in Zech 1:17 God will comfort his people again, and this time the sequel indicates that the ground of this comfort is the fact that he will once again choose Jerusalem. It is not surprising that this message is introduced in 1:13 as דברים נחמים—"comforting words." In both these contexts the substance of the comfort is the fact that the exile is over, and the covenant between God and his people is reaffirmed.

Several further instances of God comforting his people may be found in the book of Isaiah. In 12:1 the context indicates that God's former anger has now abated, and is followed by his comfort. In 49:13 the verb נחם is used in parallel with רחם, and God's people are described as his "afflicted ones" (עניו). In this passage the sense of divine compassion for human affliction predominates. In 52:9 the statement that God has comforted his people is paralleled by a statement that God has redeemed (גאל) Jerusalem. In 51:12 God affirms that he is the comforter of his people, and asks why then should they fear mere human beings. In 61:2 the verb נחם is particularly related to mourners, but the following verse specifies those who mourn for Zion, and the wider context indicates that the comfort consists in the announcement of freedom and restoration. Similarly in Jer 31:13 the verb is used in a context of turning mourning into joy and sorrow into gladness, where the passage as a whole is once again concerned with restoration and return from exile.

The sense of "compassion" seems certainly to be present in the *nip'al* in Ps 90:13, where God is asked to "return" (שׁובה) and "have compassion" (הנחם) on his servants. Another possible instance of this meaning of the *nip'al* is Judg 21:6, where the Israelites may feel compassion for the tribe of Benjamin, although it might be argued that the sense of the verb in this passage also includes the idea of "regret" and "relenting" over the previous judicial acts which had brought the tribe of Benjamin to its present situation. The same ambiguity is present later in the passage, at 21:15. A particularly interesting example is to be found earlier in the book, at Judg 2:18, where the *nip'al* may be interpreted in two different ways. God may be said to have relented repeatedly because of the groaning of the Israelites, or alternatively to have been moved repeatedly to pity and compassion by their groaning, although it is also possible that both nuances are intended.

A similar ambiguity may be found in yet another instance of the *nip'al*, in Ps 106:45. Here, however, the sense of "compassion" predominates in the wider context. In v. 44 God observes the plight of the people and hears their cry of lament. In v. 45 he remembers his covenant, and either "relents" or "is moved with compassion" according to the multitude of his "steadfast love" (where the particular nuance of חסד is also ambiguous).[5] In v. 46 he causes them to be pitied by their captors. This is followed in v. 47 by a prayer for God to save them, and gather them from the Diaspora. These passages illustrate the potential overlap of several nuances of meaning in a single passage, and it may not always be wise to try to establish a single dominant nuance in a particular context.

The abstract noun נחמים is used in Isa 57:18 in a context which strongly suggests the meaning "comfort": God will restore comfort to the mourners among his people. The passage, however, suggests that the mourning in this context is for sin rather than for bereavement or other adversity. The meaning of נחמים in Hos 11:8, however, is far less easy to determine. The parallel clause: "my heart is turned within me" perhaps suggests the sense of "relenting" as the most probable, but the meaning "compassion" is certainly germane to the thought of the verse as a whole, and it is not unlikely that both nuances are present. The noun נחם, which occurs only in Hos 13:14, also suggests primarily the

---

5   It is a question of where the emphasis should be put. If נחם in this verse means "relents" then חסד probably denotes God's faithfulness, whereas if נחם means "is moved with compassion" then חסד probably denotes his love.

meaning of "compassion," although this time in a negative context, but the nuance of "relenting" may also be present.[6]

At this point we need to return to Jonah, and to examine in greater detail the prophet's objection to God's decision to revoke the threatened judgement on Nineveh in view of the Ninevites' repentance. In the second part of 4:2 Jonah explains his initial reluctance to undertake the mission to proclaim God's message of judgement against Nineveh. He has known all along the character of God, and in particular his readiness to relent from a previously declared intention to act in judgement and inflict a penalty. How, we may ask, did Jonah know this? The answer must surely be that this was part of the traditional belief with which Jonah was familiar. A passage like Exod 34:6–7 immediately comes to mind as just such a formulation, with which the prophet might reasonably be expected to have been familiar.

Day,[7] however, argues plausibly that a more immediate source for the prophet's quasi-credal statement may be found in Joel 2:13–14. He establishes beyond doubt that there is a literary relationship between the passages in Joel and Jonah. The most crucial evidence is that the specific description of God as "repenting of evil" or "relenting from (inflicting) a penalty" (נחם על־הרעה) is found only in Joel 2:13 and Jonah 4:2. While other quasi-credal statements about the character of God, such as that in Exod 34:6–7, emphasize God's mercy and grace, his slowness to anger and his readiness to forgive, it is only in Joel 2:13–14 and Jonah 4:2 that "repenting of evil" is given as part of the characterization of God. Further evidence of a specific literary relationship between the two passages is found in the Ninevite king's question in Jonah 3:9 — "Who knows whether God will turn and relent?", with its direct parallel in Joel 2:14. Day proceeds to argue, again plausibly, that the direction of literary dependence is that Jonah is dependent on Joel.

Our study has shown that a great deal of the difficulty occasioned initially by the concept of God "repenting of evil" arises from the inherent limitations and ambiguity of human language. In both biblical Hebrew and contemporary English the terms "repent" and "evil" are patient of a wide field of semantic interpretation, and it has become clear that careful attention must be paid to the specific contexts in which such words are used if a correct interpretation is to be achieved.

---

6   For a fuller discussion of the semantic range of the root נחם, see H. Van Dyke Parunak, "A Semantic Survey of NḤM," *Bib* 56 (1975): 512–32.

7   John Day, "Problems in the Interpretation of the Book of Jonah," in *In Quest of the Past: Studies on Israelite Religion, Literature and Prophetism: Papers Read at the Joint British-Dutch Old Testament Conference, Held at Elspeet, 1988* (ed. A. S. van der Woude; OtSt 26; Leiden: Brill, 1990), 32–47 (46–47).

The importance of this methodological principle was emphasized nearly half a century ago by James Barr.[8]

Putting together the various nuances we have detected in the semantic range of נחם, and taking into account the specific situation envisaged in Jonah, it seems then that the initially shocking statement that God repents of evil is in fact to be interpreted as a particular aspect of his readiness to forgive. The evil of which God repents is not some putative moral failure on his part, but the calamity he was on the point of inflicting, with full moral justification, on those who were morally guilty. His repentance is not regret over damage he has already inflicted, but a rescinding of his earlier judicial decision to inflict it, and this relenting is occasioned, at least in the case of Jonah 3:9–10, by the repentance of the guilty parties on whom his judgement had been pronounced. The characterization of God as "repenting of evil" in Joel and Jonah may thus be seen as encapsulating the principle governing God's relations and dealings with his human creatures set out so clearly in Jer 18:7–10.

It is a privilege and a pleasure to dedicate this study in honour of Graham Davies, in gratitude for his profound, meticulous, and lucid scholarship, and for his genial friendship within the community of students of the Hebrew Scriptures.

---

8   James Barr, *The Semantics of Biblical Language* (London: Oxford University Press, 1961), e.g., 233.

Part III

Language and Literacy

Literacy, Orality, and Literature in Israel

STUART WEEKS

It is rarely assumed or asserted any more that monarchic Israel enjoyed high levels of popular literacy, and there is little evidence for any circumstance or mechanism in Iron Age Palestine which might have given rise to what would have been, by ancient norms, such a very unusual phenomenon; this new caution prevails in part, perhaps, because similar assumptions have been challenged successfully for later Roman culture and even for the famously literate Athenian population.[1] It has become more tenable these days to start with the assumption that in Israel, as elsewhere, literacy (even in the broadest sense) was probably limited to quite a small proportion of the population, and that there must have been a substantial number of Israelites, perhaps even a vast majority, whose culture remained essentially oral.

The influence of such orality on the biblical literature has long been appreciated, of course, both by those earlier scholars who thought in terms of a historical transition from illiteracy to literacy in Israel, and, in recent decades, by those who have recognized the "mixed economy" that more probably persisted. It is widely acknowledged, therefore, that certain compositional aspects of some texts have been shaped by the conventions of oral tradition, while phenomena associated with orality are often adduced in discussions of the origin or transmission of content. It seems unlikely that anyone would now seriously reject the need to consider orality as an important component in Israelite culture, but with an acceptance of that need there comes a corresponding need to think carefully about the place of writing and literature. Indeed, by emphasizing aspects of continuity between literature and oral tradition, we run the risk of ignoring significant discontinuities between the two, and of discounting the very writtenness of the biblical texts in a society where writing was not the only option.

Before turning to that broader issue, though, it would be helpful to say a little more about the historical situation, or rather to stress how little more can be said with any confidence. It is understandably tempt-

---

1   See especially William V. Harris, *Ancient Literacy* (Cambridge, Mass.: Harvard University Press, 1989).

ing to suppose that literate culture in Israel can be understood by analogy with the better-attested cultures of Egypt and Mesopotamia, or at
least that of Ugarit, which would set literacy and literature almost exclusively within the confines of a scribal and priestly élite, trained
through an educational system which combined the acquisition of literacy with a process of acculturation.[2] Israel and Judah certainly had
literate scribes and priests, moreover, and a good proportion of the
literary and epigraphic material which has survived seems to correspond to their interests. With little direct information on many aspects
of the issue, however, we have to be aware of the substantial differences which limit the usefulness of analogy as a tool here.

Scribes in the systems usually evoked were trained at length in the
classic literature of their cultures (or of the dominant local culture),
learning to read, copy, and recite texts which commonly belonged to an
earlier age, and which were frequently written in archaic languages
very different from their own. This was not a practical matter of training in foreign tongues for trade or diplomacy, but of education in the
broader sense. It did, however, entail some acquisition of practical
skills, not least of which was the ability to write at a level beyond the
merely adequate.[3] It is not a trivial matter to become proficient in the
writing of texts in any script, at least for those who begin with experience of none, and children in the modern world progress at a similar
rate in the learning of very different types of writing.[4] This learning,
however, effectively reaches a ceiling quite quickly in some scripts,
while others are more open-ended. Although any word in Japanese, for
example, can be represented using the phonetic *kana* signs, an educated
adult will be expected to know the common *kanji*, and a very educated

---

2   For an excellent overview of scribal education in the region, see David Carr, *Writing
    on the Tablet of the Heart: Origins of Scripture and Literature* (New York: Oxford University Press, 2005).

3   Of course, not even adequacy was always necessarily achieved, and we should not
    underestimate the extent to which a scribal class may become a hereditary social
    class, rather than a guild of experts.

4   The relationship between script and the acquisition of literacy is a complicated one,
    with some evidence suggesting that logographic scripts may be easier at first, with
    phonetic, alphabetic scripts providing significant advantages at a later stage, as
    word-recognition becomes quicker; correspondingly, the orthographic complexities
    of English prove somewhat harder to learn than does vowelled Hebrew. See especially Shin-Ying Lee, David H. Uttal, and Chuansheng Chen, "Writing Systems and
    Acquisition of Reading in American, Chinese, and Japanese First-Graders," in *Scripts
    and Literacy: Reading and Learning to Read Alphabets, Syllabaries and Characters* (ed. I.
    Taylor and D. R. Olson; Neuropsychology and Cognition 7; Dordrecht: Kluwer Academic, 1995), 247–63; and Esther Geva, "Orthographic and Cognitive Processing in
    Learning to Read English and Hebrew," in Taylor and Olson, *Scripts and Literacy*,
    277–91.

one a high proportion of the rarer ones. In the related case of Chinese, it is doubtful that anyone is familiar with all the signs technically available for use, but the number of logograms known will generally be in proportion to an individual's level of education and experience of reading. The writing systems used for Egyptian and Akkadian have this open-ended quality, along with other features which placed scribal orthography some way beyond basic literacy: it would have been very difficult to write like a scribe without having been trained as a scribe.

None of this, so far as we can tell, would have been an issue for scribes in Israel and Judah. Although the biblical literature shows the influence at some points of literature from various other regions, there is no evidence of any specific, intense grounding in the scribal and literary traditions of either Egypt or Mesopotamia, and we have no very good reason to suppose that there would have been sufficient cultural influence from either region in this period to motivate such an education: it is no small matter to educate one's scribes in the archaic languages and literature of a foreign country.[5] Even if education did involve the use of literature produced more locally, in Hebrew or Aramaic, these languages did not employ open-ended scripts, and to reach a high level of competence would have required much less practice in reading or copying.[6] More nebulously, although the point is no less important, it is difficult to tell what perception Israel and Judah had of their own culture in the monarchic period, and we cannot assume the strong sense of cultural and scribal tradition which underpinned the enculturating aspects of education in Egypt and Mesopotamia. There is

---

5   Carr, *Writing*, 56–59, 84–85, is able to adduce extensive cutural and political connections with both Egypt and Mesopotamia for the Late Bronze Age, but the evidence for the Israelite period in Palestine is altogether much thinner, and this is a period of significant political and cultural re-alignment, for which continuity with previous practices cannot be assumed. The literary evidence, especially, would be more persuasive if it pointed in a particular direction or dated from a particular period, but setting the influence of, say, *Amenemope* on Proverbs beside that of *Gilgamesh* on Qoheleth points to something much more atomistic than intensive influence from any one region.

6   Scribes would also, of course, have required less practice in foreign language. For Ugarit, where there seems to have been less emphasis on training in Ugaritic itself than in Mesopotamian languages and literature, Seth L. Sanders summarizes the situation: "The reason there was so little scribal training in West Semitic before the Late Iron Age is that writing was understood as linguistically transparent. Technically, learning it was thought not to require much curriculum beyond the alphabet itself" ("Writing and Early Iron Age Israel: Before National Scripts, Beyond Nations and States," in *Literate Culture and Tenth-Century Canaan: The Tel Zayit Abecedary in Context* [ed. Ron L. Tappy and P. Kyle McCarter Jr.; Winona Lake, Ind.: Eisenbrauns, 2008], 97–112 [105]).

a risk in this, moreover, of imposing entirely anachronistic notions of education.[7]

The different circumstances and requirements suggest that we should beware of looking too far abroad for models of education in Israel or Judah. Despite the absence of direct evidence for schools, it is possible that they existed, and that some scribes learned to read with a full panoply of texts and institutional support.[8] It hardly seems less likely, however, that all or many learned their basic skills at home, or in a makeshift classroom with a paid tutor, and that sort of route may have been available to others. While the average small farmer would have found little use for writing, it is possible that some members of the merchant or artisan classes would have found an education for their sons cheaper over time than, say, paying a scribe to inscribe jars.[9] If it

---

7   Of modern assumptions about education and literacy, M. T. Clanchy writes in another context: "Humanist schoolmasters propagated and reinforced all sorts of myths and dubious ideas about literacy, such as that it stems from schooling rather than the home . . . that its inspiration is secular rather than religious, that it is elitist rather than inclusive, uniform rather than multicultural, and town-centred rather than rural. All these assumptions fed into the state schooling programmes of nineteenth-century reformers . . . and thence into the beliefs of the schooled populations of today." His further comments are particularly appropriate to the discussion here: "Within their own terms of reference . . . the humanists were absolutely right; their peculiar curriculum of ancient Greek and Latin did require a special and exclusive sort of schooling, which was ultimately epitomized in the Victorian Classical Sixths of the English public schools and their equivalents in the other European nations" (*From Memory to Written Record: England 1066–1307* [2d ed.; Oxford: Blackwell, 1993], 15–16).

8   I have written elsewhere on the vexed question of scribal schools and their existence; see Stuart Weeks, *Early Israelite Wisdom* (Oxford Theological Monographs; Oxford: Clarendon, 1994), ch. 8. As Carr, *Writing*, 113, points out, such schools were not always typical of the educational systems even in Egypt and Mesopotamia. Graham Davies has, of course, written on this subject himself; see his "Were There Schools in Ancient Israel?" in *Wisdom in Ancient Israel: Essays in Honour of J. A. Emerton* (ed. J. Day, R. P. Gordon, and H. G. M. Williamson; Cambridge: Cambridge University Press, 1995), 199–211.

9   How far this actually happened is hard to determine. Ian Young ("Israelite Literacy: Interpreting the Evidence," *VT* 48 [1998]: 239–53, 408–22) suggests that the evidence points to literacy only amongst scribes, administrators, and priests, although he holds open the possibility that some craftsmen had minimal skills. His treatment of the famous Lachish Letter 3.4–13, however, shows one aspect of the difficulties. Though this text surely indicates an expectation that junior army officers be literate, Young's conclusion that this shows that "members of the upper class in Judah at this time prided themselves on being part of a literate élite" (411) assumes both an identity of the "upper class" with scribes and administrators, and membership of that class by junior officers; William M. Schniedewind ("Orality and Literacy in Ancient Israel," *RelSRev* 26 [2000]: 327–32) takes it to prove the opposite, and we really do not know about such matters. Sanders, "Writing," puts a case for trade as the context

was confined, then, neither by the complexity of the script nor by the existence of a closed educational system, the extent and the degree of literacy in Israel and Judah at any time may have been determined more by economic convenience and social expectation than by membership of any single profession, and it is difficult, furthermore, to assess quite how literacy would have related to the availability and use of literary texts.[10] Clearly, we are not in a position to say anything definite, except that we should avoid presuming *a priori* some very specific context for the biblical literature.

If the other cultures of the ancient Near East offer little help for determining the social origins of biblical literature, they do, however, provide some important indications of its nature, and help us to set some bounds to the extent of oral influence. At least since Gunkel, and the nineteenth-century romantic interest in folklore, many scholars have viewed some or all of the biblical literature in terms of a fundamental continuity with oral traditions. Whether this is seen in terms of literature "fixing" oral material or of oral-traditional practices shaping the form and presentation of literature, such a view has tended to presume a transition or continuing interaction between the two within an Israelite context. As Niditch puts it, "[t]o study Israelite literature is to examine the place of written words in an essentially oral world and to explore the ways in which the capacity to read and write in turn informs and shapes orally rooted products of the imagination."[11]

Niditch's own, influential position is more nuanced than that of many. Dundes, for instance, declares that "The Bible consists of orally transmitted tradition written down," and cites with approval the view of Koch, from a form-critical perspective, that "[n]early all the Old Testament, whether the Tetrateuch stories, the psalms, or prophetic speeches, had been passed down orally for a long period before they

---

within which literacy actually survived the Late Bronze/ Iron Age transition, being picked up only secondarily by the state.

10   We should beware of attributing modern uses of literature to ancient readers: both Near Eastern and classical practices suggest that literature was intended more for performance than solitary reading, and although a cultic, liturgical setting is probable for some, we know little about the context in which many texts were read. In any case, however, literacy would not in itself have been the prime qualification for access to literature, so much as entrance to those contexts in which literature was performed, be they the temple, the public square, or the drawing room. On "reading" as "reading out" in the biblical texts, see especially Daniel Boyarin, "Placing Reading: Ancient Israel and Medieval Europe," in *The Ethnography of Reading* (ed. J. Boyarin; Berkeley, Ca.: University of California Press, 1993), 10–37.

11   Susan Niditch, *Oral World and Written Word: Orality and Literacy in Ancient Israel* (Library of Ancient Israel; London: SPCK, 1997), 134.

came to be written down."[12] Although such statements have often been made, however, it is most unlikely that they are true. There is a historical problem here, to be sure, insofar as the dates of many texts are disputed, and the circumstances in which they arose uncertain. Even so, it is difficult to understand in some cases why the textual versions should not have appeared almost immediately, if there was a perceived need for the preservation or circulation of the material: writing was not some late development in the society, it is far the most efficient way of preserving material, and works like the psalms are generally supposed to have arisen in circles which would probably have been highly literate.[13] There are some more fundamental issues here, however, and before turning to questions about the interaction of the oral and written, let us focus for the moment on the seemingly simpler question of the extent to which biblical literature actually does have an oral origin or precedent in Israel.

Writing is far from being a simple recording mechanism: if it preserves, fixes, and disseminates material that already exists, it also creates new possibilities for composition, and we find the roots of much ancient literature amongst these. An obvious example is the law code, which can present, arrange, and fix hundreds of laws. Although individual laws and customs were certainly used before such codes (and probably continued to be used in both Mesopotamia and Greece), it is questionable whether they would, or could, have been organized in this way, and a code on the scale of Hammurabi's, or of the Great Code of Gortyn, would have been inconceivable before the invention of writing. That is, literally inconceivable: oral cultures do not sit around aspiring to create such works until the technology arrives to permit them, and the notion of fixing things in writing is consequent upon the development of writing.[14] So too, rather differently, are several types of literature which emerge in Egypt, where writing gave, for the first time, a voice to the dead among the living. It is a matter of definition whether tomb autobiographies should themselves be regarded as literary, but they were highly influential upon the development of many literary

---

12 Alan Dundes, *Holy Writ as Oral Lit: The Bible as Folklore* (Lanham, Md.: Rowman & Littlefield, 1991), 20, citing (15) Klaus Koch, *The Growth of the Biblical Tradition: The Form-Critical Method* (London: Black, 1969), 81; trans. of *Was ist Formgeschichte? Neue Wege der Bibelexegese* (Neukirche-Vluyn: Neukirchener Verlag, 1964).

13 Conversely, it is not easy to understand how or why such ephemera as prophetic oracles did come to be preserved in writing, unless, of course, the works which we have are not quite what they claim to be.

14 The development of written codes in Greece is examined in the context of orality and literacy by Kevin Robb, *Literacy and Paideia in Ancient Greece* (New York: Oxford University Press, 1994), chs. 3–5.

works.[15] One of the earliest and greatest Egyptian narratives, the *Tale of Sinuhe*, presents itself (fictionally) as such an autobiography, and the classic instruction genre, with its own testamentary flavour, seems closely related to the ethical sections of the tomb inscriptions.[16] Indeed, the very tendency of Egyptian literature to present all sorts of material as the speech of an individual seems to go back to these texts. The same point could be made, with greater or lesser degrees of certainty, about various other ancient compositions: they are not simply written manifestations of oral paradigms.

The extent to which Israelite literature emerged directly from other uses of writing within Israel itself is uncertain. Particular "literate" genres have surely been inherited from elsewhere, though, and that brings me to a second point: if a text or type of text does go back to oral prototypes, it does not necessarily do so directly, and the transition did not necessarily occur locally. We may suppose, to take an extreme case, that the basic characteristics of rhythmic poetry were developed for oral transmission in the distant past—but that does not make John Keats an oral poet. The facts that some characteristics of oral composition may persist into written modes of composition, and that literature may choose deliberately to imitate oral composition, make it difficult to assess the significance of oral traits in any given text. In Judges, for instance, we may freely acknowledge that many stories are told in a style which is oral-traditional, but that does not prove that the writer or his source heard those very stories told orally: traditional modes of expression may simply be a genre-marker for literary compositions, as in the case of many modern fairy-tales. As Niditch concedes, "[i]t is, of course, extremely difficult if not in many cases impossible to distinguish between oral-traditional imitative written works and orally performed works that were then set in writing."[17]

The issue of locality complicates matters further. Although the *use* of proverbs may be an oral phenomenon, the *collecting* of proverbs is a literary activity, and in the ancient world almost certainly gave rise to the creation of new aphorisms in the genre of sentence literature. So where this genre is picked up in the book of Proverbs, what are we dealing with? Sayings collected locally from oral tradition, sayings

---

15   See especially Jan Assmann, "Schrift, Tod und Identität: Das Grab als Vorschule der Literatur im alten Ägypten," in *Schrift und Gedächtnis: Beiträge zur Archäologie der literarischen Kommunikation* (ed. Aleida Assmann, Jan Assmann and Christof Hardmeier; Archäologie der literarischen Kommunikation 1; Munich: Fink, 1983), 64–93.

16   See Stuart Weeks, *Instruction and Imagery in Proverbs 1–9* (Oxford: Oxford University Press, 2007), ch. 1.

17   Niditch, *Oral World*, 125.

inherited from other, foreign sentence literature—perhaps originating in oral traditions elsewhere—or sayings composed *ad hoc* to create new sentence literature? There is no simple answer, and it is clearly unhelpful to rely on the original orality of proverbial performance to provide one. Once literature has itself taken up the contents or conventions of oral tradition, they may be passed on or imitated across long distances or periods of time through purely literary processes, and the recognition of their original nature may tell us little or nothing about the origins or culture of the work in which they appear.

Not all ancient literature, then, has an origin in oral tradition, and even material which seems oral in origin may never actually have existed in that form, at least in Israel. With respect to both these points, it is important to appreciate that writing and literature had been established for many centuries in the region before there even was an Israel, and that the relationship between the oral and the literary in Israel or Judah can hardly be considered without reference to a much broader picture. From the second, in particular, though, it is also clear that we cannot work with a simple binary opposition between the oral and the literate, at least in terms of what is produced by each. This problem, in fact, goes deeper: although it may seem obvious that one is spoken and the other written, difficulties arise as soon as we try to characterize, say, a written poem read out loud, or the transcript of a taped oral performance. Those difficulties become especially acute, of course, in the ancient context, where much literature was written for performance out loud, and was perhaps rarely read silently.[18] If we shift our attention from the mode of delivery to the mode of composition, though, it still remains no easier to say which someone is creating when, for instance, they improvise a speech or poem around a set of notes. These sorts of problems are not merely fanciful objections: writing of sub-Saharan Africa, Ruth Finnegan observed that "[a] poem first composed and written down . . . may pass into the oral tradition and be transmitted by word of mouth, parallel to the written form; oral compositions, on the other hand, are sometimes preserved by being written down. In short,

---

18   Although silent reading was unusual, against the common assertion that it was so rare in classical and late antiquity as to provoke astonishment see F. D. Gilliard, "More Silent Reading in Antiquity: *Non omne verbum sonabat*," *JBL* 112 (1993): 689–94. The situation for Hebrew readers is uncertain, and the dynamics of text with an unvocalized script rather different, but habit is not the only issue: the difficulties of copying a text point to performance or shared reading aloud as the simplest way to achieve distribution or publication, and the most efficient use of whatever copies did exist.

the border-line between oral and written in these areas is often by no means clear-cut."[19]

This might push us towards Niditch's idea of a "continuum between Israelite orality and literacy,"[20] but that idea actually implies a very clear distinction, and for Niditch, the two do not merge but intertwine. This "continuum" involves a discernibly oral "aesthetic," which permeates much of the biblical literature, and which can be identified through a specifically oral style and register. Alongside that aesthetic, there sits a particular set of attitudes toward writing which, in the earlier monarchic period at least, are deemed "illiterate" —more typical of oral than of literate cultures. We have already touched on the problems involving style and register, but it should be noted that Niditch is willing to associate with oral style even features that are hardly specific to oral composition, such as the use of divine epithets, or of repeated *Leitworte*. "Illiterate" attitudes to writing, moreover, are supposedly reflected in, for example, the use of monumental inscriptions that were not intended to be read—which would presumably make, say, the Vietnam Veterans Memorial Wall a testament to modern US illiteracy— whilst literacy is approached largely in terms of the practical uses of writing.[21] Such criteria load the dice in favour of orality for almost any creative composition, and others are introduced on similar lines even with respect to non-creative activities.[22] It seems pointless to quibble over precise criteria, however, when more fundamental problems of definition and distinction are involved: much of the material that Niditch seems to be discussing does not reflect the tension or connection between two separate phenomena, so much as the capacity of one thing to become another when it changes context or function.

In the end, for all that we may recognize oral influences upon much of the biblical literature, and the possibility that this literature arose through more complicated processes than those typically involved in

---

19   Ruth Finnegan, *Oral Literature in Africa* (The Oxford Library of African Literature; Oxford: Clarendon, 1970), 52.

20   Niditch, *Oral World*, 108. Carr, *Writing*, 6–7, is critical of the term and concept.

21   Cf. Niditch, *Oral World*, 58–59: "the purpose of writing in these cases is not primarily for record keeping or for future consultation or even in order that the inscription be read in its own time. . . . Such writing is monumental and iconic. It reflects a respect for the ways in which writing creates and transforms, a respect for writing more common among the illiterate than among those who are literate in the modern sense."

22   So, for instance, Niditch (*Oral World*, 68) comments on omen texts that "[t]he practical benefits of writing thus intermingle with oral-world assumptions about the efficacy of omens." It is difficult to see what, though, is specifically "oral-world" about such assumptions, unless she means simply that they may pre-date the existence of the texts.

modern authorship, what we actually have is literature, and the fact of that literature's emergence in a primarily oral culture. This is a great deal more interesting than it sounds, and potentially more significant than any question of oral influence. As Walter Ong has emphasized, we tend to look at orality from a profoundly literate perspective,[23] and one aspect of this may be that we tend to accept literature as natural or inevitable, without always recognizing its implications in a less literate society. These implications lie in various areas, and there is a whole range of ways in which scholars have understood literacy and literature to shape thought and society. Here I want to focus briefly, however, on the more specific issues concerning history-writing, which spring from the capacity of writing to fix and preserve. This capacity is vital for some purposes, but it is a cultural bias on our part to assume that it is inherently a valuable characteristic. We need, in fact, to appreciate that the absence of such a capacity in oral tradition may be no less valuable or valued.

It should be noted first that oral composition is commonly improvisational, and not intended to produce material which will be fixed. To take a familiar instance, the Parry-Lord hypothesis for the origin of the Homeric texts does not envisage verbatim memorization of long epics, but the use of a narrative framework and remembered rhythmic formulae to create a fresh poem for each performance.[24] Although shorter poems may be memorized and passed on essentially unchanged, creativity and adaptation is a hallmark of much oral performance,[25] whilst the memorization of long poems is more commonly associated with literate societies, and the notion of a fixed text.[26] Oral performance is

---

23   Walter J. Ong, *Orality and Literacy: The Technologizing of the Word* (2d ed.; London: Routledge, 2002), 7–10.

24   The hypothesis is set out most famously in Albert B. Lord, *The Singer of Tales* (Harvard Studies in Comparative Literature 24; Cambridge, Mass.: Harvard University Press, 1960).

25   So, for instance, Finnegan, *Oral Literature*, 148–49, notes in different African settings both the composition of new elegies for funerals, "using the accepted idioms and forms," and the apparent transmission of certain famous elegies over long periods. As she notes elsewhere, though (107), preconceived ideas may have led some Western observers to overlook the degree of creativity involved in much poetic performance.

26   As one psychologist puts it, "the human accomplishment of lengthy verbatim recall arises as an adaptation to written text and does not arise in cultural settings where text is unknown. The assumption that nonliterate cultures encourage lengthy verbatim recall is the mistaken projection by literates of text-dependent frames of reference" (Ian M. L. Hunter, "Lengthy Verbatim Recall: the Role of Text," in *Progress in the Psychology of Language* [ed. Andrew W. Ellis; London: Lawrence Erlbaum Associates, 1985], 207–35 [207]). Hunter defines "lengthy" as over fifty words. David C. Rubin, *Memory in Oral Traditions: The Cognitive Psychology of Epic, Ballads, and Count-*

quintessentially an ephemeral activity, through which stories or themes find constant re-expression, rather than a conscious re-presentation of established versions. Improvisation and adaptation is also found in the transmission of matter which might be considered more specifically historical or factual. Thomas's study of family traditions in Athens, for example, highlights the extent to which these were oriented to the contemporary needs and circumstances of each generation.[27] As she observes elsewhere, "If traditions are fundamental to the current social and geographical organization of a group (tribe, city, family), anthropologists find that they may change with alarming rapidity when the social divisions themselves change"; and in the case of Athenian genealogies, "undemocratic and unsuitable ancestors were quietly set aside and eventually forgotten."[28]

This warns us not to place too much reliance on oral tradition as a source for historical reconstruction, and should give pause for thought, at least, to those who see such tradition as a bridge between historical events and later biblical sources.[29] The data change, however, not

---

ing-Out Rhymes (New York: Oxford University Press, 1995) has examined the transmission of various oral genres, noting the ways in which works are formulated to assist recollection. He finds variation, though, even in very short works, and considerable "instability" in longer ones. For the handful of known or supposed counter-examples, see Ong, *Orality and Literacy*, 61–67. Professional "remembrancers" do exist in some societies, but their role is generally confined to the transmission of very specific data, or to a more general remembering of, for example, decisions reached by councils.

27 Rosalind Thomas, *Oral Tradition and Written Record in Classical Athens* (Cambridge Studies in Oral and Literate Culture 18; Cambridge: Cambridge University Press, 1989), chs. 2–3.

28 Rosalind Thomas, *Literacy and Orality in Ancient Greece* (Key Themes in Ancient History; Cambridge: Cambridge University Press, 1992), 109.

29 Certain data can be preserved for long periods in oral tradition, but it can be difficult to identify which elements have been passed down, and very difficult to disentangle fact from interpretation. As Elizabeth Tonkin puts it, "professional historians who use the recollections of others cannot just scan them for useful facts to pick out, like currants from a cake" (*Narrating our Pasts: The Social Construction of Oral History* [Cambridge Studies in Oral and Literate Culture 22; Cambridge: Cambridge University Press, 1992], 6). In her chapter 5, she provides a valuable critique of Jan Vansina's influential supposition, that oral tradition typically passes on a core of past knowledge, susceptible to critical examination as a document would be. Issues of contextualization aside, individual data are liable to what is sometimes called in the field "structural amnesia," of which the Athenian genealogies are only one example. J. Goody and I. Watt ("The Consequences of Literacy," in *Literacy in Traditional Societies* [ed. J. Goody; Cambridge: Cambridge University Press, 1968], 27–68 [33]) note an instance from Ghana, where the Gonja attributed seven sons to their founder, corresponding to the number of tribal divisions whose chiefs were eligible to become head of state; sixty years after this was recorded, two of those divisions had ceased to exist, and the founder then "was credited with only five sons." Biblical

because the transmission is unreliable, so much as because the past is subservient to the present, and the changing values or situations of the tradents are expressed, consciously or unconsciously, through changing depictions of the past (mirroring, to a great extent, the way in which human memory itself can re-shape experience). Without a fixed and canonical version of the past, moreover, a society can contain variant traditions, supporting different claims or senses of identity, which need never meet, let alone come into conflict. The introduction of written history, however, changes all that, and the promulgation of such history within a primarily oral society, especially if it is backed by political authority, not only creates tensions, but potentially re-shapes self-understanding within the society.

Shryock's research amongst the Bedouin in Jordan offers many insights into the process.[30] Seeking to collect and examine the oral histories of two tribes, Shryock found himself in a situation where different groups maintained steadfastly different accounts of the past, so that the possibility of him creating a single account, validated by publication, was perceived by his informants as profoundly problematic, even though it covered a relatively minor set of events and relationships. On a much wider scale, printed national histories of Jordan were already changing things, not only by promoting a past oriented to Hashemite interests, but by linking the past to the nation, so that the national boundary, for example, artificially excluded consideration of the cisjordanian Bedouin. This is to simplify the matter considerably, but the key point for our present purpose is the radical difference which it highlights between written and oral histories, and the tension which can exist between them. A similar cautionary tale is told by Henige of Torben Monberg, who returned to the site of his fieldwork in Oceania to discover what impact his published collection of local tales had had on the population. He discovered disquiet not only about the omission of some tales, which it was assumed would now die out, and about the inclusion of tales which put some people's ancestors in a bad light, but also about the exclusion of some perspectives: "One informant had an answer for Monberg . . . he should 'make a new book containing all the different versions of stories' since this would be a work that 'nobody

---

scholars may care to reflect on that story for other reasons, but the significant general point is that even—perhaps especially—key structural information is subject to rapid revision.

30   Andrew Shryock, *Nationalism and the Genealogical Imagination: Oral History and Textual Authority in Tribal Jordan* (Comparative Studies on Muslim Societies 23; Berkeley, Ca.: University of California Press, 1997).

would fight about.'"[31] Goody and Watt, moreover, cite the example of the Tiv in Nigeria, whose typically flexible genealogies were so widely used in court cases that British administrators made the effort to record them for posterity: in the next generation, of course, subsequent administrators found themselves seriously out of step with the Tiv, to whom the records now seemed inaccurate, and the attempt to preserve tradition became a source of deep disagreement.[32] If the other examples show the difficulties arising from acknowledged variation between traditions, this last shows something no less important: the recreated past in an oral society is not seen as recreated, and does not lack authority.

For the very different context of medieval England, Clanchy notes that,

> without documents, the establishment of what passed for truth was simple and personal, since it depended on the good word of one's fellows. Remembered truth was also flexible and up to date, because no ancient custom could be proved to be older than the memory of the oldest living wise man. There was no conflict between past and present, between ancient precedents and present practice. . . . "[T]he law itself remains young, always in the belief that it is old."[33]

His further observation, that attitudes to writing were correspondingly informed by a deep popular mistrust, could be applied to many societies in which writing has been given an authoritative role against a largely oral backdrop. In the Israelite context, it has long been understood that the creation of the Pentateuch and the historical Books was an unusual, perhaps unprecedented, move toward the creation of a national history, and that these books probably played a significant role in the establishment or shaping of identity.[34] We must also appreciate, however, that so far as those who received them were concerned, they effectively put an end to the constant reinvention of history and identity which is so characteristic of oral societies, or at least pushed it into the sort of literate channels exemplified by the reworking of the Deuteronomistic History in Chronicles. Rather than presuming simple acquiescence or enthusiasm, we must further understand that promulgation of the biblical texts imposed upon their society not only these

---

31 David Henige, *Oral Historiography* (London: Longman, 1982), 128, citing Torben Monberg, "Informants Fire Back: A Micro-Study in Anthropological Methods," *Journal of Polynesian Studies* 84 (1975): 218–24.

32 Goody and Watt, "Consequences," 32.

33 Clanchy, *From Memory*, 296. The quotation is from F. Kern, *Kingship and Law in the Middle Ages* (Oxford: Blackwell, 1939), 179.

34 See Stuart Weeks, "Biblical Literature and the Emergence of Ancient Jewish Nationalism," *BibInt* 10 (2002): 144–57.

new constraints, which may not have been welcome to everybody, but also a significantly new relationship with the past.

It is important, then, to emphasize that writing is not just the continuation of orality by other means. If literate and oral methods continued to interact throughout the Israelite period, as they did, indeed, in much later Judaism, we must recognize, nonetheless, that they were also different things, and that interaction does not imply an identity of character or function. Written texts may inherit oral features but they may also have their own separate origins; they may be performed orally, moreover, but they are memorized, not improvised. Carr writes that, "[o]rality and writing technology are joint means for accomplishing a common goal: accurate recall of the treasured tradition,"[35] but the treasured traditions of oral societies are not fixed or agreed: to copy or recite them, rather than recall and compose them afresh each time, is to alter their nature. To fix them is to change them. The written tradition no longer adapts fluidly to the changing needs of its context, and if it tells one version, then it may exclude countless others for ever. Once it had been fixed by writers, then, and promulgated as a text, the story of Israel was no longer shaped by Israel; indeed, we might say instead that Israel came to be shaped by its story.

It is a pleasure to offer this to Graham Davies on the occasion of his retirement. His thoughtful and thorough work on Israel's writings, both biblical and epigraphic, has left us all in his debt.

---

35   Carr, *Writing*, 7.

Light on ליץ

A. A. MACINTOSH

I

There have been over the years a number of attempts to give an account of the root ליץ and its derivatives.[1] None, however, can be said to have been satisfactory. Accordingly the standard dictionaries of biblical Hebrew display some uncertainty and, as a consequence, differ from one another in their treatment of the root. While all give the meaning "scorn," "mock," "*spotten*," and the like, that sense is sometimes related to arrogant, insolent speech,[2] and sometimes to foolish babbling.[3] Further uncertainty derives from attempts to describe the relationship of such meanings with an apparently very different one, universally agreed for some instances of the *hipʿil*, i.e., "mediator," "ambassador," "interpreter," "*Dolmetscher*." But here another complication presents itself: Gesenius-Buhl,[4] followed by the most recent edition of this work,[5] distinguishes two roots ליץ, the first denoting "scorn," "*spotten*," etc., together with "*übermütig behandeln*," "boasting," "*großsprecherisch sein*"; the second (*hipʿil* only) denoting "mediate,"

---

1   In what follows ליץ will serve as a general indication of the root and its various forms. I am grateful to J. A. Emerton and B. A. Mastin for helpful comments on a draft of this paper.

2   E.g., KBL, 481, *qal*, "*grossprecherisch sein*," cf. *HAL* 2:503, "*das grosse Wort führen*," "brag," "talk big."

3   E.g., KBL, 481, *hitpoʿlel*, "*sich als dummen Redner, Spötter erweisen*," cf. *HAL* 2:503 *qal*, as an alternative, "*zuchtlos sein*," "be chatterers," cf. *DCH* 4:544, which understands "scorn," "scoff" as belonging to the vocabulary of the Wisdom tradition and to constitute a contrast to the חכם or wise man. There being no references to cognate languages in this work, the judgment is made solely on consideration of the context.

4   F. Buhl, ed., *Wilhelm Gesenius' hebräisches und aramäisches Handwörterbuch über das Alte Testament* (16th ed.; Leipzig: F. C. W. Vogel, 1915), 386. For Buhl's particular treatment of ליץ, see Section II below.

5   R. Meyer and H. Donner, eds., *Wilhelm Gesenius hebräisches und aramäisches Handwörterbuch über das Alte Testament* (18th ed.; Berlin: Springer, 1987–), 3:609.

"interpret," "*Dolmetscher*," etc. Similarly Barth in *ThWAT* concludes that if מֵלִיץ is the *hipʿil* of לִיץ, it must be derived from לִיץ II.[6]

Again, BDB understands the form יְלִיץ as *qal* (of which another, perfect form is clearly attested), while Gesenius in his *Thesaurus*[7] and its successors parse it as a *hipʿil*,[8] giving it much the same meaning as the *qal* (*illusit*) as well as the meaning "interpretation."

Where the evidence of cognate languages is concerned, Schultens, writing in the eighteenth century, appealed to Arabic لاص, *lāṣa*,[9] and his suggestion has influenced scholarly opinion right up to the nineteenth and twentieth centuries (see further Section VI below). This Arabic word, then, is widely cited, but often tentatively.[10] Gesenius, in the second edition of his *Thesaurus*, states that he had originally followed Schultens in this matter, but that he had changed his mind, preferring to compare the specifically Hebrew words לוע "to swallow down" and לעע "to stammer" or "to mock."[11]

Such observations are enough to indicate the grounds on which Barth is led to characterize Hebrew lexicography as, on this matter, confused ("... spiegelt sich die Verlegenheit der hebr. Lexikographie").[12]

II

An important milestone in the modern quest was reached as a result of articles by Joüon[13] and Buhl.[14] Joüon noticed that the rendering "mock," "scorn," "*se moquer*," "*spotten*," regarded as the principal meaning of the root by most modern authorities and commonly so translated in the

---

6 C. Barth, "לִיץ *ljṣ*, לְלִיץ *lîṣ*, לֵץ *leṣ*, לָצוֹן *lāṣôn*, מֵלִיץ *melîṣ*," *ThWAT* 4, cols. 567–72 (= *TDOT* 7:547–52).

7 W. Gesenius, *Thesaurus philologicus criticus linguae hebraeae et chaldaeae Veteris Testamenti* (2d ed.; 3 vols.; Leipzig: F. C. W. Vogel, 1835–58), 2:751.

8 So the recent eighteenth edition (see n. 5 above), as well as KBL, 481, and *HAL* 2:503.

9 Albert Schultens, *Proverbia Salomonis* (Leiden: Johannis Luzac, 1748), 4.

10 See, e.g., the comments of BDB, 539.

11 Gesenius (*Thesaurus philologicus*, 2:750) supposes that the basic meaning, typified by the combinations לע, לח, לה, is the mouth opened to fulfil these functions. In respect of לוע, he suggests that the word comes to mean "*balbutire*," "*inepte loqui*," "to stammer," "to babble incoherently."

12 Barth, *ThWAT* 4, col. 567 (= *TDOT* 7:547).

13 P. Joüon, "Notes de lexicographie hébraïque," *MUSJ* 5 (1911-12): 415-46.

14 F. Buhl, "Die Bedeutung des Stammes לוץ oder ליץ im Hebräischen," in *Studien zur semitischen Philologie und Religionsgeschichte Julius Wellhausen zum siebzigsten Geburtstag am 17. Mai 1914 gewidmet* (ed. K. Marti; BZAW 27; Giessen: Alfred Töpelmann, 1914), 81–86.

later of the ancient versions, is nowhere represented in the LXX. He cites the following figures for "scorn"[15] as a rendering in the versions other than the LXX: the Vulgate, 15 times; the Peshitta, 7; the Targum, 20.[16] The conclusion reached by Joüon was that the sense "scorn" could not be detected for ליץ in the Hebrew Bible, but rather belonged to post-biblical Hebrew, to what used to be styled "New Hebrew." Buhl approved Joüon's finding and set out evidence to the effect that the common biblical adjectival form לֵץ, now supplanted by לֵיצָן, became part of the stock of Talmudic vocabulary, generating also the abstract term ליצנות.[17] The לֵיצָן was the person who mocked frivolously what was sacred. All mockery is forbidden according to *b. Meg.* 25b,[18] with the exception of the mocking of idol-worship. From this the usage was widely applied to include all immoral and frivolous activities, such as the Philistines' mocking of the blind captive Samson, or attending gladiatorial shows or watching snake charmers, magicians, clowns or dancers, so *ʿAbodah Zarah* 18b–19a.[19] All such activities constituted the "seat of the scornful" (מושב לצים), Ps 1:1.

If Buhl approved Joüon's main point, he differed from him on the question of the older and biblical meaning of ליץ. Joüon had noted that ליץ was associated with פתי and כסיל and constituted a contrast to חכם and נבון (e.g., Prov 14:6; 19:25; 21:11). Consequently he concluded that the basic denotation of the term was "fool," "foolish" and, extended to the ethical sphere, "wicked," "evil."[20] For Buhl, however, this conclusion was not satisfactory and did not accord with the evidence derived from his examination of the renderings of the LXX, including those of Ben Sira,[21] to which he attributed special importance. In the latter work the word was, he supposed, still widely used by strict Jews, and the

---

15 Hereafter "scorn" will serve as a general indication of this rendering and include all English synonyms.

16 Typical renderings may be listed as follows: (a) Targum מִיקָן, "mock," Jastrow, 778; Peshitta ܡܒܙܚܢܐ, "mocker," J. Payne Smith, ed., *A Compendious Syriac Dictionary* (Oxford: Clarendon, 1903), 279; Vulgate "*illusor*," "*derisor*," "mock," "scorn"; (b) Targum רשעין, "the wicked"; cf. Peshitta ܣܟܠ; Vulgate "*indoctus*," "*stultus*," "ignorant," "foolish."

17 Cf. Jastrow, 709: "scoffing habits," "sneering," "irony."

18 L. Goldschmidt, *Der Babylonische Talmud* (9 vols.; Berlin: S. Calvary [vols. 1–3, 7]; Leipzig: Otto Harrassowitz [vols. 4–6, 8]; The Hague: Martinus Nijhoff [vol. 9], 1897–1935), 3:641; cf. *The Babylonian Talmud, Translated Into English with Notes, Glossary and Indices* (ed. I. Epstein; 35 vols.; London: Soncino, 1935–1952), *Moʿed*, 4:154.

19 Goldschmidt, *Babylonische Talmud*, 7:858–61; cf. *Babylonian Talmud, Nezikin*, 4:94–97.

20 The laconic nature of Proverbs at times promotes a tendency towards bland, imprecise translations; thus, the LXX has κακός for לֵץ in a number of places.

21 None of the passages cited by Buhl fall within the extant fragments of the Hebrew text discovered at Masada, Qumran, and the Cairo Genizah.

translator, related as he was to the author, would have been familiar with its proper sense. The renderings for לִיץ which predominate here are ὑπερήφανος, "arrogant," "haughty"; ὑβριστής, "insolent"; καθυβρίζειν, "to insult"; ὕβρις, "insolence." It is just these terms which characterize the LXX renderings of לִיץ, and they confirm that here we have the essential, authentic, and fundamental meaning of the root. In particular Prov 21:24 constitutes an effective definition of לִיץ: זֵד יָהִיר לֵץ שְׁמוֹ, "The proud, insolent man, his name is לֵץ." Buhl believed that his conclusion as to the meaning of לִיץ fits all occurrences of the root in the Hebrew Bible, though there are understandable shifts of meaning in some verses of Proverbs in which לֵצִים are subject to correction or are set in contrast to the חכמים (e.g., Prov 15:12; 20:1; 21:11). The LXX here offers ἀπαίδευτος, "coarse," "uneducated" or ἀκόλαστος, "unbridled," "intemperate."

The transition in meaning from the basic sense of לִיץ in biblical Hebrew to the Hebrew of the Talmud is also readily explained. From uncouth arrogance to a description of the man who makes a habit of reviling divine authority or of mocking the moral law is a natural step and one which accords precisely with the increased tendency to identify Torah with wisdom.

Buhl's treatment of the problem has much to commend it. Yet there are difficulties. First, as he himself says, his theory would be considerably strengthened if there were a satisfactory etymological basis for it. Arabic لاص (lāṣa) in the meanings he cites for it[22] is, he concludes, too vague ("farblos") for the purpose, and Syriac ܐܠܨ, ʾlṣ, "to compel," "to force," "to oppress," while it is suggestive for some particular occurrences (e.g., Ps 119:51; Prov 19:28), with its initial ʾālep, cannot be said to have a clear relationship with the hollow root לִיץ. Secondly, the rendering "arrogant," "insolent," etc., does not fit every occurrence as closely as Buhl claims. Thus, for example, Hos 7:5 (on the view that לִיץ is the root involved),[23] "he stretches out his hand to the לֹצְצִים," may concern insolent, arrogant persons, but it does not certainly do so.[24] Similar arguments may be deployed in respect of Prov 20:1 and its concern

---

22   He cites "sich wenden von einer Sache weg, oder zu einer Sache hin." His other suggestion that لاص (lāṣa) represents a variant form of راص (rāṣa) is doubtful, not least because he gives no account of such a verb, of which there is no sign in, e.g., Lane or Wehr.

23   I.e., pōʿlel participle, mêm omitted.

24   Cf. the varied renderings of the versions: LXX λοιμῶν, "pests"; Aq. χλευαστῶν, "scoffers," cf. Vulgate inlusoribus; Peshitta ܥܡ ܒܝܫܐ, "with evil men"; Targum סִיעַת שִׁכְרִין, "company of falsehood." For ibn Ezra's view, supported by the present author, that the root involved is לצץ and the meaning "conspirators," see A. A. Macintosh, A Critical and Exegetical Commentary on Hosea (ICC; Edinburgh: T&T Clark, 1997), 260.

with intoxication. If "wine is a לץ, strong drink a turbulent fellow," the former is not obviously "insolent," "arrogant," or the like. In a saying where "drink is credited with the characteristics which it produces in men,"[25] arrogance is not certainly such a characteristic. In general pugnacity and trouble-making would seem to be more characteristic and with this the LXX's ἀκόλαστον, "intemperate," "licentious," agrees. Moreover, Buhl's predilection for the apparent explicit identification of the לץ with the proud and insolent man in Prov 21:24 may not be securely based. Thus, the sentence may describe the proud and insolent whose behaviour is typified by the לץ. The LXX renders the latter term λοιμός, "pest," "pestilence," thereby characterizing not the לץ but the proud and insolent.[26]

III

A later approach to the problem is that of Richardson,[27] whose work is built upon a suggestion of Canney. The latter, appreciating the difficulty of rendering the qal of ליץ as "scorn" and the hipʿil as "interpret," suggested that the verb meant "to talk freely" (qal) and "to make (others) to talk freely" (hipʿil). "Scorner" for לֵץ in Proverbs "seems to be a pure guess," and its true meaning is "babbler."[28] The theory found its way into KBL as "grossprecherisch sein" (qal) and (hipʿil participle) "Mittelsmann," "Dolmetscher" ("spokesman," "interpreter").[29] Yet KBL also gives the meaning "scorner" ("Spötter") for לץ; and for לצון "boasting prattle" ("grosstuerisches Geschwätz"), where Buhl's suggested meaning appears to be combined with that of Canney.[30] Richardson notes the ambivalence and apparent failure to come to a final decision in KBL. As a consequence he resolved to pursue Canney's suggestion in a thorough-going manner.

---

25   C. H. Toy, A Critical and Exegetical Commentary on the Book of Proverbs (ICC; Edinburgh: T&T Clark, 1899), 383; cf. ibn Ezra, חסר איש, "wine is personified."

26   For the form of the phrase, cf., with W. Frankenberg, Prov 16:21 where the wise (in thought) is he who merits the epithet נבון, "discerning" (Die Sprüche [HKAT; Göttingen: Vandenhoeck & Ruprecht, 1898], 99).

27   H. N. Richardson, "Some Notes on ליץ and Its Derivatives," VT 5 (1955): 163–79.

28   M. A. Canney, "The Hebrew מֵלִיץ," AJSL 40 (1923–24): 135–37 (136). KBL, 481, incorrectly attributes the article to W. F. Albright, and gives the wrong page number (corrected in the "Zusätze und Berichtigungen," 163). Richardson seems to have been unaware of Gesenius's suggestion in this sense; see above, n. 11.

29   KBL, 481.

30   KBL, 484.

It is not possible here to review in detail Richardson's notes on some thirty-six verses, most of which occur in Proverbs. Here it is sufficient to note, however, that Richardson regards the text of some six verses as corrupt and requiring emendation in the sense that ליץ is held to have no place in them.[31] To the rest, he attributes the sense "speak freely," "babble," etc. In many such verses Richardson's argument depends on his assertion that the traditional "scorn" may readily be replaced with "babbling" and that the latter gives at least as good a sense and usually a better. In some cases Richardson sees indications in favour of his theory in adjacent verses or in texts elsewhere which treat of the same subject. Thus, for example, Isa 29:20, "Surely the ruthless man (עריץ) shall come to naught and the לץ will vanish." He comments that the "ruthless man" is not an exact synonym, whether לץ means "scorner" or "babbler." He seeks support for the latter by turning to the next verse where the wicked (of verse 20) are described as bringing a man into condemnation "with a word" and who by an "empty plea" (so Richardson renders בתהו) effects the wresting of justice from the innocent. He concludes that "an empty plea" and "a word" which effects condemnation are "better characterizations of לץ if it means 'babbler' than if it means 'scorner.'" The argument is scarcely satisfactory in that particular difficulties arise such as Richardson's weak translation of בתהו in the context of what is clearly the perversion of justice and the wrongful conviction of the innocent.

Another example is Richardson's treatment of Prov 20:1, which he renders: "Wine is a babbler (לץ), strong drink is uproarious." Emphasizing that the parallel denotes "tumultuous noise," לץ is more likely to denote "idle, foolish or irrational talk" than "scoffing, mocking or even brawling." In support of this conclusion, he appeals to Isa 28:14 where אנשי לצון, usually rendered "scoffers" or "arrogant," should, by reference to the "entire context," properly be rendered "babblers." By "entire context" Richardson points to the preceding verses of chapter 28 and its indictment of the drunkards of Ephraim. The prophet, he claims, continues to address "these drunkards." But they are not "these drunkards"; they are the rulers of Jerusalem and there is no indication that they are drunk.[32]

---

31   The verses include Prov 14:9, where יליץ is construed with an object and is regarded as crucial evidence by ibn Janāḥ; see Section V below.

32   Richardson asserts that the opening לכן of verse 14 "would tend to relate this verse and what follows to that which precedes." It is difficult to be precise about a word so common in prophecy but the connection may, for example, imply that the fate of Ephraim should be regarded as a paradigm and warning to the Judeans.

Richardson's fundamental plea is to the effect that "babble" is a better translation of ליץ than "scorn" because the former can be substituted
in most cases for the latter.[33] This hardly amounts to a satisfactory
argument. Richardson is able to adduce no evidence from the ancient
versions, from rabbinic or other traditions, or from comparative philology in favour of his case. It should, then, be rejected.

IV

Another attempt to explain ליץ is that of de Boer.[34] For him the fundamental meaning of the root is "repetition using different words"
(*"veranderd herhalen"*)[35] and this facilitates his explanation of how ליץ
can denote "interpreter" (Gen 42:23) as well as "scorner" (e.g., in Job
16:20). De Boer, in this book, is primarily concerned to explain the juxtaposition of מליץ and מלאך in Job 33:23 and, related to it, the reference
to מליצים in Isa 43:27. He concludes that מליץ in these texts denotes
"intercessor," "mediator" (whether heavenly or, in respect of Isa 43:27,
earthly).[36] The meaning is a natural extension of the "interpreter" of
Gen 42:23. His suggestion (virtually incidental) that the basic meaning
of ליץ is "repetition in different words" is made in order to explain its
capacity to accommodate the two apparently unrelated meanings
"scorn" and "interpreting." It is made, moreover, explicitly on the
grounds that the cognate Semitic languages offer no clear guidance on
the matter.

De Boer's suggestion is, perhaps, the best of the three listed here. It
is, however, to be rejected by reference to the same arguments, *mutatis
mutandis*, advanced in respect of the suggestions of Buhl and Richardson. His is another conjectural suggestion made in respect of a mere
four occurrences and on the basis (convincingly challenged by Joüon
and Buhl) that ליץ was capable of meaning "scorn" in the Hebrew Bible.

The three attempts to determine the precise meaning of ליץ are
regarded as unsatisfactory for the particular reasons advanced above
but also by reason of more general considerations. It is the nature of

---

33 Prov 19:29 constitutes a case where the substitution cannot be said to work. Richard-
    son's (tentative) "the worthless witness babbles of justice" is particularly unconvinc-
    ing in respect of the verb and its object.

34 P. A. H. de Boer, *De voorbede in het Oude Testament* (OtSt 3; Leiden: Brill, 1943), 165–
    67.

35 Both KBL, 481, and *HAL* 2:503 in respect of de Boer's suggestion cite *"wiederholen"*
    simply; this is misleading since the adverbial *veranderd* is not represented.

36 For this, see further Section V below.

aphoristic moral sayings, and particularly of proverbs, that they oppose tersely and succinctly the good and the bad, the wise and the foolish. When, then, forms of ליץ present themselves in Proverbs, it is clear that the words are pejorative in meaning. But since the sayings are so terse, there is not the help from the context that obtains from more extended pieces such as are found, for example, in prophecy. Secondly, it is generally stated that attempts at defining ליץ by reference to cognate Semitic languages and particularly to Arabic have not proved successful.[37] In these circumstances, scholars have been reduced to making conjectures as to the precise meaning of the term. As long as the sense is pejorative, a number of possibilities present themselves. But without the independent evidence gleaned from cognate languages, the suggestions remain simply conjectural.

V

R. Jonah ibn Janāḥ (abu 'l-Walīd Marwan; tenth and eleventh centuries) in his Kitāb al-Usūl[38] frequently offers explanations for words which "belong to the sum of what I have produced of unusual thoughts and noteworthy opinions which no one else has expressed or noticed."[39] Under lāmed-wāw-ṣādê[40] he lists Prov 3:34 and Isa 28:22, stating that he has considered them in his work on weak verbs. There, too, he mentions Gen 42:23 כי המליץ בינתם, the incontrovertible, "there was an interpreter between them," and Job 33:23, where מליץ and מלאך are juxtaposed and have the apparent sense "intermediary." It is on the basis of these meanings that ibn Janāḥ believes ליץ in two verses of Proverbs is to be explained. In fact he cites a mixed text, a combination of Prov 14:9 and 19:28, setting out the words: עד בליעל יליץ אשם. In fact Prov 19:28 reads משפט for ibn Janāḥ's אשם. He understands the words to mean (author's translation): "A lying witness devises for his benefit (specific) interpretations (تأويلات, taʾawīlāt) in his false testimony, supposing that by it he has rid himself of guilt." It is also possible, he continues, that the words are characterized by hysteron-proteron thus: "he who devises interpretations[41] in justice (i.e., in a law court), he is like a lying witness; i.e., the man who perverts (حرف, ḥarrafa) the course of justice by means of some specific interpretation." Ibn Janāḥ supposes that

37   E.g., Buhl, "Die Bedeutung," 85 and de Boer, De voorbede, 165.

38   A. Neubauer, The Book of Hebrew Roots (Oxford: Clarendon, 1875).

39   Neubauer, Hebrew Roots, col. 93.

40   Neubauer, Hebrew Roots, col. 350.

41   The word "interpretations" is my translation of Arabic تأويلات.

similar considerations apply to Prov 14:9: אולים יליץ אשם ובין ישרים רצון.
He comments: "the insolent devise for each other what is requisite to
indict for sin/crime or else the godless indicts a companion for a crime
which he could not have committed. But the upright are in agreement
with each other and treat each other with justice."

It is convenient here to offer a number of comments on ibn Janāḥ's
definition of ליץ. First, the two particular verses from Proverbs are the
only instances of ליץ in the *qal* with an object. In addition the verses are
well suited by the context in which they are found to manifest the legal
nuance which ibn Janāḥ believes attaches to the word. Secondly,
though he rather surprisingly quotes a mixed text, it is clear that he
knew both the verses of which it is composed. By substituting אשם for
משפט in 19:28 he emphasizes the essential identity of these two verses.
For to pervert justice is to direct guilt away from the guilty and to
impose it upon the innocent.

Thirdly, ibn Janāḥ uses two particular Arabic words which serve to
define accurately his view of יליץ. The first is يتأول, *yatʾawwil*, the IInd
and Vth themes of the root أول, *ʾwl*, together with the cognate noun in
the plural, تأويلات, *taʾawīlāt*. Lane offers the following observations for
these forms: generally, "تأويل [*taʾawīl*] seems to me to signify the *collecting the meanings of dubious expressions by such expression as is clear, or
plain.*" In particular, a) "the *interpreting of language that has different
meanings; and this cannot be rightly done but by an explanation which
changes the expression*"; b) the "*turning a verse of the Ḳur-án from its apparent meaning to a meaning which it bears*";[42] c) although تأويل [*taʾawīl*] "*may
often be rendered by interpretation*, ... *it more properly signifies the
rendering in a manner not according to the letter, or overt sense*"; d) "*interpreting in a manner not according to the obvious meaning: or the reducing a
thing to its ultimate intent, whether it be a saying or an action*"; e) "*He rendered a word, or an expression, or a phrase ... by another word, or expression, or phrase.*"[43]

The second word that he uses is the common and well-known verb
حرف, *ḥarrafa*. Wehr lists for it: (IInd theme) "to bend off, up, down or
back, turn up, down or back, deflect; to distort, corrupt, twist, pervert,
misconstrue, falsify."[44]

---

42 Thus, e.g., the saying "He produced the bird from the egg" is the تفسير, *tafsīr* (simple)
    exposition; but "he produced the believer from the unbeliever" or "the knowing
    from the ignorant" this is the تأويل, *taʾawīl*.
43 Lane, 1:126–27.
44 Wehr, 198. Cf. Lane, 2:549, e.g., (Ist and IInd themes) "*The altering words from their
    proper meanings*"; "*He turned the thing from its proper way, or manner.*"

The two verbs used by ibn Janāḥ to define his view of the meaning of ילי in Proverbs are very revealing in respect of the root ליץ as a whole. Thus the word מליץ in Gen 42:23 denoting the interpreter acting between Joseph (ostensibly an Egyptian ruler) and his brothers is, according to context and all traditional evidence, incontrovertible. Ibn Janāḥ's description of the meaning of ליץ by his use of تأويل, taʾawīl, suggests the fundamental meaning, the *Grundbedeutung* which generates this particular meaning in the Joseph story. Similar considerations apply in respect of Job 33:23 where מליץ[45] is in apposition to מלאך and the verse expresses the yearning for the (remote—"one in a thousand"[46]) possibility of a mediator capable of giving revelation and explanation as a prelude to salvation and restoration to health. Isa 43:27, "Your first forefather sinned and your מליציך rebelled against me" may also constitute a reference to the (false) prophets as those charged with interpreting and explaining Yahweh's will to his people; or, perhaps more likely in view of the chiasmus created with the following verse, with its reference to Jacob and שָׂרֵי קֹדֶשׁ, the priests.[47] A third verse is also illuminated in this sense. 2 Chr 32:31 speaks of the מליצי שרי בבל. What is clearly intended are envoys of the Babylonian establishment, whose function was diplomatic. They are מליצים because the envoys mediate between those who commission them and the party to whom they are sent (so Rashi). Ibn Janāḥ's use of تأويل, taʾawīl, in the meaning detected by Lane (see his meaning d above), is strikingly appropriate in describing this function.

In contrast to the *hipʿil* usages so far considered, are verses in which the forms of the root, largely *qal* but sometimes *hipʿil*, are clearly pejorative. In fact all forms of the *qal* may be characterized as pejorative. Here, as has been indicated, ibn Janāḥ seems to have chosen two particular texts from Proverbs as exemplifying the precise meaning which he believes the word to bear, and that meaning is detected in the context of the perversion of justice. The second Arabic word which he uses to define ליץ is حرف, ḥarrafa, denoting "twisting," "perversion," "falsification" (see above). That this accords with the wider, more nuanced, senses of تأويل, taʾawīl, seems clear. Indeed, the definitions offered by

---

45   Cf. Targum פרקליטה, "paraclete"; Vulgate (*angelus*) *loquens*, "speaking"; Peshitta ܕܫܡܥ ܠܗ, "(an angel) who hears him." For the longer and free rendering of the LXX, see P. Dhorme, *Le livre de Job* (2d ed.; Paris: Gabalda & Cie., 1926), 456–57 (ET *A Commentary on the Book of Job* [London: Nelson, 1967], 500–501).

46   Cf. Eccl 7:28.

47   So, respectively, B. Duhm, *Das Buch Jesaia übersetzt und erklärt* (5th ed.; HKAT 3/1; Göttingen: Vandenhoeck & Ruprecht, 1968), 329–30, and de Boer, *De voorbede*, 166.

Lane from a) – e) (see above) may be said to do so in a complementary manner.

It has been observed above in relation to conjectural estimates of the fundamental meaning of ליץ, that the aphoristic, laconic nature of proverbs diminishes the possibility of gathering inferences from the context. One particular prophetic passage containing the word לץ would seem to redress this deficiency. Isa 29:20–21 runs:

> The ruthless (עריץ) shall be no more, the לץ shall cease to exist.
> All those who plan wickedness will be destroyed;
> those who condemn a man with a word;
> who make difficulties[48] for those who adjudicate in court,
> who deny justice to the righteous by falsehood (תהו).

This passage may be said to confirm ibn Janāḥ's understanding that the fundamental sense of ליץ is most readily detected in the context of twisting, perversion or falsification, and especially in the context of law courts.[49] That is not to say, however, that all occurrences of ליץ belong exclusively to this particular category, and to a number of them I will return below.

Ibn Janāḥ, though writing in his native Arabic, does not always or even frequently mention words in Arabic which are cognate with the Hebrew word which he is reviewing. Thus, he does not mention لاص, lāṣa, in connection with ליץ. In view of the substance of what he writes, however, it is worth considering again whether a useful semantic connection can be recognized by comparing the two cognate words. The widespread tendency to dismiss لاص, lāṣa, as unhelpful in this venture has been noted. That judgment depends largely on the view that "scorn" was the usual meaning of ליץ (especially, but not exclusively, in the qal).

Lane lists لاص, lāṣa, as a hollow verb with medial wāw. For the Ist theme, he records: "He turned aside, or away, from the thing, or affair; he declined from it; he avoided it." For the IIIrd theme: "He looked to the right and left as though he desired, or sought, a thing ... or he looked as though he were deceiving, or beguiling, to seek to obtain ... a thing." Further, there is: "He looked, ... or glanced, ... at him, or it, from the interstice of a door."[50]

---

48 After ibn Janāḥ (Neubauer, *Hebrew Roots*, col. 633), who understands יקוש to mean "make difficulties," "dispute," for which he cites Aramaic קושיא, cf. Jastrow, 1345; similarly the LXX with πάντας δὲ τοὺς ἐλέγχοντας ἐν πύλαις πρόσκομμα θήσουσιν. Others, cf. *BHS*, assume a form of the verb יקש "to entrap."

49 It is interesting to note that the NEB, which usually retains "scorn" for ליץ, renders Prov 19:28, "A rascally witness perverts justice."

50 Hence apparently *HAL*'s citation of "*durch Turspalt schauen.*" "To peep through a chink in the door" is cited by Wehr, 1036, and this may well reflect modern usage. According to Lane it is just one of several meanings.

A cluster of citations follow which involve deceit, guile, enticement: *"Such a one endeavoured to turn me by deceit, or guile, from such a thing"*; he *"endeavoured to turn him to, or induce him to do, such a thing."* The IVth theme merges with the IIIrd in five places, but the active participle ملاوص, *mulāwiṣ*, denotes *"a man who behaves in a loving, or affectionate, and blandishing, or coaxing, and deceitful, or beguiling, manner."*[51]

Among these meanings for لاص, *lāṣa*, those associated with the use of deceit or guile seem to suggest a convincing continuity with aspects of the meaning which ibn Janāḥ claims for ליץ in Hebrew. If a fundamental *Grundbedeutung* is required, the suggestion may be made that it is "to twist," "to turn,"[52] "to bend," "to make oblique," "to alter," "to beguile"; in short what is denoted by the Arabic verb حرف, *ḥarrafa* (see above).

VI

The word "oblique" is found in BDB's account of ליץ. In the notes on cognate languages, they cite لاص, *lāṣa*, with the intransitive meaning to "turn aside" and they speculate "hence perh[aps] prop[erly] *speak indirectly or obliquely*."[53] It seems likely that this reflects the influence of the eighteenth-century commentator on Proverbs, Schultens.[54] On Prov 1:6 and the word מליצה, he lists for the verb לאص, *lāṣa*, *flexit, deflexit, torsit* and he compares the (different) root (חיד) حاد, *ḥād, inflexit, obliquo oculo adspexit*; in the IVth theme *obliquato flexu facit circumire aliquid*. He concludes that the primary sense of לאص/ליץ, *lāṣa*, is "twisting" (*est hisce primariam virtutem in torquendo et obliquando sitam fuisse, satis liquet*). Hence the sense "scorner," "mocker" (*irrisor, ludificator*) is a natural extension of meaning.

While Schultens was clearly pursuing a useful line of inquiry, it remains the fact that he used the information he had gleaned from the *Qāmūs* (i.e., that of Fīrūzābādi) to explain that מליצה in Prov 1:6 was virtually a synonym of חידה,[55] and that elsewhere in Proverbs it had developed the traditionally accepted sense "scorn." BDB's tentative suggestion that ליץ may mean basically "speak indirectly or obliquely"

---

51   Lane, 7:2681.
52   Cf., perhaps, English "a turn of phrase" or "to turn" in the sense of "to translate."
53   BDB, 539.
54   BDB cites H. L. Fleischer on Prov 1:6. I suspect that this is a mistake for the correct Schultens (*Proverbia Salomonis*, 4). I have been unable to find a reference to Prov 1:6 in the former scholar's works.
55   I.e., a riddle; *oratio obscurior interpretatione egens*.

and that it generally denotes "scorn," has marked similarities with Schultens's conclusions. It may be said, however, to suffer from lack of precision and from inaccurate information.[56]

VII. Conclusion

It appears that ליץ and its derivatives did not, as is generally supposed, signify scoffing, scorn, mockery, etc., in biblical Hebrew. Rather the noun לץ denotes what Ps 43:1 calls "the deceitful and wicked man" (איש מרמה ועולה). The verb has as its essential meaning "twisting," "turning," specifically in relation to speech. In a good sense and in the *hip'il* it denotes an interpreter who "turns" (converts) speech in explanation/interpretation, or turns it from one language into another. In the more common, pejorative sense it denotes the "twisting" (perversion) of speech for wicked or selfish ends.

It is not possible to suggest a single English word to represent the meaning of ליץ in its various occurrences in the Hebrew Bible. Since "turning" and "twisting" are the likely fundamental meanings, each occurrence is best rendered by words which accord with this consideration but yet are suited to the particular context in which it is found. A few examples may suffice to indicate what is meant.

On the basis of the meaning "twist":

Prov 19:28: עֵד בְּלִיַּעַל יָלִיץ מִשְׁפָּט, "A diabolical witness perverts justice." Cf. "A worthless witness mocketh at judgement" (RV). See ibn Janāḥ's comments above.

Prov 22:10: גָּרֵשׁ לֵץ וְיֵצֵא מָדוֹן, "Cast out the perverse/deceiver that contention go out; that strife and ignominy cease." Compare and contrast: "Cast out the scorner . . ." (RV).

Isa 28:14: "Wherefore hear the word of the Lord, ye crooked statesmen (אַנְשֵׁי לָצוֹן), that rule this people . . ." Note v. 15 following, ". . . we have made lies our refuge, and under falsehood have we hid ourselves."

---

56   Thus, it is clear that "oblique," used in explanation of لاص, *lāṣa*, is predicated of eyes, glances, and looking, rather than of speaking. Where "turning" or "twisting" and so "beguiling" is concerned the object is a person rather than speech. That Hebrew ליץ denotes the turning, the changing of the sense of words and expressions is not, of course, denied.

Compare and contrast "Hear the word of the Lord, ye scornful men . . . etc." (RV).

Prov 3:34: עִם לֵצִים הוּא־יָלִיץ, "Surely he [i.e., God] acts perversely with the perverse, but he grants the lowly favour." (The MT is emended with BHS on the basis of Ps 18:27b[26b]: וְעִם־עִקֵּשׁ תִּתְפַּתָּל, ". . . with the perverse thou shalt shew thyself froward.") Compare and contrast "Surely he scorneth the scorners . . . etc." (RV).

Prov 20:1: לֵץ הַיַּיִן הֹמֶה שֵׁכָר וְכָל־שֹׁגֶה בּוֹ לֹא יֶחְכָּם, "Wine is a distorter/befuddler, strong drink is a noise-maker; whosoever errs/reels through them is not wise." Note the beverages are personified, and the translations suggested here seek to reflect this, though they do not accord with proper English. Compare and contrast "Wine is a mocker, strong drink a brawler . . . etc." (RV).

On the basis of the meaning "turn":

The established and traditional English renderings of ליץ (hip'il only) under this heading do not require revision.

Gen 42:23: כִּי הַמֵּלִיץ בֵּינֹתָם, "for the interpreter was between them." The official turns/converts speech from one language to another.

2 Chr 32:31: מְלִיצֵי שָׂרֵי בָּבֶל, "the envoys of the princes of Babylon," are those whose function it is to present (turn/convert) the aims and aspirations of the rulers of Babylon in (into) a form and language persuasive and understandable by the Judeans.

Job 33:23: אִם־יֵשׁ עָלָיו מַלְאָךְ מֵלִיץ אֶחָד מִנִּי־אָלֶף לְהַגִּיד לְאָדָם יָשְׁרוֹ, "If there be with him an angel, an interpreter, one among a thousand, to show unto man what is right for him." Here the intermediary between God and man is seen as an envoy capable of conveying the former's requirements to the latter. He explains (turns/converts) such requirements into a form that is readily understood. Similar considerations apply to the use of מְלִיצֶיךָ in Isa 43:27 in respect of priests or prophets (see in Section V above) who are condemned for their shortcomings in this function.

The Operation of a Syntactic Rule in Classical Biblical Hebrew and in Hebrew Inscriptions of the Monarchic Period

JAN JOOSTEN

The Use of Linguistic Evidence in Dating Biblical Texts

In the historical critical approach to the Hebrew Bible, the dating of biblical texts remains an important point on the agenda. Although it is true that a "breath of eternity" inspires many biblical writings, it is true too that if they can be related to a definite period in history, they can often be better understood, or at least that they could be. For, in our own time, the whole enterprise of dating biblical texts has become deeply problematical. Not only such literary fragments as individual psalms, but even large works in prose such as the Joseph story or the succession narrative, as well as the legal corpora, have become the object of widely divergent proposals with regard to their date. The situation is particularly critical in regard to the Pentateuch. While only thirty years ago, much of this corpus would almost unthinkingly be dated to the monarchic period, today even very serious biblical scholars stand utterly divided. It is not at all uncommon to see large parts of it dated to the Persian period.[1]

From a linguistic point of view, the late dating of the Pentateuch and historical books is problematic. Ever since Wilhelm Gesenius's work in the early nineteenth century, historical study of biblical Hebrew has led to the identification of two basic varieties of the language: Classical Biblical Hebrew (CBH), associated with the preexilic period, and Late Biblical Hebrew (LBH), typical of the postexilic

---

1   Illustrative of this tendency is J. L. Ska, *Introduction à la lecture du Pentateuque: Clés pour l'interprétation des cinq premiers livres de la Bible* (Bruxelles: Éditions Lessius, 2000), where hardly anything in the Pentateuch is dated before the exile. In English, see, e.g., J. Blenkinsopp, *The Pentateuch: An Introduction to the First Five Books of the Bible* (ABRL 7; New York: Doubleday, 1992).

period.[2] The approach has been developed by many scholars, most notably by S. R. Driver and A. Hurvitz,[3] and is still widely favoured today.[4] In this scheme, practically the entire corpus of Genesis to 2 Kings, written as it is in CBH, should be dated to the preexilic period.

Very recently, it must be said, the turmoil reigning in biblical studies has been projected into Hebrew studies as well. With varying degrees of professionalism, Hebraists or would-be Hebraists of a new generation have tried to show that the linguistic facts are not incompatible with the late dates proposed by some biblical scholars. Forsaking the usual chronological approach, these scholars have tried out a variety of angles. Some argue that the CBH–LBH divide does not exist and that the whole Hebrew Bible represents a single linguistic unit.[5] Others, while recognizing two basic varieties of biblical Hebrew, argue that the difference between them is not due to language development but to the use of different dialects or style-forms.[6] Still others argue that CBH and LBH are indeed distinct and do reflect successive periods, but must not be associated with the preexilic and postexilic periods respectively.[7]

Certainly, the most potent objection against the traditional approach is the last one. An eloquent statement of it can be found in a review of Wright's book on the language of the Yahwist by Levin. After

---

2   Wilhelm Gesenius, *Geschichte der hebräischen Sprache und Schrift* (Leipzig: Vogel, 1815), 21–30.

3   An excellent overview, with bibliographical references, is found in A. Sáenz-Badillos, *A History of the Hebrew Language* (Cambridge: Cambridge University Press, 1993), 50–160; trans. of *Historia de la lengua Hebrea* (Sabadell: Ausa, 1988).

4   E.g., P. Joüon and T. Muraoka, *A Grammar of Biblical Hebrew* (2d ed.; SubBi 27; Rome: Editrice Pontificio Istituto Biblico, 2006), 9: "we shall be content with distinguishing two main periods in the history of the Hebrew language: the pre-exilic and post-exilic periods." This statement has remained essentially unchanged since the earliest French edition of this standard grammar (1923). For a fresh evaluation coming essentially to the same conclusion, see John F. Elwolde, "Language and Translation of the Old Testament," in *The Oxford Handbook of Biblical Studies* (ed. John William Rogerson and Judith Lieu; Oxford: Oxford University Press, 2006), 135–58 (136).

5   E.g., R. Rezetko, "Dating Biblical Hebrew: Evidence from Samuel-Kings and Chronicles," in *Biblical Hebrew: Studies in Chronology and Typology* (ed. I. Young; JSOTSup 369; London: T&T Clark, 2003), 215–50.

6   P. Davies, "Biblical Hebrew and the History of Ancient Judah: Typology, Chronology and Common Sense," in Young, *Biblical Hebrew*, 150–63; M. Ehrensvärd, "Linguistic Dating of Biblical Texts," in Young, *Biblical Hebrew*, 164–88. This is also the approach defended in I. Young and R. Rezetko, *Linguistic Dating of Biblical Texts*, (2 vols.; London: Equinox, 2008).

7   This seems to be the position of Blum: see E. Blum, "Das althebräische Verbalsystem—eine synchrone Analyse," in *Sprachliche Tiefe—Theologische Weite* (ed. Oliver Dyma and Andreas Michel; Biblisch-theologische Studien 91; Neukirchen: Neukirchener Verlag, 2008), 91–142 (94–95).

giving Hurvitz credit for isolating LBH as a distinct linguistic stratum, Levin writes:

> The question is not whether by far the greatest part of the Old Testament represents the linguistic stage SBH [i.e., Standard Biblical Hebrew]—that goes without saying. The real question is when the transition from SBH to LBH can be *dated*. The assertion that the borderline was the exile is unproven and also unprovable. Of the reference texts for LBH, Chronicles, Daniel, Esther, and Ecclesiastes certainly date from the Hellenistic period, while Wright himself places Ezra-Nehemiah between 400 and 300 (11 n. 50). Consequently, a gap of two centuries yawns between the beginning of the exile and the observable beginning of LBH. Hurvitz and Wright disregard this gap. With such a *petitio principii* it is impossible to refute the opposite view, that the greater part of Old Testament literature that is written in SBH was composed precisely during these two hundred years, that is, in the sixth and fifth centuries.[8]

What is spelled out here is a very clear challenge to the regnant position among Hebraists: CBH and LBH might be successive stages of the Hebrew language, both belonging to the exilic–postexilic period.[9]

Contrary to Levin, however, it is not entirely true that the location of the borderline between CBH and LBH in the exilic period is "unproven and also unprovable." Although proof is always rare in human sciences, several considerations do indicate a basic divide in the sixth century. To begin with, the differences between CBH and LBH do not all reflect organic change. There are signs of disruption: LBH is to a certain extent artificial, with authors using classical expressions in a way that shows their real meaning was forgotten.[10] This phenomenon tends to confirm that the watershed occurred during the exile, when the literate elite of Judah were forcibly removed from their cultural

---

8   Christoph Levin, review of Richard M. Wright, *Linguistic Evidence for the Pre-exilic Date of the Yahwistic Source* in *RBL* 01/2006, 2. Further on in the same review, Levin writes: "as long as it is merely asserted and not proved that the transition from SBH to LBH was contemporary with the exilic period—and not, perhaps, with the transition from the Persian to the Hellenistic period—the dates proposed by F. W. Winnett and J. Van Seters lose none of their probability" (4–5).

9   Just to be on the safe side, Levin (review of Richard M. Wright, 1) also states that Hebrew linguistics can contribute nothing to the dating of Hebrew texts, because they were rewritten again and again by each generation: "It is not unusual for passages of only a few verses to derive from several centuries." This is a very different claim, and one which historical linguistics could answer more easily. But there is no reason to broaden the scope at the present point in this paper.

10 See Sáenz-Badillos, *History*, 112, and Ron Hendel, *Remembering Abraham: Culture, Memory, and History in the Hebrew Bible* (Oxford: Oxford University Press, 2005), 110.

matrix and confronted with very different cultural markers.[11] Secondly, some writings ostensibly composed during the exilic period, notably the book of Ezekiel, reflect a transitional type of Hebrew standing halfway between CBH and LBH.[12] The *prima facie* implication of this phenomenon is that CBH texts should be considered to be earlier than Ezekiel, and LBH texts later.

A third line of evidence, tying the CBH corpus directly to the monarchic period, emerges from a comparison between the biblical texts and Hebrew inscriptions. Several scholars have drawn attention to the proximity between CBH and the language of preexilic Judean inscriptions. To the extent this proximity can be demonstrated it strengthens the suggestion that texts written in CBH go back to the period of the monarchy.

Using the Inscriptions as External Controls in the Historical Study of Biblical Hebrew

When Gesenius developed his theory of the history of biblical Hebrew, he had no external Hebrew evidence of the preexilic period to go on. The first Judean inscription to be discovered was the Siloam inscription, which first came to light in 1880. Today, the corpus of Judean inscriptions of the eighth to sixth centuries has grown enormously.[13] And still new documents are being discovered.[14] Generally speaking, the linguistic proximity of these inscriptions to biblical Hebrew, and to classical prose texts in particular, is rather striking. Cooke, in his textbook of North-Semitic inscriptions, says about the Siloam inscription: "The style is pure and idiomatic, and reads like a good prose passage

---

11   Frank H. Polak, "Sociolinguistics and the Judean Speech Community in the Achaemenid Empire," in *Judah and the Judeans in the Persian Period* (ed. Oded Lipschits and Manfred Oeming; Winona Lake, Ind.: Eisenbrauns, 2006), 589–628.

12   See M. F. Rooker, *Biblical Hebrew in Transition: The Language of the Book of Ezekiel* (JSOTSup 90; Sheffield: Sheffield Academic Press, 1990).

13   See G. I. Davies, *Ancient Hebrew Inscriptions: Corpus and Concordance* (Cambridge: Cambridge University Press, 1991); idem, *Ancient Hebrew Inscriptions, Volume 2* (Cambridge: Cambridge University Press, 2004); J. Renz and W. Röllig, *Handbuch der althebräischen Epigraphik* (3 vols.; Darmstadt: Wissenschaftliche Buchgesellschaft, 1995–2003); F. W. Dobbs-Allsopp, J. J. M. Roberts, C. L. Leong Seow, and R. E. Whitaker, *Hebrew Inscriptions: Texts from the Biblical Period of the Monarchy with Concordance* (New Haven: Yale University Press, 2005).

14   See, e.g., S. Aḥituv and A. Yardeni, "Silver, Pistachio and Wheat: Two Letters of the Seventh–Sixth Centuries BCE," in *Zaphenath-Paneah: Linguistic Studies Presented to Elisha Qimron on the Occasion of his Sixty-Fifth Birthday* (in Hebrew; ed. D. Sivan, D. Talshir, and C. Cohen; Beer Sheva: Ben Gurion University of the Negev, 2009), 15–28.

out of the O.T."[15] Many other scholars have expressed similar judgments, and some have backed them up with specific observations. In the recent debate, it has been argued several times that such proximity indicates a relatively early date for CBH.[16]

An exception should of course be made for the script and orthography of the inscriptions, which do not resemble those of Biblical Hebrew. The square script of most biblical manuscripts reflects the customs and conventions of the postexilic period.[17] As to the orthography, the use of vowel letters and the spelling of the third person masculine singular suffix clearly set the inscriptions apart from biblical Hebrew. These differences are purely formal, however. A postexilic scribe copying a preexilic book may well have modernized the script and the orthography without otherwise modifying the text. The biblical scrolls from Qumran show that in the Hellenistic period, biblical writings were again adapted to the current orthography.[18]

A few scholars have pointed to the fact that there are more substantial differences as well between the Hebrew of the inscriptions and CBH.[19] Many biblical words and constructions never occur in the inscriptions and, conversely, some of the vocabulary of the inscriptions is unattested in the Bible. On the basis of such observations, it has been argued that CBH does not represent written Hebrew of the monarchic period but a late and artificial imitation of monarchic Hebrew,[20] or, alternatively, that linguistic data are unreliable as evidence for dating biblical texts.[21]

In the compass of the present paper, it is impossible to explore the methodological side of this question exhaustively. Briefly, however, it

---

15 G. A. Cooke, *A Text-Book of North-Semitic Inscriptions: Moabite, Hebrew, Phoenician, Aramaic, Nabataean, Palmyrene, Jewish* (Oxford: Clarendon, 1903), 16.

16 E.g., A. Hurvitz, "The Historical Quest for 'Ancient Israel' and the Linguistic Evidence of the Hebrew Bible: Some Methodological Observations," *VT* 47 (1997): 301 – 15 (307–10: "External Controls for the Classical Phase of BH"). Hurvitz here reviews much earlier literature.

17 For the use of the square script in biblical texts see Joseph Naveh, *Early History of the Alphabet* (Jerusalem: Magnes, 1997), 112–23.

18 Some of the Qumran manuscripts show occasional updating of the vocabulary and the grammar as well; see E. Y. Kutscher, *The Language and Linguistic Background of the Isaiah Scroll (1 Q Isaᵃ)* (STDJ 6; Leiden: Brill, 1974). Nevertheless, this type of modernizing remains haphazard when compared with the orthographical changes in some of the same scrolls.

19 E.g., E. A. Knauf, "War 'Biblisch-Hebräisch' eine Sprache?: Empirische Gesichtspunkte zur linguistischen Annäherung an die Sprache der althebräischen Literatur," *ZAH* 3 (1990): 11–23; I. Young, "Late Biblical Hebrew and Hebrew Inscriptions," in idem, *Biblical Hebrew*, 276–311.

20 This is the claim advanced by Knauf, "War 'Biblisch-Hebräisch' eine Sprache?"

21 See Young, "Late Biblical Hebrew."

may be said that differences between the language of the Judean inscriptions and CBH do not necessarily show that the two corpora of texts are not contemporary. Linguistic variety may be attributed to many causes. An obvious difference between the biblical corpus and the inscriptions is that the former mostly consists of literary texts while the latter are almost entirely of a documentary nature. The English used today in business documents and private letters differs from that used in literary works. Closer to the biblical period, Deissmann famously showed that New Testament Greek stood closer to the Greek of documentary papyri than to the language of contemporary authors such as Plutarch.[22] It would be no surprise to find out that in the time of the Judean monarchy, too, documentary and literary texts used slightly different varieties of the Hebrew language.

More impressive than the alleged differences are the striking resemblances between CBH and the language of the inscriptions. Of course, some methodological rules should be observed. It is not enough to find a feature attested in the inscriptions and in CBH texts, but never in later texts. One must be able show also that the distribution of the feature can reasonably be explained in terms of language evolution. An example will help to define the approach. An expression of the type ביתה אלישב, "to the house of Elyashib," with a *status constructus* followed by the locative *hê* is found in the inscriptions (e.g., Arad 17:2)[23] and in CBH (e.g., Gen 28:2 ביתה בתואל), but never in Chronicles, Ezra-Nehemiah, Daniel or Esther, nor in the Qumran scrolls or Ben Sira. What lends significance to this constellation is that the locative *hê* can be shown to disappear over the history of Hebrew: it is rather frequent in the Bible, becomes rare in Qumran Hebrew and is attested only in a few petrified expressions in Mishnaic Hebrew.[24] The general evolution of the language confirms the suggestion that the syntactic peculiarity setting apart the inscriptions and CBH from LBH is due to linguistic development.

Such instances show that CBH and the Hebrew of the Judean inscriptions essentially reflect the same *état de langue*. Several other features show a similar distribution and can be interpreted with a

---

22 See for this issue the studies by Adolf Deissmann and others in S. E. Porter, ed., *The Language of the New Testament: Classic Essays* (JSNTSup 60; Sheffield: Sheffield Academic Press, 1991).

23 Davies, *Ancient Hebrew Inscriptions*, 17 (§2.017.2); Renz, *Die althebräischen Inschriften*, 381 (§Arad (6):17.2).

24 For this example, see in more detail J. Joosten, "The Distinction between Classical and Late Biblical Hebrew as Reflected in Syntax," *HS* 46 (2005): 327–39 (337–38).

similar result.[25] The logical conclusion this leads to is that the CBH corpus and the inscriptions were put into writing at more or less the same period. Since it is difficult to know until when this type of language was practised, the connection admittedly does not give us a firm date *ante quem*. Nevertheless, the more the date of CBH texts is separated from that of the inscriptions, the less likely that date becomes from a linguistic point of view.

Case Study: Volitive Clauses with an Adverbial Phrase of Time

Meaningful similarities between CBH and the inscriptions can be collected from the realm of both vocabulary and syntax.[26] The most convincing cases are those involving syntax, because they are often more systematic in nature than lexical cases. The gradual disappearance of locative *hê*, for instance, is to be seen against the background of the more global evolution moving away from a grammatical system based on case endings toward a system using only prepositions. Syntactical changes have the added advantage that they would have been difficult to imitate, or consciously to avoid, by later authors. While it would be easy for later authors to re-use an archaic word they found in old texts, doing the same with a syntactical construction would be much harder. In what follows, one possible "isogloss" between CBH and the language of the inscriptions will be discussed.[27]

1. CBH

In CBH, volitive forms make up a distinct subsystem within the verbal paradigm. The subsystem is strangely heterosyzygistic, "yoking together" forms that appear to be etymologically distinct, but it is used in a sufficiently regular manner to have been recognized by most

---

25 Hurvitz, "Historical Quest," 307–10; Joosten, "Distinction," 336.

26 See some lexical examples in Martin Ehrensvärd, "Once Again: The Problem of Dating Biblical Hebrew," *SJOT* 11 (1997): 29–40 (38).

27 The biblical examples have been discussed in more detail in J. Joosten, "La vérité philologique dans les débats sur la datation des textes bibliques," in *Vérité(s) philologique(s): Études sur les notions de vérité et de fausseté en matière de philologie* (ed. Pascale Hummel and Frédéric Gabriel; Paris: Philologicum, 2008), 19–33.

authorities.[28] The first person is expressed by the *cohortative*, the second person by the *imperative*, and the third person by the *jussive*. The negation is in principle with אל, not לא, and in the second person the jussive takes the place of the imperative which cannot be negated. Semantically, all these forms express the will of the speaker.

As was discovered independently by Niccacci and Revell, and demonstrated more systematically by Shulman, volitive verbal forms tend to occur at the head of the clause in CBH prose.[29] In this respect, the volitives contrast with non-volitive YIQTOL (long form), which is almost entirely restricted to a non-first position in the clause. These placement rules probably reflect the necessity to distinguish homonymous forms. The jussive form and YIQTOL often coincide, and so do the cohortative and first person YIQTOL with third weak verbs. Word order helps to tell them apart. Compare ישמעו העברים, "Let the Hebrews hear" (1 Sam 13:3), with וכל העם ישמעו, "And all the people will hear" (Deut 17:13): although the forms are homonymous, their position in the clause marks them as jussive and normal YIQTOL respectively. Volitive forms may take the second position in the clause if they are preceded by a marked topic or focus. In CBH, however, this happens only in about five percent of the cases, according to the research of Shulman.[30]

The placement rules governing volitive clauses account for a rather striking syntactic rule obtaining in such clauses. Where a volitive verbal form combines with an adverbial phrase of time, the latter always follows the former. One says השכם בבקר, "get up early tomorrow" (Ex 8:16), but never *בבקר השכם. By some quirk of circumstances, almost all attested cases in CBH involve an imperative. There are twenty eight cases of the sequence imperative + adverbial phrase in the prose texts in Genesis to 2 Kings,[31] and only one exception, with the reverse sequence.[32]

---

28   See G. Bergsträsser, *Hebräische Grammatik* (2 vols.; Leipzig: F. C. W. Vogel/J. C. Hinrichs, 1918–29), 2:45: "Kohortativ, Jussiv und Imper. bilden ein einheitliches Bedeutungssystem für den Ausdruck eines Begehrens des Sprechenden irgend welcher Art"; more recently, and more extensively, see Blum, "Verbalsystem."

29   A. Niccacci, "A Neglected Point of Hebrew Syntax: Yiqtol and Position in the Sentence," *LASBF* 37 (1987): 7–19; E. J. Revell, "The System of the Verb in Standard Biblical Prose," *HUCA* 60 (1989): 1–37; A. Shulman, "The Use of Modal Verb Forms in Biblical Hebrew Prose" (PhD diss., University of Toronto, 1996).

30   See Gen 20:15; 21:12; 23:6,15; 31:16; 47:6; Exod 5:16; 16:23; Lev 8:3; Deut 1:38; 2:2–3, 24; Josh 22:8; 1 Sam 14:36, 40; 21:4; 28:11; 2 Sam 20:4; 1 Kgs 2:26; 13:31; 20:18; 2 Kgs 9:27; 10:19; 11:15; 16:15 (Shulman, *Modal Verb Forms,* 246). Shulman lists no cases where a temporal phrase precedes the volitive.

31   Gen 24:12; 25:31, 33; Exod 7:15; 8:16; 9:13; 10:17; 16:25; 32:29; Num 11:18; 16:7, 16; 22:8, 19; Josh 7:13; 24:15; Judg 9:32; 10:15; 16:18, 28; 1 Sam 9:27; 14:33; 19:2; 29:10; 2 Sam 11:12; 1 Kgs 12:12; 22:5; 2 Kgs 10:6. Note the use of the same sequence with the

2. LBH, Ben Sira, Qumran Hebrew

In Hebrew texts that are by common consent dated to the postexilic period, the picture changes completely. The three forms making up the volitive paradigm in CBH are still in use, but they no longer appear to make up a distinct subsystem. Instead, the cohortative and jussive are turning into syntactical variants of YIQTOL: they do not express a distinct function, but tend to be used mechanically whenever the verbal form occurs in first position in the clause.[33] Meanwhile, the imperative keeps its volitive meaning, but it no longer submits to the placement rules of CBH: it often occurs in second position and is found once or twice even in third position in the clause.[34] The verbal system of these texts is clearly evolving toward the situation we find in Mishnaic Hebrew, where the distinction between the volitive forms and YIQTOL has disappeared and the prefix conjugation expresses the whole range of modal meanings.

It is no surprise, therefore, to observe that the rule governing the place of an adverbial phrase of time in imperative clauses has lapsed as well. A few instances of the classical sequence imperative + adverbial phrase of time are attested, but alongside these, one finds an appreciable number of instances of the reverse sequence.

- In LBH, Esth 5:14; Eccl 7:14; 11:6 בבקר זרע את זרעך, "In the morning sow your seed"; 2 Chr 20:16, 17.
- In Ben Sira, 14:13 A בטרם תמות היטב לאוהב, "Do good to friends before you die"; Sir 33:24/30:32 E; Sir 6:18 C.
- In Hebrew texts from Qumran, 4Q200 2 3 (Tob 4:3); 4Q200 7 i 1 (Tob 13:13); 4Q418 43–45 i 4 יום ו[לילה הגה ברז נהיה, "Day and night, meditate on the mystery of existence;" 4Q418 81+81a 11; 4Q525 14 ii24; 4Q385a 18 ii 8; 4Q427 7 i 17.[35]

---

cohortative: Gen 18:32; 46:30; Jud 6:39; 1 Sam 14:36; 2 Sam 17:1; with אל + jussive: Exod 16:19; Lev 10:9; Josh 22:22; 2 Sam 17:16. There appear to be no cases in BH of a simple jussive combining with a temporal phrase.

32 Num 14:25: this verse may be a late addition designed to harmonize the text in Numbers with its parallel in Deuteronomy; see Joosten, "Vérité," 30–31. Note that cases with עתה or ועתה are not to be considered exceptions since this adverb functions on the textual and not the clausal level.

33 E. Qimron, "Consecutive and Conjunctive Imperfect: the Form of the Imperfect with Waw in Biblical Hebrew," *JQR* 77 (1987): 151–53.

34 J. Joosten, "The Syntax of Volitive Verbal Forms in Qoheleth in Historical Perspective," in *The Language of Qohelet in Its Context: Essays in Honour of Prof. A. Schoors on the Occasion of his Seventieth Birthday* (ed. A. Berlejung and P. Van Hecke; OLA 164; Leuven: Peeters, 2007), 47–61.

35 The post-biblical material has been discussed more extensively in my study on "Imperative Clauses containing a Temporal Phrase and the Study of Diachronic

While in CBH there are twenty-eight cases of the sequence imperative + adverbial time phrase and only one example of the reverse order, in LBH, Ben Sira and Qumran there are eight instances of the former and seventeen of the latter sequence. This statistical difference attests a far-reaching reorganization of the verbal system along lines that are reasonably well understood on both the factual and the theoretical level. There can be little doubt that this reorganization reflects a diachronic development within literary Hebrew. CBH, with its intricate system distinguishing two types of modality, is earlier than LBH, where inherited forms are used without distinction.

There is no way to know, however, how much earlier. The absolute date of the CBH texts cannot be determined on the basis of this type of analysis.

3. Hebrew Inscriptions

At this point, a comparison of the biblical data with the inscriptions becomes relevant. If it can be shown that the syntax of the inscriptions obeys the same rules as CBH texts, this will suggest that the two corpora are roughly contemporary.

Now, unfortunately, there appear to be no cases in epigraphic Hebrew of imperative clauses containing an adverbial time phrase. The diagnostic feature showing up the difference between CBH and the later corpora is unavailable in the inscriptions. This absence is almost certainly due to accident. The corpus of Judean inscriptions remains very small. It just so happens that no imperative clause with a temporal phrase is found in any of them.[36]

This is not the end of the story, however. Imperatives happen not to combine with temporal phrases in the inscriptions, but jussives do. While there is not even a single jussive clause with an adverbial time phrase in CBH, six such clauses occur in the inscriptions.[37]

Syntax in Ancient Hebrew," forthcoming in the proceedings of the Fifth International Symposium on the language of Ben Sira and the Dead Sea Scrolls, which will be edited by Steve Fassberg.

36   There are a few examples of imperative after עתה, but these are irrelevant (see n. 32).

37   The text is given according to the edition of Renz, *Die althebräischen Inschriften*, 411, 421, 424, 426, 428 (§§ Lak(6):1.2.1–3; Lak(6):1.4.1–2; Lak(6):1.5.1–3, 7–9; Lak(6):1.6.1–2; Lak(6):1.8.1–2). I have not sought to transcribe all the marks indicating doubtful letters.

Lachish 2:1–3 ישמע יהוה את אדני שמעת שלם עת כים עת כים
May YHWH cause my lord to hear tidings of peace even now, even now.[38]

Lachish 4:1–2 ישמע יהוה את אדני עת כים שמעת טב

Lachish 5:1–3 ישמע יהוה את אדני שמעת שלם וטב [עת כים] עת כים

Lachish 5:7–9 יראך יהוה הקצר בטב הים
May YHWH show you the harvest (completed) successfully today (or: this year)

Lachish 6:1–2 ירא יהוה את אדני את העת הזה שלם
May YHWH cause my lord to see peace in this time.[39]

Lachish 8:1–2 ישמע יהוה את אדני שמעת טב עת כים כים

These examples call for a few remarks. To begin with, it should be observed that most of these examples have a rather stereotyped form, as one would expect in the greetings at the beginning of a letter. Only one example, Lachish 5:7–9, occurs in the body of the letter and appears to have been formed more freely.[40] Secondly, the semantics of the clauses manifestly imply a wish, i.e., volition of the speaker. In Lachish 6:1, the verbal form is marked as a jussive short form. It is legitimate to conclude that the other verbal forms, too, are jussives, even if the writing does not reveal this. In Tiberian vocalisation, the form in Lachish 2:1 and parallels would be יַשְׁמַע, not יִשְׁמַע.[41] Thirdly, although the clauses manifest a certain syntactic variety, they all have the verbal form in first position while the temporal phrase follows in a later position. In this respect, the cases where the temporal phrase is repeated, in Lachish 2, 5, and 8, are especially revealing. Even where the temporal phrase is underscored, it is never fronted. This syntactic peculiarity is analogous to what one finds in imperative clauses in CBH: even when a certain insistence falls upon the temporal phrase, it is positioned after the verb. So, for example

---

38 For כים, "now, first," see S. R. Driver, *Notes on the Hebrew Text and the Topography of the Books of Samuel* (2d ed.; Oxford: Clarendon, 1913), 31.

39 The accusative of time is similarly marked by את in Exod 13:7; Deut 9:25; see GKC §118k (p. 374).

40 Reinhard G. Lehmann, "Brief oder Botschafter? Eine kotextuelle Annäherung an Lachish Ostrakon 2 und 5," in *Bote und Brief: Sprachliche Systeme der Informationsübermittlung im Spannungsfeld von Mündlichkeit und Schriftlichkeit* (ed. A. Wagner; Frankfurt a. M.: Peter Lang, 2003), 75–101 (84–85). Lehmann argues that even Lachish 5:7–9 was formed after the model of the greetings.

41 See A. Gai, "הערות לשוניות על כתובות עבריות," *Tarbiz* 65 (1996): 529–33 (529).

Exod 10:17 ועתה שא נא חטאתי אך הפעם
And now, forgive my sins *just this once*.[42]

Since placing a constituent before the verb is one of the most widely used expedients for expressing emphasis in Hebrew, the post-verbal position of the adverbial phrase is remarkable in these examples.

If it be accepted that jussives and imperatives are part of the same volitive paradigm, both semantically and syntactically, then the six examples of the sequence jussive + temporal phrase in the Lachish letters attest to exactly the same syntax as the twenty-eight examples of imperative + temporal phrase in CBH. As so often, the case study does not amount to absolute proof: if there were cases of jussive + adverbial time phrase in the Bible, or of imperative + adverbial time phrase in the inscriptions, they might exhibit a different type of syntax. More generally, if the material of ancient Hebrew, both literary and epigraphic, were much more abundant, one might find other structures throwing our scheme into doubt. The least that can be said, however, is that there is a striking analogy between the CBH data and what one finds in Judean inscriptions. The evidence, restricted as it may be, is supportive of the view that CBH and epigraphic Hebrew reflect the same *état de langue*, although in slightly different stylistic registers.

Conclusions

In the debate on the dating of biblical texts, linguistic evidence should be given a fair hearing. The distinction between Classical and Late Biblical Hebrew, schematic as it is, corresponds to a reality. The narrative prose of the Pentateuch and Former Prophets reflects, roughly speaking, a type of language different from that of Ezra-Nehemiah, Chronicles, Esther, and Daniel. The differences are not merely stylistic, nor dialectal, but point to a diachronic development.

Relating the phases of biblical Hebrew to definite periods in history is to a certain extent problematic. When Gesenius connected CBH with the preexilic period and LBH with the postexilic period, he had practically no linguistic reasons for doing so, only historical ones. In the meantime, however, many new texts have been discovered. A small but appreciable set of inscriptions illustrates the use of Hebrew in the late monarchic period. And the Qumran texts show how literary Hebrew evolved in the Hellenistic period. The undeniable fact that CBH stands relatively close to the Hebrew of the inscriptions, and LBH to Qumran

---

42 See also Judg 16:28 and 2 Sam 11:12.

Hebrew, confirms the validity of the diachronic approach. Unfortunately, between the latest Judean inscriptions and the earliest Qumran scrolls there is a gap of more than 400 years. From the beginning of the Babylonian exile to the founding of the Qumran sect, hardly any epigraphic Hebrew remains. This gap in the attestation of Hebrew makes it impossible to know for certain until when the type of language found in the inscriptions remained in use. Nor is it possible to tell when the type of Hebrew attested in the Qumran scrolls first emerged. The transition from CBH to LBH took place at some point during these 400 years or so. Linguistic evidence does not allow one to map the history of the Hebrew language with precision.

The connection between CBH and inscriptional Hebrew is sufficiently strong, however, to caution against the recent tendency to date ever more biblical texts after the Babylonian exile. Some scholars even envisage a Hellenistic date for certain parts of the Pentateuch or the older historical books. Although it impossible to disprove that skilled Judean scribes continued to write CBH during the exile and into the early Persian period, the more reasonable inference from the linguistic facts is that the CBH corpus is roughly contemporary with the inscriptions.[43]

---

43 Cf. Hendel, *Remembering Abraham*, 110: "Some scholars suggest that it would have been possible to write a work in flawless CBH during the Persian-Hellenistic periods and that such a perfect imitation would be impossible to detect. That is a logical possibility. . . . But it is not very likely, and on methodological grounds we should eschew improbable possibilities when more probable historical reconstructions are available."

The Significance of Rhetoric in the Greek Pentateuch

JAMES K. AITKEN

Any reader of the Septuagint is confronted from the first by rhetorical features in the Greek. Upon opening Genesis, we see the translator successfully accomplishing the task of representing by different means forms or sounds in Hebrew for which there are no equivalents in his target language.

וְהָאָרֶץ הָיְתָה תֹהוּ וָבֹהוּ
ἡ δὲ γῆ ἦν ἀόρατος καὶ ἀκατασκεύαστος
NETS Yet the earth was invisible and unformed (Gen 1:2)

It is possible that in the obscure but euphonic phrase תֹהוּ וָבֹהוּ the second word בֹהוּ is primarily a paranomastic pairing for the first,[1] especially given its appearance in this combination (here and at Jer 4:23; Isa 34:11). This presented the challenge of translating the pair into Greek. Accordingly the translator chose a combination that both conveyed the sense of the Hebrew and had a comparable alliterative effect, if different from that in Hebrew. The two adjectives ἀόρατος καὶ ἀκατασκεύαστος, whether or not they denote philosophical concepts,[2] are accommodated to Greek in both sound and sense. Both words begin with *alpha*-privative and both end with the adjectival -τος; neither feature inevitable given the possibilities of translating the Hebrew words. In addition the second of the pair has more syllables, and the resultant rise in syllables could be seen as euphonic, perhaps even metrical.[3]

---

1 Cf. the explanations in some of the lexica: e.g., KBL, 1556.

2 See M. Harl, *La Genèse: Traduction du texte grec de la Septante, introduction et notes* (2nd ed.; La Bible d'Alexandrie 1; Paris: Cerf, 1994), 87, on the philosophical readings of the phrase. Her contrast between the philosophical adjectives of the Greek and the rhyming adjectives of the Hebrew overlooks the effect also created by the Greek pairing.

3 Establishing metrical patterns is contentious when appearing apparently randomly in prose texts, but a trained writer would have been attuned to the sounds of the words. In this case the whole phrase is composed of a paeon and the last three feet of a hexameter, the former more suited to prose, although the latter is well attested in prose writers (see J. K. Aitken, "The Literary Attainment of the Translator of Greek Sirach," in *Texts and Versions of the Book of Ben Sira: Transmission and Interpretation* [ed. J.-S. Rey and J. Joosten; Leiden: Brill, forthcoming], 95–126 [102]). On hexameters in

It is no great surprise to find such stylistic elements in the Septuagint. Their appearance will naturally vary from one translated book to
another, but it is more surprising to find them in those translations
where there is a higher degree of lexical equivalence (for example, Song
of Songs or Ecclesiastes)[4] than in others (for example, Proverbs or Job).[5]
Nevertheless, any literate Greek writer would have been familiar to
some degree with rhetorical techniques, and their presence in the Septuagint is testimony to this. Although a different social setting or time
might account for a greater preference in some books than others,[6] evidence is accumulating to suggest that throughout the Septuagint rhetoric is a notable feature of the translations. These rhetorical features are a
reminder to us, in the first place, that the translators were literate, a
statement so obvious that it verges on tautology to state. But it is
important to remember that the translators were not merely bilingual
speakers or Jews with some knowledge of Greek. To be literate, that is
to say to be able to write in Greek, was a matter of education, which
can too often be taken for granted with contemporary western pre-
sumptions of literacy. To write in Greek required schooling, even if the
degree to which one progressed varied according to class and financial
means, and the higher levels of Greek education were not essential for
mastering the writing of Greek to a competent level. It appears, as we
shall consider below, that even the more elementary introductions to
reading and writing would have incorporated some exposure to rhetorical techniques, and that the traditional picture of three distinct levels of Greek education, with rhetoric as the ultimate goal attained by a
few, is more theoretical than the reality that is revealed from papyri.[7]
This picture also presupposes the identification of rhetorical techniques

---

LXX Proverbs, see H. St. J. Thackeray, "The Poetry of the Greek Book of Proverbs,"
JTS 13 (1911–1912): 46–66 (48–55). The translator might not have been conscious of
the metrical form, but might well have chosen it for its harmonious sound, especially
for this ending.

4   J. K. Aitken, "Rhetoric and Poetry in Greek Ecclesiastes," *BIOSCS* 38 (2005): 55–78.
Some features can also be identified in Canticles, but fewer than in Ecclesiastes.

5   On Proverbs, see H. St. J. Thackeray, "Poetry," 48; G. Gerleman, *Proverbs* (vol. 3 of
Studies in the Septuagint; LUÅ 1.52.3; Lund: Gleerup, 1956), 11–35; D.-M.
d'Hamonville, *Les Proverbes: Traduction du texte grec de la Septante, introduction et notes*
(La Bible d'Alexandrie 17; Paris: Cerf, 2000), 92. On Job, see J. G. Gammie, "The Septuagint of Job: Its Poetic Style and Relationship to the Septuagint to Proverbs," *CBQ*
49 (1987): 14–31.

6   Cf. Aitken, "Rhetoric and Poetry," 72–74, where the marked features in Ecclesiastes
are explained by an increased interest in rhetoric in the Roman period.

7   Such is the picture in older books of classical education: e.g., Stanley F. Bonner,
Education in Ancient Rome: From the Elder Cato to the Younger Pliny (London: Methuen,
1977).

only with the third level of rhetoric at school, although in reality different aspects of rhetoric would have been introduced at different stages.
This raises the question in turn as to how significant or meaningful are
the rhetorical features that can be identified in the Septuagint.

The importance of this topic lies on several fronts. In the first place
it is one aspect of translation technique that can easily be overlooked
when focus is placed on the lexical choice made for rendering individual Hebrew words. The translators were as sensitive to the target language as to the source language, and to the context on the phrasal as
much as the lexical level. As a corollary to this, it shows a sensitivity to
the genre of the Hebrew source, in that, as we shall see, some rhetorical
features appear to be more frequent in Hebrew poetic passages.

A further significance of the topic at hand is that it sheds light on
the educational background of the translators. The apparent vernacular
nature of the Greek raises issues over their training or their expectation
on the part of their readers.[8] Rhetorical features could be an indicator of
the educational level that the translators attained, or at least of the
socio-linguistic setting within which they operated. If rhetoric was
introduced in the elementary stages of learning, then the presence of
these features does not prove the higher level of education of the translators. To this question we will return at the end. The nature of translation itself, however, and the technique employed by the ancient translators, do obscure any clear picture we try to draw of the competence of
the translators. Nevertheless, as our knowledge of *koine* is expanding
we can see that their lexical choices and grammatical decisions were
usually not contrary to Greek norms,[9] and we can infer something of
their competence in Greek. Rhetoric as an indicator of their educational
background provides information that we cannot learn from a study of
grammar or semantics alone. However, it is not an easy task to evaluate
the features of the Septuagint and to present a balanced portrait of
what it means for our understanding of the translations. This investigation will consider what we may and may not infer from rhetorical evidence, using the Pentateuch as an illustrative example. The evidence
will be located within the larger context of Greek education, for which
comparison will be made with educational exercises and papyri to shed
light on the translators.

---

8   Jan Joosten has recently renewed interests in aspects of the colloquial nature of the
    Greek, concluding that its intended audience was not the Ptolemaic court ("Le
    milieu producteur du Pentateuque grec," *REJ* 165 [2006]: 349–61).

9   A standard work on Septuagint Greek language remains J. A. L. Lee, *A Lexical Study
    of the Septuagint Version of the Pentateuch* (SBLSCS 14; Chico, Calif.: Scholars Press,
    1983). Much work, nonetheless, still remains to be done.

Rhetoric in the Septuagint

There have been few studies devoted to this aspect of the Septuagint,[10] although stylistic features have been remarked upon in passing by many.[11] The difficulty lies in determining whether a feature is a choice made by the translator for stylistic effect or the result of translating a Hebrew verse that already reflected such style (for example, word order) or that naturally arose from translating the Hebrew (for example, a stereotyped rendering). Thus, to identify a feature in the Greek as rhetorical, one must first decide whether the feature could have been generated unintentionally by a translator aiming at a standard rendering of the Hebrew. For example, in Exod 5:13 there appears what could be intentional alliteration on the syllable καθ-:

Συντελεῖτε τὰ ἔργα <u>τὰ καθήκοντα καθ' ἡμέραν καθάπερ</u> καὶ ὅτε τὸ ἄχυρον ἐδίδοτο ὑμῖν.

NETS: Complete the customary tasks daily even as when the straw was being given to you.

While the effect here is striking, each expression is a natural translation of the Hebrew דְּבַר־יוֹם בְּיוֹמוֹ כַּאֲשֶׁר, rendering uncertain the intentionality of the effect. Of course other equivalents could have been chosen, such as ὡς for כַּאֲשֶׁר (Gen 18:33), but the equivalents are common enough that they do not permit definitive conclusions in this case. The translation equivalents, therefore, used by a translator for the relevant Hebrew word should be determined in order to infer whether the translator has chosen a distinctive word for its stylistic effect. Likewise, departures in syntax or word morphology from the translator's standard choices can confirm that a feature is intended.[12]

It should be made clear that the focus here is on rhetorical lexis, that is to say on rhetoric at the level of the word and phrase. This fea-

---

10 For specific books, see footnotes 4 and 5 above. See too, for Exodus, D. L. Gera, "Translating Hebrew Poetry into Greek Poetry: The Case of Exodus 15," *BIOSCS* 40 (2007): 107–20; for Sirach, Aitken "Literary Attainment," 103–4, 118–21. For a general brief introduction, see J. A. L. Lee, "Translations of the Old Testament. I. Greek," in *Handbook of Classical Rhetoric in the Hellenistic Period, 330 B.C.–A.D. 400* (ed. Stanley E. Porter; Leiden: Brill, 1997), 775–84. An IOSCS panel was devoted to the topic at its meeting in 2007, and the papers will be published in: *Et sapienter et eloquenter: Studies on Rhetorical and Stylistic Features in the Septuagint* (ed. E. Bons and T. Kraus; FRLANT; Göttingen: Vandenhoeck & Ruprecht, forthcoming).

11 E.g., I. L. Seeligmann, *The Septuagint Version of Isaiah: A Discussion of its Problems* (Leiden: Brill, 1948), 40–41; Anneli Aejmelaeus, *Parataxis in the Septuagint: a Study of the Renderings of the Hebrew Coordinate Clauses in the Greek Pentateuch* (AASF. Dissertationes humanarum litterarum 31; Helsinki: Suomalainen Tiedeakatemia, 1982), 71–72.

12 Cf. Aitken, "Rhetoric and Poetry," 58–61, on method.

ture is to be distinguished from many of the features known from tertiary Greek education, also known as rhetoric but which includes persuasion and composition of a variety of genres. We cannot draw conclusions on the translator's larger intention for his discourse, if he had
any, from the identification of lexico-rhetorical features alone. Furthermore, finding only sporadic or occasional rhetorical features
reveals some competency on the part of the translator, but it does not
by itself provide evidence of any broader intention or view of his composition, which would have to be demonstrated by a consistent use of
rhetoric.

Rhetoric in the Greek Pentateuch

It would be informative to gather all possible cases of rhetorical features in the Greek Pentateuch for a systematic analysis of the topic, and
to determine any distinctive profiles of the translators. There is neither
the space nor the need here, however. It is sufficient to note that there
are rhetorical features, but that they are by no means consistent enough
or frequent enough to indicate any particular intention on the part of
the translators. Some examples have already been long noted. Thus the
Greek translation of Numbers 22–24 displays features not reflected in
the Hebrew *Vorlage*, and notably a progression of compound forms of
ἀράομαι in Num 23:7–8: Δεῦρο ἄρασαί μοι . . . καὶ δεῦρο ἐπικατάρασαί μοι . . .
τί ἀράσωμαι ὃν μὴ καταρᾶται . . . καταράσωμαι ὃν μὴ καταρᾶται.[13] Although
this aspect of the translation cannot be shown to be systematic, it does
reflect a tendency towards variation, a common stylistic technique.
Such cases are rare, however, in the Pentateuch. There is some variation
in syntax throughout the Pentateuch, with infinitive absolutes, infinitive constructs and clause connectors, for example, being rendered in a
variety of ways. It is often not possible, however, to determine whether
variations in these renderings are due to intentional stylistic preference
or to mere inconsistency in translation technique.

As a test case we can take the first 15 chapters of Exodus, a sample
of a reasonably-sized text, and significant in the light of Gera's analysis
of the Greek of chapter 15. The Hebrew of chapter 15 is generally recognized as poetic, and Gera identifies a number of tropes in the Greek,
including the use of Homeric forms or poetic words, the avoidance of
anthropomorphisms, and verbal echoes. She points to a number of

---

13   H. Rouillard *La Péricope de Balaam (Nombres 22–24): La Prose et les «Oracles»* (EBib NS
     4; Paris: J. Gabalda, 1985), 81–82 n. 61; cf. J. W. Wevers, *Notes on the Greek Text of
     Numbers* (SBLSCS 46; Atlanta, Ga.: Scholars Press, 1998), 388.

specifically rhetorical devices including repetition (*anaphora*; for example, vv. 5 and 10),[14] preference for the κατα- prefix (*homoeoarchton*; Exod 15:4, 5, 7, 9, 12, 17),[15] and use of a key-word (δόξα and cognates).[16] Even so, these are limited in number if still frequent enough in one chapter to be noteworthy. Nevertheless, the contrast between chapter 15 and the first 14 chapters is clear, when we see that in the first 14 chapters there are few such rhetorical devices, perhaps the same number as in chapter 15 alone. Thus we can point to the repetition of cognate verbs in Exod 3:2:

καὶ ὁρᾷ ὅτι ὁ βάτος <u>καίεται</u> πυρί, ὁ δὲ βάτος οὐ <u>κατεκαίετο</u>
NETS: and he saw that the bush was burning [בֹּעֵר] with fire, but the bush was not burning up [אֻכָּל].

This reflects both repetition and variation with the κατα- prefix, comparable to the example from Exodus 15 noted by Gera. A similar case can be seen in Exod 5:18 where anaphora of the verbs is combined with the addition of a prefix to δίδωμι. Variation is also achieved in the two verbs of Exod 3:21, where the Hebrew has the same verb:[17]

MT: תֵלְכוּן לֹא תֵלְכוּ רֵיקָם
LXX: ὅταν δὲ <u>ἀποτρέχητε</u>, οὐκ <u>ἀπελεύσεσθε</u> κενοί·
NETS: Now whenever you depart, you will not go away empty-handed.

Such cases are rare and apparently random, appearing according to the opportunity afforded the translator or even to whim. This shows some sensitivity on the part of the translator to the sound of the Greek, but not to such a degree that it dominates his translation method. It also throws into contrast Exodus 15, where it seems clear that the translator paid greater attention to the poetic register of the source text.

The translator of Deuteronomy proves yet more interesting in this regard. Like the translator of Exodus, he renders the Hebrew consistently and, for the most part, without apparent attention to the sound or sense of the Greek in the prose sections, only to exhibit unexpectedly a flourish of rhetorical features. Thus, it is likely in Deut 1:30 the translator chose the verb both for its sense and its alliterative effect:

MT: יְהוָה אֱלֹהֵיכֶם הַהֹלֵךְ לִפְנֵיכֶם
LXX: κύριος ὁ θεὸς ὑμῶν ὁ προπορευόμενος πρὸ προσώπου ὑμῶν·
NETS: The Lord your God, who goes before you.

---

14   "Translating Hebrew Poetry," 116–17.

15   Gera, "Translating Hebrew Poetry," 116.

16   Gera, "Translating Hebrew Poetry," 118–19.

17   As John Lee has pointed out to me, the variation here could have been determined by Greek grammar, wherein new compound forms compensate for the loss of earlier forms in particular tenses, although it still could be intentional in this case. For verbs of motion, see Lee, *A Lexical Study*, 85–86.

A few verses later, in Deut 1:33, the translator once more had to translate the Hebrew הַהֹלֵךְ לִפְנֵיכֶם, and this time chose a different expression,
but equally alliterative: ὃς προπορεύεται πρότερος. The translator could
have chosen the simplex πορεύομαι (for example, Exod 3:19). These features are not frequent enough to be of major significance, but throw
into contrast those places where the translator uses many such tropes,
which he does in Deuteronomy 32. This is undoubtedly a response to
the nature of the poetic Hebrew of the *Vorlage*, as seen in the case of
Exodus 15. It is in these notably poetic passages of Hebrew that an acc-
umulation of rhetorical features can be found in the Greek translation.
To illustrate we may note the choice of poetic words in Deuteronomy
32, which contrasts with other more prosaic parts of Deuteronomy:

προσδοκάσθω ὡς <u>ὑετὸς</u> τὸ ἀπόφθεγμά μου,
καὶ καταβήτω ὡς <u>δρόσος</u> τὰ ῥήματά μου,
ὡσεὶ <u>ὄμβρος</u> ἐπ' ἄγρωστιν
καὶ ὡσεὶ <u>νιφετὸς</u> ἐπὶ χόρτον.

Let my saying be expected as rain
and let my words descend as dew,
as a rain storm on a grassy field
and as snowfall on grass.[18] (Deut 32:2)

The translator has chosen four words for the natural elements here, all
ending in -ος (homoioteleuton), the first and last with three syllables,
the middle two with two, producing a chiasm. Variation is already
apparent in the Hebrew where the adverb כ is used twice, followed by
עֲלֵי twice. But the translator has made the variation more striking by
choosing the adverb ὡς twice and then its variant ὡσεί twice, the latter
matching the length and sound of the final syllable of the Hebrew עֲלֵי.
The noun ὑετός "rain" is primarily epic and poetic in its appearances in
Greek literature, and corresponds to the final pair of terms in their poetic connotations. νιφετός (also found in Dan 3:68 OG and Th) "fallen
snow" appears almost entirely in Epic, while ὄμβρος is more commonly
used in koine, found in papyri, but can also be used in epic poetry. The
pairing of νιφετός with ὄμβρος as here is twice found in Homer (*Il.* 10.6;
Od. 4.56), and attested in Hesiod (frg. 266a, line 11). Before the LXX, the
only other cases are once each in Herodotus (*Hist.* 8.98) and Polybius
(*Hist.* 36.17). Such rarity suggests that there might have been a poetic
feel to it, Herodotus certainly using the words in a literary flourish and
possibly Polybius aiming at a higher register.

---

18 All translations are my own, unless indicated otherwise.

Coordination of verbs is clear from Deut 32:21. The repetition of the two verbs is dependent on the Hebrew, but the choice of verbs with the same compound prefix παρα- (cf. 32:36) is an internal Greek choice:

αὐτοὶ <u>παρεζήλωσάν</u> με ἐπ' οὐ θεῷ,
<u>παρώργισάν</u> με ἐν τοῖς εἰδώλοις αὐτῶν·
κἀγὼ <u>παραζηλώσω</u> αὐτοὺς ἐπ' οὐκ ἔθνει,
ἐπ' ἔθνει ἀσυνέτῳ <u>παροργιῶ</u> αὐτούς.

A similar coordination of verbal prefixes can be seen in Deut 32:23:

<u>συνάξω</u> εἰς αὐτοὺς κακὰ
καὶ τὰ βέλη μου <u>συντελέσω</u> εἰς αὐτούς.

I will gather evil against them,
And my arrows I shall spend on them.

Finally, the device known as *polyptoton*, the variation of related forms, is put to good use at Deut 31:11:

ὡς ἀετὸς σκεπάσαι <u>νοσσιὰν</u> αὐτοῦ
καὶ ἐπὶ τοῖς <u>νεοσσοῖς</u> αὐτοῦ ἐπεπόθησεν

As the eagle to shelter his nest
also on its young it dotes.

These examples should be sufficient to indicate that in the Greek Pentateuch there is an occasional attempt to introduce rhetorical devices in the prose sections, but that this becomes more marked in the verse sections. The translators have aimed at a heightened literary level, generated by the Hebrew genre but not by the Hebrew words themselves. It cannot be presumed that translators would have recognized poetic passages or that it would have been indicated in the Hebrew text they had before them. In the Judean Hebrew manuscripts that we have there seems to be a lack of consistency in presenting poetry differently from prose.[19] Poetic units are arranged into stichs primarily in biblical texts and in Ben Sira (both in 2QSir and the Masada scroll), but even this is not consistent. The majority of poetic compositions are not differentiated from poetry. The supposition of Tov is that there were different scribal traditions, scribes operating not so much out of personal preference but according to their school tradition.[20] Nonetheless, in early Greek biblical texts it appears that some Greek scribes as much as the Hebrew scribes tried to represent units stichographically (e.g., P.Fouad

---

19   See E. Tov, "Special Layout of Poetical Units in the Texts from the Judean Desert," in
      *Give Ear to My Words: Psalms and Other Poetry in and around the Hebrew Bible. Essays in
      Honour of Professor N. A. van Uchelen* (ed. J. Dyk; Amsterdam: Societas Hebraica
      Amstelodamensis, 1996), 115–28; idem, *Scribal Practices and Approaches Reflected in the
      Texts Found in the Judean Desert* (STDJ 54; Leiden: Brill, 2004), 155–67.

20   Tov, *Scribal Practices*, 160.

266b [848] for Deuteronomy 32).[21] The evidence of rhetorical features and vocabulary in the Septuagint supports these data in indicating that some translators did recognise passages as poetic and translated them with some attention to this feature.

That there are such moments of a higher level is not ruled out by other places where this is not the case. At times the reasons for a choice are not obvious: perhaps the translator felt there was opportunity in the Greek to incorporate a literary flourish or he merely broke from his traditional approach without aiming at consistency. The question that remains to be asked is whether or to what extent this sheds light on the educational background of the translators.

Rhetoric and Greek Educational Practice

While rhetoric could be said to have been a standard part of Greek society, enshrined in the democratic need of public speaking in the assembly, such truisms do not account for an individual's ability to write Greek to a level that incorporates such flourishes. There would have been varying degrees of literacy in antiquity, from the person who could merely sign their name at the end of a contract, to the well-known case of the semi-literate Petaus "the village scribe" (P.Petaus 121), who unsuccessfully practises copying out a formal signature,[22] and finally to the accomplished scribe of some of the Zenon papyri (e.g., P.Cair.Zen 1.59034). Although rhetoric, the art of public speaking, was only taught formally in the tertiary stage of education, to which only the most wealthy or accomplished would have aspired, rhetorical lexis could have been taught much earlier. Recent research on Greek educational practice has drawn attention to the lack of a clear demarcation between the three stages of Greek schooling and has indicated how aspects of the later stages were introduced earlier.[23] Rhetorical school texts on papyri demonstrate the way students would have been intro-

---

21 See Tov, *Scribal Practices*, 157, and further references there.

22 See *Das Archiv des Petaus (P. Petaus)* (ed. U. Hagedorn, D. Hagedorn, L. C. Youtie and H. C. Youtie; Abhandlungen der Rheinisch-Westfälischen Akademie der Wissenschaften. Sonderreihe Papyrologica Coloniensia 4; Cologne: Westdeutscher Verlag, 1969).

23 See T. Morgan, *Literate Education in the Hellenistic and Roman Worlds* (Cambridge Classical Studies; Cambridge: Cambridge University Press, 1998); R. Cribiore, *Gymnastics of the Mind: Greek Education in Hellenistic and Roman Egypt* (Princeton, N.J.: Princeton University Press, 2001). The primary sources have been collected in R. Cribiore, *Writing, Teachers, and Students in Graeco-Roman Egypt* (ASP 36; Atlanta, Ga.: Scholars Press, 1996).

duced to rhetorical features and poetic language from an early stage, not least in the copying out of passages from authors such as Homer and Attic writers. Furthermore, the aural nature of reading in Greek, the frequent reading aloud of texts, would have placed a greater emphasis on the sound than the visual similarity of words. Sound from the very start would have played a central role.[24]

To place the rhetorical features of the Septuagint in context, evidence not merely of educational traditions, but the traces that have been left in documents are vital. Morgan has drawn attention to papyri that indicate an aspect of learning to read and write was also the introduction of proto-rhetorical exercises.[25] It is clear from these papyri that quotations from literature were given as writing exercises and that part of the exercise of learning to write was the copying out of literature. At a more advanced level the composition and imitation of literary works was set. One such papyrus (P.Oxy. 79) is a composition on Alexander the Great, and another is a retelling of the return of Odysseus to Ithaca.[26] An impressive example of such exercises is an elaborate paraphrase of the opening of the *Iliad* (1.1–21) found in a school-book comprised of seven wooden tablets, now housed in the Bodleian Library.[27] The prose paraphrase is three times longer than the original epic version, and far from the poetic quality of the original; the student is still learning his art. Nevertheless, as Morgan identifies, within the exercise there are attempts at rhetorical style and in particular the adoption of poetic phrases similar to those of the *Iliad*, including "many and numberless men" and a quarrel "born from no-one other than Apollo himself."[28]

These examples suggest that in learning to read and compose, students who did not progress to the higher stages of education would have been exposed to some rhetorical training, learning through copy-

---

24   G. A. Kennedy, *Classical Rhetoric and its Christian and Secular Tradition from Ancient to Modern Times* (Chapel Hill: University of North Carolina Press, 1980), 35; P. J. Achtemeier, "*Omne verbum sonat*: The New Testament and the Oral Environment of Late Western Antiquity," *JBL* 190 (1990): 3–27 (16–19).

25   Morgan, *Literate Education*, 219–26.

26   C. H. Roberts, *Theological and Literary Texts* (vol. 3 of *Catalogue of the Greek Papyri in the John Rylands Library, Manchester*; Manchester: Manchester University Press, 1911–1952), no. 487, on Odysseus's return to Ithaca, but using no distinctively Homeric vocabulary or following closely any episode from Homer. It is possible that this papyrus is not even an exercise, though (so Morgan, *Literate Education*, 219).

27   Bodleian Greek inscription inv. 3019 (third century CE), published in P. J. Parsons, "A School-Book from the Sayce Collection," *ZPE* 6 (1970): 133–49 (135–38).

28   T. Morgan, "Rhetoric and Education," in *A Companion to Greek Rhetoric* (ed. Ian Worthington; Oxford: Blackwell, 2007), 303–19 (314); cf. Morgan, *Literate Education*, 205–8.

ing and paraphrasing. Even clerks and other officials in Egypt, without ambitions at attaining a high level of literacy, would have had some knowledge of such techniques. More significant than Morgan's examples, though, are those where in a documentary text, in which the author is not aiming at literary imitation, rhetorical features are to be found. Evidence of the knowledge of Homer or awareness of poetic-sounding words have already been noted in some papyri.[29] The identification of rhetorical features in documentary papyri, however, has not been subjected to analysis so far. It can be shown that rhetorical features were known to such scribal officials, whose most literary activity was probably writing letters of an administrative nature. For example, from the third century BCE in a letter to Zenon the author Theudoros or his scribe shows off his literary pretension:[30]

[Θεύδωρος] Ζήνωνι χαίρειν. ὅτε
ἀπὸ σοῦ ἀπῆλθον εἰς Ἄθριβιν, κατέ-
λαβον Πύθωνά τε καὶ Ἀμμώνιον
πολιορκουμένους ὑπὸ Ἀντιόχου
περὶ ἀργ[υ]ρ[ί]ου. οὐ μὴν ἀλλ᾽ ὅτε
ἀπέδωκα Πύθωνι τὴν [[την]][31] παρὰ σοῦ
ἐπ[ισ]τολ[ήν], ἐκ <u>παντὸς</u> τρόπου
<u>π[άντ]α πάρε[ργ]α</u> ποιησά[μ]ενος

Theudoros sends greetings to Zenon. When I came from you to Athribis, I found both Python and Ammonios under pressure from Antiochos over money. Nevertheless, when I delivered to Python the letter from you, exerting every effort in every manner possible. . . .[32]

This letter, dated 5 May 257 BCE, recounts how Python, a banker at Athribis, has advanced 1000 drachmae to Theudoros. The emphasis on the efforts exerted is highlighted by the alliteration of the Greek letter π in the concluding phrase παντὸς τρόπου π[άντ]α πάρε[ργ]α ποιησά[μ]ενος "exerting every effort in every manner possible." The effect is notice-

---

29 E.g., an allusion to Homer, *Od.* 11.415, noted by R. Luiselli, "Authorial Revision of Linguistic Style in Greek Papyrus Letters and Petitions (AD i–iv)," in *The Language of the Papyri* (ed. T. V. Evans and D. D. Obbink; Oxford: Oxford University Press, 2010), 71–96 (89–90).

30 P.Cair.Zen. 1.59062 (reprinted as P.Lond. 1943).

31 The scribe accidentally wrote the definite article twice, but it has been deleted in the papyrus.

32 Greek text from T. C. Skeat, ed., *The Zenon Archive* (vol. 7 of *Greek Papyri in the British Museum*; London: British Museum, 1974). The reading here is that of Skeat, following P.Hib. 44.5 that has the same phrase. In his edition Edgar (*Zenon Papyri, Catalogue général des antiquités égyptiennes du Musée du Caire*, 5 vols. [ed. C. C. Edgar; Cairo. 1925–1940], 1:87) has read παρα[χρῆμα] although the fourth letter might be an ε as much as an α.

able and probably intentional.[33] The repetition of πᾶς and the choice of the compound πάρεργα as opposed to the simplex ἔργα serve to emphasize the extent to which the subject, perhaps Python despite the change in case, has exerted himself in the task. It seems that in antiquity alliteration on π was particularly favoured, and it is no surprise to find it here (cf. Deut 1:30, 33 above).[34]

In another example, again from the same century as the Greek Pentateuch, we find a coordination of verbs with the same prefix (PLon 1954.8):

> δεόμεθα οὖν σου, εἴ σοι δοκεῖ, <u>εισκαλεσθαι</u> [read εἰσκαλέ<σα>σθαί] τ[ιν]ας ἡμῶν, καὶ <u>εἰσακοῦσαι</u> περὶ ὧν βουλόμεθά σοι ἀναγγεῖλαι.

> We therefore ask of you, if you think it fitting, to summon some of us and pay heed to the matters that we wish to report to you.

Although this papyrus is not dated, it can be located in the sowing season, that is October to November, of either the year 258 or 257, owing to its relation to other events recorded in the Zenon papyri. Arising from a dispute over land with native Egyptians, the Greek petitioners request an interview with Apollonios, effectively coordinating the verb εἰσκαλέσασθαί with εἰσακοῦσαι. Once again in the Zenon papyri we find another case of such coordination in a financial letter (P.Lond. 1979.15–17):

> . . . ἐβουκόλησεν [[εβουκολησεμ]] μὲν
> οὖν ἡμᾶς Σώστρατος· συστήσας [[συσστησας]] γὰρ ἡμῖν Πρῷτον ἵνα δῶι ἐκ τοῦ μέλιτος, πάλιν
> <u>ἀποσυνέταξεν ἀποτρέχων</u> μηκ[έτ]ι̣ [τὸ] μέλι Προίτωι προέσθαι.

> Sostratos has cheated us. For, having recommended to us Proitos to give us from the honey, he hurried off and gave orders that the honey not be delivered to Proitos.

In this letter, dated to 2 January 252 BCE, we find one of only two occurrences in the Hellenistic period of the verb ἀποσυντάσσω. The other occurence is also in a Zenon papyrus and hence from the same period (PSI 418 1.14), although in a supralinear reading. Outside the time period a further occurrence is to be found in John Moschus's *Spiritual Meadow* (189.3068). The translation given in LSJ (221), "order to be sup-

---

33 Skeat, *The Zenon Archive*, 31, notes that the same phrase πάντα πάρεργα ποιησάμενος appears at P.Hib. 44.5. This might indicate that it was a well-known expression, perhaps popular owing to the alliteration. What is striking about P.Lond. 1943, though, is the extended phrase with the alliteration of the letter π.

34 J. D. Denniston, *Greek Prose Style* (Oxford: Clarendon, 1952), 126, 129, notes the popularity of alliteration on π in Pindar and Plato. Examples from other parts of the Septuagint are noted by Lee, "Translations," 778 and n. 9. For the frequency of this feature in Greek Ecclesiastes, see Aitken "Rhetoric and Poetry," 63–64.

plied," has been described by Skeat as "guesswork."[35] Skeat proposes instead that the ἀπο- prefix be understood as privative, which would mean, in the context where it is followed by a negative and infinitive, "revoke an order; prohibit." Skeat's proposal has been adopted by the *Revised Supplement* to LSJ,[36] although the context would not seem to require the ἀπο- prefix to be privative, since the negative is conveyed by the negative particle. Whether or not Skeat's proposal is correct, the scribe might well have chosen this unusual compound form to complement the following verb ἀποτρέχω. This would then be another case of a scribe employing some basic rhetorical lexical techniques in a documentary letter.

These few examples provide us with a snapshot of the writing desk of the scribal class in Egypt. Many who learned to read and compose in their local village probably did not go on to study advanced rhetoric in the schools of the larger towns. Most would have learned to read and analyse a text, reproduce it and paraphrase it (as in the case of the Homeric exercises), perhaps with the odd flourish to show they were educated men.[37] For their educational needs, this was the minimal level of rhetorical training required: some simple literary effects were more than enough for men of middling social rank. They were unlikely to perform on the larger public stage, and their only need was to conduct business, draft and analyse legal documents, and interpret government demands. Some local scribes, such as the hapless Petaus, were not even able to do that much, but those that could aimed at writing a Greek with a certain degree of elegance, even if they were not capable of writing high literature or could only introduce such rhetorical flourishes occasionally. In conclusion, it remains to locate the Septuagint translators within the possible social strata of such scribes.

Conclusions

We have seen that the Septuagint translators occasionally employed rhetorical features in their translation, combined with the occasional word with an Homeric or epic ring. These features are generally on the level of the lexeme, and we cannot surmise a sustained rhetorical inten-

---

35 Skeat, *Greek Papyri*, 76.
36 *Greek–English Lexicon: Revised Supplement* (ed. P. G. W. Glare, with the assistance of A. A. Thompson; Oxford: Clarendon Press, 1996), 47.
37 So Morgan, "Rhetoric and Education," 314.

tion such as that of exhortation (protreptic) or denunciation (diatribe).[38] With the spread of Greek culture and the rise of a "Hellenistic globalisation,"[39] there was an added impetus to learn how to engage on a public level in Greek as individuals would learn how to express themselves more ably in achieving civic and personal goals. Greek education, of which Jews in Egypt soon began to partake,[40] allowed students to study different kinds of speeches, the theory of style, the figures to be employed for effect, and the nature of words and prose rhythm (cf. Quintillian, *Inst.* 1.4.6–7.35). In learning just to write Greek, models would be taken and memorized from the literature of the classics or the speeches of great orators of the past. But this does not mean that everyone would have reached the competency or experience of writing such literature or speeches themselves. The Septuagint translators might well have been comparable to the more skilled of the Egyptian bureaucratic scribes, having not achieved the highest level of education, but having acquired some rhetorical skills which were taught in the elementary levels of education. It is possible that in looking for a translator in the context of Ptolemaic Egypt, the most likely place to find one is among the scribal class of the Ptolemaic bureaucracy.[41] And, as we have seen, such scribes had the competence to write with the same level of rhetorical technique as the Septuagint translators.

If this thesis has some value, then the small rhetorical flourishes do not indicate anything more than a competent scribe displaying his skill at certain points. It also presupposes that the translation was not a

---

38 For one attempt to argue a Greek translation is a diatribe, see C. P. Giese, "The Genre of Ecclesiastes as Viewed by its Septuagint Translator and the Early Church Fathers" (Ph.D. diss., Hebrew Union College-Jewish Institute of Religion, Cincinnati, 1999).

39 So L. Pernot, *La rhétorique dans l'Antiquité* (Le livre de poche. Références 553; Paris: Librairie générale française, 2000); cf. J. A. Crook, *Legal Advocacy in the Roman World* (London: Duckworth, 1995), 8–9, 58–118.

40 Jewish names are already included among the recently-published salt tax papyri from the early third century BCE, where they are classed as Hellenes, a term defining their education or role in the administration rather than their origins: W. Clarysse and D. J. Thompson, *Counting the People in Hellenistic Egypt* (2 vols.; Cambridge Classical Studies; Cambridge: Cambridge University Press, 2006), 2:147–48.

41 Cf. W. Peremans, "Les ἑρμηνεῖς dans l'Égypte gréco-romaine," in *Das römisch-byzantinische Ägypten: Akten des internationalen Symposions 26.–30. September 1978 in Trier* (ed. G. Grimm, H. Heinen, and E. Winter; Mainz am Rhein: Philipp von Zabern, 1983), 11–17; B. G. Wright, "The Jewish Scriptures in Greek: The Septuagint in the Context of Ancient Translation Activity," in *Biblical Translation in Context* (ed. F. W. Knobloch; Bethesda, Md.: University Press of Maryland, 2002), 3–18; T. V. Evans, "The Court Function of the Interpreter in Genesis 42:23 and Early Greek Papyri," in *Jewish Perspectives on Hellenistic Rulers* (ed. T. Rajak, S. Pearce, J. Aitken, and J. Dines; Hellenistic Culture and Society 50; Berkeley, Calif.: University of California Press, 2007), 238–52.

grand literary enterprise, for which there was no exemplar, but the routine task of translating documentary material, of which there are many examples.[42] The one reservation to such a conclusion is the tendency for the translator to introduce more features at poetic points in the Hebrew. This in itself is further evidence of the recognition in this period of Hebrew poetic units. It also might suggest that the translators were in fact highly skilled writers, who were merely restrained by the translation technique adopted, perhaps chosen as the only model of translation they had rather than out of any particular agenda. This could be the case given the signs of increased rhetorical features when needed for poetry. But even then the examples are small, perhaps more marked in Deuteronomy 32 than in Exodus 15.

Any conclusion must therefore be reserved. The translation of Ecclesiastes still stands out as remarkable for the number and sophistication of rhetorical features in such a short work, typified by a high degree of lexical and quantitative equivalence. Study of the Pentateuch throws into contrast all the more the translation of Ecclesiastes. The latter work might well have been undertaken by someone very well educated, perhaps under the influence of the emerging Second Sophistic movement.[43] The Pentateuch by comparison is far more muted in its use of rhetorical techniques and could be compared to the documentary papyri illustrated here. It is possible that the nature of the prose material did not induce such literary flourishes in the translator, or that the translation technique inhibited the space for such elaboration. From a translation we cannot tell for sure if it reflects all that they had learnt at school, or whether it merely reflects all they were able to do within the confines of the translation discipline.

It is hoped that this is a fitting tribute for a devoted teacher and scholar who has focussed much of his scholarly activity on the Pentateuch, but whose work extends to such other areas as the ancient versions and education in Israel.

---

42 E.g., W. Peremans, "Notes sur les traductions de textes non littéraires sous les Lagides," *ChrEg* 60 (1985): 248–62.

43 See Aitken, "Rhetoric and Poetry," 73–74.

Midrash in Greek?

An Exploration of the Versions of Aquila and Symmachus in Exodus

ALISON SALVESEN

The translations of Aquila, Symmachus, and the more enigmatic Theodotion, were well known in antiquity. Although they all were the work of Jews—Aquila and Symmachus may even have been converts to Judaism[1]—they were at least as popular with Christians as with the Jewish readership for which they were apparently intended. They are all representatives of a movement centred on Palestine where the Hebrew text of Scripture was becoming more standardized in form and more central to Jewish interpretation. The books of the LXX translated in the last phase of the collection of books already show signs of this revisional movement, termed by some the kaige-Theodotion-Revision. The trend towards closer representation of the emerging MT was further developed in the literal translation of Aquila around 130 CE. However, by the end of the same century the emphasis of Symmachus's translation is not on an ever closer representation of the formal features of the text but on its currently understood meaning.

Rabbinic approval is recorded for Aquila's version in the Palestinian Talmud.[2] The widespread use of Aquila by Jews is attested by the Christian scholars Origen in the mid-third century and Jerome in the late fourth century. However, in the case of Symmachus it appears that

---

1   See for example the "biographies" given by Epiphanius, in *De mensuris et ponderibus* §13–17, written ca. 392 CE, in which Aquila, Symmachus, and Theodotion all convert to Judaism from, respectively, paganism via the Church, the Samaritan community, and Marcionism (ed. E. Moutsoulas, "Τὸ «Περὶ μέτρων καὶ σταθμῶν» ἔργον Ἐπιφανίου τοῦ Σαλαμῖνος," *Θεολογία* 44 (1973): 157–98). In the Palestinian Talmud Aquila is said to be a proselyte (e.g., *y. Meg.* 1:9 [71c], and *y. Qidd.* 1:1 [59a]).

2   *y. Meg.* 1:9 (71c): "Aquila (עקילס) the proselyte translated the Torah before (לפני) R. Eliezer and R. Joshua, and they praised him (וקילסו) and said, יָפְיָפִיתָ מִבְּנֵי אָדָם (Ps 45:3)." Also *y. Qidd.* 1:1 (59a) on Aquila translating Lev 19:20 before R. Akiva. See now the article by Jenny R. Labendz, "Aquila's Bible Translation in Late Antiquity: Jewish and Christian Perspectives," *HTR* 102 (2009): 353–88, where she questions whether these passages indicate that Aquila translated under rabbinic auspices, as has usually been assumed.

he quickly became more beloved of Christians than of Jews. Some Christians believed Symmachus was Ebionite, a Jewish-Christian here- tic, though there are few unequivocal signs of this in his translation. The notion seems to have arisen out of a misunderstanding of a state- ment by Irenaeus on the Ebionite denial of the virgin birth, a view shared of course by Jews. Epiphanius in contrast represents Symma- chus as a Samaritan sage who converted to Judaism and was recircum- cised, a tradition that for all its tendentious detail fits the affinities of Symmachus's version with the exegesis of Palestinian Judaism.[3] Lack of reference to the version or its translator in rabbinic literature may be because it represents the end-phase of respect on the part of Palestinian rabbis for Greek as a cultural and especially a religious medium: for them Hebrew should hold primacy.[4] In contrast, Aquila's more literal approach, which drew attention to the Hebrew original, ensured his continuing popularity and his recognition by the rabbis.

Certainly, in Jewish circles more has been preserved of Aquila's version than that of Symmachus.[5] We have some pages of Aquila's version of Kings in the underwriting of a palimpsest from the Cairo Geniza, dating from the fourth to sixth centuries CE,[6] and some more Cairo Genizah fragments containing verses from Aquila's version of Psalms.[7] The Jewish origin of these fragments of Kings and Psalms is likely because of the use of the paleo-Hebrew Tetragrammaton.[8] There is also a verse of Psalms in Aquila's version on a stone block from a

3   See A. Geiger, "Symmachus, der Uebersetzer der Bibel," *Jüdische Zeitschrift für Wissenschaft und Leben* 1 (1862): 39–64; D. Barthélemy, "Qui est Symmaque?" *CBQ* 36 [Patrick W. Skehan Festschrift] (1974): 451–65; repr. in *Études d'Histoire du Texte* (OBO 21; Göttingen: Vandenhoeck & Ruprecht, 1978), 307–21; A. van der Kooij, "Symmachus, 'de vertaler der Joden,'" *NedTT* 42 (1988): 1–20 (English summary, 67); A. Salvesen, *Symmachus in the Pentateuch* (JSSMS 15; Manchester: Manchester Uni- versity Press, 1991).

4   R. Simeon ben Gamaliel, who by tradition dates to the first century CE, stated that the only language into which Torah is capable of being translated is Greek. This tra- dition occurs immediately before the report about Aquila translating the Torah so successfuly before Eliezer and Joshua in *y. Meg* 1:9 (71c). Cf. also *m. Meg* 1:8 for Simeon ben Gamaliel's view that the Scriptures may only be written in Greek.

5   For full details and bibliography on the remnants of Aquila, see N. Fernández Mar- cos, *The Septuagint in Context: Introduction to the Greek Versions of the Bible* (Leiden: Brill, 2000), 113–15.

6   1 Kgs 20:7–17 and 2 Kgs 23:11–27. F. C. Burkitt (ed.), *Fragments of the Books of Kings According to the Translation of Aquila* (Cambridge: Cambridge University Press, 1897).

7   Pss 90[91]:17–103[104]:17.

8   According to Origen, *Sel. Pss.* 2:2 (PG 12, col. 1104), the most accurate manuscripts of his period had the Name in ancient Hebrew characters.

synagogue in Turkey.[9] In 1980 de Lange published some Greek glosses in Hebrew letters from the Cairo Geniza, which resemble Aquila's version.[10] The Emperor Justinian's *Novella* 146 stating that Jews were to read either the LXX or Aquila in the synagogues might be a concession to its popularity among Jews.[11] Last but not least, Azariah de' Rossi devotes a chapter of his *Me'or Enayim* to Aquila, and speaks of his work in very positive terms.[12]

The fragments of Symmachus's version are preserved mainly by Christian writers and copyists,[13] but there are also the fragments of Psalms[14] found at El Fayum in Egypt. They are dated to the third or fourth century, now in Vienna as part of the Rainer collection.[15] They

---

9   A. Salvesen, "Psalm 135(136).25 in a Jewish Greek inscription from Nicea," in *Semitic Studies in Honour of Edward Ullendorff* (ed. G.A. Khan; Leiden: Brill, 2005), 212–21.

10 N. R. M. de Lange, "Some New Fragments of Aquila On Malachi and Job?" *VT* 30 (1980): 291–94; idem, *Greek Jewish Texts from the Cairo Genizah* (Tübingen: Mohr, 1996); and idem, "*Non placet Septuaginta*: Revisions and New Greek Versions of the Bible in Byzantium," in *Jewish Reception of Greek Bible Versions: Studies in their Use in Late Antiquity and the Middle Ages* (ed. N. R. M. de Lange, J. G. Krivoruchko, and C. Boyd-Taylor; TSMEMJ 23; Tübingen: Mohr Siebeck, 2009), 39–44.

11 See the discussion of Justinian's motivation in Labendz, "Aquila's Bible Translation in Late Antiquity," and her critique of Rutgers. However, in spite of the qualms of a few patristic writers that Aquila's version was specifically designed to be anti-Christian, commentators from Origen onwards frequently cited it to elucidate the LXX. Thus by the time of Justinian it may not have represented a concession to Jews at all. Judah Goldin's humorous comment "I don't doubt that Aquila pleased several important scholars; maybe subconsciously they hoped that after one hour with such Greek, a man would cry out, Give me Hebrew or give me death" ("Reflections on Translation and Midrash," in Judah Goldin, *Studies in Midrash and Related Literature* (ed. Barry L. Eichler and Jeffrey H. Tigay; Philadelphia: Jewish Publication Society, 1988), 239–52 [247]), fails to recognise the esteem in which many Jews and Christian scholars held Aquila.

12 Azariah de' Rossi, *The Light of the Eyes* (trans. J. Weinberg; Yale Judaica Series 31; New Haven: Yale University Press, 2001), ch. 45, pp. 571–85.

13 Origen included both Aquila and Symmachus among the parallel Bible texts in the Hexapla. Thus Christians were able to access, copy, and pass on interesting readings that differed from or explained problems in the wording of the traditional LXX. Once the Hexapla disappeared sometime in the seventh century CE, only the jottings and comments of Christian writers preserved them in the Church. Only a few larger chunks in palimpsests and papyri have been found in Christian circulation, notably the Milan and Cairo Geniza fragments of folios copied from the Hexapla of Psalms: see G. Mercati, *Psalterii Hexapli reliquiae* (2 vols.; Rome: Bibliotheca Vaticana, 1958, 1965); C. Taylor, *Hebrew-Greek Cairo Genizah Palimpsests from the Taylor-Schechter Collection including a Fragment of the Twenty-Second Psalm according to Origen's Hexapla* (Cambridge: Cambridge University Press, 1900).

14 Pss 68:13–14, 30–33; 80:11–14.

15 Published by Wessely mistakenly as Aquila: C. Wessely, "Un nouveau fragment de la version grecque du Vieux Testament par Aquila," in *Mélanges offerts à M. Emile Châtelain* (Paris: A. Champion, 1910), 224–29.

are probably Jewish because they have the Tetragrammaton in paleo-Hebrew script.[16]

Since both Aquila and Symmachus are Palestinian Jewish translations dating from the Tannaitic period, a formative time for classical rabbinic midrash, what kind of relationship might they have to midrash? Years ago Geiger,[17] Liebreich[18] and Schoeps[19] all argued that Symmachus had links with midrash, and in *Les devanciers d'Aquila* in 1963, Barthélemy argued that what remains of the versions of Aquila and Symmachus reflects rabbinic interpretative techniques and even rabbinic exegesis, especially that of R. Akiva.[20] This was on the basis of the single reference in *y. Qidd* 1:1 (59a) and Jerome's remark in his *Commentary* on Isaiah 8:14, that Akiva was Aquila the proselyte's teacher.[21] Furthermore, in 1974 Barthélemy published an article that associated Symmachus with R. Meir and his exegesis. However, Grabbe raised a number of objections to Barthélemy's position with regard to Aquila.[22] He noted the existence of two traditions, one linking Aquila to Akiva for the interpretation of a single verse (*y. Qidd* 1:1 [59a] for Lev 19:20),[23] and the other with Eliezer and Joshua for the Torah more generally (*y. Meg* 1:9 [71c]). Grabbe argued that there is no reason to privilege one tradition over the other, and no evidence that Aquila's version in fact employs whatever hermeneutical devices we can safely

---

16   See Fernández Marcos, *The Septuagint in Context*, 127–28, for details of the remnants of Symmachus and bibliography.

17   A. Geiger, "Symmachus, der Uebersetzer der Bibel."

18   L. J. Liebriech, "Notes on the Greek Version of Symmachus," *JBL* 63 (1944): 397–403.

19   H.-J. Schoeps, "Symmachusstudien III: Symmachus und der Midrasch," *Bib* 29 (1948): 31–51; repr. in *Aus frühchristlicher Zeit: Religionsgeschichtliche Untersuchungen* (Tübingen: Mohr, 1950), 101–19.

20   D. Barthélemy, *Les devanciers d'Aquila* (VTSup 10; Leiden: Brill, 1963), 3–30.

21   Saul Lieberman took both statements at face value: *Greek in Jewish Palestine: Studies in the Life and Manners of Jewish Palestine in the II–IV Centuries CE* (New York: Jewish Theological Seminary of America, 1942), 18–19.

22   Lester L. Grabbe, "Aquila's Translation and Rabbinic Exegesis," *JJS* 33 (1982): 527–36 (536), and idem, "The Translation Technique of the Greek Minor Versions: Translations or Revisions?" in *Septuagint, Scrolls and Cognate Writings: Papers Presented to the International Symposium on the Septuagint and Its Relations to the Dead Sea Scrolls and Other Writings (Manchester, 1990)* (ed. George J. Brooke and Barnabas Lindars; SBLSCS 33; Atlanta, Ga.: Scholars Press, 1992), 505–56.

23   R. Jose said in the name of R. Jochanan, Aquila the proselyte translated before R. Akiva, "and she is a slave, betrothed to another man," as "with pounding before a man" דאמר רבי יוסי בשם ר' יוחנן תירגם עקילס הגר לפני ר' עקיבה (ויקרא יט) והיא שפחה נחרפת לאיש בכתושה לפני איש. No Greek reading attributed to Aquila has survived for this verse. It is just possible that the anonymous one in MS 56, καταδουλωμένη, "oppressed," is Aquila's as it corresponds roughly in sense to what the Yerushalmi reports, but this is far from certain.

attribute to Akiva, particularly in view of the very fragmentary evidence remaining from Aquila's version. At the end of his article Grabbe issued a plea for a "comprehensive study of *all* the Minor Versions in the light of *all* the various types of ancient Jewish biblical interpretation," but particularly with regard to Aquila and Symmachus. He implied that a proper methodology is required for such an investigation.[24]

It is outside the scope of a short essay to develop such an appropriate methodology. It would also be impossible here to examine comprehensively *all* the minor Greek versions in comparison with *every* type of ancient Jewish interpretation. But some preliminary reflections on the relationship of Aquila and Symmachus to midrash in general (rather than merely to one or other rabbi) may be in order.

Much depends on the definition of midrash. Following over two decades of sometimes heated debate over whether it is best regarded as a hermeneutical process, a defined corpus, or a literary genre, the general consensus today seems to be that a strict definition of midrash is confined to the classic rabbinic midrashim, the Bible exegesis of the Talmudic and post-Talmudic eras covering both halakah and haggadah.[25] At the same time it appears acceptable to describe Targum as midrashic when it displays similar interpretative stances and methods to midrash.[26]

If Aquila and Symmachus are Jewish translations of the Tannaitic period, could they too be considered midrashic? Or is Targum considered midrashic because of its high degree of paraphrase, as well as its lemmatization of the scriptural text?[27] So an important question is whether one-for-one, unlemmatized translations like those of Aquila and Symmachus are capable of reflecting midrashic traditions and

---

24 Grabbe, "Aquila's Translation," 536.

25 A recent article of Carol Bakhos helpfully compares the various definitions of the most prominent scholars of midrash: "Method(ological) Matters in the Study of Midrash," in *Current Trends in the Study of Midrash* (ed. C. Bakhos; JSJSup 106; Brill: Leiden/Boston, 2006), 161–87. In the same volume, Burton Visotzky's article ("Midrash, Christian Exegesis, and Hellenistic Hermeneutic," 111–31) looks at the other side of the coin, by noting points of similarity between rabbinic and patristic exegesis and arguing that both qualify as Hellenistic literature (125).

26 Gary Porton back in 1981 included Targum in his rather broad definition of midrash as "a type of literature . . . which stands in direct relationship to a fixed, canonical text, considered to be the authoritative and revealed word of God by the midrashist and his audience, and in which this canonical text is explicitly cited or alluded to" ("Defining Midrash," in *The Study of Ancient Judaism* (ed. J. Neusner; New York: Ktav, 1981), 62, 70.

27 Modern editions and translations of Targum tend to omit the Hebrew lemma at the start of each verse.

midrashic techniques. Grabbe denied the possibility of the latter: he said that "many aspects of [rabbinic exegesis] would simply not be reflected in a translation (e.g., such 'rules' of exegesis as *qal wa-homer* and *gezerah shawah*)."[28]

A further question concerns the implicit assumption that midrash is in Hebrew, or possibly in Aramaic, and if a text is in Greek, Latin, Syriac, or another language, it cannot be midrash. This assumption is not unreasonable, since rabbinic midrashic approaches depend so much on details of the Hebrew text that a commentary in any other language would continually have to refer back to the Hebrew wording. Grabbe also refutes the possibility that Aquila's literal translation was used as a *basis* for later Akivan exegesis since there is no evidence that this ever happened among non-Hebrew speaking Jews.[29]

What are we left with? Can we find parallels in Aquila or Symmachus to interpretations in rabbinic midrash, and if so, does that make either of them midrashic? Below are a few examples from Exodus, a book with which our honorand Graham Davies has been much associated, along with comparable material from the Mekhilta de Rabbi Ishmael.[30] I have also given the renderings of the different Targumim.

Examples

1) Exod 13:18 וַחֲמֻשִׁים עָלוּ בְנֵי־יִשְׂרָאֵל מֵאֶרֶץ מִצְרָיִם "and the Israelites went up out of the land of Egypt *prepared for battle*" (NRSV)

LXX πέμπτῃ δὲ γενεᾷ "in the fifth generation"[31]
Th. πεμπταΐζοντες "on the fifth day"
Aq. ἐνωπλισμένοι "armed"
Aq. has the same rendering at Josh 1:14 for חֲמֻשִׁים where LXX has εὔζωνοι. ἐνωπλισμένοι is used by LXX at Num 31:5; 32:17, 27, 29, 30, 32; Deut 3:18 for חֲלוּץ, and also at Jdt 15:13.
Sym. ὁπλῖται "hoplites (heavily armed soldiers)"

---

28 Grabbe, "Aquila's Translation," 527.

29 Grabbe, "Aquila's Translation," 534.

30 *Mek.* is now generally agreed to be basically Tannaitic, and not from the eighth century as B. Wachholder had argued: M. Kahana, "זמנה ואופיה של המכילתא לפי ב״צ ואכולדר – ביקורת," *Tarbiz* 55 (1986): 515–20.

31 Citations from the LXX are taken from J. W. Wevers, ed., *Exodus*, vol. 2/1 of *Septuaginta: Vetus Testamentum graecum auctoritate Academiae Scientiarum Gottingensis editum* (Göttingen: Vandenhoeck & Ruprecht, 1991). Readings from Aq. and Th. are taken from his second apparatus.

Mekilta de Rabbi Ishmael (ed. Lauterbach, 1:174 line 71–175 line 85)[32]
a) מזוינין "armed"(as in Josh 1:14);
b) מזורזין "zealous, valiant" (as in Josh 4:12–13);
c) אחד מחמש ... אחד מחמשים ... אחד מחמש מאות "(only) one in five/fifty/500" (came up, many having died in Egypt already)

Tg. Onq. מזרזין "zealous, valiant"
Tg. Neof.[33] (cf. *Frg. Tg.* MSS 440, 264, 110) מזיינין בעבדא טבא "armed with good deeds"
Tg. Ps.-J. וכל חד עם חמשא טפלין "each one with five infants"

Here the exegetical options are to take a presumed etymology from חמש, "five," or to look at other contexts in which חֲמֻשִׁים turns up. Note that Aquila does not etymologize here (unlike Theodotion and LXX, who connect חמש with the numeral). Aquila and Symmachus have similar interpretations based on other military contexts for this word: Symmachus's equivalent is used once by LXX in Num 32:21 for חָלוּץ.

The military option is shared by one strand of the Mekilta ("armed"), and by Neofiti and the Fragment Targumim, though spiritualized as "armed with good deeds." It is possible that Aquila and Symmachus reflect rabbinic midrash here but it is more likely that they are rendering in line with earlier LXX tradition, associating חמוש with חָלוּץ. In other words, their renderings are explicable within Greek biblical tradition alone, without recourse to rabbinic influence.

2) Exod 14:7 וְשָׁלִשִׁם "[Pharaoh] took six hundred picked chariots and all the other chariots of Egypt with officers over all of them" (NRSV)

LXX τριστάτας "third officers (?)"[34]
Aq. ܘܬܠܝܬ̈ܐ = καὶ τρισσούς? "thirds/threefold"
Sym. ἀνὰ τρεῖς "in threes"

Mekilta de Rabbi Ishmael (ed. Lauterbach, 1:202 line 200–203 line 218
a) גבורים "warriors" (cf. Ezek 23:23)
b) שהיו משולשים בזיין "triply armed"
c) R. Simon b. Gamaliel: זה השלישי שעל המרכבה "the third man on the chariot

32 J. Z. Lauterbach, *Mekilta de-Rabbi Ishmael: A Critical Edition on the Basis of the Manuscripts and Early Editions* (3 vols.; Philadelphia, Pa.: Jewish Publication Society of America, 1933–1935).

33 A. Díez Macho, *Biblia Polyglotta Matritensia Series IV: Targum Palaestinense in Pentateuchum additur Targum Pseudojonatan, eiusque hispanica versio,* vol. 2., *Exodus* (Madrid: Consejo Superior de Investigaciones Científicas, 1980). This synoptic edition includes *Tg. Neof., Tg. Ps.-J.,* and *Frg. Tg.*

34 Cf. also LXX Exod 15:4, and 2 Kgs 7:2, 17, 19; 9:25; 10:25; 15:25, all for שָׁלִשׁ. See J. W. Wevers, *Notes on the Greek Text of Exodus* (SBLSCS 30; Atlanta, Ga.: Scholars Press, 1990), 211, and A. Le Boulluec and P. Sandevoir, *L'Exode: Traduction du texte grec de la Septante, introduction et notes* (La Bible d'Alexandrie 2; Paris: Cerf, 1989), 55–56.

(in order to pursue Israel faster)"

d) שלשה על כל אחד ואחד "three of them against each [Israelite]"

Tg. Onq. גיברין ממנן "appointed warriors"

Tg. Neof. (cf. *Frg. Tg.* 440, 264) ורברבנין הוון ממנין על כולהון "officers/princes were appointed"

Frg. Tg. 110 וגיברין מתלתין בזיינא הוו ממנין "triply armed warriors were appointed"

Tg. Ps.-J. ומולתא תליתיתא למינגד ולמירדוף בבהילו אוסיף על כל רתיכא ורתיכא "[Pharaoh] added a third mule to each chariot to draw and pursue speedily"

שָׁלִשִׁם is comparable to חֲמֻשִׁים, in that both invite an etymology based on a numeral. In this case this is the route taken by all the recorded Greek versions, as well as three of the interpretations in the Mekilta, one manuscript of the Fragment Targum, and Pseudo-Jonathan. However, Onkelos, Neofiti, Fragment Targum manuscripts 440 and 264, and the Mekilta's first interpretation are more prosaic, and apparently look to the occurrences in 2 Kings where a שָׁלִשׁ is some kind of officer.[35] As in the previous example, it is not necessary to make midrashic influence the decisive factor in the renderings of Aquila and Symmachus, though it is possible that Symmachus reflects a view witnessed by R. Simon b. Gamaliel (three warriors on each chariot). Aquila's rendering is so literal that it requires as much explanation as the Hebrew original. It is compatible with, but does not necessarily reflect, the midrashic notion of being triply armed.

3) Exod 14:20 וַיְהִי הֶעָנָן וְהַחֹשֶׁךְ וַיָּאֶר אֶת־הַלָּיְלָה וְלֹא־קָרַב זֶה אֶל־זֶה "and so the cloud was there with the darkness, and it lit up the night; one did not come near the other." (NRSV)

LXX καὶ ἐγένετο σκότος καὶ γνόφος, καὶ διῆλθεν ἡ νύξ, καὶ οὐ συνέμιξαν ἀλλήλοις "and there was darkness and gloom and the night passed, and they did not mix with one another."

Aq. καὶ ἐγένετο ἡ νεφέλη καὶ τὸ σκότος καὶ ἐφώτισε σὺν τὴν νύκτα καὶ οὐκ ἤγγισεν οὗτος πρὸς τοῦτον "and there was the cloud and the darkness and it illuminated with [*sic*] the night, and this one did not go near this one."

Sym. καὶ ἦν ἡ νεφέλη σκότος μὲν ἐκεῖθεν φαίνουσα δὲ ἐντεῦθεν "and the cloud was darkness over there, but shining over here"

Mekilta de Rabbi Ishmael (ed. Lauterbach, 1:226 line 37–227 line 50)
היו ישראל באורה ומצרים באפלה "the Israelites were in the light and the Egyptians in the darkness" (citing Exod 10:23)

---

35 Origen gives five different explanations of the term: those able to fight against three men at once; those in the third battle rank; chariots able to carry three men, with two to fight and one to drive; those riding three horses; the third in command in the kingdom. Though he relates them to the LXX reading τριστάτας, some of the explanations are close to those in the Jewish sources, and his comments come close to midrash in form (Origen, *Sel. Exod.* [PG 12, col. 288]).

Tg. Onq.   והוה עננא וקבלא למצראי ולישראל נהר כל ליליא ולא אתקרבו דין לות דין
"there was the cloud and darkness for the Egyptians, but for Israel it shone all night and one did not approach the other."

Tg. Neof. (cf. all *Frg. Tg.*)   חשוך ופלגא נהורא חשוכא מחשך <פלגא?> והוה עננא
למצרייה לישראל ונהרא לישראל כל ליליא ולא קרבו אלין לאליין "The cloud was half darkness and half light. The darkness obscured the Egyptians but Israel had
light all night. They did not approach one another."

Tg. Ps.-J.   והוה עננא פלגיה נהורא ופלגיה חשוכא מסיטריה חד מחשך על מצראי ומסיטריה
חד אנהר על ישראל כל ליליא ולא קרבו משרי כל קבל משרי למסדרא סדרי קרבא "Part
of the cloud was light and part of it was darkness. On one side it threw
darkness over the Egyptians while on the other side it shone over Israel,
and one camp did not approach the other to draw up battle lines."

Here Symmachus clearly reflects the common midrashic interpretation,
that the cloud created darkness for the Egyptians and light for the Israelites. His reading is well attested in the manuscript sources, and is
certainly not a close translation of the difficult Hebrew text. Although
his interpretation is more succinct than those of the Mekilta and Targum, the intended meaning is the same. Aquila's translation is very
close to the Hebrew, and here we have an example of his famous use of
σύν to render אֶת plus definite article, followed by the accusative case
and not the dative required by the prepositional use of σύν. Barthélemy
had argued that by doing this Aquila was following Akiva, who interpreted אֶת as indicating inclusion. Grabbe points out that this method
was not confined to Akiva, and in contrast to Aquila's practice, not
limited to places where אֶת was followed by the definite article.[36] Certainly in this particular verse it is hard to argue that any kind of inclusive sense is intended by Aquila, and one must agree with Grabbe that
it is merely a translation device used by Aquila to indicate the presence
of אֶת plus the article.[37]

4) Exod 14:25 וַיָּסַר "He *removed* their chariot wheels" (NRSV: footnote reading)

LXX συνέδησεν "he bound" (cf. SamPent ויאסר)
Sym. μετέστησε "he removed" (reading *hip'il* of סור: Sym. is employing the
usual LXX rendering for this root.)

Mekilta de Rabbi Ishmael (ed. Lauterbach 1:241 lines 127–36)
R. Judah: מחמת האש של מעלה נשרפו הגלגלים של מטה "from the heat of the fire
above, the wheels were burned below."
R. Nehemiah: מקול רעם של מעלן נתזו צנורות מלמטן "from the sound of the
thunder above the pins of the wheels below flew off."

---

36   Grabbe, "Aquila's Translation and Rabbinic Exegesis," 529.
37   See K. Hyvärinen, *Die Übersetzung von Aquila* (ConBOT 10; Lund: LiberLäromedel-
     Gleerup, 1977), 26–29.

Tg. Onq. ואעדי "he removed"
Tg. Neof., Frg. Tg. 440 and 264 ופרק "he untied, took off"
Tg. Ps.-J. ונסר "he sawed off"

Symmachus occasionally has individual readings that reflect a Vorlage similar to the Samaritan Pentateuch, which is interesting in light of Epiphanius's "biography" of him as a defector from the Samaritans. However, here it is the LXX text that resembles the Samaritan Pentateuch, and Symmachus who follows the Masoretic Text. He does not reflect the more elaborate midrash of the Mekilta.

5) Exod 14:27 לְאֵיתָנוֹ "Moses stretched out his hand over the sea, and at dawn the sea returned *to its normal depth*" (NRSV)

LXX ἐπὶ χώρας "to its place"
Sym. εἰς τὸ ἀρχαῖον αὐτῆς "to its ancient/original state"

Mekilta de Rabbi Ishmael (ed. Lauterbach 1:245 lines 23–26)
a) תקפו (Num 24:21) "its strength"
b) R. Nathan ישן וקשה "old and hard" (via Jer 5:15)

Tg. Onq. (cf. *Tg. Neof., Frg. Tg.* 110) and *Tg. Ps.-Jon.* לתוקפיה "to its strength"
Frg. Tg. (440, 264) לאתריה "to its place"

The *Dictionary of Classical Hebrew* renders שוב לאיתנו as *"go back to its continuity,* i.e., to its normal state."[38] Symmachus resembles one element of R. Nathan's definition in the Mekilta ("old"), where the interpretations are drawn from the use of the word in other places in Scripture. ἀρχαῖος is Symmachus's standard equivalent for איתן.[39] So both Symmachus and R. Nathan are apparently using other occurrences of the word to explain this case, but this is a technique that is not confined to midrash.

6) Exod 14:27 וַיְנַעֵר "The Lord *tossed* the Egyptians into the sea." (NRSV)

LXX ἐξετίναξεν "he shook"
Aq. ἀνέβρασεν "he threw up"

Mekilta de Rabbi Ishmael (ed. Lauterbach 1:246 lines 37–43)
a) כאדם שמנער את הקדרה "as someone who stirs the pot"
b) נתן בהם כח נערות כדי לקבל את הפורענות "he put in them the strength of youth so that they could receive punishment."
c) מסרם כאילו בידי מלאכים נערים כאילו בידי מלאכים אכזרים "he handed them over, as it were, to young angels, as it were to cruel angels." (via Prov 17:11 and Job 36:14)

---

38   *DCH* 1:238.
39   Cf. also 1 Kgs 8:2; Ps 73[74]:15; Jer 50 [MT 27]:44.

Tg. Onq., Frg. Tg. 110 ושניק "he tormented"
Tg. Neof. ושבק (read ושנק: cf. *Frg. Tg.* MSS 440, 264)
Tg. Ps.-J. ועלים ייי ית מצראי בגו ימא דלא ימותון במיצעיה מן בגלל דיקבלון פורענו
דמשתלחא להון "The LORD made the Egyptians young in the sea so that they
would not die in its midst, in order that they might receive the punishment
sent for them."

The verb נער is common enough with the meaning "shake, etc.," but the
Mekilta has two fanciful interpretations deriving from the
homonymous root "to be young": either the Egyptians are made
younger so that they can endure the punishments God allots them, or
he hands them over to young, cruel angels for torment (a conclusion
reached by the use of two other verses in Scripture). The rendering
"torture" in the Targumim represents a compressed form of the explicit
haggadah in the Mekhilta. Aquila's equivalent appears only here for his
version. It is also used by the LXX in Ezek 21:26 and Nah 3:2, but for
very different verbs. It is possible that Aquila's interpretation is related
to the first one given in the Mekilta, "stir up."

7) Exod 23:19 לא־תְבַשֵּׁל גְּדִי בַּחֲלֵב אִמּוֹ "you shall not boil a kid in its mother's
milk."

LXX οὐχ ἑψήσεις ἄρνα ἐν γάλακτι μητρὸς αὐτοῦ "you shall not boil a lamb in its
mother's milk." (also at Exod 34:26 and Deut 14:21[20])
Sym. οὐ σκευάσεις ἔριφον διὰ γάλακτος μητρὸς αὐτοῦ "you shall not prepare a
kid using its mother's milk."

Tg. Onq. לא תיכלון בסר בחלב "you shall not eat meat with milk."
Tg. Neof. לא תיכלון בשר בחלב מערבין כחדא דלא יתקף רוגזי עליכון וניבשל עבוריכון צריירין
דגנה וקשה מערבין כחדא "you shall not eat meat with milk mixed together, lest
my anger grow strong against you and we boil your sheaved cereal produce, grain and chaff mixed together."[40]
Tg. Ps.-J. (cf. *Neof. Mg., Frg. Tg.* 110) לית אתון רשאין לא לבשלא ולא למיכול בשר
וחלב מערבין כחדא דלא יתקף רוגזי איבשיל עיבוריכון דגנא וקשא תריהון כחדא "you are
not permitted to boil or eat meat and milk mixed together, lest my anger
grow strong and I boil your cereal produce, grain and chaff, the two together."

σκευάζειν διὰ γάλακτος "to prepare with milk" is a regular culinary
phrase, frequent in medical writers of Symmachus's age, especially
Galen (e.g., *De rebus boni malique suci* 6.768.7: ὁ διὰ γάλακτος ἢ τυροῦ
σκευαζόμενος πλακοῦς, "a cake prepared using milk or cheese"); and
Soranus (*Gynaeciorum* 3.48.5: τὰ διά γάλακτος καὶ τυροῦ σκευαζόμενα).
σκευάζειν διὰ is also used with other substances such as styrax, drug
compounds, and cold water. The contexts of these passages do not

---

40 See R. Le Déaut, *Exode et Lévitique* (SC 256; Targum du Pentateuque 2. Paris: Editions
du Cerf, 1979), 195 n. 12.

necessarily suggest the application of heat to the preparation, but they
do imply its subsequent consumption by the patient.

In this last example Symmachus is both closer and less literal than
LXX: he renders גְּדִי correctly as "kid," but instead of employing the
word for boiling used in LXX, he employs a word with a much wider
scope, σκευάζειν, "to prepare." Geiger thought this rendering reflected
the rabbinic prohibition of mixing milk and meat generally,[41] while
Field understood σκευάζειν to imply preparation.[42] However, Onkelos's
literal version refers to the consumption of meat and milk but not culinary preparation, and surely Onkelos intended at least to hint at the
halakhic prohibition. It is likely that Symmachus is also "compressed
halakah" here:[43] σκευάζειν in this context covers all kinds of preparation,
with or without heat, and normally implies consumption afterwards.
So this may be a rare example of halakhic midrash in Symmachus.

Conclusion

In the light of the foregoing examples, it is clear that in their different
ways Aquila and Symmachus go beyond the translational approach of
LXX in terms of the standardization of renderings throughout Scripture.
Obviously this is not in itself akin to midrash, since one expects single
translators to be more consistent than translations produced in the ad
hoc manner of the LXX. Though at times Aquila and Symmachus come
close to Targum and midrash in their philological approach to the
Hebrew, yet, since we can find similar features in the LXX,
"Theodotion," the Peshitta, and even the Vulgate, as well as Targum,
we cannot say that this is a midrashic characteristic *per se*, only that it is
a general feature of interpreting Hebrew words at this period that happens to be shared by classical midrash. Individual units of halakhic or
haggadic interpretation sometimes occur in Symmachus and Targum.
These units are the product of midrashic process, and so we could perhaps say that sometimes we find "midrash in Greek."

One could test this notion from the opposite direction: if midrash
did not exist, and we only had the scattered fragments of Aquila and
Symmachus, would there be anything that we would find curious and
unexpected if we thought we were dealing with a "straight" translation? There are indications that this is in fact the case. Aquila some-

---

41   Geiger, "Symmachus, der Uebersetzer der Bibel," 51.
42   F. Field, *Origenis Hexaplorum quae supersunt; sive, Veterum interpretum Graecorum in
     totum Vetus Testamentum fragmenta* (2 vols.; Oxford: Clarendon Press, 1875), 1:121.
43   See G. Vermes, "Haggadah in the Onkelos Targum," *JSS* 8 (1963): 159–69.

times has renderings that are so tied to the apparent etymology of the word that they make no sense in context and themselves would seem to require explanation (midrash). Furthermore, the rendering σύν plus accusative is well known. By this means Aquila draws attention to the Hebrew behind it, a trait which is surely a feature of rabbinic midrash if ever there was one. For Aquila, the phenomenon of σύν plus accusative for את plus article makes sense only in the light of rabbinic hermeneutics: it is a crude device, and Barthélemy made too much of Aquila's supposed reflection of Akiva's exegesis, but there are no normal translational reasons for Aquila's practice in this respect. Aquila is not slavish, but he does have a close affinity with the Hebrew text and wants the reader to reflect on the source text, not the target language.

The recognition of the importance of the details in the Hebrew starts before the turn of the era, and grows in sophistication through the Tannaitic and Amoraic periods. Aquila's version falls about midway in that process (ca. 130 CE), and so it would be foolish to look for too much this soon, especially in Greek, where the language imposes more limits than Aramaic in representing Hebrew. According to tradition, the rabbis greeted Aquila's translation with the pun from Psalm 45:3, יָפְיָפִיתָ מִבְּנֵי אָדָם, "you have out-Japheted everyone else," and were themselves playing etymological games with *leshon haqqodesh*. Evidence from both Jewish and Christian sources demonstrates that Aquila was favoured by Jews. Given such a verdict, it must be that the Palestinian rabbis believed that Aquila's version was in harmony with their interpretation of Scripture, even in a limited way. It reflects certain attitudes towards the text of Scripture that are shared by the rabbis whose interpretations are recorded in classical rabbinic midrash, and it has stronger links with Targum, especially that of Onkelos—hence the association of the two literal renderings through the names Aquila/Onkelos.[44] If Targum Onkelos has a relationship with midrash in terms of rabbinic approval, subservience to the Hebrew text, consistency of rendering, and etymological approach, then Aquila has a similar relationship.

The case of Symmachus differs a little. Symmachus is closer to the Hebrew text than he is often given credit for (very often he is much closer to it than LXX, for instance in Isaiah and Genesis), but he pays less attention to representing the details of the Hebrew, and more to producing a readable target text that is less concerned with stereotyped etymological equivalences. This also gives him scope to give what he

---

44 However, Azariah de' Rossi rightly insisted that the two translators were distinct, in ch. 45 of *Me'or Enayim*. See Labendz, "Aquila's Bible Translation in Late Antiquity," 354.

considers to be the *sense* of the Hebrew, and often this corresponds with the interpretation of classical midrash or of Targum, perhaps because of a shared milieu. There are some expanded readings or ones that go against the clear sense of the Hebrew, for instance Gen 18:25 ὁ πάντα ἄνθρωπον ἀπαιτῶν δικαιοπραγεῖν ἀκρίτως μὴ ποιήσῃς τοῦτο for הֲשֹׁפֵט כָּל־הָאָרֶץ לֹא יַעֲשֶׂה מִשְׁפָּט, and Gen 22:1 ἐδόξασεν for נִסָּה. Again this demonstrates at least a relationship with midrashic hermeneutics, and here and there we find traces of compressed midrashic traditions, both haggadic and halakhic.

In terms of the interrelationships between the different Greek versions of Scripture, if Aquila is aware of LXX and "Theodotion" as well as rabbinic exegesis, and Symmachus is aware of all of them, could their renderings be considered a kind of *davar aher*?—in other words, the presentation of an alternative reading to an audience already aware of the other renderings? Or, in contrast to the alternatives in the Mekilta, are they trying to oust the readings of their predecessors? In which case Aquila and Symmachus would be more like Targum Onkelos, giving a single authoritative interpretation in the face of earlier possibilities.

Could Aquila and Symmachus ever have been creators rather than mere tradents of some of the etymologies and interpretations known only through their versions? Although we regard units of midrash as products of tradition, not of individuals, they must have originated somewhere. After all, the much later Targum to Psalms seems to use its own initiative from time to time, though apparently within hermeneutical constraints and the broad tradition.[45] Otherwise we have to see rabbinic midrash as the sun, and Aquila and Symmachus as moons, orbiting and reflecting but not producing the light of midrash themselves. However, if, according to Genesis Rabbah, an uneducated Jew could produce haggadah that a rabbi could find sufficiently acceptable to quote in the man's name,[46] it is theoretically possible that a Jewish proselyte translator could occasionally create original haggadic midrash and thus be a midrashist himself.

---

45 T. Edwards, *Exegesis in the Targum of Psalms: The Old, the New, and the Rewritten* (Piscataway, N.J.: Gorgias, 2007), 217–24.

46 R. Hoshaya in *Gen. Rab.* 78:12: חד עם ארע אמר ליה לר' הושעיא אין אמרית לך חדא מילה טבא את אמ' לה משמי בציבורא . . . אמר ליה חייך מילה טבא אמרת, משמך אנא אמ' לה.

LXX Exodus 23 and the Figure of the High Priest

ARIE VAN DER KOOIJ

According to Josephus, "the second of the Ptolemies, that king who was so deeply interested in learning and such a collector of books, was particularly anxious to have our Law and the political constitution based thereon translated into Greek" (*Ant.* 1.10). This passage about the Greek translation of the Pentateuch, dated to the reign of Ptolemy II (282–246 BCE), testifies to an interest in laws as a source of information on political institutions, in particular regarding the form of government. The Law of Moses is presented here as containing "the ordering of the polity" (διάταξιν τῆς πολιτείας) of the Jews.

A similar statement is to be found in the description of the Jews by Hecataeus of Abdera, a Greek scholar who lived around 300 BCE. It has come down to us in the work of Diodorus Siculus (*Bibliotheca historica* 40.3).[1] Its focus is on the laws and customs of the Jewish people. The reader is told that Moses, "outstanding both for his wisdom and for his courage," took possession of the land and founded cities, such as Jerusalem. Hecataeus then continues, "he established the temple that they hold in chief veneration, instituted their forms of worship and ritual, drew up their laws, and ordered their political institutions." Thus, also in this statement the laws of Moses are clearly related to the issue of the polity (πολιτεία) of the Jewish nation. Interestingly, as to the form of government Hecataeus tells his readers that the priests were selected (by Moses) "to head the entire nation." They should not only occupy themselves with the temple and the sacrificial cult, but were also "appointed to be judges in all major disputes." It was to them that Moses entrusted "the guardianship of the laws and customs." Hecataeus then states, "For this reason the Jews never have a king, and authority over the people is regularly vested in whichever priest is regarded as superior to his colleagues in wisdom and virtue. They call this man the high priest."[2]

---

1   For the text, see Menahem Stern, ed., *Greek and Latin Authors on Jews and Judaism* (3 vols.; Jerusalem: Israel Academy of Sciences and Humanities, 1974–1984), 1:26–29.

2   See Stern, *Greek and Latin Authors*, 1:28. On this passage, see, e.g., James C. Vander-Kam, *From Joshua to Caiaphas: High Priests after the Exile* (Minneapolis, Minn.: Van Gorcum, 2004), 1:118–22, and M. Brutti, *The Development of the High Priesthood during*

The picture as presented by Hecataeus is that the Jewish nation was ruled by priests, under the supreme direction of a high priest, a form of government which is considered to be in accord with the laws of Moses. The same view was expressed on another occasion, this time by leading Jews. I have in mind an incident that took place in the year 63 BCE when members of the Hasmonean house came before Pompey, the Roman general, in Damascus with their dispute over the kingship. As we are told by Diodorus Siculus,

> Likewise the leading men, more than two hundred in number, gathered to address the (Roman) general and explain that their forefathers . . . had sent an embassy to the senate, and received from them the leadership of the Jews, who were, moreover to be free and autonomous, their ruler being called High Priest, not King. Now, however, these men were lording it over them, having overthrown the ancient laws (τοὺς πατρίους νόμους) and enslaved the citizens in defiance of all justice.[3]

According to this passage, another party ("the leading men") appeared before Pompey, claiming that the ruler of the Jewish nation should not be a king, but a high priest, because this type of leadership was considered by them to be in agreement with the ancient, "ancestral" laws. Two forms of government are at stake here—that of kingship, and that of aristocracy. It is clear that the leading men were in favour of the latter, taken in the sense of priestly rule, while rejecting the former as being a constitution that brings about the enslavement of the citizens.

Thus, the sources just mentioned not only reflect the fact that the Jewish nation of the time was ruled by a high priest, but refer also to the claim that (high-)priestly rule was in line with the ancient laws, the laws of Moses. It may be noted that whereas the leading men are focussing on the figure of the high priest as leader—in contrast to the king— the passage of Hecataeus is more nuanced, saying that it was the high priest together with "the priests" who were ruling the nation.

As I have argued elsewhere, the Greek version of the Pentateuch (LXX Pentateuch) contains a passage that testifies to the concept of priestly rule—LXX Exod 19:6. It reads thus: "You will be for me a royal priesthood and a holy nation." The phrase "royal priesthood" (βασίλειον ἱεράτευμα), a body of priests with kingly status, is best understood as referring to the leadership of the Jewish nation. So one can say that the statements of Hecataeus and the claim of the leading men in 63 BCE were in line with an ideology that was given expression in LXX Exodus

---

the Pre-Hasmonean Period: History, Ideology, Theology (JSJSup 108; Leiden: Brill, 2006), 138–41.

3   Diodorus Siculus, 40.2. For this translation, see Stern, Greek and Latin Authors, 1:185– 86.

19:6.[4] In this contribution in honour of Graham Davies I would like to discuss another passage in LXX Exodus, 23:20–23, which, I believe, is also of great interest to the issue of leadership.

II

The LXX passage of Exod 23:20–23 reads in translation:

[20] And look, I am sending my angel in front of you in order to guard you on the way in order to bring you into the land that I prepared for you.

[21] Mind yourself, and listen to him, and do not disobey him. For he shall not hold you in undue awe, for my name is upon him.

[22] If by paying attention you listen to my voice and do all that I tell you, I will be an enemy to your enemies and will resist those who resist you.

[23] For my angel will go, leading you, and will bring you in to the Amorrite and Chettite and Pherezite and Chananite and Gergesite and Heuite and Iebousite, and I will destroy them. (NETS)

This translation is based on the edition of Wevers, but, interestingly, important MSS attest a text which includes a large plus prior to the first word of v. 22:

If by paying attention you listen to my voice and do all that I command you, and keep my covenant, you shall be for me a people special above all nations. For all the earth is mine. And you shall be for me a royal priesthood and a holy nation. These words you shall say to the sons of Israel.[5]

This passage is a plus which, according to Wevers, "at an early date (at least preOrigenian) came into the text, taken over bodily" from 19:5–6.[6] He considers the whole passage a secondary plus because of "the fact that the original plural" of 19:5–6 is "retained in its new location." I agree with Wevers that it is unlikely to assume that this doublet is due to a different *Vorlage*. The question then is whether it is due to an initiative of the translator, or whether, as is the view of Wevers, it has been added at a later stage.

---

4   Arie van der Kooij, "The Greek Bible and Jewish Concepts of Royal Priesthood and Priestly Monarchy," in *Jewish Perspectives on Hellenistic Rulers* (ed. Tessa Rajak, S. J. Pearce, J. K. Aitken and J. Dines; Hellenistic Culture and Society 50; Berkeley, Ca.: University of California Press, 2007), 255–64 (258–59).

5   Text in John William Wevers, ed., *Exodus*, vol. 2/1 of *Septuaginta: Vetus Testamentum graecum auctoritate Academiae Scientiarum Gottingensis editum* (Göttingen: Vandenhoeck & Ruprecht, 1991), 272.

6   John William Wevers, *Text History of the Greek Exodus* (MSU 21; Göttingen: Vandenhoeck & Ruprecht, 1992), 246.

It is clear that the passage under discussion has been derived from Exod 19:5–6. There are however a few differences which are not discussed by Wevers: first, the beginning of 19:5 (καὶ νῦν) is not taken over, and secondly and more importantly, there is a plus within the plus: καὶ ποιήσῃς πάντα ὅσα ἂν ἐντείλωμαί σοι. The interesting thing about this plus is that it is formulated in the singular whereas the passage derived from Exodus 19 is in the plural. It indicates that the one who added the whole passage was aware of the fact that the surrounding text of Exodus 23 is in the singular. It also means that the alternation of singular and plural did not bother him that much, which by the way is not that remarkable as one thinks of the fact that the same phenomenon is typical of the book of Deuteronomy. Hence, it is far from certain that the argument brought forward by Wevers is strong enough to state that the whole passage is secondary. Although one cannot be sure, it is at least possible that the plus in v. 22 was part of the original text, due to a literary initiative of the translator. The manuscript evidence is in favour of this option.[7]

Be this as it may, it is to be asked why the plus was added, and how it functions in the context. It is interesting to note that the first part of it (A) and the beginning of v. 22 as based on the Hebrew text (B) run parallel:

> A: If by paying attention you (plur.) listen to my voice and do (sing.) all that I command you

> B: If by paying attention you (plur.) listen to my voice and do (sing.) all that I tell you

The great similarity between both passages strongly suggests that it is intended, the more so as it is enhanced by the plus within the plus— "and do all that I command you"—being a clause which parallels the second part of B. It seems that the agreement between 19:5 and 23:22 triggered the plus in our passage. From a stylistic point of view the agreement between A and B has the effect of putting emphasis on what is stated in the verse as a whole.

The immediate context of the plus, vv. 20–23, is marked by the presence of "my angel" (vv. 20–21 and v. 23). Hence, it may well be that

---

7   In the Septuagint edition of Rahlfs the plus is part of the Greek text. For a translation including the plus, see A. Le Boulluec and P. Sandevoir, *L'Exode: Traduction du texte grec de la Septante, introduction et notes* (La Bible d'Alexandrie 2; Paris: Cerf, 1989), 239. Like NETS, LXX.D (*Septuaginta Deutsch: Das griechische Alte Testament in deutscher Übersetzung* [ed. Wolfgang Kraus and Martin Karrer; Stuttgart: Deutsche Bibelgesellschaft, 2009]) being also based on the edition of Wevers does not provide a translation including the plus, but informs the reader by giving a translation of the plus in a note.

the plus is meant to put the passage about "my angel," in one way or another, in a particular perspective. In v. 21 the people is called on to listen to the angel and not to disobey him, whereas in v. 22 Israel is urged to listen to the voice of God by keeping the covenant. This raises also the question of the relationship between the angel and God.

Before exploring this matter, one wonders what might be the meaning of the clause at the end of the plus, "These words you shall say to the sons of Israel," in the context of v. 22. In Exod 19:6 this phrase is addressed to Moses, "all these words" being the words spoken to him by God in the preceding verses (vv. 3–6). In Exodus 23 this command does not seem to fit the context, because it is Israel, not Moses, who are addressed in the rest of v. 22. However, it is arguable that it is meant to emphasize the significance of the words found in the plus.[8] The "you" may be Moses, in line with 20:22. It is interesting to note that the latter passage too contains a plus derived from Exodus 19, in this instance from v. 3: "This is what you shall say *to the house of Jacob and report* to the sons of Israel" (plus in italics). One has the impression that in both cases, 20:22 and in our passage, the plus is meant to tie together the passage of 19:3–6, on the one hand, and the laws in 20:22–23:33, on the other.

III

In LXX Exod 23:20–23 the figure of "my angel" dominates the scene. He is designated in those terms both in v. 20 (MT without suffix, but see the Samaritan Pentateuch), and in v. 23 (cf. MT). God will send him in front of Israel, and he will guard the people on the way to the land in order that they arrive in the land safely. The underlying Hebrew text is about a heavenly messenger, an angel,[9] and it is commonly assumed that this also applies to the Greek version. However, this version displays elements which seem to point in another direction. Verse 21 is of particular interest in this regard. It reads thus: "Mind yourself, and listen to him, and do not disobey him. For he shall not hold you in undue awe, for my name is upon him."

The rendering "Mind yourself (πρόσεχε σεαυτῷ)" differs a bit from MT which reads, "Give heed to him." Instead of the expression in MT

---

8   In the edition of Rahlfs the clause is presented as introducing the words that follow (cf. the edition of Swete).

9   On the figure of the angel in the Hebrew text, see now H. Ausloos, "The Angel of 'YHWH' in Exod. xxiii 20–33 and Judg. ii 1–5: A Clue to the 'Deuteronom(ist)ic' Puzzle?" *VT* 58 (2008): 1–12.

(impv. of שמר *nip'al* + מפניו), not attested elsewhere in the Hebrew Bible, LXX reflects the well-known expression of this imperative followed by לך. See, for example, MT and LXX in Gen 24:6; Exod 10:28; 19:22; 34:12.[10] The next phrase reads: "Listen to him." This is "a free though adequate rendering of the Hebrew 'hear his voice.'"[11] The verb used (εἰσακούω) is followed by "him" (αὐτοῦ), and not by "his voice" as in MT. Usually the latter term (together with "to hear") is rendered in LXX Exodus (see, e.g., 4:1). Notably, v. 21 is at variance with the next verse where the same Hebrew expression is used. In the latter the Hebrew is translated in a more literal fashion: "Listen to my voice," i.e., the voice of God ("my voice," cf. Samaritan Pentateuch; MT "his voice"). The differentiation may be due to the different figures involved, the messenger, on the one hand, and God, on the other.

The verse continues with, "Do not disobey him (μὴ ἀπείθει αὐτῷ)"; MT "do not rebel against him." The Greek version presupposes an interpretation of the Hebrew different from that of the Masoretes. The latter presupposes the verb מרד (cf., e.g., Symmachus), whereas the Greek phrase is based on the verb מהר (cf. Deut 1:26; 9:7, 23, 24 [all cases *hip'il*]; Isa 50:5; 63:10 [both cases *qal*]).

"He shall not hold you in undue awe," for MT "he will not pardon your transgressions." The Greek verb used here (ὑποστέλλομαι) means "to draw, shrink back." The idea is that "he will not refrain from judging you."[12] The Greek text alludes to the role of a judge, as is clear in the light of Deut 1:16–17 and of Job 13:8 as well.[13]

> And I commanded your judges at that time, saying: "Give a full hearing among your brothers, and judge rightly between a man and between his brother and between his guest. You shall not recognize the person when judging: like the small so you shall judge the great; *you shall not shrink from the face of a person*, for the judgment is God's. And the matter, if it be too hard for you, you will bring it to me, and I will hear it." (Deut 1:16–17 LXX)

> Or will you shrink (from his face, i.e., God)? Nay, you should be judges yourselves![14] (Job 13:8 LXX; MT: Will you lift up his face? Will you contend for God?)

As a judge, the messenger will not be overawed by you. As to the question of how the underlying Hebrew text was read I would suggest the

---

10   The Greek προσέχω as rendering of שמר *nip'al* is only found in LXX Pentateuch.
11   John W. Wevers, *Notes on the Greek Text of Exodus* (SBLSCS 30; Atlanta, Ga.: Scholars Press, 1990), 370.
12   Wevers, *Notes*, 370.
13   See also Wis 6:7.
14   NETS: "Really? Will you prevaricate? Go ahead; become judges yourselves!" I prefer a translation in line with Deuteronomy 1, because of the "judges" in the second part of the Greek text.

following: "he will not lift up (*sc.* your face [cf. נשא פנים]) as to your transgressions." The issue at stake here is the sensitive matter of showing partiality in court, pronouncing someone guilty who is not, or the other way around. Or to put it in the words of Prov 18:5: "It is not good to lift up the face of the guilty."

The final clause of Exod 23:21 reads, "My name is *upon* him," for MT "my name is *in* him." According to Wevers, the Greek text is marked here by an interpretation that is meant to avoid an identification of the angel with the Lord. His name is not within him because "he is not himself the Lord," and he cannot forgive sins because only God can do so.[15] Ausloos considers this difference as one of the elements in the Greek version that point to a weakening of the role of the angel.[16] However, neither scholar addresses the question of what the phrase "my name is upon him" might mean. It is said of the angel, or messenger, that the name of the Lord is upon him. It has to be asked as to which figure this idea might apply. In the light of the available data the most likely answer to this question is: the high priest.

As we know from Exod 28:36 and 39:30, the high priest is the one who carries the name of the Lord as part of an inscription ("Holy to YHWH") engraved on a plate of pure gold, which was fastened on the turban. In the Letter of Aristeas when describing the apparel of the high priest (§§ 96–99), the relevant passage reads thus:

> Upon his head he has what is called the "tiara," and upon this the inimitable "mitre," the hallowed diadem having in relief on the front in the middle in holy letters on a golden leaf the name of God (§ 98).[17]

In this description the focus is on the name of God as being inscribed, no reference being made to the term "holiness" (ἁγίασμα), as the first word is rendered in the LXX (28:32; 36:38). The same idea is attested by Josephus, *B.J.* 5.235; *Ant.* 3.178, the latter of which reads as follows: "the forehead . . . had a plate of gold, bearing graven in sacred characters the name of God."[18] The name was inscribed in "holy" (Aristeas) or "sacred" (Josephus) letters, that is to say, it was not put in square characters, but in the Old Hebrew script. At another place Josephus provides us with a striking illustration of the significance attached to the

---

15 Wevers, *Notes*, 370. For the idea that the rendering in Greek, which is unusual, is to be seen as an interpretation by the translator, see also R. Sollamo, *Renderings of Hebrew Semiprepositions in the Septuagint* (AASF 19; Helsinki: Suomalainen Tiedeakatemia, 1979), 241.

16 H. Ausloos, "The Septuagint version of Exod 23:20–33: A 'Deuteronomist' at work?" *JNSL* 22/2 (1996): 89–106 (102).

17 Translation of R. J. H. Shutt in James H. Charlesworth, ed., *The Old Testament Pseudepigrapha* (2 vols.; New York: Doubleday, 1983–1985), 2:19.

18 See also Origen, *Sel. Ps.*, at Ps 2:1–2 (PG 12, col. 1104); *Tg. Ps.-J.* Exod 29:6.

fact that the name of God is on the high priest. It is a story about Alexander the Great who, having taken Tyre after a long siege, and also Gaza, went up to the city of Jerusalem (*Ant.* 11.326). Alexander's meeting with the Jewish leaders, at Mount Scopus, is described as follows:

> When Alexander while still far off saw the multitude in white garments, the priests at their head clothed in linen, and the high priest in a robe of hyacinth-blue and gold, wearing on his head the mitre with the golden plate on it on which was inscribed the name of God, he approached alone and prostrated himself before the Name and first greeted the high priest ... the kings of Syria and the others were struck with amazement at his action and supposed that the king's mind was deranged. And Parmenion alone went up to him and asked why indeed, when all men prostrated themselves before him, he had prostrated himself before the high priest of the Jews, whereupon he replied, "It was not before him that I prostrated myself but the God of whom he has the honour to be high priest." (*Ant.* 11. 331–33)

According to this story, which is considered to be legendary, Alexander prostrated himself before the high priest of the Jews because of the Name inscribed on the plate worn on the head of the latter. The Macedonian king therefore greeted the high priest first, before being greeted by him as one would expect. To be more precise, Alexander did not prostrate himself before the high priest, but before God, as he himself explains. This story, which obviously reflects a Jewish view, offers clear proof of the significance of the name of God on the plate worn by the high priest, underlining the close relationship between him and God.

In the light of these data the phrase, "my name is upon him," in the Greek text of Exod 23:21 makes sense if understood as referring to the figure of the high priest. It is to be asked however whether this would also apply to the term ἄγγελος in v. 20 and v. 23. As such this Greek word need not be taken in the sense of a heavenly messenger, an angel, since it can also denote a human messenger (see, e.g., Gen 32:3). More importantly, there is evidence that a priest could be designated in that way. In Mal 2:7 the priest is called a "messenger" of the Lord: "For the lips of a priest should guard knowledge, and people should seek instruction from his mouth, for he is the messenger of the Lord of Hosts." Furthermore, in the description of the Jews by Hecataeus of Abdera (see above) the following note on the high priest is found:

> Authority over the people is regularly vested in whichever priest is regarded as superior to his colleagues in wisdom and virtue. They call this man the high priest, and believe that he acts as a messenger (ἄγγελον) to them of God's commandments. It is he, we are told, who in their assemblies and other gatherings announces what is ordained, and the Jews are so

docile in such matters that straightway they fall to the ground and do reverence to the high priest when he expounds the commandments to them.[19]

The high priest is depicted here as a "messenger" of God's commandments, who in assemblies and gatherings announces and expounds what is ordained. As we know from other sources of the time, the priests were considered to be experts in the law and hence the ones who should teach the people (see, e.g., Sir 45:17; *Jub.* 31:15).[20] This is in line with the statement of Hecataeus about the leading priests being appointed as "judges" (see above), which of course presupposes their expertise in the laws. As these priests were ruling the nation under the supreme authority of the high priest, the latter was considered the prime authority as far as the law and its interpretation is concerned. Another example of this view is to be found in the Letter of Aristeas, where the high priest Eleazar is described not only as the head of the Jewish temple state, but also as the (prime) interpreter of the law (§§ 128–69).

All this fits the Greek text of Exodus 23 well as it also sheds light on other elements (modifications) in the text. In v. 21, the people is urged to listen and not to disobey the messenger of God of whom it is said that "he shall not hold you in undue awe," which, as we have seen, alludes to his role as judge. It is true that in v. 22 it is not the messenger but God and his voice that one should listen to, but, just as in the story about Alexander the Great, our passage seems to be marked by the idea of a very close relationship between God and the high priest, particularly so because of the Name being on the latter. It is interesting to note that this is fully in line with the following statement of Josephus: "Any who disobey him [i.e., the high priest] will pay the penalty as for impiety towards God himself" (*C. Ap.* 2.194).

There is yet another remarkable feature of our passage to be mentioned. In v. 23 the phrase, "my messenger before you" has been translated thus: "my messenger leading you/your leader (ἡγούμενός σου)." This rendering of Hebrew לפניך is attested only here and in v. 27. It has been taken as the one "going before you" = leading you, being your leader (cf. Exod 13:21 [ἡγέομαι for הלך לפני]). The choice of this rendering evokes the notion of a leading figure (compare Gen 49:10; Deut 1:13),

---

19   Stern, *Greek and Latin Authors*, 1:28. For recent literature on this passage, see note 2.

20   Cf. Deut 17:9; 33:10. For evidence from Qumran, see Florentino García Martínez, "Priestly Functions in a Community without Temple," in *Gemeinde ohne Tempel / Community without Temple: Zur Substituierung und Transformation des Jerusalemer Tempels und seines Kults im Alten Testament, antiken Judentum und frühen Christentum* (ed. Beate Ego, Armin Lange, and Peter Pilhofer; WUNT 118; Tübingen: Mohr Siebeck, 1999), 303–19 (311–12 ["Priests as Judges"]).

and may well be intended to serve the idea of the messenger as high priest.[21]

IV

The modifications in LXX Exod 23:21–23, the most significant one being "my name is upon him," make perfect sense if understood as referring to the figure of the high priest as the "messenger" of God. The Greek version of our passage testifies to an interpretation which reflects particular ideas of the translator and his milieu, ideas about the figure of the high priest that are in line with Mal 2:7 and with the passage of Hecataeus of Abdera (ca. 300 BCE) quoted above.

This interpretation may help us to understand the function of the plus in v. 22. As we have seen this plus not only underlines the obedience to God, but it also speaks of "a royal priesthood." As stated above, this phrase refers to a body of leading priests having a royal status. It will be clear that this element is most interesting to our topic since the high priest is of course part of the leadership. The plus in v. 22 therefore can be seen, partly at least, as a passage underlining the issue of priestly rule of the Jewish nation.

The idea that both "priests" and the high priest are considered to be governing the Jewish people is in line with the picture of the Jews as provided by Hecataeus of Abdera (see above): "priests" are said to head the entire nation, whereas it is also stated that the high priest is the one in whom the authority ($\pi\rho\sigma\tau\alpha\sigma\acute{\iota}\alpha$) over the people is vested. This raises the question which (group of) priests are envisaged here. A large number of priests, and Levites, were engaged in the temple service, but given the strict hierarchy involved (see below) only a particular group is to be regarded as representing the leading ones. Unlike Greek $\acute{\iota}\epsilon\rho\alpha\tau\epsilon\acute{\iota}\alpha$ which denotes the priesthood and the priestly office in general (see, e.g., Exod 29:9; 35:19), the term $\acute{\iota}\epsilon\rho\acute{\alpha}\tau\epsilon\upsilon\mu\alpha$ refers to a particular group, a body, or college, of priests, which, as is indicated by the adjective "royal," has a leading position. It stands to reason to think here of the priests who are often mentioned as accompanying the high priest at official occasions. See, for example:

> [To our lord Bigvai, the governor of Judaea,] your servants Yedoniah and his colleagues, the priests who are in Yeb the fortress. (Cowley 30.1)[22]

---

21 Verse 27 reads, "$\tau\grave{o}\nu\ \phi\acute{o}\beta o\nu$ leading you" (MT "my terror before you"). The term $\phi\acute{o}\beta o\varsigma$ seems to refer here to a leading figure, an awesome person, someone to be feared, which too would fit the idea of the high priest as leader. Compare the use of $\phi\acute{o}\beta o\varsigma$ in Gen 31:42.

[We sent a letter to your lordship and] to Johanan the high priest and his colleagues, the priests who are in Jerusalem, and to Ostanes the brother of Anani, and the nobles of the Jews. (Cowley 30.18–19)[23]

[When he—the high priest—learned that Alexander was not far from the city,] he went out with the priests and the body of citizens. (Josephus, *Ant.* 11.329)

With his colleagues [συνιερέων] he [i.e., the high priest] will sacrifice to God, safeguard the laws, adjudicate in cases of dispute, punish those convicted of crime (Josephus, *C. Ap.* 2.194)

From these examples we learn that the high priest together with "the priests" is part of the leadership of the Jewish nation, the other part being the nobles, the body of citizens. The latter college comprises the representatives of the people in the sense of the lay people, referred to in other sources as the "elders" (see, e.g., 1 Macc 7:33, which speaks of "priests from the temple" and "elders of the people [= lay people]").

But who were the priests that together with the high priest were heading the nation? In my view, one has to think here of the priests who are designated, both in the New Testament and by Josephus, as ἀρχιερεῖς, "chief priests." They were the ones who constituted the highest level of the priests acting in the temple, as we know from Josephus and rabbinic sources.[24] To quote Jeremias, the "chief priests permanently employed at the Temple formed a definite body who had jurisdiction over the priesthood and whose members had seats and votes on the council [i.e., the Sanhedrin]."[25] A work from Qumran, 1QM, contains a passage which is illuminating in this regard. 1QM II, 1–3 provides the following picture of the priestly hierarchy in the temple:

- The chiefs of the priests behind the High Priest and of his second (in rank), twelve priests to serve continually before God;

- The twenty-six chiefs of the divisions;

- The chiefs of the Levites to serve continually, twelve;

- The chiefs of their divisions.

---

22 A. Cowley, *Aramaic Papyri of the Fifth Century BCE* (Oxford: Clarendon, 1923; repr. Osnabrück: Otto Zeller, 1967), 113.

23 Cowley, *Papyri*, 114.

24 See Joachim Jeremias, *Jerusalem in the Time of Jesus: An Investigation into Economic and Social Conditions during the New Testament Period* (London: SCM Press, 1976), 147–80.

25 Jeremias, *Jerusalem*, 180.

The chiefs of the priests, representing the highest rank, are to be equated with the chief priests.²⁶ It therefore is likely that they are the ones who together with the high priest were making up the priestly rule of the Jewish nation. In the light of these data it is reasonable to assume that the phrase "a royal priesthood" refers to the college of chief priests (under the supreme direction of the high priest). Hence, the interpretation of the angel as referring to the high priest accords well with the phrase just mentioned in the plus.

V

LXX Exodus 23, together with Exodus 19, reflects a great interest in the concept of priestly rule as a form of government of the Jewish nation. The interpretation involved sheds light on the large plus in 23:22 which seems to be intended as underlining the constitutional issue. As I have argued elsewhere, the translators of the Pentateuch were presumably scholars from Jerusalem.²⁷ If so, the Greek version can be viewed as testifying to the views of the authorities of the temple state in Judea. Furthermore, it is interesting to note that it shares the concept of priestly rule—the royal priesthood under the supreme direction of the high priest—with the testimony of Hecataeus of Abdera dating roughly speaking to the same period of time.

There is, however, one question left to be mentioned. The passage of Exodus 23 is not the only place in the Pentateuch containing a reference to the messenger of the Lord in a context related to the story of the liberation from Egypt, the journey through the desert, and the bringing into the land. Of particular interest are passages such as Exod 14:19; 32:34; 33:3; and Num 20:16. It would lead too far to discuss these passages in detail, but I believe these passages, in Greek as well as in Hebrew, do refer to a heavenly figure, and not to the messenger of the Lord in the sense of the high priest. In view of the military role of the angel in these instances it may well be that the translators were thinking of a heavenly figure like the one mentioned in Josh 5:14 (depicted as having a sword drawn, and being called, in Greek, "the ἀρχιστράτηγος of

---

26 See Arie van der Kooij, *Die alten Textzeugen des Jesajabuches: Ein Beitrag zur Text-geschichte des Alten Testaments* (OBO 35; Fribourg, Switzerland: Universitätsverlag Freiburg Schweiz; Göttingen: Vandenhoeck & Ruprecht, 1981), 201.

27 Arie van der Kooij, "The Septuagint of the Pentateuch and Ptolemaic Rule," in *The Pentateuch as Torah. New Models for Understanding Its Promulgation and Acceptance* (ed. Gary N. Knoppers and Bernard M. Levinson; Winona Lake, Ind.: Eisenbrauns, 2007), 289–300.

the army of the Lord"; see also Num 22:31; 1 Chr 16:31). One is reminded here of the angel who is fighting for Israel, the heavenly warrior, called Michael in the book of Daniel (Dan 10:21; 12:1).[28]

It may seem strange that our passage in Exodus 23 is not in line with the other texts mentioned. However, the shift from angel to messenger/high priest need not surprise us since, as we know from Jewish sources dating to the Hellenistic era, the priests, including the high priest, are described in the likeness of angels (see, e.g., *Jub.* 31:14; for the high priest, see 1QSb IV, 24–25).[29]

---

28 On this figure, see, e.g., John J. Collins, *Daniel: A Commentary on the Book of Daniel* (Hermeneia; Minneapolis, Minn.: Fortress Press, 1993), 374–75.

29 See, e.g., Gabriel Barzilai, "Incidental Biblical Exegesis in the Qumran Scrolls and Its Importance for the Study of the Second Temple Period," *DSD* 14 (2007): 1–24 (14–15, and the literature cited there); M. Abegg, "1QSb and the Elusive High Priest," in *Emanuel: Studies in Hebrew Bible, Septuagint, and Dead Sea Scrolls in Honor of Emanuel Tov* (ed. Shalom M. Paul *et al.*; VTSup 94; Leiden: Brill, 2003), 3–16 (11).

Robert Hatch Kennett (1864–1932)

The Old Testament in a Time of Transition

Ronald E. Clements

Robert Hatch Kennett was appointed to the Regius Professorship of Hebrew in Cambridge University in 1903 and held the post until his death in February 1932. His tenure of this important teaching position—one of the oldest in the University—marked a significant period of transition for the study of the Old Testament in the University and, as importantly, for an enlarged recognition of the place of the Hebrew language and the Old Testament in the development of western culture. The brief memoir of Kennett by Francis Burkitt published in the *Cambridge Review* shortly after his death sets the scene that prevailed in Cambridge at the time of his appointment very vividly:

> It was the great days of Semitic study in Cambridge. . . . Robertson Smith was already in Cambridge, but our great inspirer was William Wright, Professor of Arabic, a master of all branches of Semitic study. I shall never forget how Kennett took me—I think it was in the October Term of 1887—to Professor Wright's rooms to join in his class on Phoenician Inscriptions. There were only three of us, but we all became Professors, and we were all after the first two or three hours of study in those rooms at Queens', which afterwards Kennett himself occupied, united in love and veneration for William Wright.

> Biblical study was an exciting matter in those days. The great decision, *viz.* that the written Law was later than the Prophets, had indeed been accepted by nearly all those who had any right to an opinion, but Cambridge in general and the Professors of Theology in particular were at most only half-convinced. The Regius Professor of Hebrew [A. F. Kirkpatrick] . . . was sound on the critical question, but Mr Peter Mason was still alive to remind us that a few years before very different views about the Old Testament had been dominant in University circles. Now there had come a new spirit into Hebrew study, and Kennett shared it with us to the full. He had great reverence for the rules of Hebrew grammar and syntax, but very little for the transmitted text of the Hebrew Bible, and he was quite ready to emend when the sense required it. . . .

What further distinguished Kennett was that along with his modern and scientific treatment of the text he was not only sincerely religious, but drew as fully as any of the older Evangelicals his religious inspiration from the Bible.[1]

In order to appreciate the force of Burkitt's remarks and the significance of the names of the two scholars he mentions—William Wright and William Robertson Smith—it is necessary to reflect on the dramatic manner in which what was described at the time as the "Higher Criticism" of the Old Testament arrived in Cambridge during the last two decades of the nineteenth century.

Biblical Criticism in Cambridge: 1882–1903

Robert Hatch Kennett came up to Queens' College, Cambridge, in October 1882—a year that marked a major milestone for the study and teaching of the Old Testament in Great Britain. It was the year of the appointment of Alexander F. Kirkpatrick (1849–1940) to the Regius Chair of Hebrew in the University—an event that was immediately followed by that of Samuel Rolles Driver to the corresponding Regius Chair of Hebrew in Oxford in January 1883. Driver had already established an outstanding reputation in Hebrew studies for his work on the Hebrew tenses,[2] and his appointment in succession to E. B. Pusey had been delayed in order to allow for his ordination as priest of the Church of England. These appointments took place shortly after the final ending of religious discrimination in the two universities (1871)—another event which, like the new appointments, contributed greatly towards stimulating major changes in the teaching of the Bible in Great Britain.

The Old Testament was particularly implicated in the ending of religious discrimination since it occupied a prominent place in the teaching and educational interests of nonconformist Churches. Evangelicalism, Nonconformity, and concern with the Old Testament were aspects of Victorian Church life which were closely inter-related. Before this time students of nonconformist persuasion who wished to prepare for ministry—Methodists, Congregationalists, and Baptists—were

---

1   F. C. Burkitt, *The Cambridge Review* 53, no. 1305 (February 26, 1932): 287–88 (287); cf. also *The Dial* (Queens' College Magazine), Spring 1932, 5–8. Peter Mason was College Lecturer in Hebrew in St. John's College, Cambridge; cf. T. R. Glover, *Cambridge Retrospect* (Cambridge: Cambridge University Press, 1942), 81.

2   S. R. Driver, *A Treatise on the Use of the Tenses in Hebrew* (Oxford: Clarendon, 1874; further editions in 1881 and 1892).

almost wholly dependent on help to prepare themselves for ministry by private study or by attendance at the small Dissenting Academies; some fortunate few could go to Wales or Scotland. As a result of the final removal of religious tests in Oxford and Cambridge Mansfield College (predominantly Congregational) was established in 1886 and swiftly attracted a number of outstanding biblical scholars. In Cambridge Westminster College moved to the city from London in 1899 for the training of Presbyterian clergy; Cheshunt College (chiefly Congregational) followed in 1905, and the Methodist Wesley House was established in 1926. Nonconformist (i.e., non-Anglican) biblical scholars of international eminence quickly flourished in both Oxford and Cambridge, giving to both universities a renewed eminence in biblical research and greatly extending the range of its appeal to students of various religious persuasions as well as to others who were interested.

All these new institutions followed the lead set by S. R. Driver and Alexander Kirkpatrick in introducing into the forefront of theological study the methods and conclusions of the Higher Criticism of the Old Testament. This methodology had begun to establish itself half a century earlier on the mainland continent of Europe. Where earlier knowledge of the Greek and Hebrew languages had been the primary test of academic competence for biblical interpretation it now became essential to understand the basic principles of literary and historical criticism.[3] Not only did this result in changing the perception of the Old Testament as a Christian literature, but it also greatly affected the teaching of Hebrew language by recognizing its place as one of a much larger family of Semitic languages, notably Arabic and Syriac. This broadening of the scope of the teaching of Hebrew also reflected the fact that the subject was of direct interest to Jews as well as Christians.[4]

The consequence of these changes to the way the subject was studied was that, after 1882, the year of Kennett's arrival as a student in Cambridge, the place of the Old Testament in Christian theology

---

3   Several scholars, notably John Pye Smith, who taught for fifty years at Homerton College, and Benjamin Davies, a Baptist teacher at Stepney College, had built excellent reputations in the study of Greek and Hebrew. Certainly the Baptist tradition of theological education in Stepney College was based on thorough knowledge of the biblical languages but was concerned to keep abreast of contemporary studies in Germany. Cf. especially, J. H. Y. Briggs, *The English Baptists of the Nineteenth Century* (Didcot: The Baptist Historical Society, 1994), 188–98.

4   Hebrew had been introduced into the curriculum of King's College, London, from 1831 with the explicit purpose that it would assist in the development of Christian missionary activity among the Jewish communities of Europe. Cf. my essay, "A Fruitful Venture: The Origin of Hebrew Studies at King's College, London," in *Biblical Traditions in Transmission: Essays in Honour of Michael A. Knibb* (ed. C. Hempel and J. M. Lieu; Leiden: Brill, 2006), 60–79.

underwent a major re-appraisal. This period lasted until the beginning of the Second World War; and its ending was marked, so far as Cambridge was concerned, by the death of W. E. Barnes in 1939, of A. F. Kirkpatrick in 1940, and S. A. Cook in 1949. In the post-war era after the disaster of the Holocaust, questions concerning Christian interest in the Old Testament appeared in a very greatly changed perspective. Not surprisingly the first major attempts to rethink these issues were forced to turn once again to mainland continental scholarship for guidance.[5]

The first decades of the twentieth century were, in British theological circles, a time for far-reaching re-examination and re-appraisal of the structure and nature of the English Bible, with questions about the significance and place of the Old Testament heading the list. These questions had already appeared a century earlier in Germany with the work of J. S. Semler and F. D. E. Schleiermacher, but the British response to this had been negative and desultory. In Germany in 1921, in a celebrated and widely acknowledged study on the teaching of the Early Church figure Marcion, the theologian Adolf von Harnack addressed the issue.[6] He proposed the radical solution that the Christian Church of the twentieth century should follow Marcion's lead and dispense with the Old Testament in its biblical canon. Among the great majority of Protestant churches this solution was ignored, rather than rejected; the Old Testament was too well established a part of the Protestant tradition for it simply to be dropped. Nevertheless alternative solutions to the problems that had become apparent were piecemeal, limited, and generally resorted to a broad appeal to the "enduring value" of the Old Testament.[7] Only when attempts were made to spell out the content of this "enduring value" more fully could the following generation of scholars begin to re-engage with the issues that nineteenth-century biblical criticism had brought to the surface. It is this process of re-engagement that makes the work of R. H. Kennett and his contemporaries in Cambridge a subject of theological, as well as historical, interest.

---

5   The most notable exception was the figure of Henry Wheeler Robinson, who was preparing a comprehensive volume on Old Testament Theology at the time of his death in 1945. Cf. N. W. Porteous for a review of the situation in *The Old Testament and Modern Study* (ed. H. H. Rowley; Oxford: Oxford University Press, 1951), 311–45.

6   A. von Harnack, *Marcion: Das Evangelium vom fremden Gott: Eine Monographie zur Geschichte der Grundlegung der katholischen Kirche* (Leipzig: J. C. Hinrichs, 1921; rev. ed. 1924); ET *Marcion: The Gospel of the Alien God* (Durham, N.C.: Labyrinth, 1990).

7   Cf. my essay, "The Enduring Value of the Old Testament—An Interesting Quest," *BibInt* 16 (2008): 25–42.

Cambridge Theology in the Late Victorian Age

The Regius Professorships of Hebrew in both Oxford and Cambridge universities were intended from their inception in the sixteenth century to uphold and defend a distinctively Christian interpretation of the Old Testament. They therefore belonged within the broad context of the study of Divinity (until the twentieth century the preferred subject designation for a range of theological disciplines). Yet in order for fresh research to take place scholars were dependent on access to Jewish sources for the Hebrew text and knowledge of its language. The earliest Christian Bibles were in Greek.

Against this background the work of William Wright proved to be a major factor in introducing into Cambridge in the second half of the nineteenth century a greatly broadened grasp of the major Semitic languages—Arabic and Syriac—alongside comparative methodology for the study of them.[8] Wright was a remarkable pioneering figure. Born in India, he enabled Great Britain to catch up on the advances in the study of oriental languages and culture that had already taken place earlier in France and Germany. The understanding of Hebrew had been revitalized by the work of Wilhelm Gesenius (1786–1842) in noting that it required to be understood in the context of its wider linguistic setting. The task of compiling a revised modern dictionary of Ancient Hebrew, begun by Gesenius and based on advances that the new comparative methodology made possible, continued throughout the nineteenth century and eventually extended further to the end of the twentieth century.

It is also necessary to take account of a national event concerned with the Bible which had a particular impact upon the study and teaching of it in Cambridge. This was the publication in 1881 and 1885 of the Revised Version translation of the Bible, which had been undertaken with the full approval and backing of the major national Churches. Cambridge was especially involved through the participation in the project of scholars such as Westcott, Hort, and Lightfoot on the New Testament and the financial backing of the publication by the University Press. A surprisingly wide assortment of scholars from all the major Church traditions was involved. In a formal sense the finished work must be judged to have been a failure; this is largely how it was

---

8   W. Wright, *Lectures on the Comparative Grammar of the Semitic Languages* (Cambridge: Cambridge University Press) was published in 1890, edited by W. Robertson Smith in the Oriental Series of the Palaeographical Society. The importance of the contribution of William Wright to Semitic studies is noted by R. Irwin, *For Lust of Knowing: The Orientalists and their Enemies* (London: Allen Lane, 2006), 178–80.

seen at the time, to the dismay of its scholarly translators, and, in longer perspective, its lack of popularity and short life supports such a judgment.[9] It failed completely to achieve its aim of displacing the much-respected Authorized (King James) Version of 1611 in popular usage; it also failed to win more than limited respect from scholars for its academic merits since many of the proposals for changes in the interpretation of key passages were overruled. It did, nevertheless, serve to highlight the emerging gulf between the academic study of the Bible in a culturally secular context, and the use of it for liturgical and devotional purposes.

An unexpected consequence of the preparation for this new translation was that it led to the move to Cambridge in 1883 of William Robertson Smith (1846–1894). After his dismissal in 1881 by the Assembly of the United Free Church of Scotland from his professorship in Aberdeen he had continued as an editorial adviser for the *Encyclopaedia Britannica* and remained a member of the Bible revision committee. In this forum he had established a warm friendship with William Wright and other members of the panel from Cambridge. His move to Cambridge, initially to a lectureship in Arabic, enabled him to lecture more widely on religious topics and to continue his editorial work for the *Encyclopaedia Britannica*, to which Wright also contributed. As a result his relatively few years in Cambridge (his health began to fail in 1890 and he died in 1894) were among the most productive of his controversial career.[10] His Burnett Lectures, published as *Lectures on the Religion of the Semites*, proved to be among his most enduring contributions to scholarship,[11] and Stanley A. Cook, a young Cambridge scholar of the time, became his most immediate and committed follower.[12]

---

9   Cf. C. J. Cadoux, "The Revised Version and After," in *The Bible in its Ancient and English Versions* (ed. H. Wheeler Robinson; Oxford: Oxford University Press, 1940), 235–73.

10   Cf. Norman McLean, "Dr. Robertson Smith in Cambridge," *The Expositor* 9 (1894): 462–72. Cf. now also the major study of Robertson Smith by Bernhard Maier, *William Robertson Smith: His Life, His Work and His Times* (FAT 67; Tübingen: Mohr Siebeck, 2009). The Cambridge years are dealt with on pp. 217–79.

11   W. Robertson Smith, *Lectures on the Religion of the Semites, First Series: The Fundamental Institutions* (Edinburgh: A&C Black, 1889; 2d ed. 1894; 3d ed., with additional notes by S. A. Cook, 1927). The second and third series were originally left unpublished, but were published under the editorship of John Day as *Lectures on the Religion of the Semites: Second and Third Series* (JSOTSup 183; Sheffield: Sheffield Academic, 1995).

12   Cf. D. Winton Thomas, "Stanley Arthur Cook," *Proceedings of the British Academy* 36 (1950): 260–76. Cook came to Cambridge to read Oriental Languages in 1891 and, after graduation, was employed by the publishers of *Encyclopaedia Biblica* to contribute numerous articles (chiefly of minor significance). The *Encyclopaedia* had been planned by W. Robertson Smith, but after his death the editorship was put in the

In spite of the strongly Bible-focused culture of Victorian church life, at the time of Smith's arrival in Cambridge the critical study of the Old Testament had fallen far behind that which had already emerged in Germany and Holland. Major attention had particularly focused on the book of Genesis in the aftermath of Charles Darwin's *On the Origin of Species* (1859). As a result the relationship between the Bible and science had become a central point of contention for popular culture as well as theological reflection.[13]

Critical re-evaluation of the nature and origin of the Pentateuch, especially in the form which Julius Wellhausen had set out, appeared to help towards a resolution to these problems. Although critical reassessment of the form and date of the biblical writings stood in conflict with the high emphasis on biblical inspiration which contemporary theologians had affirmed, the perception of the doctrinal, rather than historical, relevance of the stories of Genesis removed an obstacle. The result was a significant re-alignment of loyalties among those members of the public who were sufficiently knowledgeable to follow the arguments. The strong biblical emphasis of Evangelicalism encouraged several of its supporters to find in the new criticism a path of reconciliation between religion and science;[14] others saw it as a further attack by "Rationalist" unbelief.

So far as Oxford and Cambridge were concerned, the teaching of the new critical approach began with great energy and seriousness in the writing and lectures of A. F. Kirkpatrick and S. R. Driver, who had become holders of the prestigious Regius Professorships of Hebrew at Britain's oldest universities. Both men embarked on a well-planned and

---

hands of T. K. Cheyne (1841–1915). Cook drafted many articles, and latterly contributed a number under his own signature, but complained of editorial interference. He drafted the original of the notorious entry on Jerahmeel in which Cheyne revealed the eccentricity of his reconstructions.

13 H. E. Ryle published a study of the early chapters of Genesis in 1892 based on lectures given in Cambridge entitled *The Early Narratives of Genesis* (London: Macmillan). He complained of the "snarling notice" it received in one newspaper, and in walking about Cambridge reflected seriously on the fate of earlier Reformation martyrs. Through his link with the publisher Macmillan he planned, with the assistance of A. T. Chapman, an impressive series of popular biblical commentaries which regrettably did not reach fruition; some of the intended contributors subsequently wrote volumes for the Westminster series of commentaries which followed many features of Ryle's guidelines. Cf. M. H. Fitzgerald, *A Memoir of Herbert Edward Ryle* (London: Macmillan, 1928), 95.

14 The most notable and acclaimed figure in this context was Henry Drummond, an ardent supporter of, and fellow worker with, the American evangelist D. L. Moody. Cf. D. W. Bebbington, "Henry Drummond, Evangelicalism and Science," in *Henry Drummond: A Perpetual Benediction: Essays to Commemorate the Centennial of his Death* (ed. T. E. Corts; Edinburgh: T&T Clark, 1999), 19–38.

theologically directed campaign, rooted in Christian faith and conviction, to explain and popularize the new understanding of the Old Testament and to defend its place in Christian education and worship.[15] In
Cambridge two major steps were undertaken. The first was the revision, and where necessary replacement, of the volumes of short commentaries on the Bible in the series "The Cambridge Bible," initially
intended for use in schools and colleges and published by the industri-
ous Cambridge University Press. The advisory editorship for the Old
Testament was placed under the guidance of Alexander Kirkpatrick,
replacing the more conservative J. J. S. Perowne (1823–1904); new volumes were commissioned reaching out beyond the original Anglican
editorial framework. The pre-eminence of questions regarding the
authorship of the Pentateuch is shown by the inclusion of an extra volume in the series, not itself strictly a commentary, by A. T. Chapman
entitled *An Introduction to the Pentateuch*.[16]

The second step towards reinforcing advocacy of the "Higher Critical" approach to the Old Testament was the appointment in 1888 of
Herbert E. Ryle, son of the popular evangelical Bishop of Liverpool, to
the Hulsean Professorship in Divinity. Ryle had been a student in
Cambridge under A. F. Kirkpatrick and was an early and enthusiastic
convert to the critical approach. He received large audiences, sometimes controversially so in view of his evangelical background, and was
particularly concerned to refute the notion that the stories of Genesis
were irreconcilable with the findings of contemporary geology and
zoology. He returned in 1900 to whole-time Church responsibilities as
Bishop of Exeter, which put an end to his active engagement in first-
level biblical scholarship.

Other changes rapidly followed in Cambridge reflecting the wide
tensions and divided loyalties that pertained to a Faculty of Divinity
which carried major responsibility for the training of Anglican clergy.

---

15   Cf. S. R. Driver and A. F. Kirkpatrick, *The Higher Criticism: Three Papers* (2d ed.; Lon-
     don: Hodder & Stoughton, 1905). These were popular addresses by the two scholars
     addressed to clergy and lay persons.
16   A. T. Chapman, *An Introduction to the Pentateuch* (Cambridge: Cambridge University
     Press, 1911). The volume was proof-read by S. R. Driver and approved by A. H.
     McNeile and H. E. Ryle. Both Chapman and A. H. McNeile were close followers of
     Ryle. It is an excellent survey of the problems and concludes with general approval
     for Julius Wellhausen's "four-document" hypothesis. It also represents a valuable
     appraisal, coupled with rejection, of James Orr's *The Problem of the Old Testament*
     (London: Nisbet, 1906), which was by far the most detailed and considered attempt
     by any British scholar to present an alternative to Wellhausen. Chapman was a Fel-
     low of Emmanuel College who died in 1913. This very useful volume appears to
     have been largely ignored in studies of the British reception of German nineteenth-
     century criticism.

Shortly after Ryle's departure A. F. Kirkpatrick relinquished the Regius Professorship of Hebrew in 1903 in favour of the more specifically theological responsibilities of the Lady Margaret Professorship. Subsequently he also returned to full-time Church affairs to become Dean of Ely Cathedral. The university appointments had for a long time been linked to local parishes and cathedral canonries which involved preaching and teaching commitments. With the move of these two scholars to full-time ecclesiastical responsibilities two of the leading proponents of the "Higher Criticism" were diverted to other fields. Ryle was later appointed Bishop of Winchester (1905–1910) and subsequently Dean of Westminster (1910) until his death in 1925. Kirkpatrick continued as Dean of Ely Cathedral until his death in 1940. Today his name is remembered on a prayer cushion in the Cathedral in that city.

Robert Hatch Kennett: Hebraist and Historian

In succession to Kirkpatrick Robert Hatch Kennett was appointed to the Regius Professorship of Hebrew in 1903 and held the position until his death in 1932. He was, by all accounts, an exceptionally well-qualified Hebrew scholar. Born into a clerical family in St. Lawrence-in-Thanet, near Ramsgate, in 1864, he had expressed from an early age his intention to seek ordination as a priest of the Church of England. He was fortunate enough to be educated at the Merchant Taylors' School, where he became a member of a remarkable Hebrew class taught by C. J. Ball. Among his contemporaries in the class was G. A. Cooke, who became Oriel Professor in the University of Oxford in 1908 and who succeeded S. R. Driver as Regius Professor of Hebrew in 1914.

C. F. Burney (1868–1925) was another, slightly later, member of the exceptional Hebrew class at Merchant Taylors' School. In turn he succeeded G. A. Cooke as Oxford's Oriel Professor in 1914. Subsequently D. Winton Thomas, who occupied the Regius Professorship of Hebrew in Cambridge (1938–1968), was also a product of this outstanding Hebrew class; another such scholar was G. H. Box (1869–1933), who for a period returned to the school to teach Hebrew (1897–1904), subsequently being appointed Professor of Hebrew and Old Testament Studies at King's College, London (1918–1926), afterwards Samuel Davidson Professor (1926–1930).

When Robert Kennett entered Queens' College, Cambridge, in October 1882 he studied Oriental Languages and quickly came under the spell of William Wright (1830–1889). He was also privileged to learn Arabic from Robertson Smith and continued throughout his life to be a much respected and devout Anglican cleric; he was ordained in 1887 and appointed Chaplain and College Lecturer in Hebrew. Like many of his contemporaries he could readily be described as a "Liberal-Evangelical." He was inclusive in his Christian loyalty and warmly welcoming to Jewish students, being representative of the revitalized ecumenical outlook of the period. He was a founder member of the Society for Old Testament Study, the planning and organization of which took place in his rooms in Queens' College in the summer of 1916.

R. H. Kennett as Scholar and Teacher

Against the background of the development of biblical studies in Cambridge at the beginning of the twentieth century Kennett's work is full of interest and unexpected contrasts. It broadly divides between three main fields: (a) his exceptional qualities as a gifted teacher of the Hebrew Bible and his eagerness to broaden understanding of the importance of the "Hebraic" character of the Christian Bible; (b) his attempts to extend and develop critical theories about the biblical writings along lines that were already well advanced in Germany; (c) the search for a fresh defence of the theological importance of the Old Testament in terms of its "contribution to mankind." Throughout his work the twofold influences of William Wright and William Robertson Smith are strikingly evident. Hebrew language required to be understood from within the family of Semitic languages and could no longer be taught and researched in isolation from this. Alongside this widened concern with linguistic matters, a major theological re-assessment of the place of the Old Testament in Christian theology was demanded. This required to be based on recognition that the Old Testament literature, like the ancient Hebrew language in which it was chiefly written, was part of an ancient Semitic culture which is unfamiliar to the modern world.

A selected bibliography of Kennett's publications is provided by Stanley Cook in the collection entitled *The Church of Israel*.[17] To some extent these writings, which are all relatively short in length, are strongly reflective of the changing face of Old Testament studies in the early decades of the twentieth century. They help to show why the subject of "Old Testament theology" almost completely disappeared

---

17   R. H. Kennett, *The Church of Israel: Studies and Essays* (ed. with an introduction by S. A. Cook; Cambridge: Cambridge University Press, 1933), lv–lvi.

from the theological agenda of British scholarship until after World War II.

Kennett's first significant publication in 1901 was a short study of the Hebrew system of tenses in which he presented, in as concise and readable a form as possible, the exposition of the system by S. R. Driver.[18] This was followed in 1907 by another book—a series of popular lectures and sermons, entitled *In Our Tongues*.[19] These were really no more than talks to clergy, aimed at showing the distinctiveness of Hebrew language and the difficulties of providing a translation in English that can express the fullness of the original text. They echo the disappointments and arguments that followed the publication of the Revised Version in 1885. Alongside this was an emphasis on the importance of the Hebrew background to the language of the New Testament—especially the Epistles of St. Paul. The theme that languages are replete with complex semantic subtleties was to prove a major one for Kennett. He twice delivered lectures to the British Academy under the Schweich Foundation and the second of these series, on the use of idiom and metaphor in the Old Testament, focused directly on this theme.[20] Language does more than simply impart information. It conveys, often incidentally, a world-view and facilitates the perception and ordering of reality. Through its metaphors, contrasts, and valuations the Hebrew language of the Old Testament reveals a distinctive way of life in which social and ethical values are embodied.

In furtherance of this high regard for the nature of language Kennett argued for the importance of Hebrew as an essential tool for understanding the New Testament and the Bible more generally. This provided a central groundwork for the new apologetic—the New Testament could not be understood without understanding of the Old! Christian ideals of righteousness and justice were rooted in Hebrew concepts and this enabled the New Testament to rise above the ethical commonality of Greek society. Kennett argued that knowledge of Hebrew was a vital tool for understanding the Bible as a whole. Moreover, familiarity with the language not only made possible a wider and more considered translation of the original, but exemplified the fact that all translations are an approximation—a "second best." Similar

---

18 R. H. Kennett, *A Short Account of the Hebrew Tenses* (Cambridge: Cambridge University Press, 1901).

19 R. H. Kennett, *In Our Tongues: Some Thoughts for Readers of the English Bible* (London: Edward Arnold, 1907).

20 R. H. Kennett, *Ancient Hebrew Social Life and Custom as indicated in Law Narrative and Metaphor* (Schweich Lectures 1931; London: Oxford University Press for The British Academy, 1933).

ideas to those of Kennett were expressed by G. A. Cooke in his inaugural address as Oriel Professor in Oxford (1908).[21]

In regard to literary theories about the origin and formation of the Pentateuch and other of the Old Testament writings, Kennett differed from his contemporary, S. R. Driver, by his willingness to embrace more radical views regarding the date of origin of the key sources. Most specifically he argued in detail that the book of Deuteronomy was a late, post-exilic, product, as evidenced by its dependence on the language of Jeremiah.[22] More broadly still, Kennett accepted a strongly developmental, evolutionary, view of the Old Testament, pointing to a late date for the Decalogue and a late (Maccabean) date for the majority of the Psalms. Unlike his contemporary F. S. Marsh (1886–1953), he took no interest in the literary approach of Hermann Gunkel and Sigmund Mowinckel. The two essays that he contributed to the Hastings *Encyclopaedia of Religion and Ethics*[23] indicate his having absorbed very fully the importance that William Robertson Smith attached to the ritual and institutional features of ancient Israelite religion. Theological and spiritual ideas are an outworking of actions and concepts that are often, in themselves, crude and repugnant. This feature led Kennett to engage in reflections on the links between the language of the Christian Eucharist and the ancient practice of animal sacrifice.

Robert Kennett among his Contemporaries

The arrival in Cambridge of William Robertson Smith in 1883, coming just a year after the appointment of Alexander Kirkpatrick to the Regius Professorship of Hebrew, marked the beginning of a new era for the place of the Old Testament in Cambridge biblical studies. At the time this took place the distinctively Protestant Anglican status of the university's Faculty of Divinity was still very much in evidence. This not only affected the status of those appointed to its Professorships, but

---

21 G. A. Cooke, "Some Principles of Biblical Interpretation," *The Expositor* 7 (1909): 193–208.

22 Kennett's views on the Old Testament literary development are noted in my essay, "The Deuteronomic Law of Centralisation and the Catastrophe of 587 BC," in *After the Exile: Essays in Honour of Rex Mason* (ed. J. Barton and D. J. Reimer; Macon, Ga.: Mercer University Press, 1996), 5–26.

23 The subjects covered were "Ark" (*ERE* 1:791–93) and "Israel" (*ERE* 7:439–56), and an entry under "Psalms" (the first part of the article being by W. Robertson Smith) appeared in the *Encyclopaedia Britannica* (11th ed.; 1910–1911), 22:534–40. The short study entitled *Deuteronomy and the Decalogue* was published in 1920 (Cambridge: Cambridge University Press).

also their responsibilities. This did not change until after 1920. The Professors were committed to ecclesiastical duties through cathedral canonries and village parishes requiring active participation in preaching and teaching. By the time that Stanley A. Cook, an Anglican layman, was appointed as Kennett's successor in 1932, the link with a canonry of Ely Cathedral had become a limitation that was no longer helpful.

In the wide administrative sense this change was one aspect of the move towards a "secularizing" of the university and its teaching,[24] but, in a wider perspective, it marked recognition of the very broad range of concerns that are reflected by the Old Testament and the Bible generally in western culture. This relates not simply to the study of Judaism, but also to other major areas of English life and literature. The fact is that the Bible, in both its Jewish and Christian forms, continues to exercise a profound influence on social, political, and cultural life. The concern to understand and monitor that influence remains a subject fully worthy of the highest scholarship that a modern university can offer. It touches the concerns of religious communities of various kinds, but it also reaches into the deepest levels of cultural values and creativity.

In its post-Reformation guise as a translation of the Hebrew Bible the Christian Old Testament profoundly influenced political thought and legal theory. Furthermore the introduction of a sharply focused Christian "Mission to the Jews" at the beginning of the nineteenth century brought about a significant revival of Christian Hebrew studies, as a form of Christian missionary apologetic. As a consequence Jewish converts and sons of converts made major contributions to Christian biblical studies in the nineteenth and twentieth centuries. Eventually a well-informed dialogue between Jews and Christians developed, and is happily continuing in Cambridge.

The Old Testament in Edwardian Cambridge

F. C. Burkitt notes in his memoir of Robert Kennett that, in the year of his appointment in 1903, the Old Testament held a prominent—almost certainly the most fervently discussed—place in the theological curriculum of the university. It was controversial; it was enlivened by remarkable and unexpected new discoveries of manuscripts and hitherto unknown ancient texts; it was the subject of new theories about the

---

24 Cf. J. Berlinerblau, *The Secular Bible: Why Nonbelievers Must Take the Bible Seriously* (Cambridge: Cambridge University Press, 2005).

authorship and dates of familiar biblical writings; it was that part of Christian tradition which appeared most sharply to conflict with the theories of Charles Darwin about the origin of the human species. Herbert Ryle had commented, not altogether in jest, that he expected a stake in the streets of Cambridge. The Old Testament was also that part of Christian Protestant tradition where traditional Anglican and Nonconformist doctrines appeared most strongly to differ. A strong Scottish influence had entered into the theology of both Oxford and Cambridge as a result of the ending of religious discrimination, which injected into it a powerful "Reformed" element. The Hebrew Bible was also a shared inheritance between Christians and Jews who, at the turn of the century, were seeking refuge in England in increasing numbers from the oppressive and intolerant regimes in mainland Europe.

The agenda was immense and a rich army of scholars became involved in the University's teaching programme to cater for its many demands. The study of the Septuagint became one such project in which the University played a major role, and the development of Jewish studies, including studies of Mediaeval Judaism, was another such development. It is also worthy of note that several of the most significant and internationally acclaimed developments in New Testament studies published by members of the Divinity Faculty arose directly as a consequence of explorations into the Jewish and Hebrew background of the New Testament writings.

The legacy of the acceptance and furtherance of the "Higher Criticism" of the Bible, which made a great leap forward as a branch of theology in 1882 and 1883 with the appointment of the new incumbents to the ancient Professorships of Hebrew at Oxford and Cambridge, received a further stimulus with the arrival of William Robertson Smith in 1883. Stanley Cook became his most significant and influential pupil and succeeded to the Hebrew Professorship in 1932; other scholars, notably J. G. Frazer (1854–1941) and Jane Harrison (1850–1928) continued to explore his anthropological interests. Robert Hatch Kennett carried the torch for Hebrew studies which William Wright had lit.

Seen in retrospect the two decades between 1883, when S. R. Driver was appointed to the Regius Chair of Hebrew in Oxford, and 1903, when R. H. Kennett was appointed to the comparable Chair in Cambridge, were two of the most remarkable decades in the history of the Hebrew Bible/Old Testament. It is a treasured privilege to have been a student of this rich heritage, and it is a pleasure to offer these reflections regarding an altogether remarkable period of British theological scholarship in tribute to a scholar who is an exemplary heir of that tradition.

Index of Modern Authors